Kitty Clive,
or The Fair Songster

Kitty Clive,
or The Fair Songster

BERTA JONCUS

THE BOYDELL PRESS

© Berta Joncus 2019

All Rights Reserved. Except as permitted under current legislation no part of this work may be photocopied, stored in a retrieval system,
published, performed in public, adapted, broadcast, transmitted, recorded or reproduced in any form or by any means, without the prior permission of the copyright owner

The right of Berta Joncus to be identified as the author of this work has been asserted in accordance with sections 77 and 78 of the Copyright, Designs and Patents Act 1988

First published 2019
The Boydell Press, Woodbridge

ISBN 978 1 78327 346 1

The Boydell Press is an imprint of Boydell & Brewer Ltd
PO Box 9, Woodbridge, Suffolk IP12 3DF, UK
and of Boydell & Brewer Inc.
668 Mt Hope Avenue, Rochester, NY 14620–2731, USA
website: www.boydellandbrewer.com

A catalogue record for this book is available from the British Library

The publisher has no responsibility for the continued existence or accuracy of URLs for external or third-party internet websites referred to in this book, and does not guarantee that any content on such websites is, or will remain, accurate or appropriate

This publication is printed on acid-free paper

Printed and bound in Great Britain by TJ International Ltd, Padstow, Cornwall

FOR ANDREW

Contents

Illustrations		viii
Preface		xi
Conventions of Transcription		xiv
1	The Siren Song: Kitty Clive in the Playhouse	1
2	'The Lovely Virgin tun'd her Voice': Henry Carey and the Production of a Native Songster	28
3	'Charm'd with the sprightly Innocence of Nell': The Metamorphosis of Miss Raftor	64
4	'HINT writes, and RAFTOR acts in Drury-lane': Clive, Fielding, and Theophilus Cibber	105
5	'The pious Daughter, and the faithful Wife': Fielding, Miller, and Clive, 1733–35	138
6	'A Likeness where none was to be found': Contested Images of Clive, 1734–37	168
7	The Patriot Soprano: British Worthies at Drury Lane	194
8	Handel and the Sweet Bird of Drury Lane, 1740–43	227
9	*The Case of Mrs. Clive*	275
10	Of Scuffles and Rivalries: The Demise of 'Kitty Cuckoe'	302
11	From Miss Lucy to Mrs. Riot: Voice and Caricature	331
12	Clive on Clive: *The Rehearsal: Or, Bays in Petticoats*	378
13	Conclusion: The Fair Songster	409
Appendix 1 Catherine Clive's Roles 1728–69		427
Appendix 2 Lines in Catherine Clive's Repertory 1728–69		461
Appendix 3 *The Case of Mrs. CLIVE* (1744)		477
Select Bibliography		482
Index		509

Illustrations

Fig. 2.1 John Faber the younger after John Ellys, *Miss Fenton*, 1728. Mezzotint. © Trustees of the British Museum. Museum number: 1902,1011.1422.   35

Fig. 2.2 Gerard Vandergucht, Frontispiece to *Damon and Phillida*, 1737. Engraving. Courtesy of the Center for Archival Collections, Bowling Green State University. Call number: rareovsz ML50.5 .D17 1737.   48

Fig. 2.3 After Godfried Schalcken (*Couple d'amoureux dans un forêt*, c.1695), *MISS RAFTER in the Character of PHILLIDA*, 1729. Mezzotint. © Victoria and Albert Museum, London. Museum number: S.3874-2009.   50

Fig. 3.1 Francis Hayman (?), Frontispiece to *The Devil to Pay*, 1731. Engraving. © The British Library Board 30/9/2018. All Rights Reserved. Shelfmark: Music Collections 11775.c.24.   99

Fig. 3.2 Francis Hayman and studio, A Scene in *The Devil to Pay*, 1730s. Oil on canvas. By permission of the owner.   100

Fig. 3.3 Gerard (?) Vandergucht after Francis Hayman. Frontispiece to *The Devil to Pay*, 1738. Engraving. © The British Library Board 30/9/2018. All Rights Reserved. Shelfmark: Music Collections 11775.c.25.   101

Fig. 3.4 Richard Parr after Francis Hayman, *From the Farce, The Devil to pay or the Wife's Metamorphos'd Jobson and Nell, 26 May 1743*, 1743. Engraving. © Victoria and Albert Museum, London. Museum number: S.4303-2009.   102

Fig. 3.5 After Richard Parr after Francis Hayman, *ROYAL AMUSEMENT or a Curious Representation of one of ye Celebrated Paintings at Vaux-Hall done by ye Ingenious MR. HYMEN, NELL and the COBLER*, c.1744. Engraving. The Bodleian Libraries, The University of Oxford. Shelfmark: Douce Prints a. 49, fol. 114, Item 90.   103

Fig. 6.1 John Faber after Pieter van Bleeck, *The Celebrated Mrs. Clive, late Miss Raftor in the Character of Philida*, 1734. Mezzotint. © Victoria and Albert Museum, London. Museum number: S.3816-2009.   172

ILLUSTRATIONS   ix

Fig. 6.2 Edward Fisher after Jonathan Richardson, *Mrs. Oldfield the celebrated Comedian*, 1758–82. Mezzotint. National Portrait Gallery, London. NPG number: D27619.   172

Fig. 6.3 Pieter van Bleeck after Pieter van Bleeck, *Mrs. Clive in the Character of Philida*, 1735. Mezzotint. © Victoria and Albert Museum, London. Museum number: S.3817-2009.   176

Fig. 6.4 Jeremiah Davison after Joseph van Aken, *Catherine Clive*, c.1735. Oil on canvas. Reproduced by permission of the Marquess of Bath, Longleat House, Warminster, Wiltshire. Longleat Collection Number: 9341.   176

Fig. 6.5 John Simon after John Richardson, *Mrs. Oldfield*, c.1730. Mezzotint. National Portrait Gallery, London. NPG number: D27620.   177

Fig. 6.6 Alexander van Aken after Joseph van Aken, 'Of all the Arts …' [Catherine Clive, 'Printed for T. Bowles'], 1735. Mezzotint. © Trustees of the British Museum. Museum number: 1902,1011.6026.   177

Fig. 7.1 William Nutter after John Boyne, *Mr. MACKLIN & Mrs. POPE in the Characters of SHYLOCK and PORTIA*, 1789. Stipple engraving. © Victoria and Albert Museum, London. Harry R. Beard Collection, given by Isobel Beard. Museum number: S.201-2009.   207

Fig. 8.1 William Verelst, *Catherine Clive*, 1740. Oil on canvas. By kind permission of the Garrick Club of London. Paintings: G0122.   231

Fig. 8.2 Simon (?) Beauvais, *Mr. Beard in the Character of a Captn of a Man of War*, c.1740. Engraving. Folger Shakespeare Library. Call number: ART Vol. d45 no.186. Used by permission of the Folger Shakespeare Library.   250

Fig. 9.1 'Historical Chronicle, October 1743', *The Gentleman's Magazine and Historical Chronicle*, vol. 13, October 1743, p. 553. The Bodleian Libraries, The University of Oxford. Shelfmark: Per.Bibl. 2.   285

Fig. 9.2 'Historical Chronicle, November 1743', *The Gentleman's Magazine and Historical Chronicle*, vol. 13, November 1743, p. 609. The Bodleian Libraries, The University of Oxford. Shelfmark: Per.Bibl. 2.   287

Fig. 9.3 *The Theatrical Contest 1743*, 1743. Etching. The Folger Shakespeare Library. Call number: PR3291.T39 Cage 1. Used by permission of the Folger Shakespeare Library.   300

Fig. 10.1 Thomas Booth, *The Green Room Scuffle, or, Drury Lane in an Uproar*. Letterpress broadside song illustrated with etching, 1746 ('Publish'd Persuant to Act of Parliament Jan. 29, 1746, by G. Foster on Ludgate-Hill, and Sold at the Print and Pamphlet Shop; in London and Westminster'). Yale Collection, Lewis Walpole Library. Call number: 746.01.29.01+. Courtesy of the Lewis Walpole Library, Yale University.   320

Fig. 10.2 Made by the Bow porcelain manufactory; Catherine Clive (?), left; Peg Woffington (?), right; c.1750. Soft-paste porcelain. Philadelphia Museum of Art, Gift of Mrs. Morris Hawkes, 1942-59-57,58. 327

Fig. 11.1 Pieter van Bleeck, *Catherine Clive as Mrs. Riot, the Fine Lady in Lethe; or Aesop in the Shades*, c.1749. Oil on canvas. By kind permission of the Garrick Club of London. Paintings: G0121. 356

Fig. 11.2 Charles Mosley after Pieter van Bleeck, *Mrs. Clive, in the Character of the fine Lady in Lethe*, 1750. Etching and engraving. Lewis Walpole Library. Call number: Portraits C642 no. 3. Courtesy of the Lewis Walpole Library, Yale University. 357

Fig. 11.3 After Charles Mosley, after Pieter van Bleeck, *Mrs. CLIVE IN THE CHARACTER OF THE LADY IN LETHE*, 1750. Watch-paper. © Trustees of the British Museum. Museum number: 1902,1018.71. 358

Fig. 11.4 Made by the Bow porcelain manufactory, after Charles Mosley, after Pieter van Bleeck, *Kitty Clive as 'The Fine Lady' in Lethe*, 1750. Soft-paste porcelain. © Fitzwilliam Museum, Cambridge. Object Accession Number: EC.3-1938. 359

Fig. 13.1 Alexander van Aken after Joseph van Aken, *The FAIR SONGSTER* [original 1735], 1763–67. Mezzotint. © Trustees of the British Museum. Museum number: K,58.180. 417

Fig. 13.2 Robert Sayer, after Johann Ludwig Fäsch (?), *Mrs. CLIVE in the Character of Mrs. Heidelberg* [in *The Clandestine Marriage*], 1769. Coloured engraving. © Victoria and Albert Museum, London. Museum number: S.440-1997. 418

Fig. 13.3 Johann Ludwig Fäsch, *Mrs. CLIVE in the Character of Lady FUZ in a Peep behind Curtain*, c.1767. Print study. © Trustees of the British Museum. Museum number: 1931,0509.252. 419

Fig. 13.4 Alexander van Aken after Joseph van Aken, *Mrs. CLIVE, from the Picture at Strawberry Hill* [original 1735], after 1793. Mezzotint. © Trustees of the British Museum. Museum number: 1902,1011.6028. 421

Fig. 13.5 William Hoare, *Mrs. Clive in the Character of Philida* [sic] *Drury Lane*, 1736. Red chalk on paper. Unknown collection. Photograph National Portrait Gallery, London. 423

The author and publisher are grateful to all the institutions and individuals listed for permission to reproduce the materials in which they hold copyright. Every effort has been made to trace the copyright holders; apologies are offered for any omission, and the publisher will be pleased to add any necessary acknowledgement in subsequent editions.

Preface

In 1735 the 'beauteous Ease' of Drury Lane star Catherine Clive and the 'heavnly Strains' of her song were extolled in the same popular press which in 1746 would call her a '*Red-Fac'd* B[it]ch!'.[1] By the late eighteenth century, stage historians typically sneered at her figure, manner, and nature. Why did Clive, who debuted in 1728 and for whom Handel, Henry Fielding, and David Garrick wrote, rise and fall so drastically in public report? Modern scholars have shown her to be an important actress and a fascinating stage writer. But what marked Clive most strongly has never been properly considered: her song – by which means she shot to first rank – and her sudden downfall.

Clive possessed a protean voice, dazzling audiences equally in exquisite airs and raw ballads. Such singing is unknown today, as is, Handel's works apart, the music she sang. Clive drew energy from playhouse audiences, who loved in particular that she could defy a playbook author's intent; she did this repeatedly, spontaneously, and often through music. Her first great success, in 1731 as Nell in *The Devil to Pay*, resulted from this skill. Until 1750, Clive used song to bond with her audiences, improvising for them, directly addressing them, and delighting them with send-ups of fashionable Italian sopranos.

Yet her dizzying climb bred her career crash of the 1740s. Clive confronted formidable biases against women, and while she tried to project herself as a witty and incorruptible model Briton, her empowerment caught up with her. While on stage she could project the self of her choosing, but she couldn't control what was said or written about her. Once her high wages and influence behind the scenes became public knowledge, her boldness was heard as insolence and her ease seen as temerity. Gaining weight as she aged made her vulnerable to charges of excess and self-indulgence; fandom, in its progeny-eating dynamic, made her into a figure of fun. To save her career Clive took up this parodic view of herself, managing thereby to reign at Drury Lane for another twenty years. What divides her first career, founded on respect, from

---

[1] On Clive's 'beauteous Ease', see [Aaron Hill], 'The Stage's Acknowledgment', *The Prompter*, no. 99 (21 October 1735), p. 331, and Chapter 6, p. 178; on her 'heavnly Strains', see Fig. 6.6 and Chapter 6, p. 177; and on '*Red fac'd* B[it]ch!' see Fig. 10.1a and Chapter 10, p. 321.

her second, founded on disrespect, is serious song. Around 1750 serious song receded from her repertory; this book, which is about Clive as songster, ends there.

I have been living with Kitty Clive for a long time. A brief description of her in Roger Fiske's *English Theatre Music in the Eighteenth Century* led to Clive becoming the topic of my 2004 PhD dissertation, supervised by Reinhard Strohm, who first emboldened me to challenge my material.[2] Writing as a post-graduate, however, I lacked long immersion in the sources and their contexts. Findings from my post-doctoral research allowed me to see beyond standard accounts of her repertory and career, and to formulate new ones. Learning and performing Clive's music brought her stage works alive to me as events. Reports about Clive, including her own, revealed themselves to me not as faithful records but as a welter of often conflicting updates from the shopfloor of playhouse stardom. That also is my subject: how playhouse stars, especially women, were made and marketed, and in particular how they could use song to produce themselves. By virtue of her stagecraft, Clive shaped stage works and stage politics. A Clive-informed view asks us to rethink both, sometimes radically.

I am deeply grateful to all those who have made this book possible. Many scholars generously shared their expertise with me in emails, conversations, and feedback on draft chapters. I especially thank Ruth Smith, David Coke, Jeremy Barlow, Felicity Nussbaum, Susan Rutherford, Thomas Lockwood, Vanessa Rogers – who kindly put the scores she had made at my disposal – Rebecca Harris-Warwick, Robert D. Hume, and Judith Milhous for their thoughtful and illuminating responses. My Handel Institute Council colleagues Colin Timms and Helen Coffey facilitated access to University of Birmingham holdings and to the forthcoming *George Frideric Handel: Collected Documents* volumes. Several discoveries came from this material.

The expert staff of, among other institutions, the British Library, the Bodleian Libraries, the National Portrait Gallery, the Harvard Theater Collection, the Folger Shakespeare Library, the Huntington Library – where Anita Weaver checked foliation against digitized sources for me – the Gerald Coke Handel Collection, and the Garrick Club of London aided my archival work. The Garrick Club has graciously allowed me to reproduce in this book, without charge, their oil portraits of Clive. During my research trip to the Lewis Walpole Library, Sue Walker helped me navigate their valuable collection. The archivists with whom I corresponded – from Eton College, Shropshire Archives, Herefordshire Record Office, Kilkenny Family Archives, the National Library

---

[2] Roger Fiske, *English Theatre Music in the Eighteenth Century* (London and New York, 1973), pp. 214–16; Berta Joncus, 'A Star is Born: Kitty Clive and Female Representation in Eighteenth-Century English Musical Theatre' (PhD diss., Univ. of Oxford, 2004).

of Ireland, and Christchurch College Library, Oxford – provided valuable evidence otherwise inaccessible to me.

For help in preparing the bibliography and music examples, I thank Chandler Hall and Christopher Gould respectively. I am particularly grateful to Natassa Varka, who meticulously checked all this book's quotations, citations and music analyses against their original sources and formulated along with me an editorial policy for transcribing words. Her absolute commitment kept my spirits high during this book's final phase. My perceptive sons, Gustav and Oliver, have helped me refine my reflections on Clive through conversation. It is, however, to my husband Andrew that I am most indebted. His brilliant editing, constant counsel, shared enthusiasm for my subject, and shrewd observations about my findings have been crucial to bringing this book into being. I dedicate it to him.

Conventions of Transcription

Eighteenth-century writing is based on phonetics. Spelling, punctuation, italicization, and capitalization typically communicate how the reader should hear words, whether spoken aloud or mentally registered. When quoting period sources – I use them even if other scholars quote the same material – I forego modernization to capture the original as far as possible. Proper nouns are, however, shorn of the italics which they automatically were given in the eighteenth century, to avoid modern readers erroneously assuming emphasis where none was intended. Where entire passages are italicized in the original, I reverse the lettering of italics to plain text, and vice versa. I follow online resources in omitting the first article from a newspaper's title (*Grub-street Journal* rather than *The Grub-street Journal*), even if the first article is in the original printed title. Clear printer's errors, such as omitted spaces, are silently corrected, except for possessive apostrophes whose variant usage – *The Beggar's Opera*, *The Beggars' Opera*, or the *Beggars Opera* – might impute different meanings. I don't insert '[sic]' unless I think its absence would confuse the reader. Superscripts are faithfully transcribed, as are contractions which are completed only where deemed necessary. Old Style dates are silently changed to New Style dates, although the former are retained in quoted material. For a person's name in my main text, I ignore variants and use the spelling of the person's headword entry in modern dictionaries such as *Oxford Music Online*. Other editorial interventions include standardizing punctuation with a full colon before the subtitles of stage works. I also omit quotation marks that in primary sources are repeated in lines that follow each other; finally, at the start of a quote, I change any lower-case letter to upper case and set it in square brackets.

I use the abbreviation *The London Stage* for *The London Stage, 1660–1800: a Calendar of Plays, Entertainments and Afterpieces, together with Casts, Box-Receipts and Contemporary Comment*, 5 parts, 11 vols; Part 2: 1700–1729, ed. Emmett L. Avery, 2 vols (Carbondale, IL, 1960); Part 3: 1729–1747, ed. Arthur H. Scouten, 2 vols (Carbondale, IL, 1961); Part 4: 1747–1776, ed. George Winchester Stone, Jr., 3 vols (Carbondale, IL, 1962). For dates of performance, original press notices, rather than *The London Stage*, have been consulted whenever possible; these announcements are cited with the issue number.

1

The Siren Song:
Kitty Clive in the Playhouse

> If therefore this Theatrical Genius was able to entertain, contrary to the Intention of the Author – what must we say of her, or what Words can describe her Merits, when she appeared in the Fulness of her Powers, and was the very Person she represented?
> Benjamin Victor on Catherine Clive, *The History of the Theatres of London, from the Year 1760 to the Present Time* (London, 1771), vol. 3, p. 145.

Who was Kitty Clive? Her earliest 'portrait' shows a bare-bosomed nymph whose song, verses below the image tell us, seduces male listeners. Like so many representations of Clive, this image was a fiction; it was taken from a canvas painted c.1695, sixteen years before she was born. Stories were spun around Clive, some of them by Clive herself. She asserted the kind of person she was through performance, which was when she had greatest control over her self-presentation. Audiences knew that what she enacted was a show, with postures and antics, but soaring above this noise was her seemingly incorruptible voice, which fascinated them. Clive became the first playhouse principal to attain and maintain stardom primarily through song.

Her ascent was improbable. She was born Catherine Raftor, to William and Elizabeth Raftor, in London in 1711.[1] She once suggested that her birthday was 15 November,[2] but her twentieth-century biographer Patrick J. Crean found evidence that she may have been baptized 'Ellenor' on 15 July 1711.[3] Her father

---

[1] Patrick J. Crean, 'The Life and Times of Kitty Clive' (PhD diss., Univ. of London, 1933), pp. 10–11. Clive's maiden name was spelled both 'Rafter' and 'Raftor'; I follow most eighteenth-century and modern dictionary entries for 'Catherine Clive' in spelling it 'Raftor'. Crean contends that the 'more correct form is Rafter, a modernisation of the ancient Irish surname "Mac Reachtagain"'. *Ibid.*, p. 1.

[2] Catherine Clive to Jane Pope, letter of 15 November 1782: 'I write to you on my Birth day, it is no matter how Long ago; I was born as Some say in the Consious lovers [*The Conscious Lovers*] in one thousand seven huendered and something or other; I little thought four months ago I shoud have lived to have seen Another.' 'Autograph Letters from Catherine Clive to Jane Pope', Bodleian Library, Toynbee b.1. Some modern sources give her date of birth as 5 November; earlier scholars appear to have misread the '15' in this letter as '5'.

[3] The entry is in the Registers of St Paul's, Covent Garden, found in *The Harleian Society Publications*, vol. 33; Crean, 'The Life and Times of Kitty Clive', pp. 10–11. The register

was the son of dispossessed Catholic Anglo-Irish landowners. Disgraced through his support of the Stuart King James II, William Raftor was on 21 April 1691 listed as one of the 'Jacobites of the County Kilkenny and Upper Ossory[,] outlawed' by England's new monarch, King William.[4] After the Crown expropriated his lands, he fled to France, like many of his compatriots. He sued for and was granted pardon, came to London, and married Elizabeth Daniell, daughter of 'an eminent Leather-seller … with whom he had a handsome Fortune'.[5] William Raftor was trained in law but as a Catholic was unable to practise his profession in London.[6]

Despite her politically compromised parentage, and without theatre connections, Clive rose to top rank at Drury Lane. This house had been the licensed home of English-language theatre since 1707, when the Lord Chamberlain sequestered spoken drama from opera and made the Queen's (later King's) Theatre the exclusive venue for 'Operas and other Musicall presentments'.[7] Yet music was crucial at Drury Lane and at London's other playhouses.[8] As celebrity production grew in scope during the century, English-language song helped both to generate and to constitute the personae of several London playhouse principals.[9] Clive spearheaded the self-production of stars through song. This book is about Clive's singing career until 1750, and is for that reason in part a study in vocal music's semantic richness, and how it might be exploited.

To understand Clive's success requires us to re-imagine her voice, engage with her technical proficiency, and identify her moments of improvisation.

---

passage reads: 'Ellenor Da[ughte]r of Wm Raster by Eliz. his Wife'. Crean, *ibid.*, points out that the 's' could originally have been 'f', the two letters being hard to tell apart in the cursive writing of the time.

[4] William Carrigan, *The History and Antiquities of the Diocese of Ossory*, vol. 4 (Dublin, 1905), p. 398 (copied from the original in the Public Record Office, Dublin); William Raftor's name appears on p. 403. Cited in Crean, 'The Life and Times of Kitty Clive', pp. 6–7.

[5] Crean, 'The Life and Times of Kitty Clive', p. 8. Crean speculates that William Raftor may have fled to the exiled court of King James II at St Germaine en Laye and repeats the assertion of Edmund Curll – an unreliable eighteenth-century writer – that William Raftor was awarded a Captain's Commission in the army of Louis XIV. As yet, these assertions are undocumented. Crean, 'The Life and Times of Kitty Clive', pp. 5–7.

[6] Crean, 'The Life and Times of Kitty Clive', pp. 8–9. William Raftor had apparently earlier practised law in New Ross, Wessex. *Ibid.*, pp. 1–7.

[7] 'The Haymarket Opera House', *Survey of London: Volumes 29 and 30, St James Westminster*, Part 1, ed. F. H. W. Sheppard (London, 1960), pp. 223–50. *British History Online* <http://www.british-history.ac.uk/survey-london/vols29-30/pt1/pp223-250>. Accessed 20 January 2017.

[8] Vanessa Rogers, 'Orchestra and Theatre Music', *The Oxford Handbook of the Georgian Theatre, 1737–1832*, ed. J. Swindells and D. F. Taylor (Oxford, 2013), pp. 304–20.

[9] Ballad opera and its cousin, pastiche comic opera, served as vehicles for producing later playhouse celebrities such as John Beard and Charlotte Brent. See Berta Joncus, 'Ballad Opera: Commercial Song in Enlightenment Garb', *The Oxford Handbook of the British Musical*, ed. R. Gordon and O. Jubin (Oxford, 2016), pp. 31–63.

The distinctiveness of her vocalism helped Clive to unify, in her person, improbably diverse stage characters. Within each character, she shaped song in ways that only she could duplicate. In stage speech also, Clive's early musical training helped to distinguish her from other actresses. She was aided in this by the spatial intimacy of Drury Lane and the freedoms its audiences enjoyed. Physically close to her public, she reached out musically to them.

Her stage productions accommodated two kinds of reciprocity: between Clive and the dramatis personae she enacted, and between her self-projections and what audiences knew and thought they knew about her. She brought a dramatis persona into being, and this persona, because it belonged to a character type, guided how audiences saw her; yet by investing this type with her 'self', she helped to shape the very audience taste that guided her performance. Clive variously bolstered, circumvented, challenged, and overturned conventions of stage production as she involved audiences in the business of her self-construction. This dynamic broke down in 1745–46 as audiences came to view her success as unseemly, and derision of Clive overtook approbation of her. To salvage her career, Clive began to play up to the negative caricature that had been imposed on her in the press. Refined song, foundational to her early career, disappeared from her stage line as she enjoyed a late flowering of success as a fat, ageing, outrageous Fine Lady.

Hearing Kitty Clive

From 1728, when she first appeared on stage, until the mid-1740s, Clive sang most nights that she performed. She led English-language musical productions across genres: masque, ballad opera, burlesque, serenata, cantata, oratorio, serious opera, and interpolated song. Of these, masque and ballad opera were the most important to Clive's career. Masque was the English-language equivalent of Italian opera: high-style, sung throughout, based on classical myth, and written by one composer. Ballad opera, by contrast, was pastiche: begun by John Gay with *The Beggar's Opera* (1728), ballad opera was essentially sentimental comedy interlarded with common tunes – that is, melodies already in the public sphere, identified by title alone. The sources of the tunes were heterodox, ranging from broadsides to opera arias. A ballad opera might contain as few as nine and as many as sixty sung numbers. Cousin to ballad opera was interpolated song. Usually newly composed, interpolated songs were independent numbers inserted into revived or new comedy. Burlesque was more a practice than a genre, and Clive specialized in applying burlesque to individual Italian arias that she interpolated; composers also wrote burlesque operas, oratorios, and pastorals which she co-led.

In the 184 roles she performed by 1750, she usually sang, as shown in Appendices 1 and 2. While Clive's post-1900 reputation has rested mainly on her acting, her most celebrated parts before 1750 – in Henry Carey's masque

Cephalus and Procris, Milton's masque *Comus*, the ballad opera *The Devil to Pay* and Fielding's ballad farces – were in musical stage works. Given Clive's evident reliance on song during her career, why have historians passed over it? Reasons for this oversight are several. Modern scholars tackling her history have mostly been theatre specialists and as such have engaged neither with reading her music nor re-imagining her execution of it.[10] Because so much of Clive's repertory is of humble origin or content, musicologists have also tended to pass it by.[11]

Yet modern ignorance of Clive as initially a celebrated songster, and then a first comedienne-soprano, stems largely from eighteenth-century writings, including Clive's. An assumption underpinning this contemporary opinion was that acting, not singing, determined a player's merit, and in early commentary about Clive her singing is almost never discussed. Obscuring our view of Clive more generally is her eventual career devolution: after 1746, not even Clive herself thought that audiences would accept her in a serious part. This made it easy for a new generation of writers, including Thomas Davies and Charles Burney, to relegate her to low comic representations.

Clive's song is hidden from us also because we have no model for such a voice. She excelled in opposing genres. Her vocal production ranged widely: in polite repertory, she was said to transport audiences with her 'meaning Raptures';[12] in ballads, her voice was compared to 'London Cries' – that is, to the raw sound of street vendors.[13] Beyond this, she hijacked the vocal identi-

---

[10] I am indebted to the findings of these scholars, who include Felicity Nussbaum, Fiona Ritchie, Matthew Kinservik, and Richard Frushell. Their publications are cited below.

[11] Because English, and because derived sometimes from common tunes, Clive's song has been marginalized in music histories. During the formation of musicology as a discipline, leading nineteenth-century German scholars identified Britain as 'Das Land ohne Musik' ('The country without music'). Although a product of nineteenth-century prejudices – *inter alia*, the centrality of great works, and of male (Austro-German) composers and scholars, to the creation of a European music history – this characterization is not uncommon today. For a pithy summary of this historiography, see Bennett Zon, 'Histories of British Music and the Land without Music: National Identity and the Idea of the Hero', *Essays on the History of English Music in Honour of John Caldwell: Sources, Style, Performance, Historiography*, ed. E. Hornby and D. Maw (Woodbridge, 2010), pp. 311–24. On the challenges with which this legacy lumbers scholars of British eighteenth-century music, see Peter Holman, 'Eighteenth-Century English Music: Past, Present, Future', *Music in Eighteenth-Century Britain*, ed. D. Wyn Jones (Burlington, VT, 2000), pp. 1–13. From 1845, when scholars began to devise British music histories, they looked to 'heroes', and to authors, rather than to 'heroines', or to performers, to rescue British music from oblivion.

[12] [Aaron Hill], 'The Stage's Acknowledgment' *The Prompter*, no. 99 (21 October 1735), p. 331; repr. in the *London Magazine, or, Gentleman's Monthly Intelligencer* [1732–1735], vol. 4 (October 1735), p. 566. Quoted in full and discussed in Chapter 6, p. 178.

[13] [Christopher Smart], 'EPILOGUE written by a FRIEND, spoken by Mrs. CLIVE', Arthur Murphy, *The Apprentice: A Farce, in Two Acts* (London, 1756), pages unnumbered. See Chapter 2, p. 33.

ties of her Italian operatic rivals, building a line for herself in the comic 'taking off' of London's reigning *prime donne*.

What is clear is that Clive commanded her instrument. Vocal production is complex, with techniques that shift according to musical genre.[14] The vocalist must control her lungs, diaphragm, chest, and abdominal muscles; raise, lower, or hold neutral her larynx and its associated muscles, nerves, and cartilage; direct air flow through phonaters (throat, mouth cavity, nasal passages) while modifying articulators (tongue, soft palate, lips).[15] For Clive to shift between common and serious song, or to ape the voice of another, will have required patiently acquired physical mastery and meticulous attention to the physics of sound production. The inner discipline needed for this seems to have registered with Clive's audiences.

Clive's facility in vocalizing diverse identities was central to her appeal, not least because in so doing she reminded audiences of what was unchanging about her. Sounding like Clive, while inhabiting multiple stage personae, was what marked her integrity. One of Clive's champions, William Chetwood, called her singing 'peculiar to herself'.[16] I understand this peculiarity of Clive's voice to have been vested in what Roland Barthes would call its 'grain', that is, the 'materiality of the body' as heard by the listener, especially the sense of the singer's own self created through diction.[17] According to Barthes, the listener

[14] In pedagogy, vocal teachers tend to categorize training into practices for jazz, gospel, popular, and 'classical' repertories. See, for instance, Scott D. Harrison and Jessica O'Bryan Springer, *Teaching Singing in the 21st Century* (Dordrecht, 2014), Chapters 3, 4, 5, 18, and 19; see especially, in Chapter 4, 'Table 4.1: Fundamental Differences between Classical and Contemporary singing', p. 37, and 'Table 4.2: Broad Generalizations of Stylistic Variation' p. 49. On the eighteenth century, Martha Feldman hypothesizes about the castrato's vocal mechanism in Martha Feldman, 'Red Hot Voice', *The Castrato: Reflections on Natures and Kinds* (Oakland, 2015), pp. 79–132. Feldman's findings are necessarily speculative because lungs, cartilage – including the soft and hard palate – and resonance cavities were altered by castration, which hasn't been practised on singers since the nineteenth century.

[15] For a good introduction to vocal science, see Johan Sundberg, 'Where does the Sound come from?', *The Cambridge Companion to Singing*, ed. J. Potter (Cambridge, 2000), pp. 231–47. Inspired by extended techniques used in contemporary music, composer and acoustician Michael Edgerton explores vocal physiology in Michael Edgerton, *The 21st-Century Voice: Contemporary and Traditional Extra-Normal Voice* (Lanham, 2004). He provides a useful glossary, and, in 'Appendix A: Voice Science', analyses of pitch, quality, and register as a consequence of airflow, the function of the larynx, vocal folds, and mucosal wave; he considers also the interaction between the voice and acoustic space. *Ibid.*, pp. 149–65, 'Glossary', pp. 169–74.

[16] 'Miss Raftor had a facetious Turn of Humour, and infinite Spirits, with a Voice and Manner in singing Songs of Pleasantry peculiar to herself.' William R. Chetwood, 'Mrs. CATHARINE CLIVE (formerly Miss RAFTOR)', *A General History of the Stage, from its Origin in Greece down to the present Time. With the Memoirs of most of the principal Performers that have appeared on the English and Irish Stage for these last Fifty Years* (London, 1749), p. 127.

[17] Roland Barthes, *Image, Music, Text*, ed. and trans. S. Heath (London, 1984), pp. 179–89.

broadly shares with the singer the experience of generating musical sounds, yet the singer's control and interpretation of music arouses the listener's wonder. Diction binds them together, the listener revelling in how the singer renders language as musical sound.[18] Eighteenth-century reports suggest that audiences listened to Clive for something like this thrill.

The high-style music she sang required inner coolness, and, as we shall see, Clive was famously unflappable on the boards. From the extended phrases of her masque music by Henry Purcell and Henry Carey through to the eye-popping melismas of John F. Lampe's burlesques and the swift patter of William Boyce's burlettas, this was music Clive could only have performed by being a brilliant technician, and could only have been acclaimed for by being a consummate artist. Polite singers in the eighteenth century were judged in part by their skill in extemporizing ornaments, cadenzas, and dynamics to enhance the words they sang; where *galant* dance rhythms occur, they were to add emphases according to the steps of *la belle danse*, knowledge of which was a social essential.[19] When she made such additions early in her career, Clive provoked great praise.

Clive was acclaimed also for her execution of the English language in song. She was a principal exponent of British Worthies – Shakespeare, Milton, Dryden, and Congreve – whose words she sang in masques, odes, and oratorios. In lower-style comic airs she married the smartness of satirical verses, Fielding's especially, to familiar playhouse tunes. Her fine rendering of the distinctive sonic elements of the English language helped to forge the idea of a polite British song. She sounded – literally, and also in the sense of plumbing depths – what it was to be British, elevating words above music to teach as well as delight. Comic song was a fertile medium for this project. In the late seventeenth century William Congreve had identified humour with Englishness: to write and perform comedy was considered an exercise of the 'great Freedom, Privilege, and Liberty which the Common People of England enjoy … under no restraint'.[20] Against this backdrop, the high regard commanded

---

[18] Barthes calls this delight 'jouissance'. Adopting Julia Kristeva's distinction between pheno-text – text adduced through rules of languages – and geno-text – text according to its material realization – Barthes links jouissance to the geno-text, where language systems meet bodies. When the singer relishes his mother tongue, for instance the bass Russian cantor whom Barthes discusses, the materiality of that mother tongue is restored. Barthes contrasts such aural impact with that of a singer like Dietrich Fischer-Dieskau, whose mastery of emotive modes he saw as being harnessed commercially rather than arising from an encounter with language through music. Barthes, *Image, Music, Text*, pp. 179–89.

[19] Such practices are important to the notion of 'rhetorical music' – that is, seventeenth- and eighteenth-century music-making that borrows from oratory – and are usefully catalogued in Bruce Haynes and Geoffrey Burgess, *The Pathetick Musician: Moving an Audience in the Age of Eloquence* (New York, 2016).

[20] Letter of William Congreve to John Dennis on 10 July 1695, cited in Stuart M. Tave, *The Amiable Humorist: A Study in the Comic Theory and Criticism of the Eighteenth*

by Clive's comic song, even when part of a slight stage work, is more readily comprehensible.

Almost from the start of her career, Clive exercised both a fearless charisma and an elaborate respect for propriety. Summing up the Clive persona as he perceived it in 1761, Charles Churchill wrote:

> In spight of outward blemishes she shone
> For Humour fam'd, and Humour all her own.
> Easy, as if at home, the stage she trod,
> Nor sought the Critic's praise, nor fear'd his rod.
> Original in spirit and in ease,
> She pleas'd by hiding all attempts to please.[21]

Note that Churchill, a theatre critic writing eight years before Clive retired, makes no mention of her singing. After 1750 Clive's musical repertory was little more than occasional song, but her skill in pleasing 'by hiding all attempts to please' owed much to a delivery she had honed in becoming Drury Lane's first songster.

On stage Clive served a representative function. She was a servant of the Theatre Royal, and part of her job was to help realize the aims stated in the prefaces to the stage works she performed: to instruct audiences about proper and improper conduct. Her playhouse song was designed around this function. Its symmetries, modest proportions, and well-behaved harmonic progressions instantiated approved models of gender and nation. When building her career, Clive only rarely flaunted a vocal virtuosity that historians would later assume she had never possessed. Yet playhouse song also offered Clive licence. Through smart ballads, she could show off her talent and intelligence in ways socially acceptable for a woman. She had a prodigious memory, to which the number of her roles, the quantity of her music, and the speed of her learning testify. More singularly, Clive had an astonishing ear, and polite song provided openings for musical ad-libbing: her ingenuity as an improviser was a major audience draw.

Reviewing the playbook of the first farce that Clive wrote as a vehicle for herself, a critic of 1753 noted: 'As the lady [Clive] cou'd not print her acting with her writing, it appears to want, in the reading, some of that spirit, humour, and

---

and *Early Nineteenth Centuries* (Chicago, 1960), p. 100, and in Lisa Freeman, *Character's Theater: Genre and Identity on the Eighteenth-Century English Stage* (Philadelphia, 2001), p. 209. 'English humor', Tave says, 'is the national shield, the mark and defense of a free nation'. Tave, *The Amiable Humorist*, p. 101. Clive moved freely between the two categories of comedy recognized by period critics, wit and humour. Wit was considered more elevated, yet artificial, and humour, while tending to lowness, expressed passions and was therefore seen as a conduit for 'Nature ... / Unhelpt by Practice, Books, or Art'. Jonathan Swift, 'To Mr. Delany' (1718); cited *ibid.*, pp. 113–14.

[21] Charles Churchill, *The Rosciad: The Third Edition, Revised and Corrected* (London, 1761), p. 18.

meaning, which it might seem to have on the stage, from the brilliancy of her performance.'[22] The key word here is 'meaning': Clive produced the meaning of her texts for her audiences through performance, and this escaped written transmission even in a work that she wrote for herself to lead. In works by others, Clive could create a meaning that overwrote that of the playwright, guiding audiences to apprehend her as she wished. The first half of Benjamin Victor's praise, quoted to open this chapter, speaks to this: her Genius lay partly in being 'able to entertain, contrary to the Intention of the Author'. She once urged her protégée Jane Pope, unnerved by the weakness of a role she had to perform, to follow this example:

> I am sorry to hear you have an indifferent part in the new Comedy, but I don't at all wonder when you tell me the author. [H]e is a wretch of wretches, however I charge you to make a good part of it[.] Let it be never so bad, I have often done so myself therefore I know it is to be done[:] turn it & wind it & play it in a different manner to his intention and as hundred to one but you succeed.[23]

This was how Clive authored her own parts in real time. With some immersion in the practices of the period, we can imagine the interpretations through which she transformed the abused housewife Nell in *The Devil to Pay* into a sentimental heroine, the harlot of *The Harlot's Progress* into a patriot and, in *Comus*, Milton's muse Euphrosyne into a divine version of herself.

Clive redesigned stage characters to her advantage; her characterizations, because hugely popular, were then ploughed back into roles designed for her, in stage works whose generic parameters altered as a result. That process is a major focus of this book. To appreciate its workings, we must consider the practices, discourses, and constraints peculiar to the creation of eighteenth-century playhouse stars.

In the Playhouse: Engagement, Reciprocity, and Stage Stars

The Stage Work and the Player

The terms 'celebrity' and 'star' are today often deployed interchangeably,[24] but it is useful to distinguish between them, not least because Clive did so. Whereas the reputation of a celebrity might rest on notoriety, a star earns her

---

[22] *The Monthly Review; or, Literary Journal*, vol. 8 (May 1753), p. 392. The passage refers to the 1753 version of Clive's farce, *The Rehearsal: Or, Bayes in Petticoats*, discussed in Chapter 12.

[23] Letter of Catherine Clive to Jane Pope of 15 December 1774, 'Copies of letters to Jane Pope from various people, 1769–1808, in the hand of James Winston [manuscript], ca. 1840', Folger Shakespeare Library, W.b.73.

[24] For an introduction to this field, see Sean Redmond and Su Holmes, ed., *Stardom and Celebrity: A Reader* (Los Angeles and London, 2007); P. David Marshall, *Celebrity and Power: Fame in Contemporary Culture* (Minneapolis, 2001); and Richard Dyer with Paul

status through unique gifts acknowledged publicly.[25] Throughout her career Clive emphasized that her top ranking depended on the 'Publick *alone*' – as opposed to private patrons – recognizing her merit.[26] By presenting herself as her audiences' servant, Clive gave playgoers the right to judge her; this helped her to forge an alliance with them through which her most outré flouting of convention could find favour.

Social identities were both reinforced and challenged in the playhouse, among audience members as well as on stage. Playhouse seating was designed to sort attendees into their proper ranks. Roughly speaking, the front and side boxes, and onstage seats, were the preserve of the *beau monde*; the pit was for intellectuals, professionals, and the less affluent; the first or middle gallery was for wealthy tradespeople; and the upper gallery was for the lower orders.[27] Because ticket prices determined these boundaries, they were fluid; royal boxes alone lay beyond purchasing power. At Drury Lane, the royal boxes were split at pit level between the King's box, to the left of the auditorium, and the Prince of Wales's, to the right; each was accessed by a private entrance near the stage door.[28] The chance to ogle royalty and their guests sometimes – but not always – boosted ticket sales.[29] Even with royals present, social conduct could break down: playhouse audiences might call for the manager, or riot; gentry, if seated onstage, could distract actors and spectators alike; audience members generally would watch and converse with each other.[30] A principal player represented this theatricalized collective – what Betsy Bolton calls 'a fantasy of communally embodied, public identity'[31] – yet also rose above it by virtue of commanding attention despite its distractions.

McDonald, *Stars*, 2nd rev. edn (London, 1998). Aspects of these writings are discussed below.

[25] Chris Rojek, *Celebrity* (London, 2001), esp. 143–98; Berta Joncus, 'Producing Stars in Dramma Per Musica', *Music as Social and Cultural Practice: Essays in Honour of Reinhard Strohm*, ed. M. Bucciarelli and B. Joncus (Woodbridge, 2007), pp. 275–93.

[26] See, for instance, her first letter to the press, in *The London Daily Post and General Advertiser*, issue 641 (19 November 1736), reprinted in Chapter 6.

[27] Jim Davis, 'Spectatorship', *The Cambridge Companion to British Theatre, 1730–1830*, ed. D. O'Quinn and J. Moody (Cambridge, 2007), pp. 57–70.

[28] Harry William Pedicord, 'Preface', *"By Their Majesties' Command": the House of Hanover at the London Theatres, 1714–1800* (London, 1991), p. x.

[29] For the period 1714 to 1800 Pedicord calculates 'approximate grosses' at London's three theatres royal, and compares the largest and smallest receipts for performances by royal command. According to his findings, 'on only five nights did the presence of royalty cause the admission receipts to exceed' a house's average gross intake. He asks modern historians to 'temper' the view that audiences were 'flocking' to playhouses to see royals. Ibid., pp. 38–41.

[30] 'In the Name of Freedom', Harry William Pedicord, *The Theatrical Public in the Time of Garrick* (New York, 1954), pp. 41–63.

[31] Betsy Bolton, 'Theorizing Audience and Spectatorial Agency', *The Oxford Handbook of the Georgian Theatre, 1737–1832*, p. 37.

On stage, social identities were dramatized for the 'Spectator', an imagined personage who in the eighteenth century stood for the subject generally. The perspective was famously cultivated by Joseph Addison, who in 1711 co-founded one of the century's essential periodicals, *The Spectator*.[32] Addison believed that subjectivity formed itself extrinsically: by watching, weighing, approving, or rejecting the conduct of others, the spectator could gain understanding and improve himself.[33] For such a selfhood, forged by observing others and being observed by them, the playhouse was an ideal forum. Claiming to instruct, playwrights invented generic 'Characters' – not simply to be copied or rejected, but, as Lisa Freeman emphasizes, to spark debate about what constituted a persuasive social performance.[34] Caught up in this dynamic, stage players proved their mettle by being fascinating *despite* being forced into a stock character. As Felicity Nussbaum shows in her important study *Rival Queens*, the playhouse star dazzled by both fulfilling and resisting expectations of ideal conduct.[35]

This achievement crystallized in the 'line', also called 'cast', or 'walk', that a principal player owned.[36] These terms referred during Clive's career both

---

[32] *The Spectator* was the continuation of Richard Steele's *Tatler*. First issued on 1 March 1711, and reprinted for decades, its impact on generations of eighteenth-century writers, from abolitionists to theatre critics, has long been a subject of scholarly debate, some of which is surveyed in Alison O'Byrne, 'The Spectator and the Rise of the Modern Metropole', *The Cambridge Companion to the City in Literature*, ed. K. R. McNamara (Cambridge, 2014), pp. 57–68.

[33] Terence Bowers, 'Universalizing Sociability: The Spectator, Civic Enfranchisement, and the Rule(s) of the Public Sphere', *The Spectator: Emerging Discourses*, ed. D. J. Newman (Newark, 2005), pp. 150–74. Bowers compares writings to show that '*The Spectator* forged a *constitutive* relationship with the public sphere *throughout* the eighteenth century' (italics original) and that, at a 'basic level, buying *The Spectator* was an endorsement of the system itself'. Ibid., pp. 152, 170. See also Freeman, *Character's Theater*, pp. 193–97.

[34] Freeman holds that the generic characters of stage drama offered audiences a 'dynamic model of identity', with which playwrights experimented. Besides being a 'rubric for shaping identities', stage character became a means to critique what was being posited as an ideal way of being. Freeman, *Character's Theater*, p. 12. Although ground-breaking in many respects, Freeman's view that dramatic performance concerned itself primarily with creating and questioning social types tends to overlook performers' creative practice, which I seek to account for in this book.

[35] Analyzing the way Freeman posits genre to have encoded subjectivity, Nussbaum notes that 'a talented actress could affect a persona that carried far beyond the surface codings typical of a particular genre, sometimes mocking these codings'. Felicity Nussbaum, *Rival Queens: Actresses, Performance, and the Eighteenth-Century British Theater* (Philadelphia, 2010), p. 20.

[36] Peter Holland shows that the 'line' was an essential element in the formation of comic stereotypes on the London stage; he cites testimony from several Restoration dramatists about their strategy when writing in this vein. Peter Holland, *The Ornament of Action: Text and Performance in Restoration Comedy* (Cambridge, 1979), esp. pp. 73–79. Building on his findings, Tiffany Stern argues that the line absorbed into itself the perceived personality of the principal player to whom it was assigned, and that this metacharacter

to the family of stock characters in which a principal player specialized and to parts within a stock type owned by a player. Appendix 2 shows the eleven stock types in which Clive specialized and, within them, which roles were hers. Her stage characters required that she excel in acting and singing. In high-style entertainment such as masques, her perceived merit depended largely on the persuasiveness with which she realized an affect and so moved audiences. In comic parts, her merit tended to be measured by the recognizability of a character type, which she could render in an incomparable yet instantly comprehensible fashion.

In tragedy, the ideals prescribed by European court and salon culture shaped corporeal display, physical movement, and stage speech. Critics found their ideals for corporeal display in history painting, for physical movement in etiquette and dance manuals, and for stage speech in classical oratory.[37] A great tragic actor synthesized these ideals to transport audiences in a moment of shared effervescence. Praise for David Garrick describes this: '[T]he Beholder feels himself affected he knows not how, and it may be truly said of him ... *His powerful Strokes prevailing Truth impress'd, / And unresisted Passion storm'd the Breast*'.[38] In farce, protagonists were two-dimensional figures said to be intended to expose persons whose conduct audiences should shun.[39] In sentimental comedy – an entertainment that sat between comedy and tragedy – actors were, in the words of Richard Steele, to 'touch the viewer's heart' by combining the ideal representations of tragedy with Restoration comedy's simulation of urban life.[40]

---

generated 'the kind of personal interest in specific actors that brings about a "star" system'. Tiffany Stern, *Rehearsal from Shakespeare to Sheridan* (Oxford, 2000), p. 149. See also Freeman, *Character's Theater*, pp. 30–32.

[37] Drawing on his book *Illusion and the Drama* (1991), Frederick Burwick deftly summarizes period and modern writings on tragic acting and ideal embodiment in 'Emotion, Expression and the Size of Theatres', *The Oxford Handbook of the Georgian Theatre, 1737–1832*, pp. 181–88. Commentary on this topic until 1760 is collated into the first two of five volumes in the reprint series, *Acting Theory and the English Stage, 1700–1830*, ed. L. Zunshine (London, 2009). Paul Goring outlines mid-eighteenth century acting methods and relates theoretical writings about acting to the practice of writing sentimental plays; see Paul Goring, *Rhetoric of Sensibility in Eighteenth-Century Culture* (Cambridge, 2005).

[38] [David E. Baker], 'Garrick, David', *The Companion to the Play-house* (London, 1764), pages unnumbered.

[39] Tave, *The Amiable Humorist*, pp. 91–100.

[40] Preface to Richard Steele's *The Conscious Lovers*; cited in Maik Goth, 'Exaggerating Terence's *Andria*: Steele's *Conscious Lovers*, Bellamy's *The Perjur'd Devotee* and Terentian Criticism', *Ancient Comedy and Reception: Essays in Honor of Jeffrey Henderson*, ed. S. Douglas Olson (Berlin, 2014), pp. 503–36. Goth argues that Steele relied on Terence's writings to formulate his of ideas about sentimental comedy. On the history and legacy of Steele's sentimental comedy, see the literature cited in note 41 of *The Oxford History of Classical Reception in English Literature: Volume 3 1660–1790*, ed. D. Hopkins and C.

Principal players were held to own those roles in which the Town had consistently applauded them. When a player's stage manner was compelling enough to become its own convention, the original performance became the benchmark against which new players in the role were assessed. With principals themselves able to forge new roles through their own reputations and stage manners, bespoke vehicles came to be written for them.[41] Strengthening a player's sense of ownership of a role were its physical manuscript parts, which the players retained for training. Preparation tended to be, as Tiffany Stern shows, largely private – by oneself, or one-to-one – rather than through ensemble rehearsal.[42]

Within each part, audiences looked for 'points', or dramatic junctures, during which a player's distinctive artistry would crystallize in performance.[43] The 'point' was a clap trap, a moment at which the audience could be nudged into applause. According to one critic, only a 'few passages' of a play were thought worthy of 'notice', and the polite theatregoer was expected to know 'where an actor is to exert his abilities.'[44] Stars were known to 'give the signal when they are to be applauded'; at such moments, 'Othello has a most languishing aspect, Monimia is all sighs and softness, Beatrice will bridle, and pretty Peggy Wildair leers you into a clap'.[45] Within this dramatic syntax, Clive had the added advantage that song was itself a kind of point which typically arrested or stood outside the narrative flow. David Garrick's later practice of holding a frozen attitude may well have been a leaf borrowed from Clive's book.[46]

Martindale (Oxford and New York, 2012), p. 475. See also Freeman, *Character's Theater*, pp. 204–19.

[41] 'The rule must be to start with the [principal] actor and consider the development of the line as an historical process in relation to that actor. The actor precedes the role.' Holland, *The Ornament of Action*, p. 79.

[42] Stern, *Rehearsal from Shakespeare to Sheridan*, pp. 260–70. In Stern's words: 'Though the value of ensemble rehearsal was constantly stated, no one, not even the managers, actually had an ensemble mentality.' *Ibid.*, p. 266.

[43] Shearer West defines the 'point' as the eighteenth-century 'actor's depiction of a specific character at a specific moment [that] obscured other concerns'. Shearer West, *The Image of the Actor: Verbal and Visual Representation in the Age of Garrick and Kemble* (London, 1991), p. 19. In practice, this meant that parts 'were ... divided into "moments" that were both key to the characterization and separate from it'. Stern, *The Rehearsal*, pp. 258–59.

[44] *A Guide to the Stage: Or, Select Instructions and Precedents ... towards forming a Polite Audience* (London, 1751), p. 13.

[45] *Ibid.*, p. 14. The actors and roles referred to are: Garrick as Othello, Susanna Cibber as Monimia in *The Orphan or The Unhappy Marriage*, Hannah Pritchard as Beatrice in *As you Like it*, and Peg Woffington as Harry Wildair in *The Constant Couple*. For Freeman, the 'art of "pointing"' consists of 'of bracketing off a set speech ... and directing that speech, along with a set of gestures, at the audience'. Freeman, *Character's Theater*, p. 31.

[46] On Garrick's practice, see Stern, *Rehearsal from Shakespeare to Sheridan*, p. 163. Elsewhere Stern discusses multiple examples of the practice of striking fixed attitudes and notes its instructive value.

If a role passed from one principal player to another, audiences looked to the new incumbent to duplicate every 'stroke'. In period parlance, a 'stroke' was a trick, as in the title to the comedy, *A Bold Stroke for a Wife*; used in relation to actors, a stroke was a stage mannerism with which a player stamped a part. Celebrated players would sometimes drill their protégées in their own strokes,[47] as Clive did when training Jane Pope, or before her, Mary Edwards. In this way, principal players used their authority to perpetuate their stage legacies. The expectation of a quasi-mechanical reproduction of a benchmark interpretation militated against innovation, or even improvement. Apothecary, would-be actor, and sometime theatre critic John Hill claimed that 'the only way to please the greater part' of the audience was 'to copy ... [the] faults' of the 'player ... to have last perform'd the same character with success'.[48] Because Clive primarily led not only new productions, but also new genres of stage work, she was unusually free to be 'Original in spirit', as Churchill described, crafting personifications to her own strengths. She then fiercely guarded these roles and passed some of them publicly onto Edwards and Pope, who tried without lasting success to duplicate her performances. In this way Clive, who throughout her career cultivated originality, embraced a system which denied it to her protégées.

In contrast to the insouciance Clive enacted on stage, offstage she cultivated the image of a woman beyond reproach.[49] Many of the period's onstage practices – of speech, song, dress, dance, and physical action – were rooted in sanctioned forms of conduct expressed as models thought proper to each

---

[47] Stern, *Rehearsal from Shakespeare to Sheridan*, pp. 260–66. Prior to the creation of early modern playhouse stars, court wits and theatre professionals trained up principals like Elizabeth Barry, the protégée of John Wilmot, Earl of Rochester, 'in essentially puppet-fashion'. *Ibid.*, p. 156.

[48] [John Hill], *The Actor: A Treatise on the Art of Playing. Interspersed with Theatrical Anecdotes* (London, 1750), pp. 178–9. This treatise was mostly a plagiarized translation of Pierre Rémond de Sainte-Albine's *Le Comédien* (Paris, 1747) that Hill passed off as his own. In 1755 he revised and expanded the treatise as *The Actor: Or, a Treatise on the Art of Playing. A new Work, written by the Author of the former, and Adapted to the Present State of the Theatres*, and named its source. The 1750 translation varies only slightly from the original, but the 1755 version is thought to 'stand as an original work'. Joseph Roach, *The Player's Passion: Studies in the Science of Acting* (Newark, 1985), p. 101; cited in Goring, 'The Art of Acting', *Rhetoric of Sensibility in Eighteenth-Century Culture*, p. 136, note 51. Earl Wasserman compares Hill's 1750 with his 1755 treatise in Earl R. Wasserman, 'The Sympathetic Imagination in Eighteenth-Century Theories of Acting', *The Journal of English and Germanic Philology*, vol. 46 (1947), pp. 264–72. John Hill is identified as an apothecary during his row in 1739 with manager John Rich, whom he accused of stealing his wordbook, for instance, in *Mr. Rich's Answer to the many Falsities and Calumnies advanced by Mr. John Hill, Apothecary* (London, 1739). See Chapter 5, p. 141 and note 8.

[49] Kimberly Crouch notes that 'Clive, circumspect in sexual matters, used chastity as an indicator of the social acceptability'. Kimberly Crouch, 'Attitudes towards Actresses in Eighteenth-Century Britain' (PhD diss., Univ. of Oxford, 1995), p. 277; for her general comments about Clive see *ibid.*, pp. 198–227.

sex.[50] The 1765 pamphlet *A Critical Balance of the Performers* rates playhouse principals according to standards of etiquette: 'Figure', 'Grace', 'Spirit *and* Ease', 'Dignity [and] Manners', 'Elocution [and] Voice', 'Dress'.[51] Striking performances of decorum on stage would sometimes be imitated by women in polite society, who, as Nussbaum observes, adorned their assemblies with stage stars whose dress fashions they copied.[52] By 1788 the custom led Richard Kimberley to protest: 'I revolt with indignation from the idea of a lady of fashion being trammelled in the trickery of the stage, and taught her airs and graces, till she is made the mere *fac-simile* of a mannerist, where the most she can aspire to is to be the copy of a copyist.'[53] Participating in this exchange of manners, Clive flagged her membership of polite circles by dressing as a Woman of Quality even in low-style roles.[54]

The business of being a well-bred woman conflicted with that of being a stage player. Guidance in treatises for those aspiring to politeness typically recommended a woman's exclusion from public and professional life, her dedication to running a household, her education only in the womanly pursuits thought to enhance home life, and her acknowledgement of the innate superiority of men.[55] By contrast, the female playhouse principal was a trained

---

[50] The means by which gender is defined by and produced for a community vary widely. For my understanding of this process within Georgian London's entertainment industry I am indebted to many scholars, including John Brewer, Elizabeth Eger, Elizabeth Howe, Vivien Jones, Jane Moody, Daniel O'Quinn, Gill Perry, Angela Smallwood, Kristina Straub, and Cheryl Wanko.

[51] *A Critical Balance of the Performers at Drury-Lane Theatre. For the last Season 1765* (London, 1765) (broadsheet). A less detailed list rates actors according to four categories (Genius, Judgment, Vis Comica, Variety). It was issued in *The Theatrical Review: For the Year of 1757, and Beginning of 1758* (London, 1758), p. 46.

[52] 'Influential patronage was often exchanged for glamorous clothing and fashion expertise.' Nussbaum, *Rival Queens*, p. 147.

[53] [Richard Cumberland], *The Observer: Being a Collection of Moral, Literary and familiar Essays*, vol. 4 (London, 1788), p. 288. Already in 1725, Horace Walpole is said to have complained – though this may be apocryphal, being from a nineteenth-century report – that 'the *young* ... adopted ... as a fashion' Cuzzoni's '*brown silk gown*, trimmed with silver', which he found vulgar and 'indecorous'. Allatson Burgh, *Anecdotes of Music, Historical and Biographical: In a Series of Letters from a Gentleman to his Daughter*, vol. 3 (London, 1814), p. 51; cited in Donald Burrows et al., ed., *George Frideric Handel Collected Documents: Volume 1 1609–1725* (Cambridge, 2013), p. 752.

[54] Crouch, 'Attitudes towards Actresses in Eighteenth-Century Britain', pp. 71, 159, 220–27. Crouch meticulously investigates the means by which Clive safeguarded her reputation after 1745 – through friendships, press reports, and epilogues. Complementing Crouch's findings, I look particularly at the reputation constructed by and for Clive before that date.

[55] To quote Vivien Jones: 'The concern of all eighteenth-century "conduct" manuals for women is how women might create themselves as objects of male desire, but in terms which will contain that desire within the publicly sanctioned form of marriage.' Vivien Jones, ed., *Women in the Eighteenth Century: Constructions of Femininity* (London, 1990), p. 14. A collation of treatises prescribing and challenging models of female

professional – rare at this time for a woman – whose prodigious gifts could secure her earnings to rival those of her male colleagues.

Tension between the female player's conduct and what was expected from a woman of breeding whet public appetite for news about actresses. Female principals were the subject of gossip, portraits, ephemera, scores ('as sung by'), fake memoirs, and memoir-like commentary that fed audience desire to know more about them. Reports about female principals are often libellous, falsified, or unfalsifiable.[56] Chetwood contributes a cautionary tale about how a woman's reputation could ruin her credibility as a player. Recommending that performers … 'be as blameless as human Nature will allow', he recalls an episode when cognitive dissonance between an actress's putatively louche behaviour and her lines as Cordelia in *King Lear* – 'Arm'd in my Virgin Innocence I'll fly' – provoked 'a Horse-laugh' from the audience that turned 'the Scene of generous Pity … to Ridicule.'[57] Yet prurient curiosity could also aid a female principal, as in the case of Peg Woffington, whose stardom owed much to her flouting of conventions both onstage and off.[58]

Unlike Woffington, Clive chose to project a blameless personal life from the start of her career. By 1733, five years after her stage debut, she had earned the soubriquet 'Miss Prudely Crotchet' in recognition of her musicianship and proud chastity. This stood at odds with the racy characters and epilogue speakers she routinely enacted on stage. From 1733 onwards authors lauded her as an exemplary daughter and wife, despite Clive reportedly having separated

---

sexuality, together with a selected modern bibliography, are reprinted in Jones's collections. A helpful overview of proscriptive seventeenth- and early eighteenth-century literature on female conduct is found in Ingrid H. Tague, *Women of Quality: Accepting and Contesting Ideals of Femininity in England* (Woodbridge, 2002); see especially 'Modesty, Chastity and Feminine Conduct in the Early Eighteenth Century', pp. 30–48. Tague compares didactic writings to correspondence among Women of Quality who, while sometimes circumventing restrictions, thanks to their rank, perpetuated social regulation as a means to demarcate rank; in Tague's words, 'Chastity was, as always, a primary concern.' *Ibid.*, p. 47. The interplay between iconography, conduct manuals, and proper female embodiment of musical performance is the subject of Richard Leppert, *Music and Image: Domesticity, Ideology and Socio-Cultural Formation in Eighteenth-Century England* (Cambridge, 1988).

[56] A primary medium of fabrication was the so-called memoir of the stage actress. In her pithy account of its narrative strategies, Wanko shows that the memoir 'assumes a Foucauldian circularity, as the celebrity develops into someone whom the spectator aspires to emulate and mutual "controlling" mechanisms result'. Cheryl Wanko, *Roles of Authority: Thespian Biography and Celebrity in Eighteenth-Century Britain* (Lubbock, 2003), p. 13.

[57] Chetwood, *A General History of the Stage*, p. 28. Discussing this same passage, Freeman concludes that audiences conflated the actress's 'publicly acted' with her 'privately lived' character. Freeman, *Character's Theater*, pp. 38–41.

[58] Nussbaum, 'The Actress, Travesty, and Nation: Margaret Woffington', *Rival Queens*, pp. 189–225, and 'The Nation in Breeches: Actress Margaret Woffington', *"The Stage's Glory": John Rich, 1692–1761*, ed. B. Joncus and J. Barlow (Newark, 2011), pp. 211–22.

from George Clive soon after their marriage. I have concluded that George and Catherine Clive in fact only pretended to be married, and that the fiction of their union may have been known to some of her peers. Whether or not this was the case, becoming 'Mrs. Clive' was an important step forward for Kitty Raftor.

The Self Staged: In propria persona

Given the glaring artifice of eighteenth-century playhouse entertainments, the star herself may well have been, as Nussbaum argues, the most credible representation on stage.[59] Clive exploited this, highlighting the artifice of her roles to make her own self seem more genuine. Physical proximity, particularly when the player stood on the forestage, encouraged a sense of intimacy between audience and star. Practices of spectatorship allowed free exchanges between players and audiences; there are for instance documented incidents of players bowing to specific patrons, and of monologues being repeated at the insistence of audience members.[60]

As both agent and commodity, a principal player like Clive participated actively in producing herself, using liminal moments in the entertainment to reveal her putatively true nature. Prologues and epilogues were among Clive's most important points, providing opportunity for her 'real' and fictional characters to meld and separate.[61] Her speeches were of course written by another, often the author of the work performed. Prologues and epilogues also had to comply with good form. Prologues were typically reserved for men, and epilogues for women. At licensed playhouses, they were usually spoken by a star, sometimes from outside the production's cast. Much less frequently a new company member might, as a novelty, be designated to speak.[62] Prologues,

---

[59] 'Brilliant actresses such as Oldfield, Clive, Woffington, and Abington pre-figured a modern subjectivity, a commoditized version of the self that they offered to consumers as an *effect* of an interiority that encapsulated and ascribed a certain value to be exchanged in the theatrical marketplace.' Nussbaum, 'Introduction: At Stage's Edge', *Rival Queens*, p. 21.

[60] The attendees of the middle gallery were charged with 'frequent and injudicious interruption of the business of the play by their applause', *The Connoisseur*, no. 43 (21 November 1754); quoted in Pedicord, *The Theatrical Public*, p. 58. Regular authors of *The Connoisseur* were Bonnell Thornton, William Cowper, Robert Lloyd and George Colman the elder. Pedicord in general defends the behaviour of mid-eighteenth-century playhouse audiences. Stern documents multiple instances of actors ad-libbing to please audiences; see Stern, *Rehearsal from Shakespeare to Sheridan*, pp. 101–5, 183–85, 232–33. For Bolton, interactivity between players and audience – which after 1750 included so-called 'spouting clubs', and enthusiasts' imitation of favourite actors' prologues and epilogues – has a parallel in the 'cultural convergence and overflow' described by present-day media theorists. Bolton, 'Theorizing Audience and Spectatorial Agency', p. 33.

[61] Nussbaum, 'Introduction: At Stage's Edge', *Rival Queens*, pp. 18–22.

[62] Mary E. Knapp, 'Speakers', *Prologues and Epilogues of the Eighteenth Century* (New Haven, 1961), pp. 34–81. As she notes: 'A minor actor might make a name for himself by his skill ... but in general only the great actors were allowed to speak.' *Ibid.*, p. 36.

spoken between the band's second and third 'music' (overtures), introduced the play's subjects and aims; epilogues, spoken immediately after the play, summed up the action and sued for audience approval.[63] In epilogues, the player spoke as her reputed self and also, if a cast member, as the fictional character she had just been enacting; her monologue was typically designed to conflate the two. Limited usually to the early part of a new production's run,[64] prologues and epilogues were a powerful draw for audiences, who occasionally insisted on hearing them again and were known to riot if they were omitted from performance.[65] To speak these texts well was, according to Chetwood, the height of the player's art: 'Prologues and Epilogues are the most difficult Tasks of both Sexes on the Stage, it is to be remark'd, but few, besides the capital Performers, are trusted with them; and a good Prologue and Epilogue have often help'd a bad Play out of the Mire, or, at least, sent the Audience home a little better humour'd.'[66] Richard Cumberland, writing decades later, saw prologues and epilogues as 'vehicles of humiliation at the introduction of a new play, and traps for false wit, extravagant conceits and female flippancy at the conclusion of it'.[67]

A prologue, due to its function, typically divulged less about its speaker than the epilogue.[68] Though pretending to first-person address, an epilogue was structured less as a window into the player's thoughts and more as a monologue on a subject prescribed by tradition, and created according to line. For an eighteenth-century female player, typical epilogue topics were patriotism, women's rights, playwrights' weaknesses, the rules of drama, and the

---

[63] Knapp, 'Presentation', *Prologues and Epilogues of the Eighteenth Century*, pp. 82–85.
[64] Discussing the function of prologues and epilogues, Knapp and Pierre Danchin link them to the opening of a run. See Knapp, 'Presentation', *Prologues and Epilogues of the Eighteenth Century*, pp. 5–6; Pierre Danchin, 'Introduction', *The Prologues and Epilogues of the Eighteenth Century: A Complete Edition* (Nancy, 1990), p. xv. There is, however, some 'debate whether whether epilogues (and prologues) were performed during the first performance only, during the first three performances, or throughout the play's entire first run; but scholars agree that revivals generally did not feature the initial paratexts.' Diana Solomon, 'Tragic Play, Bawdy Epilogue?', *Prologues, Epilogues, Curtain-Raisers, and Afterpieces: The Rest of the Eighteenth-Century London Stage*, ed. D. J. Ennis and J. Bailey Slagle (Newark, 2007), p. 172, note 18.
[65] Knapp, 'Popular Demand for Prologues and Epilogues', *Prologues and Epilogues of the Eighteenth Century*, pp. 1–33.
[66] Chetwood, *A General History of the Stage*, p. 254.
[67] [Cumberland], 'Remarks upon the Present Taste for Acting Private Plays', *The Observer*, vol. 4 (London, 1788), p. 287; cited also in Janine M. Haugen, 'The Mimic Stage: Private Theatricals in Georgian Britain' (PhD diss., Univ. of Colorado, 2014), pp. 73–74.
[68] Knapp, Holland and Solomon discuss epilogues that, for audience delectation, include seeming personal information about either the speaker or her fellow actors. See, for instance, Knapp, *Prologues and Epilogues of the Eighteenth Century*, pp. 42–85, Holland, *The Ornament of Action*, pp. 65–80, and, on Nell Gwynn, Solomon, 'Tragic Play, Bawdy Epilogue?', pp. 155–78. Solomon notes that the 'bawdy epilogue originated from the deliberate merger of the actress's character and public persona'. *Ibid.*, p. 156.

didactic value of the work just seen.[69] Because standardized, yet seemingly personalized, epilogues illustrate particularly well the contradictions inherent to playhouse star production. By cleaving to convention, the epilogue reinforced tradition; by being a platform for self-representation, it invited the player to challenge tradition in novel ways. In epilogues, a real-life performer ghosted behind a construction of self, articulating views she possibly, but not necessarily, held. Typically spoken 'in character', epilogues were efficient carriers for the 'poignant antimonies' that Joseph Roach identifies as vital to stars and stardom.[70] Stars, in Roach's view, distinguish themselves from ordinary actors by embodying seemingly opposed qualities, thereby generating a social apartness, or 'It' effect, which fans cannot penetrate.[71] Within this central conundrum, publicity then nests other oppositions, most notably the apparent intimacy but actual distance created by reproduced images of the star.[72]

In Clive's case, epilogues were moments of both risk and empowerment: while the eroticism of her early epilogues imperilled the blameless reputation she cultivated, her later epilogues allowed her to challenge the playwright's authority. Clive's epilogue characters were, as Mary Knapp has noted, as 'definite as those which she represented in the play itself',[73] and just as imposed. Neither Clive's outrageous stage action nor her defiant epilogues were necessarily taken as proof of what 'she' thought; rather, it was a teasing suggestion. That Clive was sometimes brought in for comic epilogues after tragedies bears witness to her ability to lift an audience's spirits, as well as to her top rank.

Her songs, like her epilogues, were summative points during which she proved herself 'unbiddable',[74] that is, self-confident and beyond influence,

---

[69] Danchin, 'Introduction', *The Prologues and Epilogues of the Eighteenth Century*, pp. xv–xxxiii. Surveying prologues and epilogues written from 1701 to 1720, Danchin notes the continuity between earlier and later prologues and epilogues. One may also sort many post-1720 prologues and epilogues into the four categories that he creates: 'patriotic or political manifestoes', 'competition of foreign performers', 'the "uselessness" of prologues and epilogues', and 'female revolt'. *Ibid*. The first and second categories are treated in Knapp, 'The Patriotic Prologue', *Prologues and Epilogues of the Eighteenth Century*, pp. 205–33.

[70] 'Introduction', Joseph Roach, *It* (Ann Arbor, 2007), pp. 1–44, esp. p. 11. Many of my readings are in dialogue with Roach's work.

[71] *Ibid.*, p. 4–11.

[72] On the ways that the proliferation of the star's image nourishes fandom, see, for instance, P. David Marshall, 'The System of Celebrity', *Celebrity and Power*, pp. 185–9, or John Ellis, 'Stars as Cinematic Phenomenon', *Stardom and Celebrity: A Reader*, pp. 90–97. The latter passage builds on Richard Dyer's theories. For Roach, the image is an 'effigy'; that is, a depiction rooted in, and animated by, assumed knowledge and viewer fantasy. To quote Roach, 'the consumer of celebrity icons does the work of creating the effigy in the physical absence of the beloved'. Roach, *It*, p. 40.

[73] Knapp, *Prologues and Epilogues of the Eighteenth Century*, p. 68. On Clive's epilogues, see *ibid.*, pp. 68–75.

[74] Socialite, writer and taste-broker of the 1920s Eleanor Glynn identified 'It' with being unbiddable, defining both as a state wherein the subject is 'entirely unselfconscious …

while also conforming to generic codes. She was familiar in song, speech and manner, yet remote as a goddess. She was vulnerable, yet imperious and defiant of men. She was inimitable, yet held to typify her sex, her nation, and her social position as one of the middling sort. Her transgressive conduct was a stage draw, even as she herself was thought virtuous. A wealth of portraits – in oil, print, watercolour, chalk drawing, and porcelain – adorned private spaces with likenesses of an indecipherable Clive.

It was not, however, Clive's body which fascinated audiences, but her voice. Among female stage stars of her era, she stood apart for not selling herself as a sex object; through voice, she escaped the constraints of her physical self. Voice allowed Clive, as Drury Lane's first songster, to move freely between high and low genres, between ideal English elocution and mimicry of Italian accents, between personifying herself and playing someone else. Her allure lay in hiding yet baring herself, and testing this process by repeatedly switching identities. Her mimicry, being the opposite of 'her', was evidence of her personal immutability. Her rectitude was credible because she did not pretend to appeal to the male gaze. A plain woman with an indomitable voice, Clive never had lovers that we know of – although her male promoters put out that she wanted them. Music distinguished Clive from other players, whether her song was part of the work staged or an independent interlude. In ballad opera, her song was often didactic, articulating the lessons a viewer was meant to draw from the stage action. Clive typically addressed audiences directly in her airs, which strengthened her authority. During these parenthetical moments she could bind together contradictory traits – coldness and tenderness, intelligence and stupidity, candour and cupidity – to generate tension, without owning either extreme.

The stage genres in which Clive specialized, low-style ballad opera and high-style masque, were themselves contradictory. Her ballad opera songs were points minted from 'common' tunes derived chiefly from playhouse entertainments, dance collections, and Thomas D'Urfey's song collections.[75] Because familiar to audiences, these tunes were easily recalled and usually carried a host of associations. While playwrights such as Gay or Fielding typically selected a melody, and its associations, to heighten satire,[76] players like Clive or Lavinia Fenton – the first Polly in Gay's *Beggar's Opera* – could spin a melody, and its associations, to dress their own natures to advantage.[77]

---

full of self-confidence, indifferent to the effect he or she is producing, and uninfluenced by others'. Roach, *It*, p. 4.

[75] Joncus, 'Ballad Opera', pp. 34–38.
[76] On Gay's strategies for choosing common tunes, see Dianne Dugaw, *Deep Play: John Gay and the Invention of Modernity* (Newark, 2001).
[77] Berta Joncus, '"The Assemblage of every female Folly": Lavinia Fenton, Kitty Clive and the Genesis of Ballad Opera', *Women of Fashion: Popular Culture in the Eighteenth Century and the Eighteenth Century in Popular Culture*, ed. T. Potter (Toronto, 2012), pp. 25–51; Berta Joncus, '"A Likeness where none was to be found": Imagining Kitty Clive (1711–1785)', *Music in Art*, vol. 34 (2009), pp. 89–106.

Ballad opera followed Restoration and post-Restoration mainpiece comedy in using song to stop action and ask audiences to reflect on a moral.[78] Clive appeared in mainpiece comedy revivals far less frequently than she did in ballad operas, but could realize more cultural capital from them because their songs tended to be newly composed and fit to her line, while those in ballad operas were common tunes, often of smutty renown. A new song for Clive would add lustre to any revived mainpiece she led.

Clive's high-style masque repertory was a more substantial foil to her ballad opera roles. From 1728 until 1740 her ownership of masque parts, shown in Appendix 2, rivalled that of her ballad opera parts. Stage masque was loosely related to the ritualistic masque of sixteenth- and seventeenth-century English courts. A masque could be either a stand-alone work, or part of a revived seventeenth-century drama, or a series of scenes which alternated with harlequinade in a pantomime.[79] Independent stage masques were mounted for royal celebrations and 'commanded' by their honourees, whose playhouse visits constituted their own spectacle.[80] Far more frequent in Clive's repertory were masques embedded within pantomime. Regardless of the context within which it was presented, a masque's music married the 'English Tongue' to 'the Excellencies of the Italian [operatic] Composition'[81] – while its scenes, machines, decorations, choruses, and choreographies drew on French court traditions to create dazzling spectacle. So for instance into the story of *Cephalus and Procris*, led by Clive as Procris, were shoehorned dances, choruses, ascents by chariot, Neptune's Temple rising 'out of the Sea', and 'a fine Hunting Country [scene] … painted by Tilemans of Antwerp'.[82] Clive's high-style song

[78] Dianne Dugaw, '"Critical Instants": Theatre Songs in the Age of Dryden and Purcell', *Eighteenth-Century Studies*, vol. 23 (1989), p. 175. Curtis Price categorizes Restoration theatre music according to interpolative types ('Melancholy Music', 'Music for Discoveries', 'Music for Love Scenes', etc.). Curtis Price, *Music in the Restoration Theatre* (London, 1979), pp. 1–67.

[79] Michael Burden, 'The British Masque 1690–1800' (PhD diss., Univ. of Edinburgh, 1993), pp. 1–63; Michael Burden, 'The Independent Masque 1700–1800: A Catalogue', *Royal Musical Association Research Chronicle*, vol. 28 (1995), pp. 59–62; and Michael Burden, 'Britannia versus Virtue in the Harmony of the Spheres: Directions of Masque Writing in the Eighteenth Century', *Miscellanea musicologica*, vol. 17 (1990), pp. 78–86. See also Chapter 2, p. 57 and note 130.

[80] 'The doors of the theatres were opened at were opened at 5.0[o] pm … Some time after 5.30 the royal carriage arrived at a private entrance near the stage door, and a proprietor greeted the notables with a candelabrum with which he lighted the King and Queen to the royal box ante-room at pit level … At his Majesty's first appearance from the ante-room the entire audience rose and applauded, as the King bowed to the assembled spectators. Then followed the entrance of the Queen and the rest of the Royal Family, bowing to the King and then to the house. After this brief ceremony the play commenced.' Pedicord, *"By Their Majesties' Command"*, p. x.

[81] Colley Cibber, 'The Preface', *Venus and Adonis: A Masque* (London, 1736), pp. iv–v.

[82] *Cephalus and Procris. A Dramatic Masque. With a Pantomime Interlude, call'd, Harlequin Grand Volgi* (London, 1733), pp. 13, 18.

in such works will have made her seem as remote as her low-style music in ballad operas made her seem familiar.

Until 1745 Clive also routinely sang during interludes. These performances helped established her signature tunes, such as 'Life of a Beau', which then migrated into Clive's spoken parts. Like Italian singers with their 'baggage arias', Clive was apparently able to choose when to perform her signature tunes. This liberty is suggested by what she sang, not least when in 1746 she was able to replace Thomas Arne's new songs in *The Tempest* for her with those by Willem De Fesch.[83] A signature song, once removed from its original production, flagged up its singer even more than when first performed. When Clive executed 'Life of a Beau', written by her friend and singing teacher Henry Carey, she was clearly performing 'Clive' rather than a dramatis persona. 'Life of a Beau' was in fact pure Clive product, having been created for her to sing *in propria persona* in James Miller's *The Coffee House* (1738).

The signature song and the *in propria persona* vehicle were just two of a range of eighteenth-stage practices – among them the benefit performance, the play about theatrical politics, the practice of *ad hominem* mimicry – which mainly served the production of stars, whose rank, character, taste, sympathies, off-stage antics, professional strengths and weaknesses, and social and professional networks were monitored, probed in the press, and sometimes staged. Such practices and entertainments were not so much reflections of stars as the means for making and monetizing them. Playhouse personae were continually being constructed, challenged and re-assembled on the boards, in the press, and in the minds of audience members. The star's challenge of continually constructing the self was moreover shared by members of polite society, who had constantly to negotiate between private desire and publicly approved behaviour.

Representation Offstage and On: Simulation and Authority

Although Clive could project herself from the stage, she had very little control over how she was represented outside the playhouse. Her first 'portrait', mentioned at the start of this chapter, evidences her vulnerability to misrepresentation: rather than being her likeness, it was an erotic nymph lifted from a seventeenth-century Dutch oil painting. One of this book's major concerns is to challenge how Clive has been transmitted through scores, wordbooks, press commentary, and her own writings, as well as through pictures. I intend to explore conventions, identify Clive's contributions, correct false attributions, investigate rips in received narrative surfaces, and speculate about the agendas informing her various representations. Throughout, I aim to illuminate the processes of star production, and her agency within them.

---

[83] I discuss this incident in Chapter 10, pp. 313–15.

Clive's portraits were perhaps the most potent way for audience members to recall her. Images are of course vital to the industry of stardom, and in the eighteenth century portraiture was a lodestone for writers about the theatre, as both object and metaphor. Actor-manager Colley Cibber, in his memoirs, describes the failure of an actor to copy a pioneering interpretation as an act of disfigurement akin to 'a Child's Painting upon the Face of a *Metzo-tinto*'.[84] Extending Cibber's metaphor, Clive's composite 'portrait' might be thought to consist not just of images of her, but also of written depictions by memoirists, theorists, puffers, and satirists.

The popular press, to which Clive occasionally contributed, both advanced Clive's interests and threatened them. From 1732 onwards her meteoric ascent grabbed the attention of connoisseurs and those parading as such, like John Hill. Rather than acknowledge Clive's talent, Hill explained away her success as the consequence of an overlap between the 'kinds of temper' evoked in her roles, and her own nature; no comedian, he asserted, 'ever acted a part well, who was not in some degree, of the same turn in his own mind'.[85] Hill's invention of this seemingly empirical law, and his denial of Clive's agency, were moves typical of eighteenth-century treatise writers. His observations, at first mostly plagiarized in 1750 from a French treatise and only in 1755 updated with substantial comments about London players, often provide more insight into the prejudices of their author, and his desire to be an arbiter of taste, than into what happened on stage.[86]

No less biased than the connoisseur was the puffer, whose task was to promote works – often without seeming to. Writing in *The Grub-street Journal* in 1737, 'Puffemofius' sorted puffs into five categories: 'material' (brief announcements), 'formal' (reports clearly favouring a production), 'direct' (seeming news items which then slip into praise), 'oblique' (seeming news items concluding with a strong endorsement), and 'circular' (seeming news items which

---

[84] Colly Cibber, *An Apology for the Life of Mr. Colley Cibber*, 2nd edn (London, 1740), p. 247. In this passage, Cibber denigrated his rival, the 'famous Mimick' Thomas Escourt, who for his London debut re-invented the title role in John Dryden's *The Spanish Friar* immortalized by Tony Leigh. According to Cibber, although Escourt 'remembered every Look and Motion of the late Tony Leigh, so far as to put the Spectator very much in mind of him ... the true Spirit ... was not the same, but unskilfully dawb'd on, like a Child's Painting upon the Face of a *Metzo-tinto*: It was too plain to the judicious, that the Conception was not his own, but imprinted in his Memory, by another, of whom he only presented a dead Likeness.' *Ibid.*, pp. 246–47.

[85] [Hill], *The Actor* (1755), pp. 174, 176.

[86] Bias in writings about the theatre is the subject of Robert Schoch, *Writing the History of the British Stage: 1660–1900* (Cambridge, 2016). Schoch treats mid-eighteenth century theatre writings mainly in his fourth chapter, identifying the volumes that established the viewpoint of the 'theatrical insider': Downes' *Roscius Anglicanus* (1708), Charles Gildon's *Life of Betterton* (1710), Colley Cibber's *An Apology for the Life of Mr. Colley Cibber* (1740), William Oldys's *Biographia Britannica* (1747), and Thomas Davies' *Dramatic Miscellanies* (1747).

hide the puffing altogether). In his summary he equates these announcements with flatulence ('crepitative puffs') and burping ('eructative puff[s]')[87]. Another article, 'On the Modern Art and Mystery of Puffing' likewise warns readers of the 'inextricable labyrinth of PUFFING'.[88] Like treatises, puffs tend to tell us more about strategies than they do about events, and I interpret all such testimony about Clive in this light.

Examination of creative practice grants us more immediate access to what might have taken place on stage. If, as Peter Holland claims, the modern study of past theatre is flawed in its preoccupation with the 'visual rather than the aural',[89] this would help account for the elusiveness to scholars of Clive's appeal, which lay in the performance of music and stage speech. Clive's musicianship was part of what made her as prized as an actress as she was as a singer. Just as stage appearance in the eighteenth century was measured against a painted ideal,[90] so was the actor's voice measured against the sounded ideal of high-style music.

Period stage critics routinely compared speech to high-style music, focusing on four components: tempo, timbre, rhythm, and melody. Critics tended to analyze the tempo of stage speech simplistically, recommending a slow rate in tragedy and a quick one in comedy. Affective weight bred this split: tragedy, with its 'sorrow, grief, pain, &c' required 'a voice slow, solemn and affecting, like the melancholy plaintive notes of an Adagio'; by contrast, the 'proper

[87] Puffemoffius, 'A Short Dissertation on Puffs', *Grub-street Journal*, issue 285 (12 June 1735) and Puffemoffius, 'A Short Dissertation on Puffs [part 2]', *Grub-street Journal*, issue 286 (19 June 1735).

[88] [Bonnell Thornton], 'On the Modern Art and Mystery of Puffing' (annotation in MS 'April 13, 1752'), *Have at you all: Or, the Drury-Lane Journal. By Madam Roxana Termagant* (London, 1752), p. 270.

[89] Peter Holland, 'Hearing the Dead: The Sound of David Garrick', *Players, Playwrights, Playhouses: Investigating Performance, 1660–1800*, ed. M. Cordner and P. Holland (Basingstoke, 2007), p. 249. Drawing on testimony from present-day actors and historical testimony about elocution – including Joshua Steele's 'exact' representation of Garrick's voice as he spoke Hamlet's monologue 'To be, or not to be' – Holland analyses conflicting accounts of pauses, accents and the speed of Garrick's tragic stage speech. He concludes that while the historian's grasp of vocal inflection is necessarily imprecise, such study is requisite to appreciate Garrick's artistry. *Ibid.*, 248. This view is taken up by Judith Pascoe in her study of Sarah Siddons' speaking voice. For Pascoe, how 'Sarah Siddons sounded was what made her seem so staggeringly original'. *The Sarah Siddons Audio Files: Romanticism and the Lost Voice* (Ann Arbor, 2014), p. 109. Pascoe believes that Siddons' aural impact cannot be understood today because not recorded, and that Siddons' audiences longed for such aural permanence.

[90] Actors followed a lexicon of gestural representation, famously illustrated by Charles Le Brun and based on history painting, to optimize declamation and affective expression. Foundational studies of this stagecraft include Roach, *The Player's Passion*; West, *The Image of the Actor*; Holland, *The Ornament of Action*; and Dean Barnett and Jeanette Massy-Westropp, *The Art of Gesture: the Practice and Principles of Eighteenth-Century Acting* (Heidelberg, 1987). For a useful summary of this acting legacy, see Goring, 'The Art of Acting', *Rhetoric of Sensibility in Eighteenth-Century Culture*, pp. 114–41.

execution ... [of] Joy and Pleasure', those 'marks of Comedy', called for speaking at a tempo of 'Spirituoso, or chearful vivacity'.[91] Timbre was an aspect over which the player was held to have no control: certain musical instruments, which the actor's 'pipe' either did or did not match, were thought optimal for exciting certain passions. For instance, in 1752 Bonnell Thornton praised Susannah Cibber, London's top tragedienne, for having a 'soft easy pipe' with the 'mellowness of a GERMAN FLUTE [transverse flute] ... whose sounds are adapted to the languishings of love ... exctatic mildness ... [and] wild fury of extravagant Despair'.[92] In 1759 Samuel Derrick reasoned that an actor 'whose voice has all the roughness of a base-viol' or the 'rougher tones of a bassoon' was ill-suited to love scenes, because 'Love in general requires a soft, alluring, and melodious voice'.[93] Thornton likened Garrick's voice, in its expressive range, to a 'double-key'd [two-manual] HARPSICHORD struck by the nice finger of an HANDEL' which could sound '[a]ll the powers of harmony' by virtue of being a 'various and delightful instrument'.[94] Garrick and Clive in particular became known for commanding instruments whose timbres they could change to suit their presentations.

On stage speech's proper rhythm and melody, one of the clearest writers was the politician John Burgh, an early advocate of free speech and universal suffrage. *The Art of Speaking* (1761), which he wrote to educate common readers in public address,[95] specifies and summarizes practices a speaker should follow. For the rhythms of free stage speech – as opposed to verse, whose metre would determine the rhythm – he advocates maintaining a basic pulse, just as a musician would follow a time signature's meter. When encountering punctuation, the speaker should count the pause, as would a musician a notated rest, with discretionary flexibility. 'The common rule', says Burgh, 'for holding [stops] out to their just length, is too exact for *practice*, viz. that a comma is to be held the length of a syllable, a semicolon of two, a colon of three, and a

---

[91] [Samuel Derrick], *A General View of the Stage. By Mr. Wilkes* (London and Dublin, 1759), p. 111. Thornton thought the variety that Hannah Pritchard brought to the placement and timing of rests made her superior to Susannah Cibber, whose repetitiveness in this regard dulled her declamation: 'I could wish indeed Mrs. CIBBER's stops were regulated with the judgment of a PRITCHARD, that we might not be so often tir'd with a constant and unalter'd monotony. [Thornton], *Have at you all*, p. 89.

[92] [Thornton], *Have at you all*, p. 89.

[93] [Derrick], *A General View of the Stage*, p. 111.

[94] [Thornton], *Have at you all*, pp. 87–88; likewise, Thornton equated the 'rich music' and 'harmonious utterance[s]' of George Ann Bellamy with a curious blend of the 'softness of the FLAGELLET, the mellowness of the [traverse] FLUTE, and the fullness of the HAUTBOY'. *Ibid.*, p. 90.

[95] [John Burgh], *The Art of Speaking. Containing I. An Essay; in which are given Rules for expressing properly the principal Passions and Humours, which occur in Reading, or public Speaking; and II. Lessons taken from the Antients and Moderns (with Additions and Alterations, where thought useful) exhibiting a Variety of Matter for Practice; the emphatical Words printed in Italics; with Notes of Direction referring to the Essay* (London, 1761).

period of four.' When Burgh recommends that speakers deviate or add pauses 'to render the *sense clear*' or 'shew ... beauty',[96] he could almost be coaching musicians.

It was in melody that the so-called 'natural' school of acting – a new method pioneered from 1733 by theatre impresario Aaron Hill[97] – broke most decisively from pre-existing stage practice. Characteristic of old-style acting were rant (angry pronunciation), cant (whining or loving pronunciation), and declamation or 'tone' (cadenced, intoned pronunciation).[98] Burgh, an exponent of 'natural' acting, likens all these old-style modes to 'psalmody and ballad in music, a strain consisting of a few notes *rising* and *falling* without variation, like a peal of bells, let the *matter* change how it will'.[99] He criticizes cant as 'chaunt, with which the prose psalms are half-sung, half-said, in cathedrals'.[100] For Burgh, '*canting, whining, drawling* or [an] *un-animated* manner'[101] is simply a '*uniform* humming sound', in place of which he commends the '*natural* inflections of voice'.[102]

In Burgh's view, an actor worth emulating brings out, in accordance with the action, a word's inherent melody. Like cant and its cousins, such elocution is a musical speech; but unlike cant, it generates variety. Practices borrowed from high-style song provide this variety. Burgh's practice for delivering a parenthetical phrase parallels how a musician typically marks a main theme and its return: he recommends that the stage player speak 'with a *lower* voice, and *quicker* than the rest, and with a short *stop* at the beginning, and end; that the hearer may perceive where the strain ... *breaks off*, and where it is *resumed*'.[103] Cadential resolutions – generated by either lowering or raising vocal pitch at the end of a sentence – separate one idea from another. Phrases shaped by a '*stronger* accent' highlight crucial words.[104] Burgh even tells speakers to select a home key, and be ready to apply dynamics:

---

[96] [Burgh], *The Art of Speaking*, p. 8.
[97] 'The informal advice Hill had offered the Drury Lane actors in autumn 1733 began to expand into what he himself described as his "system" of acting – a system which he developed in a series of journal articles, letters, poems, and essays between 1733 and 1746. Hill was writing during the decade before Charles Macklin and David Garrick pioneered the new style of acting which was to take London audiences by storm.' Christine Gerrard, *Aaron Hill: The Muses' Projector, 1685–1750* (Oxford, 2003), p. 167. Aaron Hill was not related to John Hill.
[98] John Harold Wilson, 'Rant, Cant and Tone on the Restoration Stage', *Studies in Philology*, vol. 52 (1955), pp. 592–98; cited in Stern, *Rehearsal from Shakespeare to Sheridan*, p. 159.
[99] [Burgh], *The Art of Speaking*, p. 8.
[100] Ibid., p. 8.
[101] Ibid., p. 9.
[102] Ibid., p. 8.
[103] Ibid., p. 10.
[104] Ibid., p. 10.

> [The speaker's] *success* with his audience, depend[s] much upon his *setting out* in a proper *key*, and at a due pitch of *loudness*. If he begins in too *high* a tone, or sets out too *loud*, how is he afterwards to rise to a *higher note*, or swell his voice *louder*, as the more *pathetic* strains may require? The *command* of the voice, therefore in this respect, is to be studied very *early*.[105]

'The *command* of the voice' is precisely what Clive demonstrated throughout her career. Due to the Town fashion for ballad opera, she was trained primarily to lead such productions as a singer. This developed not just her vocal talents, but also her musical invention. She joined music and musical knowledge with her '*natural* inflections' to make her voice stand out from all others.

Conclusion: Imagining Kitty Clive

In the playhouse, entertainment and commerce met public reputation and social convention, often redirecting the business of the evening from its stated aims. Tragedy, despite the sublime heights it was said to reach, could be followed by a comic epilogue; farce pretending to instruct often served instead to titillate, or to invert standard pieties; pantomime juxtaposed antipodal serious and comic scenes. This confusion of modes and aims helped Clive to create unseemly stage characterizations yet seem respectable, and the Barthian 'grain' of her voice provided a means for her public to recognize her through all the diverse guises she assumed on stage.

Performing performance was a big part of what Clive did, thrilling spectators in part with the risk of failure. Among what Roach calls the 'suddenly reversible polarities' of stardom,[106] perhaps none is stronger than the twinned desire of audiences to worship idols and to smash them: the fan reveres the star, but delights in her fall.[107] The power and savagery of playhouse audiences impressed even the hardened stage professional Fielding: 'In the Theatre especially, a single Expression which doth not coincide with the Taste of the Audience, or with any individual Critic of that Audience, is sure to be hissed; and one Scene which should be disapproved, would hazard the whole Piece'.[108] Whether Clive would be idolized or reviled was tested night after night at Drury Lane. She could fail in either of two ways: by leaving the audience cold, or by delivering an unpersuasive performance of self. In either case, audience disenchantment would put in question her power to induce laughter, wonder, sympathy, and reflection; it would cast doubt on her inimitability; it would

---

[105] *Ibid.*, p. 12.
[106] Roach, *It*, p. 9.
[107] As Chris Rojek explains, star idolatry functions like worship within, and rejection of, a religion: the aura of the idolized first is perceived and then denied. See Chris Rojek, 'Celebrity and Religion', *Celebrity*, pp. 51–100.
[108] Fredson Bowers and Martin C. Battestin, ed., *Henry Fielding, The History of Tom Jones, a Foundling* (Oxford, 1974), p. 571.

lead audience members to question the authority they had given her. Kitty Clive had to justify her status as a star every time she stepped out on stage. As high as she soared, it was her potential to crash that made her a signal attraction.

On the battlefield of representation, Clive often surrendered what we might call her integrity. To advance in public favour, she pandered to ugly prejudices about women, Jews, Britons, foreigners, sexual orientation, and social rank. She contributed to press wars by stealth to avoid the opprobrium that female writers provoked. She was sometimes dishonest with her audiences while pretending to a disarming directness. When negative tattle imperilled her respectability, she turned it into stage entertainments. This last was perhaps Clive's deftest manoeuvre: by appointing herself the chief critic of Clive, she ultimately helped steer audience desire to witness her own failure.

Clive gave life to her parts so persuasively that they couldn't be successfully re-imagined in any other way. Her variety of line confounded easy synthesis, allowing each spectator to imagine her differently. Her success lay not in representing a stock type, but in using each type to alternately suggest and deny who she was. Her voice was her instrument, and commanding it, she commanded her audiences. This book explores how.

2

'The Lovely Virgin tun'd her Voice': Henry Carey and the Production of a Native Songster

Enter Catherine Raftor – Carey as composer and teacher – Clive's hybrid voice – pretty Polly Fenton swoops in – Colley Cibber tries to tame Town taste – the shepherdess 'Miss Rafter' – Phillida lingers, but Arethusa is cut down – from swains to gods, or traversing musical spheres – Procris prevails

When she auditioned for Drury Lane, Catherine Raftor reportedly bowled over veteran manager Colley Cibber. The audition took place some time before 13 April 1728, when she apparently debuted on stage. More than twenty years later, Drury Lane prompter William Chetwood would recall:

> Miss Raftor had a facetious Turn of Humour, and infinite Spirits, with a Voice and Manner in singing Songs of Pleasantry peculiar to herself. Those Talents Mr. Theo. Cibber and I (we all at that Time living together in one House) thought a sufficient Passport to the *Theatre*. We recommended her to the *Laureat* [Colley Cibber] … and the Moment he heard her sing, [he] put her down in the List of Performers at twenty Shillings *per* Week. But never any Person of her Age flew to Perfection with such Rapidity … like a Bullet in the Air, there was no distinguishing the Track, till it came to its utmost Execution.[1]

Chetwood's 1749 account is the earliest we have of Clive's career. A year later, in a theatre memoir for Dublin readers, Chetwood noted that 'her teacher in music was the luckless Henry Carey and we find her furnishing her talent to entertainments given for his benefit on several occasions'.[2] Chetwood's admiration of Clive tinges all his writings about her, and seems to have been shared

---

[1] Chetwood, 'Mrs. CATHARINE CLIVE (formerly Miss RAFTOR)', *A General History of the Stage*, p. 127.
[2] [William R. Chetwood], *The British Theatre: Containing the Lives of the English Dramatic poets … Together with the Lives of Most of the Principal Actors, as well as Poets* (Dublin, 1750); entry for Catharine Clive, cited in Joseph N. Gillespie, 'The Life and Work of Henry Carey (1687–1743)', vol. 1 (PhD diss., Univ. of London, 1982), p. 84. The Dublin version of this book that Gillespie quotes differs from the Dublin print digitized on *Eighteenth Century Collections Online*, which contains no entry for Clive.

by many of the Irishmen with whom she worked. By 1740 not only Chetwood, but also Charles Coffey and James Quin, had helped boost her career. Chetwood had ties to Kilkenny and was probably from there, like Clive's father.[3]

In early 1728, two people badly needed Clive employed at Drury Lane: Colley Cibber and Henry Carey. Drury Lane nominally had three managers, but Cibber had in fact been running the business since the early 1720s,[4] competing hard against his rival John Rich, the manager of London's only other licensed playhouse. In the autumn of 1727 Cibber had made a bad decision, rejecting *The Beggar's Opera* when John Gay offered it to him.[5] Gay had then taken his 'Opera' to Lincoln's Inn Fields, Rich's house, where from its debut on 29 January 1728 it made theatre history and an overnight star of its seventeen-year-old lead Lavinia Fenton. The notoriously stingy Cibber then hired his own seventeen-year-old soprano, Clive, paying her five shillings more than Fenton had reportedly earned.[6]

Chetwood tells us that Clive's first stage appearance was in the April 1728 revival of Nathaniel Lee's seventeenth-century tragedy *Mithridates*.[7] Dressed 'in Boy's Cloaths', Clive played a page whose sole function was to sing 'One

---

[3] Patrick J. Crean has studied the public records of Kilkenny and Wessex, tracing Clive's lineage back to the Rafters of Kilkenny. Clive's father practised law in New Ross, Wessex. Crean, 'The Life and Times of Kitty Clive', pp. 1–2. Evidence of Chetwood's links to Kilkenny lies in his poem, *Kilkenny: Or, the Old Man's Wish* (Dublin, Printed for the Author, 1748), where he records his youthful haunts. Ann Tierney, the honorary librarian of the Kilkenny Archaeological Society, Rothe House, Kilkenny, notes that 'William Chetwood seems to have spent some time in Kilkenny, judging by his remarks on St Canice's, published in his 1748 *Tour of Ireland*.' Ann Tierney, personal message to author, 30 December 2016. I am grateful to Ann Tierney and Mary Flood for their research into the Chetwood family on my behalf.

[4] Colley Cibber, Thomas Dogget and Robert Wilks managed Drury Lane from 1710 on behalf of the ageing patent holder, Richard Steele. At first, Wilks trained the actors, Doggett supervised finances, and Cibber programmed and selected new plays. In 1714, Barton Booth replaced Dogget in this 'triumvirate', as it was known. Cibber's power grew as Wilks aged and Booth fell ill, finally retiring in 1728. Helene Koon, *Colley Cibber: A Biography* (Lexington, KY, 1986), pp. 112–26. Details of Cibber's managerial duties are known through a statement he gave on 16 February 1728 as part of a lawsuit. *Ibid.*, pp. 118–19. See also Robert D. Hume, 'John Rich as Manager and Entrepreneur', *"The Stage's Glory"*, pp. 38–42.

[5] John Fuller, 'Introduction', *John Gay: Dramatic Works*, vol. 1 (Oxford, 1983), p. 44. Gay finished writing *The Beggar's Opera* by 22 October 1727. Gay's patron, the Duchess of Queensberry, may have intervened to get Rich to stage the work.

[6] Impressed with Fenton's performance as Cherry in *The Beaux' Stratagem* at the New Haymarket Theatre, John Rich is said to have hired her 'by the tempting offer of *fifteen shillings per week*'. William Cooke, *Memoirs of Charles Macklin, Comedian* (London, 1804), p. 44.

[7] 'Her first Appearance was in the Play of *Mithridates* King of *Pontus* … [as] the Page … where a Song proper to the Circumstances of the Scene was introduced.' Chetwood, *A General History of the Stage*, p. 127. Notices for *Mithridates* do not carry Miss Raftor's name in cast lists.

Night when all the Village slept' whose melody, a common tune like those that filled *The Beggar's Opera*, had circulated since 1678.[8] After Clive earned 'extraordinary Applause' for her song,[9] Colley Cibber set about launching his own brand of ballad opera with Clive at the cast's helm. In coming seasons Cibber would continue to promote Clive in both serious and comic sung parts, at the same time and with equal vigour. Cibber's creation of parallel and opposed stage lines for Clive gave Carey the chance not just to compose for his pupil, but to realize his long-cherished dream of uniting, in one voice, serious and comic English song.

The Ambitions of Henry Carey

Henry Carey did more than any other single person to get Clive's career underway. He was a polymath, writing and composing for the stage, and criticizing stage productions. Today he figures only marginally in histories, whether of music, theatre, or Clive. Yet he helped create Clive's singing voice, was the first to write expressly for her, and composed some of her most celebrated songs, including 'The Life of a Beau'.[10] A champion, unusually for his time, of women's rights, Carey broke with stage formulae and wrote strong-willed characters for Clive to play. Their friendship led Carey to name his daughter after Clive.[11] But Carey was dogged by misfortune: despite the praise he earned for his writings and compositions, he never secured sustained patronage or a permanent appointment. His greatest stage successes were designed for Clive, but managers mounted them without her. Carey never got to see Clive finally lead, in 1747, the epoch-making *Dragon of Wantley* he had written for her ten

---

[8] 'One Night when all the Village slept' took its name from the song verses that Sir Carr Scrope supplied for Lee's tragedy of 1678. Carey's biographer Joseph Gillespie wrongly attributes the song to Carey. Gillespie, 'The Life and Work of Henry Carey', vol. 1, p. 85. A 'wretched' setting of the melody by Louis Grabu appeared in 1681, and the tune and verses turned up in broadsides, collections, and ballad operas from the late seventeenth century onwards. Claude Simpson, *The British Broadside Ballad and its Music* (New Brunswick, 1966), pp. 557–59.

[9] Chetwood, *A General History of the Stage*, p. 127.

[10] 'The roles of Arethusa in *The Contrivances* (1729) … and … in … *Cephalus and Procris* (1730) were specially written for her, as were numerous songs and cantatas bearing her name in their titles.' Gillespie, 'The Life and Work of Henry Carey', vol. 1, p. 84. In his analyses of Carey's high-style music, Gillespie notes the talents of Clive for which Carey was writing: on *Love in a Riddle*, pp. 84–87; on *The Contrivances* and his Italianate and burlesque cantatas, pp. 94–97; on operatic burlesque, Lampe's *Opera of Operas*, and Carey's songs for Clive in the *Colombine Courtezan*, pp. 115–21; on *The Dragon of Wantley* and the celebrated Clive songs in Carey's collections, pp. 130–35.

[11] The child was 'Catherine-Clive Carey'. Gillespie, 'The Life and Work of Henry Carey', vol. 1, p. 84. Discussing evidence for their collaboration, Gillespie, *ibid.*, observes that 'she remained his loyal friend and supporter, and their names are often associated together in theatre records'.

years earlier, because on 5 October 1743 he had hanged himself, apparently out of despair over his debts and the death of his infant son.[12]

When he trained Clive in the 1720s, Carey's prospects looked brighter than they had for years. In 1717 he had misguidedly composed 'a merry Tune for Joy' for the 'Liberty' of the treasonous Robert Harley, Earl of Oxford. This indiscretion cost Carey all three of his posts: as parish clerk at the chapel of Lincoln's Inn, as 'keeper of the library' at the Middle Temple, and as composer at Drury Lane, where he had worked from c.1714.[13] In 1723, however, he again began to provide music for the house, beginning with the spectacularly successful *Harlequin Dr Faustus*.[14] In 1724 his series of cantatas, modelled after those of John Hughes, began to appear. In 1726, Carey's song 'Mocking is Catching, or a Pastoral Lamentation for the Loss of a Man and no Man', which skewered devotees of the Italian castrato singer Senesino, became a favourite.[15]

Carey therefore had reason to hope he could fully recover from the taint of his link to Harley. Clive was his dream pupil, capable of realizing on stage the aims he had long espoused. In his 1729 poem 'Blundrella: Or, the Impertinent. A Tale', there is a character, 'Belinda', who seems clearly to have been inspired by Clive.[16] A gifted singer, Belinda has been constrained by her hostess Blundrella from performing English-language songs at a social gathering – but does it anyway:

> At length, unwilling to appear
> Affected, peevish, or severe,
> The lovely Virgin tun'd her Voice,
> More out of Complaisance than Choice:
> While all were with her Musick pleas'd,
> But she [Blundrella] who had the Charmer teaz'd;
> Who, rude, unmanner'd, and abrupt,
> Did thus BELINDA interrupt.[17]

---

[12] The deaths of Henry Carey and his son Charles Colborn Carey, born 23 May 1743, are entered in the register of St James Clerkenwell on the same day, 5 October 1743. Gillespie notes that 'Carey's death was reported in almost all the daily and weekly newspapers'. Gillespie, 'The Life and Work of Henry Carey', vol. 1, pp. 150–51.

[13] Gillespie, 'The Life and Work of Henry Carey', vol. 1, pp. 61–62; the quotation is from the *Weekly Journal* of 13 July 1717.

[14] Gillespie, 'The Life and Work of Henry Carey', vol. 1, pp. 69–70.

[15] The history of Carey's 'Mocking is Catching', known later as 'The Ladies Lamentation for the loss of Senesino', is convoluted. According to Gillespie, 'it was first published without music ... but Carey updated [it] to coincide with Senesino's second departure from England in 1736 [when he] set the poem to music. A second revision followed in 1737 when Carey adapted the lyric to Farinelli ... Mrs Roberts performed the song at Covent Garden on 14 April 1737.' Gillespie, 'The Life and Work of Henry Carey', vol. 2, pp. 17–18.

[16] Henry Carey, *Poems on Several Occasions* (London, 1729), p. 12.

[17] Carey, *Poems on Several Occasions*, p. 14. The earliest advertisement for the sale of the volume was in the *Daily Post*, 11 July 1729.

'Blundrella: Or, the Impertinent' captures Carey's aims as a composer of vocal music: to deflate pretension and supplant Italian repertory with English. Carey tried to realize these goals in his music, wordbooks, song verses, and commentary, in which he often condemns followers of Italian opera.[18] Clive had the voice and musicianship to help Carey both realize his aims and popularize his oeuvre.

Before Carey and Clive went public, they developed between them the distinctive vocal technique discussed in Chapter 1. Singing ballads, Clive was as bracing as a street crier; singing sophisticated airs, her refinement was exquisite. The first technique had the frisson of power, as well as novelty. Around 1700, the lawyer and musical amateur Roger North had written admiringly of 'the crys and ballad singers – some weomen singing in the streets with a loudness that downs all other noise, and yet firme and steddy'. By contrast, North complained, 'come into the theater or musick-meeting, and you shall have a woman sing like a mouse in a cheese, scarce to be heard, and for the most part her teeth shutt'.[19] The difference lay in the mastery of breath by those whose livelihood depended on a 'loudness that downs all other noise'.[20] Yet in Clive's day this brash, embodied loudness was considered anathema to any performance of femininity.

Emboldened by Carey, Clive integrated the 'loudness' of street singers into her ballad singing on stage. Near the end of her career, Christopher Smart wrote an epilogue for Clive to speak after *The Apprentice* (1756), Arthur Murphy's farce about so-called spouting clubs, at meetings of which apprentices would learn to imitate celebrity actors. In Smart's epilogue, Clive celebrates her own powers, citing as proof two of the ballads she had sung in *The Beggar's*

---

[18] 'Carey became the spokesman on the state of the English musical stage during the 1720s. It was not the quality of the Italian music presented of which he complained, but the antics of the fashionable society who patronised it, both in their pretentiousness and attitude toward the singers at the opera, and their distaste for anything English.' Gillespie, 'The Life and Work of Henry Carey', vol. 1, p. 179. Carey expressed his resentment in airs, cantatas, stage burlesques, commentary and satirical poems: see *ibid.*, esp. pp. 96–99, 132–37, and on his satirical poems and commentary, pp. 179–205.

[19] 'Of English Singing', John Wilson, ed., *Roger North on Music: Being a Selection from his Essays written during the Years c.1695–1728* (London, 1959), p. 215. Wilson notes that this passage is from North's rough notes written between 1695 and 1700. I am grateful to Jeremy Barlow for bringing this quotation to my attention.

[20] Wilson, ed., *Roger North on Music*, p. 215. Such street cries were, as David Garrioch notes, a feature across eighteenth-century urban Europe: 'street sellers ... developed appropriate vocal techniques, using pitch, projection and repetition to achieve a high level of audibility'. He quotes the Viennese writer Johann Pezzl who, in his 'Sketch of Vienna' (1786–90) observed that the 'voices of most of the market-women seem half-hoarse, but very sharp withal, attacking one's eardrums with piercing insistence'. David Garrioch, 'Sounds of the City: the Soundscape of Early Modern European Towns', *Urban History*, vol. 30, no. 1 (2003), p. 8.

Opera and recalling her '*Voice like* London Cries'.[21] In the 1720s Clive and Carey had helped render such rawness acceptable, and make it a means of reaching out to audiences. Her 'Cries', were heard as candour, and her voice as a vox populi. Yet Clive also transported listeners with her serious airs. She was the first London stage player to found her acclaim on the adoption of plural vocal personae. John Beard, her later singing partner, would be the second. Carey, whose youngest son would later make a career of reproducing celebrity voices,[22] trained Clive to control her vocal identity.

At the start of her career, that identity was serious. On 2 January 1729, in her first stage appearance of any substance, Clive played Dorinda, the sister of Miranda, in *The Tempest*. The part had been invented by John Dryden and William Davenant for their 1667 adaptation of Shakespeare's play, which was still a staple. As Dorinda she sang a favourite air, 'Dear pretty Youth', then thought to be by Henry Purcell, but in fact probably by John Weldon.[23] Such was her appeal that she not only retained her part, but eventually received separate billing for her air. Five days later, on 7 January, Clive stepped out in her first bespoke part: Phillida, in Drury Lane's inaugural ballad opera, *Love in a Riddle*. The work was written by Cibber himself to compete with *The Beggar's Opera*, with music arranged or composed by Carey, whom he had not employed in nearly four years.[24] Cibber's decision to take Carey back likely hinged on his casting of Clive. She was to be Drury Lane's attraction to rival Lavinia Fenton of *The Beggar's Opera*, around whom a media craze had raged during the first half of 1728.

[21] [Smart], 'EPILOGUE written by a FRIEND, spoken by Mrs. CLIVE. In this epilogue, Clive invokes the parts for which she is either infamous or celebrated: the 'scold' who thinks herself capable of playing the tragic Zara, the defiant 'daughter' who sings 'O Ponder well – and *Cherry Chase*' and fancies herself as Ophelia, a cousin who 'Acts Lady Townly – thus – in all her Glory'. Clive's speech is supposed to be about matching male spouters with female ones, but these all turn out to be manifestations of her. See also Nussbaum, 'The Economics of Celebrity', *Rival Queens*, pp. 40–41.

[22] Born the year his father died, George Saville Carey (1743–1807) had no chance to learn from him. He lectured publicly on mimicry, touring Britain to reproduce for audiences outside London the sound of celebrated actors and singers with ranges from soprano to bass. As David Brewer notes, George Saville Carey's mimicry attests to the ways which past performances bled into the reader's understanding of character in a drama. David A. Brewer, *The Afterlife of Character, 1726–1825* (Philadelphia, 2005), pp. 2–15. Henry Carey's daughter Anne was mother to the legendary Shakespearean actor Edmund Kean.

[23] Margaret Laurie argues persuasively for Weldon's authorship in Margaret Laurie, 'Did Purcell set *The Tempest*?', *Proceedings of the Royal Musical Association*, 90th Sess. (1963–64), pp. 43–57.

[24] Gillespie, 'The Life and Work of Henry Carey', vol. 1, pp. 68–84. The last full score Carey had provided was for the pantomime *Apollo and Daphne, or Harlequin Mercury*, which opened on 20 February 1725. Before the 1729 *Love in a Riddle*, Carey also supplied two songs for the January 1728 Drury Lane production of Sir John Vanbrugh's *The Provoked Husband*.

Lavinia Fenton, Stardom, and Ballad Opera

Colley Cibber had looked on for many months as *The Beggar's Opera*, which he had rejected, shattered theatrical conventions and box-office records. John Gay had written a musical stage work unlike any other. Building on the notoriety of the thief Jack Sheppard, Gay turned Sheppard's exploits and hanging into an 'Opera' that both satirized Town taste and exploded the conceits of sentimental comedy. The commonness of the tunes Gay chose mocked the fashion for Italian arias. Polite audience members, including first minister Robert Walpole at one performance, saw their conduct likened to that of criminals and bawds. The unprecedented first run of sixty-two nights, the flood of publicity, merchandise and commentary, the profits with which John Rich built Covent Garden theatre in 1732, and the many ballad operas written in imitation were all part of the storied impact of *The Beggar's Opera*.

As *The Beggar's Opera* took the Town by storm, the seventeen-year-old Fenton catapulted to stardom as the female lead, Polly Peachum. This perplexed even Gay, who came to wonder 'whether her fame does not surpass that of the Opera itself'.[25] A former coffee-bar maid, Fenton would quickly come to represent all that was wonderful, and wicked, about this new entertainment of Gay's. In print commentary and ephemera of all kinds, one question dominated: how did this easy-virtue girl come to command Town taste? Much lay in Fenton's style of delivery.

In the playbook, Polly defies her parents to marry the man she loves, the highwayman Macheath, but then devolves into a rancorous jade, fighting with a rival over the title of wife to her bigamous husband. Gay even has Polly declare that 'I know as well as any of the fine Ladies how to make the most of myself [in the sexual marketplace] and my Man too.'[26] In performance, however, Fenton's Polly was sweetly sentimental, her singing a foil to the cynicism of the text. Songs in *The Beggar's Opera*, conceived as isolated points which halted the action, allowed Fenton to make Polly's voice her own. According to an anecdote passed down by James Boswell, a latter-day fan of the work, Fenton's performance of Air 12, 'Oh ponder well', transformed an initially dubious first-night audience into enthusiasts 'much affected by the innocent looks of Polly'.[27] Supporting Boswell's report is surviving publicity around the song: on a c.1730 broadsheet, *The Whole Life of Polly Peachum ... Shewing how she jumpt*

---

[25] Chester F. Burgess, ed., *The Letters of John Gay* (Oxford, 1966), pp. 72–73.
[26] John Fuller, ed., *The Beggar's Opera, John Gay: Dramatic Works*, vol. 2 (Oxford, 1983), pp. 11, 17.
[27] See the entry for Tuesday, 18 April 1775 in R. W. Chapman ed., rev. J. D. Fleeman, with a new introduction by Pat Rogers, *Life of Johnson by Boswell* (Oxford, 1980), p. 630. I would like to thank Jeremy Barlow for calling my attention to this passage. The numbering and title of the air are taken from Jeremy Barlow, *The Music of John Gay's The Beggar's Opera* (Oxford, 1990), p. 28.

Fig. 2.1 John Faber the younger after John Ellys, *Miss Fenton*, 1728. Mezzotint. © Trustees of the British Museum. Museum number: 1902,1011.1422.

from an Orange Girl ... to be a Lady of Fortune,[28] 'O Ponder Well' is printed just below Fenton's portrait. Fenton's Polly came to be seen as 'a *natural, innocent* Girl, forming Sentiment from her own Heart'.[29] Her personal story was held to mirror that of Polly. A fake memoir gave out that Fenton's mother had sold her daughter's maidenhood to a Portuguese nobleman, to whom Fenton

---

[28] *The Whole Life of Polly Peachum ... Written by one of her Companions* (London, [1730?]).
[29] *Daily Journal*, issue 5842 (13 November 1736). This opinion was given out during what became known as the Polly Row, discussed in Chapter 6, when critics described Fenton's interpretation and argued that it was definitive.

remained loyal. Writers hotly debated whether Fenton was 'really' a heroine, or a whore.[30]

Fenton's unschooled singing was quickly extolled in print as a touchstone for her sincerity. This was the first time an untrained voice had excited large-scale critical admiration among playgoers. Fenton and her song went on to be celebrated in her mezzotint portrait, engraved by John Faber after an oil by John Ellys, and issued by 20 March 1728 (Fig. 2.1).[31] The image proliferated wildly; Alexander Pope remarked on it being 'engraved and sold in great numbers,'[32] and Henry Carey noted its inescapability for those hurrying by London's print shops and coffee houses: '& as we paß, in Frame & Glass, / We see her Mezzo=tint=o.'[33] One author raged against 'the Prints of Captain Macheath and Polly Peachum' for 'hanging in the Windows with those of the

---

[30] Berta Joncus, '"The Assemblage of every female Folly": Lavinia Fenton, Kitty Clive and the Genesis of Ballad Opera', *Women of Fashion*, pp. 25–34.

[31] A close friend of William Hogarth's and also of the actor and manager Robert Wilks, Ellys was anonymously commissioned to paint Fenton's portrait. Ellys was later, from 1736, the Prince of Wales's principal painter and was hired by Robert Walpole to help amass his painting collection, which became renowned. Ellys had friends among theatre personnel, and from 1732 until 1735 owned the actor Robert Wilks' former share of the Drury Lane patent. He also painted Wilks, and Hester Booth. Writing to Jonathan Swift, Gay noted: 'There is a mezzotinto print published to-day of Polly, the heroine of the Beggar's Opera.' Letter of 20 March 1728, cited in William E. Schultz, *Gay's Beggar's Opera: Its Content, History, and Influence* (New Haven, 1923), p. 7.

[32] Pope noted that the fame of *The Beggar's Opera* 'was not confin'd to the author only; the ladies carry'd about with 'em the favourite songs of it in fans; and houses were furnish'd with it in screens. The person who acted Polly, till then obscure, became all at once the favourite of the town; her *pictures* were engraved and sold in great numbers, her *life* written; books of letters and verses to her publish'd; and pamphlets made even of her *sayings* and *jests*'. Annotation in *The Dunciad* (Book iii, l.330), cited in Schultz, *Gay's Beggar's Opera*, p. 8. Although not error- or bias-free, Charles E. Pearce's collation of contemporary commentary about Fenton is useful. Charles E. Pearce, *"Polly Peachum." Being the Story of Lavinia Fenton (Duchess of Bolton) and "The Beggar's Opera"* (London, 1913).

[33] Henry Carey, 'Polly Peachum, to the Tune of Sally in our Alley' in *Six Ballads on the Humours of the Town* (London, 1728). Carey's song was reprinted in editions of *The Beggar's Opera* from its 'third edition' onwards and in Carey's *Poems on Several Occasions* of 1729. The mezzotint process was perfected by the engraver John Smith; its innovation lay in reproducing the effects of an oil painting – chiaroscuro, nuanced contouring, and precision – in a print medium. Mezzotints varied in size, with formats from quarto to large folio. They often cost about a shilling, and were sold at booksellers, printers, and other retailers, where they were displayed. For an account of Smith's career and a chronology of his plates, see Antony Griffiths, 'Early Mezzotint Publishing in England – I. John Smith', *Print Quarterly*, vol. 6, no. 3 (1989), pp. 243–57. On the transformative impact of Smith's mezzotints, see Amanda-Nicole Ridel, 'Modification of Market: John Smith and the Mezzotint Print in Eighteenth-Century England' (MA diss., Univ. of California, Riverside, 2011). On the print-sellers who sold pictures, see Timothy Clayton, *The English Print 1688–1802* (New Haven, 1997), pp. 3–13.

first Quality of both Sexes', that is, for occupying spaces formerly the preserve of the privileged.[34]

In her 'Mezzo=tint=o', the wigless Fenton wears a front-tassled bodice and kerchief head-dress (Fig. 2.1). These are plainer clothes than she wore as Polly,[35] and redolent of the plain dress of Quakers. Below her portrait, verses were added:

> 'Miss Fenton'
> While Crowds attentive sit to Pollys Voice,
> And in their native Harmony rejoyce;
> Th'admiring Throng no vain Subscription draws
> Nor Affectation promts a false Applause.
> Nature untaught, each Pleasing Strain supply's,
> Artleß as her unbidden Blushes rise,
> And Charming as the Mischief in her Eyes.

Pastoral conceits serve a double function here. While Fenton's 'voice' and 'Nature untaught' are held to be the ideal conduit for 'native Harmony' and 'Pleasing Strain[s]', her artlessness signals also her potential sexual adventurism, witnessed by her 'Blushes' and the 'Mischief in her Eyes'. In the picture Fenton herself appears aloof, in plain dress and with a doe-eyed sideways glance distancing her from the spectator. Critics and theatre personnel were quick to exploit the cognitive dissonance between Fenton's dress in the Faber mezzotint and her burgeoning reputation. Thomas Walker, who had played Macheath in *The Beggar's Opera* opposite Fenton, went on to write and lead *The Quaker's Opera*, whose action unfolds in a bordello and apes that of *The Beggar's Opera*.[36] In a similar vein, the satiric 'Dialogue between POLLY and PUNCH WILLIAM, in the Quaker's Dialect' had Fenton pretending piety to justify 'the Comforts of carnal Copulation'.[37]

Fenton's mezzotint verses recall at once her looks and her singing. Plain dress and plain voice conjoin as signs of an 'untaught' nature, which corrects the kind of musical 'Affectation' beloved by opera supporters – that is, the purchasers of a 'vain Subscription'. In an early salvo in the long battle between art song and popular song which continues to this day, Fenton's singing is here

---

[34] *Thievery A-la-mode: Or, the Fatal Encouragement* (London, 1728), p. 13.
[35] William Hogarth's five authenticated oils of the final scene of *The Beggar's Opera* show Fenton wearing a cap of lace, ribbon, and pendant lappets, a frilled chemise, swagged sleeves, and a choker. For details about Hogarth's oil of this scene, see note 00.
[36] Thomas Walker, *The Quaker's Opera* (London, 1728). The ballad opera ran as a summer booth entertainment during 1728, and sale of its playbook was announced on 22 June 1728. Berta Joncus and Vanessa Rogers, 'Beyond The Beggar's Opera: John Rich and English Ballad Opera', *"The Stage's Glory"*, p. 188 and note 43.
[37] *Polly Peachum on Fire, The Beggars Opera Blown Up, and Capt. Mackheath Entangled in his Bazzle-Strings* (London, 1728), pp. 21–29, esp. p. 25.

portrayed as a window into her private, convention-free inner life.[38] It clearly bewitched audience members, not least the Duke of Bolton, who, after watching Fenton onstage multiple times – William Hogarth famously painted the Duke's besotted gaze in several versions[39] – made her his mistress, and eventually his wife.

Admiration for Fenton came to stand either for the 'triumph' of the lower orders' 'deprav'd' taste,[40] or as a deliverance from suffocating Town artifice. As factions formed over whether Fenton was a notorious slut or a beguiling innocent, their debates unfurled across an unprecedented volume and variety of media: prints, ballads, broadsides, and an avalanche of commentary. Her detractors claimed that she owed her success solely to Town folly and to her manipulation of lovers; her defenders praised her charms, graces, generosity, and songs. She was treated as both a celebrity and a star: vilified for success not earned but rather conferred, lionized for possessing qualities which made her audiences 'rejoyce'. She was also a synecdoche for a broader collective introspection triggered by *The Beggar's Opera* over whether playhouse entertainments should be regulated by elite taste or by common consent.

The greater volume of commentary about Fenton was scurrilous. For instance, 'Polly's Description of a Terrible HAIRY MONSTER' is a 42-stanza verse riddle adapted from the publican Ned Ward's *The Dutch Riddle* (1708).[41] One reads here of Polly's allegedly commodious genitalia: 'Two white *Herculean* Pillars prop / The tufted *Gin*, the tempting Snare: / When they divide, then

---

[38] The seeming revelation of personality through voice is a tenet routinely probed in popular music studies. Summing up the contrast between the classical and the popular singer's relationship to the performed work, Simon Frith famously observed: 'As listeners we assume that we can hear someone's life in their voice – a life that's there despite and not because of the singers' craft.' Simon Frith, 'The Voice', *Performing Rites: on the Value of Popular Music* (Cambridge, MA, 1996), pp. 185–86.

[39] Hogarth drew his scene 'directly from the stage in 1728' and painted five versions; a sixth version earlier attributed to Hogarth was dismissed in 1997. The chronology and variants between the five accepted versions are analysed in Robin Simon, 'Hogarth and Rich: Gesture and Expression in The Beggar's Opera', *"The Stage's Glory"*, pp. 253–65.

[40] 'Yesterday I was at the Rehearsal of the New Opera Composed by Handel[.] I like it extreamly, but the taste of the Town is so deprav'd that nothing will be approved of but Burlesque. The Beggar's Opera, intirely triumphs over the Italien one.' Letter from Mary Pendarves to Anne Granville, 15 February 1728, in Donald Burrows et al., ed., *George Frideric Handel Collected Documents: Volume 2 1725–1734* (Cambridge, 2015), p. 194. See also the *London Journal*, issue 451 (23 March 1728): '[T]here is nothing which surprizes all true Lovers of Musick more, than the Neglect into which the Italian Operas are at present fallen ... The *Beggar's Opera* I take to be a Touch-stone to try the British Taste on ... Our English Audience have been for some Time returning to their Cattish Nature; of which some particular Sounds of late from the Gallery have given us sufficient Warning.'

[41] [Edward Ward], *The Riddle. Or, a Paradoxical Character of a Hairy Monster often found in Holland* (London, 1706).

in we pop, / Before we well know where we are.'[42] Nicholas Amhurst, writing under the pseudonym Caleb D'Anvers, was the fiercest slanderer of Fenton: in his *Twickenham Hotch-Potch* he called her a 'A Jew-trump Girl',[43] and elaborated on attacks he had published earlier in *The Craftsman*.[44] No fewer than twenty ballads about Fenton appeared in London between January and June of 1728. Writers often set verses to the tune 'Pretty Parrot say', sung by Macheath in *The Beggar's Opera* as he probes Polly's fidelity: 'Pretty Polly, say, / When I was away, / Did your Fancy never stray / To some newer Lover.'[45]

Standing as it did for female promiscuity, the tune 'Pretty Parrot' invited audiences to reflect on Fenton's imputed concupiscence. *A New Ballad, Inscrib'd to Polly Peachum. To the Tune of Pretty Parrot say* accused Fenton of sluttish opportunism, keeping a stable of lovers, and sexually servicing John Rich in order to be cast as Polly. Even a rebuttal to this ballad, *An Answer to Polly Peachum's Ballad*, while hailing Fenton's talent, elaborated on her allegedly easy virtue. Amhurst spitefully paraphrased the first stanza of *A New Ballad* to preface the *Twickenham Hotch-Potch*, playing with the word 'Stitch' – a cant term for 'lying with a woman'[46] – to imply that she owed her success to a targeted application of her skills as a prostitute: 'Yet, dear Poll, you may / Suffer J[ohn]y G[a]y / For to S[titc]h you for his Play, / Which has rais'd your Grandeur; / Before which / You would S[titc]h / Near Fleet-Ditch … Then don't you vaunt it over all, / Tho' you are pretty Poll.'[47] Fenton reportedly loved Jews for their 'Generosity', and was said to have had borne one Jewish lover a son, whose name was given as a mock-Hebrew amalgam of her supposed lovers.[48] A counterfeit memoir of Fenton took what passed for the middle ground in this discussion, representing her as a stereotypical good-natured harlot.[49]

---

[42] 'Polly's Description of a Terrible Hairy Monster, lately discovered by her and Sir R— F—', *Polly Peachum on Fire*, p. 17.

[43] 'Caleb D'Anvers' [Nicholas Amhurst], *The Twickenham Hotch-Potch … a Sequel to the Beggars Opera* (London, 1728), p. 37.

[44] Reviewing D'Anvers' criticism of *The Beggar's Opera* in *The Craftsman*, the leading anti-Walpole political journal of its time, Bertrand Goldgar contends that Amhurst and other Opposition writers were merely pretending: 'It is clear, I think, that the moral and aesthetic arguments against Gay's opera … were a mask for objections that were primarily political.' Bertrand A. Goldgar, *Walpole and the Wits: The Relation of Politics to Literature, 1722–1742* (Lincoln, 1976), p. 72. I disagree with Goldgar's reading.

[45] Air 14 in Barlow, *The Music of John Gay's The Beggar's Opera*, p. 30.

[46] [James Caulfield], *Blackguardiana: Or, a Dictionary of Rogues, Bawds, Pimps, Whores …* (London, 1793), pages unnumbered.

[47] [Amhurst], *The Twickenham Hotch-Potch*, p. 17.

[48] Her son's name was said 'to be a Compound of Hebrew and English Anagram thus; Rich-Red-Gay-Fraw-Hub-Stan-Fag'. *The Case between the Proprietors of News-Papers … To which is annex'd … Polly Peachum's Child; its Name, Father, &c.* (London, [1729]), pp. 20–21.

[49] 'Good-natured harlot' is a term applied by Cheryl Wanko, who analyses Fenton's reception in light of her 'memoir' *The Life of Lavinia Beswick alias Fenton, alias Polly Peachum* (London, 1728) in Wanko, *Roles of Authority*, pp. 51–62, esp. p. 60; on *The Life of Lavinia*

At least for some audience members, Fenton's sentimental performance of Polly eclipsed this scandalous public construct. A poem in *Mist's Weekly Journal* of 2 March 1728 held that Polly 'charms the present Age', such that the 'Autumnal' actress Anne Oldfield 'broils with Rage'.[50] Another poetaster in *The Craftsman* of 9 March 1728 enthused how 'Ev'n thy *own Sex* thy shining Charms extol, / And, young or old, acknowledge *pretty Poll*'.[51] Elsewhere Fenton was extolled for the 'Grace and Arts' by which she 'conquers Hearts' and 'vindicate[s] her Cause'.[52] The author of the 'Epistle Dedicatory to Miss Peachum' in *Polly Peachum's Jests* hails the 'bright Nymph' who defies her 'humble State'.[53] The author of her counterfeit memoir, after describing her early prostitution to the Portuguese nobleman, argues that her loyalty to him marked her as 'the most humble, the most affable, and the least conceited of any Woman'.[54]

Several writers blended the two perspectives, holding that Fenton's artless singing evidenced an agreeableness which sometimes, as in her mezzotint, could be sexual. For instance, her 'tuneful warbling Throat, / With native, tho' sweet harmonious Voice' is said to make her 'every Lover's Choice'.[55] According to another report, 'The House Rings, / When she Sings' as Fenton 'out-shines them all'.[56] In *Polly Peachum: A New Ballad*, set to a favourite tune by Carey, 'Sally in our Alley', Polly overwhelms not only English but also Italian rivals: 'Compar'd with her, how flat appears Cuzzoni or Faustina?' cries the poet.[57] In this ballad, jealous 'Partizans of Handel' are blamed for sullying Fenton's reputation.[58]

That Fenton was an unprecedented and divisive media sensation is clear. The intensity of the debate around her is startling, with practically all materials

---

Beswick, see also Nussbaum, 'Actresses' Memoirs: Exceptional Virtue', *Rival Queens*, pp. 97–100.

[50] *Mist's Weekly Journal*, issue 150 (2 March 1728): 'On Miss POLLY in the *Beggar's Opera*. / WHILE Polly charms the present Age, / And Venus' Train the Fair surrounds. / Autumnal O—f—ld broils with Rage, / And rugged P[o]rt[er] grimly frowns.'

[51] *Country Journal or The Craftsman*, issue 88 (9 March 1728): 'To *Miss* POLLY PEACHUM. / A TOWN PASTORAL.'

[52] *An Answer to Polly Peachum's Ballad* (London, 1728). This publication is a broadside; that is, a sheet of paper printed on one side only.

[53] 'Epistle Dedicatory to Miss Peachum', *Polly Peachum's Jests* (London, 1728), pages unnumbered.

[54] *The Life of Lavinia Beswick*, pp. 43–44.

[55] *A Letter to Polly. To one of her own Tunes* (London, 1728), p. 6.

[56] "The House Rings, / When she Sings, / Must such Things / Vanish in a Vapour, / No, she out-shines them all.' *An Answer to Polly Peachum's Ballad*.

[57] 'POLLY PEACHUM: *A* new Ballad. To the Tune of, *Of all the Girls that are so smart*', *Country Journal or The Craftsman*, issue 93 (13 April 1728). On the provenance and settings of this tune – some by Carey himself – see the catalogue no. 275 in Gillespie, 'The Life and Work of Henry Carey', vol. 2, pp. 72–73.

[58] *Ibid.*

appearing within six months. Fenton had exploited the liminality of ballad opera song to her advantage. Listening to its didactic vocal numbers such as 'Would you have a young Virgin' (Air 21), audiences may have apprehended both the coruscating scorn with which Gay shaped Polly and the shining-faced ingenuousness with which Fenton played her. Some audience members were won over, while others heard a doxy on the make. Fenton's sudden retirement to become the Duke of Bolton's mistress brought the first run of *The Beggar's Opera* to an abrupt end.[59]

Fenton was what Joseph Roach and other celebrity scholars call an 'It girl': an eroticized, indecipherable *provocateuse* whose mysteriousness spawns not just effigies of herself, but also cravings for intimacy, and character readings whose paradoxes, because unresolvable, fuel audience fascination.[60] With Fenton gone from 14 June 1728 – the night of her final public performance[61] – a vacuum opened in London's celebrity market that Colley Cibber was eager to have Clive fill.

Love in a Riddle, or Cibber confounded

Colley Cibber had drawn his own lessons from the factionalism around Fenton. While Polly's voice made some crowds attentive, others grew fractious, offended by her low singing and loose reputation. Cibber's strategy for appealing to both constituencies was to have Clive, his own young soprano, invite the Town to partake in a more elevated musical fare. Because Clive, unlike Fenton, was a trained musician, she brought sophisticated skills to Cibber's project – and Carey was on hand to help raise the tone.

In his memoirs of 1740, Cibber would explain that in 1729 he had sought to put ballad opera 'upon a quite different Foundation'.[62] As an alternative to *The Beggar's Opera*, Cibber wished for ballad opera to recommend 'Virtue, and Innocence' rather than vice and corruption.[63] To realize this project he wrote *Love in a Riddle*, which he called a 'Pastoral'. He gave it the trappings of classical

---

[59] Another female player took Fenton's role for the last performance, on Wednesday 19 June, of *The Beggar's Opera* during the 1727–28 season. Fenton's precipitous retirement was reported days later: 'On Wednesday last, being the 62d Day, the BEGGAR'S OPERA was [to be] acted at Lincoln's-Inn Fields; but to the great Surprize of the Audience, the Part of Polly Peachum was performed by Miss WARREN, who was very much applauded; the first Performer being retired, as it is reported, from the Stage'. *Country Journal or The Craftsman*, issue 103 ([Saturday] 22 June 1728).

[60] Joseph Roach, *It*, pp. 40–44. Regarding stardom and the performer's likeness, Roach elaborates a tenet now accepted among scholars that, as John Ellis puts it, 'the star image rests on the paradox … that the photograph presents an absence that is present'. John Ellis, 'The Phenomenon of Stardom', *Stardom and Celebrity*, p. 90.

[61] Schultz, *Gay's Beggar's Opera*, p. 24.

[62] *An Apology for the Life of Mr. Colley Cibber*, p. 199.

[63] Ibid.

pastoral, which for centuries had been associated with elite music-making,[64] while in fact combining farce with sentimental comedy. His dramatis personae are Arcadian shepherds with classical names – Amyntas, Corydon, Phillida – who speak in verse, as in pastoral eclogues. Between their verse lines, the players sing tunes whose low provenance is obscured by the absence of the melody's common title in the playbook sold from the day of the premiere, an omission rare among printed ballad operas.[65]

Alone among the cast Clive received new songs by Carey.[66] Cibber announced to audiences his ambitions for ballad opera in a prologue spoken by stage legend and fellow-manager Robert Wilks:

> Old England will with English Throats dispense,
> And take what's well design'd, for Excellence.
> …
> An English Song, ill sung, will please Good-nature:
> You've some Delight, to know you sing it better.
> If Songs are harmless Revels of the Heart,
> Why should our Native Tongue not bear its Part?
> Why after learned Warblers must we pant,
> And doat on Airs, which only They can chaunt?[67]

Note the resemblance between Cibber's prologue and Fenton's mezzotint verses. Just as Fenton had made 'Crowds' rejoice in 'native Harmony', Clive's 'English Song' was that night to lead 'harmless Revels of the Heart'.

Love in a Riddle may have been the worst disaster of Colley Cibber's career. There were two main problems. First was the sheer awfulness of the piece: turgid verse, stiff characters, and the irony-free deployment of common tunes starved this 'Pastoral' of the satire that had delighted audiences of *The Beggar's Opera*. Second was that Cibber, in his vanity, had given himself a principal part – and he was a terrible singer. Until that night Cibber had been known for performing airs in mimic fashion. But on 7 January 1729, he followed Fenton's lead in singing naturally, and the audience went up in flames at what it heard:

---

[64] Pastoral myth and poetry from classical antiquity depicted a time and place in which men and women lived in harmony with nature and natural instincts. This model became central to Italian Renaissance cultural production, particularly in music, a process documented in Giuseppe Gerbino, *Music and the Myth of Arcadia in Renaissance Italy* (New York, 2009).

[65] 'This Evening at Five o'Clock will be Publish'd, / LOVE in a RIDDLE. A PASTORAL'. *Daily Journal*, issue 2496 (7 January 1729).

[66] Although not named, Carey must have arranged and composed this music. Not only was Carey now composing again for Drury Lane, but *Love in a Riddle* includes Carey's 'I'll range around the shady Bow'rs', and in its 'third edition' an Epilogue 'To the Tune of Sally in our Alley', Carey's celebrated song. The musical epilogue, which was never performed, closely resembles the spoken epilogue, which was. Gillespie, 'The Life and Work of Henry Carey', vol. 1, pp. 86–88, 498–99.

[67] Colley Cibber, 'Prologue', *Love in a Riddle* (London, 1729).

The People in the Beginning of the Play seemed inclinable to attend, and give it a fair Hearing; but when you [Cibber] ... began to sing ... not in a mimick, not in a false, but in your own real natural Voice, and they found that you intended to impose this upon 'em for Harmony, which they perceiv'd hurt their Ears extremely, they did grow somewhat outrageous, and in the second Act they call'd aloud several Times to have the Curtain dropt; but Philautos [Cibber] came forward and humbly petition'd, that they would hear him one Song more. They granted his Request, and then damn'd his *new-fangled innocent Performance*.[68]

Not only was Cibber's singing voice miserable, but he was said to be too conceited to notice. In *The Egotist: Or, Colley upon Cibber*, an anonymous spoof published fifteen years later, the 'Author' (supposedly Cibber) speaks of his 'Insensibility of being ridiculous' after having had to 'fifty times *sing* before Handel, with as little Concern, as if I had been only squalling to myself'.[69] To this his interlocutor replies: 'That's true ... my Ears have as often been the painful Witnesses.'[70] On the opening night of *Love in a Riddle*, audience members reportedly called out '*Kill him, kill him*', when one of the shepherds, the cross-dressed Winifred Thurmond, pointed a spear at Cibber.[71]

Clive rescued the evening. When she began to sing, audiences heard a new kind of vocal production – fresh, direct, and striking:

[W]hen Miss Raftor came on in the Part of Phillida, the monstrous Roar subsided. A Person in the Stage Box, next to my Post, called out to his Companion in the following elegant Stile – 'Zounds, Tom! take Care; or this charming little Devil will save all.'[72]

So Chetwood, writing about twenty years after *Love in a Riddle* premiered. Corroborating his report is an anonymous writer of 1747, now thought to be John Mottley, who recalled the 'great Disturbance in every Part of the Performance' at the opening night of *Love in a Riddle*, and that 'when Miss Raftor (Mrs. Clive that now is) sung ... she was received with much Applause, and greatly encouraged for her musical Voice'.[73] At the next evening's performance, commanded and

---

[68] *The Laureat: Or, the Right Side of Colley Cibber, Esq* (London, 1740), p. 46. According to Julia Fawcett, Cibber's 'mimick' voice was part of a general strategy of over-expression, which he cultivated in order to make audiences favour his person. Julia H. Fawcett, 'The Celebrity Emerges as the Deformed King: Richard III, the King of the Dunces, and the Overexpression of Englishness', *Spectacular Disappearances: Celebrity and Privacy, 1696–1801* (Ann Arbor, 2016), pp. 23–60.
[69] *The Egotist: Or, Colley upon Cibber* (London, 1743), p. 34.
[70] Ibid.
[71] *The Laureat*, p. 46: 'I remember Mrs. Thurmond ... came on to attack Philautos with a Boar Spear; and as she held it level to his Person, some ill-natur'd Persons cried out from the Pit, *Kill him, kill him*; at which Philautos started back, a good deal frighted.'
[72] Chetwood, *A General History of the Stage*, p. 128.
[73] [John Mottley?], 'A Compleat LIST Of all the *English* Dramatic POETS', in Thomas Whincop [and John Mottley?], *Scanderbeg: Or, Love and Liberty. A Tragedy ... To which are added a List of all the Dramatic Authors* (London, 1747), p. 197. On Mottley's

attended by Frederick, Prince of Wales, a 'great Disturbance' again interrupted the action. Called forth by audiences, Cibber had to both apologize and promise not to perform the work again.[74] Following this speech, Frederick 'soon left the House'[75] while the work was 'suffered to go on' until the end.[76]

Excoriating press reports followed. *Fog's Weekly Journal* called *Love in a Riddle* a 'ridiculous Piece', opining that it 'met with the Reception it well deserv'd'.[77] The satiric poem 'To Mr. Keyber, on his Elaborate Performance of *Love in a Riddle*' was printed along with this assessment. According to its verses, Colley Cibber was an 'errant Fool', responsible for profaning 'Sonnet, Madrigal and Ballad, / Below the Pedlar to Burlesque his Wallet'.[78] According to this writer, *Love in a Riddle* gave 'Offence to none but Persons of Sense and good Taste'.[79] In this same journal a week later there was a two-page rant likening Cibber to a castrated *primo uomo*. In the form of a satiric tale, this article is an almost hallucinatory fantasy about the singing Cibber, facing judgment in the classical underworld:

> [T]he Judge enquired, if that Stranger was not KEYBER … 'My Name Sir, replied the Stranger, is SIGNOR TCHIBBERINI, *a l'Italiano*, my Lord;' beginning an Air with the Voice of an Axle-tree in an un-greased Wheel, and warbling into the breaking of the rusty Hinges of a brazen Gate, and stop'd with a 'Hem, 'Sblood, I'm hoarse with the Damps of this damn'd Country; but to shew that I am qualified for an Eunuch: – Let me see, – I hope there are no Ladies here.' He was going to give Proofs [of castration] in open Court, when Hermes interrupted him.[80]

Cringe-worthy exposure is certainly what audiences took away from *Love in a Riddle*. As Elaine McGirr notes, Cibber's failure was so spectacular that it swiftly became 'theatre legend'.[81] In his memoirs of 1740 Cibber blamed the fiasco on a cabal against him, an account credited by historians from the

---

authorship of 'A compleat LIST' see Charles Brayne, 'Whincop, Thomas (1697–1730), Playwright and Literary Biographer', *Oxford Dictionary of National Biography*, Oxford University Press, 2004; *ODNB* online: accessed 21 March 2019.

[74] 'Last Wednesday his Royal Highness the Prince went to … see Mr. Cibber's new Pastoral, call'd, *Love in a Riddle*: The Actors were for a while prevented from performing, by the great Disturbance some of the Audience made. But on a Speech from Mr. Cibber, with a Promise it should not be acted again, the Catcall, &c. ceased'. *Universal Spectator and Weekly Journal*, issue 14 (11 January 1729). See also *The Laureat*, p. 46–47.
[75] *Daily Journal*, issue 2498 (9 January 1729).
[76] *Universal Spectator and Weekly Journal*, issue 14 (11 January 1729).
[77] *Fog's Weekly Journal*, issue 16 (11 January 1729).
[78] Ibid.
[79] Ibid.
[80] *Fog's Weekly Journal*, issue 17 (18 January 1729).
[81] Elaine M. McGirr, *Partial Histories: A Reappraisal of Colley Cibber* (Basingstoke, 2016), p. 94. Elsewhere McGirr's account contains errors, but on the enormity of Cibber's flop, she is backed up by Koon, who notes that Cibber quit playwriting because of it. Koon, *Colley Cibber*, p. 121.

eighteenth century until today.[82] Not everyone was persuaded: 'the real Truth', according to Benjamin Victor, was that audience members 'had too much Reason and Justice on their Side'.[83] Yet from the ashes of *Love in a Riddle* arose the myth of Clive's Phillida. The scenes she had led were reworked that summer into what would become one of London's most popular ballad operas, *Damon and Phillida*. Just as Fenton was known in the press as 'Polly', Clive was identified with 'Phillida' in all her early portraits. Carey's intervention made this possible: his many airs delivered Clive from Cibber's dead verses, allowing the charmingly defiant yet chaste Phillida to step forward.

In *Love in a Riddle*, Phillida is a secondary character who leads a comic subplot separate from the main action. She is courted by two bumpkins, Cimon and Mopsus, but loves the philandering Damon, who also woos her. She refuses to yield to Damon unless he first marries her, which, after resisting, he agrees to. Carey deftly distinguished character types through song. To the brothers he assigned the bumptious broadside 'Tell me Jenny' and common tunes such as the aptly titled 'Phillida flouts me', while to the hero-lover Damon he gave 'Handel's Minuet' and Littleton ('Lewis') Ramondon's melody 'At Noon in a sultry Summer's Day'. To characterize Clive, he gave her first a beloved pastoral 'Scotch' tune called 'Bush o Boon Traquair',[84] and then an Italian da capo aria from one of London's most celebrated operas, *Camilla* by Bononcini.[85] Adapted by Carey, this Italian aria became a Clive-led trio with action: the opening words 'Give over your Love, you great Loobies' express Phillida's scorn, which grows until she ends the number by boxing each suitor's ear.[86] For her second solo, 'While you pursue me', in which she insists on marriage, he wrote new music. This is a minuet whose strict meter, symmetrical phrases,

---

[82] According to Colley Cibber, the cabal was organized because he was suspected of having encouraged the suppression of Gay's *Polly*. Cibber, *An Apology*, p. 201. This account is transmitted in, for instance, Chetwood, *A General History of the Stage*, pp. 127–28, Koon, *Colley Cibber*, p. 121–22, *The London Stage*, Part 2, vol. 2, p. 1007, and McGirr, *Partial Histories*, pp. 94–95.

[83] Benjamin Victor, *The History of the Theatres of London and Dublin, from the Year 1730 to the present Time. To which is added, an Annual Register of all the Plays, &c. performed at the Theatres-Royal in London, from the Year 1712*, vol. 2 (London, 1761), p. 106.

[84] Jane Barbier first popularized this song, known as 'Hear me, ye Nymphs, and ev'ry Swain: The Bush aboon Traquair … Sung by Mrs. [Jane] Barbier' (London, c.1720). It was included in William Thompson's influential 'Scotch' collection *Orpheus Caledonius* (1726); the song's composition is attributed in the collection's first edition to the court composer David Rizzio.

[85] After premiering in London at Drury Lane on 30 March 1706, *Camilla* had by 1728 been performed 111 times; from 1726 to 1728 it was performed 31 times. See the introduction by Lowell Lindgren in Giovanni Bononcini, *Camilla*, introduction and notes by L. Lindgren, Music for London Entertainment, series E, vol. 1 (London, 1990), p. xi.

[86] 'Air XV' in the third act of Colley Cibber, *Love in a Riddle*, pp. 64–65.

and knitted motifs represent Phillida's rectitude.[87] To create Clive's climactic row with Damon, Carey adapted a 1718 march from William Babell's didactic *Harpsichord Master*, using its emphatic rhythms to underscore Phillida's vehemence as she foreswears not just Damon, but men altogether ('Adieu, Mankind; I'll sigh for none').[88]

Phillida is tart-tongued, reducing Cimon to tears with her taunts of 'Simpleton, Paperskull!'.[89] She is a practical British shepherdess whose respectability, unlike the nymphs of classical or Italian poetry, masters her passion. Such representation meshed not just with Cibber's stated aims but also with Carey's very public commitment to advancing polite women. He had declared for this cause as early as 1710, when he created Britain's first-ever periodical for females, *The Records of Love: Or, Weekly Amusements for the Fair Sex*. It championed a 'Love of Virtue' for the 'Ingenious part of the World, especially those of the Fair Sex'.[90] Reflecting in its pages on the 'Miseries of a Female State', Carey argued, astonishingly, that women 'are equally as capable as the contrary Sex' and therefore deserving of 'Learned Education'.[91] Once Clive had freed herself from being marketed as an erotic nymph, she would become known for representing such outspoken views on stage.

While more propitious than Fenton as Polly, Clive as Phillida transgressed norms of femininity through her self-possession. This immediately drew criticism. The pseudonymous 'Hilarius' complained in *The Craftsman* that 'Mr. Cibber hath introduc'd a Couple of *foolish*' brothers 'on the Stage, who are both

---

[87] 'Air IX' in the second act of Colley Cibber, *Love in a Riddle*, p. 33–34, titled 'While you pursue me', p. 85.

[88] Gillespie, 'The Life and Work of Henry Carey', vol. 2, p. 144.

[89] Her protests occurs in 'Air XIV' (in Act III) sung chiefly by Mopsus and Cimon with occasional lines for Phillida. See Cibber, *Love in a Riddle*, pp. 63–64, and under 'Airs' ('Ah! poor Cimon! Dud a Cry?'), p. 94. Its correlate is 'Air XII', *Damon and Phillida ... Drury-Lane*, pp. 27–28. The air's melody, 'One long Whitson Holy-Day' is a country dance tune, and was set by Thomas D'Urfey as 'The Parson among the Pease' in his *Wit and Mirth: Or Pills to purge Melancholy*, vol. 1 (London, 1719), pp. 38–39. Richard York, ed., '8 One Long Whitson Holyday', *One Long Whitson Holyday: Country Dance Tunes from an 18th century* [sic] *Northamptonshire Hall* (Northampton, 1991), pages unnumbered.

[90] 'Numb. 1. [/] Vol. 1 [/] Saturday, January 7, 1710', in this journal's collected edition, Henry Carey, *The Records of Love: Or, Weekly Amusements for the Fair Sex* (London, 1710), p. 15. Female characters in this periodical include the gentlewoman Quaker Tabitha, and Arethusa cloistered against her will, who, like the eponymous heroine of Carey's *Contrivances*, helps to engineer her own escape and marriage union. On Carey's creation of and contributions to this periodical, see Gillespie, 'The Life and Work of Henry Carey', vol. 1, pp. 166–72.

[91] 'Vol. 1 [/] Saturday, January 28, 1710 [/] 'The British Convents', *The Records of Love*, p. 53: 'It was thus I amused my self in observing the Transactions of the pretty Devotees, not without a Thousand reflections on the Miseries of a Female State; and what tormenting Confinements render the Fair Sex abundantly more unhappy than the Men: They are not only denied a Learned Education, of which they are equally as capable as the contrary Sex; but are forbid the most Innocent and ordinary Recreations.'

outwitted and treated in a very contemptuous Manner by a WOMAN'.[92] But, Hilarius notes smugly, 'we had the Satisfaction to observe that the Audience ... were so far from giving any Encouragement to *Sedition* or *Calumny*, that They expressed an universal Resentment at them'. Such sedition, in his view, was the 'chief, if not the only Reason, of the ill Success of that most *inimitable Performance*'.[93]

Not so. Clive's sung banter in *Love in a Riddle* was precisely what a throw-together summer company pirated to make the afterpiece *Damon and Phillida*. It opened at the New Haymarket Theatre on 16 August 1729. Clive, bound to Drury Lane, lost her role, and could only look on as *Damon and Phillida* went on to become the first stage staple taken from one of London's fringe playhouses.[94] Colley Cibber, whose authorship of *Damon and Phillida* was discreetly passed over in advertisements and playbooks, put up no resistance; indeed, only royal command finally brought *Damon and Phillida* to Drury Lane, on 28 October 1729 as an afterpiece to *Macbeth*.[95] In attendance was Frederick, who, having quit *Love in a Riddle* mid-performance, perhaps wished to see what he had missed.[96] Thereafter Clive didn't perform the work until the summer season of 1731, by which time it had been lost to Drury Lane; of roughly 250 *Damon and Phillida* performances by 1760, she led only sixteen.[97]

Yet Clive's Phillida acquired its own life on the page. For the royal command performance of October 1729, bookseller John Watts prepared a *Damon and Phillida* playbook featuring the Drury Lane cast, with 'MUSICK prefix'd to each SONG'.[98] This he issued six more times, and booksellers in and outside London

---

[92] 'Hilarius', 'To Caleb D'Anvers', *Country Journal or The Craftsman*, issue 135 (1 February 1729).
[93] Ibid.
[94] William J. Burling, *Summer Theatre in London, 1661–1820, and the Rise of the Haymarket Theatre* (Madison and London, 2000), pp. 94–95.
[95] *Daily Post*, issue 3153 (28 October 1729).
[96] *Daily Post*, issue 3154 (29 October 1729): 'Yesterday their Majesties, with all the Royal Family, arriv'd at St. James's from Kensington in good Health. And Last Night their Majesties, with their Royal Highnesses Prince Frederick, the Duke, and the five Princesses, were at the Theatre Royal in Drury Lane, and saw the Tragedy of Mackbeth, with the Ballad Opera of Damon and Phillida'.
[97] Clive's performances took place on 16 August 1729 and 7 June and 9 July 1731 (with the summer companies under Theophilus Cibber's management), 6 November 1732, 2 May 1733, 26 and 31 August 1736, and, after John Beard joined the company, on 11 and 15 October and 5 and 11 November 1737. As discussed below, *Damon and Phillida* was revived for Clive on 3, 4 and 6 January 1746, and she last performed Phillida on 4 May 1748.
[98] Watts issued two playbooks in 1729, one capturing the New Haymarket Theatre cast and the other the Drury Lane cast. The advertisement of 28 October 1729 for Drury Lane's *Damon and Phillida* 'before his Majesty' announced also the first sale of Watts' playbook, presumably the one featuring Drury Lane players: 'This Day at Three o' Clock will be publish'd, DAMON and PHILLIDA. A Ballad Opera of One Act, as it is to be perform'd this Evening before his Majesty, by the Company of Comedians at the Theatre

Fig. 2.2 Gerard Vandergucht, Frontispiece to *Damon and Phillida*, 1737. Engraving. Courtesy of the Center for Archival Collections, Bowling Green State University. Call number: rareovsz ML50.5 .D17 1737.

copied his 'Drury Lane' version.[99] To his 1737 re-issue, co-published with the bookseller Jacob Tonson, Watts added a frontispiece showing Clive, engraved by Gerard Vandergucht (Fig. 2.2).[100] The scene depicted is the juncture at which Phillida, after singing the trio based on Bononcini's *Camilla* aria, speaks the lines: 'If there's a Joy comes near recovering those / We love, sure 'tis to silence those we hate'.[101] In the frontispiece, Phillida plants her staff on the ground. Slightly frowning, she turns away from Mopsus, who leans towards her on her right; with her left hand she dismisses the sobbing Cimon. Her fashionable pastoral dress strengthens her authority: a low-necked boned and frilled pointed bodice emphasizes her upright stance; a small decorative straw cap perches atop her soft coiffure; her lappets billow out behind her and a decorative garland snakes itself around her bodice and skirt. The hand gesture of Damon, who hides behind an outcrop in the background, registers his surprised approval.

Phillida would become an early Clive role-icon – that is, what Joseph Roach calls 'a part that certain exceptional performers play on and off stage, no matter what other parts they enact'.[102] It was through Watts' wordbooks, not her stage enactment of Phillida, that she was identified with a character eventually held to be her own. But not yet. Colley Cibber had other plans.

From Shepherdess to Goddess: Disguising 'native Beauty'

While dropping *Love in a Riddle* as he had promised, Cibber pressed on with his model of a polite and native Opera, headlined by Clive. In these productions, from 1729 to 1731, Clive invariably played a passive rustic heroine, saved by others from an unwanted match: Rosella in *The Village Opera* (6 February 1729, and its abridged version a year later); Flora in *The Lover's Opera* (14 May 1729); Peggy in *Patie and Peggy: Or, the Fair Foundling* (20 April 1730), Isabella in *The*

Royal in Drury-Lane' *Daily Post*, issue 3153 (28 October 1729). The English Short Title Catalogue lists Watts' later 'Drury Lane' editions of 1732, 1734, 1736, 1737, 1749 and 1765.

[99] In addition to Watts' seven 'editions', the English Short Title Catalogue lists twelve *Damon and Phillida* playbooks published in London between 1729 and 1765, only two of which feature the New Haymarket Theatre cast. Editions of the ballad opera published in Ireland and Scotland referred to both local and Drury Lane companies in their title pages.

[100] Taught to engrave by his father, Gerard Vandergucht worked for printsellers and booksellers until his father's death in 1725, when he took over his father's house and business, preparing illustrations occasionally with his brother John, also an engraver. Vandergucht created frontispieces well known by modern scholars, such as that to the 'third edition' of James Miller's *Harlequin-Horace*, showing pantomimic dance. Vandergucht contributed to other volumes printed by Tonson, who may have been responsible for bringing out the new frontispiece. On the Vanderguchts and their importance among a network of engravers and printsellers, see Clayton, *The English Print, 1688–1802*, pp. 13, 19, and 266.

[101] *Damon and Phillida* (London, 1729) [Watts edition].
[102] Roach, *It*, p. 39.

Fig. 2.3 After Godfried Schalcken (*Couple d'amoureux dans un forêt*, c.1695), *MISS RAFTER in the Character of PHILLIDA*, 1729. Mezzotint. © Victoria and Albert Museum, London. Museum number: S.3874-2009.

Stage-Coach Opera (13 May 1730), Amie in *The Jovial Crew* (8 February 1731), and Nanny in *The Highland Fair: Or, Union of the Clans* (20 March 1731). Although as banal as the others, *The Lover's Opera* by William Chetwood stands out as the only hit among these productions.[103]

---

[103] Clive was given five of thirty-two airs to sing in *The Lover's Opera*. Of more than sixty performances by 1738, Clive led the first twenty-five only; from 1731 *The Lover's Opera* passed to other houses, and was performed most frequently at Goodman's Fields.

Colley Cibber's pastoral ballad operas may have found little Town favour, but their marketing trudged forwards nonetheless. Within a year of the fiasco of *Love in a Riddle*, the mezzotint *MISS RAFTER in the Character of PHILLIDA* appeared (Fig. 2.3). As mentioned, this 'portrait' was actually a genre scene, engraved after an oil of c.1695 by Godfried Schalcken.[104] An unnamed printer has simply lettered 'Miss Rafter' and verses below a picture that, given how squeezed the lettering is, may well have been a proof before letters.[105] Although called 'in the Character of Phillida' – who, in Cibber's stage action, rejects suitors – Schalcken's shepherdess is promiscuous: her lover, his hands around her waist, pulls her towards him, pouting his lips into a kiss. The shepherdess crowns him with a chaplet to signify his conquest, yet also turns to invite the viewer to consider her future sexual availability. While the lover is fully clothed, she is dishabille, and her chemise has slipped to expose her left breast. This low-budget 'likeness', and the poem below it, invoke a Fentonesque allure:

> See native Beauty clad without disguise,
> No art t'allure a paltry Lovers Eyes,
> No stiff, sett Airs, which but betray the mind,
> But unaffected Innocence, we find:
> Happy the Nymph with charms by Nature blest,
> But happier Swain, who of the Nymph possest,
> Can taste the Joys, which she alone can bring,
> And live in Pleasures which alternate spring.

Only when Clive was able to escape Colley Cibber's ham-fisted management did she achieve sustained success. In 1729 she joined Drury Lane's summer company, directed by Cibber's son, Theophilus. Though Theophilus, like his father, would have the final say over repertory and casting, the summer company gave Clive a bit more autonomy. It was a 'young company' of junior players, the reduced numbers of which meant less competition for parts. Usually Drury Lane's summer season, with two productions weekly, ran from about mid-May to September, and from 1727 to 1732 there was no summer competition

---

Edmond Gagey rightly calls *The Lover's Opera* 'conventional and stupid'. Edmond Gagey, *Ballad Opera* (New York, 1937), p. 103.

[104] The original was an oil-on-wood painting. Thierry Beherman, *Gottfried Schalcken* (Paris, 1988), pp. 344–45. Schalcken was Dutch genre and portrait painter who worked in London at the end of his career, and was known for painting subjects in candlelight and scenes from ancient literature.

[105] Perhaps John Smith, who engraved several of Schalcken's oils, created this mezzotint, since he sold proof impressions from his print shop, and specialized in 'subject' prints after oils that connoisseurs were known to be collecting. Griffiths, 'Early Mezzotint Publishing in England I. John Smith', pp. 243–57, esp. pp. 254–57.

from John Rich's theatre.[106] The summer company was a voluntary association whose members split among themselves the running expenses – candles, announcements, patentees' fees, and the use of theatre stock (costumes, scenery, and props) – while, for new productions, the author and the summer manager shared extra costs.[107] The players divided profits in proportion to their regular salaries; Theophilus Cibber would later grumble that he 'never had an Allowance extraordinary' for his 'Care and Hazard' as manager.[108]

Summer seasons were discontinuous. Theophilus Cibber, when only twenty, had in 1723 first managed Drury Lane's summer company; he did so again in 1729, 1730 and 1732.[109] These last three seasons were significant for Clive, bringing with them stage works crucial to her progress. As a stake-holder in these summer companies, Clive will have pocketed more from her stage successes than she did during the regular season, though having money down meant that failures hit her purse directly. Aaron Hill reckoned that the summer players' 'endeavours to please the Town generally produced 'em double pay on those nights; sometimes more'.[110] These arrangements help explain how, in 1729, Clive and Carey were together able to vault over Colley Cibber's lumbering pastoral ballad operas to bring what they wanted to the boards.

At first the younger Cibber followed his father in casting Clive as a rustic heroine, in the title role of *Phebe: Or, the Beggar's Wedding*; opening on 13 June 1729, this production was poached from John Rich's theatre, where it had opened the previous month.[111] In August, the summer season's final week,[112] Carey wrote ravishing new airs for his spoken sentimental comedy *The Contrivances*, with which he had debuted as a playwright fourteen years

---

[106] Burling, *Summer Theatre in London*, pp. 54–58, 80–81. Rich's summer companies ran irregularly from 1715 to 1726, in Richmond during the summers of 1729–32, in London in 1733, and in Richmond in 1734.

[107] Burling has pieced together the arrangements between players, writers and the Drury Lane summer manager from other writings, notably Francis Hawling's preface to *The Impertinent Lovers* (1723). Burling, *Summer Theatre in London*, pp. 67–71, 83–92.

[108] *A Letter from Theophilus Cibber, Comedian, To John Highmore, Esq.* (London, 1733); also cited in Burling, *Summer Theatre in London*, p. 69.

[109] Burling, *Summer Theatre in London*, pp. 54–55, 83–91. The tradition of summer companies began in the 1670s. Drury Lane summer seasons ran from 1695 to 1702, from 1708 to 1712, and, under John Mills' management, from 1714 to 1722. Theophilus Cibber managed his last summer company in 1735, without Clive.

[110] Aaron Hill, 'Preface' *The Insolvent* (London, 1758); cited in Burling, *Summer Theatre in London*, p. 84.

[111] Burling, *Summer Theatre in London*, pp. 83–85 and *The London Stage Calendar*, Part 3, vol. 1, p. 146.

[112] This final week, unusually, featured three rather than the summer company's standard two weekly performances: 'It being the last Week of Acting till Winter; the Company will perform thrice that Week, viz. Tuesday [5 August], Thursday [7 August] and Saturday [9 August]'. *London Journal*, issue 522 (2 August 1729).

earlier.[113] Theophilus Cibber had revived Carey's play without Clive on 20 June, but Carey's 'several SONGS properly introduced in the Characters of ROVEWELL and ARETHUSA' meant that in August the singers Clive and Richard Charke took over the formerly non-sung principal roles.[114] Of Carey's ten new numbers, Clive performed six solos and one duet.[115] On the season's final night, Theophilus Cibber added to *The Contrivances* an epilogue thanking the Town on behalf of the summer company, after which the 'young Actors were dismiss'd with general Applause'.[116]

Carey didn't just give Clive the most numbers in his revised *Contrivances*, but also the best music, the sophistication of which speaks for her character's affective depth. Take, for example, Arethusa's 'Cease to perswade' (Ex. 2.1). A da capo aria, its A section, in G minor, is redolent of a passepied – with a swift compound meter, balanced twelve-measure phrases and offbeat accents – but concludes with a twelve-measure Italianate flourish building to an exclamatory leap of an eleventh to vocalize Arethusa's fear. In the B section, tonal instability depicts Arethusa's unease: having begun in B flat major (the relative major of the home key of G minor), the music passes through the subdominant (E flat major), dominant (F major), and relative minor of its dominant (D minor), all within ten measures. The final bars of the B section contain a *saltus duriusculus*, or dissonant leap, in this case of a minor ninth, to paint the word 'despair'. By contrast, Rovewell's air that follows is bland, throwing Arethusa's finer sensibility into relief: Rovewell's melody merely outlines triads, never departs from the air's home key, and his final cadence is unprepared, lurching clumsily into the tonic minor. Rovewell's bass and melody lines typically unfold in similar or parallel motion, whereas Arethusa's bass and melody lines are more independent. But when Rovewell sings with Arethusa, his music is splendid. To create their final duet, Carey fused a minuet – its triple meter, delicate syncopations and symmetrical phrases signifying nobility – with an Italian aria, within which the lovers' voices sensually chase and entwine with each other (Ex. 2.2).

Apart from having maneuvered Clive front stage, Carey was surely responsible for seeing his *Contrivances* songs to print, several times over. On 9

---

[113] Carey's original *Contrivances* opened on 9 August 1715 and achieved modest success. Gillespie, 'The Life and Work of Henry Carey', vol. 1, pp. 58–59.

[114] *Country Journal or The Craftsman*, issue 161 (2 August 1729). The performances of 5, 7, and 9 August were advertised in the *Country Journal or The Craftsman*, issue 161 (2 August 1729), *Daily Post*, issue 3082 (6 August 1729), and *Daily Post*, issue 3084 (8 August 1729). *The London Stage*, Part 2, vol. 2, p. 1042 erroneously lists a performance at Drury Lane on 16 August, which in fact took place at the New Haymarket Theatre. See the *Daily Post*, issue 3090 (15 August 1729).

[115] How the songs were split between Clive and Charke is confirmed in *The Contrivances: With the Songs, and other Additions, as now acted at the Theatre-Royal in Drury-Lane* (London, 1729).

[116] The epilogue was printed in the *Daily Post*, issue 3087 (12 August 1729).

Ex. 2.1 Words and music by Henry Carey, 'Cease to perswade', *The Songs[,] Duett and Dialogue in the Contrivances* [1729]. Copyright © The British Library Board 30/9/2018. All Rights Reserved. Shelfmark: Music Collections H.118.(2.).

August, the season's closing night, the words of the songs were 'deliver'd at the Theatre gratis' to audience members;[117] they had already appeared that day in the *Weekly Medley*.[118] On 14 September, the songs' words were again given out 'gratis'.[119] The initiative bore fruit: Carey's *Contrivances* with songs was taken up into Drury Lane's regular season, during which it was performed seventeen times. Clive and Carey each used their 1729–30 season benefits to assert their ownership of *The Contrivances*.

A player's benefit was the one evening in the year when they could choose what was mounted, who played, who wrote added sections – songs, prologues,

---

[117] *Daily Post*, issue 3085 (9 August 1729).
[118] *Weekly Medley*, issue 45 (9 August 1729).
[119] 'The Songs in The Contrivances are printed, and will be deliver'd Gratis at the Theatre'. *Universal Spectator*, 14 September 1729. Cited in Gillespie, 'The Life and Work of Henry Carey', vol. 1, p. 91 and p. 514, note 96.

Ex. 2.2 Words and music by Henry Carey, 'The Duett in ye Contrivances', *The Songs*[,] *Duett and Dialogue in the Contrivances* [1729]. Copyright © The British Library Board 30/9/2018. All Rights Reserved. Shelfmark: Music Collections H.118.(2.).

epilogues, afterpieces – and, by selling their own tickets, who was sure to be in the house.[120] This display of support networks was a major aspect of the entertainment. The benefit season began around mid-March, with evenings doled out according to rank, starting with principal players and working down to behind-the-scenes personnel. As Matthew Kinservik shows, the stakes were high: a principal could earn from one night's benefit what a mid-ranked player might earn in a year.[121] Benefits for playwrights, typically held on the

---

[120] Matthew Kinservik, 'Benefit Play Selection at Drury Lane in 1729–1769: The Cases of Mrs. Cibber, Mrs. Clive, and Mrs. Pritchard', *Theatre Notebook*, vol. 50, no. 1 (1996), pp. 15–28, esp. 'II. Choosing a Programme on the Benefit Night', pp. 20–26.

[121] Kinservik, 'Benefit Play Selection', esp. 'I. The Financial Importance of the Benefit Night', pp. 18–19. He shows that Clive, Pritchard, and Susannah Cibber each took an average of £230 per season from benefits over 1741–67, and that for the 1764–65 season the benefit intake was roughly 30 per cent of Susannah Cibber's annual income, 40 per cent of Pritchard's, and 50 per cent of Clive's.

third performance after a premiere, were less glittering, but could be just as representative.¹²²

Carey's benefit for *The Contrivances* was held on 27 October 1729. For this he composed 'Additional SONGS, and a DIALOGUE proper to the FARCE'.¹²³ He also had this music engraved, and the collection was sold from 18 November.¹²⁴ About four weeks later, audiences were also able to buy the playbook with the 'Tunes of the Songs, neatly engraven on Copper Plates'.¹²⁵ Songsheets also appeared, apparently taken from these same plates.¹²⁶ Clive selected *The Contrivances* for her benefit of 28 April 1730, when she performed 'A New Cantata' by Carey. Then, for his regular personnel's benefit of 21 May 1730, Carey took up the part of Rovewell opposite Clive's Arethusa, and leavened the evening by singing his burlesque 'Tragical Cantata' and other 'comic songs'.¹²⁷

But the next season brought only six performances of *The Contrivances*, and then they all but ceased. As with *Damon and Phillida*, the Town favour that Clive had earned was snatched away as rival houses took up *The Contrivances*.¹²⁸ That Drury Lane management tolerated this theft is mystifying.

---

[122] 'Authors were still not paid by the managers for their play manuscripts. Their rewards, if any, came from a benefit on the third, sixth, and ninth nights of the performance of their new drama ... Leading players and dramatists gained support from fashionable society, and often played to packed houses on the benefit night.' 'The Benefit Performance', *The London Stage*, Part 3, vol. 1, pp. cxi–cxii.

[123] *Daily Post*, issue 3152 (27 October 1729). See also *Universal Spectator*, issue LV (25 October 1729); cited in Gillespie, 'The Life and Work of Henry Carey', vol. 1, p. 314.

[124] Henry Carey, *The Songs[,] Duett and Dialogue in The Contrivances w[i]th their Symphonies & Basses* (London, 1729). Carey himself brought out *The Songs[,] Duett and Dialogue in The Contrivances, w[i]th their Symphonies & Basses ... The Words and Music by Mr Carey* (London, [1729]). Notice of sale on 'This Day' appeared in the *Daily Journal*, issue 2766 (18 November 1729).

[125] *The Contrivances: With the Songs, and other Additions, as now Acted at the Theatre-Royal in Drury-Lane* (London, 1729). The notice of 'This Day is publish'd' is in the *Daily Post*, issue 3195 (16 December 1729).

[126] The songsheets were: *I'll face every Danger. Song in The Contrivances*, etc. ([London], [1729?]); *Sooner than I'll my Love forego. Sung by Miss Rastor* [sic]: *in The Contrivances* ([London], [c.1730]); *The Maid's Husband. A Song in The Contrivances* ([London], [c. 1730]).

[127] *The London Stage*, Part 3, vol. 1, p. 55. 'The Tragical Cantata' was presumably 'The Tragical Story of the Mare' which Carey had composed by 1724; he had the score printed as *Cantatas for a Voice with Accompanyment* (London, 1724), pp. 11–13. Carey re-issued 'The Tragical Story of the Mare' in his collection, *Three Burlesque Cantata's* (London, 1741). See Jennifer Cable, 'How a Thrown Shooe Became a Tragedy and Other Funny Stories: A Study of the Three Burlesque Cantatas (1741) by Henry Carey (1689–1743)', *ECHO: A Music-Centered Journal*, vol. 10, no. 1 (2012), pp. 1–12. <http://www.echo.ucla.edu/thrown-shooe-became-tragedy-funny-stories-study-three-burlesque-cantatas-1741-henry-carey-1689-1743/>. Accessed 19 May 2018.

[128] George Hogarth records that 'the role of Arethusa in this opera used to be considered as a probationary part for female singers before they were bold enough to venture upon

Fortunately, Carey and Clive had an alternative genre in which they both excelled: stage masque.

Clive as first Songster: Masques and Henry Purcell

During the regular 1728–29 and 1729–1730 seasons, while her ballad operas stumbled, Colley Cibber followed up on his launch of Clive in serious song. His chief vehicle for this was playhouse masque. Just as in ballad opera, Cibber cast Clive more consistently than any other female player to lead masques. Her musicianship qualified her to preside over these musical-dramatic extravaganzas which the manager had long embraced, having himself written a masque, *Venus and Adonis* (1715).[129] As noted in Chapter 1, eighteenth-century London playhouse masque borrowed Italian opera's forms of recitative, aria, arioso, and duet, but in fact shared many more conventions with the *pièce à machines* associated with Louis XIV. Such conventions included the overture ('Sinfonia'), the parts (classical gods and goddesses), the action (pastoral myths), the choreography (based on *la belle danse*), the scenic effects (ascents, descents, transformations), and the grand finale (chorus followed by a dance and joined by instrumental music, as in a divertissement).

Masque was about spectacle, and resources were poured into lavish tableaus that overshadowed the action. Occasionally, a mainpiece masque was mounted for a royal celebration, but usually masques were small independent scenes within larger stage works.[130] These segments could appear in earlier drama still in the repertory, such as a production of Dryden or Shakespeare. More frequently, they were the 'serious' scenes of eighteenth-century pantomime, typically alternating with the danced harlequinade which London critics loathed.[131] Masque song was the inverse of pantomime's disruptive, carnivalesque pleasures, and at Drury Lane Clive quickly became masque's celebrated voice.

The masque parts of Clive's early career – Minerva, Amphitrite, Night, Fairy Queen, Venus, Diana, Mercury – departed completely from her low-style

---

characters of more consequence'. George Hogarth, *Memoirs of the Musical Drama*, vol. 2 (1838), p. 14, cited in Gillespie, 'The Life and Work of Henry Carey', vol. 1, p. 92.

[129] Colley Cibber, *Venus and Adonis, a Masque: As it is Presented at the Theatre-Royal* (London, 1715).

[130] Burden breaks down the genre into the 'Classical' masque (1609–1705), the 'Masque Burlesque' (to c.1710), the 'Italianate Masque' (1705–c.1740), the 'Pantomime Masque' (c.1710–c.1760), and the 'Occasional Masque' of the 1730s. Burden, 'The British Masque 1690–1800', pp. 44–233. He also gives an 'Overall View', ibid., pp. 221–233. See also his introduction in Michael Burden, 'The Independent Masque 1700–1800: A Catalogue', pp. 59–159.

[131] Emmet Avery collates contemporary debate over pantomime in Emmet Avery, 'The Defense and Criticism of Pantomimic Entertainments in the Early Eighteenth Century', *English Literary History*, vol. 5, no. 2 (1938), pp. 127–45.

staples. Instead of common tunes, she sang numbers rooted in Italian forms; instead of 'firme and steddy' vocal production, she will have relied on bel canto technique; instead of villages, her personae dwelt in Arcadia and Olympia; instead of submitting to others, she commanded; instead of garnering sympathy, she dazzled; instead of walking, she flew, descended, and might suddenly disappear; no longer familiar and human, she was ethereal, a goddess. Clive's leadership in masque as well as ballad opera allowed her to straddle the poles of those vocal stage works which were glossed, in prefaces and prologues, as 'native'.

On 28 May 1729, nearly six months after the *Love in a Riddle* debacle and her debut as a serious songster in *The Tempest*, Clive led her inaugural masque. For this launch, Colley Cibber again used *The Tempest*, having Clive perform not just Dorinda but also 'The Vocal Parts' of Amphitrite in the *Tempest* masque said to be by Purcell. On this night, the entertainment was 'reviv'd' with 'new Scenes, Machines, and other Decorations, and all the Original Entertainments'.[132] From 13 June 1729 Clive took the part of Bonvica, the daughter of the titular Celtic rebel queen in Jonathan Fletcher's *The History of Bonduca*. As Bonvica, she sang music truly by Purcell, including his chorus 'Britons strike Home' and his celebrated air for Bonvica, the mournful 'O lead me to some peaceful Gloom'.[133] By the 1730–31 season, her ownership of both favourite 'Purcell' parts was established.

Carey seized his chance, writing a Clive vehicle masque, *Cephalis and Procris*, which opened on 28 October 1730.[134] With this work Carey expressed his confidence both in Clive and in the fashion for Purcell, whose music had since his death in 1695 featured continuously in playhouse entertainments, in masques, scenes, and interpolated songs.[135] By the early 1720s Purcell was a British Worthy, dubbed 'our Shakespear in Music',[136] and his image had joined

---

[132] *Daily Post*, issue 3022 (28 May 1729).

[133] The 1695 score for Bonduca was Henry Purcell's last major work, which Curtis Price believes was 'in many respects the crowning achievement of Purcell's brief stage career'. Curtis Price, *Henry Purcell and the London Stage* (Cambridge and New York, 1984), p. 117; on this music, and Bonvica's air, see pp. 117–25, esp. p. 124.

[134] 'The roles of Arethusa in *The Contrivances* ... and Aurora in ... *Cephalus and Procris* (1730) were specially written for her'. Gillespie, 'The Life and Work of Henry Carey', vol. 1, p. 84.

[135] Purcell's 'greatest posthumous success' was in playhouse productions. Favourite revivals at Drury Lane from 1703 to 1731 include *Bonduca* (two), *Oedipus King of Thebes* (six), *The Indian Emperor* (one), *The Libertine Destroy'd* (four), and his music for Shadwell's 1678 adaptation of Shakespeare's *Timon of Athens* (seven). John J. Higney, 'Masques: Organic and Interpolated', in 'Henry Purcell: A Reception/Dissemination Study, 1695–1771' (PhD. diss., Univ. of Western Ontario, 2008), pp. 121–24.

[136] Richard Luckett, '"Or Rather our Musical Shakespeare": Charles Burney's Purcell', *Music in Eighteenth-Century England: Essays in Memory of Charles Cudworth*, ed. C. Hogwood and R. Luckett (Cambridge, 1983), pp. 59–77. The phrase was coined in an anonymous letter printed in *The Universal Journal* of 25 July 1724 in response to Carey's

that of other cultural titans on the ceiling of the Lincoln's Inn Fields theatre.[137] Carey had joined the veneration of Purcell from 1724, paying tribute first in verse ('The Poet's Resentment') and then in music with his 'mad songs' styled after Purcell.[138] *Cephalus and Procris*, Carey's first masque, was yet another homage to Britain's musical Shakespeare.

In the action, Procris (Clive) suspects her spouse of infidelity, and hides herself to observe him; when she realizes that he is singing to the breeze, and not to a lover, she rushes from her hiding place to embrace him. Mistaking her for an attacking beast, he shoots an arrow and kills her. Procris's numbers are more richly scored than those of other singers,[139] and rely heavily on seventeenth-century compositional procedures. For instance, in her first air, 'Go gentle Sighs', instruments echo her voice as she sings 'Eccho', and the melody features written-out agreménts (Ex. 2.3). In her second number, such devices continue: after a brief introduction the instruments stop playing, leaving Clive's unaccompanied voice to ring out as she sings 'Oh Jealousy'. In the binary air that follows, the irregular, declamation-derived rhythms of the first section contrast with the regular patterns of the second (Ex. 2.4). *Cephalus and Procris*, which opened on 28 October 1730, was Carey's first major hit for Clive that she was allowed to own. Its popularity was staggering, with 72 performances during the first season alone, and 111 in total by 1735, when Drury Lane stopped mounting the work.[140]

On 3 December 1730, five weeks after *Cephalus and Procris* opened, Carey organized an extravagant benefit to celebrate and monetize this first sustained success of his stage career. The benefit began with a grand cross-town procession that swept its participants into Drury Lane for a culminating concert. Musicians first assembled at the Haymarket, then a broad paved street where

---

poem praising Purcell, 'The Poet's Resentment', printed a fortnight earlier in the same paper. Rebecca Herissone, 'Performance History and Reception', *The Ashgate Research Companion to Henry Purcell*, ed. R. Herissone (Farnham and Burlington, VT, 2012), pp. 319–20.

[137] 'Over the Stage, Apollo and the Muses are represented, and over the Pit, a magnificent Piece of Architecture, with a Groop of Figures leaning over a long Gallery, viz. Shakespear, Johnson, Beaumont, Fletcher, Dryden, Purcell, &c. in Conference with Betterton.' *British Journal*, issue 1 (22 September 1722).

[138] On Carey's verses praising Purcell, see note 137 above. Taking up Purcell's mad song 'Bess of Bedlam' (1682), Carey wrote two imitations: 'I go to the Elisian Shade' (1724) and 'Gods! I can never this endure' (1732). These are analyzed in Jennifer Cable, '"Gods! I can never this endure": Madness made Manifest in the Songs of Henry Purcell (1659–1695) and Henry Carey (1689–1743)', *Studies in Musical Theatre*, vol. 4, no. 1 (2010), pp. 15–26. On Carey's reverence towards, and verses about, his 'great idol' Purcell, see Gillespie, 'The Life and Work of Henry Carey', vol. 1, pp. 194–96, 233–37.

[139] Henry Carey, *All the Songs in the new Entertainment of Cephallus and Procris: With their Symphonies & Basses* (London, [1731]).

[140] Gillespie, 'The Life and Work of Henry Carey', vol. 1, p. 93; Fiske, *English Theatre Music in the Eighteenth Century*, p. 122.

Ex. 2.3 Words and music by Henry Carey, 'Go gentle Sighs', *All the Songs in the new Entertainment of Cephallus and Procris: With their Symphonies & Basses* [1731]. Copyright © The British Library Board 30/9/2018. All Rights Reserved. Shelfmark: Music Collections G.220.(3.).

weekly markets for hay were held, and on which the King's Theatre was sited.[141] From there they marched to Temple Bar 'in great Order, preceded by a magnificent moving Organ, in Form of a Pageant, accompany'd by all Kinds of Musical Instruments ever in Use, from Tubal Cain to this Day'.[142] At Temple Bar, the threshold of the City, the musicians were joined by a 'great Multitude of Booksellers, Authors and Printers' to continue 'with great Decency to Covent Garden, preceded by a little Army of Printers Devils, with their proper Implements'.[143] At Covent Garden – the market, not the theatre, which was not

---

[141] In 1708 the Haymarket was described as 'a very spacious and public street, in length 340 yards, where is a great market for hay and straw'. *British History Online* <http://www.british-history.ac.uk/old-new-london/vol4/pp216-226>. Accessed 2 July 2017.
[142] *Daily Post*, issue 3497 (3 December 1730).
[143] *Ibid.*

Ex. 2.4 Words and music by Henry Carey, 'Oh Jealousy', *All the Songs in the new Entertainment of Cephallus and Procris: With their Symphonies & Basses* [1731]. Copyright © The British Library Board 30/9/2018. All Rights Reserved. Shelfmark: Music Collections G.220.(3.).

yet built – the 'two Bodies of Music and Poetry [were] joined by the Brothers of the Pencil',[144] with whom they took a 'Glass of Refreshment at the Bedford-Arms'. The entire company then made 'a solemn Procession to the Theatre, amidst an innumerable Croud of Spectators'.[145]

The procession was timed to arrive at Drury Lane after the benefit mainpiece, *Greenwich Park*, had finished. Instead of an afterpiece, the audience was presented with a benefit concert for Carey featuring exclusively Carey's and Purcell's music, and sung by Clive and Carey. Songs included 'A Dialogue of Mr. Henry Purcell's, by Mr. Carey and Miss Raftor' and 'a Cantata of Mr. Carey's by Miss Raftor',[146] this being the fifth cantata, 'Sung by Miss Raftor at the Theatre

[144] *Ibid.*
[145] *Ibid.*
[146] *Ibid.*

Royal', of Carey's *Six Cantatas* (1732).[147] His most elaborate vocal composition to date, the cantata captured fashionable Neapolitan vocal writing through its thin textures, slow harmonic rhythms, suave melodies, demanding melismas, and balanced movements (recitative–aria–recitative–aria). Carey embedded Clive's voice within carefully wrought instrumental parts. A two-movement symphony – the longest by Carey that has survived – prefaced the cantata's vocal movements, and a double obbligato in each aria winds a delicate filigree around Clive's part.[148] Introducing this music in an edition two years later, Carey cast it as evidence of his progress in composition: 'I began with *Ballads* ... I have now proceeded to *Cantatas*, and, if these find Favour ... it may probably embolden me to produce an *Opera* ... I live but to improve.'[149]

Eight months after Carey's extraordinary procession and benefit concert, *The Devil to Pay* opened. It made Clive the toast of the Town, after which Colley Cibber effectively dropped Carey. By 1735 Carey was denouncing the 'bad Taste' and 'monstrous Partiality' of Charles Fleetwood, Cibber's successor as manager,[150] who also treated him poorly. Carey's experiences make one question Chetwood's assurance of 1749 that 'the old discerning Managers always distinguish'd Merit by Reward.'[151] Questionable also is Chetwood's smooth narrative, quoted at the start of this chapter, about Clive's early career. Rather than immediate ('like a Bullet in the Air'), Clive's ascent took place two years after her stage debut. Ornate masque compositions, more than 'Songs of Pleasantry', were in fact her 'Pasport to the *Theatre*'. Carey – as Clive's music master, co-performer, and song- and vehicle-writer – did more than anyone else to help her gain Town favour. He did so in spite of, and not because of, Drury Lane's managers. In his vocal music for Clive, Carey entwined the freshness of British ballads, the elegance of *galant* dances, the sleekness of contemporary Italian opera, and the intimate expressiveness of Purcell. Leaps, line, ornaments, extemporization, dynamic and metric nuances, twists in harmony – all these he created for her. When he wrote text parts, they were respectful of her womanhood.

---

[147] Henry Carey, *Six Cantatas humbly dedicated to the Rt. Honbl Sackville Earl of Thanet The Words and Music by H: Carey* (London, 1732), p. 27.

[148] 'This was Carey's most ambitious composition to date in cantata form, with an introductory two movement symphony, and obbligato accompaniments for two instruments.' Gillespie, 'The Life and Work of Henry Carey', vol. 1, p. 94.

[149] Carey, 'Preface', *Six Cantatas*, pages unnumbered.

[150] Henry Carey, 'Preface', *The Honest Yorkshire-Man. A Ballad Farce. Refus'd to be Acted at Drury-Lane Playhouse: But now Perform'd at the New Theatre in Goodman's-Fields, with great Applause* (London, 1736), pages unnumbered. See also Henry Carey, *Of Stage Tyrants. An Epistle ... Occasion'd by the Honest Yorkshire-Man being rejected at Drury-Lane Play-House, and since Acted at other Theatres with Universal Applause* (London, 1735).

[151] Chetwood, 'Mrs. CATHARINE CLIVE (formerly Miss RAFTOR)', *A General History of the Stage*, p. 127.

Carey's most lasting gift to Clive was surely her vocal training as both ballad singer and English *virtuosa*. Carey may also have trained her in the 'taking off' of other singers. We know she mastered this technique under his tutelage from two burlesques he created for her to lead: *Chrononhotonthologos*, whose premiere at his 1730 benefit he unaccountably cancelled, and *The Dragon of Wantley*, whose wordbook he wrote and whose score he helped John F. Lampe compose, and which Fleetwood refused around 1735.[152] These works include conceits Clive likely used when, in the 1740s, she began improvising mimicry of Italian sopranos: exaggerated affective gestures (for example trills for fear and vivacious springs for hope), wrongly placed *passagi* additions (for instance, on insignificant words), and rhythmic emphases that clash with the time signature. Clive paid tribute to Carey in song: once established after 1736, she was almost certainly responsible for the repeated interpolation of his songs into her spoken roles (see Appendix 1).

Carey's acuity about Clive was lost on Colley Cibber. In casting himself to lead *Love in a Riddle*, and in ceding *Damon and Phillida* and *The Contrivances* to rival houses, the manager put his pet notions above other concerns and ended up sabotaging his own enterprise. In trying to sell his own Fenton, he foisted widely disliked entertainments on his audiences. Publications then created their own reality: print sellers made Clive the next artlessly erotic stage nymph, and bookseller John Watts broadcast that the part of Phillida was hers. Was this a victory? Not for Clive, and certainly not for Carey. They served at the manager's pleasure, and after Clive's triumph in *The Devil to Pay*, Carey was dismissed.

---

[152] '[T]he first version of *The Dragon of Wantley* was [prepared] sometime during the 1734–35 season, most probably late 1734.' Gillespie, 'The Life and Work of Henry Carey', vol. 1, p. 133. Gillespie dates Carey's preparation and submission of *The Dragon of Wantley* from comments from Henry Carey, 'To Mr. John Frederick Lampe', *The Dragon of Wantley ... the Eighth edition, with Additions* (London, 1738). On *Chrononhotonthologos*, Gillespie, vol. 1, p. 351, notes that it was announced in *Fog's Weekly Journal*, 28 November 1730, for 'Carey's benefit on 3 December'.

3
'Charm'd with the sprightly Innocence of Nell': The Metamorphosis of Miss Raftor

James Miller writes for Clive – the first Kitty persona – the 'rankest Poisons' of Oxford College Fellows – the death of Anne Oldfield – ballad opera at Drury Lane falters – Clive conjures triumph out of The Devil to Pay – Nell and Clive are one

How to escape managerial control, and how to shed Fenton's mantle: these were interlinked challenges facing Clive as the 1730–31 season opened. Help came unexpectedly from Drury Lane's principal actress, Anne Oldfield. A bold Oxford student named James Miller had written an Oldfield vehicle, *The Humours of Oxford* (1730), a spoken comedy which included a part for Clive as 'Kitty' the inn-keeper's daughter, who also sings an air. Colley Cibber was said to 'choak' novice playwrights like Miller,[1] but Oldfield apparently demanded that Drury Lane mount *The Humours of Oxford*. 'Kitty' was Clive's first *in propria persona* role – that is, a part designed to represent Clive herself – and her first scheming servant role; both kinds of part would prove essential to her later progression.

'Kitty' was also the first role to pair her with Theophilus Cibber, and as such was the start of a stage partnership whose mutual abusiveness audiences would come to adore. One critic wrote that Theophilus seemed to have inherited his father's odd appeal: 'Of all the Comedians … no one has taken a kicking with so much Humour as our present most excellent Laureat [Colley Cibber], and I am inform'd his Son does not fall much short.'[2] Miller's comedy gave Clive her

---

[1] The observation is in 'Of Aesopus [Cibber], in the Character of Corrector, and of the Delight he took in Choaking of Singing-Birds', the title of the fourth chapter in *The Laureat: Or, the Right Side of Colley Cibber, Esq*, p. 117.

[2] *Common Sense*, issue 19 (11 June 1737), attributed to Lord Chesterfield, who with George Lyttleton backed this Opposition journal; cited in Mary Nash, *The Provoked Wife: The Life and Times of Susannah Cibber* (London, 1977), p. 48. Thomas Cleary explains the mission and financing of *Common Sense* in Thomas R. Cleary, *Henry Fielding: Political Writer* (Waterloo, 1984), pp. 117–22.

first chance to kick the younger Cibber – who kicked her back – on behalf of a public which loved to loathe him.

Clive herself created a second breakthrough that season. Performing in *The Devil to Pay*, a new summer production, she turned the drab cobbler's wife Nell into a plucky sentimental heroine. In response to Town applause the playbook was swiftly cut down to focus on Clive, with enduring impact on theatrical trends in London and across Europe. The draw of Clive's Nell made Drury Lane the new home of ballad opera, and the Clive-centered afterpiece was translated into German and French, eventually seeding the *Singspiel* and the *opéra comique*. More importantly for her career, through *The Devil to Pay* Clive cracked the Fenton mould, wooing audiences with 'sprightly Innocence' rather than imposed eroticism. By the end of the 1731–32 season she was poised to become a Drury Lane principal in drama as well as song.

'Kitty' and James Miller

Even as ballad operas failed at Drury Lane, Anne Oldfield's comedies were roaring successes. Since 1703 Oldfield had reigned as first actress, and on 10 January 1728, about a fortnight before *The Beggar's Opera* opened, she triumphed as Lady Townley in a revival of John Vanbrugh's *The Provoked Husband*. Colley Cibber would later claim that its 37-night run earned him more than any entertainment of the previous fifty years.[3] Oldfield, born in 1683, was by 1730 legendary, in parts often tailor-made for her. Already in 1704 Cibber had based something he wrote for Oldfield on 'Sentiments ... originally her [Oldfield's] own, or only dress'd with a little more care, than when they negligently fell, from her lively Humour'.[4] As plausibly related by Cibber, his comedy *The Careless Husband* owed its success not just to the 'uncommon Excellence of her Action' but also to the way he had brought to the stage her 'personal manner of Conversing' in 'private Societies', which 'Women of the best Rank ... borrrow'd'.[5] This was a genuine innovation: the commercialization of a star's polite manner that was already circulating as a meme in the Town. Such lessons in social presence, and in leveraging that presence as an entertainment, were surely not lost on Clive.

In 1730, Oldfield's 'manner' inspired James Miller, a divinity student, to write for the stage. Before going up to Oxford in 1726, Miller had been apprenticed to a family relative in the City of London,[6] where he would have had

---

[3] Colley Cibber, *An Apology for the Life of Mr. Colley Cibber*, pp. 430–31; also cited in Joanne Lafler, *The Celebrated Mrs. Oldfield: the Life and Art of an Augustan Actress* (Carbondale and Edwardsville, 1989), p. 155, note 41.
[4] Cibber, *An Apology for the Life of Mr. Colley Cibber*, p. 250.
[5] Ibid.
[6] He had been placed with 'a Merchant, his near Relation in the City' [Mottley?], 'A Compleat LIST Of all the *English* Dramatic POETS', p. 261; cited in Paula J. O'Brien,

the chance to see Oldfield perform. So deftly did he capture her stagecraft in *The Humours of Oxford* that Oldfield, after reading his manuscript, reportedly 'insisted upon its being immediately brought on the Stage'.[7] Strengthening the comedy's appeal to Colley Cibber was a fop role, 'Ape-all', for his son. The fop was a stage type that the elder Cibber had forged in his own image, and Theophilus would eventually claim his father's fop parts.[8] In one of his cleverest flourishes, Miller pitted the songster 'Kitty' against Theophilus Cibber's Ape-all, 'a trifling ridiculous Fop, affecting Dress and Lewdness'.[9] This pairing accommodated the kind of 'additional graces' to scenes that John Hill identified as crucial to the success of both Clive and the younger Cibber.[10]

Miller's 'Kitty' was an *in propria persona* role for Clive in name only. The likelihood that he had seen her at Drury Lane is slim, she having debuted while he was at Oxford. Miller's Kitty, by type a 'Jilt', is based on parts from Thomas Shadwell's *The Virtuoso* (1676) and Thomas Baker's *An Act at Oxford* (1704).[11] From the former, Kitty is like Mrs. Figgup, who secretly marries Snarl; from the latter, she is like Mrs. ap Shinken, who gives herself airs beyond her social rank. To this mix Miller added the type of an Oxford 'Toast', that is, a socially groomed, low-born young woman who cruises Oxford's balls and public walks for a husband.[12] To set out her views on men, Miller gave Kitty a smart song, 'The provident Damsel'.

'The Life and Works of James Miller, 1704–1744' (PhD diss., Univ. of London, 1979), p. 16.

[7] 'Preface', James Miller, *Miscellaneous Works in Verse and Prose* (London, 1741), pages unnumbered: 'Upon her Persuasion it was put into the Hands of Mr. Cibber, Mr. Wilks, and Mr. Booth, who all concurring in their Approbation of it, it was immediately got up'.

[8] In 1696 Colley Cibber engineered his own theatrical breakthrough as Sir Novelty Fashion in his *Love's Last Shift*. John Vanbrugh then created for him the part of Lord Foppington in *The Relapse*, and this role became the subject of Giuseppe Grisoni's celebrated 1696 portrait (engraved decades later by John Simon), *Colley Cibber as Lord Foppington*. Other of Colley Cibber's fop roles include Sir Fopling Flutter in *The Man of Mode*, and Witling in his own comedy, *The Refusal*. Kristina Straub charts the evolution of this type in Kristina Straub, 'Colley Cibber's Fops: Actors and Homophobia', *Sexual Suspects: Eighteenth-Century Players and Sexual Ideology* (Princeton, 1992), pp. 53–54.

[9] [James Miller], 'Dramatis Personae', *The Humours of Oxford* (London, 1730), pages unnumbered.

[10] [Hill], *The Actor* (1755), p. 31.

[11] O'Brien, 'The Life and Works of James Miller', p. 196. According to cant, a 'Jilt' was 'a tricking woman, who encourages the addresses of a man whom she means to deceive and abandon'. [Caulfield], *Blackguardiana: Or, A Dictionary of Rogues, Bawds, Pimps, Whores*, pages unnumbered.

[12] 'She is born ... of *mean estate*, being the daughter of some insolent *mechanick*, who fancies himself a *Gentleman* [who] ... resolves to keep up his *family* by marrying his girl to a *Parson*, or a *Schoolmaster*: to which end, *He* and his *wife* ... send her to the *dancing-school* ... This foundation being laid ... she frequents all the *balls* and *public walks* in *Oxford* ... [to] meet with some raw coxcomb or other ... and is at last, with some art and management, drawn in to *marry* her.' [Nicholas Amhurst], *Terrae-Filius: Or, the Secret History of the University of Oxford* (London, 1726), p. 169; cited in Gagey, *Ballad Opera*,

Kitty has only four brief scenes; in these, she engineers her marriage to Ape-all, whom she wants for his money, to save Victoria (Oldfield), who loves another, from being forced to wed him. Kitty's longest scene is the first, in which she chastises Ape-all.[13] Here, Miller gave Clive another first: an opportunity to dial up tension onstage by alluding to theatre gossip. By 1730 Theophilus Cibber was publicly humiliating his wife Jane, cheating on her and squandering her earnings; later that year they briefly separated.[14] Jane was a friend of Clive's from childhood,[15] which can only have sharpened Clive's execution of her onstage clash with Ape-all. Here Kitty confronts Ape-all with his lies, which she says will 'mean something in the Opinion of a Judge and Jury'. Ape-all counters that if dragged to court he will pretend to be unable to write, as would be expected 'in a Person of [his] Figure and Dress' – a comment as relevant to the cocky Theophilus as it was to the generic fop. Kitty asks, 'Is that your Conscience?', a question he scorns as irrelevant: 'Why Conscience in Love, Child, is no more expected than at Cards'.[16] She observes that his thoughts turn constantly to his next conquest ('you have a lovely whirligig Pate of your own').[17] In their final scene, when Ape-all realizes he's been tricked into marrying Kitty, he promises her 'a plaguy Life, a very scurvy Life', to which Kitty archly replies: 'Then we shall live the more like Man and Wife, my Dear' – and indeed like Theophilus and Jane Cibber.[18]

Kitty's character crystallizes most clearly in her song, 'The provident Damsel'. Composed by the singer–actor Richard Charke – with whom she had led the musical version of *The Contrivances*, and who would soon marry Theophilus's sister, Charlotte[19] – its music and epigrammatic verses depict Kitty's wiliness (Ex. 3.1). In this ballad-style air, Kitty advises women to play one lover

---

pp. 167–68. Gagey notes that Amhurst, who also spearheaded the attacks on Fenton in *The Craftsman*, was expelled from Oxford.

[13] [Miller], *The Humours of Oxford*, Act 2, pp. 17–18; Act 4, pp. 53–54; Act 5, pp. 67–68, 74–75.

[14] 'Her [Jane Cibber's] marriage had been a stormy one, constantly imperilled by her husband's hasty temper and persistent infidelity.' Eric Salmon, 'Cibber, Theophilus (1703–1758)', *Oxford Dictionary of National Biography*, Oxford University Press, 2004; ODNB online: accessed 4 July 2017. See also Nash, *The Provoked Wife*, p. 43. Chetwood's comment on Theophilus Cibber's conduct as a spouse expands with disgust: 'I shall not meddle with conjugal Affairs; these short Memoirs would swell too large, and the Belly, out of Proportion for the Body, appear dropsical, and require Tapping.' Chetwood, 'Mr. THEOPHILUS CIBBER', *A General History of the Stage*, p. 121.

[15] '[S]he told me, when she was about twelve Years old, Miss Johnson ... and she, used to tag after the celebrated Mr. Wilks (her own Words) whenever they saw him in the Streets, and gape at him as a Wonder.' Chetwood, 'Mrs. CATHARINE CLIVE (formerly Miss RAFTOR)', *A General History of the Stage*, p. 127.

[16] [Miller], *The Humours of Oxford*, p. 17.

[17] Ibid., p. 18.

[18] Ibid., p. 75.

[19] They married in February 1730, a month after the run of *The Humours of Oxford*. Philip E. Barut, *Introducing Charlotte Charke: Actress, Author, Enigma* (Urbana, IL, 1998), p. 17.

Ex. 3.1 Words by James Miller, music by Richard Charke, 'The Provident Damsel' in *The Humours of Oxford*, 1730. Copyright © The British Library Board 30/9/2018. All Rights Reserved. Shelfmark: Music Collections G.306.(28.)

off against another. Like 'Fidlers' and 'Archers', maidens should have at least 'two Strings' to their bow, using their beauty to obtain one man for marriage and another for pleasure. The music of the 'The Provident Damsel' winks at the way Kitty makes men dance to her tune. The melody is a jig. Its rollicking compound meter and rhythmic emphases in the bass line pick out the dactyls (long-short-short) of Miller's verses. Charke imitates the modality of a traditional jig – heard especially in bars five to seven – and its disjunct melody. Melody and rhyme scheme share their repetitions (abab) on the words 'Merit' and 'Spirit'; here Charke fits in a so-called Scotch cadence – an ascending skip of a third – to add local colour to Miller's truncated verse-ends. The semiquaver run in the song's last line slightly elevates the tone ('And t'other poor Soul we may Marry'). Native yet poised, simple yet clever, 'The Provident Damsel' allows Kitty to display her wit and her derision of men. Printed c.1730 as a songsheet,[20] in May 1738 it was grafted, probably by Clive, onto another character Miller devised for her, Maria in *The Man of Taste*.[21]

The bookseller John Watts paid Miller an eye-watering eighty pounds to print *The Humours of Oxford*, about four times what Watts gave Henry Fielding around that time.[22] Watts knew that coy allusions to uncomfortable truths had audience pull; what he didn't know was who the main satiric butts of *The Humours of Oxford* were, and the power they had to ruin Miller's career. Miller's comedy was not just a star vehicle; it was a thinly veiled character assault on Robert Thistlethwayte, the Warden of Wadham College, Oxford, where Miller was studying. Miller's references to Thistlethwayte in *The Humours of Oxford* would eventually doom his theatrical career, although during the 1730–31 season the work strengthened his career progression.[23] Thistlethwayte was a powerful Church official,[24] who had appointed Miller's father, a rector, to one of his two benefices. Why would the 22-year-old Miller risk calling down his wrath? Miller later claimed to have written the comedy solely to amuse himself and some friends, which is scarcely credible since he sold it to Watts.[25]

---

[20] British Library, G.305.(49.).
[21] 'At the Theatre-Royal in Drury-Lane, this Day, May 13, will be presented … *The MAN OF TASTE* … In which will be introduc'd several Songs, to be sung by Mrs. Clive and Mr. Beard, particularly The Life of a Beau. The Beaux Lamentation for the Loss of Farinelli. And the Provident Damsel.' *London Daily Post and General Advertiser*, issue 1104 (13 May 1738).
[22] O'Brien, 'The Life and Works of James Miller', p. 22. In 1732 Watts paid Fielding twenty-one pounds for his mainpiece *The Old Debauchees*. Martin C. Battestin, 'Phillips, Edward', *A Henry Fielding Companion* (Westport, CN and London), p. 220.
[23] O'Brien, 'The Life and Works of James Miller', p. 19.
[24] He became Prebendary of Westminster in March 1730 and, as O'Brien points out, would have been an influential patron. *Ibid*.
[25] 'The first Production publish'd by the Author was *The Humours of Oxford*, written … with no other View than for his own Amusement and that of some of his particular Friends.' 'Preface', James Miller, *Miscellaneous Works in Verse and Prose*, pages unnumbered.

Far likelier is that *The Humours of Oxford* was Miller's protest against Thistlethwayte's sexual assaults on Wadham students and staff.

In 1739 Thistlethwayte would flee to France to escape charges that he had raped William French, a commoner at the college.[26] From testimony gathered for the trial, it appears that servants and staff had long known about Thistlethwayte's harassment. When French, supported by his barrister father, pressed charges in 1739, earlier victims came forward. Among them was the butler Robert Langford, who testified how, five or six years earlier, Thistlethwayte had acted in a 'beastly Manner; endeavouring to kiss and tongue him, and to put his Hand into his Breeches.'[27] The Warden 'persisted then, and at several other Times, and once in particular in a very violent Manner', not just with Langford but also with another (unnamed) College servant.[28] The barber William Hodges gave a similar account, describing how Thistlethwayte 'attacked him' when Hodges defended himself against his kisses and attempts to feel his 'Cock'.[29]

In representing Thistlethwayte in *The Humours of Oxford*, Miller was staging forbidden – but among College members apparently common – knowledge. Already in the prologue Miller hints at dark secrets in 'Oxford Cells':

> From Oxford Cells he brings a Group of Fools,
> Unshown before – the Vermin of the Schools;
> Not that he dares reflect the least Disgrace,
> Or hint a Satyr on that sacred Place:
> A Place that's founded on the noblest Views,
> Parent of Arts, and Nurs'ry of the Muse:
> That's truly great and good – but well you know,
> In richest Soils the rankest Poisons grow.[30]

Wadham College, as George Rousseau notes in his research on this case, distinguished itself from other Oxford colleges by having only two Fellows in residence, Thistlethwayte and John Swinton, who as surrogate parents may have generated an 'ambience of misrule'.[31] Miller's comedy suggests as much. In it, Thistlethwayte is 'Haughty', an 'imperious, Pedantick, unmannerly Pedagogue; of a vile Life, and vicious Principles'.[32] In the stage action Haughty

---

[26] George Rousseau, 'Privilege, Power and Sexual Abuse in Georgian Oxford', *Children and Sexuality: From the Greeks to the Great War* (Basingstoke, 2007), pp. 142–54, esp. 142–50.
[27] *A Faithful Narrative of the Proceedings in a late Affair between the Rev. Mr. John Swinton, and Mr. George Baker, both of Wadham College, Oxford* (London, 1739), pp. 15–16.
[28] *A Faithful Narrative*, p. 16.
[29] Ibid., p. 18. Rousseau questions the truth of these accounts, finding that of the college barber to be 'risible'. Rousseau, 'Privilege, Power and Sexual Abuse in Georgian Oxford', *Children and Sexuality*, p. 149.
[30] [Miller], 'Prologue. Spoken by Mr. Wilks.', *The Humours of Oxford*, pages unnumbered.
[31] Rousseau, 'Privilege, Power and Sexual Abuse in Georgian Oxford', *Children and Sexuality*, p. 144.
[32] [Miller], 'Dramatis Personae', *The Humours of Oxford*, pages unnumbered.

'pretends Love to Lady Science',[33] a would-be learned lady, as he has done with 'three Wives already', to gain a fortune.[34] Thistlethwayte, who was said to have hidden his same-sex orientation by being 'over-familiar with a certain Woman', was a strong model for such instrumentalizing of relationships with women.[35]

As we shall see, the fury of Miller's enemies would go on to wreck the reception of all stage works known to be his. *The Humours of Oxford* set this fury in motion. Even before it opened on 9 January 1730, 'a Report was industriously propagated' that it was an '*Invective* upon the University'; [36] in response, 'a Multitude of Enemies' were determined 'not to suffer it to be heard at all'. Protest erupted and the 'Malecontents ... permitted nothing more that Night to be heard'.[37] In February 1730 the clergyman and critic Richard Russel, a friend of Joseph Trapp ('Conundrum' in Miller's comedy), torched it in the *Grubstreet Journal*, of which Russel was editor.[38] Yet *The Humours of Oxford* actually opened doors for Clive, and even for Miller. In this mainpiece she could, for the first time, woo audiences as an intriguing servant, a critic of fops, the foe of Theophilus Cibber, and the 'Damsel' of her own *in propria persona* air. All four entertainment strands would become integral to Clive's success, and be taken up in the vehicles Henry Fielding later wrote for her. And *The Humours of Oxford* advantageously showcased Miller, who after 1734 would supersede Fielding as Drury Lane's favourite Clive vehicle writer.

The Humours of Oxford was the only time Clive ever rehearsed with or played alongside Oldfield. On 28 April 1730, playing Lady Townly, Oldfield gave what turned out to be her last performance. She died after much suffering, probably from cancer, on 23 October.[39] Oldfield was buried with pomp in Westminster Abbey, where only two other actors, Thomas and Mary Betterton, rested. Memoirs and tributes tumbled from the press. Oldfield's parts were divided mainly between Mary Heron (c.1704–1736) and Christiana Horton (1698/9–1756), the latter said to particularly excel in 'personating' Oldfield's brand of 'fine Lady'.[40]

---

[33] *Ibid.*
[34] *Ibid.* 'Dramatis personae', pages unnumbered, and p. 49.
[35] '[I]t had been suggested ... that *the Warden did not love Women* ... he took no Notice ... because it was generally believed, that the Warden was over-familiar with a certain Woman in Oxford.' *A Faithful Narrative*, pp. 4–5.
[36] Miller, 'Preface', *Miscellaneous Works in Verse and Prose*, pages unnumbered.
[37] *Ibid.*
[38] Russel was editor, primary writer, and major shareholder of *The Grub-street Journal*. Writing as 'Bavius' about Miller's comedy, he satirically invoked the Aristotelian principles of 'Unities of Time, Place and Action', pretending to praise Miller's 'greatness' of 'Art' while quoting the comedy to damn it. BAVIUS. *Grub-street Journal*, issue 7 (19 February 1730). O'Brien notes that manuscript letters from Russel evidence his friendship not just with Trapp, but also with his son. O'Brien, 'The Life and Works of James Miller', p. 23.
[39] Oldfield likely died from cancer of the reproductive system. Lafler, *The Celebrated Mrs. Oldfield*, p. 162.
[40] 'Mrs. Heron, at the Death of Mrs. Oldfield, was singled out by Mr. [Theophilus] Cibber to support his favourite Characters of Lady Betty Modish and Lady Townly. On that

The dancer Hester Santlow (1690–1773), to whom Oldfield had earlier yielded four parts, would accrue two more.[41] Yet in 1731 Santlow's husband Barton Booth wrote to Aaron Hill that a tragic part Hill had created for Oldfield 'might require great Force, and be too powerful' for his wife's voice. This helps us to understand how Clive was eventually able to compete for these roles.[42]

Clive, though a first-ranked soprano at the time of Oldfield's death, had yet to prove that her acting made her worthy of Oldfield's parts. This she would do as Nell in *The Devil to Pay*, turning the worst part she had yet been given into a stage triumph.

The Devil to Pay: Entertaining Sadism

By July 1731 the failure of ballad opera at Drury Lane was glaring. Not only did *The Beggar's Opera* still continue to draw crowds to John Rich's house, but Rich's production of *Flora*, an 'Operatical' revival of Thomas Doggett's popular farce *The Country-Wake* (1696), had since 17 April 1729 also found great favour.[43] In *Flora*, the popular tenor John Laguerre took what had been

---

Account he took extraordinary Pains, which was of singular Happiness to her.' Benjamin Victor, *The History of the Theatres of London and Dublin,* vol. 1, p. 39. By 1733, Heron was 'Head of the Female List, and in the Possession of the late Mrs. Oldfield's Parts.' *Ibid.*, p. 12. Describing Christiana Horton, Aaron Hill wrote that she was 'undoubtedly, the finest Figure on any Stage, at present', whom no other actress could surpass 'in personating the fine Lady in genteel Comedy'. [Aaron Hill], 'Friday, March 7. 1735 [no. 34]', *The Prompter* (London, 1734–36) [page unnumbered; collected vol. of *Prompter* articles]. Horton (1699–1756) was older than Heron, who first appeared in bills in 1721. Horton had enjoyed top rank since 1715, when she headed the actor's benefit season. Victor thought her 'Voice was bad' although she 'had a sensible [sensitive] Pronunciation'. Victor, *The History of the Theatres of London and Dublin*, vol. 1, p. 39.

[41] Oldfield began during 1717–18 to hand Santlow her parts, beginning with the second Constantia in Buckingham's *The Chances*, followed by Florimel in *The Comical Lovers* (from 8 October 1720), Elvira in *The Spanish Fryar* (on 1 November 1720), and, during the 1722–23 season, Dowglass, page to Mary Queen of Scots in John Bank's *The Albion Queens*. Goff notes that after Oldfield's death, managers looked to Santlow 'to take at least some of Mrs Oldfield's roles', casting her during the 1732–33 season 'for the first time as Angelica in *Love for Love*, and Indiana in *The Conscious Lovers*'. Moira Goff, 'Art and Nature join'd': Hester Santlow and the Development of Dancing on the London Stage, 1700–1737' (PhD diss., Univ. of Kent, 2000), pp. 36–37, 48, 50, 64.

[42] Letter from Barton Booth to Aaron Hill, 8 November 1731, in *A Collection of Letters … Written by Alexander Pope, Esq; and Other Ingenious Gentlemen, to the Late Aaron Hill, Esq* (London, 1751), p. 78; cited in Goff, 'Art and Nature join'd', p. 62. In 1731 Hill was revising the Oldfield title role of his 1710 tragedy *Elfrid: Or, The Fair Inconstant* in the re-titled *Athelwold: A Tragedy*. Gerrard, *Aaron Hill: The Muses' Projector*, pp. 145–48.

[43] 'Operatical' was a term was used satirically in titles and announcements, as in: 'The AUTHOR's FARCE. In which will be introduc'd an Operatical Puppet-show, call'd The PLEASURES of the TOWN.' *Daily Post*, issue 3461 (22 October 1730).

Doggett's comic role of Hob, singing numbers to enrich Hob's antics.[44] At London's main fringe playhouse, the New Haymarket Theatre, Henry Fielding had broken into London ballad opera with *The Author's Farce* (1730).[45]

Fielding was a worry for Drury Lane on two fronts. First, *The Author's Farce* made painfully clear the weaknesses of Colley Cibber's brand of 'Opera'. Fielding cashed in on the public appetite for subversion and recognizable topical references that, after Gay's sequel to *The Beggar's Opera* was banned in 1729, managers of both patent playhouses had avoided.[46] Lacking the power of Fielding's wicked pen, Drury Lane's Clive-led *Bays's Opera*, designed to compete directly with *The Author's Farce* – it opened on the same night and featured rehearsal scenes similar to those of Fielding's *Farce* – crashed spectacularly.[47] Second, the attacks in *The Author's Farce* on Drury Lane managers Colley Cibber and Robert Wilks delighted audiences. Fielding had an axe to grind: after his debut stage work had stumbled at Drury Lane, its managers had turned down his next manuscript, the ballad opera *Don Quixote in England*.[48] In *The Author's Farce*, Fielding took revenge with brilliant send-ups of the elder Cibber ('Marplay') and Wilks ('Sparkish'), targeting especially the way Cibber's alterations damaged stage works.[49]

It was against this backdrop that the 1731 Drury Lane summer company under Theophilus Cibber premiered a ballad opera patterned after *Flora*. Like *Flora*, its wordbook was a seventeenth-century farce and, like *Flora*, its author had been a renowned low comedian. The work in question was Thomas Jevon's *The Devil of a Wife: Or, a Comical Transformation* (1686), which became *The*

---

[44] On the provenance and reception of *Flora*, see Berta Joncus and Vanessa Rogers, 'Beyond *The Beggar's Opera*: John Rich and English Ballad Opera', "*The Stage's Glory*", pp. 184–204.

[45] *The Author's Farce*, after it opened on 30 March 1730, ran continuously for five nights and achieved sixteen performances that season. On its reception, see Thomas Lockwood, 'The Author's Farce. Introduction', *Henry Fielding: Plays Volume I 1728–1731*, ed. T. Lockwood (Oxford, 2004), pp. 192–97.

[46] Berta Joncus, 'Ballad Opera: Commercial Song in Enlightenment Garb', *The Oxford Handbook of the British Musical*, pp. 37–38.

[47] The Drury Lane production of *Bays's Opera* died after three nights. Led by Clive, *Bays's Opera* was, like *The Author's Farce*, a ballad opera 'in the Manner of a Rehearsal' to satirize Town taste in theatre; both opened on 30 March. Three nights later, on 2 April, a third rehearsal play/ballad opera, by Fielding's friend James Ralph, opened at Goodman's Fields; called *The Fashionable Lady*, it pilloried pantomime. Lockwood, 'The Author's Farce. Introduction', *Henry Fielding: Plays Volume I*, pp. 187–92.

[48] Due to protection by Fielding's cousin, Lady Mary Montague, Fielding's virgin stage work, *Love in Several Masques*, not only reached the boards but was given a top cast, the cost of which probably discouraged Drury Lane managers from accepting Fielding's next stage work. Lockwood, 'Love in Several Masques. Introduction', *Henry Fielding: Plays Volume I*, pp. 6–9.

[49] Fielding's attack unfolded in the first two scenes of Act II. See *ibid.*, pp. 242–44.

Devil to Pay.⁵⁰ The summer company had good reason to bank on an operatized *Devil of a Wife*: Jevon's original had been revived, and well-received, during Drury Lane's regular season.⁵¹ Two playwrights, John Mottley and the Irishman Charles Coffey, adapted Jevon's playbook into a ballad opera, although Coffey alone, by signing the dedication, identified himself as author. In Dublin, Coffey had been the first Irish playwright to write a ballad opera; once in London, his *Beggar's Wedding* had pleased audiences of the New Haymarket Theatre.⁵² Armed with this success, he shared the preparation of *The Devil to Pay* with Mottley, 'each of them' taking 'one Act and a half of this Farce, and altering some part of the Dialogue, and adding Songs'.⁵³ The composer Mr. Seedo scored up the melodies. Seedo was earlier associated with the New Haymarket Theatre, where he may have arranged the music for *The Author's Farce*.⁵⁴

But *The Devil to Pay* differed fundamentally from *Flora*: instead of sentimental union, it advocated thrashing belligerent wives. As usual in her ballad opera career until then, Clive was cast in a submissive role – in this case the cobbler Jobson's mild but nonetheless beaten wife, Nell. A minor role was

---

50   Thomas Shadwell, Jevon's brother-in-law and playhouse colleague, may have co-authored this work. The resemblances between scenes in *The Devil of a Wife* and those in Shadwell's *Squire of Alsatia* suggest as much. Alfred E. Richards, 'A Literary Link between Thomas Shadwell and Christian Felix Weisse', *Publications of the Modern Language Association*, vol. 21, no. 4 (1906), pp. 808–30.
51   The success of the play grew over time; only a few performances are recorded from its 1686 premiere until 1715, but the play was mounted annually between 1715 and 1720, an average of three times per season, and during the 1730–31 season it received nine performances. The playbook was issued six times between 1686 and 1728.
52   At Smock Alley, Dublin, Coffey's ballad operas, *The Beggar's Wedding* and *Chuck: Or, The School Boy's Opera* had failed, but in London Coffey's *Beggar's Wedding*, which ran for thirty-four performances from 29 May 1729, was the only fringe ballad opera production ever to be stolen by a licensed playhouse. During the summer season of 1730, a year before *The Devil to Pay* premiered, manager Theophilus Cibber got up Coffey's first ballad opera as *Phebe: Or, The Beggar's Wedding* with Clive in the title role. Burling, *Summer Theatre in London*, pp. 93–94 and W. J. Lawrence, 'Early Irish Ballad Opera and Comic Opera', *The Musical Quarterly*, vol. 8, no. 3 (1922), pp. 397–412.
53   [Mottley?], 'A Compleat LIST Of all the *English* Dramatic POETS', p. 199.; cited also in Yvonne Noble, 'Charles Coffey and John Mottley: An Odd Couple in Grub Street', *Restoration and Eighteenth-Century Theatre Research*, vol. 16, no. 1 (2001), p. 1.
54   On Seedo's association with Fielding in 1730, see Lockwood, *Henry Fielding: Plays Volume 1*, p. 333, note 2. On Seedo's career outside his work for Fielding, see Walter H. Rubsamen, 'Mr. Seedo, Ballad Opera and the Singspiel', *Miscelánea En Homenaje a Monseñor Higinio Anglés*, vol. 2 (Barcelona, 1958–61), pp. 776–809. 'Seedo' (1700–54) was likely the son of Samuel Peter Sydow (Sidow), a musician employed by the Elector of Brandenburg, who came to London as early as 1700, perhaps with Johan Christoph Pepusch. Graydon Beeks, 'Pepusch, Johann Christoph', *MGG Online* <https://www.mgg-online.com/article?id=mgg11831&v=1.0&q=seedo&rs=mgg11831>. Accessed 4 July 2017.

added for Theophilus Cibber who, as the aptly named Gaffar Dungfork, joins in tormenting Nell.[55] *The Devil to Pay* opened on 6 August 1731.[56]

In the action, Lord Loverule has married a woman whose wealth exceeds his. She takes over the 'Province' of her husband, shutting him out from what were formerly his spheres of authority, and rejects all forms of male control.[57] Lady Loverule's extremely bad temper, and hence need for discipline, is shown by her beating servants with a cane, slapping them and pulling their ears, flinging a glass, and hitting a blind man with a fiddle.[58] A magician arrives and requests shelter from Lady Loverule, who rudely rebuffs him. He then asks at the cobbler's house, where Nell receives him graciously, and he predicts her good fortune. When Jobson arrives and sees the magician, he suspects his wife of infidelity; threatening to whip them both, he throws the magician out. The magician revenges himself by transplanting Lady Loverule into Nell's outer form, and Nell into Lady Loverule's. What had been two pairs of socially matched but temperamentally opposed characters (Lady/Lord and Jobson/Nell) become two pairs of socially opposed but temperamentally matched characters (Lady/Jobson and Lord/Nell), freed from the social constraints that had previously governed their interactions.

In contrast to Lady Loverule's violence, which conforms to period notions of the shrew,[59] Jobson's is savage and sexual. He administers five on-stage beatings, and boasts of whipping Nell ten times a day; his threat, 'I'll run my Awl up to the Handle in your Buttocks', suggests the rapist's urge simmering

---

[55] Charles Coffey [and John Mottley], *The Devil to Pay; Or, the Wives Metamorphos'd. An Opera* (London, 1731) [mainpiece], pp. 37–38.

[56] The entries in *The London Stage* and in the *Index to the London Stage* for performances of *The Devil to Pay* from June through to October in 1731 are erroneous. The data entry in the *Index* is: 'DL, Ju 26, 28, Nov 3 …'. The Drury Lane summer company in fact performed *The Devil to Pay* on 6, 16, and 20 August. A pirated version was mounted at Southwark Fair, and advertised on 8, 9, 16, 11, 14, and 18 September; of these bills, only the first is printed in *The London Stage Calendar*. *The Devil to Pay* then ran exclusively at Drury Lane as an afterpiece, on 2, 5, 7, 9, 12, 14, 19, 21, 26, and 28 October. After 28 October, the entries for the 1731–32 season in the *Index* appear to be correct. Ben Ross Schneider, Jr., foreword by George Winchester Stone, Jr., *Index to The London Stage, 1660–1800* (Carbondale, 1979), p. 171, and *The London Stage*, Part 3, vol. 1, pp. 150–51, 159–64.

[57] Coffey [and Mottley], *The Devil to Pay* [mainpiece], p. 12.

[58] Coffey [and Mottley], *The Devil to Pay* [mainpiece]: Lady Loverule strikes the butler and 'Lugs' (pulls) the ears of the maidservant Lucy, p. 13; beats the servants collectively with the cane of a priest in her retinue, p. 14; strikes Jobson, who is visiting her servants p. 14; 'Beats the Fiddle about the blind Man's Head', p. 15; flings objects at Jobson and 'flies at him', p. 37; 'falls upon' one his colleagues, p. 38; throws a glass at the butler, p. 57; and pulls off the maidservant's head-dress, and strikes her, p. 57.

[59] As Elizabeth Foyster notes, the sorts of violence associated during the late seventeenth century with unruly wives included 'pulling wigs, hair, beards or moustaches and using household implements to inflict injury'. Elizabeth Foyster, *Marital Violence: An English Family History, 1660–1857* (Cambridge, 2005), p. 103.

beneath the surface of his dialogue.[60] Unfettered by decorum, he duly subdues Lady Loverule: their central scene begins with her verbally attacking Jobson and ends with Jobson strapping her until she begs for mercy.[61] Meanwhile, the long-suffering Nell enjoys the desserts of the rich. She crows over her rags-to-riches elevation, luxuriating in the comforts of chocolate, coaches, and fine clothing.[62] Her brief exchange with Lord Loverule confounds them both: he because the new personality of his 'wife' contradicts all his previous experience of Lady Loverule; she because his gentility is entirely new to her.[63] None of this can last, of course; the principle of recuperation requires restoration of the *status quo ante*, and the two women are returned to their own bodies. Lasting benefit, however, has been achieved by Jobson's violence: Lady Loverule is reformed, for which Lord Loverule rewards Jobson with five hundred pounds; she expresses gratitude for her beatings, because '[t]he Joy of this blessed Change sets all things right again'.[64]

Wife-beating of the kind expected among the lower orders is here the corrective for a termagant of high rank. Three of the eight ballads of Jevon's original farce celebrate the practice: 'He that has the best Wife' (sung to 'The Twitcher'), 'In Bath a wanton Wife did dwell', and 'Let the vain Spark'.[65] For *The Devil to Pay*, Jevon's words to 'The Twitcher' were preserved,[66] possibly because his double meanings were too rich to let go. Traditionally, the 'Twitcher' had been a wife's complaint about her husband, but Jevon reversed this to have Jobson lament:

> He that has the best Wife,
> She's the Burthen of his Life,
> But for her that will Scold and will Quarrel;
> Let him cut her short

---

[60] Coffey [and Mottley], *The Devil to Pay* [mainpiece], p. 21. Jobson also 'lugs and throws ... down' the priest, p. 14; beats Nell, p. 21; straps Lady Loverule twice, pp. 37–38; and 'smacks' her, p. 54.

[61] '*She flings it [the spindle] down, he straps her.* Lady: "Hold, hold, I'll do any thing."' *Ibid.*, p. 38.

[62] *Ibid.*, pp. 39–43.

[63] *Ibid.*, p. 48.

[64] *Ibid.*, p. 67.

[65] Thomas Jevon [and Thomas Shadwell?], *The Devil of a Wife: Or, a Comical Transformation* (London, 1686), pp. 2, 26–27, 40. Other songs in this play are a drinking catch 'While you Court a damn'd Vintner', p. 7; a Wassail song, p. 11, repeated on p. 50; the Doctor's conjuring song 'Praesto, all my Charms attend', p. 16; the spirits' song 'Well met, 'tis time we now be gone', p. 25; and a catch led by the butler, p. 50.

[66] *The Devil to Pay* [mainpiece], pp. 3–4. The first two stanzas of the 1688 ballad 'Let the vain Spark', which condemn women, were likewise retained; this ballad's last two stanzas, which celebrate marriage, were omitted. Air 32, *ibid.*, p. 51.

Of her Meat and her Sport,
And ten times a day hoop her Barrel.[67]

Jobson's ballad, which he sings repeatedly, pithily sums up *The Devil to Pay*'s moral.[68] Twelve more of the forty-two musical numbers in *The Devil to Pay* denigrate women, prescribe female conduct, or articulate male rights over the fair sex. The verse lines central to these songs – usually the first – capture their messages: Air 5, 'Of all the Plagues of Human Life / A Shrew is sure the worst'; Air 6, 'Tempestuous as the Seas and Winds, / Are some capricious Womens Minds'; Air 8, 'What sonorous Noise / Can equal the Voice / Of such a damn'd termagant Shrew?'; Air 12, 'Of the States in Life so various, / Marriage, sure, is most precarious'; Air 18, 'The Man who wou'd sum up in one, / All Plagues of Human Life / … Will find them in a Wife'; Air 19, 'When the Mind / Of Woman's blind, / All Demonstration's vain'; Air 21, 'But of Storms in Womens Souls, / No Mortal oft can guess the Cause'; Air 24, '[The Cobler] Has nought but his Wife / To ruffle his Life, / And her he can strap if she vex him'; Air 29, 'Fine Ladies with an artful Grace, / Disguise each native Feature'; Air 32, 'Let the vain Spark consume his Store, / In keeping an expensive Whore'; Air 34, 'If you marry a Wife … / She'll be wanton for Life'; and Air 41, 'Above the base Sphere in which she was bred, / When a Beggar is mounted, it turns her head'.[69]

The tunes of all these songs are common, primarily jigs or country dances, with modal scale patterns, typically Aeolian or Mixolydian (with a whole tone between the seventh and eighth degree of the scale). As in Jobson's 'Twitcher', the melodies contain wide skips and broken chord motifs. Each song's music is as raw as its words, fortifying the early modern argument for thrashing wives who struggle 'for the breeches'.[70]

Clive's Nell, or Violence Reformed

Clive's performance changed *The Devil to Pay* from a celebration of abuse into a sentimental love story. But how? Nell has only four brief scenes: in the first, which has two numbers for her (Air 1 and Air 4), Jobson threatens to beat her; in the second she meets the magician and sings of her pending change

---

[67] Jevon [and Shadwell?], *The Devil of a Wife*, p. 2; see also Coffey and [Mottley], *The Devil to Pay* [mainpiece], pp. 3–4. In the latter version the word 'Plague' replaces the word 'Burthen'.

[68] When Jobson sings this ballad, it is printed as two verse lines, in italics, which function as a stage direction to sing as he exits the stage: '*He that has the best Wife,/She's the Plague of his Life, &c.* [Exeunt.]'. The ballad lines are thus printed in both *The Devil of a Wife* and in early editions of *The Devil to Pay*. Jevon [and Shadwell?], *The Devil of a Wife*, pp. 2–3; Coffey [and Mottley], *The Devil to Pay* [mainpiece], p. 5. In playbooks of *The Devil to Pay* issued after 1732, Jobson's repeated air became Air 10.

[69] Coffey [and Mottley], *The Devil to Pay* [mainpiece], *passim*.

[70] Foyster, *Marital Violence*, p. 68.

of fortune (Air 15); in the third (Air 25), she finds herself in Lady Loverule's rooms; and in the last she realizes, by looking in a glass, that she inhabits Lady Loverule's form, and encounters Lord Loverule for the only time (Airs 29, 30 and 31).[71] In her dialogue, Nell is passive and simple-minded. In response to Jobson's threat to strap her 'most confoundedly', she replies 'we poor Women must always be Slaves'.[72] A duet with Jobson follows in which she begs him to 'Reel home to Nell' when he's drunk, and ends her scene with the words 'I must obey'.[73] She later excuses Jobson's loutish behaviour thus: 'my Husband is somewhat rugged, and in his Cups will beat me, but it is not much; he's an honest Painstaking Man, and I let him have his way'.[74]

Clive's songs were her opportunity to forge Nell anew. From Air 15 onwards, the tunes and words of Nell's airs project another character altogether – plucky, charming, vivacious. The ambitious Irish playwright Coffey almost certainly prepared the Nell numbers that matched Clive's line, which Clive then exploited.[75] In Air 15, Nell sings the melody 'Send home my long-stray'd Eyes', taken from seventeenth-century court composer John Coprario's setting of John Donne.[76] Richard Leveridge had in 1727 paraphrased, re-versified, and popularized this lute song, and Leveridge's version then cascaded down into *The Devil to Pay*.[77] Coprario's courtly tune and Coffey's words suggest Clive's rising rank as well as Nell's radical change of fortune: 'No more shall People call me

---

[71] Meeting Lord Loverule in Act II, scene 1, Nell promises, 'Sir, I shall always be proud to do every thing that may give you Delight, and your Family Satisfaction.' Coffey [and Mottley], *The Devil to Pay* [mainpiece], p. 48.

[72] Nell's response is to Jobson's threat, 'my Strap shall wind about thy Ribs most confoundedly'. Coffey [and Mottley], *The Devil to Pay* [mainpiece], pp. 3–4.

[73] *Ibid.*, pp. 4–5.

[74] *Ibid.*, p. 20.

[75] Yvonne Noble observes that John Mottley was 'born to live gravely in dignity and honor' and therefore likely abhorred working with Coffey, who specialized in low theatre. Noble, 'Charles Coffey and John Mottley', pp. 1–12. Extending Noble's argument, I believe Mottley would not have crafted songs that narrow the gap in social rank between Nell and Lady Loverule. In my reading, Mottley gave Nell common tunes for a common character. In Air 1, which I attribute to Mottley, Nell begs 'Dear Jobson, do not from me go', to the plaintive common tune 'True Love shall never'. I also think Mottley gave her the duet with Jobson (Air 4) in which she, to plead for his affection, sings the melody of a rude catch that depicts two persons quarrelling in a tavern ('Fie, nay, pr'ythee John'), *ibid.*, p. 2. This catch, first published in 1685, is by John Blow and has been misattributed to Henry Purcell. The misattribution arose after the catch was taken up by the Noblemen and Gentlemen's Catch Club, founded in 1761. Sandra Tuppen, *Early Music*, vol. 43, no. 2 (2015), pp. 233–45, esp. 'Table 1', p. 235.

[76] Noble, 'Charles Coffey and John Mottley', p. 4.

[77] Coprario set Donne's words in 1613 and Leveridge radically altered the music and words of the song that he inherited. See Richard Leveridge, 'The Message', reprinted in facsimile as '74' in Richard Leveridge, *Complete Songs (with the music in Macbeth) 1697–1770*, introduction and notes by O. Baldwin and T. Wilson. Music for London Entertainment, series A, vol. 6 (London, 1997), pages unnumbered. The song was initially printed as 'VII' in the second volume of Leveridge's *A Collection of Songs* (London, 1727), pp. 16–17.

Nell, / Her Ladyship will do as well, / Deck'd in my golden, rich Array, / I'll in my Chariot roll away, / And shine at Ring, at Ball, and Play.'[78]

Into Clive's final scene are squeezed three numbers whose words and musical associations frame the singer as incorruptible. In Air 29, Nell praises natural beauty over the artifices of Fine Ladies: 'But we poor Folks in home-spun Grey, / By Patch nor Washes tainted, / Look fresh and sweeter far than they, / That still are finely painted.'[79] The tune is 'Dame of Honour', early words to which had recounted Barbara Villiers' suffering at the hands of her husband, the rake and bigamist Major General Robert Fielding, incarcerated for his misdeeds in 1706.[80] Before she sings again, Nell rejoices that she has become Lady Loverule. She delights in Lord Loverule's kindness, and he in her submission to his will, as she exclaims 'what, shall I disobey my Lord and Master?'.[81] Having experienced the 'happy State' of a polite union, she resolves henceforth to challenge Jobson, concluding her next number, Air 30, with: 'Jobson, now adieu, / Thy Cobling still pursue, / For hence I will not, cannot, no, nor must not buckle to.'[82] The melody here is ''Twas within a Furlong', also known as 'The Scotch Haymakers', thought at the time to be by Purcell.[83] The music of Air 30 thus did double duty, nourishing Clive's Purcellian line and evoking a 'Scotch' pastoral scene where lovers might unite, despite the gulf between their stations.[84]

Nell's final melody comes from the c.1725 song 'The Country Lass: or the Lofty Shepherdess'. Here Clive's reputation was again invoked as the 'Lofty Shepherdess', rather than the Purcellian singer. This number combines two different ballads, both known as 'The Country Lass'. One is a broadside, whose verses ('Although I am a countrey lasse, / A lofty mind I beare-a') Coffey paraphrased;[85] the second is Henry Carey's celebrated song 'Sally in our Alley', mentioned in Chapter 2:

---

[78] Coffey [and Mottley], Air 15, *The Devil to Pay* [mainpiece], pp. 20–21.
[79] Ibid., pp. 47–48.
[80] Simpson, *The British Broadside Ballad*, pp. 155–57.
[81] Coffey [and Mottley], *The Devil to Pay* [mainpiece], p. 49.
[82] Ibid.
[83] ''Twas within a Furlong' was given the Purcell catalogue number Z 605/2. Claude Simpson believes that Charles Powell may have been the composer. Simpson, *The British Broadside Ballad*, pp. 635–38. It circulated in broadsheets, songsheets, miscellanies, and dance collections.
[84] Steve Newman discusses the ways in which, from the early 1720s, the poet, playwright, song collector, and bookseller Allan Ramsay drew together apposite 'Scots' ballads and enjoined audiences to imagine Scotland as the preserve of country pleasures elsewhere under siege. Steve Newman, 'Scots Songs in the Scottish Enlightenment: Pastoral, Progress, and the Lyric Split in Allan Ramsay, John Home, and Robert Burns', *Ballad Collection, Lyric, and the Canon: The Call of the Popular from the Restoration to the New Criticism* (Philadelphia, 2007), pp. 44–60.
[85] Simpson, *The British Broadside Ballad*, pp. 134–36. A printed ballad by Martin Parker of c.1630 begins 'Although I am a countrey lasse, / A lofty mind I beare-a'.

Tho' late I was a Cobler's Wife,
In Cottage most obscure-a,
In plain-stuff Gown, and short-ear'd Coif,
Hard Labour did endure-a:
The Scene is chang'd, I'm alter'd quite,
And from poor humble Nell-a,
I'll learn to dance, to read, and write,
And from all bear the Bell-a.[86]

An English broadside rolled into the best-known tune of Clive's music master was a shrewd, and powerful, set-up; Clive ran with it. Defying Jevon's characterization through her song, she transformed Nell, and her own career.

That Clive's great breakthrough was not as a principal in a sophisticated stage work, but as a second-tier dramatis persona in a derivative and venal farce, speaks for a talent far superior to Lavinia Fenton's. Clive followed Fenton's practice of challenging the playbook to tease sentimentality out of her part, but Clive's Nell, unlike Fenton's Polly, is upstanding: whereas Polly longs for Macheath, Nell defies her husband; whereas Polly admits to apeing a Fine Lady, Nell decries a Lady's artifice; whereas Polly's appeal is sexual, Nell's is founded on a call for justice. Clive built on these differences through performance, winning audiences over to her reading of the character. One writer, almost certainly the seasoned opera critic Aaron Hill,[87] captured audience response:

> But sure nothing has had a greater Run, than a little *Farce* called, *The Devil to Pay* … it has been perform'd almost every Night this Season; your little Favourite Miss Raftor appears a Prodigy in this Piece, it has render'd her the Darling of the whole Town.[88]

David E. Baker, writing after Clive retired, recalled that her 'Merit in this Character … not only established her own Reputation with the Audience, but fixed the Piece itself on the constant List of acting Farces, an Honour which perhaps it would never have arrived at, had she not been in it'.[89]

---

[86] Coffey [and Mottley], *The Devil to Pay* [mainpiece], p. 50.

[87] Robert D. Hume gives six persuasive reasons for Aaron Hill's authorship in his introduction to this pamphlet's facsimile reprint; Christine Gerrard summarizes Hume's evidence, and provides her own. Robert D. Hume, 'Introduction', *See and Seem Blind: Or, a Critical Dissertation on the Publick Diversions, &c.* (Los Angeles, 1986), pp. i–xii; cited in Gerrard, *Aaron Hill: The Muses' Projector*, pp. 147–48, note 9. *See and Seem Blind* was sold from 8 June 1732: 'This Day is Published, See and Seem Blind', *Daily Journal*, issue 3566 (8 June 1732).

[88] [Aaron Hill], *See and Seem Blind: Or, a Critical Dissertation on the Publick Diversions, &c* (London, [1732]), pp. 8–9.

[89] [David E. Baker], 'CLIVE, Mrs. Catharine', in *The Companion to the Play-house*, vol. 2 (London, 1764), pages unnumbered.

The Devil to Pay: Metamorphoses of Playbook and Player

As with *Damon and Phillida*, a fringe theatre immediately challenged Drury Lane with its own *Devil to Pay* production. Between 6 August, when the work premiered, and the end of the summer season, a brief competitive flurry ensued between Drury Lane (three performances) and Lee and Harper's Booth at Southwark Fair (six).[90] Once the regular season opened, Drury Lane took steps to secure *The Devil to Pay*, cutting the mainpiece down to a Clive-centred afterpiece.[91] What had begun as low farce became sentimental sung comedy, opened by Nell, not Jobson. The afterpiece version opened on 2 October,[92] and by 27 November one report boasted that 'the *Devil to pay* ... is said, according to a moderate Computation' to have 'clear'd above a Thousand Pounds already this Season' for Drury Lane.[93] Clive's success almost certainly prompted the newly operatized version of John Gay's W*hat d'ye call It*, led on 11 August by Clive as Kitty Carrot.[94]

Drury Lane then in 1732 tweaked this afterpiece, which had contained eighteen numbers, into a sixteen-air version whose wordbook survives in rare

---

[90] At Lee and Harper's Booth, a version with 'above 30 New Songs' was mounted, but no such version survives. *Daily Advertiser*, issue 196 (18 September 1731). Watts sold the mainpiece playbook from 11 or 12 August. Arthur H. Scouten and Leo Hughes, 'The Devil to Pay: A Preliminary Check List', *Library Chronicle of the Friends of the University of Pennsylvania Library*, vol. 15 (1948/49), p. 15.

[91] Since 1747, writers have erroneously claimed that *The Devil to Pay* failed as a three-act mainpiece and that this failure prompted the work's abridgement. One source of misapprehension has been the anonymous account, ascribed to the ballad opera's co-author John Mottley: 'It was performed in the Summer Season, in three Acts, but some Part of it not pleasing, particularly the Part of a Non-Conforming Pastor ... it was cut shorter, that Part left out, and so reduced to one Act.' [Mottley?], 'A Compleat LIST Of all the *English* Dramatic POETS', p. 199.. This scarcely credible story resurfaces in Sybil Rosenfeld, *The Theatre of the London Fairs in the Eighteenth Century* (Cambridge, 1960), p. 91; Leo Hughes and Arthur H. Scouten, ed., *Ten English Farces* (Austin, 1948), pp. 175–76; and Fiske, *English Theatre Music in the Eighteenth Century*, p. 112. Rosenfeld, Hughes, and Scouten argue that the omission of the priest from the Southwark Fair cast list – known only from bills – attests to the public's rejection of this dramatis persona; adaptations at fairs were, however, typically made to accommodate a throw-together company. The omissions in *The London Stage Calendar* of *The Devil to Pay*'s early productions (see notes 56 and 92) have not helped to correct the record.

[92] The index created for *The London Stage Calendar* omits the 1731–32 season performances of *The Devil to Pay* on October 2, 5, 7, 9, 14, 19, 21, 26, and 28.

[93] *Read's Weekly Journal or British Gazetteer*, issue 349 (27 November 1731).

[94] *Daily Post*, issue 3712 (11 August 1731): 'At the particular Desire of several Persons of Quality and Distinction, and Eminent Merchants of the City of London. The FOURTEENTH DAY. ... A New Play, call'd The LONDON MERCHANT ... With the Prologue and Epilogue, and Singing by Miss Raftor ... To which will be added, The WHAT D'YE CALL IT. Reviv'd. A Tragi-Comi-Pastoral-Farcical Ballad-Opera. Intermix'd with a Variety of new Songs made to old Ballad-Tunes and Country-Dances. The Part of Kitty Carrot by Miss Raftor.'

copies.[95] Of the songs cut or added, one alteration changed the action as well as the music: a new duet for Nell and Lord Loverule set to Handel's music. The occasion for the changes may have been the performance of 8 December commanded by Frederick, Prince of Wales,[96] for whom a new drinking song to the King might also have been added (see Table 3.1). In both the eighteen- and sixteen-air afterpieces, minor parts were excised and the cast slimmed from eighteen players in the mainpiece to five players in the afterpiece. Principals, which in the original version did not include Nell, lost dialogue, while most of Clive's dialogue was kept.[97] Principals' songs were also cut but Nell's were largely preserved, giving Clive the most music. Of Clive's six original solos in the mainpiece, she retained four whose order changed; once re-organized, her songs in both afterpiece versions dramatize Nell's progression from hope ('Fine Ladies with an artful Grace') to gratitude ('O charming Cunning-Man! thou has been wond'rous kind') to triumphant joy ('Tho' late I was a Cobler's Wife'). In the sixteen-air version, these three points build up to Nell's new duet with Lord Loverule, played by the Irish tenor Charles Stoppelaer, who had joined Drury Lane in September 1730.

In the mainpiece *Devil to Pay*, Clive and Stoppelaer had shared no music and only one scene. Their separation accorded with Jevon's playbook: for seventeenth-century audiences, Nell and Lord Loverule belonged to different spheres. By 1731, however, sentimental comedy was core entertainment,[98] and through her singing, Clive had dragged Nell into this tradition. In the new Clive–Stoppelaer duet, a literally harmonious union resulted. Rather than

---

[95] '[I]n 1732, an edition in one act but with sixteen songs had been printed ... it became the standard text for the later London printings until the last quarter of the century.' Scouten and Hughes, 'The Devil to Pay: A Preliminary Check List', p. 16. In Scouten and Hughes' list of editions the sixteen-air 1732 wordbook is number 5 (p. 18), but notes about this version's songs are inaccurate. To assess the sixteen-air 1732 wordbook I have consulted the copy held at the National Art Gallery, Victoria & Albert Museum, accession number Dyce M 2278. This is not listed in the English Short Title Catalogue. What seems to be the only other extant wordbook of the 1732 sixteen-air version is held at Harry Ransom Center Book Collection of the University of Texas in Austin (its catalogue wrongly links this item to the English Short Title Catalogue number T58096). Watts' 1738 *Devil to Pay* edition replicates the sixteen-air version of 1732.

[96] Notice of *The Devil to Pay*'s royal command performance appeared in the *Daily Post*, issue 3814 (8 December 1731). Advertisements for the afterpiece version do not distinguish between the version with eighteen and the version with sixteen airs.

[97] Speeches by Lord and Lady Loverule were omitted or condensed, while only five lines spoken by Nell were cut. The characters excised from Coffey's three-act version were Ranger and Valentine (friends of Lord Loverule), Lady Loverule's father, the serving boy, Gaffar Dungfork, the Fiddler, and the priest Ananias. Compare Coffey [and Mottley], *The Devil to Pay* [mainpiece] to Charles Coffey [and John Mottley], *The Devil to Pay; or, The Wives Metamorphos'd. An Opera* (London, 1731) [afterpiece], in which Nell's lines are moved to pp. 41, 45, and 48–9.

[98] Robert D. Hume, 'Drama and Theatre in the Mid and Later Eighteenth Century', *The Cambridge History of English Literature, 1660–1780* (Cambridge, 2005), pp. 316–39.

being added to Nell and Lord Loverule's unique spoken scene, the duet was inserted after Air 12 to 'Sally in our Alley' (originally Air 31), in which Nell vows not to 'buckle' to a man she despises. The duet follows a violent row between Lady Loverule and the Cobbler, setting up a contrast of bad femininity with good: after the termagant misbehaves, the intrepid Nell melts hearts through music.

For Clive's new duet, someone – possibly Seedo, or Theophilus Cibber, to whom the adaptation is attributed in modern catalogues, or even Clive herself – latched onto the aria 'Nò, non temere' from Handel's *Ottone*, earlier popularized by Richard Leveridge in a simplified version.[99] The addition matched Clive's then-nascent line in occasional Handel song. As a minor character in the original version of Gay's *The What D'ye Call It*, she had sung its only air, 'Twas when the Seas' from April 1729 until at least March 1731, and probably also during summer productions to August 1731. Handel had composed the air around 1715, probably for Gay's use.[100] From April 1731 Clive had performed 'Son confusa pastorella' from Handel's *Poro* during interludes; this was almost certainly the music of the c.1731 songsheet, *Son confuse pastorella. The celebrated Song in Porus sung by Signora Merighi*.[101] From 25 June 1731 her *Poro* air had apparently been interpolated into George Lillo's tragedy *The London Merchant* by the summer company, where she enjoyed more autonomy;[102] the

---

[99] According to Charles Burney, '[t]he number of songs in this opera [*Ottone*] that became national favourites, [was] perhaps greater than in any other that was ever performed in England', and among these Leveridge's setting ranked first. Charles Burney, *A General History of Music, from the Earliest Ages to the Present Period*, vol. 4 (London, 1789), pp. 286–87; cited in Winton Dean and John Merrill Knapp, *Handel's Operas, 1704–1726*, rev. edn (Oxford, 1994), p. 424. Besides circulating as a songsheet, Leveridge's version was reprinted in more miscellanies than any other single aria from *Ottone*, as shown in William C. Smith, *Handel: A Descriptive Catalogue of the Early Editions*, 2nd edn (Oxford, 1970), p. 46.

[100] The attribution to Handel began to appear in song collections of the 1730s; when first printed in 1716, the song was anonymous. Burrows et al., ed., *George Frideric Handel Collected Documents: Volume 1 1609–1725*, p. 310.

[101] Graham Cummings, 'Handel and the confus'd Shepherdess: A Case Study of Stylistic Eclecticism', *Early Music*, vol. 33, no. 4 (2005), pp. 575–89, esp. pp. 577–79. A 1731 English-language version of this air, also popular, was for a male voice (*When fearful Pastorella strays. Ye Bagpipe song in Porus. Ye Words by T. Brerewood junior*). Ibid., p. 588, note 14.

[102] As Erissena, Antonia Merighi premiered 'Son confusa pastorella' in Handel's *Poro* on 2 February 1731. The air was an immediate favourite, in print and at playhouses. Known also as 'the Merigghi Song', the aria was sung by Clive as an interlude on 26 and 27 April and 6 and 19 May 1731, and perhaps on 22 April 1731, when notices gave out that she would perform in Italian and English. Clive's additional song in *The London Merchant* was announced thus: 'The LONDON MERCHANT ... In which will be sung Signora Meriggi's Favourite Song in Porus, by Miss Rafto [sic]'. *Daily Post*, issue 3699 (27 July 1731). *The London Merchant* was then advertised simply with 'singing by Miss Raftor' on 25 and 30 June, 6 and 20 July, and 3, 11, 16, and 20 August 1731. Bills with the same announcement appeared on 16 October, 11 November, and 27 December 1731, and on 17

Table 3.1 Comparison of Airs in *The Devil to Pay*, 1731–32

Table 3.1 shows the three versions of *The Devil to Pay* from 6 August 1731 to the end of the 1731–32 season. Airs were cut, re-ordered, and new airs added. In this table, 'deleted' means an air was cut; a blank space to the right of 'deleted' shows the air stayed cut; air numbers show the order of airs; an added air receives a new row.

Character	Three-act mainpiece published by John Watts, 1731 Air number: Incipit Title of air	One-act afterpiece, eighteen-air version published by John Watts, 1731 Air number: Incipit Title of air	One-act afterpiece, sixteen-air version published by John Watts, 1732 Air number: Incipit Title of air
Nell	Air 1: 'Dear Jobson, do not from me go' True Love shall never	deleted	
Jobson	Air 2: 'About the great Hall Table' London Apprentice	deleted	
Jobson	Air 3: 'He that has the best Wife' The Twitcher	Air 1: 'He that has the best Wife' The Twitcher	Air 1: 'He that has the best Wife' The Twitcher
Jobson and Nell	Air 4: "Tis, I vow and swear'/ Fie, nay, pr'ythee John [duet]	Air 2: "Tis, I vow and swear' Fie, nay, pr'ythee John [duet]	deleted
Butler	Air 5: 'Of all the Plagues of Human Life' Under the Greenwood Tree	Air 3: 'Of all the Plagues of Human Life' Under the Greenwood Tree	replaced
Butler			Air 3: 'Here's a good Health to the King' [composition unattributed]
Sir John		Air 5: 'Ye Gods! you gave to me a Wife'. Set by Mr. Seedo [after Mr. Snow, *The Banquet of Music ... the First Book* (London: Henry Playford, 1688), p. 23]	Air 4: 'Ye Gods! you gave to me a Wife'. Set by Mr. Seedo [after Mr. Snow, *The Banquet of Music ... the First Book* (London: Henry Playford, 1688), p. 23]

Character	Three-act mainpiece published by John Watts, 1731 — Air number: Incipit / Title of air	One-act afterpiece, eighteen-air version published by John Watts, 1731 — Air number: Incipit / Title of air	One-act afterpiece, sixteen-air version published by John Watts, 1732 — Air number: Incipit / Title of air
Lucy	Air 6: 'Tempestuous as the Seas and Winds' / 'Twas when the Sun	deleted	
Butler	Air 7: 'Like Solon, for Wisdom, how was I rever'd' / In the Highlands of Scotland	deleted	
Cook	Air 8: 'What sonorous Noise' / There was an old Man	deleted	
Jobson	Air 9: 'No Liquor like Punch gives Delight to the Soul' / Abbot of Canterbury	deleted	
Butler	Air 10: 'Come, jolly Bacchus, God of Wine' / Charles of Sweden	Air 4: 'Come, jolly Bacchus, God of Wine' / Charles of Sweden	Air 2: 'Come, jolly Bacchus, God of Wine' / Charles of Sweden
Lady Loverule	Air 11: 'Pry'thee be gone' / Chloe, be kind	deleted	
Sir John	Air 12: 'Of the States in Life so various' / Of all Comforts I miscarry'd	Air 6: 'Of the States in Life so various' / Of all Comforts I miscarry'd	Air 5: 'Of the States in Life so various' / Of all Comforts I miscarry'd
Lady Loverule and Sir John	Air 13: 'Tell me no more of This, or That' / Contented Country Farmer [duet]	Air 7: 'Tell me no more of This, or That' / Contented Country Farmer [duet]	deleted

Character	Three-act mainpiece published by John Watts, 1731 — Air number: Incipit / Title of air	One-act afterpiece, eighteen-air version published by John Watts, 1731 — Air number: Incipit / Title of air	One-act afterpiece, sixteen-air version published by John Watts, 1732 — Air number: Incipit / Title of air
Sir John			Air 6: 'Grant me, ye Pow'rs! but this Request' Contented Country Farmer
Ananias	Air 14: 'What tho' this Punch be most prophane' Troy Town		
Nell	Air 15: 'My swelling Heart now leaps with Joy' Send home my long-stray'd Eyes	Air 8: 'My swelling Heart now leaps with Joy' Send home my long-stray'd Eyes	Air 7: 'My swelling Heart now leaps with Joy' Send home my long-stray'd Eyes
Doctor	Air 16: 'My little Spirits now appear' The Spirit's Song in Macbeth [after music from Macbeth, 1702]	Air 9: 'My little Spirits now appear' The Spirit's Song in Macbeth [after music from Macbeth, 1702]	Air 8: 'My little Spirits now appear' The Spirit's Song in Macbeth [after music from Macbeth, 1702]
Sir John	Air 17: 'Thus we'll drown all Melancholy' Bacchus one Day gayly striding	Air 17: 'Thus we'll drown all Melancholy' Bacchus one Day gayly striding	deleted
Sir John	Air 18: 'The Man who wou'd sum up in one' We all to conquering Beauty bow	deleted	
Butler	Air 19: 'When the Mind' Celadon, when Spring came on	deleted	
Butler	Air 20: 'Lyes without number' Dear Pickaninny	deleted	
Sir John	Air 21: 'When the dreadful Thunder rolls' Over the Hills and far away	deleted	

Character	Three-act mainpiece published by John Watts, 1731 — Air number: Incipit / Title of air	One-act afterpiece, eighteen-air version published by John Watts, 1731 — Air number: Incipit / Title of air	One-act afterpiece, sixteen-air version published by John Watts, 1732 — Air number: Incipit / Title of air
Nadir and Abishog	Air 22: 'The Charm on the Women is now wrought so sure' The Yorkshire Tale [duet]	deleted	
Jobson	Air 23: 'Of all the Trades from East to West' Charming Sally	Air 10: 'Of all the Trades from East to West' Charming Sally	Air 9: 'Of all the Trades from East to West' Charming Sally
Jobson			Air 10: 'In Bath a wanton Wife did dwell' Now ponder well, ye Parents dear
Jobson	Air 24: 'Let Matters of State' Come, let us prepare	Air 11: 'Let Matters of State' Come, let us prepare	Air 11: 'Let Matters of State' Come, let us prepare
Nell	Air 25: 'Sure all is Paradise around' When all was wrapt	deleted	
Lucy	Air 26: 'All unwilling, pay Submission' Whilst I gaze on Chloe trembling	deleted	
Sir John	Air 27: 'Hounds and Horns o'er Plains resounding' Whilst the Town agrees with Polly	Air 13: 'Hounds and Horns o'er Plains resounding' Whilst the Town agrees with Polly	deleted
Lucy, Butler	Air 28: 'Like Felons, or Debtors' Bath Medley [duet]		
Nell	Air 29: 'Fine Ladies with an artful Grace' When I was a Dame of Honour	Air 14: 'Fine Ladies with an artful Grace' When I was a Dame of Honour	Air 13: 'Fine Ladies with an artful Grace' When I was a Dame of Honour
Nell	Air 30: 'O charming Cunning-Man!' 'Twas within a Furlong	Air 15: 'O charming Cunning-Man!' 'Twas within a Furlong	Air 14: 'O charming Cunning-Man!' 'Twas within a Furlong

Character	Three-act mainpiece published by John Watts, 1731 Air number: Incipit Title of air	One-act afterpiece, eighteen-air version published by John Watts, 1731 Air number: Incipit Title of air	One-act afterpiece, sixteen-air version published by John Watts, 1732 Air number: Incipit Title of air
Nell	Air 31: 'Tho' late I was a Cobler's Wife' What tho' I am a Country Lass	Air 12: 'Tho' late I was a Cobler's Wife' What tho' I am a Country Lass	Air 12: 'Tho' late I was a Cobler's Wife' What tho' I am a Country Lass
Sir John and Nell			Air 15: Duetto 'Was ever a man possest' [duet, after Handel, 'Nò, non temere, o bella,' *Ottone* (1723)]
Sir John	Air 32: 'Let the vain Spark consume his Store' If Love the Virgin's Heart invade	deleted	
Lady Loverule	Air 33: 'Was Woman e'er abus'd like me' Sawny was tall	deleted	
Jobson	Air 34: 'If you marry a Wife' There was a Maid in the West		
Lady Loverule	Air 35: 'Tho' ravish'd from my Husband's Arms' The Budgeon it is a fine Trade	Air 16: 'Tho' ravish'd from my Husband's Arms' The Budgeon it is a fine Trade	deleted
Lady Loverule	Air 36: 'How truly compleat are my Woes!' Grim King of the Ghosts	deleted	
Ananias	Air 37: 'Tho' to Opinion I'll ne'er die a Martyr' Three Sheep Skins	deleted	
Ananias	Air 38: 'Of all the Joys beneath the Sun' Four and twenty Highwaymen	deleted	

Character	Three-act mainpiece published by John Watts, 1731		One-act afterpiece, eighteen-air version published by John Watts, 1731		One-act afterpiece, sixteen-air version published by John Watts, 1732	
	Air number: Incipit	Title of air	Air number: Incipit	Title of air	Air number: Incipit	Title of air
Sir John	Air 39: 'So the Wretch o'erwhelm'd with Sorrow'	Take a Kiss or twa	deleted			
Ananias	Air 40: 'Come fill about the sparkling Wine'	We've sail'd the Seas	deleted			
Jobson	Air 41: 'Then come to thy own poor Hut again'	When Orpheus tickled his Harp	deleted			
Lady Loverule and Sir John	Air 42: 'May no Remembrance of past Time'	Hey Boys up go [duet]	deleted			
Lady Loverule, Sir John and Jobson			Air 18: 'Let ev'ry Face with Smiles appear'	Hey Boys up go we	Air 16: 'Let ev'ry Face with Smiles appear'	Hey Boys up go we

great success of *The London Merchant* had delayed the opening of *The Devil to Pay*.[103]

A striking similarity between Clive's 'Son confusa pastorella' and her new duet in *The Devil to Pay* is the preservation of the detail of Handel's composition. In *The Devil to Pay* duet all of Handel's original features are intact: the instrumental introduction, the violin accompaniment, the figured bass, even the dynamic markings (see Ex. 3.2).[104] This is, according to extant notation, unique: ballad opera airs from high-style sources without exception otherwise duplicate earlier common-tune versions, like Leveridge's adaptation, here unused. In *The Devil to Pay*, the only change to Handel's original music was a new affect.

In *Ottone*, 'Nò, non temere' is sung by the brother of the opera's heroine, a bass, who boisterously assures her that his sword will defend them both.[105] In *The Devil to Pay*, Handel's music is an amorous duet, with ten fermatas inserted to linger over tender moments. The fermatas slow the pace, highlight emotional climaxes, accommodate extemporization, and give time for an exchange of kisses called for in the stage directions. To gradually heighten passion, Handel's phrases are split into ever-shorter exchanges (bars 16–35) that culminate in the cadence (bars 44–45) where the lovers finally join voice. Trills over the words 'enfold' and 'behold' (bars 55 and 57) intensify their longing.

Around the time *The Devil to Pay* took hold, Clive received the first substantive encomium of her career. Unusually, this was a high-style song rather than a poem or ballad, and its suspiciously Carey-esque music – a charming, ballad-style air in compound meter – was fitted with six stanzas by a certain George Monro (Ex. 3.3). Monro depicts Clive as a consummate artist, who 'Charms with Melody Divine', and whose 'Melting Air' causes 'all the Muses to joyn' in consort.[106] Yet she is beyond the audience's grasp: a 'Virgin', she belongs to the sphere 'Where Youth and Blooming Glories reign'.[107] Her subtlety commands

---

and 29 May, 21 August, and 26 October 1732. On the early popularity of 'Son confusa pastorella', see Cummings, 'Handel and the confus'd Shepherdess', pp. 577–79.

[103] Multiple scholars have documented the impact of this unexpected hit tragedy, which dignified and instructed the common man. See, among other writings, Lincoln B. Faller, *The Popularity of Addison's Cato and Lillo's The London Merchant, 1700–1776* (New York, 1988), pp. 88–180 and David Mazella, '"Justly to Fall Unpitied and Abhorr'd": Sensibility, Punishment, and Morality in Lillo's The London Merchant', *English Language History*, vol. 68, no. 4 (2001), pp. 795–830.

[104] I have prepared Ex. 3.2 from the manuscript collection held at the Royal College of Music, London, MS 2232. For a discussion of other manuscript and early print sources of this music, see Fiske, *English Theatre Music in the Eighteenth Century*, pp. 115–17.

[105] 'Emireno's three arias are very alike in style, rapid and rumbustious.' Dean and Knapp, *Handel's Operas*, p. 430.

[106] *A New Song Set by Mr. Monro*. University of Birmingham, Cadbury Research Library. Special Collections M 1523.C182. I am grateful to Colin Timms for having provided me with a copy of this song.

[107] Ibid.

Ex. 3.2 Words by Charles Coffey, music arranged by Mr. Seedo, 'Was ever Man possest' in *The Devil to Pay*, 1732 (2nd afterpiece version). Based on George F. Handel, 'Nò, non temere' in *Ottone*, HWV 15, 1723. Edited by Berta Joncus.

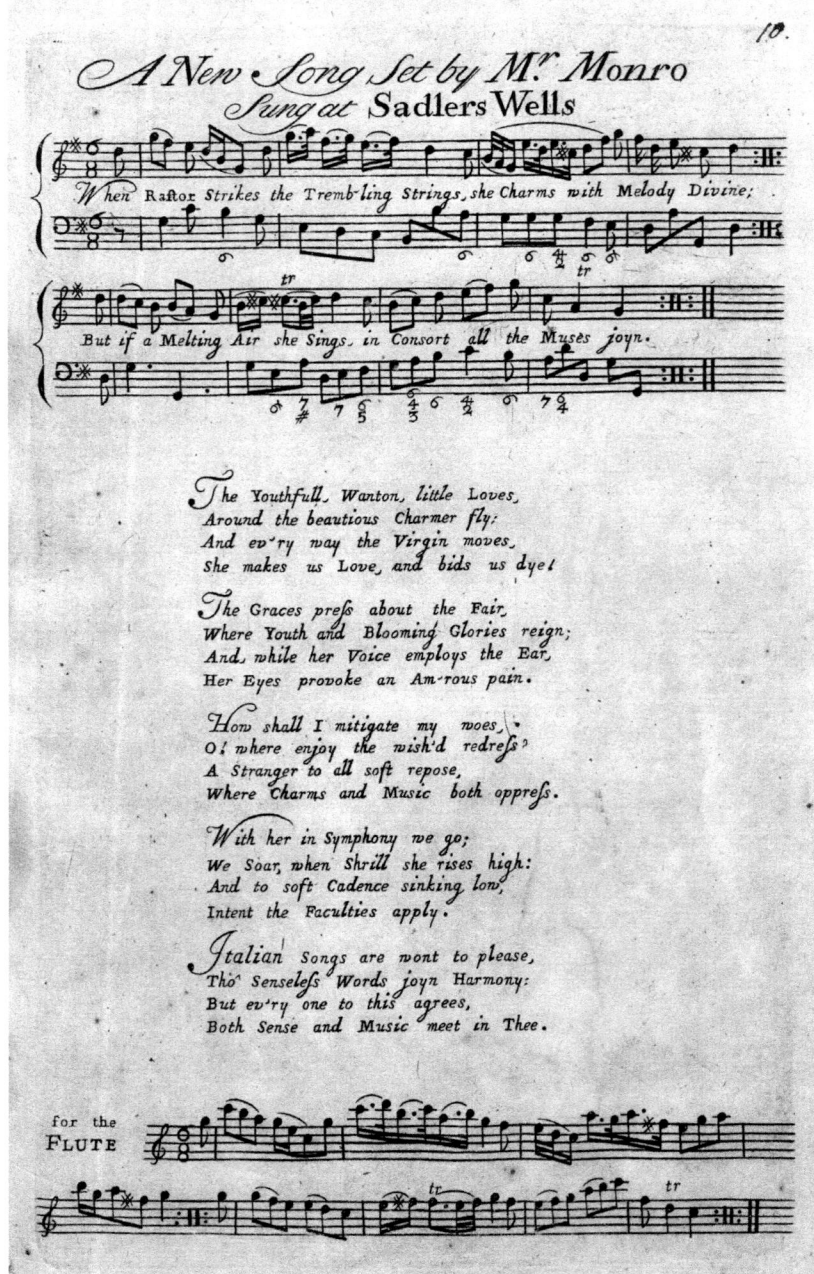

Ex. 3.3 *A New Song set by Mr. Munro sung at Sadlers Wells* ('When Raftor Strikes the Trembling Strings'), [c.1730]. By permission of the Cadbury Research Library: Special Collections, University of Birmingham. Shelfmark: M 1523.C182.

attentiveness, and the way she fuses music with the English language makes her superior to Italian singers:

> With her in Symphony we go;
> We Soar, when Shrill she rises high:
> And to soft Cadence sinking low,
> Intent the Faculties apply.
> Italian Songs are wont to please,
> Tho' Senseless Words joyn Harmony:
> But ev'ry one to this agrees,
> Both Sense and Music meet in Thee.[108]

Among others whom Clive impressed was a Prussian visitor to London, Geheimrat Wilhelm von Borcke. He translated the second afterpiece *Devil to Pay* as *Der Teufel is los*, which Johann Friedrich Schönemann staged on 24 January 1743 as part of his programme to build a German National Theatre. Seedo, who had moved to Potsdam in May 1736, was probably involved; certainly music from London featured in this seemingly 'German' entertainment. *Der Teufel ist los* became a staple of Schönemann's troupe, which brought this Singspiel to Hamburg, Lübeck, Dresden, and Leipzig.[109] The London staple version of *The Devil to Pay* likewise infiltrated the stages of Paris and Vienna. In 1756, Claude-Pierre Patu published his French translation of it in *Choix de petites pièces du théatre anglois*. From this, Michel-Jean Sedaine prepared for the Vienna Court an *opéra comique*, *Le Diable à quatre*, with music by Pierre Alexandre Monsigny. Following the warm reception of this work on 19 August 1756, Jean Monnet created out of Sedaine's libretto another version of *Le Diable à quatre*, but as an alternative kind of comic opera, the *comédie mêlée d'ariettes*; this was later revised for performance at the Parisian Foire St Laurent on 12 February 1757.[110]

The Devil to Pay was Clive's springboard to stardom. Thanks to her, Drury Lane became ballad opera's new home, and *The Devil to Pay* became the second-most performed stage work of the century.[111] This ballad opera was

---

[108] *Ibid.*
[109] Walter H. Rubsamen, 'Mr. Seedo, Ballad Opera and the Singspiel', pp. 1–35; Bertil H. van Boer, 'Coffey's *The Devil to Pay*: The Comic War, and the Emergence of the German Singspiel', *Journal of Musicological Research*, vol. 8, nos. 1–2 (1988), pp. 119–39; and Estelle Joubert, 'Genre and Form in German Opera', *The Cambridge Companion to Eighteenth-Century Opera*, ed. A. R. DelDonna and P. Polzonetti (Cambridge, 2009), pp. 184–89.
[110] See the preface by Bruce A. Brown in Christoph W. Gluck, *Le Diable à Quatre, ou La Double Métamorphose*, ed. B. A. Brown, Christoph Willibald Gluck, Sämtliche Werke, series 4, vol. 3 (Kasssel, 1992), pp. vii–xx. Kent Smith, 'Egidio Duni and the Development of opéra comique from 1753 to 1770' (PhD diss., Cornell Univ., 1980).
[111] According to the data from '*The London Stage* Data Visualisations, 1660–1800 / Most Performed Works' in the online resource *Eighteenth Century Drama: Censorship, Society and the Stage*, of the most performed works *The Devil to Pay* achieved 895 performances

Clive's legacy, and she sang it until 1765, four years before she retired.[112] The acclaim she garnered owed nothing to the Cibbbers who, whether offering soft scenes (Colley) or advocating wife-beating (Theophilus) had misjudged their audiences; it was Clive's alternative Nell that the public flocked to see. She was, as Aaron Hill wrote, the 'Darling of the whole Town', for whom *The Devil to Pay* was 'cleverly alter'd and adapted'.[113] Thirty-five years later, Clive's protégée Jane Pope earned praise for being 'so able a successor' in the role – that is, for precisely duplicating what Clive had taught her to do.[114] While composers and writers transmitted Clive's Nell on the page, Clive did so in the playhouse, defining the role for audiences even after she retired.

Nell as After-Image

Nell joined, and outlived, Phillida as a Clive role-icon. The earliest depiction of Clive as Nell was an anonymously engraved frontispiece (Fig. 3.1), perhaps by Drury Lane scenery painter Francis Hayman, in the first *Devil to Pay* playbook, sold from 10 August 1731.[115] It shows Act I, scene 3, in which Jobson (John Harper), who has burst in on Nell (Clive) and the magician (James Oates), holds his whip ready to beat him. Balancing forward on one foot, Nell twists from the waist with her left arm akimbo and smiles knowingly at the viewer while restraining Jobson by holding onto his lapel with her right hand. Her manner of dress is that of a cobbler's wife: mob cap, hitched apron, plain shift, laced bodice, petticoat with striped hem, kerchief loosely knotted. The frontispiece is crudely produced, without concern for detail or likeness.

---

during the century. The most performed work was *The Beggar's Opera*, with 1,119 performances. <http://www.eighteenthcenturydrama.amdigital.co.uk>. Accessed 22 November 2018.

[112] Her final performance was on 22 November 1765. She handed the part to Jane Pope, who appeared for the first time in this character on 26 April 1766. For data on Clive's performances of Nell, see *ibid*., '*The London Stage* Data Associations, 1660–1800 / Roles'. <http://www.eighteenthcenturydrama.amdigital.co.uk/LondonStage/CoOccurrence#rl>. Accessed 11 August 2017.

[113] [Hill], *See and Seem Blind*, pp. 8–9.

[114] 'Mrs. Clive being on the retiring plan almost on Miss Pope's commencement, gave her an opportunity to be let occasionally into some of the former's principal parts ... But what called out the full extent of her powers, was the character of Nell, in Coffey's ballad farce of *The Devil to Pay* ... Those who had seen Mrs. Clive in the character, or remembered her first appearance in it, were pleased with the thoughts of so able a successor.' 'Miss POPE', *Theatrical Biography: Or, Memoirs of the Principal Performers of the Three Theatres Royal*, vol. 1 (Dublin, 1772), p. 32. On eighteenth-century stage principals defining an interpretation for later actors and coaching them, see Chapter 1, pp. 12–13.

[115] The earliest advertisement, printed between Thursday 5 and Saturday 7 August, announced that the wordbook would be sold from Tuesday. *London Evening Post*, issue 575 (5–7 August 1731). The date of this frontispiece is erroneously said to be '1748' in David Coke and Alan Borg, *Vauxhall Gardens: A History* (New Haven, CT, 2011), p. 369.

Fig. 3.1 Francis Hayman (?), Frontispiece to *The Devil to Pay*, 1731. Engraving. © The British Library Board 30/9/2018. All Rights Reserved. Shelfmark: Music Collections 11775.c.24.

By the mid-1730s, Clive's Nell merited a large oil painting by Hayman, and a place in Europe's first-ever public exhibition of secular oils. This was at Vauxhall Gardens, London's first pleasure garden, which opened in 1732. Here, to the shock of many, visitors from diverse ranks of society mixed freely.[116] During the 1730s, Gardens proprietor Jonathan Tyers commissioned fifty-five almost life-size paintings – the canvases around seven feet by five feet – to adorn his supper-boxes, where visitors dined while others strolled by.[117] The pictures, and the manner of their display, had a double draw: besides being

---

[116] Coke and Borg, *Vauxhall Gardens*, pp. 33–48.
[117] Initially Tyers seems to have displayed the paintings only after 9 pm and put some of them on rollers by which means they rose from below, or perhaps descended from above, to 'cover all the boxes on three of their sides'; this allowed 'ladys and delicate gentlemen' to be 'screen'd from the damps of the night air'. Jacob Friedrich Bielfeld, *Letters of Baron Bielfeld, Secretary of Legation to the King of Prussia*, vol. 4 (London, 1770),

Fig. 3.2 Francis Hayman and studio, A Scene in *The Devil to Pay*, 1730s. Oil on canvas. By permission of the owner.

'very entertaining', they gave gentlemen 'unexceptionable opportunity' to gaze 'on any pleasing fair-one, without any other pretence than the credit of a fine taste for the piece behind her'.[118] Hayman designed and painted the bulk of the pictures in the supper-box series.[119] The scenes were from stage works, daily life, and rustic amusements; Clive's scene was one of seven from playhouse productions.[120] It was situated in the north range of supper-boxes, overlooking the grand walk.[121]

As Drury Lane's scenery painter, Hayman was an authoritative witness of Clive's Nell.[122] While basing his oil on *The Devil to Pay* frontispiece, Hayman

---

pp. 166–67; cited in Coke and Borg, *Vauxhall Gardens*, p. 114. By 1741 the paintings were fixed to the back or side walls of the boxes. *Ibid.*, p. 116.

[118] *Scots Magazine*, vol. 1 (August 1739), p. 363.

[119] Hubert Gravelot designed numbers 4, 6, and possibly 7; John Laguerre was responsible for number 55. Peter Monomy painted numbers 22, 31, and 39. Hayman's workshop of colleagues and students helped to paint the oils. The 'Catalogue of Framed Paintings', Coke and Borg, *Vauxhall Gardens*, p. 363.

[120] Coke and Borg's 'Catalogue of Framed Paintings' for the supper-box oils is based on the list of paintings in *The Ambulator; or, The Stranger's Companion in a Tour Round London* (London, 1774). The seven playhouse works featured in the supper-box oil series were *The Devil to Pay*, *Flora*, *The Mock Doctor*, *The King and the Miller of Mansfield*, *Falstaff*, *The Merry Wives of Windsor*, and *Pamela* (James Dance's dramatization of Samuel Richardson's novel). Coke and Borg, *Vauxhall Gardens*, pp. 363–90.

[121] *Ibid.*, pp. 363, 368.

[122] From the 1740s onwards Hayman specialized in painting Shakespearean actors mid-performance, and went on to become a founder-member of the Society of Artists, the

Fig. 3.3 Gerard (?) Vandergucht after Francis Hayman. Frontispiece to *The Devil to Pay*, 1738. Engraving. © The British Library Board 30/9/2018. All Rights Reserved. Shelfmark: Music Collections 11775.c.25.

changed the props, removing the candle and adding a low bench bearing cobbler's tools. He also subtly altered Clive's representation. Her humble costume is shown to be splendid: crisp ruffles adorn her mob cap, her apron has the weight and sheen of satin, her bodice is blue and its sleeves are trimmed with vermillion ribbon, her petticoat and kerchief are of matching vermillion, the hem stripe of her petticoat is gold, and gold stripes also adorn her kerchief. In

---

forerunner of the Royal Academy. His biography, and the centrality of Hayman to British rococo painting, is traced in the exhibition catalogue of Brian Allen, *Francis Hayman* (New Haven, 1987).

Fig. 3.4 Richard Parr after Francis Hayman, *From the Farce, The Devil to pay or the Wife's Metamorphos'd Jobson and Nell, 26 May 1743*, 1743. Engraving. © Victoria and Albert Museum, London. Museum number: S.4303-2009.

this, the only known painting of Clive mid-performance, she radiates intensity as she leans forward, serious, gazing searchingly at the magician while restraining her husband (Fig. 3.2).

Vauxhall was designed to invoke fanciful environments: Arcadia, a Roman villa's grounds, a Chinese pavilion.[123] Clive's Nell took her place in this catalogue of make-believe. In 1755, a writer would report that: 'At Vaux-hall … they have touched up all the pictures, which were damaged last season by the fingering of those curious Connoisseurs, who could not be satisfied without *feeling* whether the figures were alive.'[124] Through *The Devil to Pay*, Clive became a figure very much 'alive' in the public imagination. In 1738 one of the Vandergucht brothers engraved a frontispiece after the 1731 frontispiece, in verso, for the bookseller John Watts, who had it reprinted in 1748 and 1758 (Fig.

---

[123] Berta Joncus, '"His Spirit is in Action Seen": Milton, Mrs. Clive and the Simulacra of the Pastoral in Comus', *Eighteenth-Century Music*, vol. 2, no. 1 (2005), pp. 7–40.

[124] *The Connoisseur*, no. 68, repr. in the *Gentleman's Magazine*, vol. 25 (1755), p. 206; cited in Joncus, '"His Spirit is in Action Seen"', p. 39.

Fig. 3.5 After Richard Parr after Francis Hayman, *ROYAL AMUSEMENT or a Curious Representation of one of ye Celebrated Paintings at Vaux-Hall done by ye Ingenious MR. HYMEN, NELL and the COBLER*, c.1744. Engraving. The Bodleian Libraries, The University of Oxford. Shelfmark: Douce Prints a. 49, fol. 114, Item 90.

3.3).[125] In 1743, Richard Parr engraved the Vauxhall painting, also in verso, for the print-sellers Thomas and John Bowles, who added an inscription about the benefits of wife-beating (Fig. 3.4).[126] Shortly after, an undated pirate engraving after Parr, *NELL and the COBLER*, not in verso, appeared as one of six prints of

---

[125] As mentioned earlier, Gerard Vandergucht had engraved the *Damon and Phillida* frontispiece for Watts in 1737, and he, rather than his brother John, probably prepared *The Devil to Pay* frontispiece. When in 1738 Watts re-issued *The Devil to Pay* with Vandergucht's frontispiece, he updated the cast list to include Clive's married name. *The Devil to Pay: Or, the Wives Metamorphos'd. An Opera* (London, 1738) ['Printed for J. Watts']. The 1758 *The Devil to Pay* was '[p]rinted by Assignment from Mr. Watts, for T. Lownds, at his Circulating Library in Fleet-Street' in duodecimo format. *The Devil to Pay: Or, the Wives Metamorphos'd. An Opera* (London, 1748) ['Printed for J. Watts'] and *The Devil to Pay: Or, the Wives Metamorphos'd. An Opera* (London, 1758) [English Short Title Catalogue citation number N6406.]

[126] The inscription ends with the lines: 'This lesson much the hen-peck'd race behoves: / No wife's a shrew, whose spouse a Jobson proves.' Coke and Borg, *Vauxhall Gardens*, p. 369. I am grateful to David Coke for facilitating my access to this print, and for correcting the engraver's name from Remigius Parr to Richard Parr.

'*ye Celebrated Paintings at Vaux-Hall*'; its new inscription laments Nell's beatings (Fig. 3.5).[127] Three further versions of Parr's engraving appeared without inscription: during the 1750s Thomas (or Carrington) Bowles and John Bowles sold a print titled *Jobson, Nell and the Doctor. Scene 3 in the 'The Wives Metamorphosed'*, Benjamin Cole engraved Parr's work for the *New Universal Magazine* (1752–54), and Louis Truchy (1731–64) created *Jobson and Nell* for print-seller Robert Sayer.[128]

In the public eye of the 1730s, Nell's character merged with Clive's own: her propriety, sincerity, spiritedness, and ascent to stardom. Through song, Clive had played the conjuror, transforming a brutal farce into a vehicle for her own powers.

---

[127] 'The surly Cobler enters, and destroys / The Conj'rers Scheme, & all poor Nelly's Joys', *ibid.*, pp. 395, 369.

[128] *Ibid.*, pp. 395, 368–69.

4

'HINT writes, and RAFTOR acts in Drury-lane':
Clive, Fielding, and Theophilus Cibber

The joint interests of Theophilus Cibber and Henry Fielding – winning The Lottery – Fielding's representation of players – a trip to the bordello – reversion to Clive's line – The Devil to Pay dressed as Molière – the spectre of Fenton – Clive gets the last word

Following her spectacular success in *The Devil to Pay*, Clive began the 1731–32 season as uncontested mistress of Drury Lane's vocal stage works, serious and comic. But she had yet to shine in straight comedy, and other actresses were inheriting Anne Oldfield's celebrated roles. To advance, Clive had to eclipse her rivals in non-musical stage works. Theophilus Cibber once more intervened in her career as summer manager, bringing out Clive's first vehicles without song. These were by Henry Fielding, London's favourite new playwright. Fielding supplied Cibber with a double bill: the mainpiece *The Old Debauchees* and the afterpiece *The Covent Garden Tragedy*. They were hardly the career-boosters for which Clive might have hoped. Instead, they traded on Clive's popularity to showcase the younger Cibber, and they represented a miscalculation on Fielding's part that audiences were as interested in sex as he was.[1] In *The Old Debauchees*, Clive represented a girl nearly despoiled; in *The Covent Garden Tragedy* she played a prostitute. In all four of his Clive vehicles for the 1731–32 season (*The Lottery*, *The Old Debauchees*, *The Covent Garden Tragedy*, and *The Mock Doctor*), Fielding saw to it that if Clive had a farcical scene, it was opposite Cibber, with the jokes being at Clive's expense. In this way Fielding extended Cibber's established line even as he veered wildly away from Clive's.

Both *The Old Debauchees* and *The Covent Garden Tragedy* flopped, and the licentiousness of *The Covent Garden Tragedy* sparked outrage among critics. Damage control took the form of the hastily written *The Mock Doctor*, which

---

[1] 'The passion he felt most powerfully was sexual desire – "this all-subduing Tyrant," as he calls it in *Amelia* (VI, i), "to whose Poison and Infatuation the best of Minds are so liable." Battestin, *A Henry Fielding Companion*, p. 244.

Fielding adapted from Molière with additions redolent of *The Devil to Pay*. Rather than a cobbler, it was now Theophilus Cibber who got to abuse Clive on stage. Cibber then had Clive debut as Polly in *The Beggar's Opera*; puffs hailed her as the new Fenton, and falsely asserted that audiences loved Clive's Polly.

Fielding, as we'll see, would later brazenly claim to have authored Clive's stage success. The reverse is the case: not only was she the big pull of his only Drury Lane hits, but he flubbed her straight acting launch and put her reputation at risk, above all in epilogues and songs. In his pre-1733 epilogues, she had to pretend to a winking promiscuity; in his pre-1733 ballads, she had to perform the most vulgar songs of her career. In *The Lottery*, his first Clive vehicle, Fielding even gave another player the music of her signature interlude air, Handel's 'Son confusa pastorella', and garnished this music with words criticizing the character Clive played. Only the Cibber-led theatrical revolt of 1733 caused Fielding to change tack. Most of the company followed Cibber and quit Drury Lane; Clive, however, remained loyal to the house, as did Fielding. To galvanize the audience support he needed, Fielding now suddenly began to praise and also to invent Clive's personal virtues, and rolled these into her stage character.

The Lottery: Gambling with Reputation

Clive knew that Theophilus Cibber was unstable, and had seen his wife Jane suffer from his whoring and his gambling with her earnings. In 1730, in a joint prologue he wrote for his comedy *The Lover*, Cibber even had Jane beg audiences to overlook her husband's 'Frolick' and 'Storm', and attend his author's benefit: 'Gallants, I hope, in this [he] has touch'd your Hearts; / Let not me suffer for his weak Deserts'.[2] The applause she won led Cibber to dedicate the play to her; by Chetwood's report, she 'took away the Sting' of Cibber's 'Revelrout'.[3] During the next season, likely under pressure from her husband, Jane maintained a full performance schedule even when heavily pregnant. She died in childbirth in January 1733.[4]

---

[2] Theophilus Cibber, 'EPILOGUE. Spoken by the AUTHOR and his WIFE', *The Lover. A Comedy* (London, 1730), page unnumbered.

[3] For Chetwood, the epilogue was proof that Theophilus Cibber wrote *The Lover*, not Colley Cibber as claimed by critics of both father and son; he reprinted the epilogue in his biographical entry on Theophilus Cibber. Chetwood, 'Mr. THEOPHILUS CIBBER', *A General History of the Stage*, pp. 118–21. In his dedication to his wife, Theophilus recalled that 'Your Behaviour in the Epilogue reach'd even the Hearts of Enemies, and made them my involuntary Friends for Your Sake'. Cibber, 'To Mrs. JANE CIBBER', *The Lover*, pages unnumbered.

[4] From September 1732 onwards Jane Cibber not only acted in all in her old parts, but in December also in the new title role of *Caelia*. In a printed letter of June 1733 Theophilus Cibber blamed her death on her professional dedication, which had caused her to over-exert herself: 'What her Merits were, as an Actress, the Good-nature of the Town has

Theophilus Cibber's signature role was Pistol, Shakespeare's deceitful, licentious, spendthrift, drunken, bullying soldier. He played this part offstage as well as on. In Benjamin Victor's view, Cibber wanted 'nothing but Power to be as troublesome as any young Man living'.[5] To see him as his contemporaries did, we can rely on a counterfeit memoir, *An Apology for the Life of Mr. T— C—, Comedian ... Supposed to be written by himself.*[6] This volume, as Cibber later recalled, 'no doubt' left 'many ignorant harmless Souls' thinking he had written it.[7] In the *Apology*, 'Cibber' is made to boast of '[my] Tone of Elocution, my buskin Tread, my Elevation of Countenance, my Dignity of Gesture, and expressive Rotation of Eye-balls'.[8] The memoir's author mocks not just Cibber's manner, but the way Cibber credited himself, as Drury Lane's summer company manager, with Clive's stage successes:

> having got an Insight into the Manner of Managing, I began to think I was Equal to the Management of a young Company to play in the Summer Season. Accordingly I got Leave from Mr. Wilks, and the other Masters, to form a young Company, and, to play during the Vacation ... I generally brought out some new Pieces and Farces, which not only turned to our immediate Account, but to the Good of the *Actors* ... To Instance this, I need say no more than that *George Barnwell* [i.e. *The London Merchant*], the *Devil to pay*, the *Mock Doctor*, and the *Beggars Opera*, the Part of Polly by Mrs. Clive, were first perform'd under my Management of Summer Companies: From these young Companies see what Performers have been chiefly sprung; Mrs Clive, Mrs. Butler, and, though last,

---

often declared, and her Merits, as a good Woman, I know, and shall ever heartily Regret the Loss of ... 'Tis also well known by the whole Company, Mrs. Cibber, tho' in a very bad State of Health, big with Child, and near her Time, did attend her Business, both in Acting and Rehearsing, until the 15th of December last, when she played Angelina in *The Fop's Fortune*, which was acted by HIS ROYAL HIGHNESS's COMMAND. She was brought to Bed on the 18th of January following, died on the 25th.' Theophilus Cibber, *A Letter from Theophilus Cibber, Comedian, to John Highmore, Esq.* (London, 1733), p. 1.

[5] Benjamin Victor, *The History of the Theatres of London and Dublin*, p. 9.

[6] Joel Schechter found correspondence putatively by Henry Fielding and James Ralph on a defunct website from c.1997, and based on this, argues that Fielding and Ralph were the joint authors of *An Apology for the Life of Mr. T— C—, Comedian*. Joel Schechter, 'Treason, Wit and Scurrility: Fielding's Cibber Letters', *Studies in Theatre and Performance*, vol. 34, no. 1 (2014), pp. 53–61. Schechter admits to the tenuousness of his attribution in a revised version of the article, Joel Schechter, 'Fielding's Cibber Letters: Counterfeit Wit, Scurrility and Cartels' in Joel Schechter, *Eighteenth-Century Brechtians: Theatrical Satire in the Age of Walpole* (Exeter, 2016), pp. 134–47. I thank Thomas Lockwood for bringing the later publication, and the questions around Schechter's attribution, to my attention.

[7] 'This (though an impertinent and impudent Libel) no doubt, among many ignorant harmless Souls, passed for mine.' 'The Life and Character of ... Barton Booth ... Introduction to the General Work', Theophilus Cibber, *The Lives and Characters of the most Eminent Actors and Actresses of Great Britain and Ireland* (London, 1753), 'xiii' (p. 113, page numbering discontinuous); cited in William B. Coley, *Fielding's Contributions to The Champion and Related Writings* (Oxford, 2003), p. 423, note 6 ('Contributions to *The Champion* 12 August 1740').

[8] *An Apology for the Life of Mr. T— C—, Comedian* (London, 1740), p. 17.

not least in Love – MYSELF ...This Management of mine was an undoubted Proof of my Abilities.⁹

In truth, Cibber was not Clive's ally, but her superior, who arrogated to himself the right to fold her Town appeal into his own. Clive had only limited means with which to defend herself; one of these was to show what she excelled in. She was well-received in April 1730 as Miss Prue, an awkward country girl in William Congreve's *Love for Love*, and this may have recommended her in such parts to Fielding.

With Chloe in *The Lottery*, Fielding invented a protagonist co-extensive with Miss Prue but adorned with song. Written between mid-October and mid-December 1731, *The Lottery* opened on 1 January 1732.¹⁰ It featured newly composed songs by Mr. Seedo, who besides having worked with Fielding at the New Haymarket Theatre in 1730 had just arranged the music for *The Devil to Pay*.¹¹ Although *The Lottery* was greeted warmly, Fielding immediately revised it – a practice characteristic of him¹² – changing the final scene and giving Clive more song.¹³ Of twenty-two airs, Clive ended up with eight solos opposite the male principal's five, and most of her music was new: of the ten songs Seedo composed for *The Lottery*, she sang seven (six solos, and one duet with Stoppelaer).¹⁴ Other solos were divided among more minor parts.¹⁵ In *The Lottery* Seedo's high-style songs sat cheek by jowl with common tunes, echoing the tension between tastes that Clive's separate lines generated, and on which her charisma depended.

---

⁹ *Ibid.*, p. 85.
¹⁰ Thomas Lockwood, 'The Lottery. Introduction', *Henry Fielding: Plays Volume II 1731–1734*, ed. T. Lockwood (Oxford, 2007), pp. 130, 135.
¹¹ Seedo arranged music for Fielding's *Author's Farce* of 1730 and perhaps for *The Welsh Opera*, *The Grub-Street Opera*, and *Don Quixote in England*. Lockwood, ed., 'The Author's Farce (1734)', *Henry Fielding: Plays Volume I*, p. 333, note 2. Lockwood claims that Seedo was 'certainly the music director at Drury Lane 1731–4', an assumption difficult to square with Carey's compositions for Drury Lane during these years. See also Rubsamen, 'Mr. Seedo, Ballad Opera and the Singspiel', pp. 776–809.
¹² 'Revision of a successful new play was uncommon, but was to be characteristic of Fielding.' Robert D. Hume, *Henry Fielding and the London Theatre, 1728–1737* (Oxford and New York, 1988), p. 119. By 1732, for instance, Fielding had already re-worked *The Welsh Opera* into *The Grub-Street Opera*.
¹³ Lockwood, 'The Lottery. Introduction', *Henry Fielding: Plays Volume II*, p. 134.
¹⁴ In the second version, Seedo's newly composed airs are Airs 1, 5, 6, 8, 9, 10, 12 (Clive's duet with Stoppelaer), 13, 15, and 21. Of these, Clive sang Airs 6, 8, 9, 10, 12, 13, and 21. Her two other solos were Airs 7 and 14. Lockwood, ed. 'The Lottery', *Henry Fielding: Plays Volume II*, pp. [153]–80.
¹⁵ Songs in the second version of *The Lottery* were divided thus: Airs 1, 2 and 16 for 'Mr. Stocks' (played by John Harper), Air 3 for the Second Buyer (played by William Mullart), and Air 17 for the Coachman (actor unknown), two duets, Airs 18 and 19, for the first and second Proclaimers (actors unknown), and the duet, Air 22, for Stocks and Lovemore. *Ibid.*

Those responsible for *The Lottery* clearly sought to draw on the ongoing appeal of *The Devil to Pay*, which Fielding cited approvingly in his prologue for Cibber.[16] Except for Cibber, the principals in both works were the same, and they brought features of their *Devil to Pay* dramatis personae with them into *The Lottery*. Stocks, taken by John Harper, brutishly sacrifices a woman's well-being to his wishes – like Jobson, also played by Harper, in *The Devil to Pay*. In the action, Stocks is told by letter that Chloe (Clive) is coming into a fortune: he engineers for his brother Jack Stocks (Cibber) to trick her into marriage so that Jack can repay money he borrowed from his brother. Chloe, like Nell, is simple but aspirational: rejecting her country suitor Lovemore, she travels to London and buys a lottery ticket with a ten-thousand-pound prize, believing that the ticket guarantees her this fortune. Lovemore, played by Stoppelaer, saves Chloe from a ruinous union – as does, if only briefly, Stoppelaer's similarly named character Loverule in *The Devil to Pay*. As a libertine and predatory fortune-seeker, Jack Stocks was essentially an *in propria persona* role for Cibber.

Just two years earlier, in Miller's *Humours of Oxford*, 'Kitty' had been allowed to outwit the fop Cibber. But in Fielding's farce Chloe is duped, deflowered, and almost ruined, a tale heavily emphasized by the songs Fielding created for her and Lovemore. The words of Lovemore's first air 'Chloe is false, but still she is charming' (Air 4) expose her weakness, and its final line 'Down, down she goes' foreshadows her sexual consent.[17] Because originally a minuet from Handel's opera *Floridante* (1721), the music of Air 4 makes ridiculous Chloe's pretence to nobility – the minuet being the most noble of court dances – overlaying lines about her moral descent with musical irony.[18] The tune 'The White Joak', sung by Chloe as Air 14,[19] makes her sluttish nature indisputable, it being cousin to 'the Black Joke' – the Second Buyer's tune – and one of the lewdest ballads of the age.[20] 'Joke' was a cant term for a whore, and for female genitalia,[21] and the 'White Joke' was identified specifically with

---

[16] *Ibid.*, p. 149, note 2.

[17] Lockwood, ed., 'The Lottery', *Henry Fielding: Plays Volume II*, p. 158.

[18] The English setting to this tune (HWV 228[8], known by various titles) circulated soon after Handel's opera premiered and co-existed as a dance and an English air. Berta Joncus, 'Handel at Drury Lane: Ballad Opera and the Production of Kitty Clive', *Journal of the Royal Musical Association*, vol. 131, no. 2 (2006), p. 190. Fielding used this melody for Air 28 of his *Grub-Street Opera* (1731), as noted in Lockwood, ed., 'The Lottery', *Henry Fielding: Plays Volume II*, pp. 697–98, 736–37.

[19] Lockwood, ed., 'The Lottery', *Henry Fielding: Plays Volume II*, pp. 169–70, 746. Lockwood lists (on p. 746) the many stage works, dance, and song publications in which this melody is found.

[20] The Second Buyer sings the 'Black Joke' in Air 3. *Ibid.*, p. 155.

[21] 'The *Joke* is the noblest of all the vendible Species, and ... the Ladies who sell these, will use you much better than most of the trading Community ... The *Black Joke* ... is the best for Service ... It is commonly of a proper Temperature.' *The Female Glossary* (London, [1732]), p. 21; cited in Paul Dennant, '"Barbarous Old English Jig": The "Black

Ex. 4.1 Words by Henry Fielding, music arranged by Mr. Seedo, Air 11, 'Some confounded Planet' in *The Lottery*, 1732. Based on George F. Handel, 'Son confusa pastorella' in *Poro*, HWV 28, 1731. Edited by Vanessa Rogers. By permission of Vanessa Rogers.

the sexual organs of a prostitute 'generally young and tender'. The appellation arose because 'very few' jokes 'continue of this Colour after they are full grown'.[22] As Chloe sings 'O how I'll flame it among the Beaus!', the 'White Joke' depicts her as a fresh vulva at the service of the highest bidder.[23] By the time Lovemore sings 'Virgins beware' (Air 20), we can be sure that she has lost her maidenhood. Being another minuet (almost certainly by Henry Carey), the air's music, like that of Air 4, mocks Chloe's fate, which Chloe admits with the words 'Now I'm undone'.[24]

The musical climax of *The Lottery*, like that of *The Devil to Pay*, features a Handel composition used for Clive and Stoppelaer. It occurs as Chloe disdains Lovemore's suit for that of the fop. As in *The Devil to Pay*, the scene is mid-way through the action, but it is much longer, consisting of three numbers that run into each other: a solo song for Lovemore, a duet set by Seedo, and a reprise of Lovemore's solo (Ex. 4.1). Lovemore's music is 'Son confusa pastorella' from Handel's *Poro*, which, as noted earlier, Clive had made her signature tune during the previous summer season. In her execution, Clive had personified the lost shepherdess of its title. In *The Lottery*, Fielding gave this music to Lovemore to rebuke Chloe for her moral confusion.

Fielding's new words for 'Son confusa pastorella' upset the steady pulse of Handel's original, turning an Arcadian lament into stuttering rage at Chloe's folly. Seedo's setting amplifies Fielding's metric displacement, using displaced downbeats and leaps to highlight Lovemore's agitation ('Stoop so low') and expostulations ('Blood and Thunder! Wounds and Wonder!'). Her rebuttal (Ex. 4.2 'Dear Sir'), to new music by Seedo, interrupts Lovemore and changes the pulse from his off-beat triple pattern to a smooth duple meter, as befits her silver-tongued excuses. After Lovemore repeats the music she's just sung ('Dear Madame'), she interrupts him a second time with the words 'Ah! hideous!'; at this juncture, the music shifts to the relative minor, betraying Chloe's lack of moral compass. Their exchange descends into bickering. The final sentence is

---

Joke" in the Eighteenth and Nineteenth Centuries', *Folk Music Journal*, vol. 10, no. 3 (2013), pp. 302–3. Fielding and other ballad opera playwrights took up the 'White Joke' particularly after John Watts printed a version in his *Musical Miscellany* (1731). Edgar V. Roberts, 'An Unrecorded Meaning of "Joke" (Or "Joak") In England', *American Speech*, vol. 37, no. 2 (1962), pp. 137–140.

[22] 'The *White Joke* is generally young and tender, the being very few that continue of this Colour after they are full grown; I should rather chuse to call it a *Joquette* [little female jockey].' *The Female Glossary*, p. 22.

[23] Lockwood, ed., 'The Lottery', *Henry Fielding: Plays Volume II*, pp. 169–70.

[24] *Ibid.*, pp. 178, 750. Lockwood identifies that the melody is from Act II, scene 13 of Colley Cibber, *Love in a Riddle* (London, 1729), but he doesn't name its likely composer. On Carey's compositions in this stage work, see Chapter 2.

Ex. 4.2 Words by Henry Fielding, music arranged by Mr. Seedo, Air 11, 'Some confounded Planet' in *The Lottery*, 1732. Based on George F. Handel, 'Son confusa pastorella' in *Poro*, HWV 28, 1731. Edited by Vanessa Rogers. By permission of Vanessa Rogers.

passed on Chloe when Lovemore returns to singing 'Son' confusa pastorella', which recommences on the words 'Zounds! and Furies!'.[25]

Seedo's high-style solos for Chloe elsewhere restore some dignity to this character, traversing as they do a range of *galant* dances: bourrée (Air 6), tambourin (Air 8), and a bourrée or rigaudon (Air 9).[26] He fit his melodies to the word emphases in Fielding's verses, facilitating crisp delivery. With Air 9, Seedo gave Clive a chance to show her command of conventions, and her aptitude for bending them to comic effect. Air 9 contains downbeats in the wrong places for either a bourrée or a rigaudon, the air's quaver rests interrupting each dance's two-bar units (Ex. 4.3). These missteps are compounded by Chloe's awkward vocal line. She wrongly emphasizes, with an ugly leap of a sixth, the words 'speak for' (bar 8). We can assume Clive squeezed such moments for laughs.

However felicitous Seedo made Clive's solo songs, Fielding had Cibber, as Jack Stocks, dominate Clive in their joint scenes. Jack Stocks speaks more than Chloe, and his emotions are pitched higher than hers. Fielding seems to have transcribed onto the page Cibber's renowned bluster, as Jack replies to Chloe's musically ludicrous Air 9 with the words, 'Oh ravishing! exquisite! Exstasy! Joy! Transport! Misery! Flames! Ice! How shall I thank this Goodness that undoes me! ... Oh Madam! there is a hidden Poison in those those Eyes, for which Nature has no Antidote'.[27] A few scenes later, after Jack has confessed that he is a counterfeit fop, he curses her in another rant ('Death! Hell! and Furies! Blood! Blunders! Blanks!').[28]

Clive's epilogue, the first of her career, brought further compromises. As was standard, Clive spoke as herself ('Miss Raftor') while advancing the drama that had just ended. Predicting that Lovemore might soon discard her, she announces her willingness to 'get a third' man, inviting 'Gallants' to apply ('Well, if he does [discard me], as I have cause to fear, / To-morrow Night, Gallants, you'll find me here.').[29] This characterisation is of a piece with the

---

[25] Lockwood, ed., 'The Lottery', *Henry Fielding: Plays Volume II*, pp. 166–67, 742–743. Lockwood notes (on p. 743) that Fielding had used the melody for Air 48 of his *Grub-Street Opera* (1731), identifying it as 'sung by Antonia Merighi in Handel's opera *Porus*', and asserting that 'because of its musical complexity' Fielding was drawn to it, and gave it to Stoppelaer to sing in *The Grub-Street Opera* and in *The Lottery*. *Ibid.*, p. 716. This logic is somewhat hard to follow, given that Clive had sung the air regularly, and that *The Grub-Street Opera*, while rehearsed, was never performed. *Ibid.*, pp. 18–19.

[26] I would like thank Rebecca Harris-Warwick for confirming the dance genres. She notes that some features are attenuated: rhythmic values in Air 6 are double what is standard, Seedo omits expected syncopations, and the leaps at the start of each strain – which display Clive's abilities to advantage – are atypical of the dance. Tambourin is a genre rarely adapted for vocal music; its instrumental qualities highlight the singer's control. Personal communication of 20 July 2018.

[27] Lockwood, ed., 'The Lottery', *Henry Fielding: Plays Volume II*, p. 164.

[28] *Ibid.*, p. 177.

[29] *Ibid.*, p. 150.

Alas! My Lord, you're too severe

Ex. 4.3 Words by Henry Fielding, music by Mr. Seedo, Air 9, 'Alas! My Lord, you're too severe' in *The Lottery*, 1732. Edited by Vanessa Rogers. By permission of Vanessa Rogers.

louche Chloe who sings the common tunes Fielding had selected. *The Lottery*'s success is well-charted: after a warm reception, it became a solid rather than runaway favourite.[30] Armed with Seedo's *galant* compositions, Clive ended up benefiting from the part of Chloe, which took pride of place among her staples until 1749, when elegant song such as Seedo's vanished from her line.

Cibber, Clive, and the 1732 Drury Lane Summer Company

During the regular 1731–32 season Clive also acquitted herself in two minor spoken parts: as the servant Busy (who also sings) in the racy Restoration comedy *The Man of Mode* (1676), and as 'Miss Sprightly' in Fielding's new introduction (now lost) to his revived hit, *The Tragedy of Tragedies*.[31] By early April 1732, as the benefit season began, Fielding was writing, or had finished, the twinned comedies for Clive's launch that summer as a principal actress.[32] Clive was about to lead three separate ballad operas: *The Ephesian Matron* with

---

[30] Lockwood, 'The Lottery. Introduction', *ibid.*, pp. 135–38.

[31] The revised *Tragedy of Tragedies* at Drury Lane opened on 3 May 1732 for four performances, and competed with a rival production of this same work at the New Haymarket Theatre. In Lockwood's view, Fielding's introduction was 'in the form a pre-curtain dialogue' like those in *The Beggar's Opera* and Fielding's *The Welsh Opera*. Lockwood, 'The Tragedy of Tragedies. Introduction', *Henry Fielding: Plays Volume I*, p. 515.

[32] The copyright assignment of 4 April 1732 roughly dates Fielding's writing of both plays, but as Lockwood warns, this 'does not establish that either play was completed by this

'Tunes all New; composed in the Old English, Scotch, and Irish Style, by Mr. Seedo' on 17 April,³³ *The Country Wedding, and Skimington* on 8 May,³⁴ and *The Comical Revenge*, an operatized version of Susannah Centlivre's adaptation of Molière's *Le Médecin malgré lui*, on 12 May.³⁵ The first two were benefits, the third a production organized during the benefit season by 'particular Desire of several Persons of Quality.'³⁶

The Drury Lane 1732 summer season began on 25 May, promisingly without competition from other houses.³⁷ Fielding's two new spoken comedies for Clive opened on 1 June.³⁸ The mainpiece, *The Old Debauchees*, pandered to audience prurience and to hatred of Catholics, dramatizing contemporary reports about the Jesuit priest Jean-Baptiste Girard and his sexual abuse of Marie-Catherine Cadière. The scandal had stirred interest during the regular theatrical season just ended; *The Old Debauchees* was the third stage work to treat the subject.³⁹ Some press reports accused Girard of rape and sadism, which he was said to have convinced Cadière were necessary for her salvation; others accused Cadière of claiming rape to cover up her culpability.⁴⁰ In Fielding's dramatization of the story, Cibber was the villainous Father Martin and Clive the victim of dubious credibility, Isabella.

From the opening scene, Fielding gives cause to doubt the rectitude of Isabella, who, like Chloe in *The Lottery*, lives for 'Cards, Musick, Plays, Balls,

---

time'. Lockwood, 'The Covent Garden Tragedy. Introduction', *Henry Fielding: Plays Volume II*, p. 341.

³³ This was for Roger Bridgewater's benefit; see the *Daily Post*, issue 3926 (17 April 1732). The ballad opera was based on Charles Johnson's eponymous farce of 1730. Its music is lost, but Seedo's compositions may have been the first in 'Irish Style'. Johnson's unpublished farce is listed in *A New Theatrical Dictionary* (London, 1792), p. 77: '*The Ephesian Matron*. A Farce of one act, by Charles Johnson, 8vo. 1730.' Charles Dibdin re-scored the playbook to create a pleasure garden Italianate serenata that was engraved in 1769; this became a stage production in 1769 and 1771. Roger Fiske, *English Theatre Music in the Eighteenth Century*, pp. 354–555.

³⁴ This was a pirated production for the benefit of Edward Berry, John Roberts, and Anne (?) Brett, announced in the *Daily Post*, issue 3943 (6 May 1732). The original *Country Wedding and Skimmington*, by Essex Hawker, had opened on 6 May 1732 at Lincoln's Inn Fields, now hired out as a fringe theatre, John Rich having moved his licensed company to Covent Garden. Burling, *Summer Theatre in London*, p. 83.

³⁵ [Susanna Centlivre], *Love's Contrivance, or, Le Medecin malgre Lui. A Comedy. As it is Acted at the Theatre Royal in Drury-Lane* (London, 1703).

³⁶ *Daily Post*, issue 3948 (12 May 1732). See discussion of this ballad opera below.

³⁷ 'Only Drury Lane opened its doors this summer'. Burling, *Summer Theatre in London*, p. 86.

³⁸ Lockwood, 'The Old Debauchees. Introduction', *Henry Fielding: Plays Volume II*, pp. 290–95. The opening was slightly delayed; originally the comedies were to have opened on 29 May. *Ibid.*, p. 295.

³⁹ *Ibid.*, p. 334.

⁴⁰ Lockwood, ed., 'The Old Debauchees', *Henry Fielding: Plays Volume II*, p. 309.

Flattery, Visits, and ... a pretty Fellow'.[41] Maxims such as 'A Priest may cheat Mankind, but a Woman would cheat the Devil' imply that Isabella is necessarily more to blame.[42] The comedy's last lines, spoken by Isabella, instruct audiences: 'For when a Woman sets her self about it, / Nor Priest, nor Devil can make her go without it'.[43] The 'it' in question is of course sex. Even Isabella's oath of fidelity to Young Laroon suggest her flippancy and lust: 'I will either marry you or die a Maid, and I have no violent Inclination to the latter, on the Word of a Virgin.'[44] Her scheme to entrap Father Martin displays her lax morals, as it consists of submission to his advances. Audiences watched as Father Martin kissed Isabella while rhapsodizing Cibber-style: 'Those Eyes have a Fire in them ... there is a Sweetness in that Breath like what I've read of Ambrosia. That Bosom heaves like those of Priestesses of old, when big with Inspiration.'[45] Later Isabella, pretending to believe Father Martin's ascription of lust to numinous evil beings, describes how a 'Spirit' resembling Young Laroon has 'kissed' and 'embrac'd' her passionately.[46] Isabella's nature can be interpreted either as 'prodigious Simplicity or Cunning', as Father Martin puts it.[47]

That same evening Clive co-led the afterpiece *The Covent Garden Tragedy*. Its personae were known figures from the city's sex trade; its setting was the Rose Tavern, an infamous London brothel. For parodic effect, Fielding placed tragedy's blank verse in the mouths of its sex workers and their clients.[48] Some audience members instantly recognized 'the most notorious Bawds, Pimps, and Whores ... on the stage', and even as 'young fellows' were 'smiling' at the meaning of passages lost on 'three parts of the audience', others who knew the 'secret history, the reality of the characters, and some personal scandal' were briefing those less informed.[49]

Clive played the whore Kissinda, who may well have stood for a recognizable doxy. In a scene with her lover, Kissinda expresses her supposedly

---

[41] *Ibid.*, p. 309. Isabella also confesses to entertaining a young Cavalier during Mass (*ibid.*, p. 313); she further observes that her sins are too many to repent, and that 'to shut a Woman out from Sin is not so easy' (*ibid.*, p. 319).
[42] *Ibid.*, p. 334.
[43] *Ibid.*, p. 339.
[44] *Ibid.*, p. 315.
[45] *Ibid.*, p. 322.
[46] *Ibid.*, p. 330.
[47] *Ibid.*, p. 334.
[48] The writings that Fielding rather haphazardly parodies – above all Ambrose Philips' *The Distrest Mother* – in this pseudo-classic tragedy are analyzed in Peter Lewis, *Fielding's Burlesque Drama: Its Place in the Tradition* (Edinburgh, 1987), pp. 135–49. See also Hume, *Henry Fielding and the London Theatre*, pp. 134–36 and Lockwood, 'The Covent Garden Tragedy. Introduction', *Henry Fielding: Plays Volume II*, pp. 341–45.
[49] The report of audience reaction appeared in the *Grub-street Journal*, issue 127 (8 June 1732) and is reprinted in Ronald Paulson and Thomas Lockwood, ed., *Henry Fielding: The Critical Heritage* (London and New York, 1969), pp. 41–43.

undying passion in verses that turn tragic declaration into salacious innuendo ('With my own Hands I'll wash thy soapen'd Shirt, / And make the Bed I have unmade with thee.').[50] Fielding completed his picture of Clive in the epilogue she spoke that evening. It merged fiction with fact, as its title 'by Miss Raftor, who acted the Parts of Isabel in the *Old Debauchees*, and of Kissinda in this Tragedy' makes clear.[51] Fielding had Clive explain that both of the fictional personae she had played that evening reveal something essential about the female character. Speaking Fielding's words, 'Miss Raftor' assured male audience members:

> In short, you are the Business of our Lives,
> To be a Mistress kept, the Strumpet strives,
> And all the modest Virgins to be Wives.
> For Prudes may cant of Virtues and of Vices,
> But faith! we only differ in our Prices.[52]

Fortunately for Clive's reputation, both mainpiece and afterpiece bombed, the latter spectacularly so. *The Old Debauchees* died after six nights, *The Covent Garden Tragedy* after one[53] – indeed some audience members quit the playhouse mid-performance.[54] 'Publicus', writing in *The Grub-street Journal*, charged Fielding with having written 'the most coarse, vicious, insipid trumpery that ever was hatched'.[55] This writer identified the epilogue with Fielding rather than with its speaker, accusing Fielding of telling Ladies in the audience that they were '*downright arrant whores*'.[56] Fielding's stout self-defence – on the familiar pretext of wishing to instruct the public – prolonged the debate. In one sally, 'Dramaticus', also in *The Grub-street Journal*, condemned the 'infamous lewdness' of the afterpiece.[57] Later that summer, in the same publication, 'Prosaicus' noted that '*young C[ibber] was esteemed a judge of*

---

[50] Lockwood, ed., 'The Covent Garden Tragedy', *Henry Fielding: Plays Volume II*, p. 385.
[51] *Ibid.*, p. 373.
[52] *Ibid.*
[53] As Lockwood points out, *The Old Debauchees* was dismissed on its third night, presumably due to low audience numbers, and achieved six performances only due to the popularity of the new afterpieces appended to it. Both afterpieces were Clive vehicles, first *The Devil to Pay* and then *The Mock Doctor*. Lockwood, 'The Covent Garden Tragedy. Introduction', *Henry Fielding: Plays Volume II*, p. 295.
[54] 'All we can say for sure about the reception that night is that a few playgoers left before the curtain ... Perhaps those who walked out ... were just bored. The tone of moral outrage seems to have crept in only later.' *Ibid.*, p. 348.
[55] 'Publicus' in *Grub-street Journal*, issue 133 (20 July 1732); Paulson and Lockwood, ed., *Henry Fielding: The Critical Heritage*, p. 59.
[56] *Ibid.*, p. 58.
[57] 'I appeal to last night's new Entertainment, and particularly to that part of it, called, *The Common* [sic] *Garden Tragedy* ... Such a scene of infamous lewdness, was never brought, I believe, before on any Stage whatsoever!' 'Dramaticus', *Grub-street Journal*, issue 128 (15 June 1732); *ibid.*, p. 43.

something besides acting: but his management this vacation has not increased his reputation as a judge'.[58]

On the opening night of 1 June 1732, then, what should have been a career milestone for Clive – her launch as straight comedienne – was instead a debacle. In a revisionist account five weeks later, Fielding put out that it had been a triumph. By virtue of his mainpiece, Fielding claimed, Clive had revealed herself to be one of the 'rising Glories of the Theatre' who had 'convinced the best Judges of her admirable Genius for the Stage' by showing 'in the *Old Debauchees*, that her Capacity is not confined to a Song'.[59] Fortunately for Clive, her 'Capacity' wasn't confined to Fielding's latest spoken parts for her either. In the wake of Fielding's double fiasco, a sure-fire hit became an imperative. To supply one, Fielding turned to a Clive line of proven popularity, and raised the tone of what he wrote. Thus one of the era's most celebrated hits, *The Mock Doctor*, reached the boards.

'A Woman's Ware': Clive and *The Mock Doctor*

Puffs carefully distanced *The Mock Doctor* from *The Old Debauchees* and *The Covent Garden Tragedy*. First notice appeared on 16 June, promising 'the purest and most natural Humour'.[60] Strengthening the respectability of *The Mock Doctor* was its author Molière, whose *Le Médecin malgré lui* Fielding adapted. The nice playgoer adored Molière, in recognition of which bookseller John Watts had by 1731 enlisted James Miller to prepare a collected French-English edition of Molière's comedies.[61] Although Watts had yet to print *Le Médecin malgré lui*, its popularity had been established through earlier English-language adaptations.[62] In contrast to these works, a fuss was made around

---

[58] *Grub-street Journal*, issue 138 (24 August 1732); *ibid.*, p. 67 (italics in original).
[59] Lockwood, ed., 'The Preface [to the Mock Doctor]', *Henry Fielding: Plays Volume II*, p. 430. It was published on 11 July 1732. Lockwood, 'The Mock Doctor. Introduction', *ibid.*, p. 422.
[60] *Daily Post*, issue 3972 (16 June 1732); cited in Lockwood, 'The Mock Doctor. Introduction', *ibid.*, p. 405.
[61] Theophilus Cibber, 'The LIFE of the Revd. Mr. JAMES MILLER', *The Lives of the Poets of Great-Britain and Ireland. By Mr. Cibber and other Hands*, vol. 5 (London, 1753), p. 334; cited in O'Brien, 'The Life and Works of James Miller, 1704–1744', p. 27. Henry Baker, who collaborated with Miller several times, contributed to Watts' translation.
[62] The adaptations were James Lacy's *The Dumb Lady* (1672), Susannah Centlivre's *Love's Contrivance* (1703), and its ballad-opera version (1732) discussed below. Lockwood, 'The Mock Doctor. Introduction', *Henry Fielding: Plays Volume II*, pp. 406–8. Before *The Mock Doctor* opened, Miller was still preparing his translation of *Le Médecin malgré lui*, which would appear in Watts' second volume of Molière's plays. The first volume had been sold from 10 May: 'This Day is Published, The FIRST VOLUME of A SELECT COLLECTION of MOLIERE'S COMEDIES, in FRENCH and ENGLISH ... The Translation is entirely New, and was undertaken by several Gentlemen'. *Daily Journal*, issue 3540 (10 May 1732).

the pedigree of Fielding's source and the accuracy of Fielding's transmission. One puffer insisted that 'Le Medecin Malgre Lui, of Moliere, from whence the Mock Doctor is taken, bears the greatest Reputation of any *petit Piece* in the French Language.'[63] Fielding echoed this puff in his playbook preface ('*Le Medecin malgré Lui* of Moliere, hath been always esteemed in France the best of that Author's Humourous Pieces'),[64] vowing to have preserved 'the Spirit of Moliere'.[65]

Fielding's vow notwithstanding, *The Mock Doctor* in fact fused Molière's original with *The Devil to Pay*, just as the Clive-led ballad opera *The Comical Revenge*, which had been gotten up on 12 May, almost certainly had. The principals in *The Comical Revenge* (Harper, Clive, Stoppelaer) had been those of *The Devil to Pay*,[66] and the wife-beating and verbal abuse of its source, Centlivre's *Love's Contrivance*, presumably featured as well.[67] With hindsight it's clear that *The Devil to Pay* had initiated a new line for Clive as an abused, spirited wife that *The Comical Revenge*, *The Mock Doctor*, and other farces shown in Appendix 2 soon extended. In *The Mock Doctor*, Theophilus Cibber took Harper's place as Clive's onstage foe.

Fielding wrote under enormous time pressure, translating and adapting Molière's comedy within days, probably between 5 and 16 June. This left the players just a week to learn their parts before opening night, 23 June,[68] and the pressure seems to have forced the summer company to suspend productions, for which an apology was printed.[69] A comparison of Fielding's *Mock Doctor* with Molière's comedy makes clear that Fielding had again promoted Cibber at Clive's cost. In Molière's original, a wife outwits her abusive husband by engineering his battering without suffering reprisal. By contrast, Fielding has husband Gregory arrange the extravagant retributive abuse and possibly even rape of his wife Dorcas. Gregory, posing as the doctor, offers Dorcas money

[63] *Daily Post*, issue 3980 (26 June 1732); Lockwood, 'The Mock Doctor. Introduction', *Henry Fielding: Plays Volume II*, p. 417.
[64] Lockwood, ed., 'The Preface [to the Mock Doctor]', *ibid.*, p. 429.
[65] *Ibid.*
[66] Lockwood, 'The Mock Doctor. Introduction', *ibid.*, p. 408.
[67] *The Comical Revenge* (1732) never reached print but Lockwood notes: 'From the list of characters it [The Comical Revenge] appears to have been a cut-down version of Centlivre's *Love's Contrivance*.' *Ibid*. The advertisement for *The Comical Revenge* lists Clive as Martin's Wife, Harper as Martin, and Stoppelaer as Octavio. *Daily Post*, issue 3948 (12 May 1732). On the same evening, Clive led Carey's *Cephalus and Procris*. In Centlivre's comedy, Martin and his wife argue over his having squandered her dowry through drink; he beats her to silence her criticisms. [Centlivre], *Love's Contrivance*, pp. 10–12. As in Molière's original, she revenges herself by engineering floggings for him. *Ibid.*, pp. 35–36.
[68] Lockwood, 'The Mock Doctor. Introduction', *Henry Fielding: Plays Volume II*, p. 406.
[69] 'N.B. The Company being busily employ'd in Rehearsing several New Pieces, &c. could not perform till this Day, and they will positively continue to act twice a Week as usual.' *Daily Post*, issue 3978 (23 June 1732).

for sex;[70] she yields, but on kissing him recognizes her husband and resists, boxing his ears.[71] Once he discloses his identity to her, she confesses to having duped servants into thrashing him. In retaliation, Gregory convinces the physician Hellebor, who has come to consult him, that she is deranged. Her putative madness consists of thinking every man her husband; only maltreatment can cure her, and Gregory instructs Hellebore to 'let out thirty Ounces of her Blood ... shave off all her Hair, all her Hair, Sir ... make a very severe Use of your Rod twice a Day; and take a particular Care that she have not the least Allowance beyond Bread and Water'.[72] Hellebor promises to deliver these cures, and Gregory hands Dorcas over to him. Assaults on her, which by implication may also be sexual, take place offstage.

Abuse of Clive's character unfolded also within her song. She may have dominated as a singer – Fielding gave her character seven of the work's nine songs – but her tunes are mostly common, and laden with associations that besmirch Dorcas. By contrast, Fielding gave high-style melodies to Stoppelaer, playing the earnest lover. When Fielding revised *The Mock Doctor* for performance during the regular season from September 1732, Dorcas's tunes became even ruder.[73] In exchange for two of Seedo's new high-style airs in Fielding's original (Air 3 and Air 5, both of which contain sly Carey-esque twists[74]) she had to perform Fielding's verses to the broadside 'Thomas, You Cannot' – the title derived from its ribald refrain 'Thomas untyed his points apace'[75] – and a faux ballad by Seedo. To the latter, Clive sang of the 'Pill'

---

[70] 'Greg. I'll take this Opportunity to try her [*Aside.*] — Maye Dear ... you sal be my Physicion, and I will giva you de Fee. / Dorc. Ay my Stomach does not go against those Pills'. Lockwood, 'The Mock Doctor. Introduction', *Henry Fielding: Plays Volume II*, p. 452.

[71] 'Dorc. [*Kisses him*] As I live, my very Hang-Dog! I've discover'd him in good time, or he had discover'd me. [*Aside.*] ... And in your Ear, dat Sirrah, [*Hitting him a Box.*] *Ibid.*

[72] *Ibid.*, p. 453.

[73] Lockwood, assessing the words rather than the music, argues the opposite: 'As for the songs, Fielding kept the total number the same but replaced four of the original nine with new ones ... For the word "Slobberer" in the first song ... Fielding rather timidly substituted "Jackanapes" ... which shows something about the intended direction of revision in tone'. Lockwood, 'The Mock Doctor. Introduction', *Henry Fielding: Plays Volume II*, p. 452. Airs 3, 5, 8, 9 of the original were replaced, and numbering of the retained airs shifted (the fourth air became the third, the sixth air became the fourth, the seventh air became the fifth). Compare Lockwood, ed., 'The Mock Doctor', *Henry Fielding: Plays Volume II*, pp. 760–64 to Henry Fielding, *The Mock Doctor*, 1st edn (London, 1732). See also Berta Joncus and Vanessa Rogers, 'Ballad Opera and British double entendre: Henry Fielding's *The Mock Doctor*', *Die Praxis des Timbre in verschiedenen europäischen Kulturen: Eine musikalische Praxis zwischen Oralität und Schriftlichkeit*, ed. H. Schneider (Hildesheim, 2013), pp. 137–38.

[74] Joncus and Rogers, 'Ballad Opera and British double entendre', pp. 123 [on Air 3] and pp. 124–25 [on Air 5].

[75] This was Air 6 in the second version. Claude Simpson identifies the rude refrain, and like Lockwood and Jeremy Barlow, discusses this tune's popularity, particularly among ballad opera playwrights. Simpson, 'Thomas, You Cannot', *The British Broadside Ballad,*

that made 'Each Husband' a 'Physician'.[76] In revising *The Mock Doctor* Fielding also gave Stoppelaer a second sentimental air by Seedo (Air 7, 'Thus, lovely Patient, Charlotte') while excising Clive's lilting through-composed air by the renowned composer John Eccles.[77]

Such changes calibrated Clive's new airs to those that Fielding left untouched. In Air 1, to the tune 'Bessy Bell', Dorcas sings: 'When a Lady, like me, condescends to agree, / To let such a Slobberer taste her' (in his new version, Fielding changed 'Slobberer' to 'Jackanapes').[78] Another common title for 'Bessy Bell' was 'O Jenny, O Jenny, where hast thou been?'; it was then best known from its *Beggar's Opera* setting, in which Polly explains her slide into lust ('But he so teaz'd me, / And he so pleas'd me, What I did / You must have done).[79] In Air 2 Dorcas sings of her husband's right to 'lick' her 'Bones' to the tune of 'Winchester Wedding', whose traditional verses told about a new wife 'playing at Hoopers-hide', meaning both hide-and-seek and copulation.[80] Clive's tune 'Oh London is a Fine Town' – originally Air 4, and in Fielding's revised version Air 3 – was known as 'Our Polly is a sad slut', from *The Beggar's Opera*.[81]

Most cynical of all is the air 'A Woman's Ware', which Fielding recycled from *The Welsh Opera* and used in both *Mock Doctor* versions.[82] The melody is 'Charming Phillis', whose traditional verses tell of a shepherdess who gives

---

pp. 703–04 and Barlow, 'Air 10 "Thomas I cannot"', *The Music of John Gay's The Beggar's Opera*, p. 110. Lockwood notes that Fielding used the tune in three of his ballad operas, including *The Grub-Street Opera* (1731). Lockwood, ed., *Henry Fielding: Plays Volume II*, pp. 675–76. See also Joncus and Rogers, 'Ballad Opera and British double entendre', pp. 128–29.

[76] Lockwood, ed., 'The Mock Doctor', *Henry Fielding: Plays Volume II*, pp. 458, 759.

[77] The music stemmed from an air Eccles composed for Thomas D'Urfey's *The Comical History of Don Quixote* (1694). It was disseminated via songsheets and collections, above all D'Urfey's *Wit and Mirth*. Simpson, 'The Milkmaids, or The Merry Milkmaids, or The Milking Pail', *The British Broadside Ballad*, pp. 490–93; Lockwood, ed., 'The Mock Doctor', *Henry Fielding: Plays Volume II*, p. 684. See also Joncus and Rogers, 'Ballad Opera and British double entendre', pp. 127–28.

[78] See note 73.

[79] Joncus and Rogers, 'Ballad Opera and British double entendre', pp. 118–20. For a modern edition, and an outline of this tune's earlier prints, see Lockwood, ed., 'The Mock Doctor', *Henry Fielding: Plays Volume II*, pp. 435–36, 754–55.

[80] Joncus and Rogers, 'Ballad Opera and British double entendre', pp. 120–22. For a modern edition, and an outline of this tune's earlier prints, see Lockwood, ed., 'The Mock Doctor', *Henry Fielding: Plays Volume II*, pp. 442, 690.

[81] Joncus and Rogers, 'Ballad Opera and British double entendre', pp. 122–24; Barlow, 'Air 7 "Oh London is a fine town"', *The Music of John Gay's The Beggar's Opera*, pp. 21, 110; Lockwood, ed., 'The Mock Doctor', *Henry Fielding: Plays Volume II*, pp. 437, 755–56.

[82] Lockwood, ed., *Henry Fielding: Plays Volume II*, pp. 52, 89, 442, 690, 756. Having first set this ballad as air 17 in his *Welsh Opera*, Fielding reduced his next version to one stanza for air 19 in *The Grub-Street Opera*, and re-used this shortened setting in *The Mock Doctor*.

up her maidenhood 'on the Bank of Pinks and Lilies'.[83] To this tune Fielding had Clive sing: 'A Woman's Ware, like China, / Now cheap, now dear is bought; When whole, tho' worth a Guinea, / When broke's not worth a Groat'.[84] Here Fielding makes Dorcas the spokeswoman for one of his favourite topics: a woman's sliding valuation in London's sex trade, to which he gave frequent custom during the 1730s.[85] Fielding's epilogue, spoken by the ingénue dancer Anne Brett (not Clive), further thematizes the prostitute. Fielding has Brett assure audiences that sex is the best remedy for 'Maids' or 'Wives' who 'pine', making pimps more effective than doctors: '*Doctors*, with *some*, are in small Estimation, / But *Pimps, all* own, are useful to the Nation.'[86]

We can understand why, in 1737, Clive would yield Dorcas to Hannah Pritchard without a fuss,[87] but in the summer of 1732 she made the part her own. *The Mock Doctor* rescued the flagging summer season at Drury Lane. One critic attributed its success to the 'extraordinary good Action of him [Cibber] and Miss Raftor [rather] than to the Merit of the Writer.'[88] One puff even suggested that Cibber's talent alone had earned this afterpiece a following: 'I think it an entertaining Farcical Piece; but whether the pleasure is owing to him [Fielding], or MOLIERE, I know not. Some say it is owing only to *young* CIBBER'S playing his part so well.'[89] Young Cibber embraced his title

---

[83] One songsheet dated c.1705 ends with 'Might I tell what I could do / I would with my lovely Phillis / I would—ah would not you?' *Pinks and Lillies, or Phillis at a Nonplus* (London, [1705?]), British Library H.1601.(123.). See also Joncus and Rogers, 'Ballad Opera and British double entendre', pp. 125–26.

[84] Lockwood, ed., 'The Mock Doctor', *Henry Fielding: Plays Volume II*, pp. 442, 756.

[85] 'Arthur Murphy confirmed the view that Fielding, as a young man, was something of a rake, given to "excesses of pleasure" … having "launched wildly into a career of dissipation" … he became a favourite both "with the men of taste and literature and with the voluptuous of all ranks".' Martin C. Battestin with Ruthe R. Battestin, *Henry Fielding: A Life* (London, 1989), p. 144.

[86] Lockwood, ed., 'The Mock Doctor', *Henry Fielding: Plays Volume II*, p. 462. Sybil Rosenfeld mentions Anne Brett's dancing in 1732 at the fair booth of John Hippisley and the actor Timothy Fielding. Rosenfeld, *Theatre of the London Fairs in the Eighteenth Century*, p. 37.

[87] Pritchard's first performance of Dorcas was on 13 October 1737. Clive probably also welcomed her own absence from Francis Hayman's Vauxhall Gardens supper-box oil of a *Mock Doctor* scene. Hayman depicted 'Scene IX. Sir Jasper, Gregory, Charlotte, Maid' (Leander peeks in from behind the door), when Sir Jasper gives Gregory money; the dialogue at this point is printed in Lockwood, ed., 'The Mock Doctor', *Henry Fielding: Plays Volume II*, p. 447. Hayman depicts Cibber (Gregory), Stoppelaer (Leander), Charles Shepard (Sir Jasper), Susanna Williams (Charlotte), and Miss Mears (Maid). Coke and Borg, *Vauxhall Gardens: A History*, pp. 103–119.

[88] Thomas Cooke, 'Mr. Wilks. Some Observations on the present State of the Theatres in London, and on Elocution', *The Comedian*, no. 7 (October 1732), in *The Comedian, or Philosophical Enquirer* (London, 1732–33), p. 39; cited in Lockwood, 'The Mock Doctor. Introduction', *Henry Fielding: Plays Volume II*, p. 418.

[89] 'Prosaicus', *Grub-street Journal*, issue 138 (24 August 1732); cited in Lockwood, 'The Mock Doctor. Introduction', *Henry Fielding: Plays Volume II*, p. 418.

role, fighting off stiff competition from fringe theatres and gaining a further well-deserved soubriquet: that of the wife-abusing Mock Doctor.[90]

Of Theatric Nymphs: Fenton and Clive

Flush from the success of *The Mock Doctor*, Theophilus Cibber tried next to co-opt *The Beggar's Opera* from rival manager John Rich. Drury Lane had never mounted this seminal stage work. Not being a singer, Cibber absented himself, casting Clive and Stoppelaer as Polly and Macheath.[91] So extravagant were this production's puffs that they cover four of the five types discussed in this book's first chapter: 'material' (brief announcements), 'formal' (reports clearly favouring a production), 'direct' (putative news items which slip into praise), and 'oblique' (seeming news items concluding with a strong endorsement).[92]

On 5 July 1732 the *Daily Post* gave out a material puff, alerting readers that the 'celebrated Beggar's Opera is now in Rehearsal' at Drury Lane 'and will be speedily perform'd there'.[93] Following this were direct puffs of the upcoming performance, emphasizing that *The Beggar's Opera* was 'Never Acted there before'.[94] It opened on 11 July. Two days later an oblique puff gave out that:

> We hear the whole Performance of the Beggar's Opera (which was acted last Tuesday for the first Time at the Theatre Royal in Drury-Lane by the Summer Company) met with great Applause: There was a very handsome Audience, and every one express'd the great Delight they receiv'd from Miss Raftor, in the Character of Polly: Those who say least of her declare, they have seen nothing equal to her in that Part since the Original.[95]

A report or formal puff on 24 July seemingly confirmed Clive's ongoing triumph: 'The Beggar's Opera continues to be acted at the Theatre Royal in Drury-Lane to numerous Audiences with great Applause.'[96] The next day, a poem appeared, 'To Miss RAFTOR, on her Success in the Part of Polly in the *Beggars Opera*':

---

[90] Lockwood, 'The Mock Doctor. Introduction', *Henry Fielding: Plays Volume II*, pp. 413–14. Cibber first performed his part without Clive at the Little Haymarket, where he directed actors during their 1733 rebellion; at Drury Lane, where both Clive and Fielding remained, *The Mock Doctor* was mounted only once without Cibber, on 19 December 1733.

[91] The full cast was listed in the *Daily Post*, issue 4009 (29 July 1732), with Clive announced first: 'The BEGGAR's OPERA. The Part of Polly by Miss Raftor. Macheath, Mr. Stoppelaer; Lockit, Mr. Mullart; Peachum, Mr. Paget; Mrs. Peachum, Mrs. Mullart; Lucy, Miss Atherton; Mrs. Slammerkin, Mrs. Charke; Beggar, Mr. W. Mills; … Jenny Diver, Miss Atherton.'

[92] See Chapter 1, pp. 22–23.

[93] *Daily Post*, issue 3988 (5 July 1732).

[94] The first such announcement was in the *Daily Post*, issue 3991 (8 July 1732).

[95] *Daily Post*, issue 3995 (13 July 1732).

[96] *Daily Post*, issue 4004 (24 July 1732).

By Nature form'd to grace the British Stage,
See Raftor rise, the Darling of the Age!
Such Pow'r to Act, such strong Desire to Please,
So much Improvement, yet with so much Ease,
What have we not to hope, when rip'ning Time
Shall turn what's now Surprizing, to Sublime?
Proceed, dear Girl! thou has begun so well,
Sure as thou striv'st, so sure shalt thou excel.[97]

Fast on the heels of this poem, another appeared. Although its title was similar ('To Miss RAFTOR, on her success in acting Polly Peachum'), it robbed Clive of agency, making her the creature of Cibber ('Keyber') and Fielding (here given his customary alias 'Hint'):

By HINT and KEYBER form'd to please the age,
See little RAFTOR mount the Drury stage;
FENTON outdone, with her no more compares,
Than GAY's best songs with HINT's *Mock Doctor* airs.
Lament, O RICH: thy labours all are vain:
HINT writes, and RAFTOR acts in Drury-lane.[98]

In this elaborate puffery, Clive is held to trump Fenton in the same way that Fielding's airs – the melodies he chose, together with his words – outdo Gay's 'best songs'. While eclipsing Fenton, Clive would yet continue to 'please' as Fenton had, having been 'form'd' by her two male authors, Hint and Keyber.

On 20 July a critic let out some of this hot air: 'We hear the whole performance of the Beggar's Opera ... met with great applause: there was a very handsome audience &c. DP. – *This puffing was not occasioned by the great applause, nor by the crouding of the Audience, which might be very handsome, tho' not very numerous*'.[99] Indeed, from 27 July Theophilus Cibber began to add afterpieces to *The Beggar's Opera*, beginning with *The Mock Doctor*, a sign that houses were thin.[100] After eleven performances that summer,[101] and a three-night run against Rich's rival production in December 1732,[102] during the next four years Drury Lane staged *The Beggar's Opera* for two benefits

---

[97] *Daily Journal*, issue 3606 (25 July 1732).
[98] *Grub-street Journal*, issue 137 (17 August 1732).
[99] *Grub-street Journal*, issue 133 (20 July 1732).
[100] Lockwood, 'The Mock Doctor. Introduction', *Henry Fielding: Plays Volume II*, p. 413.
[101] Performances were twice weekly and, during this summer season, usually on Tuesdays and Fridays. *The Beggar's Opera* first played on Tuesday 11 July, Friday 14 July, Tuesday 18 July, Friday 21 July, Tuesday 25 July, and Friday 28 July 1732. Thereafter it was paired with *The Mock Doctor* on Tuesday 1 August, Tuesday 8 August, Friday 11 August, Saturday 19 August, and Tuesday 22 August 1732. This last was the final night of the Drury Lane summer company season.
[102] The three-night rival run in December 1732 was 'surely deliberate' and 'resulted in a clear victory for Rich'. Jeremy Barlow, 'The Beggar's Opera in London's Theatres, 1728–1761', "The Stage's Glory", p. 174.

only, one of which was Clive's. This gives the lie to the 'great Delight' Cibber's summer production had putatively inspired. Clive's 'success' as Polly in the summer of 1732 was, however, so persuasively faked that by 1736 she was able to weaponize it. That year, during her career-defining row with Theophilus Cibber, she vanquished him partly by claiming a triumph as Polly that she had never enjoyed. Assuming that it was Cibber who had organized the puffing of the 1732 *Beggar's Opera*, in 1736 she hoisted him with his own petard.

Clive took what steps she could to defend herself against being cast as another Fenton. Cibber mounted two other ballad operas that summer, one a Drury Lane-style pastoral (*Rural Love*, on 4 August), the other a production derived from *The Devil to Pay*, *The Devil of a Duke* (on 17 August). Like its near-namesake, *The Devil of a Duke* was an operatized seventeenth-century comedy featuring a magician, an abused wife, and swapped identities, in this case between male rather than female characters.[103] As usual, Clive sang opposite Stoppelaer. A notice appeared in the playbook: 'N.B. The [words to the] first and eighteenth *Airs* were wrote by another Hand, and inserted at the Desire of the *Performers*.'[104] The '*Performers*' were in fact Clive alone, who sang both numbers.

For her first air, she chose a setting of the aggressively high-style 'Segauci di Cupido' ('Followers of Cupid'). Its music had been the final aria for the castrato Antonio Bernacchi in Handel's light-hearted opera *Partenope* (King's Theatre, 24 February 1730).[105] In Clive's air in *The Devil of a Duke*, Handel's bright, memorable motif bounces back and forth between violins and vocal line, propelled relentlessly forward by the running bass. Only the A section of this *da capo* aria was used; in its condensed form this air, with its leaps and diminutions, made for a vigorous yet charming opening number.[106]

The unidentified music of Air 18 was Clive's final solo, and is similar in mood and style: underpinning its leaps, octave run, and high tessitura (running from middle F sharp to high A) is a continuo whose dissonant ninths on the downbeat spice up the second half.[107] In both airs, Clive sang of polite love: in the first, about how modesty forbids her to fully express her passion; in the second, about how her lover should suffer as she does. Unusually, the

---

[103] Adapted by Robert Drury, *The Devil of Duke* is based on Nahum Tate's *A Duke and no Duke* (1685), which in turn is based on Sir Aston Cockain's *Trappolin Suppos'd a Prince* (1658). Gagey, *Ballad Opera*, pp. 111–12.

[104] [Robert Drury], 'Dramatis Personae', *The Devil of a Duke: Or, Trapolin's Vagaries. A (Farcical Ballad) Opera ... To which is prefix'd the Musick to each Song, set for the Spinnet, Harpsicord, German Flute, Violin, and Hautboy; with the Thorough Base to each Tune* (London, 1732), page unnumbered.

[105] Joncus, 'Handel at Drury Lane', pp. 191, 198.

[106] [Drury], *The Devil of a Duke*, p. 2. The score appended to the playbook ('The Air's for the Violin and Harpsichord &c. in the Opera call'd the Devil of a Duke') is separately paginated; the adaptation of 'Segauci di Cupido' is on its second page.

[107] Ibid., pp. 35, 16–17.

songs in the playbook were engraved with a figured bass line; this music was both appended to the playbook, and issued as *Songs in the Farce call'd the Mock Doctor ... To which is added ye Aires ... in the Opera call'd the Devil of a Duke*.[108] Whether or not Clive had a hand in bringing this music to print, its insertion in *The Devil of a Duke* shows her sophistication – *Partenope* was obscure, having disappeared after seven performances[109] – and how she wished to be seen and heard. It was a far cry from the stage material Cibber and Fielding imposed on her during the summer of 1732.

Eleven years after *The Covent Garden Tragedy* bombed, Fielding persuaded Drury Lane management to mount his comedy *The Wedding Day*, refused by John Rich thirteen years earlier.[110] For this, his last-ever new stage production, Fielding wanted Clive to play Mrs. Useful, a procuress who facilitates the rake Millamour's seductions. But Clive was by then powerful enough to refuse parts, and in this instance reportedly did so.[111] Her reaction is the subject of 'Verses occasion'd by a Quarrel betwixt Mr. F—ld—g and Mrs. Cl—ve, on his intending her the Part of a Bawd' by Fielding's friend Charles Hanbury Williams.[112] The poem, printed 1743, skewers Clive for her vanity, temper, plump figure, and eagerness to lodge complaints in the press, and captures her voice in the outrage of its opening lines: 'A Bawd! a Bawd! where is this scoundrel Poet? / Fine Work indeed! By G—d the Town shall know it.'[113]

Clive's celebrated reverence for sexual propriety was an attitude for which she was already becoming known in the early 1730s.[114] While mocked for

---

[108] *Songs in the Farce call'd the Mock Doctor ... The Tunes proper for the German Flute, Violin & Common Flute. To which is added ye Aires for the Violin & Harpsichord in the Opera call'd the Devil of a Duke* ([London], [1732]). Lockwood mentions this 1732 score in Lockwood, ed., *Henry Fielding: Plays Volume II*, p. 754, as does Roger Fiske, *English Theatre Music in the Eighteenth Century*, p. 115. Like other scholars, they assume Seedo prepared this music, yet we have no direct evidence that Seedo ever worked for Theophilus Cibber's summer company.

[109] David Vickers, 'Partenope', *The Cambridge Handel Encyclopedia*, ed. A. Landgraf and D. Vickers (Cambridge, 2009), pp. 488–91.

[110] Fielding's different versions of *The Wedding Day* – the manuscript submitted to the censor, and Fielding's edition in his *Miscellanies* of 1743 – are published in Hugh Amory, ed., with an introduction and commentary by Betrand A. Goldgar, *Henry Fielding: Miscellanies*, vol. 2 (Oxford, 1993).

[111] Matthew J. Kinservik, *Disciplining Satire: The Censorship of Satiric Comedy on the Eighteenth-Century Stage* (Lewisburg, PA, 2002), pp. 112–16.

[112] Printed in Goldgar, 'Introduction', *Henry Fielding: Miscellanies*, p. xlvi. Goldgar calls the quarrel between Clive and Fielding 'supposed', while Kinservik accepts that it took place.

[113] *The Foundling Hospital for Wit*, no. 1 (London, 1743), p. 1; cited also in Goldgar, 'Introduction', *Henry Fielding: Miscellanies*, p. xlvi.

[114] Kimberly Crouch has traced the means by which after 1750, Clive was 'extremely careful' of her 'alliances and associations, both within the theatre and beyond ... using chastity as an indicator of the social acceptability'. Crouch, 'Attitudes towards Actresses in Eighteenth-Century Britain', p. 277.

prudishness, she may have calculated that the long-term benefits of this course were worth the passing sneers. She surely found Fielding's early parts as objectionable as she did the Bawd in *The Wedding Day*. Besides destroying her acting launch, during the 1732–33 season Fielding imperilled her good name, writing material and choosing music that clashed with her line in upright sentimental heroines and her reputation as London's finest playhouse songster. As a rising star in her early twenties, Clive had little choice but to obey the manager. With the actors' rebellion the following season, however, power relations would change.

5

'The pious Daughter, and the faithful Wife': Fielding, Miller, and Clive, 1733–35

Clive forms Fielding's parts – Clive's stage personae and Cibber's interventions – actors rebel and Hint turns publicist – the mysterious case of George Clive – exit Fielding, re-enter James Miller

In throwing together *The Mock Doctor*, Henry Fielding had in June 1732 stumbled onto something Clive excelled in: French comedy. Its banter, lightning action, stock characters, and furtive asides allowed her to blaze forth in spoken as well as sung principal parts. Fielding, alert to these strengths, converted two more French comedies for her during the regular season that followed. *The Miser* and *The Intriguing Chambermaid*, unlike *The Old Debauchees* and *The Covent Garden Tragedy*, built on talents for which Clive had won applause, integrated her comic with her musical skills, and were runaway hits.

But theatrical wars overshadowed Clive's successes of the 1732–33 season. Furious that his own father had failed to make him co-manager as he expected, Theophilus Cibber led an actors' rebellion from March 1733 against the new manager, John Highmore. In not joining Cibber's rebel company, Clive became subject to the first critical abuse of her career. A pamphlet charged her with advancing herself at the cost of others and so revealing her treacherous nature. Playwright and actor Edward Phillips blended this sketch of Clive into his hit comedy about Cibber's rebellion, casting her as 'Miss Prudely Crotchet'. Fielding, who also did not follow Cibber, stoutly defended her, testifying to her sterling qualities and rewriting the part she took in his *Author's Farce* in ways that made its fiction fit with the 'facts' he gave out about her.

Clive, then still Catherine Raftor, mounted her own defence with an advantageous personal alliance. In October 1733 she married a member of a leading Shropshire family – or did she? Evidence suggests that her 'husband' George Clive loved men, and that their marriage was a fiction from the start. In March 1734 Cibber returned to Drury Lane, negotiating a post for himself as deputy manager and bringing with him the latest comedy by James Miller. Now a respected Molière translator, Miller was ideally placed to expand Clive's line, and he eventually supplanted Fielding as Drury Lane's provider of Clive vehicles.

Clive in *comédie* parts: 'the Garrick of the ladies'

The Mock Doctor not only salvaged Drury Lane's 1732 summer season, it altered the course of Clive's career. After its success Fielding gave her other chances to blossom as a principal comedienne in works originally French, and later playwrights took up this line. The speech of such parts, regardless who adapted them for her, typically consists of rapid-fire, consonant-filled chatter, punchy aphorisms, and, most importantly, asides to the audience. To become a first singer, Clive had trained to perfect her diction, pace her accelerando passages, and make her cadences incisive. Music prepared her to excel in the speech of French-based comedies, whose strokes relied on these same skills.

The locution of Clive's asides to audiences was cousin to her renowned instructive song. In 1759 the 'variety of her powers' would cause Samuel Derrick to judge Clive the 'Garrick of the ladies'.[1] More just would have been to call Garrick the 'Clive of the gentlemen', given that her deployment of these powers preceded his. In 1736 Aaron Hill lauded Clive for the new standards of musicianship that she brought to stage speech. The way Fielding devised Clive's monologues in his mainpiece *The Miser* suggests the strengths for which he was writing. In this comedy, Clive played the scheming chambermaid Lappet, which became her earliest iconic part without song. Lappet's speeches contain three sonic patterns – patter, *accelerando* tempo, and emphatic conclusion – in whose musical correlates Clive was skilled. An instance of the first two patterns is found when Lappet alternates between wheedling and flattery. Her sudden changes confound the ageing miser Lovegold:

> I have a Law-suit depending, which I am on the very Brink of losing for want of a little Money. [*He looks Gravely.*] And you could easily procure my Success, if you had the least Friendship for me: You can't imagine, Sir, the Pleasure she takes in talking of you. [*He looks pleas'd.*] — Ah! how you will delight her, how your venerable Mien will charm her. She will never be able to withstand you. — But indeed, Sir, this Law-suit will be of a terrible Consequence to me. [*He looks grave again.*] I am ruin'd, if I lose it, which a very small Matter might prevent. Ah! Sir, had you but seen the Raptures with which she has heard me talk of you. [*He resumes his Gayety.*][2]

---

[1] 'I believe that of all Actresses who have appeared in the comic vein, Mrs. Clive's superior talents have always been pre-eminent ... She has a natural melody in her voice; and her manner of singing ballads is accompanied with a humour peculiar to herself. Mrs. Clive is not only the most useful, but the most entertaining actress on the Stage: nay, if we consider her variety of powers, and her exertion of them, I fancy we may safely allow her to be the Garrick of the ladies.' [Derrick], *A General View of the Stage*, pp. 287–88.

[2] Lockwood, ed., 'The Miser', *Henry Fielding: Plays Volume II*, pp. 512–13.

Ex. 5.1 Words and music by Henry Carey, 'Go perjurd Swain [Cantata no. 2]', *Six Cantatas humbly dedicated to the Rt. Honble Sackville Earl of Thanet The Words and Music by H. Carey*, 1732. Copyright © The British Library Board 30/9/2018. All Rights Reserved. Shelfmark: Music Collections B.380(1).

The passage demands crispness, increasing rapidity, and repeated volte-face in mannerism. After Lappet took hold, Fielding and others cultivated such banter-driven points across the charmingly roguish characters Clive brought to life, whether servants (Lettice in Fielding's *Intriguing Chambermaid*, Primrose in Miller's *Mother-in-Law*, and her *in propria persona* roles in *The Coffee-House* and *High Life below Stairs*) or disobedient daughters (Maria in Miller's *Man of Taste* or the Daughter in Miller's *An Hospital for Fools*).

Stinging conclusions typify Clive's speeches in her French comedies, demanding a build-up and flourish at which she excelled. Her first signature song, Richard Charke's 'The provident Damsel' of 1730 from Miller's *Humours of Oxford*, ends in this way. Soon after this song took hold, Carey took this procedure from Charke and refined it in the second of his 1732 cantatas for Clive (Ex. 5.1). As discussed earlier, she may have debuted this music at Carey's extraordinary benefit concert of December 1730. In the second cantata's final movement, Carey had Clive pivot from pining shepherdess to disdainful man-hater as she sang 'no more I'll pine for an Ingrate, no more my mind perplex;

/ but for thy sake I'll ever hate, / thy whole deceitful Sex.'[3] To parry before her final lunge, the music veers without preparation into the relative minor ('no more my mind'), emphasizing the word 'mind' with a Neapolitan sixth, and landing on an imperfect cadence with the word 'hate' (Ex. 5.1, bars 18–22). A fermata separates this passage from the final declaration, 'thy whole deceitful Sex', whose notes, back in the home key, emphasize rhythmically the first and last words. Such parry and thrust are strewn across Clive's spoken parts, beginning with Lappet, as where Lappet ends a short speech with 'I hope, my Dear, you will keep these Secrets safe; for one would not have it known that one publishes all the Affairs of a Family, while one stays in it.'[4] The concluding phrase pinions the appeal in place with an implied threat that is also the witty restatement of a commonplace.

Clive's best-known stroke was a kind of compound address, simultaneously giving out different messages to different characters on stage, and to the audience, which in French comedy drew on commedia dell'arte-style improvisation.[5] Clive's most virtuosic execution of this stroke was as Lettice in the afterpiece *The Intriguing Chambermaid*, Fielding's translation of Jean-François Regnard's *Le Retour imprévu*. The character of Lettice was modelled not on her cognate Lisette from Regnard's work, but on Clive.[6]

Unfortunately, the only report we have of Clive's performance in these seminal stage works is from John Hill, whom theatrical professionals – unlike modern scholars[7] – thought a pretentious stage amateur. Hill alienated many when, in 1739, he falsely accused John Rich of intellectual theft: Rich protested Hill's 'pitiful Story',[8] and Hill was excoriated for his 'vast Stock of *Pride, Vanity,*

---

[3] Carey, *Six Cantatas humbly dedicated to the Rt. Honble Sackville Earl of Thanet The Words and Music by H. Carey*, p. 12.

[4] Lockwood, ed., 'The Miser', *Henry Fielding: Plays Volume II*, p. 494.

[5] Drawing on the improvisatory skills of Italian troupes he worked with, Molière 'padded out' standard plot scenes with 'small units of back-and-forth exchanges between characters, each section in a sense autonomous, and frequently involving a strong element of repetition.' Richard Andrews, 'Molière, commedia dell'arte, and the Question of Influence in Early Modern European Theatre', *The Modern Language Review*, vol. 100, no. 2 (2005), pp. 444–63, esp. 450.

[6] 'Merlin and Lisette serve Fielding mainly as prompts for Lettice ... with the real model for the character coming from Clive herself and her earlier roles, most obviously and recently that of Lappet in *The Miser*.' Lockwood, ed., 'The Miser', *Henry Fielding: Plays Volume II*, p. 566.

[7] Paul Goring calls John Hill a 'physician' but period writers cited below called him an apothecary. Hill produced a huge corpus of works on medicine and botany. He studied with Charles Macklin, but established himself neither as actor nor playwright. Goring, 'The Art of Acting', *Rhetoric of Sensibility in Eighteenth-Century Culture*, p. 136. Passing over contemporary reaction to John Hill, Goring finds that 'John Hill could ground his science of acting in reflections' that the 'more refined' audience of the 1750s could appreciate. Goring, 'The Art of Acting', pp. 135–41, esp. 135–36.

[8] John Rich, *Mr. Rich's Answer to the many Falsities and Calumnies advanced by Mr. John Hill, Apothecary* (London, 1739), p. 7. Hill, in the preface to his *Orpheus: An English*

and *Effrontery*, blended together'.[9] The actor Henry Woodward had only disdain for Hill's 'Dress and Gallantries; your Simper and Leer from the Boxes; – your indolent Waddle along the Mall'.[10] Hill's commentary about Clive is however worth attending to: not only is it all we have, but it is credible because begrudged. In discussing Clive, Hill wished to show that the actress Jane Green (1719–91) was her superior;[11] yet such was Clive's hold on audiences that Hill found himself having to account it.

Hill describes Clive's diction, patter, and *accelerando* as an 'extreme volubility of tongue' in which, he wrote, she 'succeeded to admiration'.[12] He reports that Clive, speaking as Lettice in Act II, scene 4 of *The Intriguing Chambermaid* had 'three … parts to play at the same time' as earlier strands of action knot together.[13] The son of Lettice's master Goodall has squandered his father's wealth during his father's absence. Goodall has now returned, and because most of the household goods have been pawned, Lettice seeks to block him from entering his own home. To do so she lies, telling him that his household is being moved to Mrs. Highmore's residence, which his son has purchased. When Mrs. Highmore appears, Lettice gives out separately to each character that the other is mad, causing Mr. Goodall and Mrs. Highmore to grasp each other's contradictions of Lettice's story as a symptom of lunacy, as Hill describes:

Opera (1740) and in his pamphlet *An Answer to the many Plain and Notorious Lyes advanc'd by Mr. John Rich, Harlequin* (London, 1740) accused Rich of having rejected, then plagiarized his playbook *Orpheus* for the opera-pantomime *Orpheus and Eurydice* (12 February 1740). Hill's wordbook bears no resemblance to *Orpheus and Eurydice*, which was by the Shakespearean editor Lewis Theobald. In his wordbook, Theobald had lines cut during rehearsal printed, to ensure 'Mr. JOHN HILL' would have no room 'for continuing his chimerical Suggestions, "That such Parts were … *stolen* from his Opera."'. [Lewis Theobald], 'Advertisement', *Orpheus and Eurydice; An Opera* (London, 1739), page unnumbered.

[9] Henry Sommer, 'Preface', *Orpheus and Eurydice. With the Pantomime Entertainment* (London, 1740), p. iv. Sommer wonders if Hill 'is really out of Senses'.

[10] *A Letter from Henry Woodward … to Dr. John Hill, Inspector-General of Great-Britain, the Greatest of all Characters* (London, 1752), p. 10.

[11] Discussing Clive's most celebrated line, that of the chambermaid, Hill made the caveat that 'there is not a requisite on the female part that is not found in its utmost perfection in Mrs. Green'. [John Hill], *The Actor: A Treatise on the Art of Playing* (London, 1750), p. 151. By contrast, in *The Theatrical Review*, Green was judged 'a second edition of Mrs. Clive', and Hill's views were dismissed as 'unmeaning farrago'. *The Theatrical Review: For the Year 1757, and Beginning of 1758* (London, 1758), pp. ii, 39. Regarding Hill's plagiarism of P. R. de Sainte-Albin's *Le comédien*, see Chapter 1, p. 13, note 48 and p. 22.

[12] '[A] chambermaid is not always expected to have an air of youth and bloom; but there is another indispensible quality which she must never be without, that is, an extreme volubility of tongue … We do not forget that Mrs. Clive has succeeded to admiration in a great number of parts of this kind'. [Hill], *The Actor* (1750), pp. 150–51.

[13] *Ibid.*, p. 163.

> While the actress is here construing every look and gesture of Mr. Goodall into madness to Mrs. Highmore ... she is expressing to the audience all the while the utmost terror in the world, lest one or the other of them [Goodall or Highmore] shou'd discover her: Nay, she even adds to the necessary perplexity of the part she has to act, by blending with her very terror the pert self-sufficiency, that marks out the rest of her character ... The person who understands this merit in Mrs. Clive's playing this short character, will not wonder if it appear very insipid when perform'd by any body else.[14]

This nimble twisting between addressees is typical of Clive's didactic songs articulating lessons to be drawn from the action, such as 'The provident Damsel', or 'A Woman's Ware' in *The Mock Doctor*. The persuasiveness of such thought-sharing depended on the authority Clive could exert over stage characters and audience members alike.

Simultaneous address, whether in song or speech, was a means for Clive to forge a direct relationship with playgoers. Hill thought she showed 'too much self-sufficiency and an unnatural freedom with her betters',[15] elsewhere he called this a 'saucy and unnatural familiarity'.[16] Chetwood characterized her manner more positively, praising her 'facetious Turn of Humour, and infinite Spirits'.[17] By the end of her career, she was 'CLIVE, without the form of art, / A jolly person, with the jolliest heart'.[18] Was she artless? Was she jolly? Her frankest personal letters, written to her protégée Jane Pope, suggest instead a deep cynicism.[19] But in her spoken scenes, as in her songs, she assumed candour so effectively that audiences and critics alike presumed it be 'real' even as they knew she was acting. This seeming honesty helped Clive smuggle in her own communications. Constructing this model, and provoking admiration for it,

---

[14] *Ibid.*

[15] 'We do not forget that Mrs. Clive has succeeded to admiration ... but the nicer observers will find too much self-sufficiency and an unnatural freedom with her betters.' *Ibid.*, p. 151.

[16] [John Hill], *The Actor: Or, a Treatise on the Art of Playing. A new Work, written by the Author of the former, and Adapted to the Present State of the Theatres* (London, 1755), p. 222.

[17] Chetwood, *A General History of the Stage*, p. 127.

[18] *The Smithfield Rosciad* (London, 1763), p. 11. This was also reprinted in Charles Churchill, *The Rosciad ... The Eighth Edition. With large Additions. To which is added the Smithfield Rosciad* (Dublin, 1764).

[19] Clive could express herself with startling harshness in her letters to Jane Pope. For instance, on the subject of 'Mrs Abington's first appearance': 'I don't wonder at it, an old hussy to be playing Girls of Fiveteen'. Letter of Catherine Clive to Jane Pope, Twickenham, 12 December 1782. Bodleian Library, Toynbee b.1, 'Autograph letters from Catherine Clive to Jane Pope'. JoAllen Bradham calls Clive's letters an 'epistolary autobiography'. Bradham doesn't consider, however, the autograph letters by Clive, the majority of which are in the Bodleian Library. JoAllen Bradham, 'A Good Country Gentlewoman: Catherine Clive's Epistolary Autobiography', *Biography*, vol. 19, no. 3 (1996), pp. 259–82.

was how Clive triumphed without recourse to the sexual allure which had traditionally been key to a first actress's success.

'Happy was that author who could write a part equal to her abilities! she not only, in general, exceeded the writer's expectation, but all that the most enlightened spectator could conceive.' So Thomas Davies commemorated her in 1783.[20] Clive's abilities seem to have been rooted in a magnetism that infused both her virtuosic performances of self and her seeming revelations of a nature fascinating in its contradictions. After *The Mock Doctor*, and through the success of *The Miser*, audience enthusiasm moved Fielding and others to adapt additional French comedies that showed Clive's stage manner to advantage. Song helped her, particularly when she could carry it from one part into another. On 11 April 1738, for instance, Clive would introduce 'The Life of a Beau', her new *in propria persona* point from James Miller's *The Coffee-House*, into her performance of Lappet in *The Miser*.[21] Thanks in part to Clive's repeated interpolation of this song into other plays, it became one of the epoch's most popular.[22] The appeal of this song was reportedly the way she 'hit off' – that is, mimicked – the fop in her 'Action and Gesture'.[23] What this might have expressed or been meant to communicate about the man-loving man whose name she bore can only be imagined.

The 1732–33 Season: Success and Discontent

On stage, the 1732–33 season brought the highest peaks of Clive's career to date. Her success as Belinda in *The Man of Mode* in January 1733 prefaced her stunning debut as Lappet in Fielding's *Miser* on 17 February. She continued to reign as first songster in both serious and comic parts, singing Seedo's Thalia in the masque *The Judgment of Paris* – the last-ever production by the legendary dance master John Weaver – as well as all of Drury Lane's ballad operas.[24] She also had set-backs: the next ballad opera of Charles Coffey's that she led, *The*

---

[20] Thomas Davies, *Dramatic Micellanies*, vol. 3 (London, 1784) p. 324.
[21] '[T]his Day, April 11, will be presented … The MISER … the Part of Lappet, by Mrs. Clive, in which Character will be introduc'd a Song call'd *The Life of a Beau*'. *London Daily Post and General Advertiser*, issue 1076 (11 April 1738).
[22] 'A great deal of singing was provided … the most popular at the established theatres [was] Kitty Clive's rendition of "The Life of a Beau"'. *The London Stage*, Part 3, vol. 1, p. clviii.
[23] 'It is not from want of Spirit or Judgment to hit off the Fop or the Coxcomb, as she has evidently prov'd in the Ballad she Sings, call'd *Life of a Beau*, in which her Action and Gesture is as pleasing as in any Part she performs.' *An Apology for the Life of Mr. T— C—, Comedian*, p. 141. At the end of this counterfeit autobiography, the author shifts away from mockery to speak of 'principal Actors' who 'may be thus impartially and concisely pourtray'd'. *Ibid*., p. 137.
[24] Moira Goff, 'Weaver, Words, and Dancing in *The Judgment of Paris*', *On Common Ground 5: Dance in Drama, Drama in Dance: proceedings of the Fifth DHDS Conference*, ed. D. Parsons (London, 2005), pp. 33–40.

Boarding School – another operatized seventeenth-century farce like *The Devil to Pay* – reached a mere four nights after it opened on 29 January 1733.[25] Seeing a cross-dressed John Harper, known for playing Jobson, roiled 'Tom Cynick' of *The Auditor*: 'What is it come to this? To please an Audience, must the Stage of Great-Britain dress a fat Man in Woman's Cloaths?'[26] Cynick denounced *The Boarding School* as 'the vilest and lowest Degree of Buffoonery'.[27]

Another setback, from Clive's point of view, was that by the start of the 1732–33 season Theophilus Cibber seemed poised to be Drury Lane's co-manager for the next season. The patent of the deceased Richard Steele was due to expire on 1 September 1732, and by May 1732 the actors who had been managing Drury Lane – Barton Booth, Robert Wilks, and Colley Cibber – had secured a new patent for twenty-one years.[28] On 13 July, Booth, ill since 1728, cashed out. He sold half his share to the inexperienced and vain, but very wealthy, John Highmore for a staggering 2,500 pounds.[29] On Booth's death ten months later, the other half of his share would fall to his wife, Hester Santlow, who within months would sell her share of 'the Patent to Mr. Giffard, the Master of Goodman's Fields Theatre',[30] and retire from the stage.[31] Two months after Booth sold to Highmore, on 27 September, Wilks died; his widow enlisted the portraitist John Ellys to manage on her behalf.[32] Benjamin Victor, who had been the go-between for Highmore and Booth during their negotiations, neatly summed up the situation: Colley Cibber 'seemed greatly hurt at the Thoughts of meeting Mr. Highmore and Mr. Ellis [sic] in the Office of Managers … And to avoid the Importance of One, and the Ignorance the

---

[25] For his farce, Coffey adapted Thomas D'Urfey's *Love for Money: Or, the Boarding School* (London, 1691). Gagey, *Ballad Opera*, p. 114.
[26] *The Auditor*, no. 9 (6 February 1733); reprinted in *The Gentleman's Magazine: Or, Monthly Intelligencer* [sic] (February 1733), p. 68.
[27] Ibid.
[28] *Grub-street Journal*, issue 122 (4 May 1732).
[29] Benjamin Victor, *The History of the Theatres of London and Dublin*, vol. 1, pp. 3–4. Victor reports that Highmore's annuity was 800 pounds, and that an earlier theatrical 'Frolic' had fueled his ambition to run Drury Lane. For a 100-pound wager with Lord Limerick, Highmore had persuaded Drury Lane management to let him play the title role of *Lothario*; because Highmore's friends 'crowded' the Stage – I assume Victor means the onstage seating for patrons – the managers enjoyed 'the greatest Receipt they had ever known to a stock Play'. Highmore also 'made them [the managers] a Present of the rich Suit that he had had tailored for Lothario'. Ibid., p. 4.
[30] Santlow's patent sale was announced in the *London Evening Post*, issue 910 (18–20 September 1733); cited in Goff, 'Art and Nature join'd', p. 68. Goff describes the reactions Santlow provoked by being a patent holder – the toadying print notices of Theophilus Cibber, the charge of being 'Proud, and Foolish, scandalous and Rude', the expression of sympathy for the quarrels disturbing her husband in his grave – and the dignity that Santlow gained by her early retirement. Ibid., pp. 63–69.
[31] Goff, 'Art and Nature join'd', p. 65.
[32] Hume, *Henry Fielding and the London Theatre*, pp. 142–45, 155–57; Gerrard, *Aaron Hill: The Muses' Projector*, pp. 147–49.

Other, he would have his Deputy too; and accordingly invested his son Theophilus to sit down with those Gentlemen in his Place'.[33]

In September 1732, in a very muted paternal endorsement, Colley Cibber rented his share of the patent to his son, securing for himself 442 pounds annual payment plus two guineas for each performance that he, Colley, gave.[34] By this agreement, as the younger Cibber later reported, Theophilus gained 'full Power and Management of the Theatre as a Patentee ... for the Space of nine Months ... from the first of September 1732, to the first of June 1733'.[35] At the start of February 1733 Theophilus Cibber made a 'fresh Agreement with Mr. Cibber Sen.', who, retiring, decided to 'Farm his Share' to his son for three hundred pounds, putting management 'in Possession of his Power ... from the Expiration of [the] first Agreement' on 1 June 1733 ''till that Day Twelvemonth Inclusive'.[36]

By February 1733 Theophilus Cibber must have seemed to Clive invincible, not least due to the stage work in rehearsal that he had just written for her, *The Harlot's Progress*. It was based on the 'Story just then invented, and made popular, by that great Genius Hogarth' through his *Harlot's Progress* print series.[37] Cibber's 'Grotesque Pantomime Entertainment' was a new kind of pantomime, shorn of its masque. Instead of gods, machines, and serious song and dance, there was the ballad-singing 'Miss Kitty' in the title role. For his action, Cibber mixed the first four scenes of Hogarth's print series with harlequinade and 'Songs made (to old Ballad Tunes) by a Friend'.[38] Given Clive's prominence in the cast, the 'Friend' may well have been Henry Carey. Cibber also fundamentally altered Hogarth's story: instead of dying, the harlot triumphs in a carnivelesque inversion of the print series' moral.

To set the first scene, in which Hogarth shows a country girl enticed into London's sex trade, the Bawd sings 'What tho' I am a Country Lass',[39] best

---

[33] Victor, *The History of the Theatres of London and Dublin*, vol. 1, p. 9.
[34] Hume, *Henry Fielding and the London Theatre*, p. 144. As Hume notes, these arrangements are described in *A Letter from Theophilus Cibber, Comedian, to John Highmore, Esq.*, which was issued in June.
[35] *A Letter from Theophilus Cibber*, p. 2.
[36] Ibid.
[37] Victor, *The History of the Theatres of London and Dublin*, vol. 1, p. 10. For a detailed comparison between Cibber's playbook and Hogarth's print series *The Harlot's Progress*, see Martin Meisel, *Realizations: Narrative, Pictorial, and Theatrical Arts in Nineteenth-Century England* (Princeton, 2014), pp. 99–103. The stage works that Hogarth's *Harlot's Progress* spawned are discussed in Richard Semmens, 'John Weaver's Last Dance with Harlot', *Studies in the English Pantomime, 1712-1733* (Hillsdale, 2016), pp. 141–82. Semmens deftly summarizes Ronald Paulson's scholarship on the genesis and dissemination of Hogarth's *Harlot's Progress*.
[38] Theophilus Cibber [and Henry Carey?], *The Harlot's Progress; Or, the Ridotto al' fresco: A Grotesque Pantomime Entertainment ... The Songs made (to Old Ballad Tunes) by a Friend* (London, 1733).
[39] Cibber [and Carey?], 'Air I. What tho' I am a Country Lass', *The Harlot's Progress*, p. 6.

known to period audiences as Nell's song to Carey's 'Sally in our Alley' in *The Devil to Pay*. As the action begins, Harlequin (played by the dancer Le Brun) sneaks into Miss Kitty's trunk. For the second scene, in a boudoir provided by the Jew-fop Beau Mordecai who keeps her, Miss Kitty sings new words to Clive's *Lottery* air tune 'Oh! what Pleasures will abound'.[40] When Harlequin appears from under her dressing table, Miss Kitty yields to him, singing a riotous jig, 'Lads of Dunce', to brazen verses ('Thus finely set out, / I'll make such a Rout, / And top all the Rantipole Girls of the Town').[41] Mordecai enters, and as in Hogarth's second picture drinks tea with the harlot as her lover tries to sneak off. At this juncture Theophilus Cibber's *Harlot's Progress* departs from the story told in Hogarth's pictures: rather than escaping, the lover is discovered, and in the ensuing chaos Miss Kitty defies the Jew in song. Her melody is Thomas D'Urfey's tune 'Maidens as fresh as a Rose', whose title suggests the threat of defilement.[42] The unusually strident scoring of *The Harlot's Progress* – oboes, bassoons, horns, trumpets, and drums[43] – will have amplified Miss Kitty's message: 'Farewell, good Mr. Jew; / Now I hate your tawny Face; / I'll have no more to do / With you or any of your Race'.[44] Song and words made Clive the vanquisher, rather than the possession, of the lascivious Jew.

In the final scenes of *The Harlot's Progress*, harlequinade continues to disrupt the progress of Hogarth's story. Bridewell prison itself yields to pleasure, as '[t]he Scene changes to the Ridotto al Fresco, illuminated with several Glass Lustres, (the Scene taken from the place at Vaux-Hall)'.[45] With this, Cibber switched Hogarth's setting for that of London's most glittering celebrity event of the past year: the opening of Vauxhall Gardens. As David Coke and Alan Borg show, the Ridotto al Fresco that opened the gardens in April 1732 was a huge publicity coup, graced by Frederick Prince of Wales, his entourage, and three hundred exclusive guests.[46] In Cibber's Ridotto, 'different Characters', that is, character dancers, perform 'to English, Scotch, Irish and French Tunes'.[47]

---

[40] 'Air IV. Oh! what Pleasures will abound', *ibid.*, p. 8. As Lockwood notes, John Pepusch composed this music for the highly popular *Perseus and Andromeda* (1730), by Rich's then-favourite pantomime writer Lewis Theobald, but we don't know for which number. It is Air 7 in *The Lottery*. Lockwood, *Henry Fielding: Plays Volume II*, p. 739.
[41] Cibber [and Carey?], 'Air V. Lad's a Dunce', *The Harlot's Progress*, p. 9.
[42] Used in three earlier ballad operas, and known also as 'Chastities Conquest', the tune featured in the century's best known miscellanies and dance collections. Simpson, 'Canst Thou Not Weave Bone-Lace?', *The British Broadside Ballad*, pp. 84–85.
[43] *The Harlot's Progress* 'was given with a band that included oboes, bassoons, horns, trumpets, drums, and strings'. Fiske, *English Theatre Music in the Eighteenth Century*, p. 108.
[44] Cibber [and Carey?], 'Air VI. Maidens as fresh as a Rose', *The Harlot's Progress*, p. 10.
[45] *Ibid.*, p. 12.
[46] Coke and Borg, 'The Ridotto al Fresco', *Vauxhall Gardens: A History*, pp. 42–49. The scenery for the finale, with its 'Lustres', may have drawn on the satiric engraving *Ridotto al Fresco or the Humours of Spring Gardens* of June 1732, which shows an illuminated ballroom, presumably in the Proprietor's House. See *ibid.*, pp. 47, 53.
[47] Cibber [and Carey?], *The Harlot's Progress*, p. 12.

What was celebrated in this entertainment was not the harlot's demise, but harlotry itself, along with native song, Theophilus Cibber's appetites, Clive's musical line, and the diversions of the glitterati.

According to Cibber, *The Harlot's Progress* was ready to open by January 1733, but 'Obstructions' from Highmore and Ellys brought a three-month delay.[48] Once it finally opened, on 31 March, *The Harlot's Progress* was a runaway hit; until her March 1738 success in Milton's *Comus* put her beyond such low representations, Clive led *The Harlot's Progress* about eighty times.[49] Anti-Semitism, whose appeal for playhouse audiences has been well-charted,[50] was henceforth central to Clive's *in propria persona*. Clive's own progress slowed only when she fell afoul of theatrical politics later in the spring of 1733.

On 27 March, the *Daily Post* carried a notice that Colley Cibber had sold his patent share to John Highmore, thereby breaking his agreement with his own son.[51] Theophilus Cibber asked Highmore to appoint him deputy manager, but Highmore, due to 'the disgust he conceived to the behaviour of young Cibber', refused.[52] Young Cibber was incandescent. Within two weeks of Highmore taking over the Drury Lane management, Theophilus had persuaded most of the company to walk out along with him. Clive declined to do so, and Fielding stuck to Drury Lane as well.[53] An incentive for Clive to stay may have been that her chief rivals for Anne Oldfield's parts, Mary Heron and Christiana Horton, joined Cibber. Sure enough, once they quit Drury Lane, she finally got her first

---

[48] 'This Entertainment, (for which I was indebted to Mr. Hogarth's Designs) the Town were pleased to approve of and encourage; and it might have been performed three Months sooner than it was, but for the Obstructions I met with from my Partners.' *A Letter from Theophilus Cibber*, p. 3.

[49] Other sopranos, beginning with Miss Wilson, took over Miss Kitty from 26 September 1738.

[50] Frank Felsenstein, 'Ev'ry Child Hates Shylock', *Anti-Semitic Stereotypes: A Paradigm of Otherness in English Popular Culture, 1660–1830* (London and Baltimore, 1999), pp. 158–86, and Todd M. Endelman, *The Jews of Georgian England, 1714–1830: Tradition and Change in a Liberal Society* (Ann Arbor, 1999), pp. 128–32. Endelman points out that the negative stereotyping of the male Jew – not least his excessive wealth and lust – is common to Hogarth's series, Cibber's *Harlot's Progress*, and Fielding's *Miss Lucy in Town*. On post-1760 productions, see Michael Ragussis, *Theatrical Nation: Jews and Other Outlandish Englishmen in Georgian Britain* (Philadelphia, 2010) and Michael Ragussis, *Figures of Conversion: "The Jewish Question" and English National Identity* (Durham, NC, 1995).

[51] Hume, *Henry Fielding and the London Theatre*, p. 157.

[52] Victor, *The History of the Theatres of London and Dublin*, vol. 1, p. 10; on Theophilus Cibber's offer, and Highmore's refusal, see Hume, *Henry Fielding and the London Theatre*, pp. 156–57. Hume draws on *An Impartial State of the Present Dispute between the Patent and Players* ([London], [1733]), p. 4.

[53] Hume speculates that Fielding's fidelity to Highmore may have had three grounds: as a fellow landholder, Fielding might have sided with those who thought Cibber was overstepping his rank; he may have wished to identify, and wished others to identify him, with Highmore's gentlemanly station; and he needed a manager amenable to mounting his stage works. Hume, *Henry Fielding and the London Theatre*, pp. 168–69.

chance to appropriate roles from Oldfield's line: first Estifania in *Rule a Wife and Have a Wife* on 1 October 1733, and then Elvira in *The Spanish Fryar* on 19 October.[54] Personal loathing of Theophilus Cibber probably also weighed with Clive, as it reportedly had with Highmore. Her friend Jane Cibber's death earlier that year would have severed any lingering loyalties, especially if, as bruited in the counterfeit memoir about him, Theophilus had hosted 'a Brace of *Drurian* Doxies' the night of Jane's funeral.[55]

For the 1733 actors' benefit season, Fielding gave his first public demonstration of support for Clive: he wrote her a bespoke benefit farce, *Deborah: Or, a Wife for you All*, performed on 6 April. Scholars agree that in this farce, of which no copy survives, Fielding almost certainly burlesqued Handel's oratorio *Deborah*, which had premiered fewer than three weeks earlier, on 17 March.[56] Critics had fiercely attacked Handel's ticket price hike for *Deborah*,[57] and Fielding likely rode this wave of hostility. Clive may well have been his inspiration, commanding as she did both Handelian song and satiric delivery; her opposite was, as usual, Charles Stoppelaer.

Meanwhile Theophilus Cibber was on the move. With other leading rebel company members he secretly sought to lease the Drury Lane playhouse itself, in order to deprive the patentees of access; after this he planned to set up an actors' co-operative that would rent the patent and theatre stock and manage the house.[58] At first, Cibber succeeded: building sharers of Drury Lane proved willing to rent to him. In response, Highmore locked the rebels out. On 28 May, 'Persons arm'd' stationed themselves at Drury Lane's 'Doors and Entrances ... against the ... Company ... as also against Mr. Cibber'.[59] Thus the season ended. The inevitable print war flared. Partisans of the mutineers argued for Highmore and Ellys's incompetence; partisans of the Drury Lane managers argued for Theophilus Cibber's selfishness, and for the social imperative to

---

[54] On Oldfield's performance of Estifania and Elvira, see Lafler, *The Celebrated Mrs. Oldfield*, pp. 37, 60–61.

[55] 'Should Men say, for Instance, I used my first dear and well-beloved Wife, of ever blessed Memory, J--n--y C-----, with ill Usage: Should they affirm, that when her all pale and breathless Corps was in the Coffin laid, and I, with Sobs and Tears and interjected Sighs, had moaned to many a Witness, my too unhappy Fate, yet that same Night had a Brace of *Drurian* Doxies vile [sic] in the same House.' *An Apology for the Life of Mr. T—C—, Comedian*, p. 100.

[56] Critical reaction in 1733 to Handel's *Deborah* is reprinted and clarified in Burrows et al., ed., *George Frideric Handel Collected Documents: Volume 2 1725–1734*, pp. 602–13.

[57] Lockwood, 'Introduction. The Miser', *Henry Fielding: Plays Volume II*, pp. 469–70; Edgar V. Roberts, 'Henry Fielding's Lost Play *Deborah, or A Wife for You All* (1733)', *Bulletin of the New York Public Library*, vol. 66 (1962), pp. 567–88.

[58] The players involved were: Cibber, John Mills, Benjamin Johnson, Josias Miller, John Harper, Benjamin Griffin, William Mills, William Milward, Mary Heron, and Elizabeth Butler. Hume, *Henry Fielding and the London Theatre*, p. 157, note 119.

[59] *Daily Post*, issue 4275 (29 May 1733); cited in Hume, *Henry Fielding and the London Theatre*, p. 158.

quash defiance of managerial authority.[60] In early June the patentees fired one of the rebel players, Benjamin Griffin, whose title role in *The Miser* opposite Clive had placed him in high esteem;[61] Griffin appealed in print for redress, charging managers at the two patent houses with having formed a cartel.[62] Debate continued through the summer of 1733.

For the first time, Clive's character was openly attacked in the press. A first salvo appeared in *The Theatric Squabble: Or, the P—ntees*, sold from 10 July:[63]

> Then R-ft--r, follow'd by the Wise and Bold,
> A pleasing Actress, but a Green-Room Scold;
> Puff'd with Success, she triumphs over all,
> Snarls in the Scene-Room, Curses in the Hall:
> She'as Learning, Judgment, Wit, and Manners too;
> Ay and good Sense, — if what she say's be true.
> Her Virtue too, the purest of the Age,
> She'll scarcely be a Whore – upon the Stage:
> Yet she that rails 'gainst vicious Talk so strong,
> Makes no Objection to a Bawdy Song:
> She'll neer seek Good, nor yet from Evil flinch;
> In short, she is a *Woman*, ev'ry Inch.[64]

The sketch is highly defamatory: Clive is shrewish (a 'Scold'), arrogant ('Puff'd with Success'), prudish ('purest of the Age'), and above all, hypocritical, claiming respectability while pandering to common taste. She is therefore a typical '*Woman*': incapable of seeking good, and capable of any evil. Edward Phillips borrowed this characterization of Clive for his summer entertainment of 1733 about the actors' revolt, *The Stage-Mutineers*, titled after a satirical etching, *The Stage Mutiny*, by John Laguerre, principal at John Rich's new playhouse at Covent Garden.[65] Fresh from Cambridge, Phillips was, to quote Yvonne Noble, 'a backstage writer working under ... guidance' from the manager.[66] Without competition from Drury Lane, Rich allowed

---

[60] Hume, *Henry Fielding and the London Theatre*, pp. 158–64.
[61] In *The Miser*, Benjamin Griffin as the miser Lovegold enjoyed one of the most celebrated parts of his career. *The Miser*'s success was steady rather than spectacular. Lockwood, 'The Miser. Introduction', *Henry Fielding: Plays Volume II*, pp. 470–71.
[62] Hume, *Henry Fielding and the London Theatre*, pp. 161–62.
[63] The sale notice was in *London Evening Post*, issue 875 (7–10 July 1733).
[64] *The Theatric Squabble: Or, the P—ntees. A Satire* (London, 1733), p. 6.
[65] John Laguerre, *The Stage Mutiny*. Etching, 1733. British Museum, Museum number 1868,0808.3552. William Hogarth visually quoted Laguerre's etching as a detail in his *Southwark Fair* (December 1733). Ronald Paulson, *Hogarth's Graphic Works*, 3rd rev. edn (London, 1989), pp. 87–88. This publication includes an account of the 1733-34 actor's rebellion. The verse satire, *The Dramatick Sessions: Or, the Stage Contest* (London, 1734), establishes Phillips' authorship of *The Stage-Mutineers*.
[66] Yvonne Noble, 'Attributions and Misattributions to Edward Phillips, Theatre Writer of the 1730s, with Some Remarks on Thomas Phillips, Theatre Writer of the 1730s',

for the very last time during his management a summer season,[67] with *The Stage-Mutineers* as its main attraction. It opened on 27 July, and continued on each of the ten nights during which the summer company played. Phillips' satiric butts were instantly recognizable: according to a *Grub-street Journal* report, the 'author of the *Stage Mutineers* has drawn such characters, that every one may immediately say to whom they appertain'.[68] Cibber and Clive were described in the prologue as a '*Ranting Hero* and a *Green Room Queen*'.[69] Fielding was pilloried along with the Drury Lane players.

As the action of Phillips' farce starts, players refuse the parts written by Fielding (called 'Mr. Crambo the Author') because his writing is too vulgar.[70] The Poet's response is to boast that his comedies offer 'the Quintescence of the French join'd to the Smartness of the English Ballad'.[71] Two managers intervene, forcing the players to accept their parts.[72] Pistol incites fellow-actors to rebel but meets refusal from Miss Prudely Crotchet (Clive) and Hero Truncheon (Charles Macklin, just hired by Highmore). Pistol seduces Prudely Crotchet, who initially rejects him ('I have an Aversion to your Sex'),[73] but then relents when Pistol warns her about prudes becoming old maids.[74] On learning that the manager has barricaded Drury Lane, Pistol's followers, Prudely Crotchet included, abandon him. He pleads with her, saying 'Shall sordid Interest outballance Love?' to which she replies 'Why in Love should not Women act on the same Principle as the Men?'[75] Prudely Crotchet restates this moral in a ballad to the tune of 'Mirleton', which, being a French common tune, literally

---

Restoration and Eighteenth-Century Theatre Research, vol. 17, nos. 1–2 (2002), p. 72. Based on correspondence, Noble has shown that Rich had earlier commissioned Phillips to write the ballad opera *The Mock Lawyer* to compete with Fielding's *Mock Doctor*.

[67] Burling, *Summer Theatre in London*, p. 82.
[68] *Grub-street Journal*, issue 189 (9 August 1733).
[69] [Edward Phillips], 'Prologue', *The Stage-Mutineers* (London, 1733), page unnumbered.
[70] Squeamish constantly complains about her parts, Haughty due to her pride will play only tragic roles, and Lovemore wants to appear only in the most fashionable dress. [Phillips], *The Stage-Mutineers*, pp. 5–6. These dramatis personae may have represented Mary Heron, Christiana Horton, and Roger Bridgewater respectively. Phillips' characterization of Bridgewater accords with that of *The Theatric Squabble*: 'Hark! a loud Noise appalls the list'ning Ears! / All think it Thunder, — Br-dg-wa--r appears: / His Brazen Front he thinks will do far more / Than B[oo]th, W[il]ks, M[il]ls, or C[i]bber did before: / His noisy Pow'r the ecchoing Roofs confess; / The trembling Audience too can do no less.' *The Theatric Squabble*, pp. 5–6. For a discussion of this farce without mention of the players being satirized, see Dane Farnsworth Smith, *Plays about the Theatre in England, from The Rehearsal in 1671 to the Licensing Act in 1737* (London, 1936), pp. 161–70. Battestin identifies Fielding as 'Crambo' in Battestin, 'Phillips, Edward', *A Henry Fielding Companion*, pp. 114–15.
[71] [Phillips], *The Stage-Mutineers*, p. 8.
[72] Ibid., pp. 8–10.
[73] Ibid., p. 17.
[74] Ibid., pp. 17–18.
[75] Ibid., p. 33.

chimes with the 'Quintescence' of Fielding's French comedies for her.[76] Her ballad verses will have exemplified the then-scandalous emancipation for which Clive stood: 'If such Arts you Men will use, Sir, / With Self-Interest in your View, / Can of Folly you accuse her / Who pursues her Interest too?'[77] The Stage-Mutineers concludes, as many ballad operas do, with the tune 'Begging we will go' sung as a vaudeville – that is, with each principal taking a stanza, and joining voices in the final stanza.[78]

Defence of Clive took the form of *The Theatre turned Upside Down: Or, the Mutineers* (1733), written as a dialogue between 'Mr. Friendly' and 'Sir Charles Easy'. *The Theatre turned Upside Down* went on sale in October, the month during which Clive first played Oldfield's old roles.[79] A couplet, already quoted in part, rebuts the recent charges against Clive point for point:

> Yet in the other House doth one remain,
> Whom e'en Bracegirdle's Age would not disdain;
> R[afto]r, whose Merit might support a Stage,
> And lull the most malicious Critic's Rage.
> In every Part, with pleasure, I can trace,
> Judgment, and Humour, join'd with every Grace.
> On her soft Notes, dissolv'd in Pleasure, dwell;
> Charm'd with the sprightly Innocence of Nell.
> Others may court, but she commands Applause;
> And all become the Patrons of her Cause.
> Scorning to copy meanly, sh[e] '[h]as out-done,
> Where Oldfield, late in greatest Splendor shone.
> Such are the Parts she acts – in private Life,
> The pious Daughter, and the faithful Wife.
> R—r, by whom the Muses live, may claim
> A Muse with Justice, to assert her Fame.[80]

Not a shrew, Clive is a siren; not arrogant, she is deservedly a star; not a hypocritical singer of ribald ballads, she is Oldfield's equal; not prudish, she rather possesses a 'sprightly Innocence' – like, perhaps, Fielding's 'Miss Sprightly', written in 1732 for Clive as an addition to his *Tragedy of Tragedies*. Whereas for the author of *The Theatric Squabble* Clive had stood for the innate treachery of '*Woman*', this writer holds her to be the model of 'the pious Daughter, and

---

[76] *Ibid.*, pp. 33–34. On the tune 'Mirleton', see Vanessa Rogers, 'John Gay, Ballad Opera and the Théâtres de la foire', *Eighteenth-Century Music*, vol. 11, no. 2 (2014), p. 192.
[77] [Phillips], *The Stage-Mutineers*, p. 34.
[78] *Ibid.*, pp. 38–40.
[79] '20. The Theatre turn'd upside down … Sold by A. Dodd, price 6 d'. 'The Monthly Catalogue for October, 1733'. See the *London Magazine, or, Gentleman's Monthly Intelligencer*, vol. 2 (October 1733), p. 535.
[80] *The Theatre turned Upside Down: Or, the Mutineers. A Dialogue, occasioned by a Pamphlet, called, The Theatric Squabble* (London, 1733), p. 7.

the faithful Wife'. The similarity between the argument of *The Theatre turned Upside Down* and that of Fielding's 'Epistle to Mrs. CLIVE' the following year suggests that Fielding may well have written both.

Besides countering defamation of Clive, *The Theatre turned Upside Down* notified readers of a significant event: that Miss Raftor had become a 'faithful Wife'. Clive's union was timely: just after being called an off-stage whore, she took the name of the respected Clives of Shropshire, mainly known today from Major-General Robert Clive, aka 'Clive of India'. Decades later, congratulating her protégée Jane Pope on her decision to marry, Clive would praise especially her timing ('it is high time') and the need for her husband to be genteel ('I must hear what sort of a man he is').[81] Surely Clive followed her own advice after the 1733–34 actors' revolt had provoked the first concerted defamation of her.

The Enigma of George Clive

Clive's purported 1733 marriage is shrouded in mystery. Theatre advertisements locate her name change to between 3 October, when she was 'Miss Raftor', and 5 October, when she was 'Mrs. Clive, late Miss Raftor'.[82] But among the voluminous papers covering the Clive family there is no record of this marriage.[83] George and Catherine Clive were later said to have soon separated, but it was never said when. In his 1749 biographical entry on Catherine Clive, William Chetwood alludes darkly to 'ill Usage' in connection with her 'conjugal Affairs'.[84] We know that George Clive expressly cut her out of his will. Evidence strongly suggests that George and Catherine Clive never actually married, but instead colluded in a fiction born of mutual need. She needed a pedigree and distance from her Irish father. She may also have needed to hide the attraction to women, discussed in Chapter 11, that her later conduct and correspondence suggest she felt. He almost certainly needed what a later generation would call a 'beard': a pretend female partner to hide his same-sex orientation.

The Clive family was certainly illustrious, if limited in its range of male given names. George's namesake Sir George Clive had in 1589 served the

---

[81] Letter of 24 July 1773 [no. 5, copied by James Winston] in Catherine Clive, Folger Shakespeare Library, W.b.73, 'Copies of letters to Jane Pope from various people, 1769–1808, in the hand of James Winston [manuscript], ca. 1840'. In a subsequent letter of 26 February 1778 in the same collection, Clive insists that she vet whomever Pope selected for a partner.
[82] Crean, 'The Life and Times of Kitty Clive', p. 114.
[83] Clive family papers are held principally in the archives of Herefordshire, Shropshire, and the National Archives, Public Record Office.
[84] 'In the Year 1732. she was marry'd to Mr. G. Clive, Son to Mr. Baron Clive. I shall be silent in conjugal Affairs; but in all my long Acquaintance with her, I could never imagine she deserved ill Usage.' Chetwood, *A General History of the Stage*, p. 128. In misdating her year of presumed marriage, Chetwood follows Edmund Curll (see below).

English monarchy's rule of Ireland.[85] Another luminary of precisely the same name was George Clive, Cursitor Baron of the Exchequer and Treasurer of Lincoln's Inn Fields (1732–39), whom later biographers wrongly took to have been Kitty Clive's husband; he was in fact the uncle of the George Clive she putatively married.[86] Taking the name of Clive, a family resident in Shropshire since King Henry II, was Catherine Raftor's defence against attacks on her reputation, and an unanswerable argument for her Englishness. But George Clive (1703–1780) achieved much less than other George Clives.[87] He studied at Eton, according to the rather hazy Eton register information, around 1715, after having perhaps being admitted on 19 May 1713 as a 'student of Lincoln's Inn'.[88] He may have resided with his uncle or brother at Lincoln's Inn. There also he could have met his future partner Richard Ince. In George Clive's obituary, it is said of the deceased that:

---

[85] On the Clive family lineage, see John Bernard Burke, 'Powis', *A Genealogical and Heraldic Dictionary of the Peerage and Baronetage of the British Empire*, 7th edn (London, 1841), pp. 821–22 and Charles John Robinson, *A History of the Mansions and Manors of Herefordshire* (London, 1873), pp. 206–09. For a period source, see [Edward Kimber], *The Peerage of Ireland: A Genealogical and Historical Account*, vol. 2 (London, 1768) p. 207. I am grateful to Sarah Davis, archivist at the Shropshire Archives, and Lorna Standen, archivist at the Herefordshire Record Office, for their help with my research on George Clive.

[86] Crean, in his dissertation and later articles, clarifies George Clive's lineage: 'George Clive, second son of Robert Clive, brother of Richard, the father of the great Lord Clive … He was uncle of Lord Clive [Clive of India] and nephew of another George Clive, Cursitor Baron of the Exchequer, who died unmarried and was buried in the Temple Church, London.' Crean, 'The Life and Times of Kitty Clive', p. 118. The unscrupulous hack Edmund Curll, known for pilfering authors' writings, appears to be the earliest source of the misinformation that Clive married in 1732. 'Miss Raftor came on the Stage in the Year 1728, and married Mr. George Clive, an Attorney at Law, in 1732.' 'Thomas Betterton', *The History of the English Stage … by Mr. Thomas Betterton* (London, 1741), p. 166. William Oldys is often credited with writing this volume from papers compiled by Curll.

[87] Born to Edward and Sarah Clive, George was baptized in 1703, as recorded in the London parish register of St Martin Pomeroy. I am grateful to Lorna Standen, Archive Assistant, Herefordshire Record Office, for sending me a copy of this register in a personal communication of 6 January 2012, and for confirming that Edward and Sarah Clive had five sons and one daughter.

[88] Personal communication, Penny Hatfield, Eton College Archivist, 20 December 2011. The information comes from an annotated copy of Richard Arthur Austin-Leigh's 'Preface', *The Eton College Register 1698–1752* (Eton, 1927), pp. viii–xii, held at Eton. Entrance books at Eton are incomplete before 1753; of records from 1707 to 1725, only the 1718 school list survives. Boys typically entered Eton between eleven and fourteen years old, and left when around sixteen. Richard Arthur Austin-Leigh estimates that George Clive, whose name is not recorded in the Eton College Lists, entered Eton c.1715.

He was in the strictest intimacy with Mr. Ince, one of the writers in *The Spectator*, who left him a fortune, which enabled him to enjoy the remainder of his days in comfort.[89]

Ince's will verifies this report.[90] Ince (1684–1758) was twenty-one years older than George Clive. Although a 'Student' (stipendiary college member) of Christ Church College, Oxford from 1703, on 16 December 1702 Ince had registered at the Middle Temple,[91] where he was appointed barrister in 1711,[92] and by 6 December 1712 he had contributed 'several excellent sentiments and agreeable pieces' to *The Spectator*.[93] According to a nineteenth-century editor of *The Spectator*, Ince inherited a 'considerable fortune' from his brother, which he 'liberally' distributed among friends in his will.[94] A chief benefactor, through a codicil Ince added the year he died, was George Clive, to whom he left two thousand pounds.[95] Despite being a man of letters, Ince directed the executors of his will 'to burn all his papers', thereby destroying his own legacy of *Spectator* contributions.[96] A need to conceal his sexuality could explain this act of self-erasure: Ince's papers might have revealed his relations with men, including George Clive.

The obituary of George Clive names him 'a gentleman of extensive learning, and one of the first classical scholars of the age'.[97] That George Clive left no scholarly writings whatsoever makes this claim dubious. What the obituary describes is a gentleman scholar who partook in the type of 'epicoene

---

[89] *The Gentleman's Magazine: and Historical Chronicle*, vol. 50 (December 1780), p. 589.
[90] National Archives, Public Record Office, Prob 11/841.
[91] His appointment as a Law Faculty Student at Oxford in 1715 – a rarely granted Studentship exonerating the holder from taking holy orders – allowed him to retain his student rights until his death in 1758, despite residing in London. I thank Judith Curthoys, Archivist of Christ Church College Library, who kindly provided information on Richard Ince and the terms of his post at Christ Church in a personal communication of 22 December 2011.
[92] Herbert A. C. Sturgess, *Register of Admissions to the Honourable Society of the Middle Temple, from the Fifteenth Century to the Year 1944*, vol. 1 (London, 1949), p. 74.
[93] 'It had not come to my knowledge, when I left off the Spectator, that I owe several excellent sentiments and agreeable pieces in this work to Mr. Ince of Gray's Inn.' Richard Steele, 'Postscript', *Spectator*, no. 555; repr. in Alexander Chalmers, ed., *The Spectator. A Corrected Edition*, vol. 7 (London, 1806), p. 469. Chalmers notes: 'The present writer cannot mention particularly and with certainty the several excellent sentiments and agreeable pieces which Mr. Ince contributed to the Spectator.' *Ibid.*, p. 470.
[94] 'He inherited a considerable fortune from a brother, which at his death, October 13, 1758, he divided very liberally among his friends and domestics.' *Ibid.*
[95] National Archives, Public Record Office, Prob 11/841. Chalmers reports a different sum, saying that Ince 'left 1000l. to Mr. Clive, brother to judge Clive'. Chalmers, ed., *The Spectator*, vol. 7, p. 470.
[96] *Ibid.*
[97] *The Gentleman's Magazine: and Historical Chronicle*, vol. 50 (December 1780), p. 589.

friendship' peculiar to the age.[98] Whereas 'Sodomites' of the period were tried and, if found guilty, hanged, literary men might discreetly express the deepest affection for each other.[99] Drawing on the authority of ancient Greece and Rome, the epicoene friendship was a 'social space ... beyond the horizon of the domestic sphere'.[100] The tie between Thomas Gray and Horace Walpole, who may have been lovers,[101] was in 1786 also called one of 'strictest intimacy'.[102] At the very least, the homosocial environment in which George Clive moved helps explain why, bizarrely, no mention at all is made of his celebrated wife Catherine in his obituary of 1780.

But George Clive remembered her. He not only cut her out of his will, but ordered his executors not to communicate with her: 'concerning my Wife Catherine Clive who it is well known has been Separated from me for many years[,] I give her no part of what I shall be personally assized or possessed

---

[98] Studies on the extent to which eighteenth-century homosociability obscured, and yet was almost certainly bound up with, homosexuality, has been led by Raymond Stephanson and George Haggerty, who summarizes much of this literature in the introduction to his book, *Men in Love*. See Raymond Stephanson '"Epicoene Friendship": Understanding Male Friendship in the Early Eighteenth Century, with some Speculations about Pope', *The Eighteenth Century: Theory and Interpretation*, vol. 38, no. 2 (1997), pp. 151–70; and George E. Haggerty, *Men in Love: Masculinity and Sexuality in the Eighteenth Century* (New York, 1999), esp. pp. 1–20.

[99] After the Glorious Revolution, and the expulsion of the Stuart court, government-endorsed censure of libertinism included the persecution of mollies (practising homosexuals) under the aegis the Society for the Reformation of Manners. This yielded, however, to a nostalgia for promiscuity, and by 1700 court culture was seen by some to contain aspects of sodomitical subculture, as detailed in the 1692 satire 'Jenny Cromwell's Complaint against Sodomy'. Dennis Rubini, 'Sexuality and Augustan England: Sodomy, Politics, Elite Circles and Society', *The Pursuit of Sodomy: Male Homosexuality in Renaissance and Enlightenment Europe*, ed. K. Gerard and G. Hekma (New York and London, 1989), pp. 367–70, 379.

[100] David M. Halperin, *One Hundred Years of Homosexuality: And other Essays on Greek Love* (New York and London), p. 77; cited in Haggerty, *Men in Love*, p. 15.

[101] Gray's declarations of love survive in letters written from July 1734, when he went up to Cambridge, where Walpole joined him in March 1735. Robert L. Mack, *Thomas Gray* (London, 1996), pp. 143–66, 220–64, 330–40. Mack states, 'we possess no evidence – no proof of overt behaviour – to suggest that Gray ever ... engaged in intimate, sexual relations of any kind', but elsewhere admits that Gray felt for Walpole an attraction 'recognizably to be classified as romantic love' expressed in 'bold and unapologetic colours'. Ibid., pp. 35, 161. Less circumspect, Haggerty observes that 'what needs to be explained is not how this reclusive eighteenth-century figure kept his sexuality hidden, but rather how he could write it so large'. Haggerty, *Men in Love*, p. 113; see also George E. Haggerty, 'Horace Walpole's Epistolary Friendships', *Journal for Eighteenth-Century Studies*, vol. 29, no. 2 (2006), pp. 201–18, and George E. Haggerty, *Horace Walpole's Letters: Masculinity and Friendship in the Eighteenth Century* (Lewisburg, PA, 2011).

[102] '[H]e [Thomas Gray] contracted the strictest intimacy with two of their votaries, whose dispositions in many respects were congenial with his own.' Gilbert Wakefield, 'The Life of Thomas Gray', *The Poems of Mr. Gray*, ed. G. Wakefield (London, 1786), page unnumbered.

of ... for my Will and meaning is that she shall have nothing to do with my Executors or Representation nor they with her.'[103] Writing to Jane Pope in 1780, Catherine hinted at why George Clive had set out these conditions: 'if he had not mentioned me in that manner and they [the Executors] had attempted to have given me any trouble it wou[l]d have been hooted out of the Court – that he very well [knew?] – or he wou[l]d not have been so care-full.'[104] Should claims for debt ('trouble') have been brought against Catherine, why would they have been 'hooted out of the Court'? The simplest answer is that she and George had never married, so there were no legal ties between them. In forbidding his executors from dealing with her, George Clive had prevented this from being discovered after his death.

If Catherine Raftor had married George Clive in 1733, the legal doctrine of coverture meant that she would have lost all rights to her person, earnings and property. In the eyes of the law, 'the husband and wife are one person ... that is, the very being or legal existence of the woman is suspended during the marriage'.[105] The dangers of coverture she well knew from the fate of her friend Jane Cibber. She had probably baulked at such disempowerment even before ever meeting George Clive. A seeming union with a gentleman disinclined towards women meant that she could both safeguard her earnings and be seen as a member of a landowning family. The brevity of their assumed cohabitation also conferred deniability. After George Clive's death, she wrote about him to Lord Harcourt in 1781: 'I was in a dreadfull dangerous situation for menney years, without knowing anything of the matter.'[106] Back in 1733, however, she will likely have been disposed to accept any arguments George Clive offered for pretending to wed. She was beleaguered, and needed the part of the faithful and genteel wife.

---

[103] National Archives, Public Record Office, Prob 11/1071.
[104] Catherine Clive to Jane Pope. Letter of 25 December 1780. Bodleian Library, Toynbee b.1 'Correspondence of Jane Pope &c'.
[105] 'By marriage, the husband and wife are one person in law: that is, the very being or legal existence of the woman is suspended during the marriage, or at least is incorporated and consolidated into that of the husband: under whose wing, protection, and cover, she performs every thing ... and her condition during her marriage is called her coverture.' William Blackstone, *Commentaries on the Laws of England*, vol. 1 (London, 1765), p. 430. Although, as Helen E. M. Brooks argues, marriage might benefit the wife, a woman's loss of rights over her property may have encouraged ambitious actresses to have chosen cohabitation over legitimate matrimony. Helen E. M. Brooks, 'Negotiating Marriage and Professional Autonomy in the Careers of Eighteenth-Century Actresses', *Eighteenth-Century Life*, vol. 35 no. 2 (2011), pp. 40–57. For the propriety-obsessed Clive, cohabitation out of wedlock would have been inadmissible.
[106] Letter of 12 February 1781, Catherine Clive to Lord Harcourt. Edward William Harcourt, ed., *The Harcourt Papers*, vol. 8 (Oxford, 1880–1905), pp. 172–73; cited and transcribed in Crean, 'The Life and Times of Kitty Clive', p. 428.

The 1733–34 Season: Exit Fielding

After being locked out of Drury Lane in May 1733, Theophilus Cibber set up a rival company at the New Haymarket Theatre; this opened its doors on 26 September.[107] The Drury Lane company was reduced to fifteen regular players, from forty-five, and the house reportedly incurred weekly losses of fifty to sixty pounds from the season's start.[108] The Drury Lane patentees persuaded John Rich to co-sign a threatening letter to Cibber, warning the renegades of the Royal Patent's power; Cibber returned the letter unopened.[109] In early November the patentees had rebel actor John Harper arrested and brought to Bridewell on charges of vagrancy.[110] The public mood now swung against the managers. Harper was released 'amidst the triumphant Acclamations of his theatric Friends', and the vagrancy case was never brought.[111] The battle also manifested itself that November in rival productions at Drury Lane and the New Haymarket of *The Opera of Operas*. Being a musical version of Fielding's *Tragedy of Tragedies*, Cibber's new production of *The Opera of Operas* – scored up by Thomas Arne for Cibber to compete with Drury Lane's revival of John F. Lampe's original – was a particularly blatant act of intellectual theft. Drury Lane lost this contest, although its own *Opera of Operas* gave Clive her first chance to extravagantly burlesque Italian opera, flexing her vocal muscle with runs up to high B.[112] Later, once serious song was closed to her, burlesque operatic song would become an important part of her line.

By the start of 1734 the rebels had won their suit for possession of the Drury Lane premises, and it was clear that the patentees would have to settle with the rebel actors. On 15 January Drury Lane mounted Fielding's revised *Author's Farce* along with his new afterpiece, a Clive vehicle, *The Intriguing Chambermaid*.[113] Fielding also wrote a prologue and epilogue for Clive to pitch for audience sympathy, touched up the part she took in *The Author's Farce* to her

---

[107] Hume, *Henry Fielding and the London Theatre*, pp. 166–67. Hume quotes Victor, *The History of the Theatres of London and Dublin*, vol. 1, pp. 19–20.
[108] Hume, *Henry Fielding and the London Theatre*, p. 175.
[109] *Ibid.*
[110] *Ibid.*, pp. 175–78.
[111] *An Apology for the Life of Mr. T— C—, Comedian*, p. 90; cited in Hume, *Henry Fielding and the London Theatre*, p. 178.
[112] For decades musicologists thought that Arne had composed Lampe's three-act *Opera of Operas*, which had opened six months earlier, on 31 May 1733. This assumption was first queried in 1959 by Julian Herbage, and was later resolved by Dennis R. Martin, *The Operas and Operatic Style of John Frederick Lampe* (Detroit, 1985), pp. 28–30, and Judith Milhous and Robert D. Hume, 'J. F. Lampe and English Opera at the Little Haymarket in 1732-3', *Music & Letters*, vol. 78, no. 4 (1997), pp. 502–31.
[113] Lockwood, ed., 'The Author's Farce. Introduction', *Henry Fielding: Plays Volume I*, p. 199. Fielding had revised his *Author's Farce* before 8 December. There is no evidence of when he prepared *The Intriguing Chambermaid*. Lockwood, 'The Intriguing Chambermaid. Introduction', *Henry Fielding: Plays Volume II*, p. 561.

advantage, and testified in print to her sterling private character. The gear-shift in Fielding's characterization of Clive is felt in her appeal to reason, and to proper taste, in her prologue and epilogue to *The Author's Farce*. Uniquely in her career, she spoke both, and in both she mourns audiences' desertion of her house. In these paratexts Fielding had Clive blame the usual suspect, Italian opera, rather than the rebel company. The argument builds from the prologue, which mentions 'soft Eunuchs' who once were 'successless',[114] to the epilogue, which asserts that Drury Lane suffers from 'empty Benches' because 'none but Italian Warblers will go down'.[115]

This specious rationalization is repeated in Fielding's 'Epistle to Mrs. CLIVE', meant to lure audiences back to Drury Lane. This was printed in the playbook of *The Intriguing Chambermaid* issued by Watts shortly after *The Author's Farce* opened:[116]

> It is your Misfortune to bring the greatest Genius for acting on the Stage, at a time when the Factions and Divisions among the Players have conspired with the Folly, Injustice, and Barbarity of the Town, to ... sacrifice our own native Entertainments to a wanton affected Fondness for foreign Musick ... However, the few who have yet so much English Taste and Good-nature left ... never fail to receive you with the Approbation you deserve; nay, you extort, by the Force of your Merit, the Applause of those who are languishing for the Return of Cuzzoni.[117]

In this account, recent recognition of Clive's 'Genius for acting' merges with her high reputation in 'native Entertainments', and earlier assertions of her superiority to Italian *prime donne*. To this Fielding adds insights into her 'private Character' in terms strikingly like those in the anonymous *Theatre turned Upside Down* of the previous year:

> But as great a Favourite as you at present are with the Audience, you would be much more so, were they acquainted with your private Character; cou'd they see you laying out great part of the Profits which arise to you from entertaining them so well, in the Support of an aged Father; did they see you who can charm them on the Stage with personating the foolish and vitious Characters of your Sex, acting in real Life the Part of the best Wife, the best Daughter, the best Sister, and the best Friend. The Part you have maintain'd in the present Dispute

---

[114] 'Soft Eunuchs warbled in successless Strain', Lockwood, ed., 'Prologue. Upon the Revival of the *Author's Farce*', *Henry Fielding: Plays Volume I*, p. 297.
[115] 'For how to empty Benches can we say, / What means this mighty Crouding here To-Day?' and 'English is now below this learned Town, / None but Italian Warblers will go down'. Lockwood, ed., 'Epilogue' [*The Author's Farce* (1734)]. Lockwood, ed., *Henry Fielding: Plays Volume I*, p. 299.
[116] Battestin states that Watts began selling the *Intriguing Chambermaid* playbook in 'January' of 1734. Battestin, *A Henry Fielding Companion*, p. 182.
[117] Lockwood, ed., 'An Epistle to Mrs. CLIVE' [in *The Intriguing Chambermaid*], *Henry Fielding: Plays Volume II*, p. 581. On the prima donna Cuzzoni, see Chapter 2, p. 40.

between the Players and the Patentees, is so full of Honour, that had it been in higher Life, it would have given you the Reputation of the greatest Heroine of the Age.[118]

In his bid for public sympathy with Drury Lane's single remaining star, Fielding pretends an intimacy from which audiences are barred ('cou'd they see'). He urges readers to separate her 'foolish and vitious' stage parts – several of which he had imposed on her – from the roles she plays in 'real Life', like her marriage(!). He assures readers of the perfection with which she fulfils her womanly duties, and confers on her the merit of 'greatest Heroine of the Age'.

This noble Clive of Fielding's 'Epistle' has a correlate in the role he created for her in his *Author's Farce* of 1734. As Edgar Roberts noted in 1971, the 'colourless sentimentally-conceived romantic heroine' of Fielding's original became in 1734 the vibrant Harriot, who invites sympathy.[119] Fielding enlarged Clive's part with songs, dialogue, colour, and ironic humour. In this new version, Harriot gains credibility, agency, and nerve as she triumphs over adversity.[120] In his new afterpiece, *The Intriguing Chambermaid*, Fielding evoked the polite Clive by picking out her earlier pastoral 'Opera' numbers for her to sing as Lettice: 'Bush of Boon' (which she had sung in *Damon and Phillida* and *The Lover's Opera*) for Air 2, 'Hark, hark the cock crows' (which she had sung in *The Lover's Opera*) for Air 4, and 'As down in the meadow' (which she had sung in Theophilus Cibber's 'Scotch' Opera *Patie and Peggy*) for Air 5.[121]

---

[118] Lockwood, ed., 'An Epistle to Mrs. CLIVE' [in *The Intriguing Chambermaid*], *Henry Fielding: Plays Volume II*, p. 582.

[119] 'In the first version, Harriet [sic] had been a colourless sentimentally-conceived romantic heroine'. Edgar V. Roberts, 'The Songs and Tunes in Henry Fielding's Ballad Operas', *Essays on the Eighteenth-Century English Stage: Proceedings of the 1971 Symposium of the Manchester University Department of Drama*, ed. K. Richards and P. Thomson (Manchester, 1972), p. 31. Lockwood notes also that '[s]ince Catherine Clive was now playing Harriot ... Fielding enlarged and coloured that part accordingly'. Lockwood, 'The Author's Farce. Introduction', *Henry Fielding: Plays Volume I*, p. 200.

[120] 'In the first version ... she had the same scenes as before, but also had prominent parts in Act II, scenes, 9, 10 and 11 ... sang six solos and participated in five duets, a greater task than in the 1730 production Fielding had assigned to two actresses.' Roberts, 'The Songs and Tunes in Henry Fielding's Ballad Operas', p. 31.

[121] On 'Bush of Boon' and *Damon and Phillida* see Chapter 2, p. 45 and note 84. As noted earlier, *The Lover's Opera* was Clive's most successful ballad opera under Colley Cibber's management. As Flora she sang 'Bush of Boon' as 'Air XXXI', and 'Hark, hark, the Cock Crows' as 'Air XXXIX'. Chetwood, *The Lover's Opera* (London, 1729) pp. 25–26, 30–31. As Peggy, Clive sang 'As down in a Meadow' in 'Air VI' of T[heophilus] C[ibber] [after Allan Ramsay], *Patie and Peggy: Or, the Fair Foundling. A Scotch Ballad Opera* (London, 1730), pp. 7–8. On the provenance of all three tunes, see Lockwood, ed., *Henry Fielding: Plays Volume II*, pp. 702 ['Hark, hark, the cock crows', by the organist Jeremiah Clarke (1674–1707)], 713–14 ['Twas down in a meadow'], and 765–66 ['Bush of Boon']. For Lappet's opening air, Fielding chose another 'Scotch' tune, 'Soger Laddy': *ibid.*, pp. 765–765. Most of the melodies Fielding used in *The Intriguing Chambermaid* are pastoral and sentimental.

In his 'Epistle', the intimate knowledge of Clive claimed by Fielding shored up an assertion that she owed her success to him: 'I cannot help reflecting ... that the Town ... have one Obligation to me, who made the first Discovery of your great Capacity, and brought you earlier forward on the Theatre, than the Ignorance of some and the Envy others would have otherwise permitted.'[122] This is nonsense: Clive was already Drury Lane's first singer–actress when their collaboration began. Rather than discovering her 'Capacity', in the summer of 1732 Fielding had bungled her launch as a straight comedienne. Perhaps pushing himself forward as the supposed author of Clive's success was Fielding's way of building a case to continue writing for her.

Nine days after *The Author's Farce* and *The Intriguing Chambermaid* opened, Highmore conceded defeat. He sold his patent share to Charles Fleetwood, who, when the purchase was first being arranged, had been acting as John Rich's front-man. Wanting to control both royal playhouses, Rich had asked his friend Fleetwood to 'purchase the patent in his name, as well to secure to him the property he should disburse, as to save appearances with the town'.[123] As Rich had anticipated, the players were outraged; but what blocked Rich's plan was 'a misunderstanding', that is a falling-out, between Fleetwood and himself.[124] Fleetwood installed himself as manager by purchasing Mary Wilks' share of the patent as well as Highmore's.[125] The rebel company returned to Drury Lane, and resumed performing on 12 March 1734 with *The Mother-in-Law* by Miller.[126] Fleetwood made Theophilus Cibber his 'first Minister', while reserving to himself the right to arrange contracts and select new stage productions.[127] A new phase in Clive's career began.

The 1734–35 Season: Miller at Drury Lane

With Theophilus Cibber's return to Drury Lane, Clive's situation changed in two major ways. First, James Miller came to supplant Fielding as the house supplier of her vehicles. Second, Cibber brought with him the entire Arne family, including his betrothed Susannah, a debutante soprano who would compete with Clive for parts, and her brother Thomas, who would compose

---

[122] Lockwood, ed., 'An Epistle to Mrs. CLIVE' [in *The Intriguing Chambermaid*], *Henry Fielding: Plays Volume II*, p. 582.
[123] *The Life of Mr. James Quin, Comedian* (London, 1766), p. 47; cited in Hume, 'John Rich as Manager and Entrepreneur', "The Stage's Glory", p. 44. Based on its description, the 1766 publication *The Life of Mr. James Quin, Comedian* seems to be a reprint of the book's first edition in 1761, copies of which are rare.
[124] *The Life of Mr. James Quin, Comedian*, p. 48.
[125] Hume, *Henry Fielding and the London Theatre*, pp. 179–80.
[126] The notice of this performance says this was to be the 'first appearance of the Haymarket actors', that is, the rebel company, since its members had walked out. *The London Stage*, Part 3, vol. 1, p. 376.
[127] Victor, *The History of the Theatres of London and Dublin*, vol. 1, p. 31.

Clive's most important music. During his exile at the New Haymarket Theatre, Cibber had mounted Miller's latest comedy *The Mother-in-Law* in competition with Fielding's *Author's Farce* and *Intriguing Chambermaid* at Drury Lane. As in *The Humours of Oxford*, Miller's part for Theophilus was bespoke, but was here updated to reprise his *Mock Doctor* persona within a work that Miller cobbled together from Molière comedies he had translated for John Watts.[128] The name of Theophilus Cibber's character, 'Looby Headpiece', was happily consonant with his leadership of the revolt.

Miller had in fact written his comedy before the rebellion, as demonstrated by the record of the eighty pounds that bookseller Watts had paid him for it.[129] Miller had clearly intended for Clive to play the chambermaid Primrose, as Cibber recognized. Once back at Drury Lane, Cibber plucked the role from Mary Heron, who had performed it at the New Haymarket, and gave it to Clive; this was his only change to the cast. The Drury Lane staging featured a 'New Scene' by Miller, 'the Consultation of Physicians';[130] now lost, it surely riffed on the mutual Clive–Cibber abuse of Fielding's *Mock Doctor*. *The Mother-in-Law* was a milestone for Clive. Its reception was highly enthusiastic – a response unique in Miller's career. This was a consequence not just of talent, but of discretion: Theophilus Cibber, mindful of Miller's enemies, kept the work's authorship secret.[131]

The Mother-in-Law was also the first time Clive played alongside Hannah Pritchard. The Clive–Pritchard partnership would endure for decades, onstage and off. To quote Thomas Davies, 'though of characters extremely different', Pritchard and Clive were 'closely united in the bonds of friendship for almost forty years'.[132] Their mutual support invalidates the charge, first imputed in *The Theatric Squabble* of July 1733, that Clive brooked no rival. Not only did Clive and Pritchard persistently share the boards after *The Mother-in-Law* – their frequent co-appearances suggests that their 'extremely different' energies complemented each other – but they also shared parts. From 14 September 1734 Pritchard played Lady Loverule opposite Clive in *The Devil to Pay*, and by the 1734–35 season's end twelve of Pritchard's twenty-one productions had

---

[128] Miller translated and adapted passages chiefly from *Le Malade Imaginaire* and *Monsieur de Pourceaugnac*, but 'there are echoes of at least two more' comedies, '*Tartuffe* and *La Critique de L'Ecole des Femmes*'. O'Brien, 'The Life and Works of James Miller', p. 29. Of these, Watts had issued all but *Tartuffe* in 1732.

[129] Arthur S. Collins, *Authorship in the Days of Johnson* (London, 1927), p. 262; cited in O'Brien, 'The Life and Works of James Miller', p. 22.

[130] [James Miller], *The Mother-in-Law: Or, the Doctor the Disease*, 2nd edn (London, 1734).

[131] In a verse satire, *The Dramatick Sessions*, which appeared in August 1734, Henry Baker was attacked for what was thought to be 'his' comedy, *The Mother-in-Law*. The writer of the *Dramatick Sessions* also attacked Miller, but only for having written *The Humours of Oxford*; this attests to the effectiveness with which Miller's hand in *The Mother-in-Law* had been hidden. O'Brien, 'The Life and Works of James Miller', pp. 31–32.

[132] Thomas Davies, *Memoirs of the Life of David Garrick, Esq.*, vol. 2 (London, 1780), p. 192.

been alongside Clive.[133] On 22 October 1736, Pritchard stepped into the role of Doll Common in *The Alchemist*, first performed by Clive on 15 September 1735. After 13 October 1737, when Clive led the *The Mock Doctor* for the last time, Pritchard inherited Dorcas. Pritchard's brave appearance alongside Clive when the Polly Row climaxed in 1736, their shared success in *As you Like It* in 1740, and Pritchard's benefit notices advertising Clive's self-authored *Rehearsal* all suggest the strong sympathy between them.[134] In 1755 Pritchard even took up residence in Twickenham soon after Clive did.[135]

Miller's replacement of Fielding at Drury Lane did not happen all at once. For the 1734–35 season Fielding sold to Fleetwood – we can assume that Cibber would have refused it if it had been within his power – a new Clive vehicle, *The Virgin Unmask'd*. A brief comparison between this farce, which opened on 6 January 1735,[136] and Miller's *The Man of Taste*, which opened two months later on 5 March, illuminates the ways in which Miller's writing tended to benefit Clive, and Fielding's to compromise her.

In November 1734 Clive had triumphed in one of the playhouse's favourite defiant-daughter parts: Hoyden in John Vanburgh's *The Relapse* (1696). Fielding re-drew this stage type for Clive, thrusting it into a fictional world of greed and licence. *The Virgin Unmask'd* features sixteen-year-old Lucy, whose father wrongly believes that she 'knows nothing, and ... has no Will but' his. He wishes to choose his daughter's spouse, and invites older cousins, the apothecary Blister (John Harper) and the lawyer Wormwood (Charles Macklin) to make their suit. Their visits to Lucy alternate with those of her tutors, Coupée the Dancing Master (John Laguerre) and Quaver the Singing Master (Thomas Salway), who also court her.[137] Feigning simplicity, Lucy refuses them all,

---

[133] Pritchard's roles for each season of her career are listed in the 'Annual Checklist of Hannah Pritchard's Theatrical Roles' in Anthony Vaughan, *Born to Please: Hannah Pritchard, Actress, 1711–1768: A Critical Biography* (London, 1979), pp. 139–73.

[134] Fiona Ritchie describes Clive's and Pritchard's centrality to the success of *As you Like It* in Fiona Ritchie, *Women and Shakespeare in the Eighteenth Century* (New York, 2014), pp. 29–35. This production is discussed below. Pritchard's benefit announcements alerting audiences to Clive's farce read thus: 'DRURY-LANE. For the Benefit of Mrs. PRITCHARD ... On Monday, For the Benefit of Mrs. CLIVE, The JEALOUS WIFE, With The REHEARSAL, or, Bayes in Petticoats'. *Public Advertiser*, issue 8539 (19 March 1762). The same announcement ran again in the *Public Advertiser*, issue 8542 (20 March 1762). These two issues of the *Public Advertiser* were discontinuously numbered, presumably due to a printer's error.

[135] Clive appears to have rented a 'cottage' in Twickenham from the late 1740s, as discussed below. Pritchard and her husband bought a residence called Ragman's Castle. Vaughan, *Born to Please*, pp. 71–72. On the Clive–Pritchard partnership as actresses, see also O'Brien, 'The Life and Works of James Miller', pp. 13–26, 32–49, 61–71, 122–29, and 135–38.

[136] Thomas Lockwood, 'The Virgin Unmask'd. Introduction', *Henry Fielding: Plays Volume III, 1734–1742*, ed. T. Lockwood (Oxford, 2011), p. 85 and note 2.

[137] Lockwood, ed., 'The Virgin Unmask'd', *Henry Fielding: Plays Volume III*, pp. 106–7.

freely expressing her zest for sex and luxury and her disdain for her suitors. In the final scene, she enters with the man she has chosen: the footman Tom, whom she's secretly married. The action relates to that of two Clive-led ballad operas: Chetwood's failed *Boarding-School*, in which Jenny runs off with her dancing master Coupée,[138] and *The Livery Rake, and Country Lass*, in which the footman Tom wins the love of the 'Lass' Phillis (Clive).[139]

Heavy-handed references to Clive's earlier Fielding parts pepper *The Virgin Unmask'd*. For instance, Lucy plans how she will fritter away her inheritance of ten thousand pounds, the same sum Chloe expects to win in *The Lottery*.[140] Lucy wishes for 'a Coach' above a husband,[141] echoing Chloe's *Lottery* Air 14, set to the 'White Joak' ('In Chariot, six Horses, and Diamonds bright').[142] Quaver sings Handel's aria 'Dimmi cara' that Clive, speaking Fielding's epilogue to his *Author's Farce* of 1734, had made a symbol of the Town's enslavement to Italian opera ('And Dimi Cara rings thro' ev'ry Shop').[143] In the final air, Blister recommends the disciplining of Lucy with 'Bleeding, and Blist'ring, and Vomit, and Draught',[144] punishments that relate to those meted out to Dorcas in *The Mock Doctor*.

Fielding likewise used common tunes to remind audiences of Clive's earlier parts and current hits, while at the same time painting Lucy as immoral. Air 4, 'Now ponder Well', is, in *The Devil to Pay*, Jobson's air about female fickleness;[145] in *The Virgin Unmask'd*, Lucy sings this tune to declare that she will take lovers after marriage.[146] For Air 6, Fielding re-versified 'Bessy Bell', sung by Clive as Dorcas in *The Mock Doctor*, to have Lucy second Dorcas in

---

[138] Lockwood acknowledges that in *The Boarding-School* and *The Virgin Unmask'd* the 'Clive part is closely similar – an irrepressible teenager determined to have the forbidden man she wants'. Lockwood, 'The Virgin Unmask'd. Introduction', *Henry Fielding: Plays Volume III*, p. 87. Coffey added airs to Thomas D'Urfey's *Love for Money: Or, the Boarding School* (1691) to create *The Boarding-School: Or, the Sham Captain. An Opera* (London, 1733). Gagey, *Ballad Opera*, pp. 114–15.

[139] In the action, Tom the footman courts and wins the 'Country Lass' Phillis. But Tom's earlier lover, whom he de-flowered, takes the place of Phillis during the marriage ceremony, by which trickery Tom ends up marrying her. *The Livery Rake, and Country Lass*. Thomas Phillips, not Edward Phillips, wrote this piece. Noble, 'Attributions and Misattributions to Edward Phillips', pp. 76–77.

[140] Lockwood, ed., 'The Virgin Unmask'd', *Henry Fielding: Plays Volume III*, pp. 108–9; 'Oh what Pleasures will abound', Lockwood, ed., 'The Lottery', *Henry Fielding: Plays Volume II*, p. 161.

[141] *Ibid.*, p. 108.

[142] Lockwood, ed., 'The Lottery', *Henry Fielding: Plays Volume II*, p. 169–70.

[143] Lockwood, ed., 'Epilogue' [*The Author's Farce* (1734)], *Henry Fielding: Plays Volume I*, p. 299.

[144] Lockwood, ed., 'The Virgin Unmask'd', *Henry Fielding: Plays Volume III*, p. 129.

[145] The broadside, reused verbatim in *The Devil to Pay*, begins 'In Bath a wanton Wife did dwell'. For details on this ballad, see Chapter 3, pp. 76–77.

[146] Lockwood, ed., 'The Virgin Unmask'd', *Henry Fielding: Plays Volume III*, pp. 113–14 ('Air IV' and its preceding lines).

her desire to sample different partners.[147] In Air 11, verses betray the innocence of Lucy's 'Bush of Boon' tune (sung by Clive as Phillida), as she hints slyly at her easy virtue: 'Yet he, perhaps, without their Cloaths, / May have more Charms than they'.[148] For his finale, Fielding chose the melody of 'The Yorkshire Ballad', which, in *The Boarding-School* by Charles Coffey, had stood for intended cuckoldry;[149] in Fielding's words to this tune, Lucy's suitors bewail her weaknesses, after which Lucy, in the last two stanzas, asks audiences for their indulgence.[150]

In *The Man of Taste*, by contrast, Miller decorously expanded Clive's line in spoken French comedy. He knit together Molière's *Les Précieuses ridicules* and *L'Ecole des maris* –both of which he had translated for Watts – while dipping occasionally into other Molière comedies.[151] He preserved, in translation, some of Molière's original dialogue. The vehicle Miller created was primarily for Theophilus Cibber, who played the title role, and only secondarily for the comedy's two principal actresses, Clive and Pritchard; still, whenever Clive and Cibber exchanged barbed ripostes, Miller had Clive prevail, and Miller handed her favourite points in dialogue and song. The plot revolves around two foolish daughters whom a footman (Cibber), posing as a fop, tries to hoodwink; he ends up getting a beating. Maria, played by Clive, exposes his lies, revealing his lack of schooling and his purchase of honorary titles. She identifies his ignorance of music ('Have you learnt Musick then, my Lord?'),[152] a point she would thrust home from 1738 by interpolating two songs, 'Life of a Beau' and, from Miller's *Humours of Oxford*, 'The provident Damsel'.[153] Building on her attacks in Fielding's *Author's Farce* epilogue, she lampoons Town ladies who love Farinelli ('Oh, Ravishing! Transporting! Killing! … Dying is too little. He does more than kill one').[154] Miller's epilogue for Clive stands in stark contrast to most of those Fielding wrote for her. Speaking as 'Mrs. Clive', she explains why Miller's comedy will appeal to 'Good Wives', 'Good Husbands', and 'the Gay, unwedded Fair', and concludes with her trademark mockery of fops.[155]

---

[147] Ibid., p. 116–17 ('Air VI'); Lockwood, ed., 'The Mock Doctor', *Henry Fielding: Plays Volume II*, p. 434 ('Air I').
[148] Lockwood, ed., 'The Virgin Unmask'd', *Henry Fielding: Plays Volume III*, pp. 127–28.
[149] See under the tune's variant title 'Yorkshire Tale', Charles Coffey, *The Boarding-School: Or, the Sham Captain. An Opera* (London, 1733), p. 15.
[150] Lockwood, ed., 'The Virgin Unmask'd', *Henry Fielding: Plays Volume III*, pp. 129–30.
[151] From Molière, 'Miller makes use not only of complete scenes, but of short exchanges, minor characters and even single sentences'. Two of his characters are from *Les Femmes Savantes*, and there are 'echoes of many more of Molière's plays'. O'Brien, 'The Life and Works of James Miller', pp. 33–34.
[152] [James Miller], *The Man of Taste. A Comedy* (London, 1735), p. 28.
[153] *London Daily Post and General Advertiser*, issue 1103 (12 May 1738).
[154] [Miller], *The Man of Taste*, p. 62.
[155] [Miller], 'EPILOGUE. Spoke by Mrs. CLIVE', *The Man of Taste*, pages unnumbered.

The Virgin Unmask'd and *The Man of Taste* both succeeded, and both embedded themselves in Clive's repertory.[156] In the former, Fielding stuck to smutty innuendo, communicated through low dialogue and action,[157] the common tunes he selected, the new verses he gave these tunes, and references to his earlier parts for her. Revisiting Clive's Lucy character in *Miss Lucy in Town* (1742) Fielding made the part so offensive – Lucy finds herself in a London brothel, having her '*Bubbies*' prodded by a Jew – that one playgoer ranted for twenty pages against the farce.[158] Miller, by contrast, drew on Molière rather than male fantasy, dusting translated lines with typical Clive points and with her correctives to Town folly; in his epilogue, she is characterized as upstanding, and a defender of good taste. Seen from the perspective of Clive's career, *The Virgin Unmask'd* looks very much like the end of one era, and *The Man of Taste* the beginning of another. Clive's business sense was likely what kept her playing Fielding's Lucy:[159] this part became, as we will see, a franchise that both Miller and David Garrick extended before Fielding returned to it in 1742. But from 1735, Miller's more elevated parts dominated her line for about a decade, squeezing out the vulgarity that Theophilus Cibber and Henry Fielding had compelled her to enact on stage.

Clive's stage speech first reached full bloom as Lappet in *The Miser*, finally establishing her as a straight actress. Her vocal technique, and practices she had fostered through song – addressing audiences directly, appealing to

---

[156] On the *The Man of Taste*, see O'Brien, 'The Life and Works of James Miller', p. 34. *The Virgin Unmask'd* had twenty-seven performance during its first season, and 'established itself as a favourite'. Lockwood, 'The Virgin Unmask'd. Introduction', *Henry Fielding: Plays Volume III*, p. 91.

[157] For instance, when Lucy justifies having married a footman, Fielding's dialogue has her imply that she had to do so because she'd lost her virginity to him through her simple-mindedness: 'Indeed I should have been perjured, if I had not had him.— And I had not had him neither, but that he met me when I was frighten'd, and did not know what I did.' Lockwood, ed., 'The Virgin Unmask'd', *Henry Fielding: Plays Volume III*, p. 126.

[158] In one scene the rich Jew Zorobabel seeks to procure Miss Lucy as his mistress. A playhouse witness described what he saw thus: the Jew 'talks of all the little Preludes to the last Scene of Love, as *soft Hands, white Neck, sweet Lips*; these Provocatives, at last, make him take a Sample of her, and he fairly *kisses her*, and feels her *Bubbies*'. *A Letter to a Noble Lord* [the Lord Chamberlain] *Occasioned by … Miss Lucy in Town* (London, 1742), p. 12. Lockwood describes the writer of this pamphlet as having a 'somewhat mysterious axe to grind'. Lockwood, 'Miss Lucy in Town. Introduction', *Henry Fielding: Plays Volume III*, p. 466. The comedy had eighteen performances, and was never mounted again.

[159] *The Virgin Unmask'd* was taken up in November 1740 at Goodman's Fields and, from October 1742, at Covent Garden. Lockwood, 'The Virgin Unmask'd. Introduction', *Henry Fielding: Plays Volume III*, pp. 92–93. As other playhouses created rival productions, Clive led *The Virgin Unmask'd* primarily to open Drury Lane's season and for players' benefits, including her own. From September 1743 she led Fielding's comedy mostly when managers could impose on her – John Rich from 1743 to 1745 and David Garrick from 1747 to 1749 – as discussed in more detail below. Clive's last performance in *The Virgin Unmask'd* was on 10 May 1749.

anti-establishment sympathies – became mesmerizing in spoken parts by Molière and his successors. The blameless reputation she cultivated was turned against her when she remained loyal to Highmore over Theophilus Cibber; she was caricatured in print and on stage as a scold, and as 'Miss Prudely Crotchet', who only pretends to virtue. Her seeming marriage to George Clive, and Fielding's defence of her in his 'Epistle', spun a counter-narrative of respectability and victimhood. Although the revolt was Cibber's triumph, Clive also reaped benefits: the Oldfield parts that she had appropriated during Horton's and Heron's absence were now hers. This, together with the progress of Miller's career, was a hopeful sign that she might escape further casting in low characters, either on stage or in the public's imagination. Yet if Clive thought that working for the gentleman Charles Fleetwood would be preferable to working for Looby Headpiece, she thought wrong. Fleetwood's debts, duplicity, arrogance, and irresponsibility would damage her directly. And the now-alienated Theophilus Cibber, though he did not long retain Fleetwood's favour, had a new soprano wife to fatten his earnings. Over the next few years, London's print industry would become Clive's newest source of advancement, teaching her fresh arts of self-representation.

6

'A Likeness where none was to be found': Contested Images of Clive, 1734–37

Clive's likeness and its parts – picturing Orphic powers – the Cibbers and Thomas Arne at Drury Lane – Phaeton falls and Clive rises – rival Pollies and Clive's victory – a truce between the Tragedy Queen and the Comic Muse

After the squabbles and publicity of the 1733–34 season, Clive's likeness became more briskly traded. Drury Lane management may well have been behind this business, for just as Clive began taking over more of Anne Oldfield's comic parts, portraitists were mapping Oldfield's body onto hers. Chance now threw more Oldfield parts into her lap: her three main rivals, Hester Booth, Christiana Horton, and Mary Heron, all disappeared from the scene. Booth, née Santlow, retired after selling her husband's patent share in September 1733.[1] Horton, who had joined Theophilus Cibber's rebel company, crossed over to Covent Garden in September 1734 rather than return to Drury Lane.[2] And in May 1735 Heron, dubbed in 1733 'the Inheritrix of Oldfield's Fame',[3] had a stage accident that forced her retirement.[4] Further strengthening Clive's position, soon after March 1734 Fleetwood 'displaced' Cibber as deputy manager with someone she had no quarrels with, the Irish comic actor Charles Macklin. Brought in by John Highmore to replace actors absent during the revolt, Macklin had created 'the Drunken Colonel' in *The Intriguing Chambermaid*, stamping this work with his craft as Clive had with hers.[5] When, from January 1736, four more of

---

[1] Goff, 'Art and Nature join'd', p. 65.
[2] On Horton's appointment to the Covent Garden company, see 'rosters of principal companies … Covent Garden', *The London Stage*, Part 3, vol. 1, p. 412.
[3] *The Theatric Squabble*, p. 8.
[4] Heron last performed on 29 May 1735 and 'after a long and expensive illness' died with heavy debts in March the next year. A. C. Elias, Jr., ed., *Memoirs of Laetitia Pilkington*, vol. 2 (Athens, GA, 1997), p. 441, note 64.4. See also *The London Stage*, Part 3, vol. 1, p. 573 (under 'DL Friday 16 April 1736').
[5] 'The other triumph from the first production … was Macklin's creation of Colonel Bluff or "the Drunken Colonel", as he quickly thereafter became known.' Lockwood, 'Introduction. The Intriguing Chambermaid', *Henry Fielding: Plays Volume II*, p. 570.

Oldfield's comic roles fell to Clive over the next two seasons,[6] the casting may well have been Macklin's. As Clive appropriated Oldfield's roles, three different portraits of her appeared, all of which evoked Oldfield's person.

The portraitists faced a serious challenge. A plain woman, Clive bore as little resemblance to Oldfield as she had to Godfried Schalcken's seventeenth-century shepherdess of the 1729 'Miss Rafter' mezzotint. The truest of Clive's new likenesses, a mezzotint portrait of 1734, drew sharp criticism for being unflattering. It was from an oil by Pieter van Bleeck, who blamed the engraver for this lapse and defended his reputation by prettifying Clive in his own engraving of his oil. In 1735 an alternative portrait appeared which also made Clive's features more conventional. Later titled 'The Fair Songster', it was warmly received and circulated into the next century.[7]

While Clive portraits proliferated, composer Thomas Arne and his sister Susannah, for whom Theophilus Cibber had arranged appointments at Drury Lane, became increasingly active. The arrival of the Arnes brought Clive both opportunities and challenges. Opportunities, because Thomas Arne was a better composer than Henry Carey. It may have been for this reason that Fleetwood turned down Carey's two new Clive vehicles, the ballad farce *The Honest Yorkshire-Man* and the burlesque oratorio *The Dragon of Wantley* – Carey's pupil John F. Lampe composed its score, and Carey its playbook – both of which went on to be hits outside Drury Lane.[8] In Carey's absence, Arne's musicianship greatly enriched Clive's line in serious song. Her first Arne masque,

---

[6] These roles were: Aurelia in *The Twin-Rivals* (3 January 1736), Biddy in *The Tender Husband* (12 April 1736), Mrs. Brittle in *The Amorous Widow: Or, the Wanton Wife* (7 December 1736), and Narcissa in *Love's Last Shift* (6 September 1737). On Oldfield's performances, see Lafler, *The Celebrated Mrs. Oldfield*, pp. 40–41, 47–48, 38–39.

[7] See Chapter 13, Fig. 13.1, p. 417.

[8] In prefaces, Carey complained bitterly about Fleetwood's repeated abuse of his trust: 'The very generous Reception this FARCE has met ... is a Manifestation of the bad Taste and monstrous Partiality of the Great *Mogul* of the Hundreds of *Drury*, who, after having had the Copy Nine Months in his Hands, continually feeding me with fresh Promises of bringing it on the Stage, return'd it at last in a very ungenerous Manner.' Henry Carey, 'Preface', *The Honest Yorkshire-Man. A Ballad Farce. Refus'd to be Acted at Drury-Lane Playhouse: But now Perform'd ... with great Applause* (London, 1736), page unnumbered. Fleetwood blocked not just Drury Lane's regular company from performing Carey's farce, but also the 1735 summer company – a company without Clive but again directed by Theophilus Cibber – from doing so. In his 1738 wordbook of *The Dragon of Wantley*, Carey says his manuscript 'had lain several Years dormant in the Repository, and under the Inspection, of the most wise, most learned, and judicious, Squire *What-d'ye-call-him*, Master of Drury-Lane Play-house.' Henry Carey, 'Dedication', *The Dragon of Wantley. A Burlesque Opera*. 4th edn (London, 1738), p. v. See also Gillespie, 'The Life and Work of Henry Carey', vol. 1, pp. 120–35 (repr. preface to *The Dragon of Wantley*, p. 133) and Burling, *Summer Theatre in London*, pp. 88–90 (on *The Honest Yorkshire-Man*). Judging by when Carey wrote his wordbooks, and by the female principal's epilogue, dialogue, and song, he clearly intended Clive to lead these works.

The Fall of Phaeton, was a roaring success; so much so that Fielding chose to travesty it, and Clive, in his fringe production *Tumble-down Dick*.

Challenges, because Theophilus Cibber sought to advance his new wife Susannah Cibber, née Arne, over Clive. When Cibber persuaded Fleetwood to try Susannah out as Polly in *The Beggar's Opera*, Clive dug in. A two-month print war raged – unprecedented in its scope and subject matter – over Clive's ownership of Polly, and over her rights to her parts generally. In this conflict Clive showed herself to be a mistress of dissimulation on stage and in the press, persuading audiences of her willingness to submit to managers while defying them as far as her powers would allow. A popular comedy about the Polly row, *The Beggar's Pantomime*, sketched her as a 'fierce Amazonian Dame', but she nonetheless won over her public. She not only retained ownership of Polly, but for the first time established a following for her interpretation of the role, which emphasized spiritedness, rather than tenderness. Clive would no longer be defined in relation to Fenton.

'Of all the Arts': Stage Parts and Clive's Portraiture

Audience members want to own pictures of stars, and these pictures both satisfy a longing for intimacy and underline its absence.[9] Clive's publicity from 1733 onwards exemplifies this cycle of supply and frustration. During the actors' revolt, questions about Clive's nature had been disputed in public, and left unresolved. Was she the unscrupulous, emasculating soprano of the *ad hominem* farce *The Stage-Mutineers* and its source pamphlet? Or was she the respectable wife of a leading Shropshire gentleman, who provided for her siblings and ageing father, as she, Fielding, and others gave out? In 1734 and 1735, Clive's portraitists made their own arguments. In their representations, Clive was first songster and comedienne who, in novel ways, embodied polite English taste. The assertions were couched in the cold language of formal portraiture, accompanied by titles and epigrams. The invitation to the viewer was new: rather than an object of desire, Clive was to be admired for the graces that had enabled her rise. Strengthening this impression, and fixing her new rank, portraitists fused the imagery of first actress Oldfield with that of first singer Clive, partly by borrowing from Oldfield's posthumous publicity.

Shortly after Oldfield's death in 1730, *The Authentick Memoirs ... of that celebrated Actress Mrs. Ann Oldfield* had raced through multiple editions, and was plagiarized by Edmund Curll.[10] One of Curll's changes to *The Authentick*

---

[9] 'Introduction', Roach, *It*, p. 40.
[10] 'William Egerton' [Edmund Curll], *Faithful Memoirs of the Life, Amours and Performances, of that justly Celebrated and most Eminent Actress of her Time, Mrs. Anne Oldfield* (London, 1731). On Alexander Pope's view of Curll's career as a Grub Street writer, see Catherine Ingrassia, 'Dissecting the Authorial Body: Pope, Curll, and the Portrait of

Memoirs is noteworthy: where Oldfield had originally been described as a dazzling 'Sun',[11] Curll wrote that her 'Voice, Figure and Manner of Playing soon made *her* ... the *brightest Star*' – seemingly the first time that this term was ever used for a player.[12] Oldfield's death also provoked a barrage of encomia and mezzotints. Writers in 1730 limned their recollections of Oldfield with decency, emphasizing her professional 'Excellency',[13] her timeless beauty, and the matchless pedigree of her first long-term partner Arthur Maynwaring, while discreetly passing over Oldfield's lovers and illegitimate children.[14]

With similar care, Drury Lane management optimized which Oldfield parts fell to Clive. Generally she was given staples that Oldfield had revitalized, rather than roles specifically designed for Oldfield (Clive's 'Oldfield' roles are shown in Appendix 2). Of these, management preferred farces, in which Clive was known to excel, rather than serious or sentimental parts. By 1733, the writer of *The Theatre turned Upside Down* could praise Clive as the new Oldfield with the words: 'Scorning to copy meanly, sh[e] '[h]as out-done / Where Oldfield, late in greatest Splendor shone.'[15] The compliment was double-edged, mocking Colley Cibber's legendarily clumsy praise for Oldfield's 'outdoings' even while celebrating Clive's achievements.[16]

The artists behind Clive's portraits of 1734 and 1735 regulated how she was to be seen, just as memoirists had for Oldfield. But the artists' dilemma was different: they had to fabricate, rather than omit, in order that Clive's likeness might somehow resemble both her and her only existing portrait, which wasn't

---

a "Hack Writer"', *"More Solid Learning": New Perspectives on Alexander Pope's Dunciad*, ed. C. Ingrassia and C. N. Thomas (Lewisburg, PA, 2000), pp. 147–65.

[11] '[S]he shone in full Glory, and appeared like the Sun in its Meridian Altitude.' *Authentick Memoirs of the Life of that celebrated Actress Mrs. Anne Oldfield*, 4th edn (London, 1730), p. 22.

[12] 'But Mrs. OLDFIELD'S Voice, Figure and Manner of Playing soon made *her* shine out, even here, the *brightest Star*'. [Curll], *Faithful Memoirs*, p. 31. In 1734 'Star' would be used metaphorically to describe Farinelli. Thomas McGeary, 'Farinelli's Progress to Albion: The Recruitment and Reception of Opera's "Blazing Star"', *Journal for Eighteenth-Century Studies*, vol. 28, no. 3 (2005), pp. 339–60. According to *The Oxford English Dictionary*, the earliest usage of 'star', definition '4c. orig. Theatre. A very famous or popular actor, singer, or other entertainer; *spec.* one who has top billing or takes the leading role in a film, play, etc.' is cited as '[1751] Bays in Council 5 You may Shine the brightest Theatric Star, that ever enliveď'd or charm'd an Audience.' 'star, n.1'. *The Oxford English Dictionary*, Oxford University Press, 2017; OED Online: accessed 3 August 2017.

[13] *Authentick Memoirs of the Life of that celebrated Actress Mrs. Anne Oldfield*, p. 32.

[14] As Felicity Nussbaum has detailed, Oldfield's beauty, merits, and top salary (allegedly 500 pounds per annum) were thematized in *Authentick Memoirs* as well as by later memoirists. Nussbaum 'Actresses' Memoirs: Exceptional Virtue', *Rival Queens*, pp. 100–112.

[15] *The Theatre turned Upside Down*, p. 7.

[16] Colley Cibber was pilloried for this formulation, as chronicled in Fawcett, 'The Celebrity Emerges as the Deformed King: Richard III, the King of the Dunces, and the Overexpression of Englishness', *Spectacular Disappearances*, pp. 48–50.

Fig. 6.1 John Faber after Pieter van Bleeck, *The Celebrated Mrs. Clive, late Miss Raftor in the Character of Philida*, 1734. Mezzotint. © Victoria and Albert Museum, London. Museum number: S.3816-2009.

Fig. 6.2 Edward Fisher after Jonathan Richardson, *Mrs. Oldfield the celebrated Comedian*, 1758– 82. Mezzotint. National Portrait Gallery, London. NPG number: D27619.

of her at all, while also casting her as Oldfield. Pieter Van Bleeck, who painted other actors,[17] offered one solution. In his now-lost oil, known solely through John Faber's engraving (Fig. 6.1), he took the action of Schalcken's painting, removed its eroticism, and depicted Clive in the idiosyncratic posture of an Oldfield mezzotint (Fig. 6.2).

As in Schalcken's oil, Van Bleeck painted a shepherd at left moving toward a shepherdess whom he holds by the waist. In the Faber mezzotint (Fig. 6.1) we see that the shepherd has the same facial features, also in profile: full lips, round chin and prominent straight nose that descends from between his eyes. But Van Bleeck made the shepherd's lips closed, rather than pouted for a kiss; the shepherd steps gently towards the shepherdess, rather than seizing her, and has placed one hand behind her waist, rather than encircling her in an embrace. Van Bleeck also put the shepherd in theatrical costume, and holding a spear rather than a swain's floppy hat. Clive's unusual pose is that of Oldfield's

---

[17] Van Bleeck 'was reckoned a good painter of portraits … he painted … those excellent comedians, Johnson and Griffin'. Horace Walpole, 'Peter van Bleeck', *Anecdotes of Painting in England* (Twickenham, 1762; repr. London, 1827), p. 54.

c.1725 portrait by Jonathan Richardson the Elder, and its mezzotint by Edward Fisher (Fig. 6.2).[18] As in Richardson's oil, Clive's eyes are to front, and her left hand is raised above her shoulder. Her left elbow, like Oldfield's, rests on a support to create the same angle between upper and lower arm; like Oldfield, she raises her index finger while the other fingers droop. Clive's right arm reaches down and slightly forward along the line of her hip, like Oldfield's. The position of Clive's right hand appears to have been Van Bleeck's own invention: wrist bent back and fingers decorously spread to bar the shepherd from advancing further (Fig. 6.1). Gerard Vandergucht's frontispiece for John Watts' 1737 *Damon and Phillida* wordbook would again show Clive gesturing in this manner (Fig. 2.2).

In 1734 Van Bleeck and Faber finally presented to the public Clive's features in all their unconventionality. Her narrow lips form a slightly crooked smile; her chin is pudgy, her nostrils wide, and her nose is balled at the end. Clive's 'squinting Eyes', that Christopher Smart mentions in his 1756 epilogue about her[19] – a 'squint' being when the 'axes of the eyes [are] not coincident, so that one or both habitually look obliquely'[20] – are just perceptible. In Clive's case, the iris of her left eye seems to have been slightly further from the bridge of her nose than her right.

Compensating for her plainness, Clive is bedecked in current fashion. A dress cap sits atop her hair, which is coiffed into soft curls and pinned up. Her chemise forms a tucker, while a ribbon around her arm bands the chemise sleeves into cuffs. Her long stiffened bodice is open-fastened by cross-lacing and trimmed at the bottom; it matches the draped and swagged overskirt whose shine suggests satin, and which sits over a petticoat. Clive's finery, because contemporary, throws her into relief against the patently theatrical pastoral backdrop, shepherd included. John Faber's mezzotint is titled 'The Celebrated Mrs. Clive, late Miss Raftor in the Character of Philida' – a role which, as discussed, bookseller Watts had in his *Damon and Phillida* playbooks from 1729 falsely given out that she owned. Faber's image after van Bleeck anchored Clive's effigy both in this myth and in genteel fashion.

Fury evidently broke out, from what quarter we do not know, over this mezzotint portrait. The first we hear of the fracas is Van Bleeck's defensive

---

[18] Edward Fisher was a mezzotint engraver who moved from Dublin to London in 1758. He re-engraved other earlier mezzotints of actors, including David Garrick and Kitty Fisher.
[19] 'And in her cock't up hat, and Gown of Camblet, / Presumes on something – touching the Lord Hamlet. / A Cousin too she has, with squinting Eyes, / With wadling Gait, and Voice like *London Cries*.' [Christopher Smart], 'EPILOGUE written by FRIEND, spoken by Mrs. CLIVE', Arthur Murphy, *The Apprentice. A Farce, in Two Acts* (London, 1756), pages unnumbered. See also Chapter 2, p. 33, note 21.
[20] 'squint, v.', *The Oxford English Dictionary*, Oxford University Press, 2017; *OED* Online: accessed 2 September 2017.

response in the press against charges that he has failed to capture Clive's likeness. While he had deftly merged Oldfield's posture with Clive's actual appearance, his Clive portrait was held to break with the broader mission of an actress's representation: to perform femininity. Already in 1715 Oldfield's portraitist Jonathan Richardson had spelled out this mission, and the painter's duties within it. 'True' resemblance, according to Richardson, is that which is 'Proper', while 'Insipid Resemblance' is that which is 'said to be prodigious Like' its subject.[21] By this reading, Van Bleeck had failed in his main task, which was not to capture the subject, but to project how the subject should look. Van Bleeck defended himself by passing the blame onto the engraver John Faber:

> The Print of Mrs CLIVE, in the Character of PHILIDA (lately published by Mr. Faber) failing in the Likeness, obliged Mr. Van Bleeck, jun. (the Painter) to have the same done anew, by another Hand, and may now be had of Mr. Sympson, at the Dove in Russell-Court, Drury Lane.[22]

The accusation infuriated Faber; a week later, in the same paper, he had this notice printed:

> Mr. VAN BLEECK, jun. Painter, having asserted, that I have in a Print of Mrs. Clive, in the Character of Phillida fail'd in the Likeness, and that he has been obliged to have the same done by another Hand, meaning his own; I submit it to all Judges, which of us has most fail'd; the Painter, in his Copy after Nature, or I in imitation of his Picture; and at the same Time take Leave to acquaint the Publick, that I always acknowledge my Print unlike Mrs. Clive, it being impossible to take a Likeness where none was to be found. The Publick may soon be convinc'd of this, when they see a Print of Mrs. Clive, which, I hear, will shortly be published from a Painting by an eminent Hand; and this I think sufficiently proves that the first was never approv'd.[23]

Faber blames the painter whose work he had merely copied. But who had initially objected to this picture which, as her later portraiture makes clear, actually did look like Clive? Probably Drury Lane personnel, and possibly Clive

---

[21] "Tis not enough to make a Tame, Insipid Resemblance of the Features, so that every body shall know who the Picture was intended for, nor even to make the Picture what is often said to be prodigious Like: (This is often done by the lowest of Face-Painters ...) A Portrait-Painter must ... express their Minds as well as their Faces: And as his Business is chiefly with People of Condition, he must Think as a Gentleman ... or 'twill be impossible to give Such their True, and Proper Resemblances'. John Richardson, *An Essay on the Theory of Painting*, 2nd edn (London, 1725), pp. 21–22; cited in Marcia Pointon, *Hanging the Head: Portraiture and Social Formation in Eighteenth-Century England* (New Haven and London, 1993), p. 80.

[22] *Country Journal or The Craftsman*, issue 464 (24 May 1735). Timothy Clayton, reproducing John Faber's portrait, also cites this passage in Clayton, *The English Print, 1688–1802*, p. 60.

[23] *Country Journal or The Craftsman*, issue 465 (31 May 1735).

herself: Faber says that Van Bleeck's picture had not been 'approv'd' – by implication, by those who had commissioned it – prior to its print circulation.[24]

Van Bleeck's answer to this was to re-engrave his oil as a mezzotint, titled 'Mrs. Clive in the Character of Philida' (Fig. 6.3). Apart from reversing Faber's mezzotint, Van Bleeck emphasized the curves of Clive's breasts, straightened her nose, heightened her cheekbones, smoothed her chin, plumped her lower lip, and darkened her brows and irises. What had been cool self-assurance in her 1734 portrait became a frank appeal to the male gaze. In this tale of two mezzotints, the conceptual hollowness of the 'true likeness' of an eighteenth-century actress stands revealed. Fidelity to agendas and their concomitant pictorial conventions, rather than to the 'real' subject, seems to have preoccupied sponsor, artist, subject, and viewer alike.

Another Clive portrait was also in preparation, as Faber's response to Van Bleeck makes clear. This 'Painting by an eminent Hand' promised by Faber was apparently the now-lost c.1735 oil of Clive by Joseph van Aken that his brother Alexander engraved.[25] Van Aken shared a studio with his student Jeremiah Davison, who made a copy of the oil (Fig. 6.4).[26] It shows Clive with the posture and manner of another of Richardson's portraits of Oldfield. This alternative Oldfield portrait had circulated as a mezzotint by John Simon (Fig. 6.5),[27] and was used to make the oval facial portrait in the frontispiece to Curll's *Memoirs*. In Simon's mezzotint, Oldfield is directed towards her left, while looking front to meet the viewer's gaze. Her right hand is in her lap while her left elbow rests on a pedestal; in her upturned right palm, she cradles the bottom of an upright book's spine, while the fingers of her left hand drape themselves over the top of the book spine and its back board.

Clive's pose is the mirror opposite: she is directed towards her right, her left hand is on her lap, and her right elbow rests on a table (Fig. 6.4). Clive's coiffure is similar to Oldfield's: both sitters have hair parted in the middle, and coiled, although Clive's hair is up, while Oldfield's is plain; only in the Van

---

[24] Ibid.
[25] Joseph van Aken (c.1699–1749) was a drapery painter, as well as painter of genre and conversation pieces, who in 1720 came from Antwerp to London with his brothers Arnold and Alexander. 'As in England almost every body's picture is painted', Horace Walpole quipped, 'so almost every painter's works were painted by Vanaken.' Horace Walpole, *The Works of Horatio Walpole, Earl of Orford. In Five Volumes*, vol. 3 (London, 1798), p. 449.
[26] Jeremiah Davison (c.1695–1745) shared a studio with Van Aken until 1737, the year that he moved to Scotland under the patronage Duke of Atholl. Davison returned to London in 1740, when he set up an independent studio. Shearer West, 'Aken, Joseph van', *Grove Art Online. Oxford Art Online.* Oxford University Press: accessed 28 September 2017. Davison's oil is reproduced in Gill Perry, with Joseph Roach and Shearer West, *The First Actresses: Nell Gwyn to Sarah Siddons* (London and Ann Arbor, 2011), pp. 84–87.
[27] John Simon after Jonathan Richardson, *Mrs. Oldfield*. c.1730. Mezzotint. The curator who wrote the online catalogue entry for this portrait finds the 'characteristic expression of the eyes much weakened and altered'.

Fig. 6.3 Pieter van Bleeck after Pieter van Bleeck, *Mrs. Clive in the Character of Philida*, 1735. Mezzotint. © Victoria and Albert Museum, London. Museum number: S.3817-2009.

Fig. 6.4 Jeremiah Davison after Joseph van Aken, *Catherine Clive*, c.1735. Oil on canvas. Reproduced by permission of the Marquess of Bath, Longleat House, Warminster, Wiltshire. Longleat Collection Number: 9341.

Aken mezzotint is Clive's coil, like Oldfield's, shown on her left shoulder. In depicting Clive's gaze Davison, copying Van Aken, visually quotes Oldfield's heavy-lidded eyes. Oldfield would famously half-shut her eyes at 'some particular comic situations … when she intended to give effect to some brilliant or gay thought'.[28] Simon captured this characteristic Oldfield expression in his mezzotint after Richardson, and Van Aken seems to have borrowed it for Clive. The one significant variant between the Oldfield and Clive portraits is what each sitter holds. Rather than a book, Clive holds open, with delicately curving fingers, an oblong-format handwritten music score, with three staves on each leaf.

In the Van Aken portrait, where Clive sits and what she wears removes her from what Gill Perry rightly calls the 'dangerous zone of musical performance'.[29]

---

[28] 'Mrs. Oldfield was, in person, tall, genteel, and well shaped; her countenance pleasing and expressive, enlivened with large speaking eyes, which, in some particular comic situations, she kept half shut, especially when she intended to give effect to some brilliant or gay thought.' Thomas Davies, *Dramatic Micellanies*, vol. 3, p. 433.

[29] By displacing his subject's musical props, Perry tells us, Thomas Gainsborough in his portrait of Elizabeth Linley 'privileges feminine sensibility over musical ability, removing his sitter from the dangerous zone of musical performance, with all its connotations

Fig. 6.5 John Simon after John Richardson, *Mrs. Oldfield*, c.1730. Mezzotint. National Portrait Gallery, London. NPG number: D27620.

Fig. 6.6 Alexander van Aken after Joseph van Aken, 'Of all the Arts …' [Catherine Clive, 'Printed for T. Bowles'], 1735. Mezzotint. © Trustees of the British Museum. Museum number: 1902,1011.6026.

Clive occupies a polite interior typical of formal portraiture. Her elbow is on a pink velvet cushion, and background elements – a thick drapery in the hues of the cushion, the base of a classical column and, in the distance, a blue sky – are typical of such interiors. She is arrayed as a person of Quality. Unlike Oldfield's, her hair is powdered and entwined with bows. Her tucker, formed from the trim of her chemise, displays her breasts and neckline to advantage. Her back-fastened dress is white satin; a pearl clasp pins each short sleeve to form a swagged cuff, and a matching clasp pins the ribbons decorating the bodice. Her beauty resides in her presentation. Her facial features are, apart from her heavy-lidded Oldfield eyes, conventional; only her nose and slightly crooked mouth resemble the facial features in Faber's much-abused 1734 mezzotint of her.

---

of coquetry and feminine irresistibility'. Gill Perry, *Spectacular Flirtations: Viewing the Actress in British Art and Theatre* (New Haven and London, 2007), p. 158. Richard Leppert identifies standardized conceits for representing female music-making in Georgian painting, and how these conceits helped the sitter be seen as an ornament to her sex. Leppert, *Music and Image: Domesticity, Ideology, and Socio-Cultural Formation in Eighteenth-Century England*.

Alexander van Aken engraved a mezzotint (Fig. 6.6) after his brother's oil, issuing it in 1735 with the following verses:

Of all the Arts that sooth the human Breast,
Music (blest Power) the sweetest is confest:
Heightens our Joys, suspends our fiercest Pains:
This each One proves who hears thy heavnly Strains.

These verses resemble Aaron Hill's adulatory poem about Clive, published in October 1735 in his series *The Prompter*.[30] Hill had been a theatre and opera impresario, and had run opera at the Queen's Theatre in 1710–11; having written the libretto to Handel's *Rinaldo*, and then brought out this opera, Hill had launched the German composer in London. His authority to judge singing was unquestionable, and in a poem dedicated to her, his praise for Clive was unequivocal:

The Stage's Acknowledgment.
O NATURE! —where *thy* Sovereign POWER we see,
How *poor* a *Thing* must AFFECTATION be! —
While CLIVE, with beauteous *Ease*, the Audience *charms*,
And, with the Fire of *native* Influence, *warms*;
Pour'd from her Eyes, the meaning *Raptures* roll:
And shoot the *laughing* GRACES through the *Soul*.
 Or, when the sprightly *Song* demands her *Aid*,
How *pointed* are thy *Notes*, O MUSICK! made!
Poets, and Masters, *careless*, may *compound;*
Her Look is MEASURE: and Her Action, SOUND.[31]

The erotic nymph who had haunted Clive's iconography since 1729 was banished. In contrast to the 'Miss Rafter' mezzotint, the Van Aken portrait placed its subject beyond the viewer's reach: her gaze was now cool and authoritative, not coy with enticement; her powers were held to be Orphic, not Dionysian; her strains were deemed 'heavnly', rather than merely 'unaffected'.

The Arnes at Drury Lane

As Clive's reputation grew, so too did her competition. In 1733, while directing the rebel actors at the New Haymarket Theatre, Theophilus Cibber had become enamoured with Susannah Arne. Her 1732 debut in the title role of the

---

[30] Hill's *Prompter* was 'the only regular journal of its time devoted to theatrical affairs'. Hill's co-editor was William Popple; Hill signed his writings 'B' for 'Broomstick' – symbolic of the way Hill aspired to sweep away playhouse rubbish – and Popple signed his writings 'P'. Gerrard, *Aaron Hill: The Muses' Projector*, p. 160.

[31] [Aaron Hill], 'The Stage's Acknowledgment', *The Prompter*, no. 99 (21 October 1735), p. 331; repr. in the *London Magazine, or, Gentleman's Monthly Intelligencer* (1732–35), vol. 4 (October 1735), p. 566.

English opera *Amelia*, composed by John F. Lampe as a fringe theatre production, had made her 'the great Delight and Surprize of the whole Town', because she was 'very young, and very pretty' with a manner 'entirely modern' and 'a Warble, such a *je ne scay quoy*, as tickles my very Soul'.[32] So wrote the author of *See and Seem Blind*, who almost certainly was Aaron Hill.[33] Over the next year Susannah Arne led other independently mounted English operas – *Teraminta*, *Rosamond*, Handel's *Acis and Galatea* – and won a minor part in Handel's *Deborah* (1733).[34] By the autumn of 1733, Arne was singing during the intervals of rebel company productions at the New Haymarket.[35]

Theophilus Cibber pressed his suit, and under pressure from her impecunious father Susannah Arne yielded, marrying Cibber on 21 April 1734, about a month after his return to Drury Lane.[36] Press notice of their union refers snidely to her poverty: '[m]arried on sunday Mr. Cibber jun. comedian, to miss Arne, a celebrated singer ... Modesty *is, in some matches, a portion more necessary than* money'.[37] Thanks to Cibber, all immediate Arne family members except the mother secured employment: Susannah, her brother Thomas the composer, her brother Richard – a singer–actor who soon quit after being charged with participation in a gang rape – and her father, an upholsterer and undertaker, for whom the post of seat 'Numberer' was created.[38] The Arnes were clearly among the 'Favourites' for whom Cibber gained 'very

---

[32] [Hill], *See and Seem Blind*, pp. 12–13; quoted in Milhous and Hume, 'J. F. Lampe and English Opera at the Little Haymarket in 1732-3', p. 504. On the ways that Susannah Arne's early parts were designed to market her as a tender and pure heroine, see Jonathan Lee, 'From Amelia to Calista and Beyond: Sentimental Heroines, "Fallen" Women and Handel's Oratorio Revisions for Susanna Cibber', *Cambridge Opera Journal*, vol. 27, no. 1 (2015), pp. 1–34.

[33] See Chapter 3, p. 80, note 87.

[34] Milhous and Hume, 'J. F. Lampe and English Opera', pp. 502–31; regarding *Deborah*, see Burrows et al., ed., *George Frideric Handel Collected Documents: Volume 2 1725–1734*, pp. 602–13.

[35] For instance, on 13 October 1733 she performed 'Was ever Nymph like Rosamond', 'Mi volgo ad ogni fronda', and 'If 'tis Joy to wound a Lover'. *The London Stage*, Part 3, vol. 1, p. 326.

[36] Evidence of Susannah Arne's mother's opposition to this match, and her father's defence of it, are found in court records drawn on by Nash, *The Provoked Wife*, pp. 67–75, 338 note 6. The source she cites is 'Susannah Cibber and Anne Arne vs T. Cibber 1741, British Public Records Office, C. 11, bundle 1572, no. 15', which corresponds to the National Archives, Public Record Office C11/1572/15, 'Cibber v Cibber'.

[37] *Grub-Street Journal*, issue 226 (25 April 1734).

[38] Todd Gilman, *The Theatre Career of Thomas Arne* (Newark, 2013), p. 58. Richard Arne absconded in September 1735 'to avoid being apprehended ... for the brutal gang rape of a widow named Margaret Maccullough, which took place in an outhouse near Drury Lane, 6 July 1735'. Ibid., p. 61.

advantageous Terms' when in 1734 he negotiated with Fleetwood for the future salaries of his rebel company.[39]

By the end of 1735, around the time Fleetwood reached an agreement with Rich to even out profits and losses between their respective houses,[40] Susannah Cibber's encroachment on Clive's line had begun: on 12 November she debuted as Chloe in *The Lottery*.[41] Clive then had to watch as Susannah Cibber was spectacularly launched on 12 January 1736 as a new-style tragedienne in Aaron Hill's *Zara*,[42] making her the toast of the Town. Although Clive spoke the comic epilogue after *Zara*,[43] Susannah Cibber was its star, and one of her chief draws was, like Clive, her voice. But whereas Clive's voice and the way she used it were uniquely hers, Susannah Cibber's voice in *Zara*, and the way she used it, were reportedly the creations of Aaron Hill. Hill wrote of her as his instrument, who was 'inclinable to exert her inimitable Talent, in *additional* Aid of my Purpose'.[44] According to Thomas Davies' later account, Hill created the equivalent of a musical score to drill Susannah Cibbber in 'every accent and emphasis' of her stage speech in *Zara*.[45] The results, as William Chetwood would recall in 1749, stirred 'the Admiration of every Spectator that had their auricular Faculties'.[46]

Susannah Cibber posed a threat to Clive, as both actress and singer. Conversely, the appointment to Drury Lane of Susannah's brother Thomas Arne proved hugely advantageous to Clive. Arne took up Henry Carey's compositional procedures, generating songs for Clive that joined seamlessly with

---

[39] Victor, *The History of the Theatres of London and Dublin*, vol. 1, p. 27. Cibber bartered for the 'managing Actors' to receive 200-pound salary and 'to some [players] a clear Benefit, and to others a Benefit at a lower Rate than usual'; Cibber's counterfeit memoirist has him priding himself on a treaty so advantageous in 'a private Manner to myself'. *An Apology for the Life of Mr. T —C —, Comedian*, pp. 98, 102. Cibber would of course command his wife's earnings.

[40] Hume quotes the manuscript agreement (an 1837 facsimile in the Folger Shakespeare Library, shelfmark Folger Y.d. 135) between Rich and Fleetwood, signed 12 December 1735, in which they 'agree to divide all moneys at Each play house ... above Fifty pounds share and share like for the remainder part of this season, and to pay to Each other so much money as shall be wanting to make up fifty pounds Each Night, and to meet once a week to Ballance accounts'. That this 'profit-sharing cartel was no more than a brief experiment' was noted in 'a passing reference in a letter from Thomas Gray to Horace Walpole of November 1737'. Hume, 'John Rich as Manager and Entrepreneur', "The Stage's Glory", p. 44.

[41] *The London Stage*, Part 3, vol. 1, p. 526.

[42] Gerrard, *Aaron Hill: The Muses' Projector*, pp. 177–78.

[43] Aaron Hill, 'Epilogue, Spoke by Mrs. CLIVE', *The Tragedy of Zara* (London, 1736), pages unnumbered.

[44] Hill, 'Preface to the Reader', *The Tragedy of Zara*, page unnumbered.

[45] Thomas Davies, *Memoirs of the Life of David Garrick, Esq.*, vol. 1 (London, 1780), p.137; cited in Gerrard, *Aaron Hill: The Muses' Projector*, p. 178.

[46] Chetwood, 'Mrs. CIBBER', *A General History of the Stage*, p. 122.

Carey's earlier output for her.⁴⁷ Raiding Carey's toolkit, Arne took over his symmetrical phrasing, thin textures, fusion of English ballad with Italianate cantata writing, reserve of sequences for cadential preparation, word colouring through harmonic pivots, and heavy reliance on French galant dance meters and rhythms. But Arne's harmonic and melodic invention far exceeded that of Carey, as did his knowledge of, and respect for, fashionable Italian and German composers. Importantly for Clive, Arne's gift for word-setting was unequalled among English composers. He made words and phrases more eloquent: distilling their meaning, animating their rhythms, nuancing their expression, catching their inflection, and expanding their dramatic impact through music.

Arne's first Clive-led stage work was the 'Dramatic Masque' *The Fall of Phaeton*, which opened on 28 February 1736.⁴⁸ Its author was William Pritchard, husband of Clive's friend and onstage partner Hannah.⁴⁹ *The Fall of Phaeton* immediately hit Town taste. No music survives – Clive probably never performed the air 'Sung by Mrs Clive in The Fall of Phaeton', printed later by Arne⁵⁰ – but its wordbook and advertisement suggest why the work piqued interest. Pritchard used two means to make his form of 'Dramatic Masque' new, or 'Invented by Mr. Pritchard', as the playbook's title page has it:⁵¹ its players speak as well as sing, and Clive's part, uniquely among the dramatis personae, is comic as well as serious. Normally a masque is sung throughout, but for his masque Pritchard embedded single songs within spoken rhymed couplets in iambic pentameter. Normally a masque only has serious song,

---

⁴⁷ '[I]n fusing the features of the popular ballad with the sophistication of the Italian style Carey established the characteristics of that mid-century "English style" identified principally with Thomas Arne'. Gillespie, 'The Life and Work of Henry Carey', vol. 1, p. 217. Gillespie evidences this statement with examples, pp. 217–55.
⁴⁸ *London Daily Post and General Advertiser*, issue 414 (28 February 1736).
⁴⁹ Trained as an engraver, William Pritchard, after occasional playing at fringe theatres, was employed at Drury Lane from 1740 as house servant. According to benefit notices, he progressed from doorkeeper (notice of 24 May 1742) to office keeper (notice of 15 May 1744) to assistant box-office keeper during the 1745–46 season. He was treasurer for the summer company directed by John Hippisley in Bristol from June 1741 to September 1747. Once David Garrick became co-manager, he arranged for William Pritchard to be treasurer at Drury Lane. Vaughan, *Born to Please*, p. 23.
⁵⁰ Arne had the air 'Sung by Mrs Clive in The Fall of Phaeton' engraved when he brought out his collection, *The Songs in the Comedies called As You Like It, and Twelfth Night* (London, 1741). The air, a lilting gavotte, opens the volume; in its appeals for healing though kisses, it clashes with the part of Clymene in *The Fall of Phaeton*, for which no additional airs were advertised. Arne's derogatory pleasure garden song of 1757, 'Kitty, or, The Female Phaeton' may have been a dig at Clive; it was printed in *A Favourite Collection of English Songs sung by Mr. Beard, Miss Young &c. at Ranelagh Gardens* (London, 1757).
⁵¹ William Pritchard, *The Fall of Phaeton ... Invented by Mr. Pritchard. The Musick compos'd by Mr. Arne; and the Scenes painted by Mr. Hayman* (London, 1736).

but Pritchard mixed pensive with light-hearted airs for a goddess who shares celebrity knowledge with her audience.

Clive's part of Clymene, Phaeton's mother, neatly dovetailed with her line. Being a nymph from classical myth, Clymene resembles Clive's earlier masque parts, notably Procris – but being of questionable virtue, Clymene was a character Clive could play humorously. In the action, Phaeton doubts Clymene when she tells him that his father is the sun god Phoebus, repeating gossip that this story is a lie. Clymene urges him to visit Phoebus in his temple and procure some 'indubitable Mark' of parentage from him.[52] Phaeton goes to Phoebus, who, to prove his love for his son, promises to grant any request Phaeton makes of him. Phaeton asks to drive the chariot that carries the sun across the sky. Phoebus is appalled: he must keep his compact, yet knows that Phaeton will not be able to control the steeds that pull the chariot. When Phaeton takes up the reigns, the chariot plunges wildly, scorching the earth with the sun; to save the earth, Jupiter is forced to strike him dead with a thunderbolt. Clymene laments her son's death, as does Phoebus, whom Jupiter has to order to quit mourning and attend to his duties.

Pritchard's choice of the Phaeton myth, and the work's success, likely owed much to the story's parallels with court tattle. King George II had kept his eldest son Frederick, Prince of Wales, on a tight leash since Frederick arrived in London from Hanover in 1728 at his father's behest. Frederick's income had been restricted in an attempt to limit his influence, which he defied by going into debt. From 1729 the king had scandalously made his wife, rather than his son, regent in Britain during his visits to Hanover. During the early 1730s Frederick's parents had ignored his petition to marry, while arranging for his sister Anne to wed William, Prince of Orange. Frederick was deeply insulted: arranging Anne's marriage before his own implied that his parents preferred her to secure the throne's succession. Of all these insults, Frederick's penurious allowance cut deepest, and he was thought to have co-authored a sensational satire about his parents, *Histoire du Prince Titi* (1735), which appeared in translation just weeks before Pritchard's masque.[53]

The story of Phaeton is easily read as a cautionary tale about the need to hold Frederick in check. At several points, Pritchard seems to allude directly to common knowledge about the prince. When, on seeing Phaeton, Phoebus

---

[52] Pritchard, 'The Argument', *The Fall of Phaeton*, page unnumbered.
[53] 'Subtitled in some editions "A Royal Allegory" … the *History of Titi* … was a European *cause scandaleuse* … It came out late 1735 in Paris … [and] was published almost immediately in Amsterdam and Brussels and then "Englished" in two separate translations for publication in London in February 1736.' Kathryn R. King, *A Political Biography of Eliza Haywood* (London, 2012), p. 79. Its author, Thémiseul de Saint-Hyacinthe, had resided some years in London, and in 1736 had dedicated another work to Frederick for the prince's 'signal marks of favour' to the writer. *Ibid.*

exclaims, 'Tell, what strange Cause cou'd hither bring my Son?'[54] – he might have been George II, speaking to the renowned rarity of Frederick's appearances at court. In her second air, Clymene sings that 'if a Man of Power' pursues a maid, she shows 'Wisdom' by yielding, because her 'Fame' increases.[55] This may have been a sly poke at Maid of Honour Anne Vane, whose concurrent affairs with both Frederick and his best friend Lord Hervey, as well as her bastard son by Frederick, had provoked numerous satires.[56] That the sun king Phoebus was a travesty role – Ann Cantrell took the part – invited further parallels between the action on stage and at court, where Queen Caroline was said to govern both her husband and first minister Walpole.[57]

Pritchard's points for Clymene move from arch comedy to glittering grandeur, and Clive was their ideal mouthpiece. As the comic Clymene, Clive represented a fine woman of easy virtue, whose witty evasions to Phaeton's queries imply uncertainty about his parentage. Through Pritchard's aphoristic song verses Clymene pivots, as Clive so often did in ballad opera, from action to instruction. In her first song she upbraids 'the Prude' for censuring the maiden who yields to a lover, since the prude would also do so, given the chance.[58] In her second she explains, as mentioned above, that 'if a Man of Power' claims his lover, 'Her Frailty then her Wisdom shows'. Both songs include the word 'Fame', which could mean either disrepute or renown, and which routinely featured in comments about Vane.[59] In the masque's penultimate section, Clive took her place as first songster, executing a serious pastoral lament before the finale, a 'Grand Dance'. Thomas Arne's music and the painter Francis Hayman's

[54] Pritchard, *The Fall of Phaeton*, p. 8.
[55] 'But, if a Man of Power claim, / Her Frailty then her Wisdom shows, / More bright she from her Failing grows, / And who dares doubt her Fame?' *Ibid.*, p. 7.
[56] Robert Halsband, 'A Prince, a Lord and a Maid of Honour: A Story of Amorous Intrigue at the Court of George II', *History Today*, vol. 23, nos. 5–6 (1973), 'Part I', pp. 305–12, 'Part II', pp. 391–7.
[57] Public perception was that Queen Caroline commanded her husband, though Andrew Thompson argues that this was not true in practice. Thompson concedes that Queen Caroline shaped artistic patronage at court, as Joanna Marschner has shown, but in his view her skills were 'complementary' as befit her role as 'social hostess' and consort who helped to redefine 'what the court was and how it could function in the political and social life of the nation'. Andrew C. Thompson, *George II, King and Elector* (New Haven, 2011), pp. 71–72.
[58] 'The Prude each Maid will blame, / And censure others Fame: / Yet when some Swain prevailing / To Love has won her, / Then she in secret failing / Will yield her Honour.' Pritchard, *The Fall of Phaeton*, p. 6.
[59] To ascribe 'Fame' to a woman might be an insult or a compliment, as Kathryn King points out. On the one hand, 'Fame' could stand for 'infamy' of the female who courts ill-repute, yet the term was during the mid-eighteenth century also 'grounded in a cluster of classical and Renaissance understandings of fame … closely linked with the humanist ideal of public praise as recognition of, and thus spur to, artistic aspiration.' King, *A Political Biography of Eliza Haywood*, p. 107.

scenes set off this action.⁶⁰ With *The Fall of Phaeton* Pritchard had 'Invented' a formula for success – airs serious and comic, classical action updated with topical references, dazzling sets and dances – that would be rejigged to make *Comus*, the most important production of Clive's career.

Henry Fielding promptly skewered Clive, pantomime, and its chief exponent John Rich in his burlesque of this production, *Tumble-down Dick*. Never yet had Clive been so nastily mocked. *Tumble-down Dick* is a rehearsal play, and among the diverse scenes in rehearsal are those from *The Devil to Pay*. As *Tumble-down Dick* begins, its dramatis personae watch actors in 'A Cobler's Stall', which is where *The Devil to Pay* opens.⁶¹ Sneerwill asks Mr. Machine 'who are these extraordinary Figures?', to which Machine responds 'the Lady is Clymene; or Clymene, as they call her in Drury-Lane', a joke that will have depended on making the 'y' in 'Clymene' sound like the 'i' in Clive the second time around.⁶²

The ballads Clymene sings in *Tumble-down Dick* contain imputations about Clive in music and words. Her first tune is 'Gilliflower gentle Rosemary', known to audiences above all from Henry Carey's *Contrivances* as well as Carey's recent hit at the New Haymarket Theatre, *The Honest Yorkshire-Man*.⁶³ As such, the melody could stand for the Clive–Carey partnership and, in a shot at Carey's descent into fringe theatre, the inferiority of her music master. Clymene's next tune is that of Air 10 in *The Intriguing Chambermaid*, here used to underpin words such as 'Smaller Misses, / For their Kisses, / Are in Bridewell bang'd'.⁶⁴ Fielding's ire climaxes in his mockery of Clive's last air from *The Fall of Phaeton*, which is a serious lament. Fielding twists Pritchard's verses to insult Clive's singing:

> Thus when the wretched Owl has found
> Her young Owls dead as Mice,
> O'er the sad Spoil she hovers round,
> And views 'em once or twice:
> Then to some hollow Tree she flies,
> To hollow, hoot, and howl,

---

⁶⁰ Unusually, the names of composer and scene painter adorned the title page of the playbook (*The Fall of Phaeton ... The Musick compos'd by Mr. Arne; and the Scenes painted by Mr. Hayman*).

⁶¹ I refer here to the staple (second afterpiece) version of *The Devil to Pay*, which opens with 'Scene I. The Cobler's House'. Charles Coffey [and John Mottley], *The Devil to Pay*.

⁶² Thomas Lockwood offers a different explanation: 'Without any textual representation it is hard to be sure, but Fielding must mean "Clymene" with the first 'e' short, as it would be in Greek (epsilon), rather than long as at Drury Lane.' Lockwood, ed., 'Tumble-down Dick', *Henry Fielding: Plays Volume III*, p. 336, note 3.

⁶³ Lockwood identifies the provenance, without its associations, in notes to the airs in *Tumble-down Dick* in *Henry Fielding: Plays Volume III*, pp. 647–50.

⁶⁴ Lockwood ed., 'Tumble-down Dick', *Henry Fielding: Plays Volume III*, pp. 337, 647–48.

Till ev'ry Boy that passes, cries,
The Devil's in the Owl!⁶⁵

Fielding's last line makes his target unmistakable: the star of the *Devil to Pay* is the 'wretched Owl' whose 'hoot, and howl' provokes 'ev'ry Boy' to complain. In the dialogue that precedes this air Clymene mourns not her son's death, as in Pritchard's masque, but her barrenness: 'Art thou, my Phaey, dead? O foolish Elf ... What shall I do to get another Son, / For now, alas! my Teeming-time is done?'⁶⁶ The bait here is seemingly Clive's childless state.

As the rehearsal in *Tumble-down Dick* ends, the 'Cobler' enters. Fustian explains that he 'might have been the Father of Phaeton, if his Wife would have let him', the implication being that his wife is a termagant.⁶⁷ The Cobler rails at Clymene for cuckolding him, and for publicizing that she has done so. Clymene responds 'That every Man who wears the Marriage-Fetters, / Is glad to be the Cuckold of his Betters'.⁶⁸ Whereas in Pritchard's original, Men of Power (like Frederick) bring glory to lower women (like Anne Vane), in Fielding's parody Clymene has the effrontery to think that she raises her husband by taking lovers of superior rank. As its title insinuates, *Tumble-down Dick* is about impotence. Its laboured quips make it a stage work of dubious quality. Although briefly popular, Fielding's burlesque did not dent Clive's good standing. On the contrary, his *ad feminam* slurs signalled her star status as powerfully as her new portraiture did.

The Polly Row

From November 1736 to January 1737, one story persistently surfaced in the pages of London's newspapers: Clive's ultimately successful fight with Drury Lane management to keep the role of Polly in *The Beggar's Opera*. The so-called 'Polly Row' was unprecedented in subject and scope.⁶⁹ For the first time, a conflict between stage stars entered the front pages of newspapers and lasted for months. Press reports of the struggle would ultimately become their own stage entertainment, *The Beggar's Pantomime: Or, the Contending Colombines*. For the first time, a female player harnessed public opinion to prevail in a managerial dispute. And for the first time, a star and her supporters perpetrated a complex media hoax and got away with it.

---

⁶⁵ *Ibid.*, p. 347.
⁶⁶ *Ibid.*, p. 346.
⁶⁷ *Ibid.*, p. 347.
⁶⁸ *Ibid.*
⁶⁹ The section below draws on Berta Joncus, '"In Wit Superior as in Fighting": Kitty Clive and the Conquest of a Rival Queen', *Huntington Library Quarterly*, vol. 74, no. 1 (2011), pp. 23–42.

For Clive, the fight was over her rights to parts. She was convinced that Theophilus Cibber was plotting for his wife to take Clive's place in the company, which was indeed highly likely: top rank meant top earnings, and the spendthrift Cibber always needed money. Cibber's designs had been alleged in print already during the 1735–36 season. On 27 January 1736, it was announced: 'We hear that the Beggars Opera is soon to be acted at the Theatre-Royal in Drury-Lane; the Part of Lucy to be performed by Mrs. Clive, and that of Polly by Mr. Cibber's Wife, who is to have all the first Parts.'[70] Another announcement of this production warned that 'Mr. Cibber's Wife' would soon 'have all the first Parts, having, during the Run of Zara, shewn her natural Genius, by never any one Night varying in either Tone of Voice or Action from the Way she was taught'[71] – a sardonic echo of Aaron Hill's own claim. Did Clive plant these notices? Possibly. According to Theophilus Cibber's later pseudonymous report, written as 'A. Z.' and quoted below, around January 1736 Fleetwood had cancelled a planned revival of *The Beggar's Opera* due to Clive's fury.[72] Anger certainly simmers under the surface of the 27 January notice. In the event, Susannah Cibber's second pregnancy delayed any moves into new parts. Her lying-in and confinement stretched from early April to August 1736, as she mourned the second death of an infant child.[73]

The Polly Row erupted fully in November 1736. The very first article, by 'a SPECTATOR', in the *Daily Gazetteer* of 4 November, articulated the arguments central to Clive's defence. First, that Clive had in 1732 'shewn herself to be' an excellent Polly, having perfectly '*hit* this Character', which was intended to be '*Pathetick*, but … *Amorous*' and '*Tender*, but *passionately* so'. That is, the character of Polly was said to move between contradictions in a way for which Clive was renowned.[74] Second, that it was a 'received Maxim on the Stage, not to take a Character from an Actor, by which he has establish'd a Reputation to himself, and deservedly gain'd the Applause of different Audiences'.[75] Finally, that Theophilus Cibber, referred to as 'the Gentleman at the Head of Theatrick Affairs',[76] was 'robbing' audiences of *The Beggar's Opera*, and advancing his wife by decree, rather than allowing the Town to judge her merit.[77]

This was misleading on several points. As we have seen, the Town had in 1732 voted with its feet against Clive's Polly, despite frantic puffing in which

---

[70] *Daily Journal*, issue 5592 (27 January 1736).
[71] *London Evening Post*, issue 1278 (24–27 January 1736).
[72] *London Daily Post and General Advertiser*, issue 636 (13 November 1736).
[73] Her son Caius-Gabriel was born 5 April and died on 16 April. Nash, *The Provoked Wife*, pp. 96–97. As Nash notes, Susannah was persuaded to give two performances by royal command during the summer of 1736.
[74] 'SPECTATOR', *Daily Gazetteer*, issue 424 (4 November 1736).
[75] Ibid.
[76] Ibid.
[77] Ibid.

Theophilus Cibber probably had a hand. As shown in Clive's later letter to the press, it was Clive, not Cibber, who was responsible for blocking revival of *The Beggar's Opera* during the 1735–36 and 1736–37 seasons. And, increasingly, Theophilus Cibber was not 'at the Head of Theatrick Affairs'. Although Cibber had been Fleetwood's 'Favourite and first Minister' immediately after the 1733–34 actors' revolt, Benjamin Victor reports that he 'did not long continue in that high Office' but, being found by Fleetwood to be an 'improper and dangerous Man' was 'displaced' by Macklin.[78]

Theophilus Cibber hit back at the 'SPECTATOR' in the *London Daily Post and General Advertiser* of 13 November, under the pseudonym 'A. Z.'. Whereas the identity of the 'SPECTATOR' remained unknown, the bombast of Cibber's prose made his authorship unmistakable – as well as undermining the credibility of his report, which seems to have been far more accurate than that of Clive's boosters. According to A. Z., because Susannah Cibber's 'Talents' were 'peculiarly turn'd for the *tender* and *pathetick*', Fleetwood, not Theophilus Cibber, had decided to revive *The Beggar's Opera* during the previous season, thinking she 'might properly be cast to the Part of *Polly*'.[79] By contrast, the 'best Judges' had opined that Clive 'did *not hit* the Part of *Polly*'.[80] Clive had moreover openly defied the manager's '*sole Right* of *casting* the *Parts* of *Plays*'. According to Cibber, Clive had also refused the manager's offer to let her play Polly as well as Lucy, in order to let the Town decide which part suited her best. Cibber concluded with a damning sketch of Clive's nature:

> [I]t is of evil Tendency … when an *Actress* will from a *self-Conceit* contest Parts in all Plays, and from a *self-Vanity*, be disgusted at any Applause given to another, tho' she appears with *full Applause* in the *same Play*, yet from a *Peevishness* of *Temper* and *Narrowness* of *Thought* cannot bear any Merit to meet its Reward beside her own.[81]

This character assault flushed Clive from cover. Six days later, on 19 November, she addressed the readers of the same newspaper in an open letter on the front page. This was a risk – no polite woman opposed a male senior,

---

[78] 'Theophilus Cibber set out with him [Fleetwood], his Favourite and first Minister; but did not long continue in that high Office. The Manager [Fleetwood] had Sense enough to find that [Cibber] was an improper and dangerous Man … Cibber was therefore displaced for Macklin.' Victor, *The History of the Theatres of London and Dublin*, vol. 1, p. 31. In the counterfeit autobiography of Cibber, Fleetwood's decision is alluded to thus: 'I was a kind of Prime Minister: I say a kind of Prime Minister, for even then there was another Person shared amply in his Confidence.' *An Apology for the Life of Mr. T— C —, Comedian*, p. 102.

[79] 'To the *Author* of a *Letter* on the *Rivalship of Actors*, inserted in the *Gazetteer* of Thursday, Nov. 4.' *London Daily Post and General Advertiser*, issue 636 (13 November 1736).

[80] *Ibid.*

[81] *Ibid.*

let alone penned and published a protest against his authority – but the stakes were high:

> I am extremely sorry any Consideration should induce the Author of [the A.Z. letter] to make publick a Dispute which has happened behind the Scenes, and to put me under a Necessity of appearing in Print. The Injuries I have receiv'd at the Playhouse ... I determin'd patiently to submit to, well knowing, that by the Tenour of the Articles which I have *unfortunately* sign'd with Mr. Fletewood, I could not possibly receive any Redress until the Time for which I am engaged by those Articles is expir'd ... As to my having obstinately refus'd the Part of Lucy, I can only say in Answer, that by my Articles *it is not in my Power to refuse That or any other Part*: But that I have shewn an Unwillingness to surrender my own Part of Polly ... I confess is true ... this Unwillingness did not proceed from my Jealousy of Mrs. Cibber ... the true and only Reason is this: Not only the Part of Polly, but likewise other Parts (as could be made appear) have been demanded of me for Mrs. Cibber, which made me conclude ... that there was a Design form'd against me, to deprive me by degrees of every Part in which I have had the Happiness to appear with any Reputation ... And therefore to obviate this Design, which I apprehended contrary to a receiv'd Maxim in the Theatre, *That no Actor or Actress shall be depriv'd of a Part in which they have been well receiv'd, until they are render'd incapable of performing it either by Age or Sickness*; and for no other Reason whatsoever, have I endeavour'd to keep the Part of Polly ... if I thought it would in any Manner entertain or oblige the Publick, to whose kind Indulgence *alone* I stand indebted for all my Success as an Actress, I would not only most chearfully perform the part of Lucy, but any other inferior to that, either in the Beggar's Opera, or in any other Play or Entertainment whatsoever. As to the ill Qualities of Envy, Malice, &c. with which I am charg'd, (as I doubt not but every one who reads that Letter must conclude *who was the Author of it*) 'tis not necessary for me at present to say any thing in Justification of myself. And now ... I beg the Favour of those Gentlemen who have wrote upon this Occasion, to forbear publishing any more Letters ... which I am certain must appear extremely insignificant and contemptible to the Town ... *Your very humble Servant*, Cath. Clive.[82]

This letter was an *in propria persona* performance of extraordinary sophistication. Clive upheld prevailing notions of gender, award through merit, and the sanctity of legal systems and of private property. She offset any suspicions of her temerity by expressing humility, a sense of duty, and a reluctance to speak out. She portrayed herself as a victim robbed of a part that theatrical tradition dictated was hers. She established moral and intellectual superiority by abjuring the mudslinging to which Theophilus Cibber (A. Z.) had sunk. Clive also recalled the insinuation that Susannah Cibber's advancement was due to

---

[82] Catherine Clive, 'To the Author of the LONDON DAILY POST', *London Daily Post and General Advertiser*, issue 641 (19 November 1736).

string-pulling by emphasizing that she, Clive, owed her success to the 'kind Indulgence *alone*' of the public.

A series of front-page articles from 6 December shifted the Polly Row back onto seemingly more empirical grounds. Aping the name of the earlier 'Prompter' series by Aaron Hill about theatrical reform, 'Aequus' (Latin for 'impartial') and others penned a series called 'The Occasional Prompter'. This commentary fortified the notion that Fenton's soft, tender Polly had misrepresented Gay's intentions. According to this critique, Polly was an 'EXQUISITE JILT' whose representation was perfectly suited to Clive's temperament,[83] and Susannah Cibber 'fit for nothing else' but '*soft* and *pathetick*' parts to which Polly bore little relation.[84] Concurrently, more obviously pro-Clive reports appeared. 'A Spectator' concluded his contribution to the 'The Occasional Prompter' series with a poem, 'To Mrs. CLIVE, on the ungenerous Treatment she has lately met with'.[85] There was a '*Cantata*' on the same subject; though it was not published until 6 January 1737, a notice of 3 January ('*The Cantata is come to Hand*') implies its circulation well before:[86]

> HORACE Imitated. / Integer Vitae ['Upright of life and free from vice'], &c.[87]
> MERIT, Dear CLIVE, fears no Disgrace;
> It needs not C—'s *brasen* Face:
> It bravely dares th'envenom'd Spite
> Of *Snakes*, that *hiss*, but cannot *bite*.
>
> Whether you bravely tread the Stage,
> And dare the *hireling Catcalls* Rage;
> Or in the Green Room you abide,
> *Unmov'd*, your Rival's *envious* Pride;
>
> Assur'd remain, you'll ever find
> Each *gen'rous* Breast to *Merit kind*;
> *Merit*, which Prejudice has aw'd,
> And made *who* came to *damn*, *applaud*.[88]

There was even a report in a pro-Clive letter by 'Z. A.' that when 'a Lady in the Pit had the Misfortune to faint away; Mrs. CLIVE … in the middle of a *Song*, immediately perceiv'd it, and in great Concern ran off the Stage for a Glass of

---

[83] 'The Occasional Prompter. NUMBER III.', *Daily Journal*, issue 5865 (10 December 1736).
[84] 'The Occasional Prompter. NUMBER I.', *Daily Journal*, issue 5861 (6 December 1736).
[85] 'The Occasional Prompter. NUMBER IV.', *Daily Journal*, issue 5868 (14 December 1736).
[86] *Daily Journal*, issue 5885 (3 January 1737).
[87] Horace's 'Integer vitae scelerisque purus', the twenty-second poem in his first book of Odes, was among the author's most celebrated. Gregory O. Hutchinson, 'The Publication and Individuality of Horace's "Odes" Books 1–3', *Classical Quarterly*, vol. 52, no. 2 (2002), pp. 517–37.
[88] *The Occasional Prompter*. NUMBER XIII.', *Daily Journal*, issue 5888 (6 January 1737).

Water … [she] procur'd it to be deliver'd to the poor Lady, who by this means recover'd'.[89]

Theophilus Cibber had fewer sympathizers writing to support him. Abandoning his pseudonym, on 9 December he openly challenged Clive in a front-page press letter, just as she had challenged him. He blamed her squarely for the dispute: 'you … declared, you would rather *forfeit* those *articles* than *submit*; and would *a[l]arm* the *Town* to *discountenance any person* who should presume to appear in any character you laid *claim* to'.[90] He urged the Town '*no more to call this a Contest between two rival Actresses*, since Mrs. CIBBER *never pretended to rival any*'. In his view, this was solely 'a *dispute* between Mrs. CLIVE's *Will*, and the MANAGER's *Right*'.[91] Cibber was pushing back against an impish epigram of 25 November that had described 'the two Rival Ladies' battling as if they were Rival Queens.[92] Nathaniel Lee's eponymous tragedy had long been a favourite London drama precisely because it staged female rivalry,[93] and the Polly Row was easily made to seem its comic version. Indeed, two days before the publication of Theophilus Cibber's letter, the Polly Row had itself taken the stage as a farce about warring female principals.

Contending Colombines, or Amazonian Clive

The Beggar's Pantomime: Or, the Contending Colombines was a fringe theatre hit, reaching twenty-nine performances after it opened on 7 December 1736.[94] Shoehorned as a 'Comic Interlude' into the 1734 masque *Britannia: Or, the Royal Lovers*, this was functionally an independent ballad farce. Its climax featured 'Gossip Joan', a common tune that, like the farce's action, characterized Clive as a jealous first actress. 'Gossip Joan' is the music in *The Beggar's Opera* to which Polly and Lucy fight over who is truly Macheath's wife. Back in 1728, Gay's squabbling jades had immediately been recognized as a parody of the reigning *prime donne* Faustina and Cuzzoni, who were assumed to be rivals.[95]

---

[89] 'To the Author of the LONDON DAILY POST', *London Daily Post and General Advertiser*, issue 662 (14 December 1736).

[90] Theophilus Cibber, 'To Mrs. CLIVE', *Grub-street Journal*, issue 363 (9 December 1736).

[91] *Ibid.*

[92] 'An Epigram on the late Battle of the Female Dancers at Paris, and on the two Rival Ladies (for the part of Polly) here', *Grub-street Journal*, issue 361 (25 November 1736). The two 'Female Dancers' were Marie Sallé and Marie-Anne Camargo; see Berta Joncus '"In Wit Superior as in Fighting"', pp. 35–37.

[93] 'Actual women engaged in rivalries kept heroic tragedies such as Nathaniel Lee's *The Rival Queens* (1677), and other plays resembling it, viable.' Felicity Nussbaum, *Rival Queens*, pp. 61–62.

[94] For the opening night announcement, see *The London Stage*, Part 3, vol. 2, p. 621.

[95] William Schultz points out that this is 'clearly a reference to the quarrel between two rival singers, Cuzzoni and Faustina'. Schultz, *Gay's Beggar's Opera*, pp. 143–44. The tune circulated as a songsheet from around 1705. Barlow, 'Air 38', *The Music of John Gay's The Beggar's Opera*, p. 113.

Reset eight years later in *The Beggar's Pantomime*, 'Gossip Joan' tarred Kitty Clive and Susannah Cibber with the same brush.

The player Henry Woodward wrote *The Beggar's Pantomime*, and actor-manager Henry Giffard mounted it at Lincoln's Inn Fields, where it ran for two months, in two consecutive versions. The second version, which opened on 30 December, registered the gains made by Clive's party during the course of the month.[96] In both versions, the characters 'Colombine Lucy' (Clive) and 'Colombine Polly' (Cibber) trade insults to the tune of 'Gossip Joan', calling each other respectively 'Madam Squall' (Clive) and 'Madam Squeak' (Cibber). Clive's 'Hoarsen' throat and Cibber's 'bawling' manifest their lack of restraint.[97] In their exchange, Clive is accused of 'Affectation', 'Folly', and 'dark Design', while Cibber is accused of obduracy and inferior singing.[98] Also in both versions, Colombine Lucy shows 'Pride' and 'Spirit';[99] she claims that her rival dare not 'talk of Merit', and boasts that 'Musick was my Calling'.[100] She claims to be powerless to defend herself, despite having harnessed the press ('it shall, / In Papers soon come out').[101] And in both versions Colombine Polly discloses her ambition ('I will prevail, / And Act my Darling *Polly*'), while relying on her husband to realize her aims ('My *Little Man* / Does all he can ... / That *Polly* may be mine').[102]

Whereas in Woodward's first version Pistol (Theophilus Cibber) flaunts his power, lustily dispatching the tune 'Young Virgins love Pleasure',[103] this disappeared from 30 December. Instead an added Prologue, sung to 'Chevy-Chase', makes Clive a 'Fierce Amazonian Dame', the violence of whose rage paralyzes her opponents.[104] In the last-ever public reference to Clive being with her

---

[96] Sales of the original wordbook began on 15 December, according to a notice in the *London Daily Post and General Advertiser*, issue 662 (14 December 1736). The revised version that opened on 30 December 1736 was announced in the *London Daily Post and General Advertiser*, issue 676 (30 December 1736).

[97] [Henry Woodward], *The Beggar's Pantomime; Or, the Contending Colombines*, 2nd edn (London, 1736), pp. 15–17; [Henry Woodward], *The Beggar's Pantomime; Or, the Contending Colombines ... With New Songs, and several Alterations*, 3rd edn (London, 1736), pp. 12–13. Because the 'second edition' is in fact a re-issue of the first edition, I cite here the second edition, which has been digitized. To confirm there are no material variants between the first and 'second' editions I have compared one copy of the first edition – shelfmark PR1241 .O44 no.6 at the Kroch Library of Cornell University – with the 'second' edition.

[98] [Woodward], *The Beggar's Pantomime*, 2nd edn, pp. 15–17; [Woodward], *The Beggar's Pantomime*, 3rd edn, pp. 12–13.

[99] Ibid., 2nd edn, p. 16; ibid., 3rd edn, p. 13.

[100] Ibid., 2nd edn, p. 16; ibid., 3rd edn, p. 13.

[101] Ibid., 2nd edn, p. 20; ibid., 3rd edn, p. 16.

[102] Ibid., 2nd edn, p. 17; ibid., 3rd edn, p. 14.

[103] Ibid., 2nd edn, pp. 17–18.

[104] 'When as these Tidings came to Clive, / Fierce Amazonian Dame; / Who is it thus, in Rage she cries, / Dares rob me of my Claim.' Ibid., 3rd edn, p. 8.

husband, he is said in the 30 December version to have 'engag'd, / In Honour of his Wife ... And writ away for Life': that is, as if his life depended on it.[105] Pistol and his wife are 'discover'd, in Mourning'; he complains that 'Great Polly ... triumphant comes', and that 'My Spirit, like a Bladder swell'd with Wind, / At last will burst, and fall to—Nothing.'[106] Susannah Cibber's singing is now described as 'dismal Squeaks, and frightful Shakes, / Most shocking Squalls, and dreadful Breaks'.[107]

On the night that the revised *Beggar's Pantomime* opened, Drury Lane pushed back with a 'New Burlesque Tragi-Comic-Farcical Interlude' titled *Harlequin Restor'd* (now lost). This had little impact, apart from generating anger that it lampooned managers as well as players.[108] The Polly Row was then at fever pitch. Tremendous tension surrounded the Drury Lane production of *The Beggar's Opera*. When would it be mounted? Who would play Polly? Until the last moment, the outcome was in doubt. In the end, Clive had to comply with Fleetwood's reported earlier offer that she learn both parts and let the Town decide its preference. On 31 December, Clive, playing Polly – Hannah Pritchard took the part of Lucy – faced a hostile and potentially violent cabal. Its din brought the performance to a halt. Clive then improvised a public address:

> There was a prodigious uproar, with Clapping, Hissing, Catcalls, &c. Mrs Clive, who play'd the Part of Polly, when she came forward, address'd herself to the House, saying, Gentlemen, I am very sorry it should be thought I have in any Manner been the Occasion of the least Disturbance; and then cry'd in so moving a Manner, that even Butchers wept. Then she told them, She was almost ready with the Part of Lucy, and at all Times shou'd be willing to play such Parts as the Town should direct, and desir'd to know if they were willing she should go on with the Part of Polly; she behaving in so humble a Manner, the House approv'd of her Behaviour by a general Clap.[109]

In this speech Clive brought to the boards her earlier self-representation in the press: her powerlessness at the hands of managers, her modesty, and her willingness to submit completely to audience judgment. That evening Clive made her own history. She not only cemented her ownership of Polly, but she made her Polly the favourite of London audiences for the first time.[110] Not until 1744

---

[105] *Ibid.*
[106] *Ibid.*, pp. 22–23.
[107] *Ibid.*, p. 19.
[108] Joncus, '"In Wit Superior as in Fighting"', pp. 39–40.
[109] *London Evening Post* (1 January 1737); cited in *The London Stage*, Part 3, vol. 2, p. 626 (under the entry for Drury Lane 31 December 1736). I have not seen the primary source for this press announcement. For an alternative account of her speech see *Daily Journal* (3 January 1737); repr. in Joncus, '"In Wit Superior as in Fighting"', p. 41.
[110] After the Polly Row, the majority of *Beggar's Opera* London productions until the actors' revolt of 1743–44 took place at Drury Lane. When tenor John Beard joined the company

would Clive hand over the role, and then to a player of her choice: her protégée Mary Edwards, whom she trained in her every stroke. As for Susannah Cibber, she refused to comply when, during the next season's preparation of *Hamlet*, Theophilus ordered her to play the part of Ophelia, then owned by Clive.[111] Not until 1745 would she again challenge Clive over a part. That the prize was once again Polly, then owned by Edwards, attests less to the popularity of *The Beggar's Opera* – its draw dipped in the early 1740s[112] – than to audience desire for a Polly Row sequel.

By the end of the 1736–37 season, Clive's victory over the Cibbers, together with her portraits, bespoke vehicles, Oldfield line, and Arne songs, made her first rank as a songster and comedienne unassailable, for a time. The years that followed were her career zenith. Susannah Cibber's vulnerable heroines may have been irresistibly sympathetic, but as Clive showed on that last day of 1736, she could beat her rival at that game, too. Thanks to her voice, and the integrity it seemed to assure, Clive was poised to step into her grandest part yet: that of the Patriot Soprano.

---

in September 1737, Clive's ownership of Polly was strengthened. Barlow, '*The Beggar's Opera* in London's Theatres, 1728–1761', "*The Stage's Glory*", pp. 175–78 and Table 10.1, p. 170.

[111] See Chapter 7, p. 201.

[112] Barlow, '*The Beggar's Opera* in London's Theatres, 1728–1761', "*The Stage's Glory*", pp. 170, 176–77.

7

The Patriot Soprano: British Worthies at Drury Lane

Miller accommodates the Shakespeare Ladies' Club – the Licensing Act and Clive's short-term profit – John Beard joins voice with Clive – Frederick, Prince of Wales takes the public stage – Clive becomes Euphrosyne – Pistol vanquished by the Patriot Soprano

With the Polly Row behind her, Clive began a five-year reign as Drury Lane's first actress as well as its first singer. Otherwise unrelated circumstances came together to consolidate her position. Once Drury Lane hired Handel's young principal tenor John Beard in 1737, the house gained a vocalist whose musicianship matched hers, and he became her constant singing partner. Drury Lane continued to mount James Miller's vehicles for Clive, despite cabals organized against him. The Shakespeare Ladies' Club campaigned for Shakespeare productions, and parts with song were fitted to Clive. Not only did Theophilus Cibber's managerial powers continue to wither, but in 1738, scandal engulfed him and Susannah Cibber, and this couple, who in their separate ways had challenged Clive's progress, quit Drury Lane.

It was extra-theatrical politics that gave Clive her biggest career boost. Opposition to King George II and his first minister Robert Walpole, simmering for years, was newly inflamed in 1737 by Walpole's refusal to declare war against Spain in defence of British trade routes. Two Opposition flashpoints affected Clive directly. The first was Walpole's passing of the Licensing Act in June, which shut down all theatre companies without a royal patent and imposed censorship on any work to be mounted. The second was King George II's ejection from court in September of his son, the now-popular Frederick, Prince of Wales, who thereafter became a figurehead for the Opposition, which included a faction known as the 'Patriot Boys'.

The suppression of fringe theatres after the Licensing Act benefited Clive at first, by cutting down competition. As resentment towards Walpole's governance mounted, James Miller began to support the Opposition, writing Clive vehicles that doubled as the kind of dissent formerly expressed at fringe theatres. His first stage work in this vein was his adaptation of *Much Ado about Nothing* (1737). It was at once a call for more Shakespeare productions, the first legitimate Shakespearean sung part for Clive, and a signal of Miller's loyalty to the Opposition cause. Other writers soon joined Miller in adapting respected British poets into Opposition-styled Clive vehicles. The strategy was not without risk: the Lord Chamberlain banned Miller's final work in this vein, *The Camp Visitants* of 1740. Other Patriot comic playwrights were more careful. They toyed with playhouse sedition for an audience deprived of it, creating entertainments that ranged from harmless to discreetly provocative. Clive, the star of contrariness, was perfect for blurring boundaries between protest, which she could make seem an exercise of English Liberty, and entertainment. A prime example is *Comus*, the most prestigious stage work of her career. A seventeenth-century masque re-scored by Thomas Arne in 1738, *Comus* paid homage not only to its author Milton, but to Opposition figurehead Frederick. Yet Clive, sparkling *in propria persona* as the Goddess of Mirth, dispelled agendas.

Miller's foes from Oxford eventually silenced him even more effectively than the Lord Chamberlain could. Even without Miller, Clive would until 1743 preside in London as comic muse, Patriot soprano, queen of unruliness, and interpreter, chiefly in song, of Britain's greatest poets.

A Shakespearean Soprano at Drury Lane, 1737–41

Shakespeare had always been in the repertory of the theatres royal, but the number and quality of productions had dipped in 1720s.[1] From 1736 an initiative sprang up among 'Ladies of Quality', at whose 'Desire' Shakespeare productions were often mounted. By January 1737, the notice 'at the Desire of Ladies of Quality' littered announcements for Shakespeare plays at Drury Lane.[2] Behind these calls was almost certainly the Shakespeare Ladies' Club, led by Susanna Ashley Cooper.[3] She was the wife of the 4th Earl of Shaftesbury, and she and her husband promoted the Patriot Opposition and Prince Frederick.[4]

---

[1] Likely this was due to comparatively poor box-office receipts: from 1714 profit margins for Shakespeare plays decreased in comparison to what mainpieces by other writers earned. Hume, 'John Rich as Manager and Entrepreneur', *"The Stage's Glory"*, pp. 46–47.

[2] Ritchie, *Women and Shakespeare in the Eighteenth Century*, pp. 142–56. As Ritchie points out, Emmett L. Avery was the first to note that while 'Ladies' had earlier regularly called for Shakespeare plays, this kind of announcement was 'significantly present on every announcement of each performance of a Shakespeare play at Drury Lane in January 1737'. Emmett L. Avery, 'The Shakespeare Ladies Club', *Shakespeare Quarterly*, vol. 7 (1956), pp. 153–54.

[3] Michael Dobson identifies three of the club's members: its leader Susanna Ashley Cooper, Mary Cowper, and Elizabeth Boyd. Michael Dobson, *The Making of the National Poet: Shakespeare, Adaptation and Authorship, 1660–1769* (Oxford, 1992), pp. 146–57.

[4] According to Susannah Fleming, Susanna Ashley Cooper and her husband were 'undoubtedly influential' in the iconographic development of Vauxhall Gardens, and its 'careful promotion of the "cult" of Frederick Louis, Prince of Wales.' Susannah Fleming, 'Frederick as Apollo at Vauxhall: A "Patriot" Project?', *The London Gardener, or, The*

Clive had played Shakespeare roles before the Ladies' Club campaign, but her casting had been largely accidental. Desdemona, for instance, fell to her in 1734 only because the actors' rebellion left no one else available. Likewise, Clive ended up leading a ballad opera version of *The Taming of the Shrew* probably because James Worsdale, a portrait painter and libertine, had made Henry Carey one of his 'under Strappers in Poetical Stock-jobbing' whose work Worsdale could pass off as his own.[5] They had known each other at least from 1729, when Worsdale had painted Carey. *A Cure for a Scold* 'by J. Worsdale' was presumably Carey's adaptation of Shakespeare into a tale about an abused but spirited wife like Clive's Nell;[6] this ballad farce opened on 25 February 1735, and achieved only three performances.

James Miller's purposes were higher, as were his friends. Among the most powerful was the literatus James Harris, a fellow student from Wadham College. Harris's influential circle included the Ashley Coopers.[7] Known today for his collaborations with Handel, Harris was interested in serious stage genres, and he was a passionate advocate of Shakespeare. One of his friends, Robert Warner, asked Harris in March 1736 to 'hint ... to' Miller how best to adapt Shakespeare. Warner advocated excising the 'great absurditys' in the original while letting 'the rest stand as entire as he can'.[8] Were members of Harris's circle behind Ladies' Club productions? In the case of Miller's version of *Much Ado about Nothing*, almost certainly yes. Re-titled *The Universal Passion*, it opened on 28 February 1737 thanks to the Shakespeare Ladies' Club 'Subscription, this

---

Gardener's Intelligencer, vol. 13 (2007–08), p. 46. As Fleming explains, the Ashley Coopers contributed to debate and to 'covert oppositional activity' partly through an alliance with their neighbour George 'Bubb' Doddington, who also championed Frederick. James Thomson, in his adaptation of what had become a Patriot tract, *Alfred: An Epik Poem* (originally by Sir Richard Blackmore, as discussed below), praised the 4th Earl of Shaftesbury for his fidelity to Prince Frederick. *Ibid.*, pp. 54–55.

[5] A. C. Elias, Jr., ed., *Memoirs of Laetitia Pilkington*, vol. 1 (Athens, GA, 1997), p. 95. Matthew and Laetitia Pilkington also ghost-wrote for Worsdale.

[6] *A Cure for a Scold. A Ballad Farce of Two Acts. (Founded upon Shakespear's Taming of a Shrew) ... By J. Worsdale, Portrait-Painter* (London, [1738]).

[7] 'At the centre of the circle was James Harris ... he was related through his mother to the Ashley Cooper family, a critically important connection for his mental development.' Rosemary Dunhill, *Handel and the Harris Circle*, Hampshire Papers, vol. 8 (Hampshire County Council, 1995), p. 1.

[8] Letter of 13 March 1736, Robert Warner to James Harris, repr. in Donald Burrows and Rosemary Dunhill, ed. *Music and Theatre in Handel's World: The Family Papers of James Harris, 1732–1780* (Oxford and New York, 2002), p. 13. See also the letter of 15 November 1736, John Upton to James Harris: 'I hear from the learned world ... that Mr Miller has alter'd Shakespeares 'Much Adoe about Nothing' for our theatre this winter.' *Ibid.*, pp. 20–21. Also James Miller's letter of 1737 to Harris in which he asks Harris to look over a scene in his Clive-led comedy, *ibid.*, p. 42. Harris writes of 'Our freind [sic] Miller' and Warner expresses to Harris his sorrow at the failure in 1738 of Miller's *Art and Nature* and *The Coffee-House. Ibid.*, pp. 50, 52–53.

Winter, for the Revival of Shakespear's Plays'.⁹ Yet even with this support from Shakespeare and Opposition devotees, Miller proved more faithful to Clive's line than to the Bard.

The Universal Passion is in fact a stark lesson in the compromises that star production exacted even from a Shakespeare-loving and Patriot-minded playwright. After an adulatory prologue about Shakespeare, the Ladies' Club, and the rebirth of national taste,¹⁰ a play unfurls of which fewer than half the lines are Shakespeare's.¹¹ Clive played Beatrice, here renamed 'Liberia', which recalls her cry for liberty from managerial tyranny during the Polly Row. The non-Shakespearean lines were both Miller's and from Molière's *La Princesse d'Élide*, which Miller filleted to make points for Clive and sometimes also Theophilus Cibber – whose part, appropriately enough, was that of the jester Joculo, who defames the 'Spitfire' character played by Clive before she boxes his ears.¹²

Prior to this production, Miller had given Cibber most of the dialogue in his Cibber–Clive scenes; now, most went to Clive. But it was song above all that declared her the star of *The Universal Passion*: not only did she receive all of its six airs, but they reference her own history. For instance, to introduce her first air 'Let's sing and be merry', Liberia says, 'if I must undergo a Transformation it shall be into a Nightingale sooner than an Owl'.¹³ This clearly refers to Fielding, who in *Tumble-down Dick* had likened Clive's singing to an owl's screech. The song's refrain, 'For nothing like Rallery charms ev'ry Sense, / When we wittily laugh at anothers Expence', seems to expose Fielding's own

---

⁹ Francis Lynch, 'PROLOGUE. Spoken by Mr. HAVARD', *The Independent Patriot* (London, 1737): 'At Musick's Trunk the furious Ax he drives, / Nor fears Prevention from the Ladies Eyes. / By a late* Instance they seem well inclin'd, / To make the Ear the Passage to the Mind.' The asterix refers to the note: '*Alluding to the Ladies Subscription, this Winter, for the Revival of Shakespear's Plays.' Havard delivered the prologue on 12 February 1737, and this passage seems to refer to Miller's *Universal Passion* with its songs for Clive.

¹⁰ In his prologue Miller bemoans the corruption of British stage taste ('Britannia thus, with *Folly's Gloom* oe'rcast') and thanks 'ye Fair' – that is, the Shakespeare Ladies' Club – for their championship, begging them for their maternal favour: 'To your Protection Shakespear's Offspring take, / And save the *Orphan* for the *Father's* Sake.' [James Miller], 'PROLOGUE. Spoken by Mr. [Theophilus] CIBBER', *The Universal Passion. A Comedy* (London, 1737), page unnumbered.

¹¹ *The Universal Passion* is '15 per cent ... from Molière, 45 per cent from Shakespeare, and 40 per cent is the work of Miller.' Powell Stewart, 'An Eighteenth-Century Adaptation of Shakespeare', *Texas University Studies in English*, vol. 12 (1932), p. 100.

¹² In lying about what others say, Joculo channels past criticism of Clive: 'Joc. ... she has Beauty by the Grain, and Vanity by the Hundred-weight; Wit so light that it won't turn a Scale, but Ill-nature beyond all Weight and Measure; a Heart scantily enough furnish'd with any thing good, but most abundantly stock'd with Pride and Disdain. – And then she's such a Spitfire, such a Spitfire, said he, that whoever comes within reach of her is in danger of losing an Ear at least. Lib. [*Giving him a Box o' the Ear.*] That you may witness for him.' [Miller], *The Universal Passion*, p. 43.

¹³ [Miller], *The Universal Passion*, p. 13.

weapon of 'Rallery' as opportunism.[14] In Clive's final song, the lines 'I die for fear / Of what I must do when I'm marry'd' allude to her chastity and low expectations from marriage.[15] No notation appears to have survived from *The Universal Passion* of 1737 to show Clive's characterization in music; a single number engraved in 1741 likely derived from her benefit performance that year, and is discussed below.

What remains are the words Miller wrote for her songs, and these, as Irene Cholij notes, suggest a personality at turns spiteful and mirthful.[16] For instance, the second stanza of her first air opens with 'Let's lash and spare none, / For so modish 'tis grown'.[17] In her second song, Liberia boasts about outwitting the god of love ('None Cupid fear but Fools … He's Sweetness all … To those who're skill'd in Love').[18] For the single number that Miller didn't versify, he transplanted verses from a song in *Much Ado about Nothing* from a male character to Clive. Its words, with Miller's small alterations ('Virgins', 'Note of Woe') has the songster identify, and laugh off, the fickleness of men:

> Sigh no more, Virgins, sigh no more,
> Men were Deceivers ever;
> One foot in Sea, and t'other on Shore,
> To one thing constant never.
> Then sigh not so, but let them go,
> And be you blith and merry,
> Converting ev'ry Note of Woe,
> To *hey down, derry, derry*.[19]

For her epilogue, Miller has Clive charge 'the Poet' with omitting her best-known strokes from her epilogue. She then defends the British stage against foreign entertainers ('the squeaking, skipping Troops of Italy and France') and declares marriage to be 'the very Grave of Love'.[20] Both convictions could easily be read as Clive's own.

Protected by Harris's circle, Miller's *Universal Passion* opened on 28 February 1737 and ran successfully.[21] But even as Miller had been preparing his Shakespeare adaptation the previous year, a 'strong Opposition' had ripped off

---

[14] *Ibid.*
[15] *Ibid.*, p. 74.
[16] 'Liberia's songs reflect her personality … not just a merry, but indeed a spiteful nature.' Irena Cholij, 'Music in Eighteenth-Century London Shakespeare Productions' (PhD diss., Univ. of London, 1996), p. 61.
[17] [Miller], *The Universal Passion*, p. 13.
[18] *Ibid.*, p 27.
[19] *Ibid.*, p. 39.
[20] [Miller], 'EPILOGUE. Spoken by Mrs. CLIVE'. *Ibid.*, pages unnumbered.
[21] On 1, 3, 7, 8, 14, 21, 24, 28, and 31 March. In 1741, Clive chose *The Universal Passion* for her benefit of 14 March (see below); on 17 April that year Clive led *The Universal Passion* for Roger Wright's benefit. These performances are correctly cited in *The London Stage*, Part 3, vol. 2, pp. 642–45, 647, 650, 652–54, 897, 907.

his mask of anonymity as playwright.²² Miller was clearly the 'CLERGYMAN, who, instead of employing his Time in Works suitable to the Sanctity of his Profession, has already mispent it in writing ONE DAMNED PLAY, and TWO VILE TRANSLATIONS FROM MOLIERE, and is now making MUCH ADO ABOUT NOTHING', whom an anonymous author denounced in *The Daily Journal* in February 1736.²³ In 1738, Miller's character and stage ambitions would be savaged in two pamphlets. *The Universal Passion*, whose patronage and run were so promising, stirred up the resentments which would ultimately end Miller's playwriting career.

Clive nonetheless reaped advantages. With *The Universal Passion*, Miller proposed a model for stealing from the Bard that Thomas Arne would take up when composing for her. Four years later, tasked with supplying Shakespearean airs for Clive, Arne would also take verses from a Shakespeare character she was not playing to make songs that suited her. The practice began with *As You Like It* (from 20 December 1740), with Clive as Celia, and repeated itself in *Twelfth Night* (from 15 January 1741), with Clive as Olivia. For Olivia's 'Tell me where is fancy bred', Arne turned to *The Merchant of Venice*²⁴ for Clive to lodge another complaint against male fickleness. For Celia's 'The Cuckow', Arne borrowed from *Love's Labour's Lost* for Clive to gloat over a woman's power to cuckold a man.²⁵ The effectiveness of her singing in *Twelfth Night* was such that for sixty years after Clive, the previously songless character of Olivia was always given an air.

'The Cuckow' became one of Clive's signature airs (Ex. 7.1).²⁶ The singer of the 'The Cuckow' warns that spring heralds cuckoldry, as the cuckoo 'Mocks married men'. Downbeat emphases ('for THUS, sings HE') trip up the lilting melody just before the flute slyly echoes the dreaded 'cuckoo call' in the vocal line. The drawing out of the last two phrases (Ex. 7.1), the first through an

---

22 Miller, 'Preface', *Miscellaneous Works in Verse and Prose*, vol. 1, pages unnumbered: 'The next Dramatick Piece the Author undertook was the *Universal Passion*, against which there was a strong Opposition industriously fomented by some who were strenuous Enemies to the Writer, tho' why so, he knows not.'
23 *Daily Journal*, issue 5620 (28 February 1736); cited in O'Brien, 'The Life and Works of James Miller', p. 40. As O'Brien expains, a debate broke out in the *Grub-street Journal*, an Opposition mouthpiece, over whether Miller had contributed to its pages under the pseudonym 'Neither-side' to attack William Popple and undermine what turned out to be a stage flop, *The Double Deceit*. *Ibid.*, pp. 40–42.
24 Cholij, 'Music in Eighteenth-Century London Shakespeare Productions', pp. 13, 95.
25 *Ibid.*, pp. 22–23.
26 A snide poem of 1743, 'The SWEET SINGERS of our *Israel*', to be sung the 'To the Tune of *Blow, blow &c*.' (Arne's song, 'Blow, blow thou Winter Wind' for *As You Like It*, discussed below) acknowledges her signature airs: 'Kit Clive's all pleasing name, / When chang'd to Jobson's Nell: / The vain *Life of a Beau*; / The *Cuckow song* also.' From 'The SWEET SINGERS of our *Israel*. To the Tune of *Blow, blow, &c*', see the *London Magazine: and Monthly Chronologer*, vol. 12 (February 1743), p. 98. Other singers targeted are Thomas Lowe and John Beard.

Ex. 7.1 Thomas Arne, *The Cuckow. Compos'd by Mr. Arne, and Sung by Mrs. Clive*, 1740. Copyright © The British Library Board 30/9/2018. All Rights Reserved. Shelfmark: Music Collections H.1994.a.(67.)

ascending sequence ('O, word of fear', bars 32–35), the second through lengthening note values ('Unpleasing to a married ear', bars 34–40), heighten the teasing expressed in the words. Song can juxtapose elegance with sneering observation more readily than spoken words can. As a mocker of men in highly patriarchal contexts, Clive knew how to generate this tension, and her execution of 'The Cuckow' fixed it in this production of *As You Like It*, and in her solo song repertory.[27]

Thinking of Clive as Shakespearean songster can help explain why she owned Ophelia from 10 March 1735 into the early 1740s. Before Clive, the most celebrated Ophelia at Drury Lane had been Hester Booth (née Santlow), who, as a dancer, had brought to Ophelia 'melting lascivious motions airs and postures'.[28] In the version of *Hamlet* that Santlow and Clive performed, Ophelia has a long stretch of extemporized singing during her climactic Act IV mad scene: three stanzas of 'How should I your true love know', two stanzas each from 'Tomorrow is Saint Valentine's day' and 'And will a not come again', two lines from 'They bore him bare-fac'd on the bier', and a single line from 'For bonny sweet Robin is all my joy'.[29] Clive will have studied Santlow's manner of singing this music – in 1790 Tate Wilkinson would recall that 'Ophelia's songs were … imbibed and communicated … by the simple means of one actress conveying to the other, from recollection only' – and will have adapted its execution to her own taste.[30] Susannah Cibber's refusal in 1737 to follow her husband's orders to try to rob Clive of Ophelia, an act of defiance for which she was fined,[31] was likely due to the ballad singing by then required for this role. Also she would scarcely have wished to 'imbibe' the delivery of her rival Clive.

---

[27] Cholij, 'Music in Eighteenth-Century London Shakespeare Productions', p. 22. Clive earned a place in Francis Hayman's oil of the 1740 *As You Like It* that shows Hannah Pritchard as Rosalind and behind her Clive as Celia as they watch the wrestling scene. Ritchie, *Women and Shakespeare in the Eighteenth Century*, pp. 34–38. The painting is based on Hayman's drawing for Sir Thomas Hanmer's six-volume quarto edition of Shakespeare (1743–44) and may have been a demonstration piece for Hayman's Vauxhall supper-box decorations. Brian Allen, *Francis Hayman* (New Haven and London, 1987), pp. 16, 114, 151–5, no. 37, plate VII.

[28] 'Mrs Booth acts some things very well and particularly Ophelia's madness in Hamlet inimitably but then she dances so deliciously has such melting lascivious motions airs and postures as indeed according to what you suspect almost throws the material part of me into action too.' Letter of James Thomson in 1725; cited in Moira Goff, *The Incomparable Hester Santlow: A Dancer-Actress on the Georgian Stage* (Aldershot, 2007), pp. 122–23. Santlow, a principal dancer, took over the role from the legendary Susanna Mountfort, and earned multiple encomia for the physical grace that she brought to her Ophelia. Ibid., pp. 27–33.

[29] Cholij, 'Music in Eighteenth-Century London Shakespeare Productions', p. 131.

[30] Tate Wilkinson, *The Wandering Patentee; Or, a History of the Yorkshire Theatres, from 1770 to the present Time*, vol. 1 (York, 1795), pp. 17–18; cited in Cholij, 'Music in Eighteenth-Century London Shakespeare Productions', p. 132.

[31] The Egerton Manuscript 2320 contains the notice: 'Receipts: £82. Hamlet Posted for a week but put off upon Mrs Cibber's refusing to do Ophelia for which she was forfeited

Viewing Clive as a Shakespearean songster can also help us understand why one of her airs was probably misattributed to Handel. For Clive's benefit of 14 March 1741, Frederick commanded *The Universal Passion*, and its 'original Songs', to be performed;[32] eight months later, one air, 'I like the am'rous Youth' was issued as 'Sung by Mrs Clive in the Comedy call'd the Universal Passion. Set by Mr. Handel.'[33] Stylistically, the air bears no relation to Handel's other playhouse songs, and if Handel had provided music in 1737 his contribution would surely have been trumpeted – as it was in 1740, when he did write a song for Clive. But because by 1741 Clive was known to sing Handel's music, 'I like the am'rous Youth' could be credibly put out as 'by Mr. Handel' to improve its sales.

Clive needed to be perfect in stage speech, as well as in song, to win acclaim in her Shakespeare parts. We must imagine how her speech – its pace, crispness, exquisite diction, and natural melodies – made her feisty comic heroines persuasive. In February 1737 she led not just the *Universal Passion*, but Henry Fielding's new ballad farce for her – almost certainly commissioned by Charles Fleetwood[34] – *Eurydice: Or, the Devil Henpeck'd*, in which the gin-swilling, ballad-singing Eurydice rejects rescue by Orpheus to recklessly indulge herself in the underworld.[35] Fielding, in contrast to Miller, ignored Clive's emerging line, and his *Eurydice* lasted one night. By this point, the 25-year-old Clive stood not for licence, but for wit, youth, rectitude, sprightliness, Englishness – and above all, *propitious* sound. High-style song was a means for Clive to show audiences how best to speak, even as it permitted her to effervesce, flashing seeming insight into her own laughter-loving 'self'. That the Ladies' Club sought to define Britishness through Shakespeare strengthened her hand. She

---

five pounds – the Miser play'd instead of it.' See the entry for Drury Lane on Saturday 17 September 1737 in *The London Stage*, Part 3, vol. 2, p. 683.

[32] 'The UNIVERSAL PASSION. Alter'd from Shakespear. The Part of Liberia, to be perform'd by Mrs. Clive, in which Character will be introduc'd the original Songs.' *London Daily Post and General Advertiser*, issue 1994 (14 March 1741).

[33] '[T]his appeared in Book I of Walsh's collection *The British Orpheus* (see 11 November 1741) and surviving individual song-sheets probably derived from that source ... There is no autograph for the song, and no other source to confirm Handel's authorship. It is possible that this song had been performed in 1737, but in view of the publication date it seems more likely that it originated in 1741, for Mrs Clive's benefit performance.' Donald Burrows et al., ed., *George Frideric Handel Collected Documents: Volume 3 1734–1742* (Cambridge, 2019), p. 691.

[34] Hume, *Henry Fielding and the London Theatre*, p. 223.

[35] 'This Evening will be perform'd ... At the Theatre-Royal in Drury-Lane ... a new Entertainment call'd *Eurydice, or the Devil Hen-peck'd*.' *Daily Post*, issue 5442 (19 February 1737). According to the editors of *Eurydice*, what almost certainly provoked 'damnation' of the farce was the scene in which Eurydice, refusing to follow Orpheus, asserts 'that if she should be taken sick on the road, "no publick House dare sell me a Dram" [of gin]'. Amory and Goldgar, ed., 'Eurydice', *Miscellanies by Henry Fielding*, vol. 2, p. xlii. Goldgar and Amory omit in their critical edition the advertised subtitle '*the Devil Hen-peck'd*', which resonates, perhaps intentionally, with *The Devil to Pay*.

gave others ears to hear the music of a polite spoken English, and she translated speech into music. What truer ambassador for the Bard could there be?

'Miss Kitty' and Portia

Clive's most celebrated Shakespeare part was Portia, in which she did not sing. Her debut in the role was on 14 February 1741, the same night that Charles Macklin debuted as Shylock. Macklin is famously thought to have revolutionized acting on this night, displacing principal tragedian James Quin, who subsequently quit Drury Lane. By Macklin's own account, he had prepared for the role of Shylock through assiduous study of the 'unforeskinned race'.[36] The ferocity that Macklin brought to this character would come to be thought of as naturalist acting;[37] by our standards, as Joseph Roach has shown, it was stylized and melodramatic.[38] Audiences were riveted. King George II was reportedly unable sleep the night after seeing Macklin; later, wanting to frighten an intransigent House of Commons, the king is said to have asked Walpole, 'Vat you tink of sending dem to see dat Irishman play Shylock?'[39]

Particularly shocking was Macklin's acting in conjunction with his line, which he upended. Before 1741, Macklin had been familiar as a comic actor, known through nearly a hundred roles on the Drury Lane stage since 1733, but he had never before played a serious principal part. One of his most frequent appearances, from 27 October 1737, was as the Jew 'Beau Mordecai' in Clive's *in propria persona* hit, *The Harlot's Progress*, discussed in Chapter 5. By February 1741 Macklin had performed Beau Mordecai about forty times. The

---

[36] Francis Aspry Congreve, *Authentic Memoirs of the late Mr. Charles Macklin, Comedian* (London, 1798), p. 19. On Aaron Hill's leadership in this new school of acting, see Chapter 1, p. 25, note 97.

[37] John Hill was one of the earliest writers to take up Macklin's idea, found in Macklin's 'The Art and Duty of an Actor', that close observation and imitation were necessary to create a true stage characterization. In his influential article of 1943, Alan S. Downer was unequivocal: 'But that Charles Macklin was ever anything but a naturalistic performer cannot be questioned.' Alan S. Downer, 'Nature to Advantage Dressed: Eighteenth-Century Acting', *Publications of the Modern Language Association*, vol. 58, no. 4 (1943), p. 1012.

[38] Roach explains the means by which a mechanistic grasp of 'Nature' and of the proper depiction of 'universal passions' bred a formulaic and exaggerated stage deportment. Roach, 'Nature Still, but Nature Mechanized', *The Player's Passion*, pp. 58–86. A reflection on what 'naturalism' meant to its audiences, and Macklin's contribution to this conception, may be found in Goring, 'The Art of Acting: Mid-Century Stagecraft and the Broadcast of Feeling', *The Rhetoric of Sensibility in Eighteenth-Century Culture*, pp. 114–41, esp. p. 121, and in Robert R. Findlay, 'Charles Macklin and the Problem of "Natural" Acting', *Educational Theatre Journal*, vol. 19, no. 1 (1967), pp. 33–40 (special issue on English-Irish theatre).

[39] Edward Abbott Parry, *Charles Macklin* (London, 1891), p. 68; quoted in Emily Hodgson Anderson, 'Celebrity Shylock', *Publications of the Modern Language Association*, vol. 126 no. 4 (2011), p. 941.

1741 *Merchant of Venice* was the century's first production of this play that was somewhat true to Shakespeare, and Macklin seized his chance.[40] The Jew that Londoners had known as the Harlot's fool became on that 14 February Macklin's powerful, menacing, and unbounded Shylock. Macklin's careful preparation, which included touches of Venetian Jewish dress to his costume, helped him distinguish his Shylock from earlier representations,[41] and Shylock from Beau Mordecai. In one night, Macklin transformed himself into an affective heavyweight.

The Town also found Clive's Portia irresistible. Her nineteen appearances in 1741 alone, followed by sixty-three more performances before her retirement in 1769, helped make *The Merchant of Venice* the most frequently performed Shakespeare play of the mid-century.[42] Francis Gentleman, who idolized Shakespeare and David Garrick, thought her interpretation unacceptable:

> Mrs. CLIVE, who obtained no small share of applause, was a ludicrous burlesque on the character, every feature and limb contrasted the idea SHAKESPEARE gives us of Portia; in the spirited scene[s] she was clumsy, and spoke them in the same strain of chambermaid delicacy she did Lappet or Flippanta; in the grave part – sure never was such a female put into breeches before! – she was aukwardly dissonant; and, as if conscious she could not get through without the aid of trick, flew to the pitiful resource of taking off the peculiarity of some judge, or noted lawyer; from which wise stroke, she created laughter in a scene where the deepest attention should be preserved, till Gratiano's retorts upon the Jew, work a contrary effect.[43]

Benjamin Victor likewise complained: the '*Lawyer*'s Scene of Portia ... was certainly meant by Shakespear, to be *solemn*, *pathetic*, and *affecting* ... therefore the Comic Finishing which Mrs. Clive gave to the different Parts of the

---

[40] John Gross contends that Macklin persuaded management to replace what had been the staple *Merchant of Venice* production – George Granville's adaptation, *The Jew of Venice*, published and first performed in 1701 – with this anonymous adaptation. John Gross, *Shylock: A Legend and Its Legacy* (New York, 1992), p. 113. Cholij notes that 'we do not know exactly what text Macklin used'. Cholij, 'Music in Eighteenth-Century London Shakespeare Productions', p. 42. Below I draw on the earliest playbook printed after 1740, which appeared in 1745.

[41] Macklin added to standard costume features a short red beard and a red hat that he found out about from studying the dress of Venetian Jews. Gross, *Shylock*, pp. 94–95. The low comedian Thomas Doggett had forged and popularized the title role of Granville's *The Jew of Venice*, which was then passed onto other players. John O'Connor, 'Shylock in Performance', *The Merchant of Venice: New Critical Essays*, ed. J. W. Mahon and E. M. Mahon (New York, 2002), p. 389.

[42] Ritchie, *Women and Shakespeare in the Eighteenth Century*, pp. 30–34.

[43] [Francis Gentleman], *The Dramatic Censor; Or, Critical Companion*, vol. 1 (London, 1770), p. 297.

Pleadings (though greatly Comic) was not in Character'.[44] A decade later Thomas Davies would similarly judge Clive's Portia to have been 'buffoonery'.[45]

What was the appeal of Clive's Portia that escaped Gentleman, Victor, and Davies? Almost certainly, audiences flocked to see her perform anti-Semitism. She had in 1733 created Miss Kitty of *The Harlot's Progress*, who rejects and humiliates Beau Mordecai. In September 1738 Clive yielded the Harlot to a more junior actress, so Clive and Macklin had squared off against each other in *The Harlot's Progress* for the 1737–38 season only. The *Merchant of Venice* reprised, and dignified, a favourite onstage confrontation whose ideal casting, after having been taken away from the Town, was now restored.

While Macklin's Shylock shocked by its novelty, Clive's Portia amused and comforted with its familiarity. Clive, the patriotic wit, will have confounded the now-frightening Jew: her levity against his ferocity, her flippancy against his seriousness, her mimicry against his 'naturalism'. Their volleying had its parallel in the stage practice of '*returning the Ball*', according to which 'the Lady who acts with her Lover, plays up to him … with equal Spirit and Understanding'.[46] Clive's mock-pedantry likely swelled lines such as 'The quality of mercy is not strain'd', while her trademark vitriol will have infused her speech, 'Tarry, Jew. / The law hath yet another hold on you …', with Macklin matching her energy all the way.[47] Macklin would later describe the trial scene as one in which he 'wound up the fulness of my reputation: here I was well listened to; and here I made such a silent yet forcible impression on my audience, that I retired from this great attempt most perfectly satisfied'.[48]

Binding their stage legacies to the frisson of anti-Semitism may also have helped Macklin to escape his Irishness, and Clive to hide hers. As Kristina Straub reminds us, after 1735, when Macklin slew fellow actor Thomas Hallam in a backstage fight, his reputation was tainted for decades.[49] Macklin could be seen to personify the very worst of the intemperate low Irishman, a stage type that he indeed owned at Drury Lane.[50] Surely part of the thrill of Macklin's

---

[44] Victor, *The History of the Theatres of London*, vol. 3, p. 145.
[45] Davies, *Memoirs of the Life of David Garrick, Esq.*, vol. 2, p. 190: 'The uncommon applause which Mrs. Clive obtained in Shakespeare's Portia, was owing to her misrepresentation of the character: mimicry in a pleader … is but misplaced buffoonery.' Cited also in Ritchie, *Women and Shakespeare in the Eighteenth Century*, p. 33.
[46] *The Laureat: Or, the Right Side of Colley Cibber, Esq*, p. 43.
[47] William Shakespeare, *The Merchant of Venice. By William Shakespear* (London, 1745), pp. 56–64, at pp. 57, 61.
[48] [William Cooke], *Memoirs of Charles Macklin, Comedian* (London, 1804), p. 93.
[49] Kristina Straub, 'The Newspaper "Trial" of Charles Macklin's Macbeth and the Theatre as Juridicial Public Sphere', *Eighteenth-Century Fiction*, vol. 27, nos. 3–4 (2015), pp. 395–418.
[50] Macklin first played the character of Teague, the quintessential low Irishman, in the Restoration comedy *The Committee* on 26 September 1734. While the stage 'Irishman' was by no means uniform, London's stage productions were powerful means to classify and disempower according to ascribed national characteristics. Claus-Ulrich Viol notes

Shylock, as he prepared to cut out his pound of flesh, was knowing him to be a killer. Being vilified as the Jew onstage may also have been a means for Macklin to pass his sins onto a people held in even lower esteem than the Irish. Macklin's dark arts in identity politics disturbed German visitor Georg Lichtenberg, who after watching him in 1775 wrote: 'It cannot be denied that the sight of this Jew is more than sufficient to arouse once again in the mature man all the prejudices of his childhood against this race.'[51]

As Portia, swooping in to stay Shylock's knife, Clive brought more than just comic relief. Being disguised as a man, and robed as a barrister, will have added to her authority. That she was robed, and not in breeches as is often assumed – not least by Frances Gentleman in the quote above – seems clear. According to stage directions of 1745, Portia enters 'dress'd like a Doctor of Laws',[52] and an engraving of Jane Pope in the role for which Clive coached her surely captures Clive's own bearing and stage dress (Fig. 7.1). She will have spoken as the voice of English anti-Semitism as she brought Shylock up short: 'Thou shalt have nothing but the forfeiture, / To be so taken at thy peril, Jew.'[53]

---

a shift from about 1715 away from the Irishman as a wild, libidinous Papist to more gentrified types, such as the fortune hunter and the dueller. By 1760 the earlier defamatory characterizations had given way to the Irishman as an object of sentimental humour, though revivals meant that these stage characters were enacted concurrently. Claus-Ulrich Viol, *Eighteenth-Century (sub)versions of Stage Irishness: Prevalent Anti-Irish Stereotypes and their Dramatic Functionalisation* (Trier, 1998), pp. 38–52. Macklin later articulated differences between the Jew and the Irishman in an afterpiece he wrote, *Love à la Mode* (1759). Created to follow *The Merchant of Venice*, Macklin expanded Portia's first-act ridicule of her suitors to create a parade of ethnic types that court his comedy's heroine: the Jew 'Beau Mordecai', the Scotsman 'Sir Archy Macsarcasm', the Irishman 'Sir Callaghan O'Brallaghan', and the Englishman 'Squire Groom'. By turning ethnicity into spectacle, Macklin questions the ways the spectator sees, and thereby creates, identity. Michael Ragussis, 'Jews and Other "Outlandish Englishmen": Ethnic Performance and the Invention of British Identity under the Georges', *Critical Inquiry*, vol. 26, no. 4 (2000), pp. 773–97.

[51] Quoted without original source citation in O'Connor, 'Shylock in Performance', p. 390. See also Hans Ludwig Gumbert, ed., *Lichtenberg in England: Dokumente einer Begegnung* (Wiesbaden, 1977), vol. 1, p. 150. Lichtenberg watched Macklin's performance of 18 May 1775. The production that night was special because, as Gumbert explains, it was Macklin's first performance since October 1773, when theatre politics had forced him into temporary retirement. *Ibid.*, vol. 2, p. 93. Lichtenberg details in his report Macklin's dress and manner: 'On 18 May I saw Mister Macklin as Shylock. When he appeared on the boards, the clapping and calling was incredible, the whole house seemed to rejoice in the resurrection of such a worthy actor. He performed with much naturalness, and his yellow face, and the huge, artificially enlarged eyebrows gave him a kind of devilish Jewish appearance, which his own action made even more abhorrent. I could hardly hear him say the word *bond* and *three thousand Ducats* without horror.' *Ibid.*, vol. 1, p. 150, translation my own.

[52] Shakespeare, *The Merchant of Venice* (1745), p. 56.

[53] *Ibid.*, p. 61.

Fig. 7.1 William Nutter after John Boyne, *Mr. MACKLIN & Mrs. POPE in the Characters of SHYLOCK and PORTIA*, 1789. Stipple engraving. © Victoria and Albert Museum, London. Harry R. Beard Collection, given by Isobel Beard. Museum number: S.201-2009.

The Goddess of Mirth and the Celebrity Prince

The passage of the Licensing Act on 21 June 1737, and the banishment of Prince Frederick from court three months later, were stations along a slow build-up of opposition to what critics said was governance by Queen Caroline and her corrupt henchman Robert Walpole.[54] Anger at Frederick's dismissal was partly muzzled by the stage censorship which had been imposed in June. Audiences hungry for stage works critical of the government were denied them. In the masque of *Comus*, which opened on 4 March 1738, literary pedigree and celebrity dazzle hid the Opposition sympathies of its playbook and paratexts.

As the most important work of Clive's singing career, *Comus* fixed and celebrated her rank as London's first songster and comedienne. By 1738 Milton was revered by literati as an author equal in merit to Shakespeare and ancient classical writers,[55] and Clive led the very first playhouse adaptation of this poet.[56] Opposition writers, including *Comus* adaptor John Dalton, also viewed Milton as champion of civil liberties whose output could be harnessed to promote their aims.[57] Dalton teased out from Milton's wordbook a story of corrupt powers threatening virtuous youth that chimed with the rhetoric of Opposition leader Viscount Cobham and his 'Cubs'.[58] Dalton also worked closely with

---

[54] A scurrilous story in the *Grub-street Journal*, and its even more infamous engraving, both titled *The Golden Rump*, represent Queen Caroline as the 'High Priestess' of a court whose members worship King George's buttocks and receive his flatulence. Walpole would later claim that an anonymous playwright tried to mount a ballad opera version of *The Golden Rump* at Goodman's Fields theatre. The threat of such an offensive production – no copy survives, and it may never have existed – helped Walpole persuade Parliament to pass the Licensing Act. Vincent J. Liesenfeld, *The Licensing Act of 1737* (Madison and London, 1984), pp. 91–149.

[55] Dustin Griffin, *Regaining Paradise: Milton and the Eighteenth Century* (Cambridge, 1986), pp. 33–44.

[56] Berta Joncus, '"His Spirit is in Action Seen": Milton, Mrs. Clive and the Simulacra of the Pastoral in *Comus*', *Eighteenth-Century Music*, vol. 2, no. 1 (2005), pp. 7–40.

[57] Dalton also had a personal agenda: he was the lover of Henrietta Knight, half-sister to Henry St John, first Viscount Bolingbroke, the éminence grise of Jacobite Opposition. After bearing Dalton's bastard child in 1736, Henrietta was banished by her husband from her home and children to deepest Warwickshire, where she formed a 'Coterie' that included the Patriot poet William Shenston, whose output includes the pro-Frederick poem, *The Chace* (1735). W. P. Courtney, 'Dalton, John (bap. 1709, d. 1763)', rev. John Wyatt, *Oxford Dictionary of National Biography*, Oxford University Press, 2004; *ODNB* online: accessed 26 July 2017; Joan Lane, 'Knight [née St John], Henrietta, Lady Luxborough', *Oxford Dictionary of National Biography*, Oxford University Press, 2004; *ODNB* online: accessed 18 June 2018.

[58] Blaine Greteman, '"To secure our Freedom": How *A Mask presented at Ludlow-Castle* became *Milton's Comus*', *Milton in the Long Restoration*, ed. B. Hoxby and A. Baynes Coiro (Oxford and New York, 2016), pp. 143–58. As Greteman explains, Dalton's additional characters of Comus's followers turn the title character into the head of a court whose corruption and terrorizing of youth mirror the view of the royal court held by Opposition leader Viscount Cobham and his youthful adherents.

bookseller and Opposition protégé Robert Dodsley to disseminate the *Comus* wordbook, which Dodsley printed.[59]

Dalton assured audiences that Milton's spirit infused the stage action of *Comus*: 'His the pure Essence, Ours the grosser Mean, / Thro' which his Spirit is in Action seen.'[60] Even the title page of the 1738 *Comus* playbook printed by Dodsley and sold in the theatres aped that of 1637, naming Milton's seventeenth-century patron the Lord President of Wales in self-evident parallel with Frederick, Prince of Wales. The conflation of Opposition with Miltonic loyalties will have been more apparent to those in the know about Frederick's hand in earlier Milton projects: he had gifted a hundred punds to the poet Paolo Rolli to make the first Italian translation of *Paradise Lost*.[61] Rolli had dedicated to Frederick not just his *Paradise Lost* translation, but also his rendering of the *Comus* source text as an Italian opera libretto, entitled *Sabrina*.[62] The opera ran during the 1737 season of the Opera of the Nobility, which Frederick patronized in defiance of his family's loyalty to Handel and his rival opera company.[63]

Comus was a production devoted not just to Milton, and to current politics, but also to a cluster of celebrities among whom its pretended patron Frederick was only one. Because the playbook mixed serious with comic parts, and sung with spoken roles (as in *The Fall of Phaeton*), it could easily accommodate all the stars in its cast. The celebrated tragedian James Quin – Frederick's private tutor in elocution[64] – and Susannah Cibber took the lead speaking roles, and Clive and Beard sang. They were joined by Arne's wife Cecilia, whom Arne

---

[59] Greteman, '"To secure our Freedom"', pp. 153–57. Formerly a footman, Dodsley had received a vital leg-up from Alexander Pope, who, besides recommending his early poems, asked John Rich to mount Dodsley's first comedy, *The Toy-Shop* (1732), which was warmly received. Harry M. Solomon, *The Rise of Robert Dodsley: Creating the New Age of Print* (Carbondale, 1996), pp. 7–53, esp. pp. 40–44.

[60] [John Dalton], 'PROLOGUE', *Comus, a Mask: (now adapted to the Stage) as Alter'd from Milton's Mask at Ludlow-Castle ... Second Edition* (London, 1738), page unnumbered. The prologue and epilogue to *Comus* were first published in Dodsley's 'Second Edition' of the wordbook.

[61] Christine Gerrard notes that Rolli eventually pioneered Milton's reception in Italy, on the Prince of Wales's payroll. Christine Gerrard, *The Patriot Opposition to Walpole: Politics, Poetry, and National Myth, 1725–1742* (Oxford, 1994), pp. 61–63. On Rolli's translation, see also Greteman, '"To secure our Freedom"', pp. 150–52.

[62] Paolo Rolli, *Sabrina. An Opera for the Theatre Royal in the Hay-Market* (London, [1737]). Although in his preface Rolli called Milton an 'English Homer', he did not shrink from radically altering his text. See the introduction by Julian Herbage in Thomas Arne, *The Masque of Comus*, ed. J. Herbage, Musica Britannica, vol. 3 (London, 1951), p. x.

[63] Frederick never stopped supporting Handel, but broadcast his patronage of a company set up to destroy Handel's operas to provoke his parents. Carole Taylor, 'Handel's Disengagement from the Italian Opera', *Handel: Tercentenary Collection*, ed. S. Sadie and A. Hicks (Basingstoke, 1987), pp. 165–81.

[64] Frances Vivian, *A Life of Frederick, Prince of Wales (1701–1751): A Connoisseur of the Arts*, ed. R. White (Lewiston and Lampeter, 2007), p. 324.

decked out with four extravagant compositions.[65] Yet Clive's first rank as songster and comedienne was clear: she sang nine numbers, six of which were solo airs, and she was given two separate parts, the second of which was *in propria persona*. In the first two acts, she played a pastoral Nymph opposite Beard as a Bacchanal, and in the final act she played Euphrosyne, the Goddess of Mirth. This character Dalton took from a separate Milton source, the poem *L'Allegro*.[66] Clive alone among cast members both sang and spoke.

In the action, Comus (Quin), a son and cup-bearer of the god Bacchus, is disguised as a shepherd to lure to his palace a Lady (Susannah Cibber), who wanders lost in the woods. A Spirit warns her two brothers that their sister's virtue is imperilled. As they search, Comus's crew accosts them, but they prevail over the Bacchanals (led by Clive and Beard) thanks to a magic potion given to them by the Spirit. At Comus's palace the Lady, bound by a spell, watches a spectacle of airs and dances. Comus presses her to drink his enchanted wine, but her brothers arrive and drive him away. The nymph Sabrina (Cecilia Arne) releases the Lady from her spell, and in a finale the triumph of virtue is celebrated. Dalton and Arne made music dominate over spoken text, to Clive's benefit. In the first two acts, her songs are those of an Arcadian Nymph, who seeks to waken love through pastoral dance types and keys interlaced with dance numbers.[67] In the second act, Clive sang 'Fame's an Eccho' which is an air about her stardom: its fickleness, its fragility, its openness to manipulation. Here Arne darkened the siciliano – a dance typical of pastoral scenes – with a G minor tonality, and with phrases whose changing tonal centres depicted the shifting sands of public taste as Clive sang: 'To the best she's [Fame's] oft unkind, / And the worst her Favour find.'[68]

[65] Cecilia Arne sang 'Sweet Eccho', but 'behind the Scenes', intended to be heard as if sung by 'the Lady' (played by Susannah Cibber); 'Would you taste the noontide Air?', during which Clive gestured as if she were singing (see below); and two airs and a recitative ('How gentle was my Damon's Air!', 'By the rushy-fringed Bank', and 'Shepherd, 'tis my Office best'). The singers are indicated in the titles to Thomas Augustine Arne, *The Musick in the Masque of Comus. Written by Milton* (London, [1740]) and its subsequent issues.

[66] Michael Burden and Blaine Greteman have summarized the alterations that Dalton made to the 1637 wordbook. Besides adding air verses (his only notable contribution as an author), Dalton divided the First Spirit's long passages (originally performed by the composer William Lawes) between two Spirits and added individual lines in Acts II and III. Burden, 'The British Masque, 1690–1800', vol. 1, pp. 153–60; vol. 2, pp. 75–76. Besides re-arrangements and divisions of Milton's original, Dalton 'adds new characters, including several luxuriant members of Comus's rout' – followers of Comus, sung by Clive, Cecilia Arne, and John Beard – whose temptations 'heightened the effect of youth in peril and claimed it as an oppositional trope'. Greteman, '"To secure our Freedom"', pp. 146, 148.

[67] Joncus, '"His Spirit is in Action Seen"', p. 15. The duet for Clive and John Beard, 'From tyrant laws and customs free', relies on pastoral signifiers.

[68] The key shifts are from relative major, bars 10–12, to dominant minor, bars 13–19 and back to relative major, bars 21–24. Joncus, '"His Spirit is in Action Seen"', pp. 19–20.

The attempted Act III seduction of the Lady through enforced theatre-watching brings on Euphrosyne, whom Comus heralds as 'thou Goddess fair and free'. Descriptors identify Euphrosyne as Clive: she is the 'Nymph' of 'youthful Jollity' whose 'Quips and Cranks' provoke 'Laughter holding both his Sides'.[69] These words were Milton's own, borrowed from his poem *L'Allegro*. The joining of *Comus* with *L'Allegro* equipped Clive with an *in propria persona* role of the first rank. Clive's duties at Drury Lane were Euphrosyne's: to banish melancholy through illusion, as Arne's music suggests. Clive's opening Act III air, 'Come, come, bid Adieu to Fear', is a light-hearted gavotte in G major, celebrating her power to summon an imaginary empire of 'Love and Harmony' free from social constraints. In one of Dalton's additions, Comus then orders his followers to depict a lament scene designed to move the captive Lady to 'Pangs of gentle Love'. The stage directions read:

> After this Dance the Pastoral Nymph [Cecilia Arne] advances slow, with a melancholy and desponding Air, to the side of the Stage, and repeats by way of Soliloquy the first six Lines, and then sings the Ballad. In the mean Time she is observ'd by Euphrosyne, who by her Gesture expresses to the Audience her different Sentiments of the Subject of her Complaint, suitably to the Character of their several Songs.[70]

So while Cecilia Arne sang, Clive, standing centre stage, mimed, or more probably mimicked, the emotive content of Cecilia Arne's music – presumably for laughs. Euphrosyne then rebuts the lament, singing in the manner of an unruly daughter who mocks fops: 'Farewel Lovers, when they're cloy'd; / If I am scorn'd, because enjoy'd, / Sure the squeamish Fops are free / To rid me of dull Company'.[71] This and her subsequent air, 'Preach not me your musty Rules', sit uneasily with Milton's verses but snugly within Clive's line of outrage against fops and bores.[72] She spoke her epilogue 'in the Dress of Euphrosyne, with the Wand and Cup' of *Comus*.[73] Having appropriated Comus's props, the Goddess of Mirth celebrates her control of audiences and her power to destroy any fop that crosses her path: 'The mealy Fop, that tastes my Cup, may try, / How quick the Change from Beau to Butterfly.'[74]

Comus became the century's most performed masque, with Clive leading three-quarters of its roughly sixty performances by 1760.[75] Advertisements

---

[69] [John Dalton], *Comus, A Mask: (now adapted to the Stage) as Alter'd from Milton's Mask at Ludlow-Castle*, 1st edn (London, 1738), pp. 33–34.
[70] Ibid., p. 36.
[71] Ibid., p. 39.
[72] Ibid., p. 45.
[73] [Dalton], 'EPILOGUE, To be spoken by Mrs. Clive, in the Dress of Euphrosyne, with the Wand and Cup', *Comus … Second Edition*, [p. 62].
[74] Ibid.
[75] Roger Fiske characterizes the success of *Comus* as 'constant' from the third season onward, with eleven performances in its first season, and sixty performances at Drury

indicate the vocalists' gradual ascendance over speaking principals Quin and Susannah Cibber: on the opening night of 4 March 1738, notice of the singers was only 'Vocal Parts by Mr. Beard, Mrs. Clive' and others,[76] but by December 1739, Milton's 'New Masque' had become a 'Dramatic Opera', whose singers were listed as dramatis personae.[77] In 1741, as the vocal star of *Comus*, Clive travelled with Quin for a special summer season production in Dublin, where she took over Cecilia Arne's songs.[78] Here, Clive's 'Cuckow' song became the *Comus* finale.[79] Revising his masque *Alfred* in 1751, David Mallet would create for Clive a masque within a masque in which she, Euphrosyne-like, conjures scenes with her wand.[80] In November 1758 Clive finally stopped singing in *Comus*,[81] but at her 1761 benefit she chose *The Island of Slaves* by Marivaux with its part of 'Euphrosine', adding to that work 'a comic Opera Song in Character'.[82]

Lane alone by 1760, of which forty-three took place between the work's premiere on 4 March 1738 and the end of the 1743–44 season. As Michael Burden points out, *Comus* was the only masque composed as a full-length entertainment and the only masque to achieve box-office success during the eighteenth century. Fiske, *English Theatre Music in the Eighteenth Century*, p. 181 and Burden, 'The British Masque, 1690–1800', p. 74. As Ruth Smith emphasizes, *Comus* was a milestone in eighteenth-century Milton reception. Ruth Smith, 'Milton moderated: *Il moderato* and its Relation to *L'Allegro* and *Il Penseroso*', *Händel-Jahrbuch*, vol. 56 (2010), pp. 139–64.

[76] *London Daily Post and General Advertiser*, issue 1043 (3 March 1738).

[77] *London Daily Post and General Advertiser*, issue 1593 (3 December 1739).

[78] The dispensation of airs is partly captured in *All the Songs of Comus a Mask, as sung at the Theatre in Aungier-street. By Mr. Worsdale, Mr. Layfield, Mrs. Clive, and Mrs. Reynolds* ([Dublin], [1741]).

[79] I discuss Clive's ownership of Euphrosyne, and her deployment of the part to popularize herself during her summer 1741 tour to Dublin, in Berta Joncus, 'From "Ellen a Roon" to "Aileen aroon": Kitty Clive and the Irish Ballad'. Paper delivered at the conference *The Irish and the London Stage: Identity, Culture, and Politics, 1680–1830*, Trinity College Dublin, 17–18 February 2017.

[80] [David Mallet], 'EPILOGUE. Spoken by Mrs. CLIVE', *Alfred: A Masque* (London, 1751), pp. 67–72. Mallet revised *Alfred* – the original version of which I discuss below – under guidance from Aaron Hill, who advised him to increase the action. On the context for this version, see Michael Burden, *Garrick, Arne and the Masque of 'Alfred': a Case Study in National, Theatrical and Musical Politics* (Lewiston, NY and Lampeter, 1994), pp. 48–53.

[81] According to advertisements, she last performed Euphrosyne on 6 November 1759. On 23 November 1759, Clive's 'Indisposition' was announced, and the part of Euphrosyne was taken by a 'GENTLEWOMAN, who never appear'd upon the Stage before'. *Public Advertiser*, issue 7815 (23 November 1759). Thereafter, *Comus* passed to Covent Garden until 1777.

[82] 'The ISLAND of SLAVES … With a comic Opera Song in Character', *Public Advertiser*, issue 8234 (26 March 1761); cited in *The London Stage*, Part 4, vol. 2, p. 851. See also Victor, *The History of the Theatres of London*, vol. 3, p. 13: 'ISLAND OF SLAVES – a Farce, translated from Marivaux, brought to the Stage by Mrs. Clive, for her own Benefit, and performed that Night only.' Crean describes the post-performance paper war between Clive and Ned Shuter, who accused her of undermining English with French comedy. Crean, 'The Life and Times of Kitty Clive', pp. 320–33. In the 1930s, Crean corrected the

Presenting Clive to his readers in 1771, theatre historian Benjamin Victor would quote Comus's third-act speech. 'I cannot better introduce this Lady' Victor wrote, 'than by the following Lines from MILTON. "Haste thee, Nymph, and bring with thee / Jest and youthful Jollity— / Quips, and Cranks, and wanton Wiles, / Nods, and Becks, and wreathed Smiles— / *Sports*, that wrinkled Care derides, / And *Laughter*, holding both his Sides." As strong Humour is the great characteristic Mark of an English Comedy, so was it of this Laughter-loving, Joy-exciting Actress! – To enumerate the different Parts in which she excelled, would be feebly describing, what the Audiences have felt so powerfully'.[83] Thanks to Dalton's additions, Clive carved out a unique legacy for herself as London's singing goddess of mirth.

The Tragedy of James Miller

On 26 January 1738, fewer than six weeks before *Comus* opened, Drury Lane had mounted Miller's afterpiece *The Coffee-House* as its first new production after the Licensing Act. Adapted from a French comedy, it was a seemingly harmless *in propria persona* vehicle about how 'Cibber' (Theophilus) connives to release 'Miss Kitty' from her unwanted match to the money scrivener Harpie, probably so called to identify him as a Jew.[84] Theophilus fleeces Harpie at gaming; being stingy, Harpie refuses to pay, and being cowardly, refuses Theophilus's challenge to a duel. Harpie takes up the offer of Gaywood, Theophilus's co-conspirator, to fight on his behalf, and Gaywood pretends to kill Theophilus. Kitty's suitor Hartly then threatens to call the constable unless Harpie gives up Kitty; cue happy ending. Novelty took the form of the coffee-house guest Lord Bawble, accompanied by Lord Bubble. Beard took the part of Bawble, an effeminate worshiper of Italian opera who laments the real-life departure from London of the castrato Farinelli. Kitty counters Bawble's lamentation with 'Life of a Beau', a musical point during which she derides fops. Because it is the only number in Miller's farce by the then-marginal Henry Carey,[85] 'Life of a Beau' was probably added at Clive's behest. So closely did

---

misunderstanding at the time that Clive had been the author of *The Island of Slaves*. Patrick J. Crean, 'The London "Prentice"', *Notes and Queries*, vol. 163 (1932), pp. 346–47.

[83] Victor, *The History of the Theatres of London*, vol. 3, pp. 141–43. Line breaks have been inserted in the Milton quotation; Victor omits them.

[84] As he said in his playbook preface, Miller translated and adapted the comedy *Le Caffé* (1695) by Jean-Baptiste Rousseau to create this comedy. On its reception, see O'Brien, 'The Life and Works of James Miller', pp. 45–49. 'Harpie', homonym to the female Harpy of classical literature, is a noun meaning 'a rapacious, plundering, or grasping person; one that preys upon others'; in choosing this name Miller likely intended the dramatis persona to stand for a money-lending Jew. "Harpy, n.". *The Oxford English Dictionary*, Oxford University Press, 2018; *OED Online*: accessed 10 April 2018.

[85] The song is catalogued as '148. How brimful of nothing's the Life of a Beau' in Gillespie, 'The Life and Work of Henry Carey', vol. 2, pp. 44–45.

The Coffee-House cleave to its principals' stage personae that one critic scoffed: 'Mr. Cibber and Mrs. Clive, (as the *Irishman* says) *play'd their own Dear Shelves in Person*, and did it to so great a Charm that they resembled the Characters to the nicest Exactness.'[86]

Yet Miller, as an emerging Patriot writer,[87] tucked into Beard's first song, 'What dire Misfortune hath befel', some not-so-subtle agitation for war with Spain.[88] Farinelli, in leaving London, had broken his season's contract in order to enter the service of the King of Spain; Beard's song equates this with the action of the Spanish coastguards who had caught and punished British crews trespassing into Spanish waters in the West Indies. Bawble, as Thomas McGeary has shown, stood for supine submission to incursions on British rights.[89] This is almost certainly why, from the manuscript submitted to the Examiner of Plays for a licence, certain lines were struck through, such as 'Take all our Ships, take all our Men, / So we Enjoy but him again.'[90]

Into Clive's part Miller sneaked some subversive sexual politics: Kitty longs to own her own coffee house, where she will create 'a Room for the Women', arguing that ''tis an unreasonable thing that Women should not come to the Coffee-House.'[91] She sneers at men even in her envy at their rule-breaking: 'I should like such Doings my self; gallant all the Day, drink all the Evening, scour the Streets all the Night, break Lamps, knock down Watchmen, and make the

---

[86] 'APPENDIX', *The Usefulness of the Stage to Religion, and to Government ... with Reflections on the Taste of the Times* (London, 1738), page unnumbered.

[87] Although identified with incipient Opposition playwrights in 1735 – he derided Walpole in his *Seasonable Reproof* of 1735 – Miller only clearly expressed his views in stage works after the Licensing Act. See O'Brien, 'The Life and Works of James Miller', pp. 63–65; Ruth Smith, *Handel's Oratorios and Eighteenth-Century Thought* (Cambridge, 1995), pp. 192–94; and Thomas McGeary, *The Politics of Opera in Handel's Britain* (Cambridge, 2013), p. 347, note 134.

[88] [James Miller], *The Coffee-House. A Dramatick Piece. As it is Perform'd at the Theatre-Royal in Drury-Lane* (London, 1737 [1738]), pp. 8–9. O'Brien assumes this air to be a duet, but the song was announced in early advertisements as 'I. The Beau's Lamentation for the Loss of Farinello, by Mr. Beard'. The same advertisements show also that the year of publication in the playbook is a misprint; see the *London Daily Post and General Advertiser*, issue 1015 (30 January 1738): 'To-morrow will be published, With a Curious Frontispiece, THE COFFEE-HOUSE.'

[89] Thomas McGeary, 'Farinelli in Madrid: Opera, Politics, and the War of Jenkins' Ear', *The Musical Quarterly*, vol. 82, no. 2 (1998), pp. 383–42.

[90] John Larpent Plays, The Huntington Library, LA3, James Miller, 'The Coffee House', fol. 6r. Words in the final line are corrected. The Examiner appears to have made this correction and dated the manuscript 12 January 1737. See also O'Brien, 'The Life and Works of James Miller', p. 64; and Smith, *Handel's Oratorios*, p. 205. Citing Miller's *Coffee-House* as an example, Matthew Kinservik discusses the difficulty of identifying whether the mark-up in play manuscripts submitted for licence belong to the hand of the playwright, the two Examiners William Chetwynd and his deputy Thomas Odell, or other parties. Kinservik, *Disciplining Satire: The Censorship of Satiric Comedy on the Eighteenth-Century London Stage*, p. 113.

[91] [Miller], *The Coffee-House*, p. 37.

Constable drunk; rare, by the Stars! This is what they call *Raking*, isn't it, Captain? ... by the Stars, I'll rake with him.'[92] Much more shockingly, Miller makes clear that Bawble and Bubble are lovers. Apart from their emblematic names, Bawble's first air, when announced in the press, carried the title 'The Beau's Way of making Love'.[93] In Bawble's other air, 'Learn all from me to treat the Fair', his revulsion against the idea of conquering a woman is made explicit: 'For if to me they yielding prove, / From them I'm sure to fly'.[94]

The music of this second air is a snappy, through-composed bourrée that misbehaves. Following an unprepared lurch from G minor into its dominant minor, a high tessitura turns the words 'And how their Pride to stem' into a squeaky protest, while melismas on the words 'fly' and 'them' flounce around ridiculously (Ex. 7.2). Carey's music for Kitty's 'Life of a Beau' falls between Bawble's two airs, musically countering his excesses (Ex. 7.3). A minuet in the same key, Kitty's song is a model of correctness in symmetric four-bar phrases that comfort the ear with their predictability of rhythm and harmonic progression. But its formal qualities melt under the heat of Kitty's rising disgust, expressed in ascending sequences ('a Beau, / a Beau'). The climax is a sustained high note, on which Clive will almost certainly have improvised. After this expression of rage, her vocal line adheres strictly to the triad as control is regained. In the fourth stanza, Kitty recognizes that Bawble and Bubble are lovers: 'For they still must be beasted, who've – Nothing at all.'[95] 'Life of a Beau' became a Clive trademark, introduced to interludes and comedies, and published in songsheets, miscellanies, and collections,[96] its homophobia

---

[92] *Ibid.*, pp. 29–30.
[93] '5. The Beau's Way of making Love, by Mr. Beard'. *London Daily Post and General Advertiser*, issue 1015 (30 January 1738); see also *Daily Gazetteer*, issue 803 (30 January 1738).
[94] The stanzas in full read: 'Learn all from me to treat the Fair, / And how their Pride to stem; / For if for me they do not care, / No more care I for them. / Amidst a Thousand Belles I rove, / And a true Beau still am I; / For if to me they yielding prove, / From them I'm sure to fly.' [Miller], *The Coffee-House*, p. 32. Miller's characterization is an early example of a fop preferring men, rather than sexually preying on women, a transition treated in Straub, 'Colley Cibber's Fops: Actors and Homophobia', *Sexual Suspects*, pp. 47–68.
[95] [Miller], *The Coffee-House*, pp. 30–31.
[96] 'The Life of Beau' was grafted onto five stage works: Fielding's *The Miser* (11 April 1738); Miller's *The Man of Taste* (13 May 1738, Miller's benefit); *The City Wives' Confederacy* (29 May 1738), at the 'End of the Farce' (*London Daily Post and General Advertiser*, issue 1117, 29 May 1738); *The Amorous Widow* (19 May 1739), which included 'new Song in Character' by Carey and 'The Life of a Beau' at the 'End of the Play' (*London Daily Post and General Advertiser*, issue 1422, 19 May 1729); and Garrick's *Lethe* (15 April 1740), 'The *Life of a Belle*, &c. in Imitation of The *Life of Beau*' (*London Daily Post and General Advertiser*, issue 1708, 15 April 1740). Engravers sold 'Life of a Beau' in multiple songsheets and in collections, two of which featured illustrated songs with headpieces. George Bickham engraved the first song with headpiece in his series *Musical Entertainer*, issued in fascicles (usually of four songs) from 1737 to 1739, which were then gathered into volumes. Bundled into the second volume, on page '50', the song is titled 'The Beau' with the

Ex. 7.2 Words by James Miller, music by Henry Burgess, 'SONG' in *The Coffee House*, 1738. The Bodleian Libraries, University of Oxford. Shelfmark: Douce M 198* (1).

For the rest of the epilogue, 'Mrs. CLIVE' implores the Ladies for justice: 'We're Sure you cannot See a Guiltless Play / Judg'd Cast & Executed in one day.'[102]

Clive's onstage appeal was brilliant, but futile. In his playbook's dedication, Miller describes the vindictiveness with which that night's cabal targeted him rather than his work. Even before the opening night, 'Destruction was loudly threatn'd.'[103] A gentleman told Miller afterwards that 'he never knew a Play destroy'd with so much Art; its Enemies suffering those Things to pass without Disturbance which were of an indifferent Nature … but giving no Quarter to the Parts which they thought would entertain.'[104] By these means, his 'Opposers' ensured 'that others should not judge whether [*Art and Nature*] pleas'd them or not', which kept it from 'being perform'd a second Time.'[105] As Miller notes, second-night performances had rescued several of London's 'best Plays' – *The Provok'd Husband*, *The Drummer*, *The Way of the World* – which like his comedy, had faced first-night cabals.[106] By disrupting only the best scenes, Miller's enemies made sure that *Art and Nature* died on its first night.

In two nasty pamphlets of 1738, Miller's enemies revealed themselves to be intimates from Miller's university days. The first, which appeared on 18 March 1738, was *The Pigeon-Pye, or a King's Coronation*.[107] Formed as 'an Oratorio, Opera or Play, according to the Modern Taste', its action takes place at Wadham College and its dramatis personae are the fellows whom Miller had lampooned in *The Humours of Oxford*.[108] Its plot revolves around the humiliation of Miller ('Windmill') when he is discovered by his peers eating pigeon pie instead of attending the king's coronation. Miller's past and present merge when Clive appears on the page as 'Jenny Whettum' – an emblematically sluttish name – who coquettes with Windmill.

In a dig at Clive's recent debut as Euphrosyne, the writer has Jenny Whettum appear 'Dress'd like one of the Muses, in a tatter'd Garb' to deliver a

---

[102] Ibid.
[103] [Miller], 'To the Right Honourable the LADY ***', *Art and Nature. A Comedy*, pages unnumbered.
[104] Ibid.
[105] Ibid.
[106] Ibid.
[107] '*This Morning was drawn piping hot out of the Oven*, The Pigeon-Pye, or a King's Coronation: Proper Materials for forming an Oratorio, Opera or Play, according to the Modern Taste; to be represented in Opposition to the *Dragon of Wantley*.' *London Evening Post*, issue 1613 (16–18 March 1738).
[108] Ibid. O'Brien identifies the protagonists: 'The *Pigeon-Pye* tells a story that involves Miller and a character named "Guzzlewight", who has a servitor called "Jo Trapes". The first name obviously suggests the Warden and the second, Joseph Trapp, who was also a Fellow of Wadham … The Warden in the *Pigeon-Pye* is called Dunster. Thomas Dunster had been Warden of Wadham from 1689–1719. He was succeeded by William Baker, and four years later by Thistlethwayte.' O'Brien, 'The Life and Works of James Miller', p. 17.

pro-Opposition epilogue, which she sings.[109] The affective tomfoolery of Jenny hints at Clive's own practices as a vocalist: she 'laments (in *Piano*) the ... Act of Parliament [the Licensing Act] ... Then she drops into a melancholy Exclamation (to the Sound of the Lute) how polite Sense will be abandon'd, lost, forgotten ... at the Conclusion of which, the Muse bids adieu ... expiring.'[110] In the 'DIRECTIONS FOR A PREFACE' to *The Pigeon-Pye*, Windmill is depicted using his own 'Dung' to fertilize his works ('Flower-Pots'), and the drama concludes with him making 'an horrible Stink' by hiding his pigeon pie under his mattress.[111] *The Pigeon-Pye* also takes a swipe at Handel: the second scene's 'Chorus of ... Tutor, Pupil, and Bed-maker' is 'set to Music by Mr Handel, *before 'tis compos'd*'.[112] Normally, a wordbook was first written by a librettist, then set by a composer. To suggest that Handel reversed this process – that is, wrote the music before the words were written – was intended perhaps to mock his habit of recycling his own music. Overblown musical rhetoric is the target in Windmill's 'Sighs and throbbing Accents, whilst the Music plays something out of Handel's *Esther*, not improper for a Person going to *suffer*',[113] and in the 'Lamentation for Windmill's Misfortune', which is set to 'one of Handel's Organ-Tunes' – this being an allusion to the organ solos Handel wrote to play in his subscription series.[114] Such comments may perhaps have taken aim not just at the composer, but at 'brother Handelists', led by James Harris, who had patronized Miller.[115]

The second pamphlet, *The Breeches, a Tale. Inscribed to the Fair of Great-Britain*, appeared six months later, in October 1738.[116] The pamphlet is in three parts. A prose 'Dedication' is followed by two poems – an 'Introduction' and a 'TALE. / Inscribed to the FAIR of Great Britain, by a Friend to the Sex'. In the

---

[109] 'Christopher Columbario', 'THE EPILOGUE. BEING AN Epilogue *upon all* Epilogues; Or, a final Period to all STAGE-PLAYS. Spoken by Miss JENNY WHETTUM, *Dress'd like one of the Muses, in a tatter'd Garb*, &c. *Vide* the Muses in Lord Cobham's Gardens', *The Pigeon-Pye, or, a King's Coronation* (London, 1738), p. 49–50.

[110] *Ibid*.

[111] *Ibid*., pp. 11–14, 48. I disagree with O'Brien's characterization of *The Pigeon-Pye* as 'a light-hearted parody of an opera scenario purporting to be based on an incident of Miller's student days a decade earlier'. O'Brien, 'The Life and Works of James Miller', p. 52.

[112] *The Pigeon-Pye*, pp. 22–23.

[113] *Ibid*., p. 37.

[114] *Ibid*., p. 41. By 1738, Handel had performed his organ concertos at performances in March and April 1735 at revivals of *Esther, Deborah*, and *Athalia*, and in 1736 to *Alexander's Feast*.

[115] The term 'brother Handelists' comes from a letter of 11 January 1739 from the 4th Earl of Shaftesbury to James Harris. See Burrows and Dunhill, ed., *Music and Theatre in Handel's World*, p. 68. Commentary about Handel in *Pigeon-Pye* is reprinted in Burrows et al., ed., *George Frideric Handel Collected Documents: Volume 3 1734–1742*, pp. 371–74.

[116] 'This Day is publish'd ... THE BREECHES'. *London Evening Post*, issue 1705 (17–19 October 1738).

dedication, we read that Miller has just '*half* a *College* Education got'; further, he is a 'half *Parson* ... Jacobite and *Jew*' who loads his own '*Dung*' onto writings stolen from others, for example in his *Man of Taste* and *Humours of Oxford*.[117]

The introduction that follows is an imaginary dialogue between the thresher-poet Stephen Duck and his wife Sarah Big, a housekeeper to Queen Caroline. Duck was a grotesque figure for many: a farm labourer who had taught himself poetry, and whom Caroline had in 1735 made resident 'hermit' in her Gothic installation, 'Merlin's Cave', in the Royal Gardens at Richmond.[118] Alluding to the authority of her mistress Queen Caroline, Big asks her husband to 'unfold, / Who rul'd the *Roast* in Times of *Old*? / To whom the *Breeches* did pertain, / Whether to *Woman*, or to *Man*?'[119] Duck accordingly relates the third part of *The Breeches*, a 'TALE. / Inscribed to the FAIR of Great Britain'.[120] This garbled misogynist rant, which maligns Miller as well as public women like Queen Caroline and the authoress Eliza Haywood,[121] is of a scurrility that shocks even by early Georgian standards. In the pamphlet's final lines, the author ridicules the '*scribling* M[iller]' whose nonsense belies that he is Oxford 'bred'. Suggesting that Miller thinks that Eve dominated Adam, the pamphleteer depicts Miller as the servant of sex- and power-hungry women.[122]

It was not Miller's Patriot sympathies that killed his playwriting career, it was *The Humours of Oxford*. Its 'lively representation of the follies and vices of the students of that place', Theophilus Cibber would later write, 'procured the

---

[117] *The Breeches, a Tale. Inscribed to the Fair of Great-Britain. With a Satyrical Introduction* (London, 1738), pp. v–viii, esp. pp. v, vii. Each of the three sections ('Dedication', 'Introduction', 'Tale') is separately paginated.

[118] Ibid. Queen Caroline appointed Duck to be Yeoman of the Guard and Keeper of Duck Island in St. James's Park. She worked with others from 1731 to 1735 to create a library in Merlin's Cave through which Duck could continue his self-education. Joanna Marschner, *Queen Caroline: Cultural Politics at the Early Eighteenth-Century Court* (London and New Haven, 2014), pp. 84–85, 135–36. Writings critical of Duck are discussed in William J. Christmas, '"From Threshing Corn, He Turns to Thresh His Brains": Stephen Duck as Laboring-Class Intellectual', *The Working-Class Intellectual in Eighteenth- and Nineteenth-Century Britain*, ed. A. Krishnamurthy (Farnham, 2009), pp. 25–48.

[119] 'Introduction', *The Breeches*, p. 10.

[120] 'The Breeches, a Tale', *The Breeches*, p. 1. The 'Tale' tells of John and his wife Sukey, an 'am'rous *Dame*' of unquenchable lust. Besides endless copulation, Sukey desires to write, but John fears that '*Three dull Dupes*' – Eliza Haywood, James Ralph, and Henry Carey – may 'instruct her' and take '*Poetica Licentia*'. The mention of Carey and his 'dull *Tune*' may have been a swat at Carey's former pupil, Clive. Ibid., pp. 4, 8.

[121] Alexander Pope's attack on Haywood in his *Dunciad* is typical of defamation of her, capturing the 'familiar figure of the woman writer that Susan Gubar calls the female Augustan monster'. Christine Blouch, 'Eliza Haywood and the Romance of Obscurity', *Studies in English Literature*, vol. 31, no. 3 (1991), pp. 535–52, esp. p. 540. The abuse that Haywood faced is charted in King, *A Political Biography of Eliza Haywood*.

[122] The 'Tale' ends with John saying that Eve 'wore the BREECHES' made from '*Fig-tree Leaves*'. John knows this because he was 'at Oxford ... bred' and apes the '*scribling* M[iller]'. Ibid., p. 9.

author many enemies'.[123] Chief among the 'follies and vices' in question were surely the sex crimes of College Warden Robert Thistlethwayte, which soon caught up with him. He quit his wardenship in February 1739 and his other posts soon thereafter, fleeing to France that summer to escape prosecution.[124] His exile may have further stoked the fury of Miller's opponents, who on 15 November 1739 quashed his last Clive vehicle to reach the stage, *An Hospital for Fools*, discussed in Chapter 11.

Even after *An Hospital for Fools*, Miller kept trying. But his next comedy, *The Camp Visitants* (1740) was a misstep: Miller put Opposition politics so much before good sense that, exceptionally, the Lord Chamberlain banned his comedy outright; not even Clive's diversions could hide Miller's intentions.[125] Clive's 'Lucy' in *The Camp Visitants* is descended from Fielding's Lucy in *The Virgin Unmask'd*. But in *The Camp Visitants* Miller took over Clive's voice to pointedly impugn the manhood of British soldiers. In the action, Lucy is a fruit-seller among encamped troops waiting to be dispatched against Spain. She helps Captain Freelove escape an unwanted match with the rich Miss Molly Sparkish, who has pursued him since falling in love with him at Bath. While Sparkish could settle Freelove's debts, he is in love with Harriet, who hides within the camp. Lucy helps Freelove escape his creditors, whose corrupt practices she reveals.

While the plot itself is harmless, the verses to Lucy's opening song question the courage of the British troops in salacious terms: 'Pray look at my Peach here, you Warriors so stout, / Which, like you, is so red & so rough all without, / But trust me, fierce Sirs! if you strip off its Skin, / 'Tis, like You too, quite harmless & melting within'.[126] Equally inflammatory is the 'MARTIAL SONG for Mr LOWE', which complains about Walpole not dispatching troops that have been levied: 'Maids, for War content to part, / Think their Lovers stay

---

[123] Theophilus Cibber, 'The LIFE of the Revd. Mr. James Miller', *The Lives of the Poets of Great-Britain and Ireland. By Mr. Cibber and other Hands*, vol. 5 (London, 1753), p. 332. Doubts around whether or how much Cibber contributed to this five-volume series are outlined by O'Brien, who gives strong evidence that Cibber indeed wrote the entry on Miller. O'Brien, 'The Life and Works of James Miller', pp. 10–12.

[124] Rousseau, 'Privilege, Power and Sexual Abuse in Georgian Oxford', *Children and Sexuality*, pp. 147–49. Rousseau explains that Thistlethwayte tried to obstruct the investigation before the case became a criminal matter rather than merely one of university discipline. When the tutor Swinton failed to show by command of the university's Vice Chancellor, the witness who came forward in his absence was a college servant, who testified that Thistlethwayte had raped him. By the summer of 1739 Thistlethwayte had resigned all his posts, in Oxford, Westminster, and Wiltshire, and fled to Boulogne, where he died on 4 February 1744.

[125] Manager Charles Fleetwood applied for this play's licence on 11 December 1740. Its refusal and the grounds for its refusal are undocumented, which is not without precedence. O'Brien, 'The Life and Works of James Miller', pp. 72–73.

[126] John Larpent Plays, The Huntington Library, LA23, p. 1.

too long'.[127] Not only did *The Camp Visitants* never reach the boards, it never even reached print. As a translator, a crafter of vehicles respectful of Clive's line and her concerns, and a writer who was in turn respected by the Harris circle, Miller helped Clive's progress – for a time. By 1740 he had become a liability.

'Songs' and 'Publick Affairs': Life after Miller

Clive's other Opposition farces measure the distance between Miller's activism and other writers' commercialism. Patriotism was invoked by their titles, but their action was derived from native ballads. As a sequel to his hit *The King and the Miller of Mansfield* (1737), Robert Dodsley wrote *Sir John Cockle at Court* (1738). Whereas the former, based on the eponymous ballad, openly lionizes Frederick,[128] the latter is an empty sentimental tale with Clive *in propria persona*. Clive led also Dodsley's next comedy, *The Blind Beggar of Bethnal Green* (1741). Based on another ballad of same name, its plot is as vacuous as that of *Sir John Cockle*, in this case showing the conduct of an ideal daughter.[129] While ballad-derived comedy may have aimed to consolidate an imagined community of Britons, as Suzanne Aspden argues, when Clive stepped forward her own self-performance tended to drown out other messages.[130]

Nowhere is this clearer than in *Britons, Strike Home* (1739), which opened on 31 December 1739. Taking its title from a chorus by Henry Purcell,[131] this

---

[127] *Ibid.*, p. 27.
[128] Solomon describes this comedy as both an 'egalitarian manifesto' and a moral tale depicting Frederick as the Patriot King. Solomon, *The Rise of Robert Dodsley*, pp. 53–60. *The King and the Miller of Mansfield* became part of Vauxhall's iconographic programme when Francis Hayman's oil of its final scene was hung in Prince Frederick's private pavilion. The political implications of this and other Vauxhall installations, most notably of the Prince's 'Patriot' Pavilion, are described in Teri J. Edelstein, 'The Paintings', *Vauxhall Gardens*, ed. T. J. Edelstein (New Haven, CT, 1983), pp. 31–32.
[129] Clive took the part of the daughter Bess who, refusing the advances of Lord Ranby, stands by her blind father. Robert Dodsley, *The Blind Eeggar of Bethnal Green* (London, 1741).
[130] Suzanne Aspden, 'Ballads and Britons: Imagined Community and the Continuity of "English" Opera', *Journal of the Royal Musical Association*, vol. 122, no. 1 (1997), pp. 24–51. Aspden writes that the rash of entertainments after 1728 based on oral ballads found in *A Collection of Old Ballads* (London, 1723–25) helped to articulate notions of Britishness, in music and in words. Another conduit for representing the nation was the She-tragedy, which flourished after Glorious Revolution. As Brett Wilson has shown, its playwrights designed heroines to shape 'a political discourse of national feeling and national belonging'. Brett D. Wilson, *A Race of Female Patriots: Women and Public Spirit on the British Stage, 1688–1745* (Lewisburg, PA, 2012), p. 193.
[131] Purcell's chorus came from John Fletcher and Francis Beaumont's *Bonduca* (Act II, scene 2). Curtis Price considers the chorus music vacuous, as befit a 'cheap' revival designed to incite patriotic fervour. Price, *Henry Purcell and the London Stage*, pp. 119–25.

has all the trappings of an Opposition *cri de coeur* for war with Spain.[132] In 1731 a Spanish coastguard patrolling off Florida was said to have cut off the ear of one Captain Jenkins – Jenkins reportedly displayed his ear, in a jar, to Parliament as evidence – and this incident became a flashpoint in the Opposition campaign for war with Spain. Against Walpole's wishes, on 23 October 1739 Britain declared what became known as the War of Jenkins' Ear. After Admiral Vernon's victory at Porto Bello on 22 November, Purcell's 'Britons strike Home' became a quasi-national anthem in celebrations across the nation honouring Vernon.[133] But the Drury Lane *Britons, Strike Home*, led by 'Miss Kitty', was in rehearsal before news of Vernon's victory reached London, and the work was never revived after the cult around Vernon sprang up.

That's because *Britons, Strike Home* is really just about Clive. The action takes place on a captured Spanish boat moored in the English Channel. The sailors have prepared a comedy for Miss Kitty to lead. She baulks at the part she has been given, Donna America, because it is allegorical and seemingly Spanish. She is particularly miffed at having no airs to perform. 'I have observed', she says, 'that Tunes and Songs have a very great effect on Publick Affairs'.[134] To prove her point she performs Purcell's 'Britons strike Home' from the seventeenth-century *Bonduca* – in whose revival she had performed – with new verses describing Farinelli's admirers as spineless appeasers of the Spanish, as in Lord Bawble's air in *The Coffee-House*.[135] The farce being rehearsed is a disconnected series of scenes, among them a jolly chorus, the disarming of a Catholic priest, and Kitty's advice on how to choose a husband ('Since we are born to be controul'd, / Reward the Generous and the Bold').[136] These culminate in the actor Richard Yates taking off Theophilus Cibber.

In truth, the liberty celebrated in *Britons, Strike Home* is Clive's from Cibber, whom Fleetwood had finally sacked at the end of the 1738–39 season. Fleetwood's break with Cibber had two grounds: back-stabbing and wife-pimping. By the summer of 1737 Fleetwood had discovered, so it was alleged, that Cibber had been spreading discontent among '*Grumbletonians*' who like him believed '*no Gentleman* is proper for the *Master* of a *Theatre*'.[137] After the Licensing Act of 1737, Fleetwood had hired Henry Giffard, his wife, and several now-unemployed actors from Giffard's fringe company, firing Dury

---

[132] For an outline of this chorus's many patriotic settings, see Martha Vandrei, '"Britons, strike Home"': Politics, Patriotism and Popular Song in British Culture, c.1695–1900', *Historical Research*, vol. 87, no. 238 (2014), pp. 679–702.
[133] Kathleen Wilson, *The Sense of the People* (Cambridge, 1998), pp. 140–64, esp. pp. 142–45.
[134] Edward Phillips, *Britons, Strike Home: Or, the Sailor's Rehearsal* (London, 1739), p. 6.
[135] On the relation between this air and Beard's Farinelli-themed air in *The Coffee-House*, see McGeary, 'Farinelli in Madrid', pp. 387–88.
[136] Phillips, *Britons, Strike Home*, p. 26.
[137] *An Apology for the Life of Mr. T— C—, Comedian*, p. 107. No date is mentioned, but it can be pinpointed by the reference in the same passage to the collapse of Henry Giffard's company, which happened early in May 1737.

Lane members to make room for them. The Drury Lane company then split into two factions, the '*Riff-Raffs*' for Fleetwood and the '*Scabs*' against him, as Theophilus Cibber again sought to 'raise a Rebellion'.[138] In response, Fleetwood 'clip'd' Cibber's wings, passing onto James Quin the job of presiding over rehearsals,[139] and, according to Quin's biographer, the 'persual of such new plays as were offered'.[140]

Theophilus had also pimped his wife from the spring of 1737, forcing her to become the mistress of one of her admirers, a gentleman named William Sloper. After a year of living in a menage à trois, William and Susannah fell in love, she became pregnant, and the couple ejected Theophilus from the household Sloper had been bankrolling. Theophilus Cibber, deeply in debt, sued Sloper for damages in early December 1738. The public followed the trial's every motion; courtroom audiences piled in, and a full report of the proceedings – including the detailed testimony of an eyewitness sent by Theophilus Cibber to catch Susannah Cibber and William Sloper *in flagrante* – hit the press. Susannah Cibber broke off her stage appearances in the spring of 1738 to bear her child, and later removed to Dublin to restart her career. Theophilus Cibber returned to acting in January 1739, but his presence offended company members, particularly Quin, and by June 1739 Fleetwood had fired him.

Edward Phillips, the author of *Britons, Strike Home*, was the writer who had defamed Clive in his 1733 *Stage-Mutineers*; now he served her. In the action of his comedy, when the sailors are pressing Kitty to lead their play, Lieutenant Meanwell (Charles Macklin) asserts that her 'many Airs' – that is, assumed manners, but also a pun on 'songs' – are proof that she 'wou'd make an excellent Actress'.[141] One character observes that Kitty conducts herself 'as if … a Favourite of the Town these six Years'.[142] Meanwell comments on her fine elocution, and says she 'puts in, or leaves out o'th' Part, what she thinks proper'.[143]

Apart from Purcell's 'Britons strike Home', the tunes in *Britons, Strike Home* bear no title. We can, however, identify the sixth air: 'Now learn from me, ye wealthy Fair', for Kitty. Phillips took its music from Clive's latest *in propria persona* air, composed by Arne for Miller's *Hospital for Fools*, shouted down on 15 November 1739.[144] Titled originally 'How smoothly glides the Fool thro' Life', this song is Carey-esque in its rollicking triple meter and 'native' touches such

---

[138] *Ibid.*, pp. 107–08.
[139] *Ibid.*, p. 109.
[140] *The Life of Mr. James Quin, Comedian*, p. 50. In this account, Cibber is said to have plotted against Fleetwood during the latter's fit of the gout, putting out that Fleetwood was too ill to return to theatre management, and trying to get his father to procure him a licence from the Lord Chamberlain.
[141] Edward Phillips, *Britons, Strike Home*, p. 5.
[142] *Ibid.*
[143] *Ibid.*, p. 17.
[144] Miller's characterization belongs to that of Clive's Lucy series, which I discuss in Chapter 11, pp. 333–38. For the air, see [James Miller], 'AN ADDITIONAL SONG. The Musick by

as a modal inflection for the cadence in the eighth bar, followed by a swing beyond the fifth scale degree to shift to the home key's dominant. Setting Miller's words, Arne showed his superiority to Carey in his skipping offbeat ascents: 'whis-TLES, ON and CRIES, / What Fol-LY, it IS / To be wise'. This is the same kind of flourish through which Kitty drives home the epigrammatic point in her Cuckow Song. In *Britons, Strike Home* her song is likewise a warning, this time to Ladies that lovers are venal: 'They sigh, they wish – to have and hold, / Not the Lady – but the Gold.'[145]

Phillips made the war against Spain a metaphor for Clive's war against Theophilus Cibber, who is recalled as that 'little, shuffling, tricking, strutting, domineering Fellow, the Spanish Representative in Europe', Don Superbo Hispaniolo Pistole.[146] An epilogue shared by Macklin and Clive, during which Clive mocked Cibber's braggadocio ('Then – not their *Pleasures* and their *Hopes* to balk, / Then he would talk – Ye Gods! how he would talk!'), rounded off the vilification.[147] The 'political Part'[148] that Kitty had demanded collapses into Clive's personal story; her desire for an 'effect on Publick Affairs' proves but the caprice of Drury Lane's comic goddess. In her allegorical part as Donna America in the play within the play, Kitty is a low-style Euphrosyne – both parts being essentially about their star, regardless of their Opposition-styled packaging. To quote Phillips, 'she will do as she will, and is of too much Consequence for an Author to contradict her.'[149] This was true: after *Comus*, Clive briefly ruled the house.

Mr. ARNE. Sung by Mrs. CLIVE', *An Hospital for Fools. A Dramatic Fable. The Musick by Mr. Arne. Sung by Mrs. Clive* (London, 1739), pages unnumbered, preface to the playbook.
[145] Phillips, *Britons, Strike Home*, p. 25.
[146] *Ibid*., p. 26.
[147] 'EPILOGUE. Spoke by Mrs. CLIVE and Mr. MACKLIN', *ibid*., pages unnumbered.
[148] Phillips, *Britons, Strike Home*, p. 5.
[149] *Ibid*., p. 20.

8

Handel and the Sweet Bird of Drury Lane, 1740–43

Clive, Milton, and Drury Lane's application masques – Beard's ascendance at Drury Lane – Handel meets Clive – hearing the vocalists in L'Allegro – the Sweet Bird captured in portrait – Rosamond in the labyrinth and Alfred in the Garden – Beard, Clive, and the making of Samson – oratorio triumphs – Handel, De Fesch, and Clive's voice

Comus had opened a new chapter for Clive. The goddess of masque had formerly dwelt apart from the smart ballad-singing comedienne; in Euphrosyne, they combined. The backstreets patriotism for which Clive had been known – her sneers at Jews, beaux, and opera singers, all standard for playhouse entertainment – crystallized in *Comus*, whose songs and epilogue staged her resistance to authority. After *Comus*, Clive was a patriotic Opposition soprano in stage works both comic and serious. After *Comus* also, Clive gained gravitas in a new line of sung 'application' stage works. Traditionally, an application work was a tragedy or historical play whose action could be seen to parallel events in the political arena. *Comus* had been a new kind of application play in that, in addition to featuring celebrities and song, it joined a story about sexual morality to one about public grievances. Other such works led by Clive followed: *Rosamond, Alfred,* and *Samson.* In each, the ideal Patriot leader, Frederick, ghosted behind the stage hero; Clive necessarily took second place. The career advantage of these works for Clive lay in their elitism. Their wordbooks were from Addison and Milton, their appeal was to power-brokers who could decode messages, and their music was the most sophisticated Clive ever sang. She welcomed this elevation, taking up opportunities to promote both herself and her protégée Mary Edwards.

First Encounters

Few were more fired up by the success of *Comus* than James Harris. His veneration of Milton matched his love of Shakespeare,[1] which as discussed had led his circle to involve itself with James Miller's Clive-led version of *Much Ado about Nothing*. It matched also his respect for Handel, who belonged to his inner circle.[2] Harris was living in Salisbury when *Comus* opened on 4 March 1738, but about a fortnight later his friend the scholar–cleric John Upton wrote urging him to purchase Thomas Arne's *Comus* score, not least because Arne 'woud be glad of some money'.[3] Harris did so. By late 1739, Harris had adapted Milton's poems *L'Allegro* and *Il Penseroso* into a wordbook for Handel; as Ruth Smith shows, when preparing this wordbook Harris left out the same verses from *L'Allegro* as Dalton had when using it for *Comus*.[4] Charles Jennens wrote to Harris on 29 December that he had made Handel 'impatient to see' Harris's wordbook,[5] which Harris sent to Jennens for Handel's perusal on 6 January 1740.[6]

Unlike Dalton, Harris cleaved strictly to his literary source.[7] Milton's two poems express respectively the moods of liveliness ('allegro') and pensiveness ('penseroso'). To arrange them for the stage, Harris alternated verses taken

---

[1] Harris's 'Miltonick' activities included critical commentary on *Paradise Lost* (in Harris's *Hermes: Or, a Philosophical Inquiry concerning Language and Universal Grammar*), and preparing a wordbook for setting by Handel of *Paradise Lost* that never materialized. Rosemary Dunhill and Geoff Ridden, 'Milton's Nightcap: The Correspondence of James Harris', *Milton Quarterly*, vol. 32, no. 3 (1998), pp. 95–97.

[2] By January 1736 'the Harrisses and Shaftesburys formed a group of devoted and articulate supporters' of Handel, contributing to the composer's career as patrons, music amateurs, and literary consultants. Dunhill, *Handel and the Harris Circle*, p. 2.

[3] Letter of John Upton to James Harris, 18 March 1738: 'If you or any of your freinds will subscribe for the musick of Comus (which is 6s) pray let me know & I'll pay the money for you to Tom Arne, who I beleive [sic] at this present would be glad of some money.' Burrows and Dunhill, ed., *Music and Theatre in Handel's World*, p. 45. The engraved collection was probably *The Songs, Duetto and Trio in the Masque of Comus ... dispos'd ... for a Harpsicord [sic] & Voice* (London: Printed by Wm Smith, n.d.). Notably, in this score the performers' names are not engraved alongside each movement, as in other *Comus* printed music.

[4] Smith, 'Milton moderated: *Il moderato* and its Relation to *L'Allegro* and *Il Penseroso*', pp. 139–64.

[5] Letter of Charles Jennens to James Harris, 29 December 1739, in Burrows and Dunhill, ed., *Music and Theatre in Handel's World*, pp. 82–83.

[6] Letter of James Harris to Charles Jennens, 6 January 1740, *ibid.*, p. 85. On this work's genesis, and its three distinct versions, see Donald Burrows, 'From Milton to Handel: the Transformation of Milton's *L'Allegro and Il Penseroso* into a Musical Work for Concert Performance in the London Theatres', *Musique et théâtralité dans les îles Britanniques*, ed. C. Bardelmann and P. Degott (Metz, 2005), pp. 73–89, repr. in David Vickers, ed., *Handel* (Farnham, 2011), pp. 273–89.

[7] As Smith notes, in Dalton's *Comus* only five of Arne's twenty numbers contain Milton's verses. Ruth Smith, 'Milton Modulated for Handel's Music', *Milton in the Long Restoration*, pp. 159–79.

from each poem, contrasting an affect from the first against another from the second. In so doing, as he explained to Jennens, he 'assigned the several singers [from Handel's projected oratorio company] to each song'.[8] He did this by annotating beside each movement either a first singer's name, or a voice type, writing for instance 'Song by Beard', 'the Boy', 'a Base [Bass] voice', 'Chorus, to be opened by Francesina alone'.[9] He called this a 'liberty which I hope Mr Handel will excuse' and asked Jennens to invite Handel to 'alter & invert' his selection of voices 'in that respect just in what manner he thinks proper'.[10] Yet when setting Harris's wordbook, Handel stuck to his selection of singers and voice types.[11] At Handel's request Jennens afterwards added a third section, 'Il moderato', to Harris's original two-part structure, even though Harris had entrusted his wordbook to Jennens precisely because he wanted to 'prevent any of Handels minor poets' making 'presumptious additions to marr Milton'.[12]

Handel's *L'Allegro, il penseroso ed il moderato* opened in February 1740, during one of the century's most severe winters. Faced with a freezing playhouse and a concomitant fear of not filling seats, Handel may at the last moment have enlisted Clive to sing.[13] Handel's change to his autograph score

---

[8] Letter of James Harris to Charles Jennens, 6 January 1740, in Burrows and Dunhill, ed., *Music and Theatre in Handel's World*, p. 85.

[9] [John Milton, arranged by James Harris], Transcription of Harris's draft wordbook ('L'Allegro & il Penseroso), in Burrows and Dunhill, ed., *Music and Theatre in Handel's World*, pp. 1075–85. A facsimile of the first page of Harris's wordbook is reproduced on p. 1076.

[10] James Harris to Charles Jennens, letter of 6 January 1740, Burrows and Dunhill, ed., *Music and Theatre in Handel's World*, p. 85.

[11] Handel's most far-reaching changes were to turn five alternating sections into sixteen to quicken the alterations between moods, and re-order Harris's selections to heighten contrasts. For a summary of Handel's different versions of *L'Allegro ed il Penseroso*, and each version's singers, see Donald Burrows, 'Reconstructing Handel's Performances of *L'Allegro*', *The Musical Times*, vol. 154, no. 1922 (2013), pp. 69–76. For Handel's 'most significant' revisions to Harris's draft, see Burrows, 'From Milton to Handel', pp. 285–87.

[12] James Harris to Charles Jennens, letter of 6 January 1740, Burrows and Dunhill, ed., *Music and Theatre in Handel's World*, p. 85. In a letter of 15 January 1740, Jennens explained to Harris why he had made 'additions & Omissions' to Harris's selection of Milton's lines; he also informed Harris that Handel 'has a mind ... to add a 3rd part and that 'Handel's opinion' was 'that the piece will be more perfect, if after the extremes of mirth & melancholy have been shown ... a Moderator should interpose, & reduce the Disputants to reason'. Burrows discusses Jennens' letter, which he reprints in full, in Burrows, 'From Milton to Handel', pp. 282–85. On Jennens' *Il Moderato*, see Smith, 'Milton Moderated: *Il Moderato* and its relation to *L'Allegro* and *Il Penseroso*', pp. 139–64, and Ruth Smith, '"In this Ballance Seek a Character": The Role of 'Il Moderato' in *L'Allegro, il Penseroso ed il Moderato*', *Music in the London Theatre from Purcell to Handel*, ed. C. Timms and B. Wood (Cambridge, 2017), pp. 175–89.

[13] Announcements ran in *The Daily Advertiser* for performances on 27 February, 6, 10, and 14 March, and 23 April. The debut performance was at 6 pm, and the starting time changed to 6.30 pm on 6 March, then to 7 pm from 10 March; the performance on 23 April began at 6.30 pm. Burrows et al., ed., *George Frideric Handel Collected Documents: Volume 3 1734–1742*, pp. 577–78.

is the first indication we have of her presence. James and Martin Hall, who prepared the critical edition of *L'Allegro, il penseroso ed il moderato*, note that around 1740 Handel wrote Clive's name beside the third section's recitative 'No more short Life'. Because the third section was not included in the truncated version of *L'Allegro* that Clive sang under Handel's direction in 1743,[14] his annotation might mean either of two things. Handel may have abandoned the third section in 1743 after assigning its music to singers, as Donald Burrows believes.[15] Or, as James and Martin Hall assume, Clive performed the music during *L'Allegro*'s first run, in 1740. If so, it can only have been on 27 February and 6 March, because on other *L'Allegro* evenings she was already engaged at Drury Lane.

Why would Handel bring in Clive, unheralded and just before the premiere, to sing so briefly?[16] Handel's autograph score gives a hint: she sang the same music as John Beard. By 1740 Beard was Clive's constant singing partner. He had good reason to want Clive beside him in the 1740 *L'Allegro* cast: his playhouse stardom was built on hers, and his debts were mounting. A quick glance backwards allows us to see Beard's reliance on Clive. After debuting at Drury Lane in *The Devil to Pay* in August 1737, within eighteen months he had sung opposite Clive in all her most renowned hits: *The Virgin Unmask'd*, *The Beggar's Opera*, *The Fall of Phaeton*, *The Harlot's Progress*, *The Lottery*, and *The Intriguing Chambermaid*; that season Drury Lane even revived *The Con-*

---

[14] 'Ihr Name steht, mit Tinte geschrieben, in Hs. A … bei Nr. 38 und dem vorangehenden Recitativ. Da diese beiden Stücke des Moderato wahrscheinlich nicht in dieser Aufführung gesungen wurden, ist zu vermuten, dass dies 1740 geschah.' (Her name is written in ink in Handel's autograph score … beside No. 38 and its preceding recitative. Because these two pieces in *Moderato* probably weren't sung in this production [of 1743], it is to be assumed that this happened in 1740.) James S. Hall and Martin V. Hall, *L'Allegro, il penseroso ed il moderato: Kritischer Bericht*, Hallische Händel-Ausgabe: Kritische Gesamtausgabe, ser. 1, vol. 16 (Kassel, 1969), p. 61; see also pp. 72–73; translation by present author.

[15] 'Handel probably initially planned to perform *L'Allegro* in three parts, including "Il Moderato". In his autograph he wrote Mrs Clive's name in ink at the beginning of the recitative 'No more short life': autographs of other 1743 scores have similar annotations, presumably because the performing scores were temporarily unavailable to him.' Burrows, 'Reconstructing Handel's Performances of *L'Allegro*', p. 72, note 12.

[16] James and Martin Hall suggest that in 1740 she may also have sung no. 10, 'Mirth, admit me of thy Crew', and no. 16 with its preceding recitative, 'If I give thee Honour due / Let me wander'. Their suggestion does not clearly correlate with the information they give elsewhere about first singers named in Handel's autograph and other early sources. Hall and Hall, *L'Allegro, il penseroso ed il moderato: Kritischer Bericht*, pp. 69–72. Only the last number definitely was sung in 1740 and not in 1743, and I therefore discuss only this music. In the score, Handel's assignment of numbers to her is in an ink that, according to James and Martin Hall, dates from 1740, and that according to Donald Burrows may date from 1743. See notes above, and Joncus, 'Handel at Drury Lane', p. 208, note 61.

Fig. 8.1 William Verelst, *Catherine Clive*, 1740. Oil on canvas. By kind permission of the Garrick Club of London. Paintings: G0122.

trivances and *Damon and Phillida*, both of which Clive had previously lost to other houses, for the duetting pair. He was also her partner for the first two acts of *Comus*. During the 1739–40 season in which *L'Allegro* opened, extended runs of *Comus* and *The Fall of Phaeton* had evidenced Clive's star power.[17] By

[17] *Comus* performances recommenced on 28 November, continuing on 29 and 30 November ('By Command of Their Royal Highnesses the Prince and Princess of Wales'), on 1,

February 1740 Beard was, as we'll see, running up legal costs and needed to make a good impression on the Town. Conscripting Clive for the debut of *L'Allegro* might entice the elite, who didn't need notices to learn of Handel's activities, to a freezing house. As owner of his score part, Beard will have been able to share it with her to learn at short notice.

Accepting that Clive participated in the 1740 run of *L'Allegro* can explain three otherwise inexplicable occurrences. First, Handel contributed a song to Clive's 1740 benefit just a few weeks later; second, Handel hired Mary Edwards for his 1740 season; and third, Clive holds music from *L'Allegro* in her lavish oil portrait of 1740 (Fig. 8.1). Let's consider each matter in turn.

According to benefit season pecking order, Clive at this time was Drury Lane's highest-ranked female player, and second in the company as a whole only to James Quin. For her benefit of 17 March 1740, Clive chose the iconic Oldfield role of Millamant in William Congreve's *The Way of the World*. This was a bold attempt to wrest Millamant from Christiana Horton, who had taken the part with her to Covent Garden in 1735 and still owned it.[18] It was also shrewd self-casting on Clive's part: Congreve was an esteemed playwright, and the words to his song, 'Love's but the Frailty of the Mind', written for a precocious chambermaid, fit her perfectly. What better composer than Handel to set it? Clive managed to get Handel to gift her a song – an artistic and publicity coup. Her participation in *L'Allegro*'s first run would explain why Clive, who in 1740 had otherwise never worked with Handel, could suddenly call on his services.

Fielding called attention to Clive's achievement in a puff of her upcoming Handelian song that seems quickly to descend into parody. Here he is encouraging London audiences to attend her benefit, rather than the pantomime *Orpheus and Eurydice* at Covent Garden:

> Whereas Mrs. Clive, the best Actress of this, and perhaps of any preceeding Age, hath chosen for her Benefit on Monday next one of the best Plays of the late celebrated Mr. Congreve, and intends to sing a very pretty Song on that Occasion, which is now first set to Musick by the greatest Master in Europe, so that a rational Entertainment may be expected on that Night; on which Account, it

---

3, 4 December (with Clive's epilogue 'by Desire'), 5 December (with her epilogue), and 6 December and 10 January (again with her epilogue). The advertisements are reprinted in *The London Stage*, Part 3, vol. 2, pp. 805–7, 814.

[18] In 1718 Oldfield, blazing forth as Millamant, made Congreve's then-forgotten comedy into a staple. Lafler, *The Celebrated Mrs. Oldfield*, p. 134. Edmund Curll and William Oldys noted that 'Mr. Booth often declared that *no one was so capable of playing* Mrs. Oldfield's *Parts, after her Decease*, as Mrs. Horton. Mr. Wilks was *of the same Opinion*, and proved it, by chusing her to play with him in several Comedies, where she appeared in Mrs. Oldfield's Characters. The Part of Millamant, in the *Way of the World*, was one of the foremost.' [Curll and Oldys], *The History of the English Stage ... by Mr. Thomas Betterton*, p. 164.

is probable, all the People of Sense will then assemble at Drury-Lane; the Fools are therefore all desired to be present at the other House, where *Orpheus* and *Eurydice* will be prepared for their Entertainment.[19]

In 'Love's but the Frailty of the Mind', Handel elegantly sketched the irrepressible Clive (Ex. 8.1). As Donald Burrows points out, the song is 'his most ambitious essay in English secular song-writing outside his own dramatic productions'.[20] Three sources capture this music: Handel's roughly-written autograph,[21] and two later fair copy manuscripts.[22] Of these, the copy by one of Handel's scribes, titled 'Sung by M$^{rs.}$ Clive in The Way of the World, for her own Benefit, 1740', post-dates Clive's performance most closely. Prepared around 1740 for Charles Jennens, this copy contains a figured bass by Jennens, who knew her voice.[23] The music (see Ex. 8.1) highlights three classic Clive traits: ambition, rejection of men, and boundless self-confidence, and varies its musical material to give Clive opportunity to commune with her audiences.

Handel's melismas are judiciously placed to highlight relevant words 'Ambition join'd' (bars 14–17), 'sickly Flame [of love]' (bars 27–30) and 'Glory' (bars 73–75). The melody climaxes on the word 'Glory', where a fermata over the top

---

[19] Coley, ed., *Henry Fielding: Contributions to The Champion and Related Writings*, p. 237. Coley notes that Fielding had earlier disparaged the pantomime *Orpheus and Eurydice*: ibid., note 3.

[20] Donald Burrows, ed., *G.F. Handel: Songs and Cantatas for Soprano and Continuo: Including the Complete English Songs for Soprano* (Oxford, 1988), p. x.

[21] Burrows, ed., *G.F. Handel: Songs and Cantatas*, pp. x–xi. He based his edition on autograph sketches in the Fitzwilliam Museum, Cambridge MS 262. John Fuller-Maitland describes the Handel autograph collection that Burrows used as a 'set of sketch-books and miscellaneous manuscripts': John A. Fuller-Maitland and Arthur H. Mann, 'Preface', *Catalogue of the Music in the Fitzwilliam Museum, Cambridge* (London, 1893), pp. v–vi; cited in Donald Burrows and Martha J. Ronish, 'Preamble', *A Catalogue of Handel's Musical Autographs* (Oxford, 1994), pp. xx.

[22] The two fair copies are: Gerald Coke Handel Collection, Foundling Museum, acc. no. 1286, fols 137–39 (the song is bound with Handel's *L'Allegro*) and British Library, R.M.19.d.11, fols 141–44 ('Sung by M^{rs}. Clive in the way of the world. Love's but the frailty'). John Roberts shows that the latter was copied from the former: John H. Roberts, 'The Aylesford Collection', *Handel Collections and their History*, ed. T. Best (Oxford, 1993), pp. 51–52 and 69. I thank Natassa Varka for bringing Roberts' book chapter to my attention.

[23] '[S]ometime in the early to mid-1740s Jennens decided to embark on ... a sort of complete edition of Handel's music, for the most part necessarily in manuscript form.' *Ibid.*, p. 41. Of the copyists, S1 prepared the Gerald Coke Handel Collection score of *L'Allegro* but S2 contributed significantly to the copying of Jennens' collection. *Ibid.*, pp. 40–46. I am grateful to Varka, a specialist in Jennens' musical handwriting, for confirming to me in a personal communication of 20 August 2018 that Jennens figured Handel's bass line. Jennens in fact 'supplied many additional bass figures' to the manuscript copies of Handel's music that he ordered. *Ibid.*, p. 42. Jennens' musicianship, and his boundless confidence in it, is discussed in the exhibition catalogue by Ruth Smith, *Charles Jennens: The Man behind Handel's Messiah* (London, 2012) and by Ruth Smith, 'The Achievements of Charles Jennens 1700–1773', *Music & Letters*, vol. 70, no. 2 (1989), pp. 161–90.

Ex. 8.1 Words by William Congreve, music by George F. Handel, 'Love's but the frailty of the Mind', HWV 218 in *The Way of the World*, 1740. Gerald Coke Handel Collection, Accession Number 1286, fols 137–39. Edited by Chris Gould.

238 KITTY CLIVE, OR THE FAIR SONGSTER

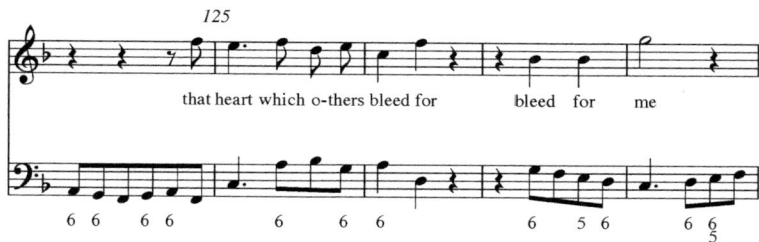
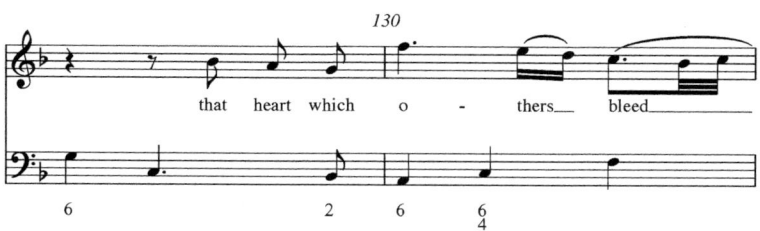
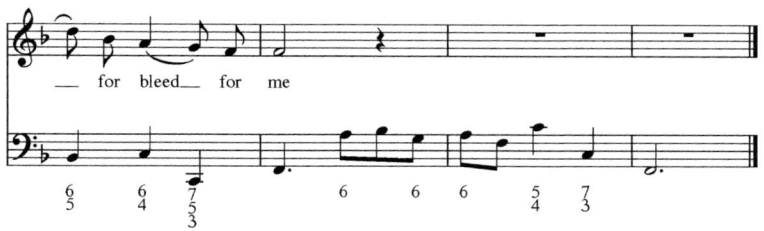

note will have accommodated Clive's improvisation. Of all songs created for her, this air alone captures her 'facetious Turn of Humour'[24] primarily through harmonic progressions. The air opens with straightforward triadic chords, but Jennens' realization – surely reflective of his own impression of Clive – quickly defies standard practice, with a proliferation of extra notes climaxing in bars 51–70, and again in bars 99–117. The superabundance of seventh chords, and chords saturated with non-triadic notes (7-3 and 5-4 chords being the most common), vividly conveys Clive's storied onstage impudence. Although Clive's bid for Millament did not take hold, she sang 'Love's but a Frailty' once more, after the second act of Shakespeare's *Timon of Athens* at William Milward's benefit two days later.[25]

That Handel was seen to be donating to Clive's playhouse benefit increased her cultural capital. She was, in fact, the only playhouse star ever to receive this distinction. The advertisement loudly announced the two Worthies, Congreve and Handel, whom Clive was to represent: 'The Part of Millament, to be perform'd by Mrs. CLIVE; *In which Character will be introduc'd the Original Song, the Words by Mr. Congreve, and new set to Musick by Mr. Handel.*'[26] Acting as Clive's benefactor may have helped Handel as well. Clive's onstage attacks on music at the King's Theatre had targeted Handel's works specifically, first in her 1733 benefit farce, *Deborah: Or, a Wife for you All* – Fielding's lost work that most probably ridiculed Handel's oratorio *Deborah* – then in the epilogue to *The Intriguing Chambermaid* (1734), in which she sneered at admirers of his aria 'Dimmi, cara' (from *Siroe*, 1726).[27] In James Miller's *An Hospital for Fools* (1739), Clive's character of the Daughter, as discussed in Chapter 11, mocks Handel's recently premiered oratorio *Saul*. Detente was to their mutual advantage.

The second hard-to-explain event for which Clive's presence at the 1740 *L'Allegro* would account is Handel's hiring of Mary Edwards. She was Clive's protégée and career dependent; her advancement was at this time entirely indebted to Clive. A 'little girl that belongs to Mrs Clive' is how James Harris's brother Thomas characterized her.[28] Edwards was originally a dancer trained by Charles Leviez; only after 1737 did she move gradually into singing parts.[29]

---

[24] Chetwood, 'Mrs. CATHARINE CLIVE (formerly Miss RAFTOR)', *A General History of the Stage*, p. 127. The full passage is quoted in Chapter 2, p. 28.

[25] Notice of this performance is in the *London Daily Post and General Advertiser*, issue 1685 (19 March 1740).

[26] *London Daily Post and General Advertiser*, issue 1674 (6 March 1740). Italics in original.

[27] See Chapter 5, p. 164 and note 143.

[28] 'I have just now bin at Mr Handel's operetta [*Imeneo*] ... I don't think it mett with the applause it deserves ... His performers are Franchescina, Andrioni, a little girl that belongs to Mrs Clive'. Thomas Harris to James Harris, letter of 22 November 1740. Burrows and Dunhill, ed., *Music and Theatre in Handel's World*, p. 108.

[29] Philip H. Highfill, Kalman A. Burnim, and Edward A. Langhans, 'Mozeen, Mrs Thomas [Mary?], née Edwards', *A Biographical Dictionary of Actors, Actresses, Musicians, &*

In late 1740 Edwards, then about sixteen, had to her credit just one legitimate role, the Page in the Clive-led English opera *Rosamond*. Yet it was Handel, dedicated to the most exacting standards, who gave Edwards her career break. Late in 1740 she joined his company for his second season (1740–41) and the last two Italian operas of his career, *Imeneo* and *Deidamia*.[30]

Jennens commented acidly to Harris in a letter of December 1740 that *Deidamia* 'will be turn'd into Farce by Miss Edwards[,] a little Girl representing Achilles'.[31] After hearing Edwards in *Deidamia*, Elizabeth Robinson wrote to her sister on 10 February 1741 that 'the Singers were vile, I can compare them to nothing that will not set your teeth on Edge[;] a little English Girl is the best [i.e. worst] & the true Brittons in the Upper Gallery never fail of giving her more a National than a Critical applause'.[32] Despite such opprobrium, in 1743 Handel had Edwards join the Beard- and Clive-led company for *Samson*.[33] After 1743, once theatre politics blocked Clive from singing with Handel, he dropped Edwards: when the success of his oratorio *Samson* led Handel to schedule a second oratorio season, she was to have sung in the London debut of *Messiah*, but was replaced.[34] Edwards was clearly expendable, and only Clive's appearance in *L'Allegro* would seem to justify Handel's having employed this weak teenage soprano in the first place.

The third matter which would be explained by Clive's singing in the 1740 *L'Allegro* is the music featured in her 1740 portrait. Painted by William Verelst, this oil was the most sumptuous of her career (Fig. 8.1). In it, she holds a folio of the aria 'Sweet Bird' from *L'Allegro*, the first two words and first few bars of which are legible, thereby staking a claim to this work in a most formal

---

Other Stage Personnel in London, 1660–1800, vol. 10 (Carbondale, 1984), pp. 370–72. Her father may have been the chapel royal singer Thomas Edwards, appointed early 1699/1700 (d. 1730), whose membership is noted in Donald Burrows, *Handel and the English Chapel Royal* (Oxford, 2005), p. 564. Between 1712 and 1730 Handel provided music sporadically for royal occasions at which the Chapel Royal sang. Having died in 1730 when Mary Edwards was six, and having only rarely worked with Handel, Thomas Edwards is unlikely to have brought her talents to Handel's attention – and he may not even have been her father.

[30] Edwards sang Clomiri in *Imeneo* on 22 November 1740 and Achille in *Deidamia* on 10 January 1741. Handel rented Lincoln's Inn Fields for his season. She may also have taken the parts either of Clori or Calliope in *Parnasso in Festa* on 8 November 1740. Burrows et al., ed. *George Frideric Handel Collected Documents: Volume 3 1734–1742*, p. 659.

[31] Charles Jennens to James Harris, letter of 29 December 1740, ibid., p. 666.

[32] Burrows confirms that the 'little English girl' was 'Miss Edwards'. Ibid., pp. 677–78.

[33] In *Samson*, Edwards took the parts of the Israelite and the Philistine Woman. Ibid.

[34] 'There is considerable doubt as to whether Miss Edwards sang in *Messiah*: her name appears on Handel's scores, but was replaced by another singer (or another movement for a different singer) in every case.' Donald Burrows, *Handel: Messiah* (Cambridge, 1991), p. 112, note 21.

context.[35] Although she never sang 'Sweet Bird',[36] she *was* the sweet bird of the English playhouse, celebrated since her 1735 portrait for her 'heavnly Strains'. Holding Handel's setting of *L'Allegro*, Clive could represent herself as the Euphrosyne of Handel's work as well as Arne's. Only those who could both read music and recognize Handel's *L'Allegro* from score would know what she is holding. This folio forges a bond between Clive and the kind of viewer with whom she most wanted to associate.

Other props, and her pose, emphasise Clive's ease among connoisseurs. The double manual harpsichord – unusual in formal portraits of ladies, or of musicians of either sex – is the instrument of a serious musician. Seated at the keyboard, she turns towards the viewer, as if she will soon return to her music-making. The background, and the empty music stand behind her, suggest a private rehearsal in a fine interior. Clive's gentility is shown through her accoutrements, which echo those of the Van Aken 'Fair Songster' portrait. As in that 1735 picture, Clive's hair is entwined with bows, although here it is unpowdered and loosely plaited around her head. As in 1735, her chemise is trimmed, but more richly than in Van Aken's oil, with lace festooning the tucker and sleeves. Her dress resembles what she wore when sitting for Van Aken: back-fastened, ivory (rather than white) satin, with short sleeves swagged with pearl clasp pins. Pearls rather than ribbon decorate her bodice in a looped rococo ornament that clasps a lace insert at the tucker, and extends to the waist, terminating in a pearl pendant.

What surprises is the honesty with which Verelst, utterly unlike Van Aken, rendered Clive's actual facial features. Here Clive's likeness is restored from her first 1734 mezzotint that, because faithful, had at the time been publicly rejected as not 'true'. We recognize the pudgy chin, flared nostrils, thin lips, and slight squint. Verelst even shows the ruddy complexion, or 'rubicundity' on which later writers would remark.[37] In light of the furore her likeness provoked in 1734, the unflinching quality of Verelst's gaze begs the question: for whom was this portrait intended? Clive herself may have commissioned it. We know that sometime before her death she acquired the c.1735 oil portrait that

---

[35] The painting is signed and dated on the back of the canvas, 'Wm. Verelst Pinxit 1740'. Geoffrey Ashton, *Pictures in the Garrick Club: A Catalogue of the Paintings, Drawings, Watercolours and Sculpture*, ed. K. A. Burnim and A. Wilton (London, 1997), p. 70.

[36] The singers whose names appear in early sources beside this aria are: Francesina (that is, Elizabeth Duparc), Christina Maria Avoglio, Mary Edwards, Giulia Frasi, and Charlotte Brent. Hall and Hall, *L'Allegro, il penseroso ed il moderato: Kritischer Bericht*, p. 70.

[37] 'The Clive has been desperately nervous, but I have convinced her it did not become her, and she has recovered her rubicundity.' Horace Walpole to George Montague, letter of 31 July 1767, electronic version of *The Yale Edition of Horace Walpole's Correspondence* (New Haven, 1937–83). <http://images.library.yale.edu/hwcorrespondence/page.asp?vol=10&seq=269&type=b>. Accessed 30 November 2018. On this comment and others on Clive's complexion, see Crean, 'The Life and Times of Kitty Clive', p. 297.

Jeremiah Davison had copied from Joseph van Aken.[38] By 1740, as a top-paid company member, Clive could afford to hire the fashionable Verelst.[39] The Verelst portrait never circulated in print. Its last private owner was the actor Charles Mathews.[40] One of Mathews' sources for his collection was the Drury Lane actor-manager James Grant Raymond, who played opposite Clive's later protégée Jane Pope.[41] Pope was Clive's closest friend, and she and her sister Susanna were the executors and legatees of Clive's brother James, inheriting the 'Rest and the Residue' of his estate when he died in 1790.[42] It is not difficult to imagine Jane or Susanna Pope selling or bequeathing Clive's portrait to Raymond at Drury Lane.[43]

This provenance is of course highly speculative. Certain is that the ambition of Verelst's oil matches that of its subject. Equally certain is that in 1740 she sang the first music that Handel had ever written for her, and that someone was determined to capture this achievement. The song of Clive's 1740 portrait

[38] Evidence of her ownership is found in the catalogue for the auction of Horace Walpole's estate in 1842. It describes Davison's portrait thus: 'A Portrait of the celebrated MRS. CLIVE, the actress, with a music book, a clever original picture. *A present from her brother, Mr. James Raftor*'. Strawberry Hill, the renowned Seat of Horace Walpole ... to sell by Public Competition, the Valuable Contents (London, 1842), p. 208 ('The Twenty-First Day's Sale' on 18 May 1842, Lot 13 'J. DAVISON'). The purchaser of the portrait was Beriah Botfield (1807–63) of Norton Hall near Daventry in Northamptonshire. On the death of his aunt, Lady Beatrice Thynne of Norton Hall, Davison's portrait passed to the 6th Marquess of Bath in 1941. 'Jeremiah Davison', Folder sh-000273, Lewis Walpole Library. John Thynne built Longleat House, where the portrait is now held, between 1567 and 1580.

[39] William Verelst (bap. 1704–1752) is probably best known for his grand 35-figure group portrait, *Audience Given by the Trustees of Georgia To a Delegation of Creek Indians* (1734) in the Winterthur Museum, Delaware. Verelst came from a family of painters, and 'was practiced in portraiture and conversation pieces'. Kalman A. Burnim and John Baskett, with contributions by Edward A. Langhans, *Brief Lives: Sitters and Artists in the Garrick Club Collection* (London, 2003), p. 269.

[40] Mathews' 'collection was finally sold to the newly formed Garrick Club for the ... sum of £1,000'. Jim Davis, *Comic Acting and Portraiture in late-Georgian and Regency England* (Cambridge and New York, 2015), p. 220. Mathews built his career on impersonating dead celebrities in one-man shows that he called 'At Homes' and he put on stage the portraits that he owned of dead actors as part of his show. Mathews encouraged private visits to his collection – to house it, he had a gallery built at his home in Uxbridge – and his visitors included Charles Lamb, who wrote movingly about seeing dead actors, Clive included, in an article in the *London Magazine* of 1822. Mathews exhibited his portraits publicly at the Queen's Bazaar in May 1833, but response to this show was tepid. Ashton, 'Charles Mathews's Gallery of Theatrical Portraits', *Pictures in the Garrick Club*, p. xxxix–l.

[41] The four main collections that Mathews acquired to create his own were Raymond's in 1818, John Philip Kemble's in 1821, Garrick's in 1823, and Thomas Harris's in 1818. *Ibid.*, pp. 214–15. On Raymond's acting with Pope, see 'James Grant Raymond 1769–1817' *The Annual Biography and Obituary*, vol. 2 (London, 1818), p. 335.

[42] National Archives, Public Record Office, Prob 11/1196/171 [James Raftor].

[43] 'James Grant Raymond 1769–1817', *The Annual Biography*, p. 335.

befits the Euphrosyne who could warm the coldest house, and give life to Milton's verses.

Rosamond: Clive in Application Stage Works

The week before Clive's 1740 benefit as Millamant in *The Way of the World*, she played the title role in a revival of *Rosamond. An Opera*, with music by Thomas Arne. This production departed sharply from any in her line at the time. As Rosamond, she played a serious and sentimental heroine facing death, singing opposite Beard, who for the first time in their joint productions had the more important role. As with *Comus*, the literary pedigree of *Rosamond* helped hide its messaging.

Rosamond was the first-ever English-language opera wordbook: written in 1707 by Joseph Addison, its action came from the eponymous oral ballad that Addison would later champion in *The Spectator* as a native 'epic'.[44] In 1733 the young Thomas Arne had with some bravura re-scored Addison's 1707 *Rosamond* to debut as a composer.[45] His sister Susannah, who had hit Town taste as a debutante soprano just weeks earlier, took the title role. The opera's six-night run helped to establish them both, although Arne's score did not reach print.[46] The work had been political from the start: in 1707 Addison had wedged into the tale of Rosamond a scene celebrating the Duke of Marlborough's recent victory over the French at the Battle of Blenheim.[47] In the source ballad, Rosamond is the mistress of King Henry II, who has just returned from battle. She resides in a bower hidden within a labyrinth on his estate. The king's wife Queen Eleanor, having discovered Rosamond's secret residence, decides to remove her rival. In Addison's added scenes, the sleeping king dreams of future British military glory; angels sing to 'Britannia's Heroes yet unborn' and of 'fancy'd Fields' where 'the Gaul shall bleed', as the scene transforms to show the 'glorious Pile' of the still-under-construction Blenheim Palace, gifted to Marlborough by Queen Anne for his services.[48] The king awakes and finds

---

[44] Brean Hammond, 'Joseph Addison's Opera "Rosamond": Britishness in the Early Eighteenth Century', *English Literary History*, vol. 73, no. 3 (2006), pp. 601–29; Lawrence Klein, 'Addisonian Afterlives: Joseph Addison in Eighteenth-Century Culture', *Journal for Eighteenth-Century Studies*, vol. 35, no. 1 (2012), pp. 101–118. Klein argues that Addison was a 'culture hero' in the ethnographic sense, functioning as a 'model of British self-perception, a kind of cultural legislator'. *Ibid.*, 102.

[45] Advertisements emphasised Arne's fidelity to Addison, and fealty to native taste: the opera cast consisted entirely of native English vocalists, and Arne was called the 'Proprietor of English Operas'. Gilman, *The Theatre Career of Thomas Arne*, p. 44.

[46] On Arne's *Rosamond* of 1733, see (besides Gilman, cited above) Lee, 'From Amelia to Calista and Beyond', pp. 1–34, esp. pp. 8–10.

[47] [Joseph Addison], *Rosamond. An Opera. Humbly Inscrib'd to her Grace the Dutchess [sic] of Marlborough* (London, 1707), pp. 27–30.

[48] *Ibid.*, pp. 27–28.

Rosamond seemingly dead, but the queen has not, as in the traditional ballad, killed her rival; she has only drugged her. She has the sleeping Rosamond removed to a nunnery. Reconciled to his wife, the king swears that he will henceforth put duty and honour before amorous passion.

For the 1740 *Rosamond*, the mainpiece became an afterpiece, and Addison's Blenheim scenes were replaced with numbers suggesting the rise of Opposition figurehead Prince Frederick.[49] His stage proxy King Henry II receives the musical centrepiece 'Rise, Glory, rise' that replaces Addison's scene about Gauls and Blenheim. Announcements gave out that in 1740 Arne's music was 'new' except for 'two or three Favourite Songs'.[50] This was probably not true. The manuscript of Arne's *Rosamond* score is incomplete and post-dates the 1733 production; scribal evidence suggests it was made for Drury Lane's 1765 revival of *Rosamond*.[51] Stylistically, Rosamond's music – yielding, plaintive, and innocently sensual – is optimal for the seventeen-year-old debutante that Susannah Arne was in 1733, and is wholly unsuited to Clive's line, suggesting that in 1740 Arne simply recycled music from his unprinted 1733 version.[52] On the other hand Beard's part, having been sung by Jane Barbier in 1733 and so needing to be masculine as well as topical, will have had to have been revised.[53] A comparison between the wordbooks of the mainpiece and the 1740 afterpiece

---

[49] Ruth Smith details the analogies between Addison's King Henry II and Frederick, the imagined Patriot King: the protagonist progresses in knowledge of good kingship, and shares with his audience revelations of national glory. Smith, *Handel's Oratorios and Eighteenth-Century Thought*, pp. 294–95.

[50] 'An English Opera, written by the late Mr. Addison, and new set to Musick by Mr. Arne, reserving two or three Favourite Songs, out of his former Opera.' *London Daily Post and General Advertiser*, issue 1681 (14 March 1740). The 'Favourite Songs' were likely those issued as songsheets around 1733.

[51] The title 'Music in Rosamond, 1733' is added in a hand unlike the copyist's to the only source we have for Arne's music, held in the British Library, Add. MS 29370, fols 33r–85r. According to the catalogue entry, the manuscript was made from 1736 to 1746. But bound into the same manuscript collection containing *Rosamond* is Arne's cantata of 1762, 'The kind Appointment', and it shares the paper, ink type, and copyist's hand of the *Rosamond* manuscript. When Drury Lane revived *Rosamond* in 1765, advertisements gave out that the original music was used. See, for instance, *Public Advertiser*, issue 9505 (19 April 1765): 'not acted these twenty Years'. On Add MS 29370, fol. 33r, the title 'Music in Rosamond, 1733' is in a script and ink more typical of a nineteenth-century scribe. Of twenty-two vocal numbers in the 1740 *Rosamond*, only ten survive, along with one dance. The earliest manuscript of Rosamond's music would appear to be a c.1745 arrangement of an air in 'Minuets & airs for the violin & harpsichord. Vol.I' ('Minuet, D major', p. 12) held at the Gerald Coke Handel Collection, Foundling Museum, acc. no. 2550.

[52] Lee, 'From Amelia to Calista and Beyond', pp. 8–10. To quote Lee: 'The producers of these works [*Amelia* and *Rosamond*] clearly tried to repeat the formula that had generated *Amelia*'s success; Cibber was repeatedly cast as a sentimental heroine battling to maintain (or in the case of *Rosamond*, reclaim) chastity.' *Ibid.*, p. 8.

[53] Gilman, *The Theatre Career of Thomas Arne*, p. 45.

– only one copy of which seems to have survived[54] – shows that Beard's part also expanded, while all others were cut down (Table 8.1).

As with *Comus*, the prologue and wordbook of *Rosamond* made it an application work, smuggling in Opposition sentiments under accepted pieties. The 1740 prologue was a 1708 poem by Addison's editor Thomas Tickell, who had hailed the poet as the 'Great Monarch of the British Lays' – a line easily grasped as referring also to that patron of poets, Frederick.[55] As with *Comus*, the dedicatee of the original wordbook remained the same, in a way that was politically charged. The 1707 dedicatee of *Rosamond* had been Sarah Churchill, Duchess of Marlborough, who by 1740 was an Opposition grandee. Through marriage she was allied with leading members of the Opposition, and she supported its campaign against Walpole's proposed Excise Tax, which he had to withdraw on 11 April 1733.[56] The Duchess of Marlborough was also rumoured to have tried in 1730 to engineer a marriage between her granddaughter and Frederick.[57]

Rosamond opened on 8 March, four days after news began to fill the press that Admiral Vernon had defeated Spanish forces at Porto Bello, in present-day Panama.[58] This first victory for British forces since the War of Jenkins' Ear had been declared made Vernon a national hero. Which real-life leader did Beard's King Henry II stand for? When it came to hero worship, Drury Lane

---

[54] The only catalogued 1740 wordbook is held in the Victoria & Albert Museum, Theatre Collection. *Rosamond. An Opera … Written by the late Mr. Addison, and new Set to Musick by Thomas Augustine Arne* (London, 1740). Victoria & Albert Museum, Blythe House (Theatre & Performance), Press mark: PLAYS ADD PAMPHLET.

[55] 'A Copy of Verses to the Author of Rosamond. By Mr. Tickell', *ibid*. Tickell's encomium was first printed in Thomas Tickell, 'To the Author of Rosamond, an Opera', *Poetical Miscellanies: The Sixth Part. containing a Collection of Original Poems … By the most eminent Hands* (London, 1709) p. 413.

[56] Clyve Jones, 'The House of Lords and the Excise Crisis: The Storm and the Aftermath, 1733–5', *Parliamentary History*, vol. 33, no. 1 (2014), pp. 160–200 (special issue, *Parliament, Politics and Policy in Britain and Ireland, c. 1680–1832: Essays in Honour of D.W. Hayton*, edited by C. Jones and J. Kelly). The Duchess of Marlborough worked tirelessly in the 1730s to strengthen support for Opposition causes, hosting gatherings of Cobham's 'Cubs', whose leaders Viscount Cobham and George Lyttelton were her cousins. Frances Harris, *A Passion for Government: The Life of Sarah, Duchess of Marlborough* (Oxford, 1991), pp. 294–333.

[57] While historians doubt whether this engagement was sought, the Duchess of Marlborough did certainly befriend Prince Frederick, offering to host him at Marlborough House after the debacle of 31 July 1737, when Frederick removed his wife from his parents' purview while she was giving birth, for which King George II banished Prince Frederick from court. Harris, *A Passion for Government*, pp. 294–312.

[58] The *London Evening Post*, issue 1921 (4–6 March 1740) hinted at Vernon's 'Secret' expedition, while the *London and Country Journal*, issue 42 (6 March 1740) and the *London Daily Post and General Advertiser*, issue 1675 (7 March 1740) reported on Vernon's imminent engagements. The *Universal Spectator and Weekly Journal*, issue 596 (8 March 1740) appears to have broken the news in the press of Vernon's victory: 'For two or three Days past it has been reported, that Porto Bello was taken, and several rich Spanish Prizes; so much good News, *all at once*, makes People doubt the Truth of it.'

Table 8.1 Rosamond (1707) versus Rosamond (1740)

Table 8.1 is a comparison between the original production of *Rosamond* in 1707, a mainpiece opera with music by Thomas Clayton (1673–1725), and the 1740 afterpiece version *Rosamond*, with music by Thomas Arne. Both productions are settings of Joseph Addison's wordbook *Rosamond* (1707). Scores and wordbooks have been collated to confirm the numbers sung by dramatis personae.

Sources consulted 1707 version:	Sources consulted 1740 version:
Thomas Clayton, *Songs in the new Opera called Rosamond* (1707)	Thomas Arne, 'Music in Rosamond, 1733' Add. MS 29370, ff. 33r-85r [copied c.1765?]
[Joseph Addison], *Rosamond. An Opera* (1707)	Joseph Addison, *Rosamond: An Opera. As it is perform'd at the Theatre-Royal in Drury-Lane* (1740)

Dramatis persona / Songs [spelling as in the wordbook]	*Rosamond* (1707) wordbook pages	*Rosamond* (1740) wordbook pages
Act I	Act I	Act I
Queen / 'As o'er the hollow Vaults we walk'	p. 2	excised
Page / 'Behold on yonder rising Ground'	pp. 2–3	p. 10
Queen / 'I feel, I feel my Heart relent'	pp. 3–4	p. 11 [abbreviated]
Page / 'He comes, Victorious Henry comes!'	p. 4	excised
Queen / 'No, no, 'tis decreed'	p. 4	p. 11
Sir Trusty / 'How unhappy is he'	p. 5	p. 12
Sir Trusty, Grideline / 'O Grideline! consult thy Glass'	p. 6	p. 12–13
Grideline / 'O how blest were Grideline'	p. 6	excised
Sir Trusty, Grideline / 'Thou art ugly and old'	p. 7	p. 13
Sir Trusty / 'How hard is our Fate'	pp. 7–8	p. 14
Rosamond / 'Was ever Passion cross'd like mine?'	p. 9	excised
Rosamond / 'Ye Pow'rs I rave'	p. 10	excised
Rosamond / 'From Walk to Walk', 'Beneath some Hoary Mountain'	p. 10	p. 15
King / 'Was ever Nymph like Rosamond'	p. 13	p. 16
King / 'O the pleasing, pleasing Anguish'	p. 14	excised
Act II	Act II	Act II
King, Rosamond / 'O may the present Bliss endure'	p. 15	pp. 17–18
Rosamond / 'They're Fantoms all, I'll think no more'	p. 16	excised
Grideline / 'Prithee Cupid no more'	p. 18	excised
Page / 'A thousand fairy Scenes appear'	p. 19	excised
Queen / 'I cannot see my Lord repine'	p. 20	p. 19
Queen / 'Wild and frantick is my Grief!'	pp. 20–21	excised
Rosamond / 'Transporting Pleasure!'	p. 21	excised

Dramatis persona / Songs [spelling as in the wordbook]	*Rosamond* (1707) wordbook pages	*Rosamond* (1740) wordbook pages
Rosamond / 'O how dreadful 'tis to die!' (title in *Songs*; first line: 'When Tides of youthful Blood run high')	p. 22	excised
		SCENE, A Grotto. King / 'Rise, Glory, rise', p. 20
Rosamond / 'Think on the soft, the tender Fires'	p. 22	p. 22
Queen / 'Moving Language, shining Tears'	p. 23	p. 22
Rosamond / 'Accept, Great Queen, like injur'd Heav'n'	p. 24	pp. 22–23
Rosamond / 'Think not, thou Author of my Woe'	pp. 24–25	p. 23
Queen / 'When vanquish'd Foes beneath us lye'	p. 25	excised
Sir Trusty / 'The Bow'r turns round'	pp. 25–26	pp. 24–25
Queen / 'My Henry shall be mine Alone'	p. 26	excised
Act III	**Act III**	**[in only two acts]**
Scene a Grotto. First Angel, Second Angel / 'Behold th'unhappy Monarch there …'	pp. 27–28	excised
Scene a Grotto. First Angel, Second Angel / 'Glory strives, The Field is won'	p. 28	excised
Scene a Grotto. First Angel, Second Angel / 'Let Grief and Love at once engage'	p. 29	excised
Scene a Grotto. King / 'Adieu, ye wanton Shades and Bow'rs'	p. 29	excised
Scene a Grotto. King / 'Rise, Glory, rise'	p. 30	p. 20
Queen / 'Misterious Love, uncertain Treasure'	p. 30	excised
King / 'What means this solemn silent Show?'	p. 31	p. 25
King / 'Distracted with Woe'	p. 31	excised
Queen, King / 'A Heart so unrepenting'	p. 32	excised
King / 'So bright a Bloom'	p. 32	excised
Queen / 'If 'tis Joy to wound a Lover'	p. 33	p. 27
King, Queen / 'No more I'll change'	p. 34	p. 27
Grideline, Sir Trusty / 'Since conjugal Passion'	pp. 34–36	p. 28
King, Queen / 'Who to Forbidden Joys would Rove'	p. 36	excised
		Chorus, 'Hymen, thou source of chaste Delights', pp. 28–29

was a broad church. On 25 March, during the eight-night run of *Rosamond*, managers got up an interlude number for Beard 'in the Character of a Captain of an English Man of War ... upon the taking of Porto Bello'.[59] This entertainment sparked Beard's earliest portrait, titled *Mr. Beard in the Character of a Captn of a Man of War* (Fig. 8.2). Beard is shown in uniform singing to the sailors he leads: 'May all English Lads like you Boys / Prove on Shore true Hearts of Gold. / To their King and Country true Boys / And be neither bought nor Sold.'[60] Beard had the advantage over Clive of his sex: he could stand as a surrogate for a leader such as Vernon or Frederick. More broadly, he could personify the qualities ascribed to these heroes – courage, fortitude, incorruptibility, virility, and rationality – which Opposition writers held requisite to a robust body politic.[61]

Arne's agile, muscular music for Beard in *Rosamond* manifests such characteristics. Consider 'Was ever Nymph like Rosamond', a dazzling da capo aria. Arne deftly varies its sequences, partly by inserting roulades, and setting the words 'her Embrace' to an eye-popping seventh leap up to a sustained middle F sharp against the G sharp major chord in the bass (Ex. 8.2, bar 48). In the repeated A section, he tucks in new material set to rapid harmonic rhythms, finishing on a top A. The aria's B section sizzles with the 'Desire' of which the king sings: on each crotchet, the dynamics change from one extreme (*forte*) to another (*piano*), imitating palpitations. Beard was also given the opera's show-stopper, 'Rise, Glory, rise'. This is a full da capo aria sung by King Henry II upon his vision of future victories, replacing Addison's 1707 tableau sung by spirits. The aria's trumpet and kettle drum, expansive line, and dizzying sequential ascents are as bellicose and triumphalist as any music can be.[62]

---

[59] *London Daily Post and General Advertiser*, issue 1690 (25 March 1740); cited in *The London Stage*, Part 3, vol. 2, p. 827.

[60] Beard's song was also engraved as a songsheet 'Come my Lads with Souls befitting. A Song on the taking of Porto Bello. Sung by Mr. Beard' ([London], [1740]), held in the British Library, GB-Lbl G.303.(9.). The verses, with additional stanzas, were printed in the *London Magazine and Monthly Chronologer*, vol. 9 (April 1740), p. 187 as the poem: 'On the taking of PORTO BELLO. Written by the Lord G-- G--me. Tune, *The Sailors Song*'.

[61] Brett D. Wilson discusses the ways in which legitimate drama, tragedy especially, registers changes in political philosophy. According to his findings, patriot heroines created between the Glorious Revolution until roughly 1730 represented the Third Earl of Shaftesbury's notion of 'sensus communis', or political belonging. Playwrights designed tragic heroines to exemplify affects and actions by which loyal subjects forged bonds within the body politic. After 1730, however, figureheads for the Patriot Opposition and Hanoverian apologists became 'the sign of and synecdoche for sentimental merger and union', replacing 'female patriots' with a 'paternal figurehead' through whom civic bonds might be strengthened. Wilson, *A Race of Female Patriots: Women and Public Spirit on the British Stage*, pp. 193–200.

[62] 'Rise, Glory, rise' is recorded, and its opening bars are published in Gilman, *The Theatre Career of Thomas Arne*, pp. 53–54.

Fig. 8.2 Simon (?) Beauvais, *Mr. Beard in the Character of a Captn of a Man of War*, c.1740. Engraving. Folger Shakespeare Library. Call number: ART Vol. d45 no.186. Used by permission of the Folger Shakespeare Library.

Rosamond, by contrast, languishes, singing music in which Arne clearly exerted himself – but probably for his sister. Rosamond's central number is the recitative arioso 'From Walk to Walk' (Ex. 8.3), followed by the minuet-based air 'Beneath some hoary Mountain' (Ex. 8.4). Rosamond is essentially an Arcadian shepherdess, who, lost in her tender amours, laments her lover's absence. The power of Arne's musical rhetoric in 'From Walk to Walk' pulls us into her affective world. His rhythms submit to syllabic emphases to pace the singer's delivery. For instance, while dotted quavers shadow the iambic meter of 'From Walk to Walk, from Shade to Shade' (Ex. 8.3), accompanying strings, hovering in higher register, cascade gently down in smaller note values (bars 9–12). Arne sticks rests between verse lines to make Rosamond hesitate, break off, and eventually, at her cadence, break down. Besides rhythm he also uses intervals to mine words for their effect. The repeated falling fifths on the words 'Turning, Burning, Ranging, Changing' emphasise the seventh and its instability (bars 15–17). Rosamond's turmoil climaxes as she holds a

Ex. 8.2 Words by Joseph Addison, music by Thomas Arne, 'Was ever Nymph like Rosamond' in *Rosamond*, 1740. British Library Add. MS 2937, fols 80–81. Edited by Chris Gould.

diminished seventh against the bass while singing 'Grief'; after this, the music relaxes, on the word 'love', into a home key triad (bars 18–20). As her recitative ends, the strings shadow her voice, heightening through their runs the contrary motions of her melody and her heart as her voice leaps up at 'I rave', and down at 'I mourn' (bars 21–23).

The air which follows is equally well-crafted (Ex. 8.4). A lachrymose F minor key and minuet meter set the mood: Rosamond is mournful, yet poised. Pastoral conceits abound in strings and voice alike: slurred descending note pairs of equal value, Lombard rhythms that catch like a lover's sobs ('I'll lay me down' bars 6–7). With trills imitating 'murm'ring Streams', Arne builds symmetry into what, on the surface, seems an outpouring. He repeats musical gestures to match word-rhymes ('Mountain', 'Fountain', bars 4 and 13), while stretching out statements to contrast one effect against another. Delays in the vocal line – for instance, holding a middle F two bars on the word 'Weep' (bars 8–9) – are offset by an insistent forward momentum of runs in the violins. At the start of the second section, Rosamond calls out to 'feather'd Quires [choirs]' in an octave leap (bar 27); here Arne suggests an optimistic F major key, yet tinges the phrase with the mournfulness of the flattened seventh degree of the scale, which pulls the music towards B flat minor. In this second section minor cadences are Rosamond's inevitable fate. What this music requires for

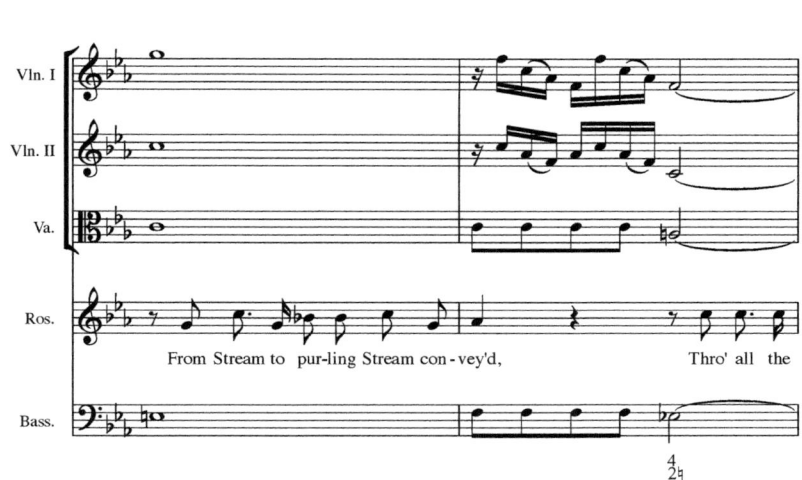

Ex. 8.3 Words by Joseph Addison, music by Thomas Arne, 'From Walk to Walk' in *Rosamond*, 1740. British Library Add. MS 29370, fols 62–66. Edited by Chris Gould.

Ex. 8.4 Words by Joseph Addison, music by Thomas Arne, 'Beneath some hoary Mountain' in *Rosamond*, 1740. British Library Add. MS 29370, fols 66–73. Edited by Chris Gould.

256　　　KITTY CLIVE, OR THE FAIR SONGSTER

impact is attentiveness to detail and the ability to subtly vary similar gestures; Rosamond must possess both control and a limpid sincerity.

Over the eight nights that it ran, *Rosamond* showed Clive capable of reining in her normally irrepressible self. Her shift from comic Patriot soprano to serious one appears to have recommended Clive to the two most illustrious employers of her career: Handel and Prince Frederick.

'O Peace' vs 'Rule Britannia': The Masque of *Alfred*

After retiring in 1769, Clive lived on Horace Walpole's estate, where her residence came to be called 'Cliveden' – a play on her surname and the actual name of Prince Frederick's residence, where she co-led *Alfred* on 1 August 1740. Clive was a playhouse star, but one of her peak appearances on stage was ironically for a private party. Frederick's under-secretary David Mallet and the poet James Thomson wrote *Alfred*, modelling its protagonist after the subject of *The Idea of the Patriot King* by Henry St John, 1st Viscount Bolingbroke. Bolingbroke's seditious Opposition work, which had circulated secretly from 1737 in manuscript copies and in Alexander Pope's ten-copy print run, outlined the qualities of the ideal ruler.[63] Frederick hired John Rich to manage the evening and had *Alfred* mounted as part of the birthday celebrations for his youngest daughter, this being a pretext for representing his aspirations among a select company.[64]

---

[63] Gerrard characterizes this late-1730s treatise as 'a coterie text with a deliberately limited circulation'. For her discussion of its transmission before 1740, see Gerrard, *The Patriot Opposition to Walpole*, p. 185–87. For the 'fullest account of the textual history' of Bolingbroke's treatise Gerrard cites Giles Barber, 'Bolingbroke, Pope and the *Patriot King*', *Library*, 5th ser., vol. 19 (1964), pp. 67–89; *ibid.*, p. 185, note 3. The poem was not printed until 1749. Frederick's private secretary and George Lyttleton, nephew and supporter of Viscount Cobham, are said to have persuaded Frederick to employ Mallet, and give a hundred-pound annual pension to Thomson. Burden, *Garrick, Arne, and the Masque of 'Alfred'*, p. 15.

[64] The politics embedded in *Alfred*, in all its versions, is the subject of Burden, *Garrick, Arne, and the Masque of 'Alfred'* and Oliver J. W. Cox, 'Frederick, Prince Of Wales, and the First Performance Of "Rule, Britannia!"', *The Historical Journal*, vol. 56, no. 4 (2013), pp. 931–54. Cox has found a letter by Martin Madan (one of Prince Frederick's equerries), in which Madan describes to his wife the evening's festivities. Besides summarizing the action in *Alfred*, Madan reported that after the masque was a 'great Dance' featuring the 'the celebrated Barbinni [Signora Le Barbarini]... a French Farce & a Pantomime Scene ... and the Judgement of Paris, of Congreve, set to Musick by Martini'. Martin Madan to J. Madan, letter of 10 August 1740, Bodl. MS Eng. lett. c. 285 fo. 28 r–v; *ibid.*, p. 944. 'Martini', as Cox notes, refers to the composer Sammartini, who set Congreve's wordbook *Judgement of Paris*. Notably, Prince Frederick himself sang Paris, whose devotion to his 'Queen' (Helen) was almost certainly an enactment of Prince Frederick's love for his wife. Donald Burrows and Berta Joncus, 'Music and Representation', *Enlightened Princesses: Caroline, Augusta, Charlotte, and the Shaping of the Modern World*, ed. J. Marschner with D. Bindman and L. L. Ford (New Haven, 2017), p. 205. Other performers in *The Judgement of Paris* were Lady Falconberg (Juno), Lady Middlesex (Pallas), and

Alfred the Great, the ninth-century King of Wessex who drove invading Danes from Britain, was a figure with whom Frederick had long been identified, and with whom he identified himself. Frederick's mentor Sir Richard Blackmore had penned an 'Epick' about King Alfred to create a model for Frederick when he was fifteen.[65] Frederick had in 1735 installed a bust of Alfred by Michael Rysbrack in the garden of Carlton House, his London residence, possibly in the garden's Octagon Temple.[66] The pro-Opposition *Craftsman* had puffed the installation and Frederick in one breath, noting that with it Frederick 'declares his Intention of making *that* AMIABLE PRINCE *the Pattern of his* OWN CONDUCT'.[67]

Although a masque, *Alfred* was largely spoken, with just six numbers and its final 'Rule Britannia' chorus, all composed by Arne. James Quin, in a spoken part, led the acting company, playing the wise Hermit who instructs Alfred in kingly ways. The role was apropos, since Quin regularly tutored Frederick and his family in their domestic theatrical productions.[68] Clive's part, uniquely among cast members, was both spoken and sung. She alone performed two solos; the other vocalists each had only one.[69] All vocalists sang the rousing

---

Prince Lobkowitz (Mercury). Mariateresa Dellaborra, 'The Judgement of Paris (1740), pastorale di Giuseppe Sammartini', *Rivista Italiana di Musicologia*, vol. 48 (2013), p. 43.

[65] In his words, Blackmore designed his poem for the young Prince Frederick (then resident in Hanover) to explain 'imperial Authority' through a 'Narration after the Epick Manner' of a 'Prince sprung from the ancient Saxon Race of your own native Land'. Richard Blackmore, 'Dedication', *Alfred. An Epick Poem*. (London, 1723), pages unnumbered.

[66] The Alfred bust was erected on 31 July 1735 along with a bust of the Black Prince, son of Edward III. Where it was sited is unclear, but press reports and craftsmen's bills indicate that the bust was likely placed in the Octagon Temple. Prince Frederick was following Viscount Cobham, who had in 1733 installed a bust of Alfred in his 'Temple of British Worthies' at Stowe Gardens. On the bust that Prince Frederick erected, the inscription read: 'This Prince was the Founder of the Liberties and Commonwealth of England.' Following Prince Frederick, Lord Bathurst erected Alfred's bust in his gardens in Cirencester. Kimerly Rorschach, 'Frederick, Prince of Wales (1707–1751) as a Patron of the Visual Arts: Princely Patriotism and Political Propaganda' (PhD diss., Yale University, 1985), vol. 1, pp. 135–40.

[67] *Country Journal or The Craftsman*, issue 479 (6 September 1735); cited in Rorschach, 'Frederick, Prince of Wales (1707–1751)', p. 139. For further press reports on Frederick's installation of the Alfred bust, see Cox, 'Frederick, Prince Of Wales, and the First Performance of "Rule, Britannia!"', pp. 939–40.

[68] Vivian, *A Life of Frederick, Prince of Wales*, p. 324.

[69] Clive sang 'O Peace' and 'If those, who live in shepherd's bower'. Arne's wife Cecilia performed 'Sweet valley, say' offstage, pretending to be the voice of Alfred's wife Eltruda, performed by Christiana Horton (who retired the next year). Isabella and Esther Young were a first and second spirit respectively in the first tableau, and sang one air each, joining voices for one stanza in the second air. The bass Henry Rheinhold, introducing the second tableau with the air 'From those eternal regions', sang in character as The Genius of England. The vocalists were announced in the *London Daily Post*, issue 1802 (2 August 1740). Burden, 'Table 22: Allocation of Parts in Alfred', *Garrick, Arne, and the Masque of 'Alfred'*, p. 128. Burden indicates that Eltruda was both sung and spoken, but this is

finale 'Rule Britannia', each taking one of the six solo stanzas in turn and joining in the refrain.[70] Thomson and Mallet took their story from Paul de Rapin-Thoyras's *L'Histoire d'Angleterre* (1724–27).[71] The shepherdess Emma (Clive) and her husband Corin have sheltered a stranger, who unknown to them is King Alfred. He and the Earl of Devon, also disguised as a commoner, defeat the Danes by having Devon and his soldiers secretly penetrate the Danish camp, and then rally Alfred's demoralized troops for a final rout. Interwoven with this tale are visions of Alfred's greatness (the first tableau), advice on monarchical greatness (by the Hermit), declarations of spousal love and mutual admiration (between Alfred and his wife Eltruda), visions of Alfred's future grandeur (the second tableau), and the revelation of Alfred's rank to Emma and Corin.

Clive opened the action with one of the most irresistible songs she ever performed: 'O Peace, thou fairest Child of Heav'n' (Ex. 8.5). Emma begs Corin to forswear warring against the Danes, and then sings 'O Peace' to dissuade him from battle. Arne's music evokes serenity and deep melancholy, anticipating the warfare that will prevail. The minor key, largo tempo, and whispered dynamics set the mood. A walking bass underpins an extended introduction that gently trudges forward. Before the voice enters, all accompaniment ceases: the words 'O Peace' are a cry that breaks the silence. The longest note of the entire song, on the word 'Peace', is held for four bars, during which the accompaniment creeps back in. From this point, violins follow each verse line with a dejected motif. This consists of a written-out ornament of a slide, first up, then down, foregrounding the mournful minor third interval. After its arresting opening, the voice moves in counterpoint to a bass line, throwing the serene beauty of its melody into relief. The violins tend to double and parallel the melody, and their occasional dissonances against the voice deepen the aching lyricism of Arne's song.

The original masque of *Alfred* was in fact shown once to the public, at a single dress rehearsal at Drury Lane on July 25.[72] Some sections seem like public statements: the blustering 'Rule Britannia' is after all about Frederick's

---

not the case; as he points out elsewhere, Cecilia Arne performed Eltruda's only air. *Ibid.*, p. 32.

[70] The tenor Thomas Salway, who played the non-singing role of the shepherd Corin, reappeared suddenly as The Bard to sing the bellicose first stanza of 'Rule Britannia'. He is sometimes erroneously said to have sung the whole ode as a solo, rather than just the first stanza. [David Mallet], *Alfred. A Masque. Represented before Their Royal Highnesses the Prince and Princess of Wales at Cliffden, on the First of August, 1740* (London, 1740). The voices are correctly allocated, according to standard finales, in the recording of 'Rule Britannia' directed by Peter Holman on *Fairest Isle*, Hyperion CDA67115.

[71] Cox, 'Frederick, Prince Of Wales, and the First Performance of "Rule, Britannia!"', p. 945.

[72] 'This day was rehears'd, at Drury-lane Theatre, a Masque entitled Alfred, in order to be represented before the Prince and Princess, at Cliefden-house, on the First of August.'

Ex. 8.5 Words by James Thomson and David Mallet, music by Thomas Arne, 'O Peace, thou fairest Child of Heav'n' in *Songs in the Masque of Alfred* [1757]. Source: Bibliothèque nationale de France, Département Musique, D-420. Notice no: FRBNF39780240.

endorsement of an aggressive maritime policy and Britain's slave trade. At Cliveden, where the open-air stage was 'compos'd of Vegetables, and decorated with Festoons of Flowers',[73] *Alfred* will also have hinted at domestic harmony and Frederick's love of gardening. At both venues, Frederick's longing for a tranquil prosperity for himself and his country will have crystallized in 'O Peace': calm, delicate, and refined, the air's effectiveness depends on its singer's subtlety and sensitivity. Clive alone was trusted with this moment.

Samson: Playhouse Stars made Sacred

While Arne's *Comus* continued to delight audiences, Handel brought out his next Miltonic production, *Samson* (1743). The idea for this oratorio appears to have come out of a gathering with Handel hosted by the 4th Earl of Shaftesbury

---

The Gentleman's Magazine: and Historical Chronicle. vol. 10 (July 1740), p. 356 (28 July); cited in Burden, *Garrick, Arne, and the Masque of 'Alfred'*, p. 32.

[73] *London Daily Post and General Advertiser*, issue 1804 (5 August 1740); cited in Gilman, *The Theatre Career of Thomas Arne*, pp. 121–22.

on 24 November 1739. In a letter to fellow Miltonian James Harris, the earl reported that his brother-in-law James Noel had 'read through the whole poem of Sampson Agonistes and whenever he rested to take breath Mr Handel (who was highly pleas'd with the peice) played'.[74] Shaftesbury found that Handel's 'harmony was perfectly adapted to the sublimity of the poem.'[75] *Samson Agonistes* was eventually adapted by Handel's friend Newburgh Hamilton,[76] rather than by one of James Harris's circle, which signalled a change of aims from *Comus*. While the concerns of Harris and his circle transcended commercial success, Hamilton, being a steward to the Earl of Strafford, will have welcomed it – and have been more tractable to Handel's will. As Ruth Smith shows, Hamilton, too, was committed to the Opposition cause, and the Earl of Strafford for whom he worked was a staunch Jacobite.[77]

The Opposition resentment Hamilton vented in *Samson* was as overt as coded language could make it.[78] By the time Handel began to set the *Samson* wordbook in June 1741, Parliament and the press were in an uproar over the conduct of the war with Spain.[79] Since the victory at Porto Bello, Britain had suffered humiliating defeats: in June 1740, the British besiegers of Florida had been repulsed after two weeks, abandoning their artillery; this had been followed in the spring of 1741 by Vernon's bungling of a massive 67-day assault on Cartagena, in present-day Colombia, which left 18,000 of the 26,000 British invading force dead, at least half from disease.[80]

---

[74] 4th Earl of Shaftesbury to James Harris, letter of 24 November 1739, repr. in Burrows and Dunhill, ed., *Music and Theatre in Handel's World*, p. 80.

[75] *Ibid*.

[76] On the basis of the Strafford papers, Ruth Smith confirms that Newburgh Hamilton was justified in calling Handel 'my friend' in the prefatory poem to *Alexander's Feast*. Ruth Loewenthal [Smith], 'Handel and Newburgh Hamilton: New References in the Strafford Papers', *The Musical Times*, vol. 112, no. 1545 (1971), p. 1065.

[77] The 3rd Earl 'was named as commander-in-chief of the Pretender's forces ... and one of the Lords Regent in the Pretender's absence; he was a leading conspirator in both the Atterbury Plot (1720–2) and the Cornbury Plot (1731–5) to restore the Stuarts, and was also involved in negotiations on behalf of the Stuart cause in 1725.' Smith, *Handel's Oratorios*, p. 192.

[78] As Smith rightly emphasises, polite audiences were well-schooled in decoding implied meanings, in part due to so much eighteenth-century writing – in satires, newspapers, and especially stage works – being conducted in this discourse. Smith, *Handel's Oratorios*, pp. 187–88. The ways Hamilton's changes to Milton's poem made the oratorio *Samson* relate to Opposition protest are outlined in Ruth Smith, 'National Aspiration: *Samson Agonistes* transformed in Handel's *Samson*', *Edinburgh Companion to Literature and Music*, ed. D. da Sousa Correa (Edinburgh, 2019). I am grateful to Ruth Smith for sharing her manuscript with me in advance of its publication.

[79] Wilson, *The Sense of the People*, pp. 141–42.

[80] Blame for these defeats fell on Walpole, held responsible for delays in dispatching British forces out of fear that France would enter the war and attack the homeland. Philip Woodfine, '"Suspicious Latitudes": Commerce, Colonies, and Patriotism in the 1730s', *Studies in Eighteenth-Century Culture*, vol. 27 (1998), pp. 25–52.

The story of *Samson* represents hope for a new order, led by Bolingbroke's Opposition Patriot king. *Samson* and *Alfred* share features, as Smith discusses, typically ascribed to this figure: a hero under threat from hostile forces who is forced to be passive, who reflects on nation and governance, and whose sympathetic fellow-sufferers guide him to fulfil his destiny, saving the nation.[81] Milton's literary authority cloaked the inflammatory message of these points. Hamilton of course humbly pledged his service to the poet:

> Several Pieces of Milton having been lately brought on the Stage with Success, particularly his *Penseroso* and *Allegro*, I was of Opinion that nothing of that Divine Poet's wou'd appear in the Theatre with greater Propriety or Applause than his SAMSON AGONISTES ... In adapting this POEM to the Stage, the Recitative is taken almost wholly from Milton, making use only of those Parts in his long Work most necessary to preserve the Spirit of the Subject, and justly connect it.[82]

This preface hides not only the politics, but also the playhouse commerce informing this production. Despite the fidelity promised to Milton, in his *Samson* wordbook Hamilton followed the stage lines of Beard the Patriot hero and Clive the Goddess of Mirth.

Gossip during the 1739–40 season had sharpened audience appetite to see Beard. On 8 January 1739 he had secretly married the young Catholic widow Lady Henrietta Herbert of Powis, known as 'Lady Harriet', the daughter of Earl Waldegrave.[83] Lady Harriet's grandmother was an illegitimate daughter of James II by his mistress Arabella Churchill; Lady Harriet's father was a first cousin of the 'Young Pretender' Charles Edward Stuart.[84] In allying himself with Lady Harriet, Beard undermined his credentials as a Hanoverian loyalist. Beyond this, Beard challenged social propriety. As the first-ever marriage between a Lady of Quality and a playhouse principal, his union sent shock waves through the Town.[85] In retaliation for marrying Beard, the Herbert family broke Lady Harriet financially, emotionally, and socially. They denied her the annual jointure of six hundred pounds which Lady Harriet's father had secured from her late husband

---

[81] Ruth Smith, 'Intellectual Contexts of Handel's Oratorios', *Music in Eighteenth-Century England: Essays in Memory of Charles Cudworth*, pp. 115–33, esp. pp. 116–18.

[82] [Newburgh Hamilton], 'Preface', *Samson. An Oratorio ... Alter'd and adapted to the Stage from the Samson Agonistes of John Milton* (London, 1743). When Hamilton's wordbook was re-issued that year, the preface was omitted. Donald Burrows, 'The Word-books for Handel's Performances of *Samson*', *Musical Times*, vol. 146, no. 1890 (2005), pp. 9–12.

[83] John Beard married Henrietta in the Fleet Prison. The marriage is recorded in the notebooks of John Burnford, clerk and register keeper. Neil Jenkins, *John Beard: Handel and Garrick's Favourite Tenor* (Bramber, 2012), p. 54, note 33.

[84] Jenkins, *John Beard*, p. 47. I am grateful to Ruth Smith for calling my attention to this reference.

[85] They may have met at court, where Beard performed royal birthday odes from 1733. Robert Halsband, 'The Noble Lady and the Player', *History Today*, vol. 18, no. 7 (1968), pp. 464–72.

Lord Powis when negotiating the marriage of the 17-year-old Lady Harriet to the 45-year-old peer.[86] This made it impossible for Beard and Lady Harriet to pay debts they had both incurred prior to their marriage.[87] Costly and extended litigation, which the Beards ultimately lost, began in 1740 after Lady Harriet's father rejected her pleas for forgiveness as his 'Kneeling weeping Child'.[88]

Apart from their debts, the scandal of the Beard-Herbert *mésalliance* made Lady Harriet a pariah. Lady Mary Montagu – who was herself secretly courting the opera impresario Algarotti[89] – wrote witheringly of Lady Harriet's union with 'Beard, who sings in the farces at Drury-lane', and how the family was 'violently surprized at … her … recourse to the church in her necessities'.[90] Lord Egmont reported that Lady Harriet's brother had written to him predicting that Beard would disappoint 'of the only thing she married him for', leading Egmont to conclude that 'there is no prudence below the girdle'.[91] Lady Harriet eventually died in 1753 under the obloquy of both Town and family. She perhaps believed what Beard routinely enacted in his sentimental comedies, that love conquers all; she may not have noticed that the happy ending in such works typically depends on the hero's hidden noble birth.

Beard dropped all work outside Drury Lane after joining the house in 1737, but from early 1739 began to concertize frantically everywhere he could, taking up, among other engagements, the work Handel offered.[92] As Hamilton prepared the *Samson* wordbook in 1741, he had every reason to expect that Beard would once again join Handel's oratorio company. Handel also anticipated re-engaging Beard. In a letter of December 1741, Jennens recorded that Beard 'should have gone with Handel into Ireland' a month earlier, but that

---

[86] Powis died intestate, undermining the settlement's legal purchase. Being refused access to her jointure forced Lady Harriet to mortgage it that year. Halsband, 'The Noble Lady and the Player', pp. 466–68.

[87] Thomas Harris to James Harris, letter 10 May 1740: 'I hear that Beard is gone off together with his lady[,] who I believe had contracted debts before her marriage.' Burrows and Dunhill, ed., *Music and Theatre in Handel's World*, p. 97. Halsband reports that Beard and Lady Harriet each had debts of around two hundred pounds. Halsband, 'The Noble Lady and the Player', p. 468.

[88] Lady Henrietta Herbert of Powis to Earl Waldegrave, letter of 9 July 1740; quoted without attribution in Halsband, 'The Noble Lady and the Player', p. 468. Jenkins identifies this letter as part of the Waldegrave Family Papers, Chewton House, Chewton Mendip, Somerset. On the twelve-year litigation that the Beards embarked on in 1740, see Jenkins, *John Beard*, pp. 56–57.

[89] Montagu's impassioned letters to Algarotti from late 1738 and early 1739 are reprinted in Robert Halsband, ed., *The Complete Letters of Lady Mary Wortley Montagu* (Oxford, 1966); see esp. vol. 2, pp. 104–11.

[90] Lady Mary Wortley Montagu to Lady Pomfret, letter of November 1738, *ibid.*, pp. 126–28.

[91] *Ibid.*, p. 128, note 4.

[92] Of Handel's works, apart from *L'Allegro* in 1749, Beard sang Jonathan in *Saul* at King's Theatre on 16 January 1739, principal tenor in *Israel in Egypt* from 4 April 1739 at King's Theatre, and Acis in *Acis and Galatea* from 13 December 1739 at Lincoln's Inn Fields.

Fleetwood had refused to release the tenor.[93] Having started setting *Samson* on 29 September 1741, Handel broke off this work on 9 October, picking it up again after his 1741–42 Dublin tour when he could procure Beard.[94]

Samson was the first English oratorio title role created for a tenor, and was almost certainly designed for Beard to play opposite his professional partner Clive. Hamilton's most radical changes to Milton's poem were in Clive's role of Dalila, which borrowed heavily from her line. Hamilton's Dalila offers Samson easy pastoral love, indeed the 'Voice of Love',[95] like that of Rosamond, or the Nymph in *Comus*. She is the effeminizing Other who, as in *Rosamond*, imperils the hero's commitment to public duty. Like Euphrosyne of *Comus*, Dalila celebrates joy for its own sake. This range of characterizations bears little relation to Milton's Dalila, who is rapacious and deceitful.[96]

Hamilton's Dalila tempts Samson with visions redolent of those in *Comus*. These are of a private court of love, which, as in *Comus*, serves to dissolve participants' moral purpose. In *Samson Agonistes*, Milton has the Philistines keep watch over Samson; Hamilton instead has Dalila guard Samson and describe the pleasures of her home ('How charming is domestick Ease!').[97] The correlate to such temptation is the 'cool Grotto' where Rosamond dwells, and where she and King Henry celebrate their 'Bliss' in a duet.[98] Dalila has attendant virgins, like Euphrosyne's attendants in *Comus*. Dalila offers pleasures redolent of Rosamond's and Euphrosyne's: 'redoubled love' and the 'Delight' of non-visual senses, as well as 'nursing Care' should Samson again yield to her.[99]

Samson's words, 'I know thy warbling Charms, / Thy Trains, thy Wiles, and fair enchanted Cup', surely evoked for playhouse audiences London's celebrated cup-wielding Euphrosyne.[100] Samson's altercation with Dalila concludes with the duet 'Traitor to Love', which has no correlate in Milton. Its structure and theme relate closely to the Beard–Clive *Comus* duet 'From Tyrant Laws and

---

[93] Charles Jennens to James Harris, letter of 5 December 1741: 'Beard is come home again [from France], & should have gone with Handel into Ireland, but Fleetwood said he should want him to sing in an English opera.' The 'English opera' may have been the new setting of Congreve's famous wordbook *The Judgement of Paris*. Burrows and Dunhill, ed., *Music and Theatre in Handel's World*, pp. 129–30.

[94] The phases of Handel's preparation of the score are analyzed by Hans Dieter Clausen in George F. Handel, *Samson: Oratorio in Three Acts, HWV 57*, ed. H. D. Clausen, Hallische Händel-Ausgabe, series 1, vol. 18 (Kassel, 2011), pp. xx–xxii.

[95] [Hamilton], *Samson*, p. 14.

[96] Mary Ann Radzinowicz characterizes Dalila as 'masterful … and sensually aggressive' who 'is no fit conversing mate' and who 'perpetually drives toward dominance'. Mary Ann Radzinowicz, *Towards Samson Agonistes: The Growth of Milton's Mind* (Princeton, 1978), p. 48. Milton's and Hamilton's verses are compared line by line in Clausen, 'Introduction', *Samson*, pp. xxxv–xlvii.

[97] [Hamilton], *Samson*, p. 14.

[98] *Rosamond … new Set to Musick by Thomas Augustine Arne*, p. 18.

[99] [Hamilton], *Samson*, pp. 13–14.

[100] Ibid., p. 14.

Customs free' – but whereas in *Comus* Beard revelled with Clive, as Samson he has to resist the 'Charmer's Voice'.[101] The score also bears traces of Clive's Euphrosyne. Handel's selection of galant dance metres, which mirror Clive's in *Comus*, signify Dalila's relish in amusement. Her dances associated with the pastoral belong to the soft temptress sketched by Hamilton, and distinguish Dalila from *Samson*'s other soloists, who sing principally in aria, recitative, and recitative arioso. In confining terpsichorean strains to Clive, Handel followed Arne, who had set nearly all her airs in *Comus* as dances.[102] In their song, the Virgin Attendants liken Dalila to a cooing dove, in lieu of Milton's power-hungry harlot. When Samson condemns Dalila ('Your Charms to Ruin led the way'),[103] Handel overrides his words with an Arcadian setting: the siciliano, undulating vocal line, and drone bass of Samson's air do not express rage, rather they conjure up an idyll. For playhouse audiences, this pastoral mood, and her air's subtexts, were stock Clive content.

In her central musical scene, Dalila, her entourage in train, weaves her magic by singing a leisurely choral rondo. For this, Handel wrote exclusively dance forms: a minuet ('My Faith and Truth') is followed by a bourrée ('To fleeting Pleasures'), which both then repeat.[104] This type of dance-based rondo, while unusual for Handel, is essentially the form of Euphrosyne's central scene, in which the Goddess of Mirth directs her followers; indeed, the necessary excision of staged dance from Handel's *Samson* account for many of the differences between Handel's rondo scene and Arne's.[105] Through keys and dance types, Handel evokes the character of Euphrosyne: her feistiness (the bravura of D major), her gaiety (the minuet), and her promises of 'heart-easing' entertainment (the bourrée).[106]

Samson was Handel's first sustained success in oratorio in a decade, and a career turning point. The public response surely owed something to the top playhouse stars who led the work, and the ways in which Hamilton and Handel accommodated them. It was for instance an important evening for Susannah Cibber. After scandal had forced her to quit the stage in 1738, *Samson* was part of her first season back. To revive her career she had gone to Dublin, where in 1741–42 Handel had unexpectedly run an oratorio season. Needing singers, he hired her, and she never looked back; the éclat of the debut of *Messiah* was particularly helpful.[107] For the 1742–43 season she returned to London,

---

[101] *Ibid.*
[102] See Arne, *Comus*. Arne set Euphrosyne's airs as follows: 'By dimpl'd brook' (gavotte, *ibid.*, pp. 24–26); 'Fame's an Eccho' (siciliano, *ibid.*, pp. 66–70); 'Come, Come, bid Adieu to Fear' (gavotte, *ibid.*, pp. 96–99); 'Ye Fawns, and ye Dryads' (minuet, *ibid.*, pp. 124–27).
[103] [Hamilton], *Samson*, p. 13.
[104] *Ibid.*
[105] Joncus, 'Handel at Drury Lane', p. 224 (Table 2).
[106] Arne, *Comus*, p. 96.
[107] Burrows, *Handel: Messiah*, p. 21.

where Handel again hired her. In *Samson* Cibber sang the part of the sober male counsellor Micah; as Jonathan Lee discusses, Handel fit this role to her post-1738 sentimental line.[108] Handel's submission to his stars is measurable by its absence as well as its presence: in response to an unrevised part that Susannah Cibbber took in another oratorio (Jael in *Deborah*), the Earl of Radnor grumbled in 1744 that 'Mrs Cybber' was not 'any thing like to what' she was 'formerly, when parts where made on purpose for' her by Handel.[109]

The response to *Samson* was very different. Thomas Harris wrote to his brother James: 'I did not imagine that any other piece would go off so well, because none could suit the voices so well.'[110] The warmth of *Samson*'s reception in 1743 encouraged Handel to organize a second oratorio season a few weeks later. Led by Beard, Clive, and Susannah Cibber, it featured his two-section version of *L'Allegro ed il penseroso* and the London debut of *Messiah*. While the former was favourably received, *Messiah* drew sharp rebuke. Critics objected to Handel placing the Holy Word in the mouths of playhouse stars.[111] This may have led Handel to scrap his plans to revive his scripture-based oratorio *Athalia*, with Clive in the title role of yet another politics-fuelled production from years earlier.[112] In this oratorio, which premiered in 1733, the daughter of King Ahab and Queen Jezebel of Israel seizes the throne of Judah, orders the execution of other potential claimants to the throne, and establishes the worship of Baal – all outcomes of a woman holding unbridled

[108] Lee, 'From Amelia to Calista and Beyond', pp. 18–26. In his dissertation, Lee reflects that: 'The rise [after 1739] of this actress depended upon the audience's belief that she held a "natural" and "chaste heart," and a change in that perception demanded a change in public persona.' Jonathan Lee, 'Virtue Rewarded: Handel's Oratorios and the Culture of Sentiment' (PhD diss., Univ. of California, Berkeley, 2013), p. 60. As Burrows notes, 'Hans Dieter Clausen has suggested that Handel may have revised the score in two stages, incorporating Mrs Cibber first, and then making provision for Edwards, Avolio and Lowe.' Burrows, 'The Word-books for Handel's Performances of *Samson*', p. 10, note 13.
[109] Letter from the 4th Earl of Radnor to James Harris, 6 November 1744, in Burrows and Dunhill, ed., *Music and Theatre in Handel's World*, pp. 204–05. Some scholars have claimed that Susannah Cibber sang Jael at its premiere in Oxford in 1733, but Celeste Gismondi did; in 1744 Handel transposed Gismondi's part down for Cibber. Lee, 'Virtue Rewarded', p. 73, note 62.
[110] Letter from Thomas Harris to James Harris, 25 March 1743, in Burrows and Dunhill, ed., *Music and Theatre in Handel's World*, p. 160.
[111] Burrows, *Handel: Messiah*, pp. 25–28. For the documentation in full, see Donald Burrows et al., ed., *George Frideric Handel Collected Documents: Volume 4, 1742–1750* (Cambridge, 2019), pp. 80–82, 87, 94–96.
[112] Deborah W. Rooke, 'Jezebel, Joash, and Jesus Christ: Aspects of *Athalia*', in *Handel's Israelite Oratorio Libretti: Sacred Drama and Biblical Exegesis* (Oxford, 2012), pp. 53–73. According to Rooke, the librettist Samuel Humphreys altered Racine's *Athalie* to parallel the victory of Protestant Hanoverians over Catholic Stuarts; Smith argues that, for Oxford's High-Church audience, Humphreys meant to celebrate the rule of God-given law in Britain – exemplified by the protest in 1733 against Walpole's proposed Excise Tax – as against the 'disgusting perversions' of law among Britain's neighbours. Smith, *Handel's Oratorios*, pp. 324–25.

authority. One of her grandsons is saved, and becomes the figurehead of a rebellion against her. In preparing this part for Clive Handel made few changes to his earlier score, apart from lowering its tessitura.[113] Perhaps he felt that the outspoken Clive could animate *Athalia* without changes, for which, in any case, he would have had little time.

Clive's powers were then at their height. Handel's selection of *L'Allegro* for his second run that season spoke for his business sense: how could any Town member miss the chance to hear Clive as Handel's Euphrosyne, as opposed to Arne's? Clive's performance of the *L'Allegro* aria 'Mirth, admit me of thy crew' would surely have been heard as an *in propria persona* representation.[114] Handel also altered his score to add a 'segue' from his organ solo into Clive's last air, 'Straight mine Eye', joining his playing to Clive's singing.[115]

His changes to *Messiah* to accommodate Clive were equally deft. With her busy Drury Lane schedule, Clive had little time to learn new music, but Handel extended the soprano part in the shepherd's scene to give Clive a cameo appearance. Augmenting his original 11-bar recitative ('And lo, the Angel of the Lord'), he wrote a lyrical 31-bar arioso section ('But lo') in which the soprano describes the reaction of the shepherds. Despite this insertion's brevity, Clive was announced as a soloist.[116] She sang this arioso at the single *Messiah* performance during Handel's second 1743 oratorio season, and was

---

[113] 'The performing score of Athalia (D-Hs M C/264) reveals that he also at some stage planned to revive that oratorio, with the following cast: Avolio (Josabeth), Cibber (Joad), Clive (Athalia), Beard (Mathan), Savage (Abner), Edwards (Joas) and Lowe (Israelite). This can only have been in 1743.' Burrows et al., ed., *George Frideric Handel Collected Documents: Volume 4, 1742–1750*, p. 60. The changes made to the part of Athalia for the 1743 version are collated in George F. Handel, *Athalia: Oratorio in Three Parts, HWV 52*, ed. S. Blaut, Hallische Händel-Ausgabe, series 1, vol. 12 (Kassel, 2006), pp. 428–85.

[114] Burrows lists the casting of the affective personalities in *L'Allegro ed il penseroso*: 'Penseroso was represented by Avolio and Cibber, Allegro by Clive, Beard and Reinhold; Edwards was mainly cast as Allegro but may have sung Penseroso's "Sweet bird", and Lowe apparently commuted between the two sides.' Burrows, 'Reconstructing Handel's Performances of *L'Allegro*', p. 73. According to the critical edition of *L'Allegro*, Clive sang airs no. 10 ('Mirth, admit me of thy crew'), no. 16 ('If I give thee honour due / Let me wander'), and no. 17 ('Straight mine Eye'), intended originally for tenor and soprano parts.

[115] Fol. 39v in the British Library, R.M.20.d.5, contains the instruction 'Org ad libit il soggetto della fuga seguente', and under the staves which follow is written 'Segue straight mine Eye Mrs Clive & accomp. Da capo'. Hall and Hall, *L'Allegro, il penseroso ed il moderato: Kritischer Bericht*, p. 10. 'Straight mine Eye' (an additional song) was first introduced at Dublin performances in December 1741.

[116] Larsen, in his painstaking reconstruction of the different *Messiah* versions (1741–60), stresses that Clive sang only the arioso. Jens P. Larsen, *Handel's Messiah: Origins, Composition, Sources* (London, 1957), pp. 194, 235.

the only soprano ever to perform it in Handel's lifetime.[117] Yet this bespoke passage for Clive circulated for decades in print, a persistence which has long puzzled musicologists.[118] The explanation suggested by Clive's story is that music lovers were as loyal to vocal stars as they were to master composers.

The afterlife of Dalila

Clive's battles with the managers of both patent playhouses over the next two seasons made it impossible for her to rejoin Handel's oratorio company. During this difficult period, Willem De Fesch provided her with alternative masque and oratorio parts. One of his compositions for the 1745 season was the oratorio *Joseph*, whose run dovetailed with Handel's revival of his own *Joseph and his Brethren*, with wordbook by James Miller, from his previous season. Beard took the title role in both De Fesch's *Joseph* and Handel's, singing opposite Clive in the former. Winton Dean's assertion that this 'music has disappeared' is incorrect:[119] a c.1745–75 fair copy of De Fesch's score is held at the Royal Academy of Music. A brief comparison of De Fesch's parts for Beard and Clive with their joint scene in *Samson* illuminates the extent to which celebrity parts might cascade. De Fesch borrowed features from Clive's and Beard's *Samson* numbers, just as, for *Samson*, Handel had borrowed Clive and Beard points from Arne's *Comus* and *Rosamond*. Furthermore, Clive's part in De Fesch's *Joseph* shows the authority she had acquired over the composer whose music she was to sing.[120]

As Potiphar's Wife in *Joseph*, like Dalila in *Samson*, Clive is a temptress who tries to persuade the hero (Beard) to indulge in amorous pleasures. Potiphar's Wife, like Dalila, appears only in the second act.[121] The clustering of Clive's numbers in both *Samson* and in *Joseph* was in each case likely an expedient to minimize rehearsal time. Potiphar's Wife traverses the same affects as Dalila, from politely urging the hero on ('Such a lovely prudent youth … Behold a gratefull Friend in me, / Esteeming your fidelity') through to quarrelling with him.[122] The couple conclude, as in *Samson*, with a brief warring duet; in *Joseph*,

---

[117] Burrows has corrected Larsen's earlier assertion that Francesina sang the passage in 1745. Compare Burrows, *Handel: Messiah*, p. 13 to Larsen, *Handel's Messiah*, p. 219.

[118] Between 1743 and 1785 no fewer than eleven of seventeen *Messiah* manuscripts and six of eleven period editions retain this section. The manuscripts and editions containing the arioso are listed in Appendix A, 'Table of Manuscript Sources and their Contents' and 'Table of Contents of the Principal Editions from 1749 to 1854' in John Tobin, *Handel's Messiah: A Critical Account of the Manuscript Sources and Printed Editions* (London, 1969), pp. 168–70.

[119] The basis for Dean's assertion, 'Defesch's oratorio, though put on at cheap prices, was not a success, and the music has disappeared' is unclear. Winton Dean, *Handel's Dramatic Oratorios and Masques* (London, New York and Toronto, 1959), p. 407.

[120] Robert L. Tusler, ed., *Willem de Fesch: Joseph. Oratorio. 1745* (Amsterdam, 1995).

[121] Ibid., pp. 48–65 (Act II, scene 4); pp. 66–70 (Act II, scene 5).

[122] Ibid., pp. 48–52.

Ex. 8.6 Willem De Fesch, 'You see what I dare not say' in *Joseph*, 1745. Edited by Robert L. Tusler. © 1995 by Donemus, The Netherlands.

this duet is 'You see what I dare not say', whose affect and structure mirror *Samson*'s 'Traitor to Love'.[123] In both, anger mounts until the final cadence. As the hero protects his virtue, the soloists interrupt each other and re-use each other's words and melody; these fragments dovetail to make a complete statement, the two melodic lines fusing in the bars just before the cadence (Ex. 8.6). In *Joseph*, however, it is the male rather than the female protagonist who quits the scene in frustration.

De Fesch went beyond Handel in giving Clive two lengthy numbers after her duet with Beard. The first is a revenge aria,[124] and the second a revenge duet.[125] Such song was new to Clive's repertory, and winked at her very public two-season conflict with playhouse managers just as this was coming to a head. Calls for justice in both her solo and duet resound with the outrage of Clive's pamphlet *The Case of Mrs. Clive submitted to the Publick* (1744). Listening to Clive, audiences familiar with her grievances will have filled in for themselves why she was suddenly singing such uncharacteristic music, and who the targets of her ire really were.

High-style revenge arias are usually wild, Italianate, and stuffed with vocal extremes of register, leap, run, and diminution. A chugging bass line typically propels momentum forward until, at the final cadence, the singer hurls a volley of notes and storms off. De Fesch chose another way: the vocal lines of Clive's revenge solo and revenge duet both shadow natural declamation. The accompaniment sometimes acts like an Italianate voice, as in the recitative arioso 'Furies, death and torture!', where runs in the strings tumble over each other.[126] To preserve the verses' clarity, De Fesch arranged motives and phrases symmetrically, and created musical rhyme; that is, he would weld a motif to a line's end-rhyme, and where that end-rhyme occurs, so does its motif. The primacy of word sense and controlled expression had always been hallmarks of Clive's song; to preserve them, De Fesch put sense before sound even at Clive's most impassioned moments.

Clive's battle against Fleetwood, which began weeks after *Samson* opened, was the juncture at which the credibility of her public persona began to erode. This process continued until, in 1746, a supposed 'scuffle' with Peg Woffington turned Clive into something of a public joke;[127] after this, to restore herself to favour, Clive had to corroborate the most damning views of herself. The Clive whom London's best composers had dressed to advantage – pastoral, mirthful, patriotic, engaging, commanding, protean – was soon forgotten.

---

[123] *Ibid.*, pp. 58–62.
[124] *Ibid.*, pp. 61–65 (rehearsal no. 27, 'Furies, death and torture!').
[125] *Ibid.*, pp. 66–70 (Act II, scene 5).
[126] *Ibid.*, pp. 61–62.
[127] The purported altercation was the subject of a broadside *The Green Room Scuffle* (London, 1746), discussed in Chapter 10.

9

The Case of Mrs. Clive

Fleetwood fleeces the company – a cartel is formed and the Lord Chamberlain falls in – the players protest but Fleetwood's 'Estimate' prevails – Garrick, Macklin, and 'Kitty Cuckoe' part ways – Clive meets De Fesch – Rich abuses, Clive protests; Garrick abuses, Macklin protests – audiences fire Fleetwood

In 1743 Clive was caught up in the second actors' revolt of her career, but this time her involvement damaged her reputation irreparably. After the Licensing Act of 1737 had closed all but the two royal playhouses, the ensuing duopoly was a temptation to form a cartel that Charles Fleetwood and John Rich did not resist. Fleetwood also stole from the Drury Lane payroll to cover his gambling debts, and the unpaid actors walked out. David Garrick and Charles Macklin headed one rebel faction, Clive another. The players' only recourse was to the Lord Chamberlain, who had the power to allow players to act outside either licensed playhouse. The Lord Chamberlain, presented with strong evidence of Fleetwood's malfeasance and petitioned by the actors for protection, sided with Fleetwood, whose story was that the exorbitant salaries of his principals had caused a modest deficit at Drury Lane, and that players were public servants who should know their place. Garrick and Macklin then turned enemies, each blaming the other in the press for spearheading the rebellion and betraying his fellows. Macklin lambasted Garrick for returning unilaterally to Drury Lane; Garrick defended this move as a means to help other rebel players return.

Clive fought her image war differently, downplaying her involvement at every opportunity. As in the 1736 Polly Row, she described herself as a victim of managers, now joined in a cartel to exploit players. She was the first of the rebel leaders to publicly charge Fleetwood with lying about their high salaries, her own especially, which she appears to have anticipated could lose audience sympathy for their cause. On the Garrick–Macklin conflict Clive was silent, refusing either to side openly with Macklin, or to return to Drury Lane with Garrick. Instead she took a breakaway group to Covent Garden. Outside the regular Covent Garden season, she led brief runs of masques and oratorios by Willem De Fesch.

As Garrick, Macklin, Clive, and Fleetwood each jockeyed to win over the public, they represented and misrepresented themselves. Critics lampooned them in print. Screeds were written in the form of stage burlesques, in which the leading personalities engage in dialogue exposing their folly. As in the Polly Row, critics carried out so-called impartial Examens of the issues. New since the Polly Row were a series of 'Cases' – including one written by Clive herself – resembling the many petitions of 1735 against anti-theatrical legislature debated in the House of Commons.[1] There was one other change since the Polly Row: almost no one complained that stories about actors weren't newsworthy.[2] A satirical engraving, *The Theatrical Contest* (1743) captured the square-off between disputants and took a view on the justice of their causes. When, after a long struggle, Fleetwood ultimately lost in the court of public opinion, it wasn't because he mistreated players, but because he hiked admission prices.

For Clive, this battle of contrasting public representations was a career tipping point, as she feared at the time. However adeptly she courted public sympathy, nothing could undo the damage of published revelations of her large earnings and her command among her peers.

The 1743–44 Actors' Rebellion

When the rebellion broke out, Fleetwood, Macklin, Garrick, and Clive each had a well-established reputation, not necessarily flattering, that they would have to negotiate in their public appeals during the rebellion itself. Fleetwood was known to be profligate – he had reportedly lost his inheritance of six thousand pounds through gambling even before he entered theatre management in 1734 – and was said to be dim-witted.[3] The wildness of Macklin's temper was renowned, and bound him to Fleetwood, who since 1734 had been quietly

---

[1] For examples, see the 'The Case of the Subscribers to Goodman's Fields', 'The Case of Henry Giffard', 'The Case of the Comedians of Goodman's Fields', 'Mr. Rich's Case', and 'The Case of the Comedians of Drury Lane and Covent Garden', all of which were submitted in defence against, or as argument for, Sir John Barnard's proposed bill in 1735. The cases are reprinted in Liesenfeld, *The Licensing Act of 1737*, pp. 168–74.

[2] I have found only one complaint about the prominence of the 1743–44 actors' revolt in print media of the day; its author wrote of 'an idle, fruitless, personal Squabble between Messieurs Garrick and Macklin'. *Old England or The Constitutional Journal*, issue 47 (24 December 1743). Clive, Garrick, and Macklin each apologized in their 'cases' (cited below) for wasting the public's time with their grievances, but nonetheless wrote at length. James Ralph acknowledged that playhouse politics had become embedded in public discourse and suggested how to change this state of affairs in [James Ralph], *The Case of our Present Theatrical Disputes, fairly stated ... wherein, the only Method is Suggested, that can prevent all future Debate* (London, 1743), pp. 1– 2.

[3] 'Mr. Fleetwood ... came a ruined Man into the Management of the Theatre ... The sudden Ruin of this once amiable young Gentleman happened ... when ... [he and] his Companion ... were surrounded and destroyed by a Set of honourable Sharpers.' Victor, *The History of the Theatres of London and Dublin*, pp. 33–35. See also the five-page pamphlet, Robert W. Buss, *Charles Fleetwood, Holder of the Drury Lane Theatre Patent ... Reprinted from Fleetwood Family Records* ([London], 1915).

assigning him Theophilus Cibber's managerial duties, and who, after Macklin killed Thomas Hallam in 1735, stood by him at his trial.[4] By the end of the 1740–41 season Macklin's co-managers Cibber and Quin were gone, leaving him as Fleetwood's sole support.

Together, Macklin and Garrick represented a new generation of actors. Garrick had witnessed Macklin's electrifying Shylock, and seems to have absorbed some of his methods.[5] Following his storied London acting debut on 19 October 1741, Garrick swiftly established himself as even more impressive than Macklin. Garrick was engaged for the 1742–43 season at Drury Lane, and his top rank registered immediately in his casting, salary, prominent billing, and staggering box-office draw.[6] With his mistress Peg Woffington, a London stage sensation since 1740, by March 1743 Garrick had set himself up at no. 6 Bow Street – in a house where Macklin also resided with his partner, a former stroller named Ann Grace whom he never married, and their child.[7] So while Garrick and Macklin may have rivalled Clive in rank, her reputation was more respectable than theirs. Along with propriety, by this point Clive also had authority. By 1743, William Chetwood could report that Clive had her 'own Choice of Parts, and appeared in whatever Characters' that she 'liked best'.[8] This chimes with the observation in *Britons, Strike Home* that Clive was 'like the real great Actresses; she will do as she will',[9] suggesting that already in 1739 the right to choose roles – the signal mark of first rank in the company – was hers.

Since 1742, Fleetwood had been systematically robbing Drury Lane personnel of their salaries, as Judith Milhous and Robert D. Hume show. Company members would later claim that by the end of the 1742–43 season they were collectively owed 3,417 pounds by Fleetwood, who had appropriated this

---

[4] William W. Appleton, *Charles Macklin: An Actor's Life* (Cambridge MA, 1960), pp. 32–33; see also James Thomas Kirkman, *Memoirs of the Life of Charles Macklin, Esq. Principally compiled from his own Papers and Memorandums* (London, 1799), vol. 1, p. 204. On the division of managerial duties between Quin and Macklin, see Chapter 7, pp. 224–25.

[5] How, and to what extent Garrick modelled himself on Macklin is debatable, as pointed out by Denise S. Sechelski, 'Garrick's Body and the Labor of Art in Eighteenth-Century Theater', *Eighteenth-Century Studies*, vol. 29, no. 4 (1996), pp. 369–89, esp. pp. 377–78.

[6] At Goodman's Fields theatre, where Garrick debuted, 'Garrick's impact on the box office is evident at a glance … The company was making a fat profit every night Garrick played, and losing money every night he did not'. Judith Milhous and Robert D. Hume, 'David Garrick and Box Office Receipts at Drury Lane in 1742–43', *Philological Quarterly*, vol. 67, no. 3 (1988), pp. 332–33.

[7] Appleton, *Charles Macklin*, pp. 22–23. Macklin's early biographers maintain that Macklin did in fact marry Grace.

[8] [William Chetwood], *The Dramatic Congress. A Short State of the Stage under the Present Management. Concluding with a Dialogue* (London, 1743), p. 20.

[9] Phillips, *Britons, Strike Home*, p. 20.

money to pay his huge gambling debts.[10] As the season closed Fleetwood refused to pay salaries in arrears, and fired some personnel who protested.[11] Over the summer of 1743, according to Macklin, Garrick explored an 'Agreement to act together' with Quin at Covent Garden, despite having pledged the season before always to play at the same theatre as Macklin.[12] By the end of the summer about a 'dozen' players, according to Garrick's early biographer Thomas Davies, 'entered into an association, to which others were invited', to act only in unison in their relations with Fleetwood.[13] Garrick reportedly asked Macklin to secretly negotiate leasing Lincoln's Inn Fields from Rich, who refused to tie the house to Garrick for only one season.[14]

Garrick's agreement with Quin never materialized, but it alarmed Fleetwood, who, recognizing the value of Macklin's friendship with Garrick, tried to buy Macklin's fidelity. According to Macklin, Fleetwood offered him an advance of two hundred pounds to 'check all Combinations' among players to resist the manager.[15] Macklin 'declined' Fleetwood's offer, 'out of a strict Regard' for his *Engagement* with Mr. Garrick'.[16] This marked a point of no return. As Macklin later bitterly recalled, Garrick had 'seduced' him from an 'easy Situation' with promises of solidarity in a common cause for justice. Fleetwood had been Macklin's *'Friend'*, but Garrick 'forc'd him to make [Fleetwood] his *Enemy*'.[17]

---

[10] Details of this event are first examined in Judith Milhous and Robert D. Hume, 'The Drury Lane Actors' Rebellion of 1743', *Theatre Journal*, vol. 42, no. 1 (1990), pp. 57–80. In their important study, Milhous and Hume explain the cryptic and disorganized contents of the 'Precedent Book', which in 1990 was a previously unknown manuscript (PRO LC 5/204). The 'Book' is an archival copy of many original documents that passed between disputants, particularly between Charles Fleetwood and the Lord Chamberlain. As Milhous and Hume point out, all 'further interpretations of the rebellion will have to rest' on this evidence, and I am indebted to their research. See also Milhous and Hume, 'David Garrick and Box Office Receipts at Drury Lane in 1742–43', pp. 323–44.

[11] Milhous and Hume, 'The Drury Lane Actors' Rebellion of 1743', pp. 60–61; 'Appendix', pp. 78–80.

[12] 'At the Beginning of the last [1742-3] Season, Mr. Garrick and I entered into a strict Friendship together, and mutually *engaged* to adhere to each other, and not to act upon separate Stages.' Charles Macklin, *Mr. Macklin's Reply ... to which are prefix'd, All the Papers ... in regard to this Important Dispute* (London, 1743), pp. 4–5.

[13] 'A formal agreement was signed, by which they obliged themselves not to accede to any terms which might be proposed to them by the patentee, without the consent of all the subscribers.' Davies lists 'Garrick, Macklin, [William] Havard, [Edward] Berry, Mrs. [Hannah] Pritchard and Mrs. Clive'; note that this misrepresents Clive's role, as explained below. Davies, *Memoirs of the Life of David Garrick, Esq.*, vol. 1, pp. 66–67.

[14] Macklin, *Mr. Macklin's Reply*, p. 5.

[15] 'Fleetwood ... offer'd me an extraordinary Sum of 200l; provided I would do my utmost to check all Combinations for opposing such a Reduction.' *Ibid.*, p. 29.

[16] *Ibid.*, p. 5.

[17] *Ibid.*, p. 26.

Fleetwood was not only failing to pay salaries owed, he was also conniving with Rich to drive these salaries drastically lower.[18] A pamphleteer, possibly Garrick, accused Fleetwood of preparing the public's acceptance of this cartel by 'insinuating Falsities by private Whispers and Coffee-house Harangues, endeavouring to magnify [his] Distresses, and setting forth the Insolence and Unreasonableness of his Actors'.[19] As the summer of 1743 drew to a close, Garrick penned an 'Application for Redress' against Fleetwood that the rest of the company, by Macklin's report, backed as one 'oppressed Body'.[20] This was presumably the communication demanding payment before the next season, which was sent to Fleetwood on 12 September.[21] Fleetwood ignored it.

At least twenty actors then signed a petition, sent on 19 September to the Lord Chamberlain, the Duke of Grafton, evidencing Fleetwood's abuses and requesting the duke's protection. They pleaded for redress against salaries in arrears, and warned against Fleetwood's 'pretence of ... salaries being (as he says) [too] Exorbitant' to pay in full – presumably a reference to Fleetwood's earlier rumour-mongering.[22] Garrick conducted himself like a company spokesman. He almost certainly wrote the anonymous pamphlet *Queries to be Answer'd*, sold from 20 September. This revisited the previous day's petition to the Lord Chamberlain, vividly relaying sentiment under the guise of forensic interrogation: Fleetwood had created a cartel to enforce players' compliance,[23] siphoning off profits while withholding payments in arrears,[24] and squandering money on French and Italian performers while failing to mount Shakespeare productions.[25] The pamphlet concludes with anecdotes about the lower sorts of people on the Drury Lane payroll starving, and second-tier actors such as Elizabeth Butler being all but arrested for personal debt. This was certainly

---

[18] As Robert D. Hume notes, 'Four cartels are known to have been put in operation for varying lengths of time – dating from the 1720s, 1730s, 1740s, and 1770s', and gives an overview of them. He confirms that 'an active cartel was in operation at the time of the 1743 actors' rebellion at Drury Lane', citing as evidence two pamphlets discussed below, *Tyranny Triumphant* and *The Dramatic Congress*. Hume, 'John Rich as Manager and Entrepreneur', *"The Stage's Glory"*, pp. 43–45.

[19] [David Garrick?], *Queries to be Answer'd by the Manager of Drury-Lane Theatre* (London, 1743), p. 16.

[20] 'It was agreed by us [Garrick and Macklin] both, to receive the Assistance of other Actors, which they voluntarily offered; In order to give the more weight to an Application for Redress, by the united Petition of an oppressed Body.' Macklin, *Mr. Macklin's Reply*, p. 25.

[21] The writings that passed between the players and manager were transcribed into the Lord Chamberlain's 'Precedent Book'. Milhous and Hume, 'The Drury Lane Actors' Rebellion of 1743', pp. 57–80. In the first petition, the list of twenty signatures ends with '&ca &ca &ca'.

[22] The petition is transcribed in Milhous and Hume, 'The Drury Lane Actors' Rebellion of 1743', pp. 59–60.

[23] [Garrick?], *Queries to be Answer'd*, p. 14.

[24] *Ibid.*, p. 16.

[25] *Ibid.*, pp. 9–10.

true: as Milhous and Hume show, during late September five such cases were 'formally sworn before a notary', which by 10 October had been joined by 'eight new ones'.[26]

Clive corroborated Garrick's charges in a letter she had printed in the *Daily Gazetteer* of 23 September. She had not addressed the public in the press since the Polly Row of 1736. Like Garrick, she founded her complaint on the need to counter gossip; in her case, she had not yet performed that season, and this had sparked 'Reports' to her 'Disadvantage'. Unlike Garrick, her protest was factual and brief, and she spoke only for herself:

> I think it incumbent on me to let the Publick know (to whom I am alone obliged for all the Advantages I have receiv'd in my Profession) the true Reason for my not performing as usual. It is ... reported, that my Demands on the Manager are so exorbitant, that it is impossible for him to comply with them. In answer to these Insinuations, or Assertions, (which I suppose are intended to injure me) they being false; I am obliged to say, that I have not a Fortune that can support me independent of the Stage; and so far from making extravagant Demands, that I have not made any. My Reason for not performing, is, That I have a very great Sum due to me from the Manager, for which I have often apply'd to him to no Purpose; therefore I hope, I shall be justified in not entering into fresh Agreements with one, who has broke through his Bonds and Promises of paying me, what is justly my Due. As to the Sallery I was to have receiv'd last Year, it was no more than he had given to another Performer for Seven Years together; and not as much as I was offer'd by the Manager of Covent-Garden Theatre, by a Person, whose Veracity is to be depended on, which I refus'd; being unwilling to quit the only Stage I have yet appear'd on. As the good Opinion of every One is not only my Ambition, but of the greatest Consequence to my Interest, I hope my endeavouring to shew I am not in the Wrong, will not be thought improper. I am, SIR, *Your humble Servant*, CATH. CLIVE.[27]

Clive's sharp denial that her salary was either exorbitant or causing her to clash with Fleetwood is the main thrust of her letter. As in the Polly Row, she represents herself as an isolated member of the middling sorts who must earn a living, in this instance bullied by a manager who hasn't paid for her services; in fact, Fleetwood owed her 160 pounds and 12 shillings.[28] She submits that she has no recourse but, as in 1736, to appeal directly to her public, to whom she owes everything, to explain why she can't perform. As in the Polly Row, her

---

[26] 'Between 26 and 29 September five of these cases were formally sworn before a notary, together with eight new ones, and delivered to the Lord Chamberlain's office (ca. 10 October?), where both informal and sworn testimony was later recorded in LC 5/204'. Milhous and Hume, 'The Drury Lane Actors' Rebellion of 1743', p. 61.

[27] *Daily Gazetteer*, issue 2586 (23 September 1743).

[28] Milhous and Hume compare the 'Monies owing' of the player's third petition with Fleetwood's account on 'pages 64–65 and 75–76 of LC 5/204', which they unscramble. Milhous and Hume, 'The Drury Lane Actors' Rebellion of 1743', pp. 68–71.

particular performance of femininity in print combines mild plain-speaking with sober submission.

On 22 September, the day before Clive's letter, a damning pamphlet about Fleetwood and Rich appeared.[29] Entitled *The Case between the Managers of the Two Theatres*, its author imagines a dialogue between them, alias 'D. L.', for Drury Lane and 'C. G.', for Covent Garden. Having sworn to serve *'Dulness'*, D. L. and C. G. agree to form a cartel. D. L. pretends to reluctance as he describes pocketing profits; he and C. G. laugh over depriving their respective company members of their wages.[30] C. G. talks D. L. into halving the salaries of players, and convincing the Town that the players are to be blamed if they refuse to perform. D. L. worries about having boasted to 'a hundred People' of his profit of three thousand pounds.[31] C. G. says that D. L. need only assert having lost that sum on other expenses. Other schemes jointly hatched include passing off old productions as new, raising prices, and foreswearing Shakespeare. The 'Brothers' nearly come to blows, however, when D. L. accuses C. G. of lying inconsistently. The comic point of this passage is redolent of Garrick's pen:

> D. L. ... you are a little unfortunate sometimes – you are apt to –
> C. G. To what, Sir? to what!
> D. L. Why, to let one Lye, Sir, come slap upon the back of another, and contradict it as flat as a Flounder, I'gad – You are very apt to do that indeed, Brother – very apt, upon my Honour.
> C. G. Upon my Veracity, Brother, there is no one in England lies with more Consistency than myself ... S'death, Sir, d'ye give me the Lye?
> D. L. No, Brother, no, I only say that you give yourself the Lye.
> C. G. Sir, you are a Scoundrel, Sir.
> D. L. If you come to that, pray, what are you, Sir?
> C. G. A Man of Honour, Sir – one that scorns to take the Lye, even from himself, Sir – And so, Sir, I demand instant Satisfaction.[32]

Around 25 September the players sent a second petition to the Lord Chamberlain, requesting the right 'to act a few Plays, in order to support the large Body of People now entirely out of Business'.[33] On 4 October, the pamphlet *Tyranny Triumphant! And Liberty Lost* went on sale.[34] In it, a malcontent 'Poet'

---

[29] Sale of the *The Case between the Managers of the Two Theatres* was announced in the *Daily Post*, issue 7504 (22 September 1743). In the volume, the title page bears the wrong year of publication: 'Printed for J. Roberts in Warwick-Lane. MDCCXIII'. *The Case between the Managers of the Two Theatres* (London, [1743]).
[30] *The Case between the Managers*, pp. 7–11.
[31] Ibid., pp. 11–12. This charge is also in *Queries to be Answer'd*, and the players' second submission to the Duke of Grafton (see below).
[32] *The Case between the Managers*, pp. 15–16.
[33] 'Fleetwood's strategy was simply to stall ... After a week or so the rebel actors sent the Lord Chamberlain a second petition'. Milhous and Hume, 'The Drury Lane Actors' Rebellion of 1743', p. 64.
[34] This was first advertised in the *Daily Advertiser*, issue 3966 (4 October 1743).

contends that theatre managers deprive audiences (and playwrights) of quality theatre 'out of the Wantonness of their Hearts ... by some enormous Acts of Cruelty to their Comedians' – though the Poet also echoes objections to players' 'extravagant Salaries'.[35]

Also on 4 October, Fleetwood finally responded to the actors' first petition of 19 September to the Lord Chamberlain, which the Lord Chamberlain had forwarded to him. Writing to the Lord Chamberlain, Fleetwood simply lied. He claimed not to be in arrears with salary payments, said that lower-tier theatre personnel were not in distress, and above all asserted that the 'exorbitant Salarys' of star players were the cause of Drury Lane's distress.[36] To substantiate his account, Fleetwood gave the Lord Chamberlain an 'Estimate of the salaries & Benefits of some of the Principal Performers in the Years 1708 and 1709 with those of sum [sic] of the Petitioners in the years 1742 & 1743 calculated at 200 Nights Playing'.[37]

Fleetwood then issued his first pamphlet, *Queries upon Queries, to be Answer'd by the Male-content Players. For the Satisfaction of the Publick, in regard to the present Dispute between them and the Manager*. This response to *Queries to be Answer'd* of 20 September was sold from 24 September.[38] Here Fleetwood denies having made any profit at all and blames principals' fees and vanity for his economic woes. Asserting Garrick's inferior 'Breeding', Fleetwood likens him to Wat Tyler, leader of the 1381 Peasants' Revolt, against whom he, Fleetwood, safeguards the Crown's patent.[39] According to Fleetwood, the 'Indolence, Exorbitance and Misbehaviour' of principals – he alludes specifically to Garrick's refusal to perform in May 1743 – is to blame for declining profits and production standards.[40] Garrick is a rebel, who, by forming his own 'Cartel' with Macklin, seeks to 'bring the Manager to ... exorbitant Terms'.[41] Fleetwood also blames principals' bloated fees for the 'lower Sort' of theatre personnel not getting paid.[42]

---

[35] *Tyranny Triumphant! And Liberty Lost ... Or, Historical, Critical, and Prophetical Remarks on the Famous Cartel lately agreed on by the Masters of Two Theatres. In a Letter to a Friend in the Country* (London, 1743), pp. 17–18.

[36] Fleetwood's letter to the Lord Chamberlain is transcribed from LC 5/204 (pp. 73–74) in Milhous and Hume, 'The Drury Lane Actors' Rebellion of 1743', pp. 62–63.

[37] This appeared on page 82 of LC 5/204 and is transcribed in Milhous and Hume, 'The Drury Lane Actors' Rebellion of 1743', pp. 66–67.

[38] *Daily Advertiser*, issue 3957 (23 September 1743): '*Tomorrow Noon will be pubish'd* [sic], (Price Six Pence) QUERIES upon QUERIES, to be answer'd by the Malecontent Players...'.

[39] [Charles Fleetwood], *Queries upon Queries, to be Answer'd by the Male-content Players* (London, 1743), pp. 3–4.

[40] Ibid., pp. 7–8, 12–13, 14.

[41] Ibid., p. 13.

[42] Ibid., pp. 17–18.

By this time Fleetwood had already won his case with the Lord Chamberlain. The latter's denial of the actors' petition was announced in the *Daily Advertiser*, also of 8 October.[43] Writing decades later, Thomas Davies would claim that the Duke of Grafton had refused the license because he was incensed at star players' earning power.[44] Around 10 October the players submitted a third petition, and at some point provided evidence that Fleetwood was cheating them of money ('Monies received at the Theatre Royal in Drury Lane for the Use of Charles Fletewood Esqr.').[45] But the Lord Chamberlain continued to accept Fleetwood's story, according to which unprincipled principals not only caused losses but threatened the social order.

William Chetwood defended the actors in a pamphlet called *The Dramatic Congress*, issued on 10 October. This describes 'two Wings' of rebels, one led by Clive, and the other by Garrick and Macklin.[46] Pretending to report on a meeting between rebels and managers, Chetwood names its participants after celebrated roles, thereby glossing their nature. 'Kitty Cuckoe' (Clive, the Shakespearean songster) bustles in alone. Accompanying 'Cato' (Garrick as a favourite stage hero who defends liberty) is 'Calista' (Susannah Cibber, the tragedy queen), while 'Bayes' (Macklin, as the Author in the Town's favourite rehearsal play) struts 'forward with Sylvia' (the breeches-wearing Peg Woffington of *The Recruiting Officer*).[47] Addressing the players are 'Basha' (Fleetwood, the Oriental-styled despot), Fleetwood's deputy 'Mr. Dash' (identity unknown), 'Volpone' (Rich as Ben Jonson's sly, greedy fox), and his deputy manager 'Mosca' (James Lacy as Volpone's toadying servant).[48] Of these characterizations, Clive's is the most complimentary, and designed to defend her high salary:

---

[43] 'We hear that the Lord Chamberlain has refus'd granting a Licence to the seceding Players to act in the Theatre in the Hay-Market,' *Daily Advertiser*, issue 3970 (8 October 1743).

[44] 'The duke of Grafton ... received the petition of the players with coldness; instead of examining into the merit of their complaints, he desired to know the amount of their annual stipends. He was much surprised to be informed, that a man could gain, merely by playing, the yearly salary of 500l. His grace observed, that a near relation of his, who was then an inferior officer in the navy, exposed his life in behalf of his king and country for less than half that sum. All attempts to convince the duke that justice and right were on the side of the petitioners were to no purpose.' Davies, *Memoirs of the Life of David Garrick, Esq.*, vol. 1, pp. 67–68.

[45] Milhous and Hume, 'The Drury Lane Actors' Rebellion of 1743', p. 65.

[46] [Chetwood], *The Dramatic Congress*, p. 19.

[47] Ibid.

[48] According to Victor, James Lacy 'became an Assistant Manager to Mr. Rich; during which Interval it was, that Mr. Fleetwood's Patent was advertised for Sale'. Victor, *The History of the Theatres of London and Dublin*, vol. 1, pp. 66–67. Victor notes also that Lacy enjoyed 'great and powerful Patrons' among the nobility, including the Lord Chamberlain, the Duke of Grafton, and the First Lord of the Treasury, Henry Pelham. Ibid., pp. 81–82.

> Dash. Good Manners oblige us to enquire of the Ladies first; therefore, Miss Kitty ...
> Kitty. I have, by my Assiduity endeavoured to please the Town; if ever I met with any Favour it was from *them*, not *him* [Fleetwood] ... To-morrow he would have no more Regard for me than a common Candle-Snuffer ...
> Dash. ... But ... you must acknowledge ... that he encreased your Salary so extravagantly as made it much above any Woman's now upon the Stage ...
> Kitt. Not near so much Esteem as he shew'd for his Foreigners ...
> Mosc. Hold, Madam, let me ask you a Question – Do you really think he could reasonably afford to give you the Salary he did?
> Kitt. I am surprized, Sir, you, of all People, should ask that, when you know you offered me a much larger [...].[49]

Did Clive have a hand in this passage by her champion Chetwood? Quite possibly. Its motifs – herself as the victim of Fleetwood's caprice, her application to the public, enmity towards foreign entertainers – are classic Clive.

Fleetwood hit back by arranging for the 'Estimate of the Salaries and Benefits' he had submitted to the Lord Chamberlain to be published on 15 October in the *Daily Advertiser* and the *London Daily Post and General Advertiser*.[50] It was also published in the October issue of *The Gentleman's Magazine* (Fig. 9.1), although a notice queried its accuracy: 'The Actors say this Account is very fallacious and give another – of which in our next.'[51] As Milhous and Hume explain, Fleetwood fiddled the numbers. The acting season of 1708–09, which Fleetwood compared to the 1742–43 season to show the players' rise in earnings, had been shortened by three months due to royal mourning, and actors' 1708–09 earnings were correspondingly reduced.[52] For the salaries of actor-managers Wilks, Cibber, and Booth in 1708–09, Fleetwood omitted the profits that they divided among themselves at the season's end, making Garrick's income seem roughly double that of the triumvirs.[53]

Cooked or not, Fleetwood's 'Estimate' made a damning impression on the public, as it evidently had on the Lord Chamberlain. Clive's income in

---

[49] [Chetwood], *The Dramatic Congress*, pp. 20–22.

[50] *Daily Advertiser*, issue 3976 (15 October 1743) and *London Daily Post and General Advertiser*, issue 2782 (15 October 1743). Milhous and Hume state that the 'Estimate' was printed in 'various other London papers on 15 October'; I have only found these two. As they note, it was reprinted a year later as well. Milhous and Hume, 'The Drury Lane Actors' Rebellion of 1743', p. 67 and note 34.

[51] 'Historical Chronicle, October 1743', *The Gentleman's Magazine and Historical Chronicle*, vol. 13 (October 1743), p. 553.

[52] '[S]omewhat misleading ... since the theaters lost about three months' acting time to royal mourning and an order of silence during the 1708–09 season, significantly reducing the actors' salaries. Fleetwood's use of a season of "200" acting days exaggerated the actors' income for 1742–43: the norm was closer to 180 days, and the precise total in 1742–43 had been 183.' Milhous and Hume, 'The Drury Lane Actors' Rebellion of 1743', p. 67 and note 33.

[53] *Ibid.*, p. 68.

BIRTHS, MARRIAGES, &c. OCTOBER.   553

Next to *Faction Detected*, the Affair which has made the greatest Noise, is a Dispute between a Proprietor of the Theatre and some of the principal Actors.

The Case in short is this——The Gentlemen of the Inns of Court insisted early in the last Season, that the Price of the Pitt should be reduced from 3 s. to the common Price of 2 s. 6d. and the Gallery from 2 s. to 1 s. 6d. but it was urged in favour of the Proprietors that they having engaged foreign Dancers at high Rates to entertain the Town, they must fulfill their Contracts, but that another Year they would not require the advanced Price. To enable them to keep their Promise, they not only forbear to hire foreign Dancers, but refuse to give to the Actors their former Salaries; without which several of them determined not to act. The following Account was therefore publish'd to shew their Exorbitant Demands in Comparison of former Actors.

Computed at 200 Days playing.

In the Year 1708 and 9.	*l.*	*s.*	*d.*
Mr Wilks's *Acting and Management*	250	0	0
By *Benefit, paying Charges*	90	14	0
Mr Betterton 4*l.* a *Week*, and 1*l.* a W. his Wife, tho' she did not act	166	13	4
By a *Benefit, paying Charges*	76	0	0
Mr Estcourt 5*l.* a *Week*	166	13	4
By *Benefit, paying Chargeo*	51	8	0
Mr Cibber, 5*l.* a *Week*	166	13	4
By *Benefit, paying Charges*	51	0	0
Mr Mills, *sen.* 4*l.* a *Week*	133	6	8
By *Benefit, paying Charges*	58	1	0
Mrs Oldfield, 4*l.* a *Week*	133	6	8
By *Benefit, paying Charges*	62	7	0
Cloaths	13	5	9
	1419	13	1

In the *Year* 1742 and 3.	*l.*	*s.*	*d.*
Mr Garrick *for acting only* 2	630	0	0
clear Benefits, and 1 *paying* 50*l.*	500	0	0
Mr Macklin 9*l.* 9*s.* a *W. and* 6*l.* 6*s.* a *W. certain, for his Wife, who acted a few Times*	525	0	0
A clear Benefit, and her's paying 50*l.*	230	0	0
Mrs Woffington 7*l.* 10*s.* a *W. cert.*	250	0	0
By a clear Benefit	180	0	0
Cloaths	50	0	0
Mrs Pritchard 7. 10*s.* a *W. certain*	250	0	0
By a clear Benefit	180	0	0
Cloaths	50	0	0
Mr Mills, *jun.* 6*l.* a *Week certain*	200	0	0
By a Benefit, paying 25*l.*	140	0	0
Mrs Clive, 15*l.* 15*s.* a *W. certain*	525	0	0
By a clear Benefit	200	0	0
Cloaths	50	0	0
Ticket at her Benefit, as by Agreem.	21	0	0
N. B. *The Benefits are computed by the Account of the House, and*	4001	0	0
to Computation made of Gold Tickets, which are sometimes very considerable.	1419	13	1
	2581	6	11

The Actors say this Account is very fallacious and give another — of which in our next.

A LIST of BIRTHS *for the* Year 1743.

Sept. 29. THE Wife of *John Evelyn*, Member for *Helston, Cornwall*, was deliver'd of a Daughter.

OCT. The Wife of *Strelley Pegge*, Esq; —of a Son and Heir at his Seat *Bello Carite* or *Beauchiff* in the County of *Derby*.

3. The Wife of Aldm. *Baker*, —of a Son. At *Rate, Perthshire*, one *Jean Galloway*, —of 2 Boys and 2 Girls, 3 of whom were living.

The Wife of the Rev. Mr *George Whitfield*, —of a Son.

17. The Lady of Lord Visc. *St John*, — of a Son.

A LIST of MARRIAGES *for the* Year 1743.

Sept. 29. THE Hon. Capt. *Lee* of the Guards and Brother to the E. of *Litchfield*, married to Miss *Derander* of *Putney*.

OCT. 4. Mr *George Ross* of *Sweeden*, — to Miss *Katbrine Ross* of *St Mary Axe*, with 10,000 *l.*

Herbert Tryst of *Crauham-hall, Essex*, Esq; —to the Widow *Hanbury* of *Monmouthshire*, with 20,000 *l.*

7. *Capel Hanbury*, Esq; Member for *Leominster*, —to the Ld *Tracy* s eldest Daughter.

8. —— *Cock* of *Camberwell*, Esq; —to Miss *Freer* of *Lewisham*, with 7000 *l.*

13. *Richard Asheton* of *Gray's Inn*, Esq; —to Miss *Asheton* of *Cuercale, Lancasher*.

14. Mr *Bridgman* of *Cheapside*, —to Miss *Molly Mixey* of *Greenwich*, with 4,000 *l.*

The Rev. Mr *Martin*, —to Miss *Mary Duncannon*, with 7000 *l.*

20. *James Halsey* of *Tunbridge, Kent*, Esq; —to Miss *Anne Davis* of *Lime-street*, with 10,000 *l.*

22. *James Forest* of *Sywood, Yorkshire*, Esq; —to the eldest Daughter of Sir *Samuel Armytage*, Bart, of *Kirklew*.

26. Mr *Pratt*, a Merchant of the City, — to Miss *Glanville* of *Mark-lane*, with 10,000*l.*

A LIST of DEATHS *for the* Year 1743.

Sept. 27. AT *Bourdeaux*, *Henry Popple*, Esq; formerly Cashire to the late Q. and Agent to several Regiments.

At *Edinburgh, William Millar*, the Quaker, aged 81, who by renting a G.rden of a few Acres, and selling Ale, call'd the *Quakers Ale*) acquired a Fortune of 5000 *l.*

At the Village of *Veniel* in the Kingdom of *Murcia*, —one *Peter M'Stanea*, aged 130, he liv'd a Batchelor, never tasted Wine, worked hard and bath'd every Morning in the River *Segura*, from the beginning of Spring till it froze : His Teeth were sound, and he had never been attack'd by any acute Distemper.

OCT. 3. At *Sudbrooke, Surry*, the Duke of *Argyle* and *Greenwich, &c. (see* p. 102, 270.) one of his Majesty's Privy Council and a Knight of the Garter ; succeeded in Estate and Honours by his Brother, the Earl of *Ilay*, except that the Title of D. of *Greenwich*, descends (by a late Grant) to his eldest Daughter, the Countess of *Dalkeith*, and her Heirs for ever.

Henry Cooke of *Shropshire*, Esq;

particular was seen as an affront to propriety: among the whole of the company, only Garrick's wages topped hers, and her income was seen to be vastly more than Oldfield's: £525 per annum as opposed to Oldfield's putative £133 6s 8d.[54] Clive's benefit was reported as 'clear' of the house charges that both she and Oldfield had to pay, with the result that Clive was shown earning £200 for her benefit against Oldfield's £62 7s.[55] Clive's 'Cloaths' were said to cost £50 per annum, compared to an outlay for Oldfield of £13 5s 9d – perhaps intended to measure the vanity, as much as the expenditure, of the two female principals.[56] To prejudice readers further, Fleetwood attached a preface to his 'Estimate', asserting that the '*Dignity* of the Characters they [the principal players] represent on the Stage is apt to intoxicate them with too great an Opinion of their *own*'.[57]

A rebuttal of Fleetwood's 'Estimate' appeared, as promised, in the November issue of the *Gentleman's Magazine* (Fig. 9.2).[58] Its preface pointed out the error of comparing the intake of actors from the full season of 1742–43 with that of the truncated 1708–09 season. '[T]o place the Salaries of the present Actors in a true Light', a new comparison was drawn with '7 of the principal Actors in 1729'.[59] This report painted a radically different picture of Clive. Her £525 income 'for Acting in Plays, Farces and Singing, from September to June' was set against Oldfield's £420 'for Acting only to the End of April' 1729. Likewise, Oldfield's weekly earnings were changed to '12 Guineas a Week', making Clive's 15 guineas seems more reasonable. Clive's 1743 benefit earnings, now net of house charges, dropped to £63 – that is, to less than a third of what Fleetwood had claimed – while Oldfield's 1729 benefit earnings were given as £60.[60]

What was undisputed, and now public, was that Clive made a lot of money. Whereas her onstage impudence and excesses had earlier served comedy's aims, they now seemed evidence of unbridled appetites. In his summary of the dispute published two months later, James Ralph inveighed against Drury Lane's top earners, who at public expense lived at the 'Rate of an English Duke, or a German Prince'.[61]

---

[54] *Daily Advertiser*, issue 3976 (15 October 1743).
[55] *Ibid.*
[56] *Ibid.*
[57] *Ibid.*
[58] 'Historical Chronicle, November 1743', *The Gentleman's Magazine and Historical Chronicle*, vol. 13 (November 1743), p. 609.
[59] *Ibid.*
[60] *Ibid.* A guinea was £1 and 1 shilling, so Oldfield's weekly earnings were £12 and 12 shillings, and Clive's were £15 and 15 shillings.
[61] [James Ralph], *The Case of our Present Theatrical Disputes, fairly Stated* (London, 1743), p. 4; see also *ibid.*, pp. 26–31, on the greed of contemporary players compared to earlier ones.

Historical Chronicle, *November* 1743.

THE Players in answer to the Account of Salaries, p. 553, alledge, that the Stage both of *Drury-lane* and the *Hay-market*, were in so wretched a Condition in the Year 1708-9 as not to be worth any body's Acceptance; its Receipts being considerably under the current Expence, while those of the Year 1742-3 amounted to above 15,000 *l.* of which 2,000 *l.* were neat Profit, and with common Oeconomy might, by retrenching exotic Expences, have been 4000 *l.* The Players farther observe the Fallacy of the above Account, in setting down besides the Manager's Charges, every benefit Night, what is got by the Actor's own private Interest in Money and Tickets, as also the Article of 50 *l.* for Cloaths, added to the Actresses Account, which is absolutely an Advantage to the Manager, as they always lay out considerably more.—— But to place the Salaries of the present Actors in a true Light, let them be compared with 7 of the principal Actors in 1729, when the Stage was in its most flourishing Condition, under the Direction of *Steele, Booth, Wilks* and *Cibber,* when the three last had each a Fourth of the Profits of the Patent as Actors, which amounted, one Year with another to 1000 *l.* besides 10 *l.* per Week for Management.

In the Year 1729   *l. s. d.*
Mr *Wilks's* Acting and Management   753 06 8
By a clear Benefit   60 0 0
Mr *Booth* as Mr *Wilks*
Mr *Cibber* ditto
Mrs *Oldfield* at 12 Guineas a Week for Acting only to the End of *April*   420 0 0
By a clear Benefit   60 0 0
By a Present   52 10 0
Mrs *Porter's* Salary   266 0 0
By a clear Benefit   60 0 0
Mr *Mills* sen. Salary   200 0 0
By a clear Benefit   60 0 0
Mrs *Thurmond's* Salary   166 0 0
By Benefit paying 40 *l.*   20 0 0
   3,746 13 4

In the Years 1742-3.   *l. s. d.*
Mr *Garrick's* Salary   630 0 0
By two Benefits   126 0 0
By another paying 50 *l.*   13 0 0
Mr *Macklin* for Acting and Managem.   315 0 0
By a clear Benefit   63 0 0
Mrs *Macklin's* Salary   210 0 0
By a Benefit paying 50 *l.*   13 0 0
Mrs *Woffington's* Salary   250 0 0
By a clear Benefit   63 0 0
Mrs *Pritchard's* Salary   250 0 0
By a clear Benefit   63 0 0

Mr *Mills's* Salary   200 0 0
By a Benefit paying 25 *l.*   38 0 0
Mrs *Clive* for Acting in Plays, Farces and Singing, from September to *June*   525 0 0
By a clear Benefit   63 0 0
   2,822 0 0
   3,746 13 4
   924 13 4

Extract of a Letter from Surinam, *dated* Aug. 15, 1743.

THREE *Portuguese Negro* Sailors on board the *Rising Sun* Schooner, bound from *Barbadoes* to the Island *Cyanna,* rose in the Night and murdered Captain *Newark Jackson,* Commander, Capt. *George Ledain,* Supercargo, an Apprentice Boy, and the Merchant's Clerk and wounded the Mate and Boatswain, leaving them and 2 Lads alive, whom they ordered to carry Ship to *Oronoque*; but they made for *Curranteen,* a *Dutch* Settlement, when two of the Villains were secured by the Governor and the third swam ashore, who being discovered by some *Indians* in the Woods, endeavoured by stabbing himself with a Knife to put an End to his Life, upon which the *Indians* seeing his Obstinacy severed his Head from his Body. The other two were afterwards executed as follows, the Vessel in which the Fact was committed being brought near the Town, and a Yard flung across her Mast, and as many Vessels, as could conveniently, coming round her with all their Crews, the Criminals were brought on Board and each slung by the Arm-pits were hoisted up to each Yard-arm; where after hanging some Time, the Executioners with redhot Pinchers pull'd off Pieces of their Flesh; then they were un-hung, and an Iron hook put into each of their Sides, by which they were hung up again for 24 H. u s, and afterwards their Heads were cut off (their Bodies being buried) and stuck up in a publick Place. One was alive when they come to cut off his Head.

Extract of a Letter from on board the Bonetta *Privateer, Capt.* Drumgold, *dated at* St Christophers, *Sep*. 18.

WE have this Instant brought in here a *Spanish* Sloop, which we took off *Laguerra:* She was bound for *Carthagena* and is esteem'd a valuble Prize; her Cargo consists of 40,000 D llars, and upwards of 50 Tons of C coa, C chineal, J suits Bark, *&c.* The *Mary,* Capt. *Wood.*

Fig. 9.2 'Historical Chronicle, November 1743', *The Gentleman's Magazine and Historical Chronicle,* vol. 13, November 1743, p. 609. The Bodleian Libraries, The University of Oxford. Shelfmark: Per.Bibl. 2.

Kitty Clive at Covent Garden, 1743–44 Season

Without a licence, the rebel players languished. According to Macklin, before the 1743–44 season started Garrick had promised as a *'Dernier Resort'* to quit London for Dublin in company with Macklin. But instead Garrick (according to Macklin) went and *'currie[d] Favour'* with Fleetwood, breaking his 'solemn Agreement' with Macklin – something no 'Gentleman of Honour' would do. To justify trafficking with the enemy, Garrick – again according to Macklin – in early November urged the stranded players to sign a letter dissolving former resolutions. By Macklin's report, Clive, having 'Honour and Spirit', chose to 'refuse, upon any Consideration, to be made so ridiculous a Tool to so base a Purpose'.[62]

Before the 1743–44 season began, Clive and her followers – including her singing partner Beard – agreed to cross over to Covent Garden.[63] Clive had no financial incentive to quit Drury Lane, apart perhaps from the hope that Rich might actually pay her – although, as it turned out, he mostly didn't. Clive finally started her 1743–44 season on 17 November, at Covent Garden. Announcements of Clive's appearances bear out her later protest that under Rich, her 'Labour, and Application' were 'greater than any other Performers on the Stage ... very frequently [in] two Parts in a Night'.[64] She performed favourite Shakespeare roles (with song) and *Comus*, which opened on 3 March 1744, and was announced as having 'Never Acted ... before' at Covent Garden.[65] This production featured 'all NEW HABITS' and 'a New Grand SCENE of The PALACE of COMUS'.[66] Other Clive standards that season were *The Devil to Pay* and Fielding's vehicles (*The Miser, An Old Man taught Wisdom, The Lottery*). She led also the hit 'opera' – in fact a pantomime – *Orpheus and Eurydice*, composed three years earlier by John F. Lampe and originally led by Lampe's wife, Isabella. The production's draw was a seventeen-foot clockwork serpent that 'being wholly a piece of machinery ... performs its exercise of head, body and tail, in a most surprising manner ... and far exceeds the former custom of stuffing a boy into such likeness'.[67] The serpent of course attacks and kills Eurydice. One wonders how Clive felt in the role.

---

[62] Macklin, *Mr. Macklin's Reply*, pp. 26–27.
[63] Catherine Clive, *The Case of Mrs. Clive* (London, 1744), p. 10. For a modern facsimile of this pamphlet with an introduction, see Richard C. Frushell, ed., *The Case of Mrs. Clive* (Los Angeles, 1973).
[64] Ibid., p. 19.
[65] *London Daily Post and General Advertiser*, issue 2902 (3 March 1744).
[66] *London Daily Post and General Advertiser*, issue 2903 (5 March 1744).
[67] *Scots Magazine*, vol. 2 (March 1740), pp. 113–14. Cited in Martin, *Operas and Operatic Style of John Frederick Lampe*, pp. 59–60. The work opened on 12 February 1740 and was a favourite at Rich's theatre. See Chapter 5, pp. 141–42, note 8. Only one song, 'The Parent Bird', survives from *Orpheus and Eurydice*.

That Clive did not join Handel's oratorio company during the 1743–44 and 1744 seasons was almost certainly due to Rich. To work with Handel, she would have needed Rich's permission, which she wasn't going to get. With her salary slashed, new productions in her line suspended, and a Handel oratorio season blocked, Clive took two steps for self-advancement while at Covent Garden: she exploited benefits as never before, and began collaborating with an alternative to Handel, the high-style composer Willem De Fesch. Because self-organized, benefits allowed Clive to replace Rich's interest with her own: she could choose the programme and the contributing authors or composers, and, by selling tickets herself, its attendees. The evening's entertainment thereby became a public declaration of loyalty to Clive. As well as holding a benefit for herself, Clive led benefits for friends and family: her protégée Edwards, the family of Henry Carey, and her brother Jemmy (James) Raftor, who owed his post at Drury Lane to her, and later in life became her dependent.

Clive's work with De Fesch enhanced her reputation as an exponent of oratorio, a genre at this time representing elite taste.[68] Like Handel, De Fesch anchored his career in patronage; indeed, he worked almost exclusively for the English aristocracy.[69] A Dutchman, he had arrived in London in 1732 from Antwerp – where he had been fired from his post as chapel master at the cathedral – and was appointed organist to the Venetian Chapel in London. Apart from important Catholic families, his patrons included Prince Frederick – the dedicatee of his Opus 10 sonatas – and the 'Society of the Gentlemen Performers of Musick', which included Handel's patron James Brydges, First Duke of Chandos, and William Huggins, the poet of De Fesch's first oratorio, *Judith*.[70] When De Fesch mounted *Judith* in 1733, it was one of the earliest oratorios to be heard in London, and was warmly commended by the Duke of Chandos.[71]

---

[68] David Hunter, 'Patronizing Handel, Inventing Audiences: The Intersections of Class, Money, Music and History', *Early Music*, vol. 28, no. 1 (2000), pp. 33–49.

[69] He travelled to London probably under the protection of Lady Frances Erskine (d. 1776, married to James Erskine, d. 1785) and Sir Francis Head (1694–1768). His list of patrons grew quickly after he arrived in England. Robert L. Tusler, *Willem de Fesch: 'An excellent Musician and a worthy Man'* (Den Haag, 2005), pp. 109–11, 137–42.

[70] De Fesch mounted *Judith* for the public at Lincoln's Inn Fields. Tusler, *Willem de Fesch*, pp. 117–24. It ran during the Lenten season of February, possibly inspired by Handel's first publicly performed oratorio *Esther* the year before. De Fesch rented Lincoln's Inn Fields; *Judith* was to have opened on 8 February 1733 but due to a singer's illness was deferred until 16 February. It was advertised but dismissed for a performance on 27 February. *The London Stage*, Part 3, vol. 1, pp. 270, 272–73. William Hogarth made a well-known satirical engraving of the 'Chorus of Singers' rehearsing *Judith*. Tusler, *Willem de Fesch*, pp. 118–19.

[71] '[I]t will be heard with as much pleasure as it was read with by me.' Charles H. C. Baker and Muriel I. Baker, *The Life and Circumstances of James Brydges, First Duke of Chandos* (Oxford, 1949), p. 91; cited in Tusler, *Willem de Fesch*, p. 117.

After *Judith*, De Fesch withdrew almost entirely from public performances to work for patrons.[72]

Only during Clive's career crisis did De Fesch return to stage composition. She, along with Beard and Edwards, led all four of his next stage works. Clive's clout and needs in 1743 strongly suggest that she enlisted him. He brought several advantages: he stood outside stage politics, he moved in the best circles despite being Catholic, and he composed only polite music. Clive refers in her *Case of Mrs. Clive* to the 'very great Expence in Masters for Singing' that she bore, that her colleagues who were speaking principals did not;[73] De Fesch may have been among her 'Masters'. Their collaboration lasted until 1754, with her benefit production of *The London 'Prentice*, an 'English Operetta' whose wordbook Clive may have written.[74]

On 17 November 1743, to open her first-ever Covent Garden season, Clive gave a benefit for Henry Carey's 'Distress'd' family, left destitute by his suicide six weeks earlier, on 4 October.[75] She chose Fielding hits, *The Miser* and *An Old Man taught Wisdom*. As was by then customary, Clive inserted into *The Miser* her signature air 'Life of a Beau', that Carey had composed for her.[76] A prologue spoken by Sacheverel Hale celebrated Carey's greatest stage legacy: Clive's singing. In praising Carey, Hale's words echoed those of Aaron Hill in 1735:

> His double Muse diverts us from the Stage,
> Whilst Nature, Humour, ev'ry Ear engage:

---

[72] An exception was when De Fesch directed one revival of *Judith* on 29 February 1740. Ibid., p. 135.

[73] Clive, *The Case of Mrs. Clive*, p. 19.

[74] *Public Advertiser*, issue 6355 (12 March 1755). Horace Walpole reported in March 1754 that he had attended the 'rehearsal of Mrs Clive's new farce, which is very droll, with very pretty music'. Horace Walpole to George Montague, Letter of 19 March 1754, electronic version of *The Yale Edition of Horace Walpole's Correspondence* (New Haven: Yale University Press, 1937–83). <http://images.library.yale.edu/hwcorrespondence/page.asp?vol=9&page=160>. Accessed 2 December 2018. This letter is cited in Crean, '"The London "Prentice"', pp. 346–47. Because lost, the work can't be assessed, but Crean asserts that she wrote it. Clive wrote other benefit farces for herself, and I discuss her output in Chapter 12.

[75] The benefit's advertisement read: 'The Unfortunate Widow humbly hopes that the Good Nature and Humanity of her Friends will … continue the favours, formerly shown to her late Husband, to her and her Distress'd Family, being left entirely destitute of any provision.' *The London Stage*, Part 3, vol. 2, p. 1072 (under the entry for Covent Garden on 17 November 1743).

[76] Notices of Clive's 'Life of a Beau' in *The Miser* appeared in the *London Daily Post and General Advertiser,* issue 1076 (11 April 1738). Later announcements of Clive's 'Life of a Beau' in *The Miser* ran in this paper in issue 1252 (2 November 1738), issue 1355 (2 March 1739), issue 1402 (26 April 1739), issue 1427 (25 May 1739), issue 1567 (2 November 1739), issue 1678 (11 March 1740), issue 1691 (26 March 1740), issue 1694 (29 March 1740), issue 1709 (16 April 1740), and issue 2199 (9 November 1741).

> She sooths in private, whilst the Fair-One [Clive] sings
> Gayly responsive to th' harmonious Strings.[77]

Clive's generosity, and her gratitude to Carey – one of whose offspring carried her name – was here on show, giving the lie to Fleetwood's complaint of her avarice and arrogance.

On 18 November, the day after her benefit, Fleetwood's camp attacked her afresh. The pamphlet *Theatrical Correspondence in Death* censured her leadership of the actors' rebellion and her assumption since 1733 of Anne Oldfield's roles. Partly an 'Epistle' – possibly a dig at Fielding's 'Epistle' to Clive in *The Intriguing Chambermaid* – and partly a dialogue, *Theatrical Correspondence* features Oldfield and other dead celebrities castigating Clive for her social and professional arrogance:

> I cannot bear with Patience … that *Sing-Song* Girl there; notwithstanding her Sex, I believe we may justly say, she is one of the chiefs of these *State Revolters* … Self-Sufficiency, and Self-Conceit, Sir, said Mr. Wilks, with their natural Offspring Arrogance and Insolence, are too often the Attendants on human Nature … For Heaven's sake Mr. Wilks, replied the G—n—l sharply, what is her Merit, when compared … with many her Predecessors … If the *Sing-Song* Girl bears any Resemblance of Mr. Wilks's Painting – if she appear the Self-Sufficient – the Self-Conceited – the Arrogant – the Insolent – let us impute it to the Weakness of her present State.[78]

So the ghosts of Oldfield's last lover Charles Churchill and the legendary actor Robert Wilks. Joe Miller (1684–1738), who in life had played alongside Clive, takes a similarly dark view:

> I once knew very well, and had some Respect for, when in her Infancy upon the *Stage* – I always thought her a pretty, pert Lass – I own I never thought she would arrive to her present Ambition – but that plaguy part NELL has actually overset the Girl – She is *metamorphosed* indeed with a Witness, and fancies herself the real Lady Loverule off the Stage, she represents on – add to this the little Gypsy's natural Temper is inclinable to be *Shrewish* – the Servants, her

---

[77] '(Spoke by Mr. Hale) to the *MISER*; acted at the Theatre Royal in Covent-Garden, for the Benefit of the Widow of the late Mr. HENRY CAREY, and her four small Children.' *Daily Advertiser*, issue 4016 (1 December 1743).

[78] *Theatrical Correspondence in Death. An Epistle from Mrs. Oldfield, in the Shades, to Mrs. Br--ceg---dle, upon Earth: Containing, a Dialogue between the most Eminent Players in the Shades, upon the late Stage Desertion* (London, 1743), pp. 2–4. 'Mr. Wilks's Painting' refers apparently to the passage in Wilks' 'memoir', authored by Edmund Curll, that describes the justice with which Oldfield inherited the parts of earlier principal actresses, and vanquished, through her merit, objections to her appropriation of roles: 'When Mrs. Oldfield's demonstrable *Merit*, put her in just Possession of Mrs. Mountfort's (afterwards Mrs. Verbruggen's) Parts; a false, ridiculous, and Party-Clamour was raised and fomented.' [Edmund Curll], *The Life of that eminent Comedian Robert Wilks, Esq.* (London, 1733), p. 27.

high Salary enabled her to keep, if unembodied and with us, would justifie my Assertion.[79]

While revisiting tropes from the 1733 satire on Clive as 'Miss Prudely Crotchet' – that she is vain, shrewish, self-interested – *The Theatrical Correspondence* also echoes Fleetwood's charges: Clive 'fancies herself the real Lady Loverule'. Her characterization as 'one of the chiefs of these *State Revolters*' was equally damning.

At this point, Clive may well have felt that her hands were tied. Further engagement in paper battles would, following this and other accusations of 'Arrogance and Insolence', only have reflected negatively on her. She was not, however, without influential supporters. Frederick, Prince of Wales, stepped in to command her benefit on 13 March 1744; she was placed second in the Covent Garden benefit season, after Quin, as she had previously been placed at Drury Lane. At Frederick's command Clive performed her celebrated Portia in *The Merchant of Venice*, announced as 'Never acted ... Before' at Covent Garden.[80] Frederick also called for the Opposition Patriot anthem, 'Britons strike Home', which was 'done, with the Chorus's, accompanied by Trumpets, Kettle-Drums, &c. and met with the greatest Approbation'.[81] Collective song united the struggle of the Opposition with Clive's own. Clive used the event to help Edwards, who that night debuted in a spoken part.

Soon after her March 1744 benefit, Clive led a special production along with Beard and Edwards outside of Covent Garden: De Fesch's *Love and Friendship*, 'after the Manner of an Oratorio' – that is, not staged. This 'new English Pastoral Serenata' had actually been composed by De Fesch in 1734, but never publicly performed.[82] *Love and Friendship* found its audience at the Crown and Anchor Tavern on 21 March 1744 'At the Desire of several Ladies of Quality'.[83] The plot of *Love and Friendship* happened to chime with Clive's role

---

[79] *Theatrical Correspondence in Death*, p. 7.
[80] *The London Stage*, Part 3, vol. 2, p. 1094 (entry for Covent Garden 13 March 1744).
[81] 'Last Night their Royal Highnesses the Prince and Princess of Wales were at the Theatre-Royal in Covent-Garden, to see the Merchant of Venice; when the Song of *Britons strike home*, &c. was Commanded to be sung, which was accordingly done, with the Chorus's, accompanied by Trumpets, Kettle-Drums, &c. and met with the greatest Approbation.' *General Advertiser*, issue 2911 (14 March 1744).
[82] Only the anonymous wordbook survives from the 1744 production: *Love and Friendship. A Serenata. Set to Musick by Mr. W. Defesch* (London, 1744). On De Fesch's original composition of *Love and Friendship* of 1734, see Tusler, *Willem de Fesch*, pp. 131–36. Apart from one cut, the action in the 1744 wordbook is the same as that of 1734; the music for both versions is lost. Tusler has transcribed the 1734 wordbook, of which only one copy apparently survives; the 1744 version is digitized. Cuts from the 1734 version include recitative for Aegeon, Camillo, and Philander, and one air for Philander. *Ibid.*, pp. 274–75.
[83] The first notice in the *Daily Advertiser*, issue 4096 (3 March 1744) gave the date of performance ('Wednesday the 21st instant') and it was also announced in the *General Advertiser*, issue 2917 (21 March 1744). According to both press notices, the cast members

in the actors' revolt. In the story, the shepherds Philander (Beard) and Camillo (Edwards) both love the shepherdess Clorinda (Clive), but Philander, ignorant of Camillo's passion, asks him to court Clorinda on his behalf. As Camillo woos for Philander, Clorinda reveals that she loves Camillo, and he admits that he loves her. Enraged at Camillo's betrayal, Philander challenges Camillo to a duel. To defend Camillo, Clorinda disguises herself as a male combatant and intervenes to halt the clash, reconcile the friends, and gain her suitor. With Edwards in a male role and Clive's character impersonating a man, the story of *Love and Friendship* tests the work's assertion that honour is a bond unique to men. Camillo finally swears allegiance to this bond with the words 'Social Love my Soul does bind, / Never found in Woman's Mind'.[84] For those attending *Love and Friendship*, the 'Ladies of Quality' especially, consideration of Clive's superior 'Social Love' – that is her 'Honour and Spirit' in refusing collusion with Garrick at Drury Lane – was surely intended by the performers to be part of the evening's entertainment. Perhaps the 'Ladies' in attendance also enjoyed listening to Edwards and Clive express their mutual ardour. The work's single performance in a tavern will, however, have been cold comfort to Clive as she watched French soprano Elizabeth Duparc take over her part of Dalila in *Samson* during Handel's 1743–44 oratorio season.

Public Taste, Private Vendettas, and the 1744–45 Covent Garden Season

Relations between Macklin and Garrick had turned toxic about a fortnight after Clive belatedly began her Covent Garden season in November 1743. Garrick had returned to Drury Lane, but Fleetwood refused to have Macklin back. Macklin speculated that Fleetwood, by refusing to hire him, aimed to humiliate Garrick, who was not yet 'sufficiently *humbled* to the Manager's *Content*'.[85] In a letter in the press of 2 December, Garrick did battle with the '*Picture*' of his (Garrick's) '*treacherous*' and '*avaritious* Disposition' which had circulated even before Macklin's report of Garrick's betrayal was published.[86] Garrick put out that he was merely trying to reach a 'Reconciliation' on behalf of a starved company.[87] The pseudonymous 'LEONIDAS' derided this posture the next day; sneering at Garrick's 'honest Appeal to the Publick', Leonidas pointed out that 'separate Measures' were 'contrary' to the '*solemn Engagement*' that Garrick was said to have entered with Macklin.[88] Macklin echoed

---

were Clive, Beard, Edwards, and William Savage, a bass. Given each vocalist's line and seniority, we can assume the assignment of parts as discussed below. A former chorister, William Savage had sung treble parts until 1740, after which he took bass parts.

[84] *Love and Friendship*, pages unnumbered; Act 1 scene 2, air 1, third page of verse.
[85] Macklin, *Mr. Macklin's Reply*, p. 30.
[86] Ibid., p. 26.
[87] *London Daily Post and General Advertiser*, issue 2823 (2 December 1743).
[88] *London Evening Post*, issue 2507 (1–3 December 1743).

Leonidas on 5 December in a broadsheet in which he raged against Garrick. He rejected Garrick's offer to give him six pounds of his weekly pay or arrange for Ann Grace to work at Covent Garden, deeming these a 'pretence of a *tender* Feeling'.[89] Macklin rolled all their exchanges into the work which has already been quoted, *Mr. Macklin's Reply to Mr. Garrick's Answer. To which are prefix'd, All the Papers, which have publickly appeared, in regard to this Important Dispute,* issued on 19 December 1743.

That same month, Macklin's party rioted to upend the return to Drury Lane of Garrick, who on 6 December attempted to lead the Duke of Buckingham's burlesque, *The Rehearsal*. According to one report, at this performance 'Many Heads were broke in the Pit, Benches torn-up, and Candle, Sconces, Bottles, &c. thrown upon the Stage'.[90] A Fleetwood sympathizer protested that the agitators, whose 'Insolences' the Town should not tolerate, were merely 'robbing the Manager of all the Money of the Boxes'.[91] On the next night, 7 December, Garrick delivered from the stage a 'proper Apology' to the Town – as Clive had in 1736. His humbleness quieted audience hostility; spectators 'received [his apology] with the greatest Marks of Approbation' and allowed the performance to continue.[92]

As the 1744–45 season began, Clive was desperate. Not just Fleetwood, but now also Rich had not paid her salary. Then, at the season's start, Rich dismissed Clive without warning, justification, or payment. In October 1744 she played her last card: not another letter to the press, but a pamphlet, *The Case of Mrs. Clive*, reprinted as Appendix 3. Here she explained that Rich and Fleetwood had forged a cartel to 'reduce the Incomes' of players,[93] and that the two managers had colluded to put out the falsehood that 'Actors Salaries' were 'too great'.[94] 'Necessity' alone had prompted her and others to cross over to Covent Garden in September 1743.[95] Between them Fleetwood and Rich had lowered her salary to £200. Both managers had failed to pay her: Fleetwood owed her £160 12s for the 1742–43 season,[96] while Rich owed her most of her

---

[89] Macklin, *Mr. Macklin's Reply*, p. 7.
[90] *Country Journal or The Craftsman*, issue 911 (10 December 1743).
[91] 'A BY-STANDER', 'To the AUTHOR, &c', *London Daily Post and General Advertiser*, issue 2828 (8 December 1743).
[92] *London Daily Post and General Advertiser*, issue 2829 (9 December 1743).
[93] Clive, *The Case of Mrs. Clive*, p. 8.
[94] *Ibid*. Milhous and Hume rightly observe that Clive wrote cagily about her earnings: 'Clive admitted to having made £300 per annum and having been offered "an additional Salary"'. Milhous and Hume, 'The Drury Lane Actors' Rebellion of 1743', pp. 67–68, note 34.
[95] Clive, *The Case of Mrs. Clive*, p. 11.
[96] *Ibid*., pp. 17–18. Milhous and Hume, analyzing the 'Precedent Book' (LC 5/204), note that in his record of 'Monies Owing' for the 1742–43 season Fleetwood 'uncharacteristically recorded a higher total: £162 12s' owed to Clive. Milhous and Hume, 'The Drury Lane Actors' Rebellion of 1743', p. 69, note 39.

1743–44 salary,[97] and had made her pay costs for her 1744 benefit. Her last-minute firing by Rich had left her without employment.[98] She argued furiously for her modesty, repented the need to publish her 'Case', assured readers that they were the 'proper Judges' of any performer, and apologized for referring to her merit: 'I am sorry I am reduced to say any thing in favour of myself ... I am not in the least vain of my Profession.'[99] In stark contrast to Garrick and Macklin, Clive emphasized that she had submitted 'intirely' to the managers, whom she accused of abusing players and public alike.[100]

A fortnight later, in the *Daily Gazetteer* of 26 October, none other than 'WILLIAM HINT' – one assumes this was Fielding writing under his usual pseudonym[101] – sided with the managers and with the writer of *The Theatrical Correspondence*. He noted that 'Mrs. Clive has been censur'd, and, perhaps, justly, for throwing herself into *genteel* Comedy; and particularly, into the Character of Lady Townley' – Oldfield's most celebrated role. The problem, according to Hint, was Clive's arrogance: 'Managers ... lay the Fault at her Door, and say, She would.'[102]

Eight days later Clive mounted her own out-of-season benefit concert, renting the Little Haymarket Theatre from an unlikely ally, the now-disgraced Theophilus Cibber.[103] Again, Prince Frederick came to her aid, attending with the Princess of Wales. Their presence was headlined in eight of nine announcements, from 23 October to 2 November, during which Hint's slander of Clive appeared. The concert, on 2 November, represented Clive's rank in London as a first musician. Performers included violin virtuoso Niccolo Pasquali and tenor Thomas Lowe – Beard, being articled to Rich, was for this reason probably unavailable – and of course Edwards. The music was firmly high-style, including, besides a violin sonata and a solo, the 'most favourite Airs from the last new Operas and Oratorios'.[104] Clive again turned to De Fesch, featuring three of his concertos – two for the bassoon and one for harpsichord – in the programme.[105]

---

[97] The 'Manager sent an Office-keeper to me with some Salary that was due ... I told him a very great Part of my Agreements were yet due ... and ... he has not paid me.' Clive, *The Case of Mrs. Clive*, pp. 12–13.

[98] Ibid., pp. 13–17.

[99] Ibid., pp. 18–19.

[100] Ibid., p. 12.

[101] On Fielding's use of the pseudonym 'William Hint' in publications other than those discussed in this book, see Lockwood, 'The Covent Garden Tragedy. Introduction', *Henry Fielding: Plays Volume II*, p. 351.

[102] WILLIAM HINT, 'To the AUTHOR, &c', *Daily Gazetteer*, issue 3264 (26 October 1744).

[103] 'Mrs. Clive ... took a Concert for her Benefit, and to that End hired the Little Theatre of me.' Theophilus Cibber, *A Serio-Comic Apology for Part of the Life of Mr. Theophilus Cibber, Comedian* (Dublin, 1748), p. 9.

[104] *General Advertiser*, issue 3111 (2 November 1744).

[105] Four pre-1745 concerto sets by De Fesch survive. Opus 10, 'VIII Concerto's in seven parts' for strings, transverse flute, harpsichord, and continuo (1741) is dedicated to

Following this high-level endorsement, Rich hired her back. A notice appeared on 27 November that Clive would rejoin Covent Garden 'as soon as she is recovered from her present Indisposition'.[106] Given that she had just sung at her own benefit, this illness was clearly invented. She opened her Covent Garden season, like the season before, as Lappet with 'Life of a Beau'.[107] With Clive back on the boards, 1744–45 at Covent Garden was, according to Theophilus Cibber, 'an extraordinary successful Season; which was not at all the case at Drury-Lane', despite Garrick, Woffington, and Susannah Cibber all performing there.[108] The singers at his disposal likely prompted Rich to mount John Gay's *What d'ye Call It* as a 'Tragi-Comi-Pastoral-Farcical Opera' with a 'Variety of Songs adapted to several of the Characters'.[109] Lampe supplied this music for a cast that included Clive as 'Kitty' appearing along with Beard. Theophilus Cibber's participation in this and other Covent Garden productions – he had joined the company in January 1745 – explains his later puffing of Rich's season.

One highlight for Clive was a three-night oratorio subscription in 1745 that De Fesch organized and she led during Covent Garden's benefit season. The first of De Fesch's three evening entertainments, on 6 March, featured the previous season's *Love and Friendship*; the other two, on 20 March and 3 April, his new oratorio *Joseph*.[110] Performances of the latter dovetailed with Handel's revival that season of *Joseph and his Brethren* on 15 and 22 March. Not having been able to join Handel's oratorio company the season before, in March 1744 Clive may well have conscripted De Fesch to organize her own. As discussed in Chapter 8, De Fesch obliged Clive and Beard by composing music co-extensive with their parts in Thomas Arne's *Comus* (1738) and Handel's *Samson* (1743).

Frederick, Prince of Wales; this music may have been adapted for Clive's benefit concert commanded by Frederick. Tusler, *Willem de Fesch*, pp. 150–52.

[106] 'We hear Mrs. Clive has engaged to act this Season at the Theatre-Royal in Covent-Garden, as soon as she is recovered from her present Indisposition.' *Daily Advertiser*, issue 4398 (27 November 1744).

[107] *General Advertiser*, issue 3135 (30 November 1744).

[108] Cibber, *A Serio-Comic Apology*, p. 23

[109] *Daily Advertiser*, issue 4436 (4 April 1745). In this notice, Clive is not listed in the cast; for the work's second and last performance, on 22 April 1745, she is recorded in *The London Stage*, Part 3, vol. 2, p. 1169 as having as having played 'Kitty'. Lampe's composition is briefly mentioned in Martin, *Operas and Operatic Style of John Frederick Lampe*, p. 69.

[110] 'By Subscription for three Nights … For the Encouragement of such Persons as shall please to favour Mr. De Fesch by subscribing One Guinea, they shall be entitled to six Tickets, each of which will admit one into the Boxes, or two into the Gallery. No Body to be admitted into the Boxes without printed Tickets, which will be delivered at the Theatre. Subscriptions to be taken in till the 5th instant [i.e. 5 March], at Mr. De Fesch's, at the Sign of the Angel and Trumpet in St. Martin's Lane; at the Bedford Coffee-House, Covent-Garden; and at Mr. Page's, Stage-Door-Keeper'. *Daily Advertiser*, issue 4410 (5 March 1745).

Clive ended her Covent Garden season with a *coup de théâtre*. On 29 May 1745, at the joint benefit of Mary Edwards and Clive's brother Jemmy, Clive handed to Edwards the coveted part of Polly in *The Beggar's Opera*, herself playing Lucy for the '*first Time*'.[111] For its afterpiece Clive performed again as Lucy, but now in *The Virgin Unmask'd*, to which she added a *galant* song, a 'Minuet' proper to the part.[112] 'By particular DESIRE', *The Beggar's Opera* led by Edwards and Clive was repeated two nights later, concluding the 1744–45 season.[113] Clive never trod Covent Garden boards again.

Exit Fleetwood

While Clive was having her 'extraordinary successful' 1744–45 season, Drury Lane audiences were in an uproar. Fleetwood had raised ticket prices, but was offering only creaky old productions (pantomimes particularly), refusing to hire back favourite comic players (Clive and Macklin),[114] and not allowing principal players – including Susannah Cibber, who had crossed from Covent Garden back to Drury Lane upon Clive's departure – 'to play together' in optimal pairings.[115] Higher ticket prices were the big complaint. Fleetwood justified this 'advanc'd' tariff' as a price hike traditionally imposed to cover the high costs of new pantomime productions – but his old productions were costing him nothing extra.[116] Garrick was also implicated in this price-gouging, according to one critic who lambasted Fleetwood for supplanting Macklin with 'this Tool, this Puppet' Garrick.[117]

In November 1744, riots again broke out; Fleetwood responded by hiring thugs to subdue the crowd. During the week of 11 November 'some Persons [began] flinging ... Sconces and Candles on the Stage', and a blameless 'Mr. Baynes' was mistakenly arraigned and brought before the magistrate Sir

---

[111] 'The Part of Lucy, to be perform'd by Mrs. CLIVE, (*Being the first Time of her performing it;*) ... And the Part of Polly, by Miss EDWARDS, (*Being the first Time of her appearing in that Character.*)'. *General Advertiser*, issue 3287 (29 May 1745).
[112] 'The Part of Miss Lucy (with a Minuet in Character) by Mrs. Clive.' *Ibid*.
[113] *General Advertiser*, issue 3288 (30 May 1745). The notice appeared the day before the season's final night.
[114] *Daily Post*, issue 7873 (26 November 1744). The notice mentions also Theophilus Cibber, who since the scandal of his court case against his wife in 1738 had yet to return to Drury Lane.
[115] *Daily Gazetteer*, issue 3289 (24 November 1744).
[116] *Stage Policy Detected; Or Some Select Pieces of Theatrical Secret History laid Open* (London, 1744), pp. 18–22, 34–36.
[117] '[W]hy have you [Fleetwood] taken into your so select Company that miserable Creature, with nothing to recommend him but his Infidelity ... they [audiences] should ... not ... suffer this Tool, this Puppet, any longer to supply the other's [Macklin's] Place.' *Ibid*., pp. 45–46.

Thomas de Veil.[118] For the performance that Saturday 17 November Fleetwood hired '*Bruisers*' to 'beat, insult, or intimidate' the audience into submission.[119] Horace Walpole, in the audience that night, to his surprise found himself leading audience protest against Fleetwood, whose 'blackguards armed with bludgeons' filled the stage; indignant, Walpole galvanized audience members when he interrupted an actor apologizing for Fleetwood by shouting 'He is an impudent rascal!'[120]

On 22 November, Fleetwood published a blatantly false account of the riots and of his actions. He attributed the 'Disturbances' to particular parties who had turned a minor resentment towards pantomime into a cabal-led persecution; he blamed his '*Advanc'd Prices*' on raised operating costs; he claimed to be responding to a demand for pantomime; he denied that he had hired '*Bruisers*', whom he variously described as '*Peace Officers*' and '*Servants*'; any individuals who had received injuries, he asserted, were trespassers in his theatre.[121] His lies provoked many printed denunciations, but the 'base' and 'despicable' Fleetwood had already planned his retreat.[122] By 24 November he had put the theatre patent up for sale.[123] Two bankers bought it on borrowed money and installed James Lacy as manager.[124] Fleetwood retired from the stage and then quit England early the following summer, leaving his household to be auctioned.[125]

Before the dispute fully subsided from the press, a report ran that the Town would have been 'willing to Reconcilement' if Fleetwood had asked 'those

---

[118] [Charles Fleetwood] 'To the PUBLICK', 'Last Week, upon some Persons flinging the Sconces and Candles on the Stage, a Quarrel arose, 'midst the Confusion of which, this Gentleman was secur'd.' *General Advertiser*, issue 3128 (22 November 1744).

[119] *Daily Post*, issue 7873 (26 November 1744).

[120] Horace Walpole to Sir Horace Mann, letter of 7 December 1744 (Old Style date 26 November 1744), electronic version of *The Yale Edition of Horace Walpole's Correspondence*. <http://images.library.yale.edu/hwcorrespondence/page.asp?vol=18&seq=565&type=b>. Accessed 2 December 2018.

[121] *General Advertiser*, issue 3128 (22 November 1744). This report was printed separately as a broadside, *To the Publick. As the Extraordinary Disturbances which have lately happen'd at this Theatre* (London, 1744).

[122] Fleetwood was condemned in *Daily Gazetteer*, issue 3289 (24 November 1744), *Daily Post*, issue 7873 (26 November 1744), *Daily Gazetteer*, issue 3293 (29 November 1744), and in a 53-page diatribe, *Stage Policy Detected*, cited above and issued 24 November 1744: 'I know nothing more base and mean, nothing than can render a Man more justly despicable in the Eyes of all Men of Sense of Spirit, than the writing what one's self knows to be false.' *Stage Policy Detected*, p. 10.

[123] *London Gazette*, issue 8382 (20 November 1744).

[124] Robert D. Hume, 'Garrick in Dublin in 1745–46', *Philological Quarterly*, vol. 93, no. 4 (2014), p. 530.

[125] '*To be Sold by* AUCTION ... THE entire Houshold Goods, &c. of CHARLES FLEETWOOD, Esq; who is lately gone abroad.' *Daily Advertiser*, issue 4531 (1 July 1745).

Gentlemen's Pardon he had affronted'.[126] Yet Fleetwood denied 'he gave any Cause of Affront'.[127] If true, Fleetwood's failure to apologize proved costly indeed. Perhaps he was too proud; perhaps he had failed to grasp the power of the apology from the stage, exploited brilliantly by Clive in 1736 and Garrick in 1744. Even today, enacting submission to an audience flatters its members with the power to rehabilitate.[128] Was defeat for Fleetwood a victory for the rebel players? Only incidentally. Audiences rejected Fleetwood because they felt exploited and insulted, not because they empathized with the plight of Drury Lane company members.

Epilogue: The Theatrical Contest

A satirical engraving, *The Theatrical Contest* (Fig. 9.3), with verses and an 'EXPLANATION', was issued on 24 October 1743, a fortnight after the Lord Chamberlain refused to support the Drury Lane actors.[129] As a summary of the 1743–44 actors' rebellion, and a perspective on the disputants' public images, this engraving, from which all quotations below are taken, rewards close reading.[130]

The scene shows the Covent Garden piazza with a waterway passing through it, in which the players flounder. The water is the players' 'Pride'. The key names the players, who are also identified by their 'favorite [stage] Characters' written on the bladders which buoy them up. According to verses attached to *The Theatrical Contest*, the 'mimic *Monarch's* ... Patriot like' who lead the company 'Against Oppression' are 'Richard' (Garrick), 'Shylock' (Macklin), and 'Nell' (Clive). A 'Current' carries them and other company members, some clinging to splintered planks, towards the Lord Chamberlain, who holds the licence in his hands. Fleetwood kneels in front of the Lord Chamberlain, pleading that 'he can't support the Charge' of players' salaries. Macklin is the 'grand Inventor

---

[126] 'Yet such was the good Nature of the Town, so prone, so willing to Reconcilement, that it gave the M--r the most easy Terms to acquit himself. What could he do less than ask those Gentlemen's Pardon he had affronted in this Manner?' *Daily Gazetteer*, issue 3293 (29 November 1744).
[127] Ibid.
[128] 'Historically, they [celebrities] may be damaged ... But a variety of devices of rehabilitation, such as the ritual of a public apology ... go a long way towards restoring public approval.' Chris Rojek, *Fame Attack: The Inflation of Celebrity and its Consequences* (London, 2012), p. 159.
[129] *The Theatrical Contest 1743*. [London] 1743 ('Publish'd according to Act of Parliament, Octobr. 24th 1743. by G. Foster at the White horse on Ludgate Hill') [etching]. Fig. 9.3 is the only copy of this print with verses that I have found, held at the Folger Shakespeare Library.
[130] The subjects in this scene are identified in the British Museum online catalogue entry for the print: <http://www.britishmuseum.org/research/collection_online/collection_object_details.aspx?objectId=3074039&partId=1&searchText=theatrical+1743&page=1>. Accessed 2 December 2018.

Fig. 9.3 *The Theatrical Contest 1743*, 1743. Etching.
The Folger Shakespeare Library. Call number: PR3291.T39 Cage 1.
Used by permission of the Folger Shakespeare Library.

of the *Scheme* … Like Satan tempting others into Sin'. He sinks up to his armpits, dragging along other 'Wretches he drew in'.

On the right, Garrick is up to his waist in water astride a splintered plank; despite thinking that he 'on his own Merit might rely', he nonetheless finds that Woffington 'is plac'd commodious by'. Woffington, by holding onto Garrick's wrist, keeps him from sinking further, while Hannah Pritchard, pictured as Woffington's rival ('sure with [Woffington] may vie') stands to the left of Garrick. Behind Garrick, in the doorway to Covent Garden, Rich 'exults to see his Audience pouring in'. Lacy, the 'Person who negociated [sic] the Cartell between Mr. R-ch and Mr. Fl—tw--d', presents Rich with this agreement; standing above them, on the door lintel, Quin and Susannah Cibber protest. Theatregoers, some of whom have animal heads, throng under Covent Garden's arcade, pressing to enter Rich's theatre. They are whipped by a horseman in the top left corner.

Speech bubbles animate this scene. The Lord Chamberlain pretends to judge fairly, declaring 'I'll hear both Sides', but justice may come too late for Garrick, who gasps 'I am almost ax'd' as his plank splinters. Macklin cries 'Never flinch and we shall get it' even as the water overcomes him. Fleetwood's ally Paul Whitehead speaks for Fleetwood's sympathizers: 'Twill do, D---mn my Liver, they must come to the Squire's [Fleetwood's] own Terms.' Another Fleetwood ally, the boxer George Taylor, declares 'I wish they may [have the Lord Chamberlain hear 'both sides'] but I fear the Squire is Bugg[r]'d'. These conversations are secondary to the satire's main thrust: 'Their Income small, as plainly may appear, / Some having scarce a *Thousand Pounds* a Year'.

Clive stands in the centre, on the water, holding a letter – presumably hers of 23 September in the *Daily Gazetteer* – and says 'I have given my reasons'. Her 'favorite characters' are listed: Polly, Ophelia, Nell, and The Virgin – this last being Lucy in *The Virgin Unmask'd*, although the name likely refers also to Clive's reputation for chastity. What keeps Clive from sinking? The poem below the picture tells us: 'such as highest float they act the best'. The word 'act' refers to personal as well as stage performance. The poem both praises and satirizes Clive in two lines: 'Alone and self superior modest Kate / Swims on the Surface and defies her Fate.' Even as it derides Clive's pride and channels outrage at her salary, *The Theatrical Contest* asks the viewer to respect her.

The Theatrical Contest evokes many of the opposing narratives spun during and after the 1743–44 confrontation; sometimes it can be hard to choose between them. Was Macklin the hot-headed, obstinate Irishman whose rashness in quitting Fleetwood for Garrick can't be blamed on Garrick? Or was he the warm-hearted, ingenuous victim of Garrick's wiliness, who, out of solidarity with his fellow-actors, refused to compromise? Was Garrick a leader of integrity, anxious to protect fellow rebels threatened with destitution? Or was he an ambitious chameleon, ruthlessly casting aside colleagues to advance into theatre management? Was Clive a blameless victim of managerial abuse, acting alone when she crossed over to Covent Garden? Or was she chiefly concerned about her purse, in defence of which she forced her dependents to follow her? For all Clive's skill in navigating the 1743–44 Drury Lane rebellion, it radically altered how audiences saw her.

10

Of Scuffles and Rivalries: The Demise of 'Kitty Cuckoe'

Doubts linger after the actor's revolt – Susannah Cibber seeks revenge – the Polly Row renewed – Peg Woffington at Drury Lane – ressentiments and tales of scuffles – Charles Burney gets the last word

Referring to Clive, the author of *Theatrical Correspondence in Death* quotes Virgil's *Aeneid* on the subject of Dido, Queen of Carthage: '*Dux Fæmina facti*' – 'A woman led the exploit'.[1] These words preface the author's charges that Clive is 'Self-Sufficient', 'Self-Conceited', 'Arrogant', and 'Insolent'.[2] The author also denies her 'Merit': 'what is her Merit, when compared and put in the Scale, with that of many her Predecessors?'[3] Even the generally pro-Clive creator of the print *The Theatrical Contest* labels her 'self superior modest Kate', suggesting that Clive's modesty is hokum. By the start of the 1745–46 season, 'Kitty Cuckoe' was no longer universally held to represent fine taste. The tipping point seems clearly to have been Fleetwood's account of her earnings, which while misleadingly presented was in fact fairly accurate. Disclosures about her leadership of the actors' revolt further implicated her in unfeminine activities. Changing politics and stage fashions were also working against her. But it was Green Room tattle that would most overtly damage Clive's reputation over the next two seasons.

---

[1] *Theatrical Correspondence in Death*, p. 3. Dido's 'exploit' was taking treasure horded by her brother, who had murdered her husband, and leading the Libyan people out from under her brother's tyranny. Virgil, *Aeneid*, trans. with notes Frederick Ahl, with an introduction by Elaine Fantham (New York, 2007), p. 15 (Book 1, line 364). Ahl translates the phrase as 'a bold coup, led by a woman'. Quoting this line in the title of her first chapter, Marilynn Desmond shows the starkly different ways that ancient and medieval authors personified Dido, from noble leader to abandoned woman undone by desire. Marilynn Desmond, *Reading Dido: Gender, Textuality, and the Medieval Aeneid* (Minneapolis, 1994).

[2] *Theatrical Correspondence in Death*, p. 3.

[3] Ibid.

Celebrity culture feeds on the desecration of the star no less than on her veneration.[4] As a known quantity with top earnings and professional clout, Clive now found that criticism of her flourished while praise dried up. Humiliation came in the form of Green Room 'peeps', or inside gossip. The Green Room, the performers' backstage retiring space, defined rank and boundaries: only playhouse principals, high-level theatre personnel, and men of Quality were admitted.[5] As the century and its celebrity marketing progressed, audience appetite for Green Room 'peeps' grew. Among the responses to this was Garrick's rehearsal comedy *A Peep behind the Curtain* (1767), featuring Clive as Lady Fuz. Yet decades earlier Clive was already the subject of this kind of story, which pretends to intimacy with the star, and carries the authority of events witnessed – whether or not they actually occurred.[6] In Clive's case, revelations about her empowerment had whet popular appetite for stories about her aggressive nature; audiences lost their ear for Clive's sweet harmonies.

Sweet Bird at Drury Lane 1745–46: Farewell Songs

The Fading of a Celebrity Prince

What affected Clive's career most immediately at the start of the 1745–46 season was the Jacobite Rebellion. This uprising erupted with little warning and impacted on London playhouse repertory generally. Summoned to put down the rebellion, the Duke of Cumberland displaced Prince Frederick as the nation's hero. Pro-Frederick stage works at Drury Lane ceased, denying Clive a rich part of her line.

---

[4] Chris Rojek calls this the 'Icarus complex'. He describes the process in which stars at their zenith are typically then castigated for what are suddenly perceived as excesses. Rojek, *Fame Attack*, pp. 142–60. See also Chapter 1, pp. 26–27.

[5] I have yet to find any written reference to a female audience member visiting an eighteenth-century Green Room. In George Cruikshank's *The Green Room at Drury Lane Theatre* of 1821 – perhaps the earliest picture of this space – only men are present. See the digitized reproduction of the print held at the Victoria & Albert Museum, <http://collections.vam.ac.uk/item/O1243732/the-green-room-at-drury-print-george-cruikshank/>. Accessed 2 December 2018.

[6] Anna Kretschmer, 'Gossip: Backstage Space in the Eighteenth-Century Theatre'. Paper presented on 2 June 2011. *Queen Mary Centre for Eighteenth-Century Studies Graduate Conference 2011. New Directions in Eighteenth-Century Studies*. Kretschmer examines the print, *The Green Room Scuffle* and Clive's farce *The Rehearsal: Or, Bays in Petticoats* (1753), both discussed below, in relation to 'truth' and spectatorship practices. Before memoirs and press reports built in volume, gossip was enacted in plays about the Green Room, as discussed below. Lesser-known early Green Room reports include David Garrick, 'Mouse in the Green Room', Folger Shakespeare Library W.b.475, p. 24 (Autograph manuscript signed by David Garrick), 'Green room chit-chat' (c.1750, Folger Shakespeare Library, D.a.53), and *Bays in Council: Or, a Picture of a Green-Room: A Dramatic Poem* (Dublin, 1751).

The uprising, mounted to reclaim the British throne lost by James II in 1688, shook the establishment. His grandson, the 'Young Pretender' Charles Edward Stuart, landed in Scotland in July 1745 and raised forces to invade England. On 23 September his army routed British forces in Scotland at the battle of Prestonpans, to the shock of government and populace alike. On 8 November, the Young Pretender and his forces marched into England. Prince Frederick begged for a military appointment, but King George II conferred this honour on his more favoured son, the Duke of Cumberland, at the time leading British forces against the French in the War of the Austrian Succession. Unruffled by Cumberland's blunders and defeat at the Battle of Fontenoy on 11 May 1745, the King appointed him to put down the Jacobite uprising in October that year. The Duke of Cumberland's British campaign proceeded with looting, rape, the arrest of women and children, and the summary execution of suspected traitors.[7] In Scotland he was known rightly as a war criminal; in England he was a war hero, showered with titles and publicly celebrated with parades, receptions, gun salutes, and public assemblies. Medals, tavern names, and even Handel's oratorios glorified him.[8]

'The Rebellion is so far from being a disadvantage to the playhouses, that, I assure you, it brings them very good houses', Susannah Cibber wrote to David Garrick on 24 October 1745.[9] But Clive was deemed unfit to help bring such houses, her pro-Frederick, pro-Opposition line ill-suiting her to represent collective loyalty to George II. Patriotic parts were repeatedly denied her: first soprano in the masque-pantomime *The Royal Chace*, which paid homage to

---

[7] After the campaign the Duke of Cumberland would argue on legal grounds that Jacobite rebels were both criminals who stood outside military law, and military enemies who, because living on British soil, needed to be crushed. By such means he sought to justify orders by which his troops summarily executed suspected traitors, raped women, arrested woman and children, and plundered households freely. Scottish regions were plunged into economic crisis due to indiscriminate killing of livestock and the burning of ploughs, fields, and homes. John L. Roberts, *The Jacobite Wars: Scotland and the Military Campaigns of 1715 and 1745* (Edinburgh, 2002), pp. 181–97. On the Duke of Cumberland's shifting argument for his orders, see Geoffrey Plank, 'Savagery: Military Execution and the Inhabitants of the Highlands', *Rebellion and Savagery: The Jacobite Rising of 1745 and the British Empire* (Philadelphia, 2005), pp. 53–76. Plank makes the important point that the Duke of Cumberland rendered acceptable, in the name of 'defence', violations of then-current war etiquette; these transgressions set a precedent for justifying misconduct by British forces during imperial adventures that followed.

[8] On the honours paid to the Duke of Cumberland, see Rex Whitworth, *William Augustus: Duke of Cumberland: a Life* (London, 1992), pp. 97–105. Handel commemorated the duke's victory with two oratorios, the *Occasional Oratorio*, HWV 62 and *Judas Maccabaeus*, HWV 63, which are among Handel's seven post-1745 oratorios that allude to crushing the Jacobites. Handel also composed two occasional songs, 'Stand round, my brave Boys', HWV 228^{18} and 'From scourging Rebellion', HWV 228^9.

[9] Susannah Cibber to David Garrick, letter of 24 October 1745, transcribed in James Boaden, ed., *The Private Correspondence of David Garrick with the most Celebrated Persons of his Time* (London, 1831), vol. 1, pp. 36–37.

Queen Caroline, a vocal part in *Henry VIII* and its 'Military Ceremony of the Champion in Westminster-Hall',[10] and Isabel in Henry Fielding's anti-Jesuit *Debauchees*.[11]

Patriotic song was denied her as well. After Prestonpans, Drury Lane's new manager James Lacy commissioned Thomas Arne to compose a chorus expressing loyalty to the king. On 28 September 'the Audience at the Theatre Royal in Drury Lane were agreeably surprized by the Gentlemen [players] ... performing the Anthem of God save our noble King. The universal Applause it met with, being encored with repeated Huzzas, sufficiently denoted in how just an Abhorrence they hold the arbitrary Schemes of our invidious Enemies.'[12] For this, the Catholic Arne re-used – perhaps as a private joke – an anthem reportedly written during the 1688 Glorious Revolution praising the soon-to-be-deposed James II. This seems not to have registered with audiences, and Arne himself claimed to have been unaware of the origin of the tune.[13] Instead of Clive, Arne's sister Susannah Cibber was allowed to join the 'Gentlemen' in the debut of Arne's chorus, in a trio section arranged by her brother.[14] 'God save the King', and the practice of prefacing entertainments with it, spread.

As Philip Bohlman notes, it is the world's oldest and most resilient national anthem, embedding a historical chronicle within the ambiguities of myth.[15] Like Henry Purcell's 'Britons strike Home', its bold, easily memorable tune facilitated a collective effervescence during which differences between those assembled might dissolve. But 'God save the King' was self-consciously crafted as a collective song, rather than acquiring its popular function by consensus,

---

[10] *London Daily Post and General Advertiser*, issue 1887 (10 November 1740).
[11] '[F]or a revival in October 1745 he shortened the play [The Old Debauchees] by about one-fifth ... now called simply *The Debauchees*, [it] was given at Drury Lane from 17 October 1745 with considerable success – a total of twenty-five performances from October to December.' Lockwood, 'The Lottery. Introduction', *Henry Fielding: Plays Volume II*, p. 296.
[12] *General Evening Post*, issue 1874 (28 September–1 October 1745); see also *The London Stage*, Part 3, vol. 2, p. 1183.
[13] '[T]welve days after the first performance at Drury Lane ... of "the Anthem of God save our Noble King," Benjamin Victor ... [wrote] to David Garrick on October 10th, 1745, saying that they were "the very words and music of an old Anthem that was sung at St. James's Chapel for King James the Second when the Prince of Orange was landed." ... [according to] Dr. Charles Burney ... when Arne was interrogated ... he answered that "he had not the least knowledge, nor could he guess at all, who was either the author or the composer [of that tune]"'. John A. Fuller-Maitland, 'Some Theories about "God Save the King"', *Proceedings of the Musical Association*, 43rd Sess. (1916–17), p. 131.
[14] Otto Erich Deutsch, *Handel, A Documentary Biography* (London, 1955), p. 623; cited in Fuller-Maitland, 'Some Theories about "God Save the King"', p. 134.
[15] Philip Bohlman, *Focus: Music, Nationalism, and the Making of the new Europe* (New York, 2011), p. 116.

as 'Britons strike Home' had done in 1739 when it was spontaneously sung across Britain to celebrate Admiral Vernon.[16]

The charisma of Miss Kitty, tied as it was to Opposition disgruntlement and hopes for Frederick, was now out of fashion.

Drury Lane: Leading a Ragged Militia

As in the royal household and the country at large, 1745–46 was a season of struggle at Drury Lane. Upon quitting as manager in November 1744, Fleetwood had left behind a deficit of about 8,800 pounds in debts and unpaid salaries.[17] With Fleetwood gone, Garrick had hoped to take a share in the patent and become a manager, but as mentioned earlier, two bankers – Norton Amber and Richard Green, in a partnership backed by the Lord Chamberlain – borrowed money to buy the patent from Fleetwood and made Lacy manager.[18] Like Fleetwood before him, Lacy tried to drive down Garrick's salary for the coming season. Deeply upset, and still owed money for 1743–44, Garrick quit Drury Lane and went to play in Dublin.[19] Refusing to play opposite any tragedian but Garrick, Susannah Cibber also quit Drury Lane at the start of the 1745–46 season.[20] Clive may have delayed returning to Drury Lane to know where other principals would be employed. Such a strategy was imputed in the press to Quin, Woffington, and Susannah Cibber, and with good cause.[21] Writing to Garrick on 9 November 1745, Cibber deployed a topical military metaphor to explain her own reluctance to sign articles. Complaining of the 'ragged regiment' that Lacy had so far assembled, she observed: 'I should be very glad to command a body of regular troops, but I have no ambition to head the Drury-lane militia.'[22]

It was Clive who ended up leading this 'militia', together with Macklin, who had returned to Drury Lane a year earlier. By waiting until late November, Clive was in a much stronger position to negotiate with the now-desperate Lacy. Trailing Clive was Mary Edwards, who upon Clive's return began appearing

---

[16] See Chapter 7, p. 224 and notes 132, 133; on 'Britons strike Home' and the Vernon cult; also Kathleen Wilson, 'Empire, Trade and Popular Politics in Mid-Hanoverian Britain: The Case of Admiral Vernon', *Past & Present*, vol. 121 (1988), pp. 74–109; and Bohlman, *Focus: Music, Nationalism*, pp. 109–17 ('Quasi-National Anthems and Unofficial National Anthems', and 'National Anthems').

[17] Hume, 'Garrick in Dublin in 1745–46', pp. 508–33, esp. pp. 510–11.

[18] Judith Milhous and Robert D. Hume, 'Receipts at Drury Lane: Thomas Cross's Diary for 1746–47', *Theatre Notebook*, vol. 49 (1995), pp. 12–26, 69–90; and Hume, 'Garrick in Dublin in 1745–46', pp. 508–33 esp. pp. 530–33. See also Buss, *Charles Fleetwood, Holder of the Drury Lane Theatre Patent*, p. 4.

[19] Hume, 'Garrick in Dublin in 1745–46', pp. 510–11.

[20] Nash, *The Provoked Wife*, pp. 210–11.

[21] *Daily Gazetteer*, issue 5111 (5 September 1745); cited in Nash, *The Provoked Wife*, p. 210.

[22] Susannah Cibber to David Garrick, letter of 9 November 1745. Boaden, ed., *The Private Correspondence of David Garrick*, vol. 1, pp. 38–39.

regularly for the first time. And despite Drury Lane's woes, the 1745–46 season began auspiciously for Clive. Lacy came from a family of dispossessed Anglo-Irish gentry, and this common background may have eased Clive's dealings with him. The season programme, like that of her Covent Garden seasons, reviewed her greatest hits. Lacy seems to have followed Fleetwood in giving Clive her 'own Choice of Parts'.[23] And Lacy paid her, while not always paying her colleagues. As Susannah Cibber sniffily observed to Garrick, 'the Manager pays what he calls his principal actors, but the others make a virtue of necessity, and wait his leisure'.[24]

The Polly Row Renewed: Susannah Cibber and *The Beggar's Opera*

As we have seen, the more stringent enforcement and exploitation of the patent duopoly following the 1737 Licencing Act left all players subject to the arbitrary rule of managers, and therefore to overwork, withheld salaries, and salary-fixing. Yet stars were also agents, helping to produce their commodified selves for an entertainment industry driven by the demand for them. Public hunger for stars was what brought Clive back to Drury Lane on what seem to have been her own terms, and what enabled Susannah Cibber to recover from obloquy that would have killed the career of any lesser stage personage.

After her scandals of 1738, Susannah Cibber had gotten no parts with song for years; from 1742, thanks to Handel's oratorios, she was singing again, now in concert rather than stage drama. Indeed, her post-1740 de-sexualized sentimental parts in oratorios – three of her four named parts for Handel were male, and all were of course biblical – became, as Jonathan Lee shows, indispensable to her rehabilitation after her scandals of 1738.[25] Susannah Cibber was just as shrewd in career management as Clive and Garrick were. Having established herself as Garrick's opposite in tragedy during the 1743–44 season, Cibber did so again during Clive's 1744–45 absence from Drury Lane, where

---

[23] [Chetwood], *The Dramatic Congress*, p. 20. See also Chapter 9, p. 277.
[24] Susannah Cibber to David Garrick, letter of 26 February 1746. Boaden, ed., *The Private Correspondence of David Garrick*, vol. 1, p. 39–40. Drawing on a newly discovered season account book for Drury Lane in 1745–46, Robert D. Hume gives a snapshot of what Lacy owed: 'No wages at all for actors or house servants were paid on 15 and 22 of February; half wages on 1 and 8 March; nothing on 15 and 22 March. As of 8 March the treasurer notes "26 Days arrears due to the performers."'. Hume, 'Garrick in Dublin in 1745–46', p. 528.
[25] Cibber sang Micah in *Samson* (which opened 18 February 1743), discussed earlier, the herald Lichas, which Handel expanded for Cibber, in *Hercules* (first performed 5 January 1745), and Daniel in *Belshazzar* (first performed 7 March 1745). She sang Jael, the virtuous wife of Heber, in the 1744 revival of *Deborah*. Lee, 'From Amelia to Calista and Beyond', pp. 1–34.

Cibber remained despite threatening to cross over to Covent Garden.[26] As she then sat out the 1745–46 season while Garrick was in Dublin, Susannah Cibber sought to turn her acting alliance with Garrick into a business partnership, inviting him to join her in two ventures: the co-purchase of the Drury Lane patent and a 1745–46 'benefit season' of upwards of fifty nights to be held at the King's Theatre in favour of British guards.[27]

On stage, Susannah Cibber was cast in a relatively restricted range of types,[28] but in her correspondence with Garrick her dramatic range widened: she played the coquette and the best friend as well as the theatre critic and the professional equal. In his correspondence to and about her, Garrick also wore many masks. Writing to Cibber, he praised her plans for a benefit season; writing to his friend Somerset Draper, he called her idea a 'chimerical and womanish' scheme.[29] Her lingering notoriety, and Theophilus Cibber's legal claim to her assets, likely also made Garrick reluctant to align his fortunes with hers. He urged Draper to report on her progress with the patent, while reaching out to other business partners to try to snatch its purchase from her.[30]

Clive's 'own Choice of Parts' during the 1745–46 season shows her diversity of repertory and business acumen. She opened the Drury Lane season opposite Macklin in *The Merchant of Venice*. She played five Shakespeare roles – Portia, Ophelia, Celia, Olivia, and, for the first time, Ariel – all, save Portia, featuring

[26] According to Nash, Susannah Cibber intended to cross over to Covent Garden for the 1744–45 season was in order to facilitate what she saw as a winning partnership with Quin, who was still at Rich's theatre. Nash, *The Provoked Wife*, pp. 194–96. On 9 June 1744, Handel wrote to Charles Jennens of his hopes to engage Cibber, whom he assumed, due to assurances from her, would be at Covent Garden for the 1744–45 season: 'I have some hopes that Mrs Cibber will sing for me … I think I can obtain Mr Riches's permission (with whom she is she is engaged to play …)'. George Frideric Handel to Charles Jennens, letter of 9 June 1744, Burrows et al., ed., *George Frideric Handel Collected Documents: Volume 4, 1742–1750*, p. 207.

[27] Helen Brooks, '"Your sincere Friend and humble Servant": Evidence of Managerial Aspirations in Susannah Cibber's Letters', *Studies in Theatre and Performance*, vol. 28, no. 2 (2008), pp. 147–59. On the financial situation under which Garrick eventually purchased the Drury Lane patent, see Hume, 'Garrick in Dublin in 1745–46', pp. 527–33.

[28] Although her line became more complex after the scandal of her trials, Susannah Cibber's range of roles was always more restricted than Clive's, encompassing chaste sentimental heroines, and after her return to the stage, fallen women. Lee, 'Appendix 2.1: Calendar of Susanna Cibber's Professional Activities, 1732–1749', 'Virtue Rewarded', pp. 193–209.

[29] David M. Little and George M. Kahrl, ed., *The Letters of David Garrick* (Oxford, 1963), vol. 1, p. 66; cited in Brooks, '"Your sincere Friend and humble Servant"', pp. 150–51.

[30] '[Garrick's] "real sentiments" were precisely what Garrick could not reveal [to Susannah Cibber]. For all the while he was showering her with letters and urging Draper to pay court to her and keep an eye on her activities lest she pull off the purchase of the patent, he had other nets in London's theatrical waters and other business partners he preferred.' Nash, *The Provoked Wife*, p. 217. Garrick's biographers are less pointed than Nash is about Garrick's dissimulation, but this is, as Nash points out, richly evidenced in the correspondence.

singing. Her mainpiece roles were typically either high-stakes repertory staples, usually with song – Lady Fanciful in *The Provok'd Wife*, Miss Hoyden in *The Relapse*, Miss Prue in *Love for Love*, Biddy Tipkin in *The Tender Husband*, Aurelia in *Twin Rivals*, Lucinda in *The She Gallant*, Mrs. Edging in *The Careless Husband*, Flippanta in *The Confederacy* – or Clive vehicles such as *The Miser*, *Comus*, and, new that season, De Fesch's *Love and Friendship*. Her afterpieces were crowd-pleasers, and without exception musical stage works; *The Devil to Pay* and Fielding's ballad farces (*The Intriguing Chambermaid*, *The Virgin Unmask'd*, *The Lottery*) were prominent. To vary the offerings, Henry Carey's *The Contrivances* was dug out for a Clive-led revival. Columbine Cameron in the ballad-pantomime *Harlequin Incendiary* was yet another iteration of Clive's 'Miss Kitty' character from *The Harlot's Progress*, and featured Columbine and Harlequin conniving to humiliate the Young Pretender. Her interlude performances of Dalila's 'My Faith and Truth' from Handel's *Samson* returned this music to its original owner.

After leading a special benefit for the distressed actor John Miller, Clive's own benefit on 10 March 1746 was the first of the regular season. On this evening, she began what would become a trademark: adding an improvised 'Mimic Italian Song'. At her March benefit, she joined her mimic Italian song to the 'proper' songs she sang as Melantha in *The Comical Lovers*. Her addition was cousin to the take-off of Lucia Panichi, called 'La Muscovita', that she had brought to Fielding's *Miss Lucy in Town* (1742). For the afterpiece of her benefit she chose *Damon and Phillida*, long since co-opted by rival theatres.[31] Clive used the benefit night for her brother and Edwards to present herself as the new Oldfield, speaking one of Oldfield's most celebrated epilogues, 'recommending the Cause of Liberty to the Beauties of Great Britain'.[32] The epilogue had been fashioned after the monologues of heroines of seventeenth-century she-tragedies, revivals of which had been mounted in the wake of the failed Jacobite plot of 1715.[33]

Clive's advancement of Edwards proceeded apace. Having handed over Polly in *The Beggar's Opera* to her at Covent Garden, Clive repeated this moment for Drury Lane audiences on 30 November. Notices alerted audiences

---

[31] *General Advertiser*, issue 3547 (10 March 1746); cited in *The London Stage*, Part 3, vol. 2, p. 1223.

[32] *An Epilogue recommending the Cause of Liberty to the Beauties of Great Britain. Spoken by Mrs. Oldfield, at the Theatre-Royal* (London, [1716]).

[33] The benefit was on 15 April 1746, and she again spoke Oldfield's epilogue on 21 April at the benefit for the prompter Richard Cross, which he shared with Charles Blakes and Mr. Bridges. In response to the arrest of the leaders of the foiled plot of 1715, Oldfield first performed this epilogue on 5 March 1716; besides being published in three editions (two in London, on in Edinburgh), 'the epilogue enjoyed its own successful run'. Lafler, *The Celebrated Mrs. Oldfield*, pp. 127–28. On the rhetorical means by which '"Royal George" emerges as guarantor of women's happiness' in this anonymous epilogue, see Wilson, *A Race of Female Patriots*, pp. 9–11; on its revival in 1746, see *ibid.*, p. 195.

that Edwards and Clive would perform Polly and Lucy respectively for the 'first Time ... upon that Stage'.[34] Besides singing Handel's 'My Faith and Truth' from *Samson* with Edwards, Clive played alongside her in two further ballad operas, *The Jovial Crew* and a new work, featuring an Irish comic character, *The Double Disappointment*.[35] The latter was a vehicle for Edwards and the Irish actor John Barrington as 'Phelim O'Blunder'.[36]

Perhaps it was Edwards' re-affirmed accession to Polly that stirred Susannah Cibber into action. Almost immediately afterwards, Cibber took steps to claw back the role denied her since 1736. For the evenings of 14, 16, and 17 December 1745 she organized a three-night 'benefit season' – a much-reduced version of what she had proposed to Garrick – for the Veteran Scheme, a high-profile fund-raising initiative led by Frederick, Prince of Wales, whose interests Clive normally represented on stage. The Scheme was set up 'to furnish the Soldiers with all the Necessaries they had Occasion for, to defend them against the Hardships and Inconveniences of a Winter Campaign, and the Severities of the Northern Climate'.[37] As Helen Brooks notes, Cibber's choice of *The Beggar's Opera* 'was a clear provocation to her rival [Clive] ... [and] also a direct challenge to Lacy, forcing him to choose between his leading actress that season and the significant benefits to be gained from supporting Susannah's venture'.[38] Brooks errs, however, in thinking that Clive still owned this role: as we've seen,

---

[34] *General Advertiser*, issue 3460 (30 November 1745).

[35] [Moses Mendez]. *The Double Disappointment: Or, the Fortune Hunters. A Comedy in Two Acts written by a Gentleman* ([London], 1755). It was advertised as: 'a new Ballad-Opera, (never perform'd before) ... With a new PROLOGUE to the Opera to be spoke by Mrs. CLIVE' and was mounted for Mrs Giffard's benefit.' *General Advertiser*, issue 3549 (12 March 1746). The original 1746 playbook and prologue in the Huntington Library, John Larpent Plays, LA 57 (submitted 1 March 1746, first performed 18 March 1746), was never published. Another version of this farce for Covent Garden, with a different prologue, was printed in 1755.

[36] Since 1739 Barrington had earned praise for his line in raw Irish characters on the London stage, especially for his benchmark Teague in *The Committee*, a London stage staple since the seventeenth century. On *The Double Disappointment* in connection to the stage type of the Irish fortune hunter, see Susan Cannon Harris, 'Mixed Marriage: Sheridan, Macklin and the Hybrid Audience', *Players, Playwrights, Playhouses*, pp. 189–212, esp. p. 202. The only music from *The Double Disappointment* that survives is 'Balin a mona', a traditional Irish tune perhaps taken from Burk Thumoth, *Twelve Scotch and Twelve Irish Airs with Variations set for the German Flute, Violin or Harpsichord* (London, c.1742).

[37] James Ray, *A Compleat History of the Rebellion* (Manchester, [1747]), p. 251. 'The Veteran Scheme was now in high Esteem ... large Sums were daily entered into the Subscription-Books, which were opened the 27th of November, in the Chamberlain's Office at Guildhall. His Royal Highness the Prince of Wales sent ... a Bank Note of 500 l. the Lord Chief Justice Lee, the Master of the Rolls, and the Judges subscribed 1200 l. the Chamber of London 1000 l. the Gentlemen of the City of London paid in 523 l .19s. the Body of Civilians in Doctors Commons 500 l. the *Drapers* Company 300 l. the *Fishmongers* Company 300 l. and several other Companies 100 l. each, besides abundance of other Donations both publick and private.' *Ibid.*, pp. 250–51.

[38] Brooks, '"Your sincere Friend and humble Servant"', p. 154.

she had passed it to Edwards, whom she had trained in 'producing her own taught Polly'.[39]

Mounting *The Beggar's Opera* was not Susannah Cibber's only move against Clive and Lacy; she also tried to discredit them. Instead of asking Lacy privately if Drury Lane could host the three benefits, she published a notice in the *Daily Advertiser* of 7 December offering to perform gratis if she could procure Drury Lane.[40] This was bizarre: normally the organizer of a benefit would negotiate directly with the patentee, leaseholder, or their agent, as Clive had done the previous season with Theophilus Cibber for her benefit at the New Haymarket Theatre. 'The same Morning' of 7 December Susannah Cibber wrote Lacy a letter asking him confirm the arrangements.[41] Lacy was happy to oblige and sent her his consent that night.[42]

Clive went up in flames, at least according to Susannah Cibber, who reported to Garrick that 'the Green-room was in an uproar: I was cursed with all the elegance of phrase that reigns behind the scenes, and Mrs. Clive swore she would not play the part of Lucy'.[43] The next day, 8 December, John Rich approached Cibber and offered her Covent Garden free of house costs for the three benefits, to which she agreed in order to reap the largest possible profits for the Veteran Scheme. That, at least, is the account she gave to Garrick in Dublin, and published in the press.[44] Her estranged husband Theophilus later contradicted this version of events, affirming that he himself 'had not been a little assiduous and instrumental, in bringing about her acting Polly at Covent-Garden Theatre'.[45] Though Theophilus is a highly unreliable witness, in this instance his account seems likelier than hers, given that Rich would have needed time to arrange for the postponement of productions already planned. In any case, Susannah clearly never intended to mount the benefits at Drury Lane, but simply to embarrass Lacy by teasing him publicly with her proposition and then denying him any chance to match Rich's offer to donate house charges. This made Lacy appear to be at once less committed than Rich to the British cause, and under Clive's thumb.

In the *General Advertiser* of 9 December, Susannah Cibber justified the removal of her three-night benefit run to Covent Garden in the following terms:

---

[39] Tate Wilkinson, *Memoirs of his own Life* (York, 1790), vol. 3, pp. 215–16.
[40] Brooks, '"Your sincere Friend and humble Servant"', pp. 154–55; see also below.
[41] *General Advertiser*, issue 3467 (9 December 1745).
[42] *Ibid.*
[43] Susannah Cibber to David Garrick, letter of 11 December 1746 (actually 1745). Boaden, ed., *The Private Correspondence of David Garrick*, vol. 1, p. 45–46; cited also in Brooks, '"Your sincere Friend and humble Servant"', pp. 154–55.
[44] *Ibid.* 'Mr. Rich having yesterday sent me the Offer of his House.' *General Advertiser*, issue 3467 (9 December 1745).
[45] Theophilus Cibber, *A Serio-Comic Apology*, p. 32.

> Whereas I publish'd an Advertisement ... making an Offer of playing the Part of Polly in the Beggar's Opera, at Drury-Lane Playhouse ... provided the Manager agreed, that the Profits of the House for those three Nights should be paid to the Veteran Scheme at Guildhall; I accordingly wrote a Letter the same Morning to the Manager for that Purpose; but receiving only a verbal Message from him late at Night ... and Mr. Rich having yesterday sent me the Offer ... proposing generously to give the whole Receipts ... into the said Scheme, I think it my Duty to accept of it.[46]

Directly below Susannah Cibber's 9 December notice ran another, claiming to have seen through her 'Double-Dealing'. Written by a 'VETERAN PROTESTANT', it imputed treachery on the grounds of her family's Catholicism.

> Mrs. Cibber is Lady I wish well as an Actress; but as I know that she and her whole Family are ... most rigid Roman Catholicks, I cannot help thinking but that her Proposal to act for the Benefit of the Veteran Scheme hath more Vanity than Loyalty in it; or rather it is a Jesuitical Stroke of a Papist Actress in Pursuit of Protestant Popularity. I make no doubt but the Design is seen thro' ... Double-Dealing may hurt us ... let us treat their Flattery, and the Art of this Lady's Proposal in particular, with the Contempt they Deserve.[47]

Susannah Cibber's rebuttal appeared in the *General Advertiser* the next day:

> I little regard the having given Offence to a particular Person, by the Offer I made of playing the Part of Polly in the Beggars Opera, but I am most sensibly hurt with an Advertisement Yesterday, which maliciously endeavours to represent me as a secret Enemy ... The Author of it knows I am no Stranger to him ... I have nothing to do with the Religion of my Family, which I take to be neither his Business, nor mine.[48]

The 'Person' offended by Susannah Cibber's 'Offer ... of playing the Part of Polly' was of course Clive, whose alleged and highly probable anger Cibber coolly dismisses as unworthy of her notice. Charged with being Catholic, Cibber implies that Lacy (the 'Veteran Protestant') has both libelled her and intruded on her privacy. She depicts herself as a rational and injured citizen, as Clive had represented herself in her earlier press letters.

Should the reader not have trusted Susannah Cibber's word, a certain 'SOCIUS' (Latin for 'ally'), inserted in that same paper of 10 December a notice just below hers.[49] According to Socius, 'some malicious Parasite, who envies her superior Merit' – by imputation, Clive – had written the 'Advertisement

---

[46] *General Advertiser*, issue 3467 (9 December 1745).
[47] *Ibid.* Susannah Cibber wrote to Garrick that 'the advertisements against me ... are the united works of Lacy, Macklin, and Giffard'. Susannah Cibber to David Garrick, letter of 11 December 1745. Boaden, ed., *The Private Correspondence of David Garrick*, vol. 1, p. 45.
[48] *General Advertiser*, issue 3468 (10 December [1745]).
[49] 'Socius', '*To the* VETERAN Protestant SUBSCRIBERS*', ibid.*

against Mrs. Cibber'.[50] Socius addresses 'GENTLEMEN', and warns them that 'To do well, is, to the Envious Mind, a Crime', and that 'such envious, detracting Advertisements' may 'Pervert' the 'most laudable Designs'.[51] A week later, on 17 December, Henry Fielding also defended Cibber in the periodical *The True Patriot*: 'This Ghost [Lacy] had the Assurance ... to spit Fire and Brimstone at a very pretty Woman, and incomparable Actress, whose Generosity and Goodness charm us more than even *her* Beauty and Talents cou'd have done.'[52]

Susannah Cibber's performances brought in some six hundred pounds for the Veteran Scheme.[53] She reported to Garrick that she had 'played it ... to the fullest houses that were ever seen';[54] he congratulated her extravagantly, but wrote to Draper that others had informed him 'that she was not so excellent in the character'.[55] Lacy kept Drury Lane dark on 14 December, the first night of the Veteran Scheme run. The announcement of this palliative move implied Drury Lane's solidarity with the benefit without naming the work that it featured: 'The Reason of the Company's not acting To-Night, is owing to the Play at Covent-Garden, the Receipt of which is to be subscrib'd to the VETERAN Scheme at Guildhall.'[56] On the two other nights of the benefit, 16 and 17 December, Drury Lane mounted Clive staples, *The Lottery* and *Comus* respectively. Cibber warned Garrick that 'Mr. Lacy's friends' were preparing a defamatory 'pamphlet' against them both, but this never materialized.[57]

One of the 1745–46 season's rare new mainpiece productions, from 30 January, was *The Tempest*, with Clive debuting in the part of Ariel. This version

---

[50] *Ibid.*
[51] *Ibid.*
[52] William B. Coley, ed., *Henry Fielding: The True Patriot and Related Writings* (Oxford, 1987), p. 382. Fielding wrote and issued this weekly periodical from 5 November 1745 to 10 June 1746.
[53] 'The whole amount of 3 nights acting the *Beggar's Opera*, proposed by Mrs Cibber, who acted Polly gratis, making 600 l. was paid by Mr Rich, into the chamber of London, for the encouragement of the soldiers. Every comedian play'd gratis, and the tallow chandlers gave the candles.' *The Gentleman's Magazine*, vol. 15 (London, [December] 1745), p. 666.
[54] Susannah Cibber to David Garrick, letter of 19 December 1745. Boaden, ed., *The Private Correspondence of David Garrick*, vol. 1, pp. 47–48.
[55] Little and Kahrl, ed., *The Letters of David Garrick*, vol. 1, pp. 71–72; cited in Brooks, '"Your sincere Friend and humble Servant"', pp. 156–57.
[56] *General Advertiser*, issue 3480 (14 December 1745).
[57] 'You could scarce believe the malice and inveteracy of Drury-lane against me ... there is a pamphlet preparing by Mr. Lacy's friends against your honour and me.' Susannah Cibber to David Garrick, letter of 19 December 1745. Boaden, ed., *The Private Correspondence of David Garrick*, vol. 1, p. 48. See also Susannah Cibber to David Garrick, letter, 'perhaps January 1746-7': 'The bad success Lacy had in his advertisements, has made him drop his design of attacking us both.' *Ibid.*

of the play, now lost,[58] was purportedly 'As written by Shakespeare', rescuing the Bard's verses from the William Davenant–John Dryden *Tempest* used on London stages since 1687. House composer Thomas Arne had prepared a substantial amount of new music, including 'proper' songs for Clive as Ariel[59] – but Clive refused to sing Arne's music, insisting that Willem De Fesch re-set her numbers. Despite Drury Lane's parlous finances, Lacy complied; Arne's songs were shelved, and De Fesch furnished her with alternatives, and Edwards with a new song.[60] Notices for the *The Tempest* omitted mention of the second composer.[61] Strategic concerns about self-representation likely figured into Clive's refusal to perform Arne's music. Particularly since the Shakespeare Ladies' Club campaign, the Bard was considered Britain's hallowed poet, and *The Tempest* was Clive's most prestigious stage appearance of the 1745–46 season. By procuring De Fesch's anonymous songs in lieu of Arne's, she avoided any association with the known Catholic Arne, brother of Susannah Cibber. More important for Clive will have been that De Fesch's songs for her were better than Arne's: fresher, more sophisticated, and more closely tailored to her line.[62]

---

[58] By comparing wordbooks with the printed airs, Cholij establishes that the 1746 Drury Lane production was very likely based on the contemporary edition of the Tempest 'corrected by' Lewis Theobald. Cholij, 'Music in Eighteenth-Century London Shakespeare Productions', pp. 79–80. Cholij identifies this production as 'the one attempt in the first half of the eighteenth century to stage Shakespeare's original version of *The Tempest*, as opposed to the alteration by Davenant and Dryden'.

[59] The British Library Add MS 29370 includes three of Arne's songs; a fourth, 'Where the bee sucks' survives in print only and was first issued in Thomas Arne's second book of Vauxhall Songs published as *Lyric Harmony ... As perform'd at Vaux Hall Gardens by Mrs: Arne and Mr: Lowe* (London, 1746). Cholij, 'Music in Eighteenth-Century London Shakespeare Productions', pp. 75–80.

[60] Unlike Arne's songs, De Fesch's were engraved following their performance. In 1986 Evan Owens and Elizabeth Gibson drew Irene Cholij's attention to the unique copy of De Fesch's songs for *The Tempest* in the Ashbridge Collection, Marylebone Public Library: *The Songs in the Tempest or the Enchanted Iisleland As they were perform 'd at the Theatre Royal in Drury Lane by Mrs. Clive and Mrs. Mozeen. Set to Musick by W. Defesch.* (London [1746]). The modern edition is a facsimile of this source. As Cholij explains, the songs are from the 1746 production and not, as Owens had opined, from later productions. Irena Cholij, 'Defesch's "Tempest" Songs', *The Musical Times*, vol. 127, no. 1719 (1986), pp. 325–27.

[61] Notices duplicated the information of the *General Advertiser*, issue 3514 (30 January 1746): 'The Part of Miranda, by Miss Edwards; and the Part of Ariel (with the proper Songs) by Mrs. Clive. With the Original Decorations, particularly The GRAND MASQUE, new set to Musick by Mr. Arne. The Part of Juno by Mrs[.] Arne; Iris, Miss Young; Ceres, Mrs. Sibella; With proper Chorus's and Dances.'

[62] About the quality of Arne's songs for Ariel, Cholij observes: '"Come unto these yellow sands" is a simple, lyrical enough, but not terribly inspired composition ... "Behold your faithful Ariel fly" ... starts with some exciting flourishes, before settling down to more conventional sustained chords ... Ariel's rather sing-song words "E'er you can say come and go" (IV i 44–47) ... [is] rather ballad-like ... not a very notable composition.' Cholij, 'Music in Eighteenth-Century London Shakespeare Productions', pp. 76–77.

For the 1746 *Tempest* De Fesch set two of Shakespeare's songs for Ariel, 'Where the bee sucks', and 'While you here do snoring lie'. To compensate for two original Ariel songs he cut, De Fesch set the speech that begins 'Before you can say'. He also added two airs with anonymous verses: 'Oh bid your faithfull Ariel fly' for Clive, and, for Edwards as Miranda, 'All fancy sick'. In his *Tempest* songs for Clive, De Fesch revisited her past musical idioms. 'Oh bid your faithfull Ariel fly' is redolent of Purcellian masque music: the first part is a duple-meter recitative arioso inflected with 'French' gestures (dotted quavers followed by demisemiquaver flourishes), and the second part is a syllabic melody based on a lilting minuet whose concluding word receives a melisma. In 'While you here do snoring lie', slow dotted rhythms for the violins, a pulsing bass line, and an obbligato oboe borrowed from slumber scenes of eighteenth-century French stage works, which Handel also imitated.[63] The entry of Ariel breaks this mood: the vocal part's minuet-style rhythm, balanced phrases, and artful lyricism are redolent of *Comus*.

Where Arne had set 'Where the bee sucks' as a simple binary air – it became a standard at Vauxhall Gardens, of which Arne was music director from 1745[64] – De Fesch's setting gave Clive a full da capo aria replete with Carey idioms. One sequence expands over an eight-bar statement culminating in a fermata on the word 'fly', where Clive could extemporize. In the B section, the arching sequence that overreaches the triad by one scale degree typifies Carey's melodic writing for Clive in his Italian cantatas. But De Fesch's scoring is much richer, with witty exchanges akin to those of Clive's 'Cuckow', composed earlier for Clive by Arne. As in 'The Cuckow', instruments seamlessly take over and complete the soprano's musical statement. As Cholij points out, 'these songs represent a landmark in the 18th-century performance history of *The Tempest*',[65] while the music's modern editor David Tusler credits Clive with a 'musical taste ... in advance of many of her contemporaries' for having chosen De Fesch to compose for her.[66]

Clive could do nothing to diminish the success of the Veteran Scheme benefit performances of *The Beggar's Opera*. For three nights Susannah Cibber owned Polly. Yet this was her preference, not the Town's. She neither robbed Edwards of this newly acquired role nor shook Clive from her place as Drury Lane's singing principal. Cibber succeeded, however, in very publicly insinuating that the theatre's manager was in Clive's thrall. Cibber's machinations set

---

[63] Cholij, 'Defesch's "Tempest" Songs', p. 326.
[64] 'In the summer of 1745 ... [proprietor Jonathan] Tyers appointed ... Arne as official composer' at Vauxhall pleasure gardens 'a position Arne would retain until 1773'. Gilman, *The Theatre Career of Thomas Arne*, p. 228.
[65] Cholij, 'Defesch's "Tempest" Songs', p. 327.
[66] Robert L. Tusler, 'Introduction', *Willem de Fesch: The Tempest Songs or the Enchanted Island ... 1745*, ed. R. L. Tusler (Amsterdam, 2003), p. iii.

the scene for a more open conflict between Clive and the actress who in 1746 would threaten her reign as comedy queen: Peg Woffington.

The Beggar's Opera revisited: 'Gossip Joan' in the Green Room

Woffington's progress, like Susannah Cibber's, may well have worried Clive. Before coming to London, Woffington had played many parts first created by, for, or about Clive – Arabella in *The Honest Yorkshireman* (by Henry Carey, which Clive never got to play), Miss Crotchet in *The Rival Theatres* (the 1733 satire of Clive by Edward Phillips), and Lappet in *The Miser*. Writing in 1803, Charles Lee Lewes recollected that Charles Coffey, author of *The Devil to Pay*, when training Woffington in Dublin 'was particularly assiduous in teaching her every applauded stroke he had observed in Miss Raftor's performance.'[67] Since her London debut at Covent Garden on 6 November 1740, Woffington had swiftly ascended through the company's ranks.

In their strengths and professional strategies, Clive and Woffington were opposites. A renowned beauty, Woffington flouted conventions in her performance of social and corporeal grace. Her movement, comportment, gestures, dress, manners, and witty repartees excited both men and women, with a simmering eroticism that reportedly laid waste to sexual mores. Preferring male company, she boldly appropriated the liberties of men, taking and dropping lovers, forging and exploiting networks, and eventually amassing considerable wealth.[68] Laudatory verses of 1740 summarize Woffington's appeal:

> When first in *Petticoats* you trod the Stage,
> *Our* Sex with *Love* you fir'd, your *Own* with *Rage*:
> In *Breeches* next so well you play'd the Cheat,
> The pretty Fellow, and the Rake compleat,
> Each Sex were then with diff'rent Passions mov'd,
> The *Men* grew envious, and the *Women* lov'd.[69]

Enhancing her exoticism was, as Felicity Nussbaum has shown, her Irishness. Woffington was the native of a kingdom controlled by the British monarch, but whose rebelliousness, Catholicism, and (banned) Celtic language enhanced her Otherness.[70]

Clive had built her success in a very different way. She courted public favour through her chasteness, intelligence, wit, and self-assurance. She stood for

---

[67] Charles L. Lewes, *Memoirs of Charles Lee Lewes* (London, 1805), vol. 2, p. 13.
[68] Nussbaum, 'The Actress, Travesty, and Nation: Margaret Woffington', *Rival Queens*, pp. 189–225.
[69] 'To Miss WOFFINGTON, on her playing the Part of SYLVIA', *London Daily Post and General Advertiser*, issue 1887 (10 November 1740).
[70] Nussbaum, 'The Actress, Travesty, and Nation: Margaret Woffington', pp. 189–225, esp. pp. 199–204.

Englishness, which she projected above all vocally, in music and words. Song was crucial to this enterprise, allowing her to straddle common and high-style taste, from her smart ballads to her airs by Britain's first poets. Her vocal technique evidenced fine command; her physical plainness was presented as a mark of virtue; and her musicianship embedded her as an equal in a field dominated by men. Disregarding the male gaze, she won respect through the ear.

Woffington was, vocally, not so well-endowed. Aaron Hill complained to William Popple in 1740 about her 'Sharps at the top'.[71] The author of *A Guide to the Stage* (1751) noted how 'Peggy, form'd by nature ... for the softest scenes ... has the misfortune of a grating voice to allay the tenderness of the impression'.[72] Theophilus Cibber observed that Woffington's voice 'has not that Silver Tone some possess'.[73] Francis Gentleman in 1770 referred to her 'croaking', saying that her 'dissonance of tones' made her the 'screech-owl of tragedy'.[74] Tate Wilkinson recalled her 'most unpleasant squeaking pipe'.[75] Thomas Davies fretted how 'she never could attain to that happy art of speaking'.[76]

This vulnerability was not lost on Clive. In 1741 she had concluded a brief summer visit to Dublin with an extraordinary gesture: singing in Irish Gaelic, for the first time ever on a licensed playhouse stage. What she sang was 'Aileen aroon', whose words were phonetically transcribed from the Irish ballad Eileanóir na Rún. Its melody had been absorbed into English country dance collections in the late seventeenth century, and from these into one fringe ballad opera production.[77] While in Dublin, Clive had learned the ballad's Gaelic words 'in Compliment to the Irish Ladies and Gentlemen, for the Civilities which she hath received',[78] and worked with band leader Matthew Dubourg to turn the common tune into a graceful set of sung variations.[79] In so doing

[71] Aaron Hill to William Popple, letter of 8 December 1740. *The Works of the Late Aaron Hill, Esq.* (London, 1753), vol. 2, p. 99.
[72] *A Guide to the Stage: Or, Select Instructions and Precedents from the Best Authorities* (London, 1751), p. 27.
[73] Cibber, *A Serio-Comic Apology*, p. 39.
[74] [Francis Gentleman], *The Dramatic Censor; Or, Critical Companion* (London, 1770), vol. 2, pp. 171, 271.
[75] Wilkinson, *Memoirs* (1790), vol. 1, p. 25; cited in Laura J. Rosenthal, 'Entertaining Women: The Actress in Eighteenth-Century Theatre and Culture', *The Cambridge Companion to British Theatre, 1730–1830*, p. 166.
[76] Davies, *Memoirs of the Life of David Garrick, Esq.*, vol. 1, p. 309.
[77] Joncus, 'From "Ellen a Roon" to "Aileen aroon": Kitty Clive and the Irish Ballad'. Paper presented at *The Irish and the London Stage: Identity, Culture, and Politics, 1680–1830*.
[78] George Faulkner, *The Dublin Journal* (8–11 August 1741); cited in Brian Boydell, *A Dublin Musical Calendar 1700–1760* (Dublin, 1988), p. 72.
[79] *Select Minuets. Collected from the Castle Balls, and the Publick Assemblies in Dublin ... to which is added Eleena Roon by Mr. Dubourgh* (Dublin, [1746]), National Library of Ireland, Add. Mus. 9013; cited in Barra Boydell, '"Whatever has a Foreign Tone / We like much better than our own": Irish Music and Anglo-Irish Identity in the Eighteenth Century', *Music and Identity in Ireland and Beyond*, ed. M. Fitzgerald and J. O'Flynn (Farnham, 2014), p. 32, note 66.

Clive forged her own kind of Irishness, one that cocooned an exotic tongue in the musical idioms of polite English song. The whole enterprise can also be seen as a means of out-Irishing Woffington, with whom she began sharing the Green Room some weeks later. Clive brought 'Aileen aroon' back with her to London and trotted it out at her benefit that season. Thereafter, 'Aileen aroon' became one of London's most interpolated stage songs until 1760.[80]

Woffington joined the Drury Lane company in September 1741. For all of 1742 we hear nothing of their rivalry. Then, on 23 January 1743, Lady Hertford wrote to her son:

> About ten days ago Mrs. Woffington and Mrs. Clive met in the Green Room. Mrs. Woffington came up to Mrs. Clive and told her she had long looked for the favor of a visit from her ... Mrs. Clive paused a little and then answered, "Madam, I have been thinking of it, and upon consideration find I have a reputation to lose." "Madam," said Mrs. Woffington, "so should I have too if I had your face."[81]

William Chetwood, in his *Dramatic Congress* (1743), asserted that rumours of strife between Clive and Woffington were Fleetwood's fabrication. Whatever its origin, Lady Hertford's story evidences public awareness of the two comediennes' respective strengths and choices of conduct. Did sexual allure imperil a female player, or empower her?

Woffington signed the petition against Fleetwood in the 1743 rebellion but stayed put at Drury Lane, thereby inheriting others' parts, including Clive's Portia. When Clive returned to Drury Lane for the 1745–46 season, she bumped Woffington from top rank. In the popular press, Clive and Woffington were soon cast as comic Rival Queens – that is, as in the Polly Row satire *The Beggar's Pantomime*, two powerful women who lose their composure and hence authority due to mutual jealousy. Reports broke out in January 1746 of an affray between them in the Green Room. The only prose account we have of the contretemps is that of Thomas Davies, writing decades later. According to Davies, Woffington and Clive traded insults in the Green Room during a performance of Shakespeare's *Henry IV*.[82] Their slander of each other moved their defenders, the 61-year-old Owen Swiney (Woffington's protector) and Jemmy Raftor (Clive's brother) to exchange blows.[83]

---

[80] Nollaig Casey, 'Eibhlin a Ruin and the Impact of Fashion in its Dissemination in Eighteenth and Nineteenth Century Ireland' (MA diss., Queen's University, Belfast, 2011).

[81] Lady Hertford to her son Lord Beauchamp, letter of 23 January 1743. Helen Sard Hughes, ed., *The Gentle Hertford* [Frances Seymour, Duchess of Somerset]. *Her Life and Letters* (New York, 1940), pp. 236–37. Cited in *The London Stage*, Part 3, vol. 2, p. 1028 (17 January 1743).

[82] Thomas Davies, 'King Henry IV. First Part. Chapter XII', *Dramatic Miscellanies: Consisting of Critical Observations on several Plays of Shakspeare: With a Review of his Principal Characters ... a New Edition* (London, 1785), vol. 1, pp. 231–34.

[83] *Ibid.*

Just such an event is the subject of a broadside, titled *The Green Room Scuffle, or, Drury Lane in an Uproar*, printed on 29 January 1746 (Fig. 10.1).[84] It illustrates the alleged combat, and its verses, set to the tune 'Gossip Joan', dramatize the scene. The tune 'Gossip Joan' was selected, ballad-opera style, for its earlier associations: to this music Polly and Lucy battle in both *The Beggar's Opera*, and in the 1736 takeoff of the Polly Row, *The Beggar's Pantomime*. Reset in the 1746 *Scuffle* broadside, 'Gossip Joan' invoked Susannah Cibber's recent appropriation of Polly for the Veteran Scheme benefits. The italics added to end the verse line, 'But 'twas about their *Duty*' pointedly lampooned Cibber's 9 December notice about her 'Duty' to play Polly at Covent Garden.

The first stanzas of *The Green Room Scuffle* set the scene with a reference to the protagonist Roxana of Nathaniel Lee's *The Rival Queens* (1677). The action of Lee's tragedy revolves around two queens, Statira and Roxana, struggling for the love of King Alexander; the wild Roxana, pregnant by the king but abandoned by him, eventually murders the pure-hearted Statira. Clive ('Kate') is likened to Roxana:

ROXANA, on the Stage,
Wou'd but appear a *Baby*,
Shou'd she with KATE engage;
Yet she's Nought to a Lady
              Call'd Peggy;
...
KATE, who was long ill-us'd,
Depended on her *Merit*,
But PEG, by all abus'd,
Said, She had only *Spirit*
              Pretty Girl!

None knew from whence it rose,
But 'twas about their *Duty*:
To rise by *Wit* one chose,
And 'tother by her *Beauty*:
              Both are Vain!

After this contextualizing, the broadside tale begins: as in Lady Hertford's report of 1743, Woffington opens the 'Battle', and the two are soon trading insults.

---

[84] Thomas Booth, *The Green Room Scuffle, or, Drury Lane in an Uproar*. Letterpress broadside song illustrated with etching, 1746 ('Publish'd Persuant to Act of Parliament Jan. 29, 1746, by G. Foster on Ludgate-Hill, and Sold at the Print and Pamphlet Shop; in London and Westminster'). The author of the article on Woffington in the *Biographical Dictionary of Actors* gives the wrong date of 1748 for the putative Clive–Woffington Scuffle. Highfill, Burnim, and Langhans, 'Woffington, Margaret', *A Biographical Dictionary of Actors, Actresses Musicians, & Other Stage Personnel in London, 1660–1800*, vol. 16 (Carbondale, 1993), p. 209.

Fig. 10.1 Thomas Booth, *The Green Room Scuffle, or, Drury Lane in an Uproar*. Letterpress broadside song illustrated with etching, 1746 ('Publish'd Persuant to Act of Parliament Jan. 29, 1746, by G. Foster on Ludgate-Hill, and Sold at the Print and Pamphlet Shop; in London and Westminster'). Yale Collection, Lewis Walpole Library. Call number: 746.01.29.01+. Courtesy of the Lewis Walpole Library, Yale University.

PEG, in a taste Polite,
At once began the Battle:
Says she, "You may be right;
But this is Tittle Tattle,
   Red-Fac'd B[it]ch!"

Now bristles bonny Kate;
All ready, fierce and fiery,
Such BRIMS cries she," I hate –
Could DAVEY[85] e'er admire Ye? –
   PROSTITUTE!

"My Beauty Me defends,
Cries *lovely pretty* PEGGY;
Whilst you abuse your Friends [i.e. 'Davey'];
And so – no more – I beg you –
   HELL'S DUCHESS!

At this point in the story, the dramatis personae broaden to include the contestants' male defenders, Swiney and Raftor. Raftor was renowned for his mild manners and absence of stage talent; his membership in the Drury Lane company was a sinecure arranged by his sister. Swiney is 'Limpo', unable to walk without two canes, as shown in the headpiece.

Up starts the *grey-hair'd Sage* –
Says Kate – "'tis most provoking!
Why should you *rule* the STAGE?
Mind *Building, Pimping, Joaking*,
   Old STAGE-GOAT!

From this, sad Work ensued:
Old LIMPO got a slap, Sir?
Which he return'd; quite rude!
And fell'd an *harmless Chap*, Sir,
   Sad JEMMEE

"My Child sha'n't be abus'd"
Says limping am'rous S[wine]y
Though POLLY me refus'd –
Shou'd you,–The Devil's in Ye,
   Saucy *Peg*!

Oh L[a]cy! Then beware
How you such *Belles* do trust to;
For, tho' they speak you fair,
They treat you as a BUSTO,
   PLAYERS ALL!

---

[85] As a pejorative term, 'Brims' probably refers to a working man's cap whose bottom was turned up all the way around to form its brim. 'Davey' is David Garrick.

The headpiece depicting all this sets the scene not in the Green Room, but backstage, under a scroll bearing the Shakespearean motto 'Totus mundus agit histrionem' ('All the world's a stage'). Three male onlookers snigger from behind the flats as a coiffured, bejeweled Woffington (left), in a formal mantua gown – probably with a thrown-back domino, although the image is hard to read – raises clenched fists above her shoulders. In the middle is a gentleman in a frock coat and full bottom wig, almost certainly Lacy, who separates Woffington from Clive, who screams, her mouth wide open. She is dressed as Nell from *The Devil to Pay*: cap, low-heeled shoes, untrimmed gown, looped petticoats, cutaway bodice, kerchief tucked around shoulders, as in the first playbook frontispiece of 1731. Beyond Clive stands Swiney, his brushed-back hair hanging as in his 1737 portrait by Pieter van Bleeck,[86] raising one of his canes, with which he has felled Jemmy Raftor. Jemmy, in breeches and long frock coat, lies on his back between his sister and Swiney, shocked and open-mouthed, his arms stretched out, hair spread, and legs in the air.

Hilarious, but did it happen? The print's date of 29 January 1746, together with Woffington's formal dress, suggests that no such altercation can have taken place at a production of Shakespeare's *Henry IV* as Davies reported because this play did not run at Drury Lane that season. It might have been on one of the nights of Macklin's *King Henry the VII*, which Woffington led that month, and which was 'entirely new-dressed'.[87] But no afterpiece followed this mainpiece, and neither Clive nor Jemmy Raftor were in the cast, so why would either of them have been at Drury Lane during its performance? Equally inexplicable is that Susannah Cibber fails to mention any such set-to when writing to Garrick of Macklin's *King Henry the VII*.[88] Given Cibber's hostility to Clive, and her eagerness to share theatre gossip with Garrick, it seems inconceivable for her not to have told him about the Clive–Woffington 'scuffle', had it taken place. The simplest explanation is that it did not.

Davies' error-filled and obviously embellished 1785 recollection of the episode strengthens this impression. By crediting period reports of a 'Scuffle', and imagining its context as Shakespeare's *Henry IV*, Davies could cast Woffington, the ex-mistress of his hero Garrick, in a more favourable light than Clive. Under Davies' pen, Woffington comes to share Lady Percy's libidinous but self-sacrificing nature in the Shakespeare play: 'beautiful and accomplished',

---

[86] After Pieter van Bleeck, *Owen MacSwinny / Peter van Bleeck Pinx.t 1737*. Mezzotint, 1749. National Portrait Gallery. Record no. NPG D5204.

[87] Susannah Cibber to David Garrick, letter, 'perhaps January 1746–47'. Boaden, ed., *The Private Correspondence of David Garrick*, vol. 1, p. 49. Charles Macklin's *King Henry the VII: Or, the Popish Impostor* (London, 1746) played on 18, 20, and 21 January 1746; press notices announced its new costumes.

[88] 'I shall say nothing of the piece, because you may read it; but, be as vain as you will about your playing Bayes, you never made an audience laugh more than Harry the Seventh has done.' Susannah Cibber to David Garrick, letter, 'perhaps January 1746–47'. Boaden, ed., *The Private Correspondence of David Garrick*, vol. 1, p. 49.

she submits to playing a 'trifling character' to 'give strength to the play' that Drury Lane never offered during the 1746–47 season.[89] He depicts Clive as a malicious rival who taunts Woffington for thin houses, rather than, as in the 1746 'Scuffle' ballad, for her whorish nature:

> A very celebrated comic actress triumphed in the barrenness of the pit and boxes; she threw out some expressions against the consequence of the Lady Percy. This produced a very cool, but cutting, answer from the other; who reminded the former of her playing, very lately, to a much thinner audience ... And now ... a most terrible fray ensued ...their altercation would not have disgraced the females of Billingsgate ... an old gentleman who afterwards bequeathed her a considerable fortune, and the brother of the comic lady, were more seriously employed. The cicisbeo struck the other with his cane: thus provoked, he very calmly laid hold of the old man's jaw ... The print-sellers laid hold of this dispute, and published an engraving called 'The Green-room Scuffle'.[90]

Davies has the biases and licence typical of theatre historians of the period: he name-checks storied actors; reports with seeming authority on verbal exchanges for which there is no record, and ascribes to women an emotional incontinence which he then mocks ('their altercation would not have disgraced the females of Billingsgate'). He pretends to discretion by not naming the participants – though he had in fact named names five years earlier, in his *Memories of the Life of David Garrick*. By this telling, 'Clive and Woffington had clashed on various occasions, which brought forth squabbles, diverting enough to their several partizans amongst the actors'.[91] Davies' conclusion is that 'No two women of high rank ever hated one another more unreservedly than these great dames of the theatre'.[92] The source of this endless strife Davies holds to be their opposing natures: 'Woffington was well-bred ... at all times mistress of herself', while 'Clive was frank, open, and impetuous.'[93]

In 1749 Chetwood related another Clive-Woffington Green Room clash. In his story, for 'Envy' of Clive's 'Merit', Woffington boasts of the persuasiveness of her characterization of Sir Harry Wildair in George Farquhar's *The Recruiting Officer*. Clive's alleged retort inverts Woffington's self-praise into a witty evocation of her reputed sexual availability:

> As Merit too often creates Envy, the little World the Theatre is not free from it. This agreeable Actress [Woffington], in the Part of Sir Harry, coming into the Green-Room, said, pleasantly, *In my Conscience! I believe Half the Men in the*

---

[89] Davies, 'King Henry IV. First Part. Chapter XII', *Dramatic Miscellanies*, pp. 233–34.
[90] Ibid., pp. 233–34.
[91] Davies, *Memoirs of the Life of David Garrick*, vol. 1, pp. 310–11.
[92] Ibid.
[93] Ibid.

> *House take me for one of their own Sex.* Another Actress reply'd, *It may be so; but, in my Conscience! the other Half can convince them to the contrary.*[94]

Chetwood also passes over the ladies' identities, which would only need to be spelled out for later generations, beginning with readers of Tate Wilkinson's sniggering 1791 version of Chetwood's anecdote.[95]

Of Scuffles and Queens

Whether or not it actually happened, the 'Green Room Scuffle' was a watershed in Clive's career. Before 1746, as Drury Lane's first-ever principal songster-comedienne, Clive had been the voice of British taste, qualities, and aspirations: crisp, fearless, and irreducible to one character. Now, in the wake of her two-year struggle with managers, the disclosure of her earnings, and Prince Frederick's retreat from public view, prejudices against Clive began to build, and her earlier identity to wither. Her reported clash with Woffington authenticated Clive as drama queen: conceited, arrogant, insolent, and self-sufficient – like her characterization in *Theatrical Correspondence in Death*. Above all, she was no longer elusive; on the contrary, her personality now seemed all too knowable.

The difference between recollections of Clive before and after 1746 is striking. Compare, for instance, the Scuffle broadside with the following backstage report on Clive from 1739. It appeared in the second issue of *The Country Correspondent*, a periodical that Theophilus Cibber was said to have founded.[96] This sketch's author, who may have been Cibber himself, claims to have had a 'good deal of Chat' with Clive in this clearly fictionalized account:

> I know you'll be impatient to hear what Progress Mrs. Cl— has made in Playing; she whom you saw … about Nine Years ago, when you foretold she would make an excellent Actress, and admir'd her strong Spirits, natural Humour, and quick Sense, &c. – I can only tell you, you were a true Prophet — Her Progress has been quick, and her Performance is extraordinary; and you may be sure her

---

[94] Chetwood, *A General History of the Stage*, p. 252.
[95] 'Dame Clive and that lady [Peg Woffington] were ever at variance: Mrs. Woffington coming into the green-room, after a favourite scene in Sir Harry, in high spirits, exultingly said to Mrs. Clive – She had got so much applause, that by the living God! she believed one half of the audience took her for a man. – "O!" says Clive, *archly* – "do not be uneasy, as you are satisfied the other half know the contrary". Tate Wilkinson, *Memoirs of his own Life, by Tate Wilkinson, Patentee of the Theatres-Royal, York and Hull* (Dublin, 1791), vol. 1, p. 30. The dig at Woffington reappeared in various nineteenth-century sources, and its speaker was said variously to be Clive, John Rich, and James Quin. Highfill, Burnim, and Langhans, 'Woffington, Margaret', *A Biographical Dictionary*, p. 202.
[96] 'Well, there [Charing-Cross] it was I composed my *Country Correspondents*, in all which I continued my Attack on Mr. Fl[ee]t[woo]d; and in a miscellaneous rhapsodical Way defended the P[rime] M[iniste]r Tooth and Nail'. *An Apology for the Life of Mr. T— C—, Comedian*, p. 118.

> Success and Encouragement are not unequal, for the Town delights in her ... I had a good deal of Chat with her (as I found her one of the most conversible Creatures there) ... but faith she is, in herself, as entertaining as a Comedy; and I did not care to be out of the *Green-Room*, when she returned from her Part, nor to be from the Scenes, when she was on the Stage – You'd be pleas'd with her in both Places — I was mentioning her to Mr. Thomas ... He told me, he should never, for the future, fail being at her Benefit, because he heard she was as honest a Girl, as she was a pleasing Actress. He said, there were some Characters became her in private Life, as well as any she appeared in on the Stage. 'Tis no small Merit to play the Parts of a dutiful Daughter, a just Wife, a loving Sister, an agreeable Companion, and a Friend to the Oppressed; all which, to do her Justice, she has made a good Figure in.[97]

Here Clive's sparkling charms and female virtue, especially in the private sphere, are a long way from her characterization, just seven years later, as a '*Red-Fac'd* B[it]ch!'. Likewise, the 1740 sketch of Clive in the counterfeit memoir of Theophilus Cibber praises her 'prodigious Fund of natural Spirit and Humour off the Stage'. What makes her excel in 'gay Characters of high Life' are her 'Air, Mein [sic], and Action, as speak the Gay, the Lively and the Desirable';[98] she is 'by far the most excellent Actress of the Drury-Lane Company ... and ... the only Actress who has any *Excellence* in it'.[99]

In later decades the 'B[it]ch' would be projected back in time via other Green Room anecdotes. At some point between 1734 and the summer of 1737,[100] for instance, James Quin, then in his forties, reportedly made sexual advances to Clive, then in her twenties:

> [T]he first disgust Quin took to this lady, was upon his offering some indecencies to her in her dressing-room; she made a complaint to the manager, who rebuked him for his conduct. This lady's virtue had never been impeached, and he ought not therefore to have supposed, that so brutish an attack, as it is said, he made upon her, could meet with success; but Sir John Falstaff would not give himself much time or trouble in his amours; and it was a rule with him, if he did not succeed at the first onset, never to rally his forces.[101]

In this passage of 1766 it is Clive who is the object of 'disgust', as the winkingly designated 'Falstaff' shrugs off what is suggested to be an excess of prudery.

---

[97] *The Country Correspondent ... with a Sketch of a Green Room. Number II* (London, 1739), pp. 16–17.
[98] *An Apology for the Life of Mr. T— C—, Comedian*, p. 140.
[99] Ibid., p. 141. This volume's author sets aside lampooning to assess players anonymously and 'impartially'. Ibid., p. 137.
[100] We can date this purported incident to between Quin's engagement at Drury Lane in 1734 and his rise to management in the summer 1737, as the anecdote makes clear that he was not yet Fleetwood's deputy at Drury Lane. *The Life of Mr. James Quin, Comedian* (London, 1766), pp. 49–50 and Chapter 7, p. 225.
[101] *The Life of Mr. James Quin*, pp. 70–71.

The memoirist then imputes that Clive is at least equally to blame for ensuing Clive–Quin Green Room tension, asserting that Clive and Quin thereafter 'could never agree while they were united in the same company'.[102]

Post-scuffle derision of Clive, while it did not favour her, benefited trade in her person. Consider the following luxury collectible: paired soft-paste porcelain figures of Greek sphinxes bearing the likenesses of Clive and Woffington (Fig. 10.2). The Chelsea porcelain factory produced the sphinxes before 1750, as did the Bow factory after 1750,[103] when it was manufacturing another figurine of Clive, as Mrs. Riot in *Lethe*.[104] The Clive and Woffington sphinxes defy visual codes standard for this mythical beast, at that time perhaps most familiar to London's polite playgoers from John Cheere's garden installations at Chiswick House.[105] Reading the Clive and Woffington sphinxes against Cheere's we can see sly imputations being made about the natures of the two actresses: their pose is casual, rather than hieratic; their dress is fashionable, rather than ancient; they cling to an ornamented, slanted base, rather than resting on a plinth; their forearms are tucked under their breasts, instead of being outstretched and symmetrical; their bodies and particularly their haunches are sensual, not muscular, an effect emphasized by being draped rather than armoured. They draw back their heads, which they turn to meet the viewer's gaze, proudly displaying their breasts.

Although the bodies and plinths of the sphinxes are in fact almost identical, the heads of Clive and of Woffington clearly differ. Clive's is larger than Woffington's, and as in her *Lethe* portraiture discussed in the next chapter she

---

[102] *Ibid.*, 70.

[103] Peter Bradshaw suggests that both sphinxes in this pair are after Clive's likeness, but as discussed below the face of each figurine is distinct. Apart from the Clive–Woffington sphinxes, the Bow factory also produced a pair of sphinxes after Woffington's portrait by Arthur Pond. Peter Bradshaw, *18th Century* [sic] *English Porcelain Figures 1745–1795* (Woodbridge, Antique Collectors' Club, 1981), p. 57: 'Bow porcelain "Sphinxes" [after Arthur Pond] ... said to be in the likeness of Peg Woffington ... are totally dissimilar from others in the likeness of Kitty Clive mounted upon wedge shaped bases that have drapery over the back and breasts and which are known in both Chelsea triangle marked (A15) and Bow (G24) versions.' In his appendices ('Appendix A, Chelsea Figures made prior to 1750' and 'Appendix G, Bow Figures made between 1750 and 1754'), Bradshaw lists the subjects of the sphinx figurines A15 (Chelsea) and G24 (Bow) as unidentified. *Ibid.*, pp. 290, 297.

[104] The catalogue entry for the Bow 'Female Sphinx' held at the Fitzwilliam Museum notes that the profile of one figurine is 'comparable to that of another famous actress of the day, Kitty Clive ... reproduced as a Bow figure in the character of "The Fine Lady" in Garrick's farce, "Lethe"'. <http://webapps.fitzmuseum.cam.ac.uk/explorer/index.php?qu=PD.340-1973&oid=42280>. Accessed 3 December 2018. The figurines of Clive as Mrs. Riot are discussed in the next chapter.

[105] Of French descent, John Cheere worked until about 1740 with his more famous brother, the sculptor Sir Henry Cheere; John Cheere then set up an independent studio, specializing in garden figures. Margaret Whinney, *Sculpture in Britain, 1530 to 1830* (Harmondsworth, 1964), pp. 122–24.

Fig. 10.2 Made by the Bow porcelain manufactory; Catherine Clive (?), left; Peg Woffington (?), right; c.1750. Soft-paste porcelain. Philadelphia Museum of Art, Gift of Mrs. Morris Hawkes, 1942-59-57,58.

is shown running to fat – jowly, rounded chin, thick neck, heavy lids – with lips slightly parted as if about to sing. The head of Woffington is smaller, graceful and attractive, with a delicate nose, wide-open eyes, fine cheekbones, and closed, smiling mouth.[106] Created for home decoration, their opposition on the mantelpiece was clearly meant to raise a smile, at both actresses' expense.

From the 1745–46 season, Clive experienced how easy it is for a star to slide from veneration to vilification. Words, pictures, and the tune 'Gossip Joan' registered this descent. Critics who had earlier concerned themselves with assessing her skill now focused on embarrassing reports about her. Her portraiture devolved into lampoon. *The Green Room Scuffle* broadside discredited Clive's refinement, manifested in song above all, by means of precisely the kind of tune that had once proven her musical breadth and won Town applause.

Afterword: Charles Burney and Backward 'Peeps'

In Clive's immediate posterity her greatest detractor was Charles Burney (1726–1814), the indefatigably prolific music historian and godson of Charles Fleetwood.[107] In his definitive Burney biography, Roger Lonsdale emphasizes

---

[106] Irish artist Thomas Frye, who founded the Bow factory, may have been responsible for the decorative motifs in the Peg Woffington Sphinxes (c.1750). Heather McPherson, 'Theatrical Celebrity and Porcelain', *The Oxford Handbook of the Georgian Theatre, 1737–1832*, p. 201.

[107] Roger Lonsdale, *Dr Charles Burney: A Literary Biography* (Oxford, 1965), p. 2.

his subject's unreliability and obsession with self-advancement;[108] yet historians still treat Burney as an objective authority. For Burney, who had been an apprentice composer under Thomas Arne, Clive stood for a repertory he rejected. Initially, in his self-published *General History of Music* (1789), Burney simply dismissed Clive as incompetent: in 1744, by his telling, Arne's wife Cecilia was Drury Lane's 'serious singer'.[109] According to Burney, Clive became ludicrous when she ventured beyond the repertory Burney confined her to: 'Her singing, which was intolerable when she meant it to be fine, in ballad farces and songs of humour was, like her comic acting, every thing it should be.'[110]

As he aged, however, Burney took to regaling readers with his own fantastical 'peeps' into Clive's Green Room clashes. In his entry for Abraham Rees's *Cyclopaedia*, prepared from 1801 to 1805, he offered a colourful story about Clive's refusal in 1746 to sing Arne's songs for *The Tempest*, which he attributed to caprice:

> Mrs. Clive, after a quarrel and battle with Dr. Arne, behind the scenes of Drury-lane theatre, would perform none of the doctor's music; and when he had new set the Tempest, and prepared for her his charming air in the part of Ariel, 'Where the bee sucks,' she refused to sing it, and employed Defesch to set the same words, and whatever else she had to perform in all her parts, which was a greater loss to the public, than disgrace to Dr. Arne, who was as superior to Defesch in genius, as [Regina] Mingotti was to Clive in the art of singing.[111]

This account bristles with falsehood and cliché: the erroneous assertion of the superiority of Burney's teacher Arne over a rival composer, the assumption that the composer was, or should have been, the main of arbiter of what was performed, the willfulness of the comic soprano, and the excellence of the Italian prima donna compared to her.

---

[108] *Ibid.*, p. 483: 'temperamental extremes of depression and exultation were, indeed, characteristic of Burney's state of mind ... His happiness lay ... in ... all that he had achieved by his own efforts ... and social success.'

[109] 'Mr. Arne, afterwards Dr. Arne, on his return from Ireland in Autumn 1744, was engaged as composer to Drury-lane playhouse ... where Mrs. Arne was likewise engaged as serious singer, while Mrs. Clive was in high favour in the comic style of ballad farces and songs of humour.' Charles Burney, *A General History of Music, from the Earliest Ages to the Present Period* (London, 1789, 'Printed for the Author'), vol. 4, p. 663. Arne was in 1744 re-engaged at Drury Lane, where he had been employed since 1734.

[110] Burney, *A General History of Music*, p. 654.

[111] [Charles Burney], 'DEFESCH', in Abraham Rees, *The Cyclopaedia; Or, Universal Dictionary of Arts, Sciences, and Literature* (London, 1819), vol.11, pages unnumbered; cited in Cholij, 'Music in Eighteenth-Century London Shakespeare Productions', p. 209, note 25. Burney began preparing his *Cyclopaedia* entries from mid-July 1801, and continued working on them until 1805. Lonsdale notes that his contributions are 'difficult to isolate' because they are 'scattered ... through ... hundreds of anonymous articles'. Lonsdale, *Dr Charles Burney*, p. 430.

In his *Memoirs*, prepared from 1806, Burney embellished on Clive's supposed 'quarrel' with Arne:

> When one night Mrs Clive having undertaken a song in wch she was imperfect: as she was given to be out of time as well as tune; at a hitch, she calls out loud to the band, 'why dont the fellows mind what they are ab^t?' At the end of the Act Arne went up stairs in the name of the whole band to remonstrate against her insolence, when the only satisfaction he obtained, was a slap on the face. In return, he literally turned her over his knee and gave her such a manual flagellation as she probably had not received since she quitted the nursery; but as a proof that she had made a good defence, he came back without his wig, all over blood from her scratches, & his long point ruffles torn & dangling over his nails.[112]

Here Burney lards his account with a 'HELL'S DUCHESS' characterization of Clive, breezily recounting sixty years later an altercation that only he knows about. By Burney's telling, she is insolent, vain, violent, ill-tempered, and emotionally incontinent. As a singer, she is incompetent and unprofessional. Male authority prevails thanks to Arne's willingness to administer a good spanking. Musicologists, insofar as they have mentioned Clive at all, have tended to uncritically accept Burney's stories of the conceited, tantrum-prone Clive whose deficiencies limited her to singing ballads.[113]

Scuffle-inspired fantasies cascade down to us through twentieth-century scholars of Clive and Woffington. The article on the latter in the *Biographical Dictionary of Actors and Actresses* purports to duplicate the 1746 *Green Room*

---

[112] Burney's passage is transcribed in Klima Slava, Garry Bowers, and Kerry S. Grant, ed., *Memoirs of Dr Charles Burney 1726–1769* (Lincoln, 1988), p. 63 (fragment 40); cited in Cholij, 'Music in Eighteenth-Century London Shakespeare Productions', p. 209, note 24. The manuscripts for the *Memoirs of Dr Charles Burney* consists of fragments for Burney's first version of his *Memoirs*, free of interventions by Fanny Burney, who destroyed and redacted Burney's papers to prepare a redacted version of the *Memoirs of Dr. Burney* (1832).

[113] 'Kitty Clive made her reputation in ballad opera ... According to Burney, "her singing, which was intolerable when she meant it to be fine, in ballad farces and songs of humour was ... every thing it should be"'. Winton Dean. 'Clive, Kitty'. *Grove Music Online. Oxford Music Online*. Oxford University Press. <http://o-www.oxfordmusiconline.com.catalogue.libraries.london.ac.uk/subscriber/article/grove/music/O597>. Accessed 15 September, 2017. Or: 'A pupil of Carey, she was primarily a comedy actress and ballad opera singer; according to Burney "her singing, which was intolerable when she meant it to be fine, in ballad farces and songs of humour was, like her comic acting, every thing it should be". Handel wrote songs for her in the thirties, but she was in his company only in 1743.' Winton Dean, 'Appendix I: Handel's Oratorio Singers', *Handel's Dramatic Oratorios and Masques* (London, 1959), p. 654. Or: 'Clive [née Raftor], Catherine ['Kitty'] (1711–85), of Anglo-Irish descent, was primarily an actress, and particularly successful in ballad operas.' Donald Burrows, 'Personalia', *Handel*, 2nd edn (Oxford and New York, 2012), p. 582. While admitting its weakness as evidence, Cholij quotes in full Burney's story of Arne spanking Clive to substantiate dating De Fesch's songs in *The Tempest* in 1746. Irena Cholij, 'De Fesch and the Tempest', *Willem de Fesch (1687–c.1760): voordrachten gehouden in Alkmaar, September 1987* (Alkmaar, 1987), pp. 65–66.

Scuffle etching – but the image it offers is misidentified, and from 1782. Instead of Clive and Woffington, its subjects are Sarah Siddons and Mary Yates. Whereas in 1746 the etching showed the two women's male defenders exchanging blows, the false identification lets readers think that they see Clive and Woffington attacking each other. In the 1782 etching, titled *The Rival Queens of Covent Garden and Drury Lane Theatres, at a Gymnastic Rehearsal*, Siddons' breasts are exposed as well as her temper.[114] The 1746 and 1782 images tellingly share many components: the subjects' stage costume, the amused onlookers, the hapless male arbiter (in 1782 he clutches a lemon), the humiliation made explicit (in 1782 a satyr holds a fool's cap over Siddons' head), the imagined dialogue printed below the scene. Although separated by two generations, Siddons and Clive had in common a reputation for putting ambition before amours.[115] The enthusiasm with which humiliation and physical violence are invoked in the Siddons–Yates image resonates with Burney's later story of Arne spanking Clive; both smack of the prurience and voyeurism intrinsic to the very concept of the 'peep'.

Seeing which way the wind was blowing, Clive had to largely abandon her line in high-end song and serious parts. From September 1747, in collaboration with new manager David Garrick, the 36-year-old Clive embraced farce and burlesque for her vehicles. In doing so, she sacrificed her dignity to regain control of her self-representation, and the admiration of her public.

---

[114] Highfill, Burnim, and Langhans, 'Woffington, Margaret', *A Biographical Dictionary of Actors, Actresses, Musicians, Dancers, Managers & Other Stage Personnel in London*, vol. 16 (1993), p. 199.

[115] On Siddons' representation in the 1782 etching see Cindy McCreery, *The Satirical Gaze: Prints of Women in Late Eighteenth-Century England* (Oxford, 2004) pp. 128–29. For an alternative reading of this image, see Séverine Lancia, 'The Actress and Eighteenth-century Ideals of Femininity', *Invisible Woman: Aspects of Women's Work in Eighteenth-Century Britain*, ed. I. Baudino, J. Carré, and C. Révauger ([London?], 2017), online resource published by Routledge, pages unnumbered.

11

From Miss Lucy to Mrs. Riot: Voice and Caricature

Clive's laurels wither – advice from an unexpected source – a look back at Lucy – Mrs. Riot drinks Lethe's waters – the bid of a gaming woman – Mrs. Edwards leaves the stage – the many forms of Mrs. Riot – caricature from ceramic into song – pastoral with a twist

By the 1747–48 season Clive's reputation was in free fall. Her professional and financial power had become unseemly, and her struggles with managers had imposed upon good taste. Accounts during the 1745–46 season of conflicts, first with Susannah Cibber and then with Peg Woffington, destroyed the earlier impression that, in private, Clive was a 'dutiful Daughter, a just Wife, a loving Sister, an agreeable Companion, and a Friend to the Oppressed'.[1] In March 1747 a writer registered the implosion of Clive's public image:

> Mrs. C[liv]e, who has had her Share of Popularity, and once was esteem'd the Phaenix of the Age, seems now to be of little Consequence; her Laurels are all wither'd; her Friends grown cold; and the repeated Acclamations that us'd to welcome her Appearance, are now no more.
>
> *Ah, how fall'n! how chang'd!*[2]

The italicized quotation is from *Paradise Lost*, Book 1, line 84. The reference to Milton, and therefore to Clive's signature role in *Comus*, was pointed: she had fallen from Goddess of Mirth to object of pity.

By this time, March 1747, even the comedian Samuel Foote – who had squandered his wife's fortune, twice been confined to the Fleet debtors' prison,

---

[1] *The Country Correspondent ... with a Sketch of a Green Room. Number II* (London, 1739), p. 17; cited also in Chapter 10.

[2] *A Letter of Compliment to the ingenious Author of a Treatise on the Passions ... with a critical Enquiry into the Theatrical Merit of Mr. G—k, Mr. Q—n, and Mr. B—y, &c. ... And a few Hints on our modern Actresses, particularly Mrs. C—r and Mrs. P—d* (London, [1747]), p. 33. This volume is misidentified as '*A Letter of Complaint*', although the date of its issue is correctly cited, in *The London Stage Calendar*, Part 3, vol. 2, p. 1296, entry for Drury Lane on 19 March 1747.

and would soon be renowned for his grotesque take-offs of celebrities[3] – felt comfortable condescending to her. In his account of current stage fashion, Foote reminded his readers of Clive's alleged Green Room scuffle: 'the Lady has ... (owing to an Earnestness for the Success of the Business) expressed herself behind the Scenes in too loud and forcible a Manner.'[4] As a result, 'some part of the Audience', Foote notes, has 'not a very favourable Opinion of her Temper.'[5] Beyond her 'Temper', Foote says, 'Mrs. Clive has been a little unhappy in her Choice of some Parts.'[6] A notorious instance of this, though Foote doesn't say so, was her appearance as Bayes in the Duke of Buckingham's *Rehearsal* for her brother's benefit of 6 May 1743. On this evening, she had performed in breeches. So 'wretchedly' did she appear to her audience that her performance was nearly stopped mid-way in front of a 'great house'.[7]

Clive's 1743 performance in *The Rehearsal* probably failed because she was putting on weight. The major draw of an actress in breeches lay in ogling her tightly sheathed legs.[8] Already in 1740, and even while anointing Clive as Drury Lane's best actress, one author had scoffed that her 'Turn of Make' made her better suited to the 'concealing Petticoat ... than the Breeches'.[9] By 1747 Clive's figure, in Foote's view, disqualified her from any 'Characters in Comedy which require a Delicacy of Figure, and an Elegance of Behaviour'. Further:

> as both Nature and Habit have denied Mrs. Clive the Possession of these Requisites. I would advise her never to think of personating a fine Lady of any Kind or

---

[3] On the career of this actor who built his career on celebrity mimicry of questionable taste, see Jane Moody, 'Stolen Identities: Character, Mimicry and the Invention of Samuel Foote', *Theatre and Celebrity in Britain, 1660–2000*, ed. M. Luckhurst and J. Moody (New York, 2005), pp. 65–89.

[4] Samuel Foote, *The Roman and English Comedy consider'd ... and an Examen into the Merit of the present Comic Actors* (London, 1747), pp. 42–43. Notice of sales for this volume appeared from 27 March 1747. *The London Stage*, Part 3, vol. 2, p. 1299, 'Comment' for Friday 27 March 1747.

[5] Foote, *The Roman and English Comedy consider'd*, p. 43.

[6] Ibid., p. 42.

[7] *The London Stage*, Part 3, vol. 2, p. 1055, under the entry for Drury Lane 6 May 1743. The actor Michael Dyer claimed that Theophilus Cibber had urged Clive to take up Bayes. Ibid.

[8] Building on Kristina Straub's findings, Helen Brooks notes that it was 'with the emerging model of the two-sex body that the breeches role resonated with its foregrounding of the character's (and actress's) biological sex over her performance of masculinity.' Helen E. M. Brooks, *Actresses, Gender, and the Eighteenth-Century Stage: Playing Women* (Basingstoke, 2014), p. 82. As Straub points out in her seminal study, 'male parts and, frequently, a whole play' in Restoration theatre 'were cast with female players in order to entice spectators with women's bodies in revealing male dress.' Straub draws on the findings of Judith Milhous, who first identified the late seventeenth-century trend of turning the actress's sexuality into spectacle. Kristina Straub, 'The Construction of Actress's Femininity', *Sexual Suspects*, pp. 89–108, esp. p. 101.

[9] *An Apology for the Life of Mr. T— C—, Comedian*, pp. 140–41.

Condition, unless the Author (with a View of rendering the Part ridiculous) has endowed it with some whimsical Peculiarity.[10]

Foote begged Clive to reign in her conceit, show better judgement, and salvage her reputation:

> You have already, Madam, a Cast of Characters in which your Action will always command the Attention and Applause of an Audience; don't, therefore, suffer an idle Ambition to destroy that Consequence; which, if you pursue the Bent of your Genius, you have it still in your Power to preserve.[11]

Foote also had more specific recommendations on how to handle rumours about her temper:

> when the Public are assured, that this Vehemence is assumed in order to procure a more decent Entertainment for themselves, I doubt not but they will convert their Resentment to Approbation.[12]

Foote counsels Clive to regain control of her reputation by channelling her 'Vehemence' into 'Entertainment'. From 1749, with David Garrick's support, this is exactly what she did.

Garrick was instrumental in helping Clive revitalize her languishing career, working with her to turn damning perceptions into comic points that Clive could leverage. The initial vehicle for this project was a revision of the first stage work that Garrick ever wrote, the afterpiece *Lethe*. Conceived in 1740 partly as a Clive vehicle, and before Garrick was an actor, *Lethe* was revised in 1749 to accommodate the fallen Clive and the risen Garrick. Clive's *Lethe* parts of 1740 and 1749 were both devised in order for her to effervesce: in 1740, as a daughter whose outrageousness Clive wielded for awe and for laughs; in 1749, as a blousy Fine Lady whose outrageousness stood for Clive's own. The demarcation between pre-1746 and post-1746 Clive – the former: sparkling, witty, and mysteriously contrary; the latter: ludicrous, predictable, and over-exposed – is made overt in Clive's two *Lethe* parts. Both illuminate the kind of Clive character that Garrick thought audiences would embrace, and the kind of material that he thought Clive could turn to her advantage.

Lethe of 1740: The Legend of Lucy

When he wrote his first *Lethe*, Garrick was still a wine merchant, conducting business in London in partnership with his brother in Lichfield. Garrick's 1740 *Lethe* was an afterpiece for the season benefit of his friend Henry Giffard,[13]

---

[10] Foote, *The Roman and English Comedy consider'd*, p. 42.
[11] Ibid.
[12] Ibid., p. 43.
[13] For an account *Lethe*'s different versions, and the background to each version, see Harry William Pedicord and Frederick Louis Bergmann, 'Commentary and Notes. Lethe; or,

who had secured Garrick wine orders from the Bedford Tavern near Covent Garden.[14] *Lethe* evidenced not just Garrick's friendship but also his playhouse skills, and in 1741 Giffard admitted Garrick into his summer touring company for his first theatric employment.[15] The following season Giffard brought Garrick onto the London stage, engaging him to perform at Goodman's Fields, a fringe theatre that Giffard used intermittently from 1740 to 1742.[16]

One mark of Garrick's talents is the way he fit his 'Lucy' in *Lethe* to Clive's artistry.[17] Lucy was Clive's personification of the unruly daughter, first brought to audiences in Fielding's *Virgin Unmask'd* (1735) and taking on its own life thereafter. Garrick's 'Lucy' was the second of four Lucy characters created for her after 1735 in various comedies: James Miller's *Hospital for Fools* (1739), where Lucy is called 'the Daughter', *Lethe* (15 April 1740), Miller's *The Camp Visitants* (banned in December 1740), and Fielding's *Miss Lucy in Town* (1742). In 1739 Miller and Clive together had re-branded Lucy, and in 1740 Garrick built on their Lucy rather than Fielding's.

Why? In 1740 audiences still flocked to Fielding's *The Virgin Umask'd*, while Miller's enemies had killed *An Hospital for Fools* on its first night in 1739. Garrick's preference was likely due to the vulgarity of Fielding's Lucy – a vulgarity that could have compromised Garrick. As discussed earlier, Fielding's Lucy chooses a footman over more well-heeled suitors, dispatching innuendo-laden common tunes while toying with her wooers. Miller, by contrast, dressed Clive's part with dignity. He derived his action from William Walsh's *Aesculapius: Or, the Hospital of Fools* (1714), an Aristophanean prose dialogue in which the Greek god of medicine, Aesclepius, exposes the follies of visitors to Hades, and has them drink from Lethe, the river of oblivion.[18] Drawing on Walsh, Miller created a comedy with two Clive *in propria persona* roles: the Actress in an introductory Green Room 'peep' scene, and the Daughter, based on Fielding's Lucy.

Esop in the Shades', in *The Plays of David Garrick*, ed. H. W. Pedicord and F. L. Bergmann, vol. 1, *Garrick's Own Plays, 1740–1766* (Carbondale, 1980), pp. 377–84.

[14] Ian McIntyre, *Garrick* (London, 1999), pp. 35–38.
[15] *Ibid.*
[16] *Ibid.*
[17] In his analyses of Garrick's various versions of *Lethe*, Peter Holland rightly emphasizes the mutability of this afterpiece. To quote Holland: '*Lethe* went through innumerable versions; at the very end of his life and retired from the stage, Garrick was still revising the piece, adding a German Jew and other characters in a version he read before the royal family in 1777.' Peter Holland, 'Unpublished Scenes in David Garrick's "Lethe"', *Huntington Library Quarterly*, vol. 57, no. 3 (1994), pp. 300–11, esp. p. 302.
[18] Pedicord and Bergmann, 'Commentary and Notes. Lethe; or, Esop in the Shades', pp. 377–79. Pedicord and Bergmann assert that Miller's 'play had in turn been based partially on [Jean Joseph] Vadé's *L'Hopital des Foux* [sic]' (*ibid.*, p. 377); in fact, Vadé lived from 1720 to 1757, and the earliest print of *L'Hôpital des Fous*, which is an anonymous French translation of Walsh, seems to have been issued in 1760. On Miller's source, see also O'Brien, 'The Life and Works of James Miller, 1704–1744', pp. 57–59; O'Brien compares Walsh's to Miller's fable, and Miller's to Garrick's comedy.

Both parts are pure Clive fizz: in the introduction, the Actress mimics a tragedian, scoffs at the playwright Miller, and warns that his enemies are 'pounding ready to bring the House down'.[19] As the Daughter, Clive did the mocking, rather than being mocked as the other characters are. Lines such as 'O charming *Oratorio!* O dear, dear Saul! I expire at that *Duetto*, and the *Dead March* brings me to life again', laugh at Handel's most recent work, *Saul*, and the pretensions of its audiences.[20] When she complains to her father that he is too miserly to let her see the performance of a castrato, whom she calls a 'ravishing Foreigner', he responds, 'ah, 'tis well they [castrati] can't ravish, you Slut you'.[21] In this moment, Clive will have stepped out of character to address her audience with her question: 'Now which is the greatest Fool of the two?'[22] Besides four smart airs by Thomas Arne, Miller had Clive execute Handel's aria 'The Prince, unable to conceal his Pain' from *Alexander's Feast*. It was the first time this music had ever been heard at Drury Lane. On finishing the air, Clive courted approval in her own voice, saying 'Well, Gentlemen, what! ne'er an *Encore!* So many People here, and not a single *Encore?* My Stars! these Folks are absolutely void of all Taste'.[23] This was a dazzling display of the many-faceted Clive.

In his 1740 *Lethe*, Garrick borrowed Miller's action and Clive's characterization, renaming Miller's Daughter 'Lucy' and adding to the *dramatis personae* Lucy's husband from Fielding's *Virgin Unmask'd*. Garrick also changed the name of Miller's Aesclepius to 'Aesop', thereby giving out that Sir John Vanbrugh's eponymous comedy had been his source.[24] Garrick imagines Lucy and

---

[19] [James Miller], *An Hospital for Fools. A Dramatic Fable ... To which is added the Songs with their Basses and Symphonies ... The Musick by Mr. Arne. Sung by Mrs. Clive* (London, 1739), 'Introduction. Scene, The Green Room', pages unnumbered, pp. 1–4, and pp. 14–18, 24–28.

[20] *Ibid.*, p. 14. *Saul* had opened on 16 January 1739 for a six-night run. The 'Dead March' later broke off from *Saul* to become an instrumental interlude. There are two duets in *Saul*, 'O Fairest of ten thousand Fair', or 'At Persecution I can laugh'; both were sung by the soprano Francesina and the male alto Mr. Russell. On the history of the 'Dead March' see Donald Burrows, 'Handel, the Dead March and a newly Identified Trombone Movement', *Early Music*, vol. 18, no. 3 (1990), pp. 408–16.

[21] [Miller], *An Hospital for Fools*, p. 15.

[22] *Ibid.*

[23] *Ibid.*

[24] Holland traces the argument, mooted in the 1749 puff *Lethe Rehears'd* (attributed to Garrick himself, as discussed below) that 'WALSH's *Hospital for Fools*, and Sir JOHN VANBRUGH's *Aesop*, furnished the Materials' for *Lethe* and that 'DODSLEY's *Toy-Shop* was the Original, and this but a Copy'. [David Garrick], *Lethe Rehears'd: Or, a Critical Discussion of the Beauties and Blemishes of that Performance* (London, 1749), pp. 2–3; cited in Holland, 'Unpublished Scenes in David Garrick's "Lethe"', p. 301. O'Brien notes that Garrick made 'no acknowledgement of any debt to Miller', which is understandable given Miller's toxicity; she notes also that Garrick 'may well have been shown the script of Miller's afterpiece' due to his habit, mentioned in letters, of seeking 'the company of

her footman-husband (played by Clive's brother Jemmy) visiting Aesop soon after the betrothal that concluded *The Virgin Unmask'd*:

> Miss: Why don't you come along, Mr. Thomas? Is the Devil in you?
> Aesop: Don't be angry, Lady; the Gentleman is your Husband, I suppose.
> Miss: How do you know that, eh?
> Aesop: By your Manner of addressing him.
> Miss: Why I was as free with him before Marriage as I am now; I never was Coy in my Life.
> Aesop: I believe you, M^{dm}. How long have you been marry'd? You seem to be very young.
> Miss: I am old enough for a Husband; & have been marryed long enough to be tir'd of him.
> Aesop: How long, pray?
> Miss: Why a Month. I married M^r. Thomas without my Father's Consent ... We are come to drink some, some Leithe, to forget one another & to be unmarried again ... Several young Ladies of my Acquaintance ... tell me they are not angry at me for marrying a Footman, but being fond [of] a Husband.[25]

The dialogue revisits Clive's best-known strokes: wit, candour, unruliness, defiance of male authority, and sharp pokes at sentimentality. Garrick then shifts Clive's discursive position to have her damn Lucy's character through a re-versified and lengthened version of Clive's signature song, 'Life of a Beau' (Ex. 11.1).[26] Garrick's eight-stanza 'Life of a Belle' mocks Lucy's pretensions to fineness, a criticism amplified by this song's minuet form. To conclude his comedy, Garrick brings Lucy back to the stage with a new husband, a Beau, in tow. In this finale, Lucy and Mercury (sung by John Beard), banter musically in the duet 'Be wise, giddy Creature' that runs into a drinking-song chorus.[27]

Garrick also wrote an 'Epilogue. Spoke by Miss Lucy, and Mr. Thomas'. In fact, Clive spoke almost alone, and her speech mixes motifs from stage types across her repertory: the patriot, the fop-hater, the mocker of men, and the champion of middling sorts. In the epilogue, Lucy pretends to search for a potential husband in the audience. Surveying the theatre she rails against the

---

actors' and visiting 'the green rooms of both Drury Lane and Covent Garden'. O'Brien, 'The Life and Works of James Miller, 1704–1744', pp. 58–59.

[25] David Garrick, 'Lethe; Or, Esop in the Shades' [dated 1 April 1740?]. The Huntington Library, John Larpent Plays, LA22, fols 4r–4v.

[26] 'For the Benefit of Mr. GIFFARD ... a new Dramatic Satire, call'd LETHE; *or*, ESOP *in the* SHADES. In which will be Introduc'd Singing by Mr. Beard, and Mrs. Clive, particularly *The Life of a Belle*, &c. in Imitation of *The Life of a Beau*, by Mrs. Clive'. *London Daily Post and General Advertiser*, issue 1703 (9 April 1740). Later announcements in 1740 for *Lethe* carried this same information without cast names.

[27] Garrick, 'Lethe; Or, Esop in the Shades', LA22, fols 8v–9r. Neither the advertisement for the 1740 Lethe nor the manuscript playbook identify the casting, but this is self-evident from the songs, and from the 1749 version.

Ex. 11.1 Words by David Garrick, music by Henry Carey, 'The Life of a Belle' in Lethe, 1749. *The Agreeable Amusement, a Collection of Ancient & Modern Songs*, Plate XLVIII [1743–44]. Copyright © The British Library Board 30/9/2018. All Rights Reserved. Shelfmark: Music Collections K.5.b.11.

men she finds there: the footmen in the Gallery ('I'll pass the Footmen, they're not worth my Care; / I married one – and lazy Rogues they are!'); the effeminate beaux in the Boxes ('Besides, of all Things, I abhor a Beaux; / For, when try'd, 'tis doubtful, whether Man, or no'); and the writers in the Pit ('The surly Critic; and the thread-bare Wit'). She decides to take two husbands, the Merchant and the (naval) Soldier, archly claiming thereby to promote the Patriot cause:

> No doubt, you'll all approve my Patriot Passion;
> My Heart is fix'd, for Trade, and Navigation:
> I hope you'll not refuse your gen'rous Voice;
> Applaud me, Britons; and approve my Choice'.[28]

The 1740 *Lethe* evidences Garrick's nose for celebrity promotion, not least in his characterization of Lucy and in his epilogue for Clive. Though Giffard owned the production,[29] Clive owned 'Life of a Belle', which she sang in entr'actes and two of her other parts.[30] 'Life of a Belle' was illustrated and engraved (Ex. 11.1), honours that Garrick's 1740 *Lethe* itself never received.

Lethe of 1749: A Reputation run Riot

On 9 April 1747 Garrick became co-patentee and artistic director of Drury Lane, while James Lacy continued to manage the business.[31] Opening the 1747–48 season with a prologue by his friend Samuel Johnson, Garrick announced his plans to expurgate the 'Folly' that had too long held 'sway' at his new home theatre.[32] His speech prefaced *The Merchant of Venice* with Macklin

---

[28] The epilogue was not included in the playbook manuscript submitted to censors, the Larpent MS. It was printed in the later pirated playbook (London, 1745).

[29] Once Giffard took Garrick's afterpiece with him to Goodman's Fields theatre, it was felt necessary to point out in notices that 'the Part of Miss Lucy' being played by Jane Green (then called Jane Hippisley) belonged to a 'Scene being a Sequel to the *Virgin Unmask'd*'. *London Daily Post and General Advertiser*, issue 2233 (18 December 1741).

[30] Clive sang 'Life of a Belle' for two benefits during the season *Lethe* premiered: her brother's benefit of 14 May 1740, and that of the box-keeper Taylor on 29 May 1740. She interpolated the song into her role of Flippanta on 10 December 1744 at Covent Garden, and again, after returning to Drury Lane, on 24 February 1746. Next season, on 30 December 1746, she introduced 'Life of a Belle' into her part of Lappet in Fielding's *Miser*. All these performances are correctly noted in *The London Stage Calendar*, Part 3, vol. 2.

[31] Garrick and Lacy's agreement of 9 April 1747 to be co-owners and co-managers on a fifty-fifty basis is preserved in the Forster Collection in the Victoria and Albert Museum. The agreement's content is transmitted in Boaden, ed., *The Private Correspondence of David Garrick*, vol. 1, pp. 50–53; Little and Kahrl, ed., *The Letters of David Garrick*, vol. 3, pp. 1344–49; and Hume, 'Garrick in Dublin in 1745–46', pp. 507–40.

[32] Samuel Johnson, 'PROLOGUE SPOKEN AT THE OPENING OF THE THEATRE IN DRURY-LANE … For years the pow'r of tragedy declin'd; / From bard, to bard, the frigid caution crept, / Till declamation roar'd, while passion slept. / Yet still did Virtue deign the stage to tread, / Philosophy remain'd, though Nature fled. / But forc'd at length

and Clive, whose Portia exemplified what Garrick, speaking Johnson's words, had just derogated as 'caprice'.[33] Yet Garrick was willing to accommodate Clive's excesses from the very first performance under his management, and in his 1749 *Lethe* would give them something like a permanent home.

For this work, Garrick spun Clive's celebrity persona anew: she was now to exaggerate what was said and written about her, rather than how she had earlier projected herself. Yet despite the ultimate success of this gambit, it was only with enormous effort, and within a market that Garrick controlled, that his new *Lethe* took hold. It opened on 2 January 1749 with Clive as the intemperate gaming lady Mrs. Riot and no fewer than three roles for Garrick. The prompter Richard Cross observed it 'was but indifferently receiv'd' on its first night, and met with 'some little Hiss' on the second.[34] On 1 February, a 52-page anonymous 'circular' puff – that is, a puff which hides its puffing – appeared.[35] Now attributed to Garrick, this pamphlet contains many seemingly empirical observations about what *Lethe* teaches its audiences.[36] Regarding Clive's character, one comment stands out: 'Mrs. Riot's is not a Character but a *Caracatura* ... all Outrage, Insolence, and Distortion [of] ... Liberties of Women in a *superior Sphere*, who enjoy their *Freedom* and take such Liberties as keep the *Cares* of *Life* at a Distance.'[37] This is indeed the case. Mrs. Riot is a grotesque lampoon of that Clive who, having risen to a '*superior Sphere*' – professionally, socially, and financially – was now despised for it.

In his 1749 *Lethe*, Garrick made Riot replace Lucy as one of the underworld's visitors. As in his 1740 *Lethe*, Aesop exposes the foolishness of his interlocuters through witty repartee; only the forgetfulness induced by taking Lethe's waters offers escape. In Garrick's words for Clive, Riot's pronouncements chime with post-1746 characterizations of Clive in the press. We find the overconfidence of which Foote complained in 1747: 'I am so perfectly satisfied with myself, that I will not alter an Atom of me.'[38] Riot is utterly convinced of her rights

---

her antient reign to quit, / She saw great Faustus lay the ghost of wit: / Exulting Folly hail'd the joyful day, / And pantomime, and song, confirm'd her sway.' *The Yale Digital Edition of the Works of Samuel Johnson*. <http://www.yalejohnson.com/frontend/sda_viewer?n=107812>. Accessed 3 December 2018.

[33] *Ibid*.

[34] Richard Cross, MS diary, cited in *The London Stage*, Part 4, vol. 1, p. 86 (entry for Drury Lane Monday 2 January 1749); Cross, MS diary, cited *ibid*., p. 87 (entry for Drury Lane Tuesday 3 January 1749).

[35] *The London Stage*, Part 4, vol. 1, p. 94 (repr. from the *General Advertiser* under the entry for Drury Lane Wednesday 1 February 1749).

[36] George Watson, ed., *The New Cambridge Bibliography of English Literature*, vol. 2 (London, 1971), column 805.

[37] [Garrick], *Lethe Rehears'd: Or, a Critical Discussion of the Beauties and Blemishes of that Performance*, p. 22.

[38] I quote from the printed playbook which, for Clive's part, matches the contents of the censor's manuscript copy. David Garrick, *Lethe. A Dramatic Satire* (London, 1749), p. 33. Variants – most of which are found in Garrick's part of Fribble – between the printed

('Liberties'), like the Clive in *The Case of Mrs. Clive* (1744). Riot's complaints that her husband has 'presum'd to contradict' her and 'refuse [her] money' are redolent of Clive's rows with managers.³⁹ Riot claims to belong to Quality, but, as was suspected of the post-Scuffle Clive, stoops to vulgar insults, for instance calling Charon a 'filthy Boatman' and Aesop an 'ugly Creature'.⁴⁰ In response to the question whether she has a husband, Riot responds, 'Yes – I think so – an Husband and no Husband ... if I must forget something, I had as good forget him'.⁴¹ Garrick's 1740 Lucy had also been dismissive of her husband,⁴² but Riot's words cast doubt on whether she is married to the man at all, a mystery perhaps evocative for those who suspected her own non-union.⁴³

When Riot discovers that no Italian operas are available in Hades ('What! no Operas! eh! no Elysian then!') we are told that she '*Sings fantastically in Italian*'.⁴⁴ This stage direction threw the door open for Clive to mimic a reigning Italian soprano. Clive's first *prima donna* take-off – in which she had lampooned an individual rather than, as in her burlesque opera parts, a genre – had earned Horace Walpole's praise,⁴⁵ and she had inserted a similar number into a later benefit.⁴⁶ It was, however, thanks to *Lethe* that mimic Italian song now became one of Clive's staple points. Although no notation survives to show what she sang, we do have one description of such a performance, from the mid-1750s:

> I was particularly diverted by her *Italian Song*, in which this truly humorous actress parodies the air of the Opera, and takes off the action of the present favorite female at the Hay-Market [Signora Mingotti], with such exquisite ridicule, that the most zealous partisans of both, I think, must have applauded the comic genius of Mrs. Clive, however they might be displeased with this application of it. I am a lover of music, am no enemy to the Opera, have seen and

---

    version and the manuscript submitted to censors (the Huntington Library, John Larpent Plays LA 72, date of application 25 October 1748, first performed 2 January 1749) are detailed in Holland, 'Unpublished Scenes in David Garrick's "Lethe"', pp. 304–11. Holland finds Garrick's 1749 version superior to his original 1740 *Lethe*.

³⁹ Garrick, *Lethe* (1749), p. 30.
⁴⁰ Ibid., p. 28.
⁴¹ Ibid., p. 30.
⁴² 'What signifies what he says?', Garrick, 'Lethe: Or, Esop in the Shades', LA22, fol. 4v.
⁴³ Garrick, *Lethe* (1749), p. 30.
⁴⁴ Ibid., p. 28.
⁴⁵ Horace Walpole to Horace Mann, letter of 6 June 1742 (Old Style date 26 May 1742): 'There is a little simple farce at Drury Lane, called *Miss Lucy in Town*, in which Mrs Clive mimics the Muscovita [Lucia Panichi, the mistress of Charles Sackville, Earl of Middlesex] admirably, and Beard [Angelo] Amorevoli intolerably.' Electronic version of the *The Yale Edition of Horace Walpole's Correspondence*. <http://images.library.yale.edu/hwcorrespondence/page.asp?vol=17&page=435>. Accessed 3 December 2018. An Italian tenor, Amorevoli was engaged at the King's Opera, London in 1741 for the fabulous sum of 850 guineas.
⁴⁶ *The London Stage*, Part 3, vol. 2, p. 1223 (entry for Drury Lane, Monday 10 March 1746).

heard this performer [Mingotti] with pleasure, but have still been a good deal surprized ... [by the] praises of this Foreigner's action ... when we have more than one actress on our own stage so infinitely superior to her.[47]

If accurate, this report contains important information. First, that Clive interpolated an entire aria ('the air of the Opera'). Second, that Clive kept abreast of musical fashion, procuring scores – in this case almost certainly Niccolò Jommelli's *Four Songs in the Opera call'd Il Demofoonte sung by Sigra Mingotti* (c.1755) – to do so.[48] Third, that Clive took off Mingotti's gestures ('action') as well, and so must have seen Mingotti perform. Fourth, that Clive's virtuosity was formidable, because besides her ridicule being 'exquisite', her execution is held to be 'infinitely superior' to Mingotti's. So popular did Clive's mimic Italian song become that it eventually received separate billing.

Clive's second number in Garrick's 1749 *Lethe* was 'The Card invites' by Thomas Arne.[49] 'Card' refers both to the invitation card that Mrs. Riot flourishes, and the gaming to which it beckons her.[50] The latter was almost certainly an *in propria persona* reference: Clive loved card gambling, as emerges in her descriptions of Horace Walpole's gatherings at Strawberry Hill, written after she retired in 1769.[51] In 1783, Clive would exult in a letter to Jane Pope that at cards 'the Raffanies ... hold their own – that is not all their own for I win their money which is their lifeblood; they can't have it.'[52] But her gaming surely began earlier, possibly even before her first known visit to Walpole on 11 August 1748, when Walpole wrote in a letter that 'the Clive was very good

---

[47] [Frances Brooke], 'Numb. 26. Saturday, May 8, 1756', *The Old Maid. By Mary Singleton, Spinster* (London, 1764), pp. 219–20. The volume consists of selections reprinted from the periodical paper of the same name, published weekly in London from 15 November 1755 to 24 July 1756.

[48] *Four Songs in the Opera call'd Il Demofoonte sung by Sigra Mingotti* ([London], [1755]). Mingotti sang these arias from 9 December 1755 to 7 February 1756. This was one of few published scores from the works that Mingotti appeared in during the 1755–56 season. On Mingotti's repertory that season, see Michael Burden, *Regina Mingotti: Diva and Impresario at the King's Theatre, London* (Farnham, 2013), pp. 41–45.

[49] Roger Fiske wrongly asserts that the stage directions '*Sings fantastically in Italian*' meant that Clive embellished 'The Card invites'; he also wrongly assumes that this song was included in the 1740 *Lethe*. Fiske, *English Theatre Music in the Eighteenth Century*, p. 206.

[50] Riot announces her song by '(*Drawing out a Card*)' to show it to Aesop and reading it out: 'Lady Rantan's Compliments to Mrs. Riot'. Garrick, *Lethe* (1749), p. 31. The song makes clear that the invitation is to a rout where ladies gamble at cards. As Jerry White observes: 'Card tables were the main attraction of fashionable "routs" or "drums" in the 1740s and after. Given by lady hostesses for mixed company, these evening assemblies also combined dancing, food and conversation.' Jerry White, *London in the Eighteenth Century: A Great and Monstrous Thing* (London, 2012), p. 340.

[51] Some of Clive's descriptions of her card-playing are transcribed in Crean, 'The Life and Times of Kitty Clive', pp. 381–82, 394–97, 433–34.

[52] Catherine Clive to Jane Pope. Letter of 21 [January?] 1783. 'Autograph Letters from Catherine Clive to Jane Pope', Bodleian Library, Toynbee b.1.

company' at a dinner he had recently hosted.⁵³ Into Clive's part in *Lethe* Garrick absorbed not just her probable gambling, but also its associations: because she gained or lost money, the gamestress was thought to have forsaken her proper gender role.⁵⁴

In 'The Card invites' (Ex. 11.2), Garrick and Thomas Arne jointly travesty the gaming lady by turning her into a male hunter. The authors parody the hunting song, a genre that tenors popularized through entr'acte and pleasure garden concertizing.⁵⁵ Its verses invoke the myth of Diana, the goddess of the hunt, who rejects men and consorts only with other huntresses. Riot's effusions refer to the chase ('we fly', 'jovial Rout, full Cry', 'Hark-away'),⁵⁶ perverting wholesome masculine outdoor pleasures into those of the midnight parlour, where female rule is absolute:

> The Card invites, in Crouds we fly
> To join the jovial Rout, full cry:
> What joy from Cares and plague all day
> To hie to the Midnight Hark-away …
>
> When tir'd with sport, to Bed we creep
> And hide the tedious Day wth sleep
> Tomorrow's welcome Call obey,
> Sing again again to ye Midnight Hark away.⁵⁷

---

⁵³ According to Paget Toynbee, Clive 'makes her first appearance at Strawberry Hill in Walpole's letter to Montagu of Aug. 11, 1748, in which he says: "Our dinner passed off very well; the Clive was very good company"'. *Strawberry Hill Accounts: A Record of Expenditure in Building, Furnishing, &c., kept by Mr Horace Walpole from 1747 to 1795 now first printed from the Original MS, with notes and index by Paget Toynbee* (Oxford, 1927), p. 136.

⁵⁴ 'The stereotypical gamestress was a highly problematic figure … an agent of disorder, disobedience, and dysfunction, of financial and sexual agency that threatened the stability of family and society alike'. Janet E. Mullin, *A Sixpence at Whist: Gaming and the English Middle Classes, 1680–1830* (Woodbridge, 2015), p. 102. Comparing Hogarth's prints to stage characters, comments in the press, and characters in early novels, Jessica Richards concludes that from 1700 until late in the century the 'female gambler's passions were imagined as utterly absorbing, eclipsing the affections that bound her to her duties, her sexual honor, and her social functions'. Jessica Richard, 'Arts of Play: The Culture of Gambling in Eighteenth-Century Britain' (PhD diss., Princeton Univ., 2002), p. 5.

⁵⁵ Hunting songs, because a favourite entertainment in playhouses and gardens, would become the platform for a central scene in eighteenth-century London's most popular comic opera, *Love in a Village* (1762). Berta Joncus, 'Borrowings: Air 9, "Let gay ones and great"', *Love in a Village* (1762), ed. B. Joncus, with V. Rogers and Z. Ozmo (Kassel, in press), OPERA – Spektrum des europäischen Musiktheaters in Einzeleditionen, Akademie der Wissenschaften und der Literatur, Mainz (hybrid hard copy and electronic critical music edition).

⁵⁶ Garrick, *Lethe* (London, 1749), p. 32.

⁵⁷ David Garrick, 'Lethe', The Huntington Library, John Larpent Plays, LA 72, p. 33.

Ex. 11.2 Words by David Garrick, music by Thomas Arne, 'The Card invites', 'Sung by Mrs. Clive in LETHE', 1749. Printed in *The Agreeable Musical Choice*, volume 6 [1754]. The Bodleian Libraries, University of Oxford. Shelfmark: Harding Mus. E 177 (6).

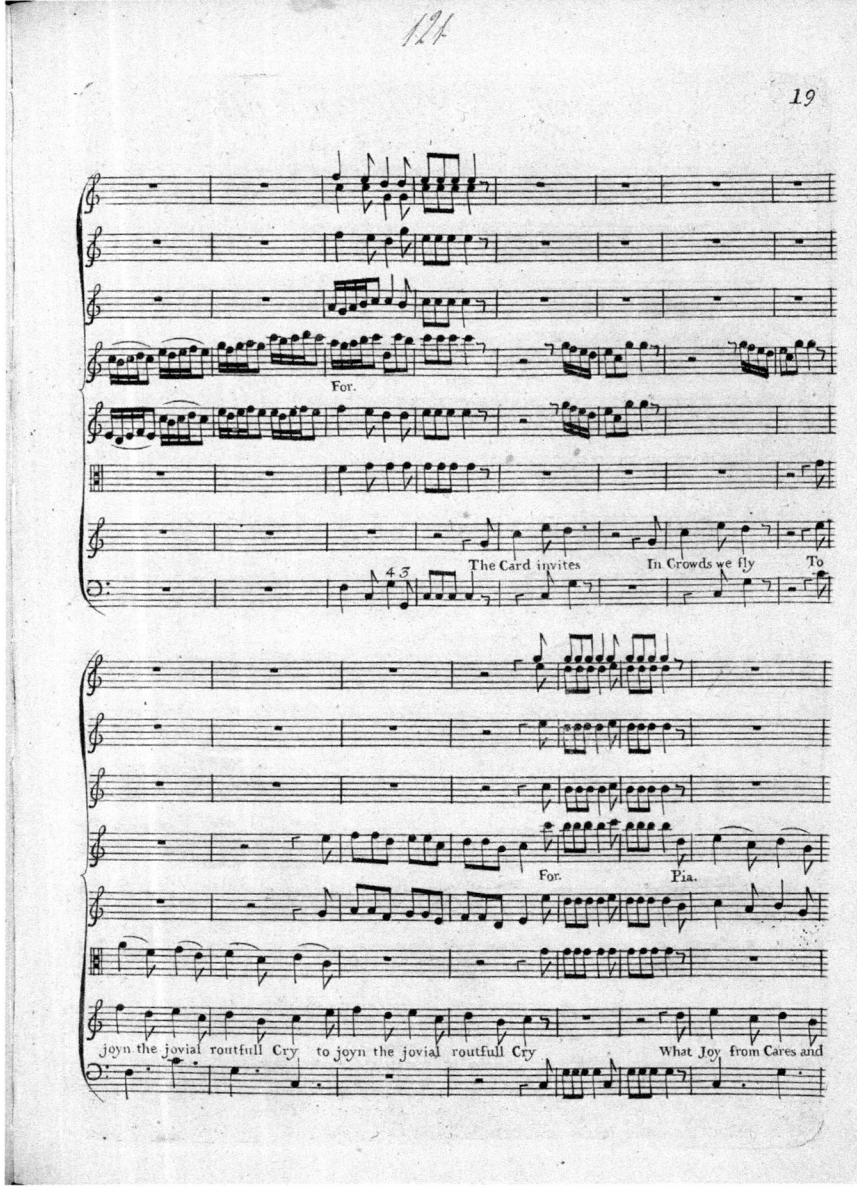

Of the dramatis personae in Garrick's 1749 *Lethe*, only Riot and the god Mercury, played by John Beard, sing. By 1749 Beard was well-known for his hunting songs,[58] so Clive's appropriation of 'his' genre in *Lethe* will have heightened the satire. Arne's music to 'The Card invites' shadows Garrick's verbal parody. As is typical in such airs, Arne's triple meter and continuo part propel the song forward. Clive's melody is trumpet-like, imitating the horn calls that precede her opening words, 'The Card invites, in Crouds we fly'. Interjections by the strings likewise emphasize hunting motifs. At the words 'Hark-away', voice and band join in braying flourishes.[59] The absence of lyricism or of any harmonic progression makes this music the antipode of a woman's soft notes, as Riot takes over a sonic territory usually the preserve of men.

Beyond the evident parody, another level of meaning may have lurked for those in the know: the mannish Mrs. Riot seems to wink at Clive being a Sapphic lover.

Gaming with Reputations: Clive and Edwards

When the 1749 *Lethe* opened, Clive had just terminated her nine-year protection of Mary Edwards. Edwards had 'sprung up under the Care of that eminent Actress Mrs. Clive',[60] who re-directed Edwards' career from dance to song. Her first major role was 'Margerinia' ('the little Margery') in a Lilliputian production of *The Dragon of Wantley* at the benefit of the Irish singer-actress Sarah Hamilton, on 16 May 1738.[61] Edwards was then about fourteen years old. From then on, Clive appears to have been responsible for all of Edwards' work, and probably for Edwards getting a regular Drury Lane post from October 1745. The process began when Arne's *Rosamond* opened on 8 March 1740, with Clive in the title role; in this production, the sixteen-year-old Edwards received her first legitimate part, as the Page.

---

[58] Beard and Thomas Lowe competed fiercely for pre-eminence in hunting songs in playhouse interludes and pleasure garden concerts. From the early 1740s, Beard was principal tenor at Ranelagh Gardens, while Lowe was principal tenor at Vauxhall Gardens. Joncus, 'Borrowings: Air 9, "Let gay ones and great"', *Love in a Village* (1762), forthcoming.

[59] Fiske identifies this air's manuscript score for oboes, horns, and strings. It is held at the Royal College of Music and not listed in open access catalogues. Fiske, *English Theatre Music in the Eighteenth Century*, p. 206. There is also is a second source, in vocal score, in the Special Collections, Main Library, University of Birmingham, 5008, fols 61v–62v.

[60] Chetwood, 'Mr. MOZEEN', *A General History of the Stage*, p. 194.

[61] 'Margerinia' was the diminutive name of the dramatis persona listed in the announcement for this production in the *London Daily Post and General Advertiser*, issue 1106 (16 May 1738). William Hallam remounted this Lilliputian *Dragon of Wantley* at his booth at Bartholomew Fair during that summer season. Rosenfeld, *The Theatre of the London Fairs in the Eighteenth Century*, pp. 44–45.

From 1740 to 1743 Edwards appeared only in Drury Lane benefits, and only those over which Clive had some control.[62] The most illustrious was Thomas Arne's 1742 benefit, for which Arne had reset William Congreve's masque *The Judgement of Paris*,[63] with bespoke music for Clive as the Goddess of War, Pallas. Handel hired Edwards, as we've seen, only during the three years in which he had professional contact with Clive. Edwards followed Clive to Covent Garden when the latter quit Drury Lane during the actors' revolt.

While at Covent Garden, Clive found ways around the fact that Edwards was a marginal player. She pulled Edwards into De Fesch's productions – over which Clive surely had a controlling hand – and benefits, not least to bequeath her Polly in *The Beggar's Opera*. Edwards was Clive's vocal partner in interlude performances of 'My Faith and Truth' from *Samson*, echoing back the words that Clive had sung as Dalila's 'Voice of Love'.[64] When Clive returned to Drury Lane in late November 1745, Edwards became, for the first time, a regular company member. Even then, if Edwards was on stage so too usually was Clive. This went on for two seasons: of fourteen casts that Edwards joined from November 1745 to the summer of 1747, only five were without Clive, and those most frequently performed – *The Tempest*, *The Beggar's Opera*, and *The Dragon of Wantley* – had Clive as a principal.

Clive's patronage abruptly ceased at the end of 1747. On 12 December Susannah Cibber took over the part of Polly from Edwards; finally, Clive and Cibber played in the same production of *The Beggar's Opera*, and with remarkably

---

[62] During the 1740 benefit season, Edwards sang at the benefits of Clive, Hannah Pritchard, Clive's brother, and, singing with Beard, Nancy Giffard. During the 1741 benefit season, Edwards sang at the benefits of Clive, Clive's brother, and the Pall-Mall tavern owner Mr. Connor, in a production of *Rosamond* led by Clive. During the 1742 benefit season, Edwards sang at the benefits of Clive and of Thomas Arne, taking the part of Juno in his resetting of William Congreve's *Judgement of Paris*. During the 1743 benefit season, Edwards sang at the benefit of Clive, for which Clive mounted *Comus* with Edwards for 'the first Time' as Sabrina, usually sung by Cecilia Arne. *Daily Advertiser*, issue 3768 (15 February 1743). Edwards sang also at Clive's brother's 1743 benefit (the evening Clive bombed as Bayes in the Duke of Buckingham's *Rehearsal*), and that of the Irish actor Dennis Delane, performing the *Comus* air 'Would you Taste the Noontide Air'. *London Daily Post and General Advertiser*, issue 2665 (6 May 1743) and issue 2619 (14 March 1743).

[63] Thomas Arne, *The Judgment of Paris*, ed. I. Spink, Musica Britannica, vol. 42 (London, 1978). The bellicosity of Clive's music – its fanfares, strumming, and implied drumbeats – underpinned a typecasting in which Arne's wife, as Venus, was Clive's opponent and vanquisher.

[64] Presumably the duet version of 'My Faith and Truth' sung by Clive and Edwards at Covent Garden on 13 March and 2 April of 1744, and at Drury Lane on 4 January and 10 April 1746, was the number 'Sung by Mrs. Clive' for two vocal lines engraved in Walsh's four editions of *Samson* until 1749. See George F. Handel, *Samson. An Oratorio* (London, 1745), pp. 51–54. On Samson's early editions, see William C. Smith, assisted by Charles Humphries, *Handel: A Descriptive Catalogue of the Early Editions*, 2nd edn (Oxford, 1970), pp. 134–36.

little fanfare.⁶⁵ Had Clive suddenly refused to perform with Edwards? On 17 September 1747 Edwards had opened her season opposite Clive in *The Beggar's Opera*; once Susannah Cibber began playing Polly, Edwards virtually ceased appearing alongside Clive.⁶⁶ In May 1748 Garrick ejected Edwards and her husband, the actor Thomas Mozeen, from the company. What had happened? Tate Wilkinson, in his *Memoirs* of 1790, is the only writer to discuss the rift:

> I met with little neat Mrs. Mozeen … [in] 1758, who … had been bred carefully up, and introduced to the London audience by Mrs. Clive, who was so partial to her adoption, that she for the first time gave up Polly … but Mrs. Mozeen's powers were weak, and she fell by tasting the apple like her mother eve, and the chaste, the comical, the enraged Clive discarded her … and let her pupil down the wind to prey on Fortune … Mrs. Mozeen had a plurality of lovers, and always put me in mind of Shakespear's lines: – Behold yon simpering lady, she who starts at / Pleasure's name, and thinks her ear prophaned with / The least wanton word; wou'd you believe it? &c.⁶⁷

The passage from Shakespeare, spoken by King Lear, continues thus: '[The] fichew nor the soyled horse goes toot, / With a more riotous appetite. / Down [from] the wa[i]st tha're centaures, though women all aboue'.⁶⁸ Wilkinson's quote implies that once the upstanding Clive discovered the 'riotous appetite' of the fallen Edwards, she recoiled. 'Down [from] the wa[i]st tha're centaures' signifies a liminal sexuality, meaning perhaps that Edwards' 'plurality of lovers' included women.

Wilkinson was of course writing much later, and all of this could be second-generation slander. Yet Chetwood, describing Edwards back in 1749, had also chosen verses that suggest unusual cravings. He is far more cryptic than Wilkinson:

> If her innate Modesty keeps her back as an Actress, Time may get the better of her Timidity. Modesty may assume a proper Spirit, when it is assured of being justly right in what is undertaken; for Virtue has ever Courage, and is its own Guardian.

---

⁶⁵ 'As the Publick has often desir'd to see Mrs. CIBBER in the Part of Polly, and Mrs. CLIVE, in that of Lucy, the Beggar's Opera will be perform'd (with the usual Dances) To-morrow, at the Theatre-Royal in Drury-Lane.' *General Advertiser*, issue 4096 (11 December 1747).
⁶⁶ Clive and Edwards did share the stage twice more, in *The Tempest* on 26 December 1747 and in Arne and Congreve's *The Judgment of Paris* on 20 April 1748. The roles in each require two trained sopranos, which explains why Clive would have had to perform with Edwards.
⁶⁷ Wilkinson, *Memoirs*, vol. 3, pp. 215–17.
⁶⁸ The speech is from Act IV, scene 4 of *King Lear*, in John Jowett, ed., 'King Lear', *The New Oxford Shakespeare: The Complete Works*, ed. G. Taylor, et al. (Oxford, 2016), p. 1320.

Virtue could see to do what Virtue would / By her own radiant Light, tho' Sun and Moon, / Were in the flat Sea sunk. Milton.[69]

In so exaggeratedly attributing 'innate Modesty' to Edwards, with a homily about the power of Virtue and a quote from Milton thrown in, Chetwood likely meant the reader to understand the reverse. Milton's words are from a scene in *Comus*: here, the Elder Brother comforts the Younger, who fears that their sister, lost in the woods, must be frightened. The Elder Brother assures him that their sister's 'Goodness' will keep her 'calm Thoughts' from falling 'into misbecoming Plight'. Then come the lines that Chetwood quotes, about Virtue lighting its own way, and the Elder Brother notes that 'Wisdom' and 'Contemplation' themselves seek out 'sweet retired solitude'.[70] Chetwood's characterization of Edwards seems to invite the reader to stand Milton's famous verses on their head: so that for virtue we are to read vice; for calm thoughts, excited ones; and for solitude, company.

If such readings seem far-fetched, consider that same-sex love was unmentionable at the time. Edwards and her husband Thomas Mozeen separated permanently in late 1749 while in Dublin, and apparently never again worked in the same city. In 1758 Thomas Mozeen wrote a Drury Lane benefit afterpiece called *The Heiress*, about a woman posing romantically as a man. By his report, *The Heiress* should have kicked off the benefit season, but 'an unforeseen Accident' relegated it to the season's end. Introducing readers to his play, Mozeen defends it against a 'Gentleman' who had objected to its 'unnatural' plot, arguing to the contrary that its action 'might probably happen'.[71]

The Heiress is Harriot Bellmour, who is raised as a boy and enters Town life as Aston Bellmour. Mozeen persuasively dramatizes Harriot's attractions as a man, first through the 'growing Passion' between Harriot and Letitia (Letty), the sister of Harriot's London host Mr. Briton junior,[72] then through a dispute between Miss Penn and Miss Dolly over 'his' virility.[73] Miss Dolly gushes: 'he has a good Complexion ... a soft Manner of Expression: But his Deportment is far from effeminate.'[74] Letty grows jealous, accusing Bellmour of courting Miss Languish.[75] Harriot's sex is disclosed in a letter to Mr. Briton's father, the pretence having been the means for her to inherit a fortune that, as a women,

---

[69] Chetwood, 'Mr. MOZEEN', *A General History of the Stage*, p. 194.
[70] Arne, *Comus*, p. 62.
[71] Thomas Mozeen, 'To the Public', *The Heiress; Or, Antigallican. A Farce*, in *A Collection of Miscellaneous Essays* (London, 1762), pp. vii–ix.
[72] 'Briton, jun. Did you never drop a Hint, Sir, of any Surmise you had concerning the growing Passion between 'em [Harriot and Letty]?' *Ibid.*, p. 246.
[73] *Ibid.*, pp. 260–62.
[74] *Ibid.*, p. 261.
[75] *Ibid.*, pp. 283–84.

she could not legally claim.⁷⁶ She declares love for Briton junior, and he for her. She comforts Letty with the words 'cheer up, my Dear ... tho' I can't marry you, I shan't go out of the Family you see. As Sisters we may agree perhaps better than as Husband and Wife'.⁷⁷ The fluidity of sexuality in *The Heiress*, and the ease with which one woman excites another, do indeed seem 'unnatural' compared to other sentimental afterpieces – but perhaps they were less so for Mozeen, after his union with Edwards. Clive was notably absent from the 1758 cast of *The Heiress*. Among the work's dramatis personae, Lady Everbloom is typical of Clive's post-1746 line of ageing, ridiculous, controlling women. Was Clive's refusal of the part the 'unforeseen Accident' that bumped this benefit to the season's end?

A pamphlet printed shortly after the 1749 *Lethe* opened, *Satan's Harvest Home*, could easily have been read as a gloss on the mannish Clive of 'The Card invites', and her past relations with Edwards.⁷⁸ Its author writes of 'a new and most abominable Vice' that 'has got footing among the W[ome]n of Q[ualit]y'.⁷⁹ This abomination is the 'Game at Flats', named after a card-game with counters called 'flats'.⁸⁰ The author of *Pretty Doings in a Protestant Nation* had in 1734 made flats stand for another game: that of pudenda rubbing together, a pastime said to be 'practis'd frequently in Turkey, as well as at Twickenham at this Day'.⁸¹ *Satan's Harvest Home* reprinted this claim. As noted above, Clive had since the summer of 1748 been socializing with Horace Walpole at his Twickenham estate. By December 1749 Clive was residing in a house on Walpole's estate, taking only temporary London lodgings for her theatre seasons.⁸² Might 'Flats' have been the imputed game of 'The Card invites'?

---

⁷⁶ *Ibid.*, pp. 286–87.
⁷⁷ *Ibid.*, p. 288.
⁷⁸ This pamphlet is mentioned in Katherine Crawford's account of lesbianism in the eighteenth century. She identifies that the term 'lesbian' was first used to describe same-sex female love in William King's 1736 satire *The Toast*, as fear grew of its contagion. The pamphlet *Satan's Harvest Home* was a best-seller, and fanned fears that a vogue for lesbianism threatened to corrupt households across Europe. Katherine Crawford, 'Deviancy and the Cultures of Sex', *European Sexualities, 1400–1800* (Cambridge, 2007), pp. 213–14. See also note oo below.
⁷⁹ *Satan's Harvest Home: Or the present State of Whorecraft, Adultery, Fornication, Procuring, Pimping, Sodomy, and the Game at Flatts ... and other Satanic Works, daily propagated in this good Protestant Kingdom* (London, 1749), p. 60.
⁸⁰ *Ibid.*
⁸¹ *Pretty Doings in a Protestant Nation. Being a View of the present State of Fornication ... in Great-Britain ... Written originally in French by Father Poussin* (London, 1734), p. 24.
⁸² Clive moved first to a cottage on Walpole's property, and then at some unknown point to 'Little Strawberry Hill'. Based on her change of London addresses (from permanent to temporary lodgings), and on a letter of 3 December (year not stated) asking Walpole to recommend a gardener, Crean shows that 'that by December, 1749, Kitty Clive possessed a house at Twickenham, and that from March, 1750, she contented herself with lodgings in town convenient to the theatre'. Patrick J. Crean, 'Kitty Clive', *Notes and Queries*, vol. 162 (16 April 1932), pp. 272–73. I have not yet found any record of the arrangements

Whether Edwards and Clive were lesbian lovers, or whether Clive's attachment to Edwards was purely sentimental and she was genuinely shocked by Edwards' alleged carnality, or whether the situation between them was some other, is of course unknowable. The point of this discussion is, first of all, to show the environment of rumour and scandal around these issues that undergirded Garrick's 1749 *Lethe*. We should also acknowledge Clive's later passion for her protégée Jane Pope. By her own declaration, Clive loved Pope deeply. Her letters to Pope are mostly innocuous requests, inquiries, professional counsel, personal news, and theatre gossip.[83] But then there is this:

> I am in mind to thank you for the oysters which were excellent; but why wou'd you give the bread out of your own mouth, particularly as I know you are remarkably fond of them, that certainly is an instance that looks kinder than if you had bought them, and accordingly they taste to me so much the sweeter; for I love every morsel of your affection sent me and always eat it up my self. I will not let anybody pertake with me; for in that only I am a Churle; pray have I not got a little into the Clouds.[84]

Clive ends in a flutter, fearing she may have gone too far, but sending the letter anyway. The consumption of oysters had long been associated with sexual arousal.[85] The implied image of an oyster passing from Pope's mouth into Clive's, the oyster as symbol of sweet 'affection' which Clive eats up, and Clive's fierce possessiveness of this token are all suggestive.

Finally we should consider, without in any way crediting, *A Sapphick Epistle, from Jack Cavendish to the Honourable and most beautiful Mrs. D—*. In this

---

between Walpole and Clive for her residency on his estate. The notion that Walpole gifted a home to Clive stems apparently from a note of 1927 by Paget Toynbee in his edition of the *Strawberry Hill Accounts*, p. 85: 'Little Strawberry Hill, between Strawberry Hill and Teddington, which Walpole bought and gave to Mrs. Clive ... and which, as her residence, he used to call "Cliveden"'.

[83] JoAllen Bradham contends, to a certain extent rightly, that in her letters Clive cast herself in the part of the Country Gentlewoman. As previously mentioned, Bradham doesn't account for Clive's autograph letters; nor does she cover copies of letters by Clive held at the Forster Collection of the Victoria & Albert Museum (outside those published by Percy Fitzgerald), at the Garrick Club of London, in supplements to Horace Walpole's letters, and in the Harcourt papers. Bradham, 'A Good Country Gentlewoman: Catherine Clive's Epistolary Autobiography', pp. 259–82.

[84] Catherine Clive to Jane Pope c.1784. No date ('no. 52') Bodleian Library. Toynbee b.1, 'Autograph letters from Catherine Clive to Jane Pope'.

[85] Oysters were among foods thought to increase desire; for instance, Miss Bland was noted for her use of aphrodisiacs such as oysters in *Harris's List of Covent Garden Ladies* (1764). Jennifer Evans, *Aphrodisiacs, Fertility and Medicine in Early Modern England* (Woodbridge, 2014), p. 102. Invoking classical myth, especially the story of Aphrodite's conception in an oyster shell, and drawing on established pictorial symbolism, Dutch painters made the oyster into a favourite signifier of concupiscence. Liana De Girolami Cheney, 'The Oyster in Dutch Genre Paintings: Moral or Erotic Symbolism', *Artibus et Historiae*, vol. 8, no. 15 (1987), pp. 135–58.

pamphlet of c.1778, Clive is squarely accused of participating in 'Taste, elegance and Sapphick love' at Strawberry Hill.[86] The lesbian antics there, according to 'Jack Cavendish', were spearheaded by Walpole's ward, the sculptress Anne Seymour Damer (1749–1828).[87] Along with the slander, in the account of 'Jack Cavendish' we find a late iteration of the manlike Mrs. Riot, first put into circulation by Garrick's 1749 *Lethe*.

Mrs. Riot Commodified

As co-head of London's playhouse duopoly, Garrick had the means to make *Lethe* a hit, despite the work's initially tepid reception. He mounted sixteen performances during its first season and wrote the 52-page puff discussed above. He may also have had a hand in the production of figurines of *Lethe*'s two principals, Clive and Henry Woodward. Each star represented a new kind of Drury Lane entertainment: Garrick had just crowned Clive queen of '*Caracatura*', and Woodward, a recent hire, was Drury Lane's new principal of low comedy. Besides taking farcical characters like the 'Fine Gentleman' of *Lethe*, Woodward was Drury Lane's new Harlequin, lured by Garrick from Covent Garden to outshine Woodward's teacher, the ageing John Rich.[88] We have already encountered Woodward as the author of the Polly Row parody

---

[86] *A Sapphick Epistle, from Jack Cavendish to the Honourable and most beautiful Mrs. D—* ([London], [?1778]), p. 15 (first published from c.1771).

[87] 'Apart from Anne Damer, the only other contemporary woman named as having lesbian sex in the *Sapphick Epistle* is Kitty Clive … we are told that Strawberry Hill has found in Kitty ***** "Taste, elegance and Sapphick love (Stanza 26)"'. Emma Donoghue "'Random Shafts of Malice?': The Outings of Anne Damer', *Lesbian Dames: Sapphism in the Long Eighteenth Century*, ed. J. C. Beynon and C. Gonda (Farnham and Burlington, 2010), p. 131. Damer was the only child of Walpole's close friend Henry Seymour Conway. An army officer, Conway frequently went abroad with his wife, leaving Damer in the custody of Walpole, who cultivated her remarkable gifts. Despite marriage to 1767 Hon. John Damer – from whom she separated in 1774 – she became known for her outré consorting with other women. In 1789 she entered a partnership with Mary Berry, to whom Walpole introduced her. Throughout her life she frequented Strawberry Hill. See, inter alia, Alison Yarrington, 'The Female Pygmalion: Anne Seymour Damer, Allan Cunningham and the Writing of a Woman Sculptor's life', *Sculpture Journal*, vol. 1 (1997). On Damer and her household, see also Susan S. Lanser, 'Sapphic Sects the Rites of Revolution, 1775–1800', *The Sexuality of History: Modernity and the Sapphic, 1565–1830*, pp. 193–221. Like Clive, Damer also won professional acclaim, becoming in 1784 the first female sculptor to exhibit at the Royal Academy.

[88] In an apocryphal nineteenth-century report, John Genest, paraphrasing Arthur Murphy, has Garrick saying 'if people would not come to Lear and Hamlet, he must give them Harlequin'. John Genest, *Some Account of the English Stage from the Restoration in 1660 to 1830* (London, 1832), vol. 4, p. 314. This is, in fact, what Garrick did: after luring Woodward away from Rich, in the 1750s Garrick spearheaded pantomime production, creating the post-Christmas pantomime season still followed in Britain. Fiske, *English Theatre Music in the Eighteenth Century*, pp. 229–39, esp. p. 232. On the ways Rich had earlier made his harlequinade compete with that of Drury Lane, see Marc Martinez,

The Beggar's Pantomime (1736), in which he had pilloried Clive and Susannah Cibber as the 'Hoarsen Throated' Madam Squall and 'bawling' Madam Squeak.

The commerce in Clive's *Lethe* character was substantially more extensive than in Woodward's. Mrs. Riot products were unique for the volume and diversity in which they were produced, from the five-centimetre print miniature to the connoisseur's hand-painted porcelain statuette. This proliferation of Clive's likeness had no equal in her career. Clive-as-Riot effigies seem to have been rolled out roughly as follows. Clive's portrait painter of 1734, Pieter van Bleeck, made an undated full-length oil portrait of Clive as Riot (Fig. 11.1), from which in 1750 Charles Mosley made a stipple etching, in reverse, with one of her lines from *Lethe* printed below the image (Fig. 11.2). Mosley's stipple etching was then used to make a medallion print miniature, sold from 17 September 1750,[89] which functioned also as a watch-paper (Fig. 11.3),[90] and porcelain figurines.[91] The figurines were initially produced from 1750 by the Bow factory (Fig. 11.4) but then 'instantly copied' by the porcelain factories of Derby and Chelsea.[92] Bow also produced a Woodward figurine, copied by the Chelsea factory but not by Derby.[93] Most of these figurines were white, but some were hand-painted, whether at the Bow factory or by an independent china painter. The account book of the painter William Duesbury contains an entry for decorating Clive figurines.[94] Further, the artist Thomas Worlidge painted a watercolour of Clive as Riot that Horace Walpole owned.[95] According

---

'The Tricks of Lun: Mimesis and Mimicry in John Rich's Performance and Conception of Pantomimes', *Theatre History Studies*, vol. 29 (2009), pp. 148–70.

[89] Sale of this item was announced thus: 'This Day at Noon will be published, and sold by the Proprietor and the Print-Shops, two Portraits of those celebrated Comedians, Mr. Woodward and Mrs. Clive, in the Characters of the fine Gentleman and Lady, in Lethe, (as they are to perform them to Night, at the Theatre-Royal in Drury-lane) curiously engraved (in Miniature) from Original Drawings of the same Size. By J. Brooke: Engraver of Silver and Copper Plate … &c. opposite Nando's Coffee-house, Temple-bar'. *General Advertiser*, issue 4964 (18 September 1750). A copy of the miniature is held at The Garrick Club of London. Catalogue no. PM0286.

[90] A watch-paper was a print designed to be pressed into the inside of a pocket-watch cover.

[91] Jan Seewald, *Theatrical Sculpture: Skulptiere Bildnisse berühmter englischer Schauspieler, 1750–1850, insbesondere David Garrick und Sarah Siddons* (Munich, 2007), pp. 35–45.

[92] Heather McPherson, 'Theatrical Celebrity and Porcelain', p. 197; on the manufacturers, see *ibid.*, pp. 197–201. The date of 1750 is incised on the base of the Bow model in the Fitzwilliam Museum.

[93] Peter Bradshaw, *18th Century* [sic] *English Porcelain Figures*, p. 57.

[94] 'For enamelling Mrs. Clive and Henry Woodward three shillings', cited in Seewald, *Theatrical Sculpture*, p. 42, note 97. Geoffrey Godden discusses the rarity of these painted figurines in comparison to unpainted figurines in Geoffrey Godden, *Eighteenth-Century English Porcelain: A Selection from the Godden Reference Collection* (London, 1985), pp. 24–27, with black-and-white plate no. 19 on p. 25.

[95] The only record of Worlidge's watercolour seems to be in Walpole's inventory of Strawberry Hill, which mentions that it hung in Green Closet. Horace Walpole, *A Description*

Fig. 11.1 Pieter van Bleeck, *Catherine Clive as Mrs. Riot, the Fine Lady in Lethe; or Aesop in the Shades*, c.1749. Oil on canvas.
By kind permission of the Garrick Club of London. Paintings: G0121.

Fig. 11.2 Charles Mosley after Pieter van Bleeck, *Mrs. Clive, in the Character of the fine Lady in Lethe*, 1750. Etching and engraving. Lewis Walpole Library. Call number: Portraits C642 no. 3. Courtesy of the Lewis Walpole Library, Yale University.

Fig. 11.3 After Charles Mosley, after Pieter van Bleeck, *Mrs. CLIVE IN THE CHARACTER OF THE LADY IN LETHE*, 1750. Watch-paper. © Trustees of the British Museum. Museum number: 1902,1018.71.

to Jan Seewald, Worlidge based his watercolour on one of the hand-painted Bow figurines, rather than the watercolour being a model for the figurine, as is usually stated.[96] Finally, an undated, anonymous pastel was drawn of the same subject, possibly based on Worlidge's watercolour.[97]

---

of the Villa of Horace Walpole, youngest Son of Sir Robert Walpole Earl of Orford, at Strawberry-Hill, near Twickenham (Strawberry-Hill, 1774–86), p. 130.

[96] McPherson follows most catalogue entries in erroneously asserting that Mosley's engraving is after Worlidge's watercolour, rather than after Van Bleeck's oil. McPherson, 'Theatrical Celebrity and Porcelain', p. 197. Seewald confirms both that Mosley copied Van Bleeck and that Worlidge painted from figurines. Seewald, *Theatrical Sculpture*, p. 43.

[97] After Charles Mosley, after Pieter van Bleeck, *Portrait of Kitty Clive*. Pastel drawing. No date [before 1785?]. Lewis Walpole Library, Yale University. Call number: Drawings Un58 no. 83. Local Record Number: lwlpr31239.

Fig. 11.4 Made by the Bow porcelain manufactory, after Charles Mosley, after Pieter van Bleeck, *Kitty Clive as 'The Fine Lady' in Lethe*, 1750. Soft-paste porcelain. © Fitzwilliam Museum, Cambridge. Object Accession Number: EC.3-1938.

As ever, specifics of consumption – who commissioned the likenesses, who bought them, where they were displayed commercially and privately – remain obscure.[98] Because Van Bleeck had produced Clive's earlier Phillida portraits, collaboration with Garrick seems likely, especially in view of Garrick's determination to popularize *Lethe*. Helen McPherson believes that Garrick facilitated production of the Bow figurines, working with Thomas Fry, an Irish portrait painter who was the co-founder and director of the Bow factory.[99] Garrick's words certainly guided what those viewing Mosley's etching (Fig. 11.2) were to think about Clive. Instead of an epigram, as in her previous portraits, Mosley placed a line from *Lethe* below *Mrs. Clive, in the Character of the fine Lady in Lethe*: 'Shew me to the Pump Room then, Fellow __ where's the company? __ I die in Solitude &c.'.

Porcelain figurines were luxury items, and those of Clive and Woordward were the very first to be made of players.[100] With its frontal pose, the Riot figurine was likely meant for display against a wall – on a wall bracket, mantelpiece, or a dressing table. In some versions, Riot is on a stand decorated with sheet music, flute, and masks, and, as McPherson observes, appears to be singing, unlike her tight-lipped Van Bleeck-Mosley portrait.[101] The figurine's detail is highly articulated: one can see and touch Clive's pet-en-l'air (pleated) jacket, silk muff, ornamental ruching, laced-up bodice, ruffled collar, pinner (a frilled head dress), and small dog – possibly the toy spaniel traditionally associated with English court ladies[102] – clamped under her right arm. McPherson justly argues that the Riot figurine was a means of 'reincarnating in miniature the living, breathing' player after the performance.[103] If Mrs. Riot on stage was a '*Caracatura*' of Clive, her presence in the home was a commodity fetish recalling Clive's self-mockery.

---

[98] Shirley Strum Kenny asserts that the visual artists themselves may have independently invested in production. Shirley Strum Kenny, 'Theatre, Related Arts and Profit Motive', *British Theatre and the Other Arts, 1660–1800*, ed. S. Strum Kenny (Washington, 1984), pp. 20–23.

[99] McPherson, 'Theatrical Celebrity and Porcelain', pp. 201–2.

[100] Seewald, *Theatrical Sculpture*, p. 37.

[101] McPherson, 'Theatrical Celebrity and Porcelain', pp. 197–98.

[102] Barbara Harris notes that by the 1550s 'spaniels were very much in vogue as pets' at the Tudor court. Barbara J. Harris, 'Women and Politics in Early Tudor England', *The Historical Journal*, vol. 33, no. 2 (1990), p. 267. Toy spaniels – not infrequently used in eighteenth-century satires to underscore a woman's excessive luxury – were traditionally used as muffs, a usage which depictions of Clive as Mrs. Riot may imply. In the Mosely print, the toy dog looks more like a pug, with which toy spaniels were cross-bred in the eighteenth century.

[103] McPherson, 'Theatrical Celebrity and Porcelain', p. 199.

Clive's Musical Caricatures: *The Chaplet* (1749) and *The Shepherd's Lottery* (1750)

On 2 December 1749, Clive and John Beard opened the last musical stage hit of Clive's career: *The Chaplet*, an all-sung pastoral afterpiece with Clive as Pastora. The wordbook was by Moses Mendez, whose ballad opera *The Double Disappointment* (1746) had shown his aptitude for fitting vehicles to the player. To clothe Mendez's *Chaplet* in music, Garrick bypassed Arne and commissioned William Boyce, a composer to the Chapel Royal from 1736 and conductor for the Three Choirs' Festival from 1737.[104] Boyce's professional reputation together with his renowned geniality recommended him over Arne, between whom and Clive there was famously no love lost. Boyce had composed Beard's music for both the 1740 and the 1749 *Lethe*, while Arne wrote for Clive; now, for *The Chaplet*, the commission for both Beard's and Clive's song fell to Boyce.[105]

Writing in 1838 about playhouse 'Musical Drama', George Hogarth would single out *The Chaplet* as the only opera 'worthy of notice' in London in the 1750s.[106] *The Chaplet* was an immediate and enduring hit, with thirty-one London performances in its first season and eighty-six more during the decade; it reached Dublin in 1750, New York in 1767, and Philadelphia in 1768.[107] This enthusiasm meant rapid print transmission: the full score was engraved and sold only a month after *The Chaplet* opened, and was reissued in 1755, while selections and arrangements from *The Chaplet* circulated until 1787.[108]

---

[104] Fiske, *English Theatre Music in the Eighteenth Century*, p. 213. Fiske quotes Burney's comment that Arne and Boyce 'were frequently concurrents at the theatre and in each other's way'.

[105] The *Lethe* 1740 manuscript (John Larpent Plays, LA22, fol. 1v) shows that Beard opened the comedy with the air 'Come, Mortals, come, unlade your Grief'. In 1749, 'Come, Mortals, come' replaced the duet finale of 1740, and Beard was given a new song at the start, also by Boyce, 'Ye Mortals whom Fancies and Troubles perplex'. As Ian Bartlett notes, Boyce's two songs for Beard are preserved in the fourth volume of Boyce's songs, engraved by John Walsh in William Boyce, *Numb: IV. Lyra Britannica: A Collection of English Songs … In which are inserted some songs in Lethe* (London, [1754]). In his catalogue of William Boyce's compositions, Bartlett erroneously assumes that both Beard's songs in *Lethe* came from the 1749 version. Ian Bartlett with Robert J. Bruce, *William Boyce: A Tercentenary Sourcebook and Compendium* (Newcastle upon Tyne, 2013), pp. 39, 55–56, 93–94, 245, 296. We don't know the composer of the final duet in the 1740 version of *Lethe*.

[106] George Hogarth, *Memoirs of the Musical Drama* (London, 1838), vol. 2, p. 100.

[107] Bartlett with Bruce, *William Boyce*, pp. 68–69; Fiske, *English Theatre Music in the Eighteenth Century*, pp. 213–14.

[108] The engraved score was sold from 4 January 1750. Bartlett with Bruce, *William Boyce*, pp. 68–69. These authors note that the absence of variants between the fair copy MS (British Library RM.22.b.8) and the printed full score, and the fact that the original cast names appear beside each part, suggest that the copy was likely made during the first or early runs of *The Chaplet*.

Striking about *The Chaplet* is its burlesque of celebrity personae, as much in music as in words. Boyce shadowed Mendez's nimble stylistic shifts, and composer and playwright alike lampooned pastoral conventions to refresh Clive's shop-worn persona.[109] *The Chaplet* is a mash-up of three distinct genres: ballad opera, pastoral serenata, and pleasure garden song. This last was the speciality of Beard, who was principal tenor at Ranelagh Gardens. Beard was simply handed songs of the type he had popularized at garden concerts; Clive's airs, by contrast, caricature pastoral conceits. As a sardonic comment on itself, Boyce's music for Clive sneers at the high-style song for which she had once been celebrated.

The Chaplet surely owed some of its initial success to Miss Norris. She had premiered at Covent Garden the season before, and *The Chaplet* was her Drury Lane debut. On the opening night, male spectators seated on stage clamoured to get close to her, forcing her to ask a certain Captain Johnson to leave, and the prompter to draw 'lines with chalk' on the boards to keep gentlemen spectators from 'crowding'.[110] Norris's opposite, George Mattocks was also a novelty, his role in *The Chaplet* being the second of his career. For its humour, however, *The Chaplet* depended on Clive and Beard making the most of material designed for them. In writing their parts, Mendez travestied the title roles of *Damon and Phillida* (1729), first performed by the Clive–Beard duo in 1737, then revived by Clive in 1746 for her benefit. Clive's ridiculousness as a shepherdess is *The Chaplet*'s central gag. For Beard, Mendez joined his part of a Bacchanal in *Comus* to his persona at Ranelagh Garden concerts, where he routinely urged visitors to indulge in their amorous passion.[111]

As *The Chaplet* opens, Damon (Beard) chides Laura (Norris) for thinking his love vows earnest: 'How could you believe all the Nonsense I spoke?'[112] His opening air signals the Britishness of this pastoral tale, with its bluff meter, predictable progressions, and Scotch snaps arranged to emphasize the words

---

[109] Earlier scholars who comment on this work appear deaf to its referents. 'The Chaplet is a conventional Pastoral of the type John Hoadly wrote for Greene': Fiske, *English Theatre Music in the Eighteenth Century*, p. 214. 'The great appeal of *The Chaplet* … lay in the deftly managed comedy of the pastoral plot': Bartlett with Bruce, *William Boyce*, p. 68.

[110] At the premiere, the prompter Richard Cross noted: 'Some gentlemen crowding behind yͤ scenes, yͤ Audience resented it & yͤ farce was stop'd for half an hour – I drew lines with chalk, but Miss Norris applying publickly to Capt. Johnson, desiring he wou'd retire, He did and yͤ farce went on with great Applause.' *The London Stage*, Part 4, vol. 1, p. 158 (entry for Drury Lane Saturday 2 December 1749), and Bartlett with Bruce, *William Boyce*, p. 68.

[111] Berta Joncus, '"To propagate Sound for Sense": Music for Diversion and Seduction at Ranelagh Gardens', *London Journal: A Review of Metropolitan Society Past and Present*, vol. 38, no. 1 (2013), pp. 34–66.

[112] [Moses Mendez], *The Chaplet. A Musical Entertainment … The Music Compos'd by Dr. Boyce* (London, 1749), p. 4.

'know' and 'meant'.[113] After Laura laments to herself, Damon re-enters, with 'several Shepherds Drinking', and sings a moralizing strophic ballad, each of whose stanzas speak of the idiocies of a stock character – the Lover, the Miser, the Beau etc. – and end with the refrain 'Deserves to be reckon'd an Ass'.[114] Mendez modelled his verses directly on Beard's celebrated 'Masquerade Song', almost certainly performed at the Jubilee Ball of 26 April 1749.[115] Boyce kept the key, pick-up, triple meter, and triadic outline of the song, whose first two phrases give way to downward triadic leaps in the final bars to ram home the refrain's words. Mendez likewise borrowed metric schemes, linked to the refrain 'Sing tantararara'.[116] Mendez subtly altered the meter of Beard's song, alternating tetrameter with trimeter lines, and folding the refrain into a four-line stanza.[117] Together, Boyce's and Mendez's borrowings caused the 'Masquerade Song' to ghost behind Beard's *Chaplet* song, which then became another Town favourite.[118]

After Beard's rollicking moralizing, Pastora (Clive) and her suitor Palaemon (Mattocks) enter quarrelling. References to Clive's biography abound: she asks her suitor to 'set due Value on my Truth'.[119] She rages against him ('Perfidious Boy!'),[120] then decides to try and capture Damon's heart. Among her reasons, Damon's money is a major consideration: 'A handsom Youth he is, and rich they say'.[121] Palaemon quits Pastora, singing a *galant* air about being 'sick of his Bondage'.[122] In Clive's next scene, Damon tries half-heartedly to seduce Pastora: 'The Devil's in her if all this won't do'.[123] Her rebuff is a distillation of Clive tropes: 'Away, false Man, no more your Tale I'll hear; / The black Attempt offends my rigid Ear: / The Joys I taste shall be without a Crime; / I'll ne'er be fool'd by Man — a second Time'.[124] Between Damon's approach and Pastora's

---

[113] William Boyce, *The Chaplet. A Musical Entertainment ... Compos'd by Dr. Boyce* (London, [1750]), pp. 9–10.
[114] *Ibid.*, pp. 14–15.
[115] The song is Willem De Fesch's arrangement of the common tune 'You mad caps of England'. It was printed as a songsheet: [Willem De Fesch], *Ye Medley of Mortals that make up this Throng: The Masquerade Song / Sung by Mr. Beard at Ranelagh* ([London, 1749?]). Claude M. Simpson, 'Sing Tantara Rara', *The British Broadside Ballad and its Music*, pp. 664–67. Beard sang the air at the masquerade where Elizabeth Chudleigh, a maid of honour to the Princess of Wales, displayed her breasts in a translucent bodice that was part of her costume as Iphigenia. The scandal of this incident likely boosted the sales and popularity of Beard's 'Masquerade Song'. Joncus, '"To propagate Sound for Sense"', pp. 55–59.
[116] Boyce, *The Chaplet*, pp. 14–15.
[117] *Ibid.*
[118] Bartlett with Bruce, *William Boyce*, p. 95.
[119] [Mendez], *The Chaplet*, p. 8.
[120] *Ibid.*
[121] *Ibid.*, p. 9.
[122] Boyce, *The Chaplet*, p. 17.
[123] [Mendez], *The Chaplet*, p. 9.
[124] *Ibid.*, p. 11.

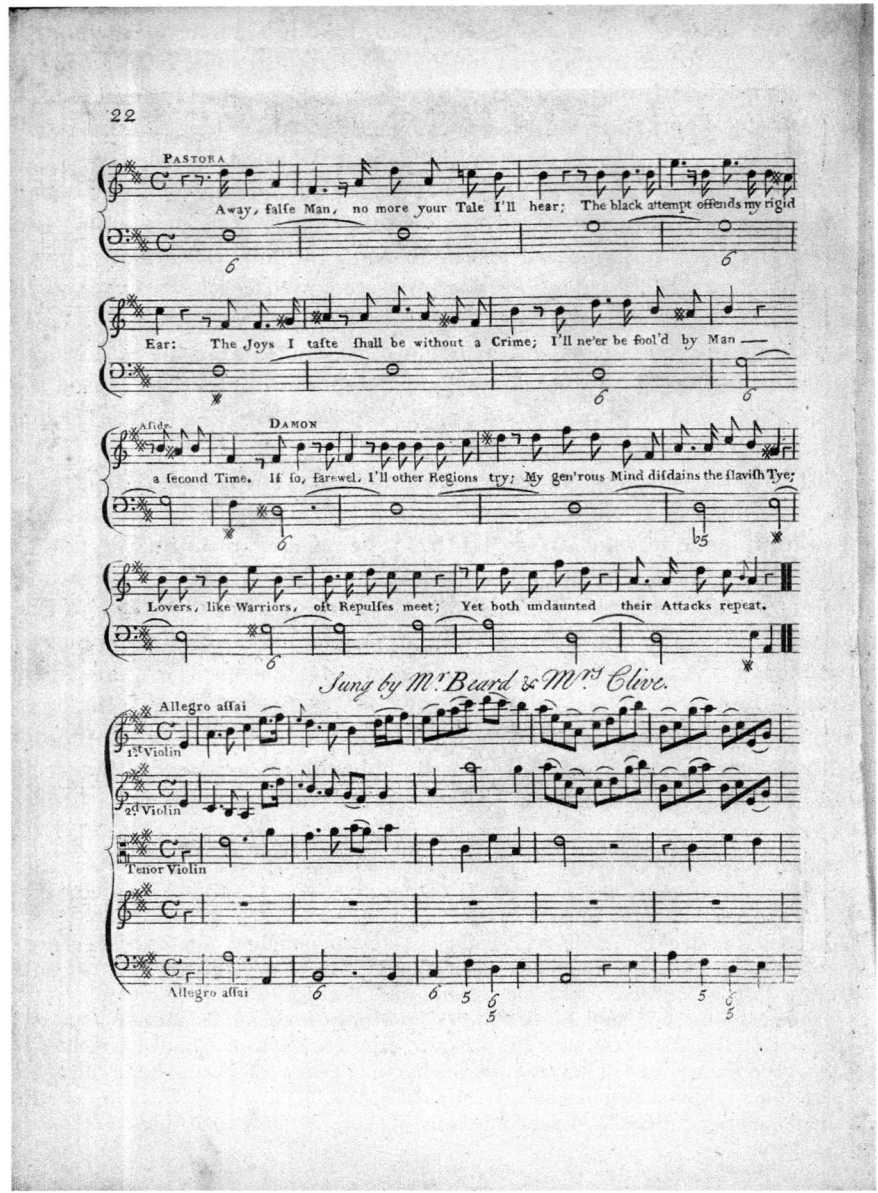

Ex. 11.3 Words by Moses Mendez, music by William Boyce, 'From Flow'r to Flow'r, his Joy to Change' in *The Chaplet*, 1750. The Bodleian Libraries, University of Oxford. Shelfmark: Harding Mus. D 72.

rejection the couple duel in the duet that starts 'Beauteous Maid, reward my Passion'. A minuet air in D minor, its singers alternate verse couplets to snub each other.[125]

To conclude the first act, a finale for Clive and Beard skewers the conventional pastoral vow between lovers (Ex. 11.3).[126] The ternary structure (ABA) is a series of strophic bourées, the first two of which have two stanzas, the last of which has only one. Pastora and Damon each sing one of two stanzas in the A section, and again in the B section, whose tonic minor contrasts the A section. When the singers return to the A section and their voices finally join, the two vocal lines are often in contrary motion (Ex. 11.3, pp. 23–25). Boyce occasionally pits motifs from the B section against the melodic subject first heard in the A section. Instead of the melting sensuality typical of a duet for lovers, this air crystallizes, especially in its final section, as a metrically rigid frame for two competing voices. Where Boyce used music to dramatize the anti-lovers' celebration of autonomy, Mendez did so in words, inverting conceits normally used to declare eternal fidelity: "Till from the Rock bursts forth the Rose".[127] He also wrote verses in which Damon and Pastora rejoice in being single: 'You'll find me blith and free'.[128] Their voices unite only when they express their mutual happiness at getting rid of each other: 'Then let's divide to East and West, / Since we shall ne'er agree'.[129] Clive and Beard may have further differentiated their respective vocal lines through extemporization.

The second act of *The Chaplet* provided Clive even more openings for laughs. After another lament by the long-suffering Laura, Pastora enters and, in the strophic air 'In vain I try my ev'ry Art' (Ex. 11.4), reflects on why she has no husband.[130] She is mystified: 'I'm not old or ugly', she sings, 'Methinks I look full smuggly' and 'bless'd with ... powerful Charms'.[131] The fault, of course, lies with men. In this air Boyce tears a leaf straight from Clive's ballad opera book: as in a common tune, he starts with an anacrusis, uses a 6/8 key signature, and builds a melody out of broad skips. His tune slips swiftly from B minor into the relative major, and cadences on 'ugly' by a skip of the fourth, as if the song were a traditional ballad. Each of Clive's next two phrases implies a different key: first, A major, 'Let me consult my faithfull Glass', and then B minor, 'Methinks I look full smuggly'. Because the two keys are unrelated, the shift between them represents how Pastora has lost her perspective as she sings 'Let me consult my faithful Glass / A Face much worse than this might

---

[125] Boyce, *The Chaplet*, pp. 19–22.
[126] Boyce, *The Chaplet*, pp. 22–25.
[127] [Mendez], *The Chaplet*, p. 12.
[128] *Ibid.*
[129] *Ibid.* and Boyce, *The Chaplet*, p. 25.
[130] Boyce, *The Chaplet*, pp. 28–29.
[131] *Ibid.* and [Mendez], *The Chaplet*, p. 15.

Ex. 11.4 Words by Moses Mendez, music by William Boyce,
'In vain I try my ev'ry Art' in *The Chaplet*, 1750.
The Bodleian Libraries, University of Oxford. Shelfmark: Harding Mus. D 72.

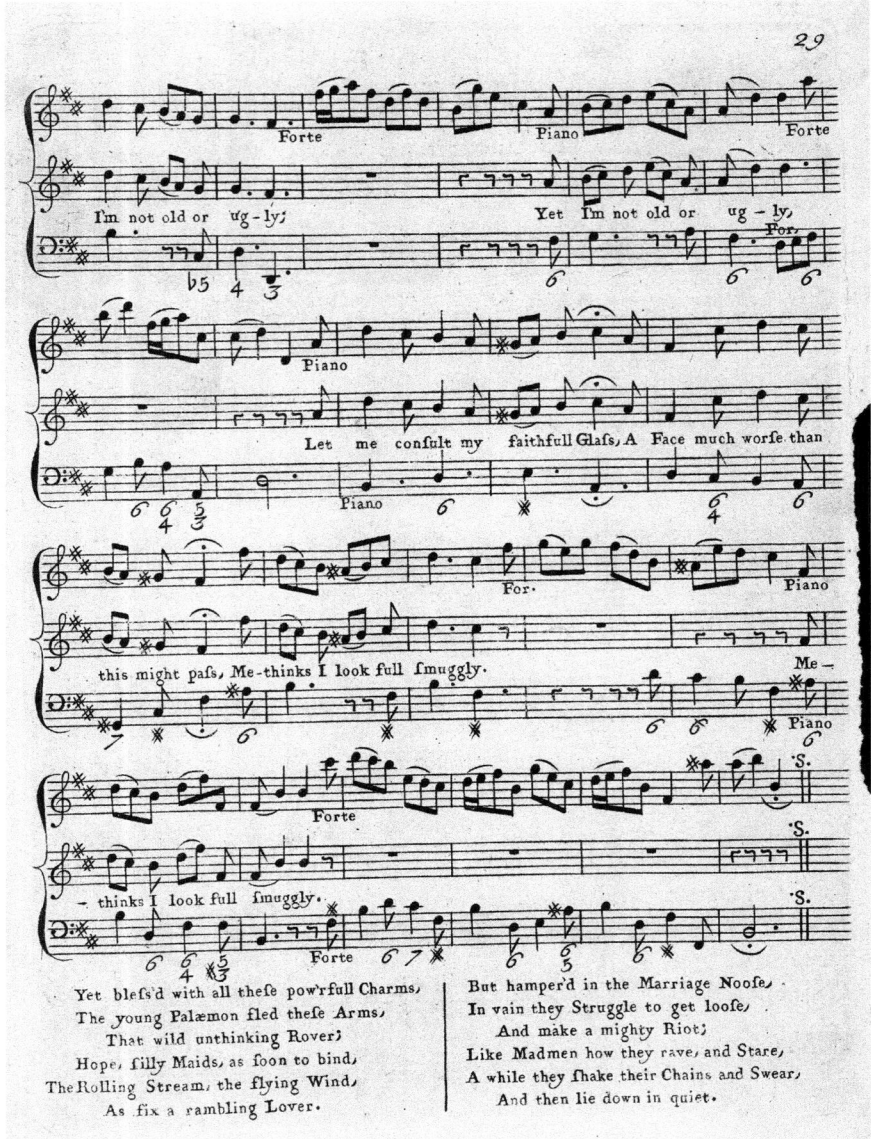

Yet bless'd with all these pow'rfull Charms,
The young Palæmon fled these Arms,
That wild unthinking Rover;
Hope, silly Maids, as soon to bind,
The Rolling Stream, the flying Wind,
As fix a rambling Lover.

But hamper'd in the Marriage Noose,
In vain they Struggle to get loose,
And make a mighty Riot;
Like Madmen how they rave, and Stare,
A while they shake their Chains and Swear,
And then lie down in quiet.

pass'. Each phrase ends with a fermata, at which Clive surely let loose with an Italianate cadenza.

Damon enters to sing another Ranelagh-styled ballad whose mottos repeat themselves in each stanza: 'I'll toy, I'll kiss and play' followed by 'hang me if I marry'.[132] After Pastora shrinks from his advances, Damon reveals that he has witnessed her amours with another shepherd. 'Pastora, fam'd for Truth / And rigid Virtue' turns out to be a prude in name only.[133] After Laura joins them Damon decides that he must, after all, choose a bride, and takes Laura. Pastora's final number, which descends from self-satisfaction to fury, is a Green Room Scuffle of a rage aria (Ex. 11.5):

> I know that my Person is charming,
> Beyond what a Clown can discover:
> That Dowdy your Senses alarming,
> Proves what a blind Thing is a Lover.
> I'll quit the dull Plains for the City,
> Where Beauty is follow'd by Merit;
> Your Taste, simple DAMON, I pity;
> Your Wit, who would wish to inherit?
> ...
> How Odious they look, I can't bear them:
> I wish you much joy of your Fury,
> My Rage into pieces could tear them.[134]

Vain, jealous of rivals, dismissive of men, intent on being an urban celebrity, confident of her wit and merit, and unable to control her anger: in December 1749 this character was unmistakably thought to be Clive's, and here she owned it indeed.

In creating this last Clive number, Mendez and Boyce experimented, combining a strophic air with what we today we would call a patter song. In a verse line crafted out of a grab-bag of meters – dactyl, anapest, spondee – the strong beat at the end of the first phrase is misplaced ('charm-ING'). The rhythms are not just ungainly, like Clive's person, they undermine the predictability of each stanza, as emphases and note-value alternations trip up the pulse, tipping it forward. In the last stanza, the erupting rage of Pastora animates the instruments: while she repeats her final phrases – probably with embellishment in performance – the first and second violins tremble in repeated semiquavers at registerial extremes against the viola and continuo, which play accented quavers. The result is a kind of metric scuffling. After Pastora storms out, peace is restored, and *The Chaplet* closes with a charming 'Scotch'-styled duetto – its

---

[132] Boyce, *The Chaplet*, pp. 30–31.
[133] [Mendez], *The Chaplet*, p. 18.
[134] Boyce, *The Chaplet*, pp. 37–39; [Mendez], *The Chaplet*, pp. 20–21.

Ex. 11.5 Words by Moses Mendez, music by William Boyce, 'I know that my Person is charming' in *The Chaplet*, 1750. The Bodleian Libraries, University of Oxford. Shelfmark: Harding Mus. D 72.Ex. 12.3.

melody recalls 'The Lass of Patie's Mill', arranged by Michael Festing as a Beard concert song – in which Damon, Laura, and a chorus praise marriage.

The success of *The Chaplet* spawned a copy-cat afterpiece, *The Shepherd's Lottery*, also by Mendez and Boyce, which opened Drury Lane's next season. Its three principals, and their character types, were the same as in *The Chaplet*: the philandering Beard, the man-hating Clive, and Norris who loves sincerely. For Joseph Vernon, new to the Drury Lane company, Mendez introduced the part of Norris's lover. As its title implies, *The Shepherd's Lottery* is a pastoral riff on Fielding's *Lottery*. Boyce set Mendez's finale as a vaudeville – an air in which each protagonist sings a solo stanza in turn – as Seedo did when setting the finale of *The Lottery*.[135] *The Shepherd's Lottery* achieved only modest success, due probably to its conventionality. The plot revolves around an imperilled union between the lovers Phillis (Norris) and Thyrsis (Vernon). In their village, an annual lottery determines marriage partners, and the two lovers fear that they will not draw each other's names. This device is the excuse for several airs in which Norris and Vernon declare undying passion for one another, and lament their loss should they not be matched, which of course they are.

Cynicism and Clive-bashing give comic relief. Daphne (Clive) tartly dismisses Phillis's love for Thyrsis. She declares that she distrusts men – a conviction she shares with the audiences by direct address, as in a ballad opera – and takes pleasure not in love, but in duping and then discarding suitors.[136] To this end, she pursues Colin (Beard). He rebuffs her in a duet that descends into an exchange of insults. Daphne casts doubt on Colin's virility, saying 'I doubt you're a Rover; if so, a young Maid / May fear to be with you, within this thick Shade',[137] to which he retorts 'Such Beauties as yours need be never afraid'.[138]

The Shepherd's Lottery contains only ballads and pleasure garden-styled songs for Clive and Beard, with high-style writing reserved for Norris and Vernon.[139] Except for the ebullient overture and a grand Norris number ('Goddess of the dimpling Smile'), over-reliance on formulae – strophic songs balanced against ornament-laden *galant* airs – make its numbers predictable.

---

[135] As Vanessa Rogers has shown, Fiske was wrong to assert that *The Shepherd's Lottery* was the 'first English opera to have a finale of the type later known as "vaudeville"'. In her words: 'Bringing all of the main characters onstage to sing a couplet or verse was also a common way of ending ballad operas. For instance, Fielding's *An Old Man Taught Wisdom* ends with an air similar in structure to a *vaudeville final*.' Compare Fiske, *English Theatre Music in the Eighteenth Century*, p. 221 with Vanessa L. Rogers, 'Writing Plays "In the Sing-Song Way": Henry Fielding's Ballad Operas and Early Musical Theater in Eighteenth-Century London' (PhD diss., Univ. of Southern California, 2007), p. 123.

[136] [Moses Mendez], *The Shepherds Lottery. A Musical Entertainment ... The Music Compos'd by Dr. Boyce* (London, 1751), pp. 5, 7.

[137] [Mendez], *The Shepherds Lottery*, p. 17.

[138] *Ibid*.

[139] William Boyce, *The Shepherds Lottery. A Musical Entertainment ... Compos'd by Dr. Boyce* (London, [1755]).

Some wit seeps into the concluding duet between Clive and Beard ('O say! must I sigh and pine');[140] here Boyce's smart little bourée crisps up the final spat between them, with syllabically-set semiquavers that generate a patter, and Boyce gives Clive two fermatas in the final stanza in which to expostulate musically.[141] Although quickly forgotten, *The Shepherd's Lottery* achieved twenty-seven performances during the three seasons it ran. Even if Clive's and Beard's star images impacted less on *The Shepherd's Lottery* than on *The Chaplet*, the musical forms, hybrid pastoral-*Lottery* scenes, and brief popularity of this afterpiece are incomprehensible without re-imagining Clive and Beard in their roles.

Describing *The Chaplet*, Tate Wilkinson wrote: 'Pastora cannot be known but by those who had the pleasure of seeing Mrs. Clive.'[142] Much of that pleasure surely derived from Clive's self-ridicule. In *The Chaplet* and *The Shepherd's Lottery*, Mendez and Boyce gave Clive the music and the allusions to run with, and song itself gave her the means to run with them.

From Portrait to Caricature

In 1747, four years after Fleetwood had published her earnings and two years after her clashes with Susannah Cibber and Peg Woffington, Clive's reputation had been in tatters. This was not the only personnel crisis with which Drury Lane's new manager David Garrick had to contend: in September 1748 Woffington, from whom he was now estranged, crossed over to Covent Garden, and by September 1750 Susannah Cibber, Spranger Berry, and Charles Macklin had followed. Clive, at daggers drawn with John Rich, was wedded to Drury Lane: she had no option but to take up whatever opportunities Garrick gave her. In so doing, she became Garrick's ally in his fight to put the house on a solid financial footing.

In reviving *Lethe* in 1749, Garrick made Clive's role as grotesque as her new reputation. By herself enacting the caricature others held her to be, Clive verified this view of her and its suggestion that the pre-1746 Clive – offstage a paragon, onstage a fascinating minx – had been a hoax. Garrick knew that his Pivy, as he affectionately called her, could bring this off, and he was right. Clive turned self-repudiation into an art, rallying, entertaining, and complimenting audiences in an extravagant guilty-as-charged act. What a crushing comedown for Euphrosyne! Having to enact Riot's tawdry insolence night after night was a surrender to calumny against her, to male views about femininity, and to common taste in entertainment. Clive had fought throughout her career to establish the opposite: her virtue, her version of a spirited womanhood, and, in

---

[140] Boyce, *The Shepherds Lottery*, p. 48.
[141] *Ibid*.
[142] Wilkinson, *Memoirs* (1790), vol. 4, p. 150.

sound, her fine sensibility. Riot's image pandered as much to male fantasy as the 1729 'Miss Rafter' mezzotint had, though now inviting not lust but derision. If Mrs. Riot looks sullen and resigned in Mosley's print, we can understand why. In memoirs, theatre chronicles, and musical studies, post-1746 authors made Clive out to be so foolish that to suggest she once moved audiences deeply today invites incredulity.

Clive's last refuge was mock Italian song. Mimicry, so intrinsic to eighteenth-century stage practice, questioned the perception of identity. Garrick's ability to imitate 'everything to perfection' frightened Denis Diderot, who understood this talent as evidence that the actor himself was 'nothing'.[143] After 1745, Clive's problem was the opposite. She had a surplus of self, in flesh as well as reputation. Her complexity, intelligence, and inner discipline had not changed, but now that she was seen as ludicrous, what did audiences have ears to hear? Mimic song at least allowed her to bait someone else, and let off her vocal fireworks. In 1750 she began to write afterpieces to lead at her benefits, channelling her gift for self-invention during performance into parts for herself. In her first-ever such work, *The Rehearsal: Or, Bays in Petticoats*, she re-tuned her voice to mimic song and bid her serious vocal repertory farewell.

---

[143] Denis Diderot, *Selected Writings on Art and Literature*, trans. Geoffrey Bremer (London, 1994); cited in Roach, *It*, pp. 141–42.

12

Clive on Clive:
The Rehearsal: Or, Bays in Petticoats

Clive plays Hazard – her farewell song – a last engagement with Susannah Cibber – Henry Woodward complains – on being a female Scribbler – Clive claims her parts

The Rehearsal: Or, Bays in Petticoats of 1750 was Clive's boldest stage experiment, the first stage work she ever wrote – and, in retrospect, a farewell to her career in serious song. My account of Clive's career ends here, with her musical adieu to the Fair Songster.

Like all 'rehearsal' burlesques, Clive's derived from the Duke of Buckingham's *Rehearsal* (1671), led by the poet-critic Bayes.[1] Clive wrote *The Rehearsal* for her benefit of 15 March 1750, recorded by Drury Lane prompter Richard Cross as 'A new farce partly singing, part speak^g. Went off well'.[2] After her *Rehearsal*, Clive wrote other benefit farces, channelling into words the ear and stage instinct she had first developed through song.[3] This chapter focuses on

---

[1] The 156 revivals of Buckingham's *Rehearsal* from 1671 to 1777 bear witness to its impact. For a list of titles, see Dane Farnsworth Smith, 'Appendix D: 'Revivals of The Rehearsal', *Plays about the Theatre in England from The Rehearsal in 1671 to the Licensing Act in 1737* (London, 1936), pp. 259–65.

[2] (MS Diary Richard) Cross, Folger Shakespeare Library. *The London Stage*, Part 4, vol. 1, p. 182 (under the entry for Drury Lane, 15 March 1750).

[3] Besides *The Rehearsal*, Clive prepared the following benefit farces, all of whose manuscripts are housed at the Huntington Library, John Larpent Plays collection: 'Every Woman in her Humour' (undated; first performed 20 March 1760), LA 174; 'The Sketch of a Fine Lady's Return from a Rout' (dated 12 March 1763; first performed 21 March 1763), LA 220; and 'The Faithful Irish Woman' (dated 9 March 1765; first performed 18 March 1765), LA 247. 'The Faithful Irish Woman' is a revised version of 'A Fine Lady's Return from a Rout'. Clive also may have helped to adapt a translation of Marivaux's 'The Island of Slaves' (dated 9 March 1761, first performed 26 March 1761), LA 190. As mentioned in Chapter 9, p. 290 and note 74, Patrick J. Crean argues that Clive wrote the wordbook of the now-lost 'Operetta' *The London 'Prentice*, set by Willem De Fesch, for her benefit of 23 March 1754. This stage work likely borrowed from the eponymous traditional ballad, typically printed as 'The Honour of a London 'prentice; Being an Account of his matchless Manhood and brave Adventures done in Turkey', to create a vehicle for Beard. Laetitia Pilkington was initially rumoured to be the author; Clive's notice to the contrary attests perhaps more to her repugnance at being associated with

the ways that Clive, in the first of four versions of her *Rehearsal* in particular, did this. In the third (1753) version of this work, Clive used burlesque to take a final shot at Susannah Cibber.

Buckingham's *Rehearsal* of 1671 was effectively a Green Room 'peep' whose vantage point he controlled. He mixed correction with malice: seemingly empirical, the writer burlesques a genre to correct its excesses, while also baiting recognizable celebrities. Others, most famously Henry Fielding, followed Buckingham.[4] By contrast, Clive twisted Buckingham's model to make herself the celebrity under attack. Already the subtitle *Bays in Petticoats* makes Clive the joke, alluding as it does to the fiasco of the 1743 benefit at which she wore breeches to lead Buckingham's *Rehearsal*: it is the fatty Clive's admission that she had overstepped herself. Yet the subtitle signals also Clive's defiance. Determined to play the critic on her terms, she reverses the travesty that had made her an object of derision at her benefit. By conceding her faults, Clive grants herself licence to criticize others, her male peers in particular.

Buckingham based his *Rehearsal* on Molière's *L'Impromptu de Versailles* (1663).[5] That Clive embraced Buckingham's farce reminds us how much Molière's dizzy, commedia-inspired action suited her. Writing her own vehicle, she follows Molière's ploy of pitting one character's grasp of what's going on against another's, and draws wit from these conflicting viewpoints. Into this she inserts herself, *in propria persona*. The main protagonist in Clive's *Rehearsal* is Mrs. Hazard, a female Scribbler who struggles to get her musical stage work mounted. Hazard is Clive's surrogate, derided by other dramatis personae for her foolishness. This self-disparagement excuses the fact that Clive has dared to write. By also having Hazard curse the conceited 'Mrs. Clive', who is engaged to sing Hazard's work, Clive strengthens her position as her own harshest critic. Yet Hazard also courts her audience with wit, wicked comments about her peers, and the exposure of grossly unjust attitudes to women. Splitting herself in two in this way, Clive both endorsed and outfaced her critics.

Clive followed Buckingham in dramatizing a stage rehearsal to pillory a genre. Whereas Buckingham had attacked tragedy, Clive in 1750 assailed the latest operatic craze: Italian 'Burletto'. This was an early form of opera buffa,

---

the adventuress Pilkington than to her own authorship. For a commentary on, and a critical edition of, Clive's 1753 version of her *Rehearsal*, and of 'Every Woman in her Humour', 'The Sketch of a Fine Lady's Return from a Rout', and 'The Faithful Irish Woman', see Richard C. Frushell, 'An Edition of the Afterpieces of Mrs. Clive' (PhD diss., Univ. of Duquesne, 1968).

[4] Lewis, *Fielding's Burlesque Drama: Its Place in the Tradition* analyzes the many works modelled after Buckingham's burlesque, Fielding's especially. The legacy of Buckingham's *Rehearsal* is deftly summarized in Robert D. Hume and Harold Love, ed., 'Reception and Influence', *Plays, Poems, and Miscellaneous Writings Associated with George Villiers, Second Duke of Buckingham*, vol. 1 (Oxford, 2007), pp. 386–95.

[5] Lewis, *Fielding's Burlesque Drama: Its Place in the Tradition*, p. 11.

featuring characters and plots akin to those of commedia dell'arte, and sometimes mockery of serious opera's conceits.[6] In another twist, the genre attacked in Clive's dialogue never materializes in a staged rehearsal. In its place, Clive got up a masque, re-deploying music from Boyce's earlier *Corydon and Miranda*.[7] This was the last new production in which Clive slipped between serious and comic song.

More than any vehicle for her up to then, Clive's *Rehearsal* depended on Clive. 'Hazard' was an eighteenth-century card game; Mrs. Hazard was the gaming lady Clive, and her *Rehearsal* was a gamble on herself as playwright despite the odds stacked against female writers.

Clive's *Rehearsal*, 1750: The Argument

To people *The Rehearsal*, Clive borrowed characters, and their players, from her recent hits *Lethe* and *The Chaplet*. Hazard is cousin to Mrs. Riot in *Lethe*, while the masque's love triangle of shepherdesses and shepherd, sung by Clive, Norris, and Beard, is the same as in Boyce's *Chaplet*. The action of the 1750 *Rehearsal* is straightforward.

Act I opens with servants complaining about their employer, the rich widow Mrs. Hazard. Since taking up writing for the theatre she has become abusive; they say also that she reads her work aloud to all her visitors, and that they find her and her writing ridiculous. As she prepares for the rehearsal of her 'Burletto', for which she has written the wordbook, her friend Witling visits her. He is courting Hazard solely for her fortune, a fact of which she is aware; she suffers him only because he leads the party supporting her opening night. He lets slip that some of those who plan to attend her rehearsal think that she is an idiot. She explains that her work is likely to succeed because burletto is in fashion and because Mrs. Clive is to be the principal singer. A young

---

[6] On itinerant Italian comic troupes as ambassadors of buffa opera, see Barbara D. Mackenzie, 'The Creation of a Genre: Comic Opera's Dissemination in Italy in the 1740s' (PhD diss., Univ. of Michigan, 1993). A brief introduction to this subject is found in Gianni Cicali, 'Roles and Acting', *The Cambridge Companion to Eighteenth-Century Opera*, pp. 85–98; on the legacy of commedia dell'arte masks, see esp. pp. 88–90.

[7] William Boyce, Bodleian Library MSS Mus c.3, 'Corydon & Miranda, A Pastoral Interlude' (autograph). The masque is one of several works gathered and bound; it is in fol. 44r to fol. 69v, and is undated. The setting is for two sopranos, a tenor, a 4-part chorus (soprano, alto, tenor, bass), first and second violin, viola, first and second oboes, and basso continuo. The playbook manuscript is Catherine Clive, 'No Title' (The Rehearsal; or, Bays in Petticoats; dated 5 March 1750), The Huntington Library, John Larpent Plays, LA 86. In his cover note to the submission, David Garrick dated the manuscript 'March 5th. 1749/50'. In giving an alternative year, Garrick was referring to old-style dating, according to which the year began on Lady Day (The Feast of the Annunciation), 25 March. Lady Day was the first of four 'quarter days' dividing the year for tax and rent collection, hiring servants, and teaching schools. The Calendar (New Style) Act 1750 was passed to regularize the dating system used in Britain.

woman without stage experience arrives requesting to audition for a part, but her conversation and song expose her vanity and unprofessionalism. Hazard mocks her, and, by singing herself, ridicules the kind of taste this would-be debutante represents.

Act II takes place at Drury Lane. Expecting to watch her rehearsal, Hazard checks with the prompter Richard Cross (who played himself) that everything is ready. She is furious to learn that Clive has sent word that she can't attend. Cross entreats Hazard to put on Clive's shepherdess costume and join Beard and Norris for the rehearsal. She agrees, and goes off to change. Instead of a burletta, they perform Clive's adaptation of Boyce's *Corydon and Miranda*.[8]

In Hazard, essential 'Fine Lady' negatives combine, among which the arrogance and ill-temper so often ascribed to Clive after 1746 dominate. For instance, Hazard dismisses Witling's suggestion that she might be nervous about her stage work's first night, explaining to him that the town 'never hiss any thing ... by a Person of Consequence'.[9] In her immodesty, Hazard assumes that she can co-opt and anglicize an Italian genre: 'I'm about a new Burletto'.[10] In naming burletto, Clive took aim at the visiting artists who had introduced it to London: the troupe of Giovanni Francesco Crosa.

Crosa's brief career in London had begun on 8 November 1748 with Rinaldo di Capua's *La commedia in commedia*, 'a Burletta, or Comic Opera' that was 'the first of this Species of Musick Drama ever exhibited in England'.[11] In the opera season that followed, only Crosa's buffa opera was mounted. Crosa had brought with him prize singers, the castrato Gaetano Guadagni and two of the century's most celebrated buffa artists, Filippo Laschi and Pietro Pertici.[12] But by the time Clive brought out her 1750 *Rehearsal* the Town was wearying of Crosa, whose latest troupe was less starry. In November 1749, a contributor to the *London Evening Post* called Crosa 'Dr. John Francisco Charlatano' and the 'Emperor of the squealing Regions' whose 'theatrical ... Sparrows' command 'little Harmony'.[13] By ridiculing Crosa's burlettos in 1750, Clive endorsed

---

[8] Bartlett with Bruce, *William Boyce*, pp. 72–73; CD sleeve notes by Peter Holman for 'William Boyce: Peleus and Thetis and Other Theatre Music, Opera Restor'd', Hyperion CDA 66935.
[9] Clive, [The Rehearsal], fol. 3v.
[10] *Ibid.*, fol. 4r.
[11] *General Advertiser*, issue 4374 (1 November 1748); cited in Richard G. King and Saskia Willaert, 'Giovanni Francesco Crosa and the First Italian Comic Operas in London, Brussels and Amsterdam', *Journal of the Royal Musical Association*, vol. 118, no. 2 (1993), p. 250. Di Capua's comic opera was one of several favoured in Rome in the 1730s. *La commedia in commedia* is the Italian equivalent of a rehearsal play, burlesquing as it does preparation of an *opera seria*. Warmly received at Rome's Teatro Valle, di Capua's 'Burletto' was repeated in Florence (1741), London (1748), Venice (1749), Munich (1749), and elsewhere.
[12] *Ibid.*, p. 248.
[13] *London Evening Post*, issue 3439 (14–16 November 1749); cited *ibid.*, pp. 257–58.

rather than corrected current Town taste. Extending this joke in her usual way, Clive wove mock Italian song into Hazard's stage speech.

The Rehearsal opens with Hazard's extreme abuse of Nelly the chambermaid, invoking both Nell and the shrewish Lady Lovemore from *The Devil to Pay*. These were now both Clive's roles – the former on stage, the latter in the public's imagination. Hazard insults Nelly ('why you move like a Snail, that has been trod upon; you Creeping Creature; Let me Die but she has provok'd me into a fine Simile'),[14] then, as Nelly waits to help Hazard dress, Hazard 'repeats some of her Recitative' as she writes.[15] When Witling arrives, Nelly asks 'Madam will you please to have your Cap on', at which Hazard explodes, saying 'No you Idiot; how durst you Interrupt me, when you saw me so Engaged' – that is, engaged in singing the lines of her recitative as she hears them mentally, and writing them down.[16] Hazard blames Nelly for having 'ruin'd' one of her 'Finest Conclusions'.[17] After ordering Nelly from her sight, Hazard 'Repeats her Recitative again', then upbraids Nell for not helping her dress.[18]

Witling brings Hazard the latest Town tattle. He says that at Lady Brag's rout the evening before, the assembled 'were all taking off' Hazard's 'new piece'; 'as soon as ever it was mentioned' everyone 'Burst out a laughing ready to kill' themselves.[19] Everyone, that is, except Hazard's fiancé Frank Surly. Surly, reports Witling, on hearing of her writing, has broken off their engagement, declaring that 'there's not ten Women in the Creation that has sence Enough to write a Consistent N.B.'.[20] Unlike Surly, Witling doesn't mind Hazard writing, but only because, as he admits, Hazard has 'Eight Hundred [pounds] a Year' that he's pursuing[21] – a pointed reference, as Felicity Nussbaum notes, to the 1744–45 controversy around Clive's high salary.[22] Hazard is in turn manipulating Witling: as she confides to the audience, she tolerates him only because he is to 'carry a party for' her stage work 'on the first Night'.[23]

Witling presses Hazard to describe the new-fangled genre, Burletto. Being herself unsure, Hazards stands revealed as a Town fashionista who hurries to display an accoutrement she lacks the wit to understand. She ends up guessing that Burletto is a 'poor Relation to an Opera'[24] – another shot at Crosa and his troupe. Next comes a jab at Henry Fielding: Hazard claims that she has drawn

[14] Clive, [The Rehearsal], fol. 1v.
[15] Ibid., fol. 2r.
[16] Ibid.
[17] Ibid.
[18] Ibid.
[19] Ibid., fol. 2v.
[20] Ibid., fol. 3r.
[21] Ibid.
[22] Nussbaum, 'The Actress and Performative Property: Catherine Clive', *Rival Queens*, p. 181.
[23] Clive, [The Rehearsal], fol. 3v.
[24] Ibid., fol. 4r.

on the 'high humour' of his ballad opera *Don Quixote in England*.²⁵ One of Fielding's forgotten works, *Don Quixote* is in fact filled with low humour.²⁶ David Garrick is next: at a loss for vocalists, Hazard laments, 'oh! if that Dear Garrick cou'd but Sing what a Don Quixote he'd make'.²⁷ Hazard also ventriloquizes the common view that the tragedian Spranger Berry had a better build for heroic parts than did the diminutive Garrick, saying: 'Don't you think Barry wou'd be a better, he's so tall you know, and so finely made for 't.'²⁸ Hazard tells Witling about the three singers she has hired, two 'rational' and one 'mad', this last being none other than 'Mrs. Clive':

> I wish she [Clive] don't spoil it; for she's so Conceited and Insolent that she won't let me teach it her. You must know when I told her I'd a part for her ... says she Indeed Madam I must see the whole Piece, for I shall take no Part in a new thing without Chusing that which I think I can Act best. I have been a great Sufferer already by the Managers mistaking my Genious, but I shall convince the Town of their fine Judgment next Year: for I Intend to Play a Capital Tragedy part for my own Benefit.²⁹

Hazard's speech is a neat collation of what Clive was known for: her ownership of favourite parts, her sometimes unhappy self-casting, and her first-actress foibles – arrogance, over-confidence, and self-obsession – on show also in *The Chaplet*, which had opened only weeks earlier.

---

²⁵ *Ibid.*
²⁶ For this comedy, Fielding reworked student juvenilia of 1728. During the 1733–34 actors' revolt, the distressed players of Drury Lane reportedly solicited a new play from Fielding, who presented them with *Don Quixote*, which was put into rehearsal. Clive was not among the cast members. After unexpectedly taking over management, Charles Fleetwood shelved the production. *Don Quixote* and its Drury Lane cast ended up at the New Haymarket Theatre, opening on 5 April 1734. Reception was tepid: it achieved eight performances during its first run, was picked up for the New Haymarket's summer season and a few fringe productions, and then forgotten. The action treats chicanery during a Somerset election and ridicules social types – a squire, a lawyer, a physician – whom Don Quixote and Sancho join at an inn. The last two dramatis personae, borrowed from Cervantes, are 'costumes more than characters'. Lockwood, 'Don Quixote in England. Introduction', *Henry Fielding: Plays Volume III*, pp. 1–29, esp. p. 4. Scholarship on this comedy tends to focus on political subtexts and pass over its misogyny and sexual innuendo. See, for instance, 'Air IX. Lilllibulero', about the inevitability of cuckoldry, 'Like Gold to a Miser, the Wit of a Lass, / More Trouble than Joy to her Husband may bring ... But Wit will conceal it; / And if you don't feel it, / A Horn's but a Pimple scarce seen on your Head.' *Ibid*. pp. 58–59. Or see Fielding's Act II verses to the infamous 'Black Joke': 'Air X. Black Joke. There's not one honest Man in a Score, / Nor Woman true in Twenty-four', *ibid*., pp. 64–65. Such ballads raise the question of why Fielding, writing a farce in protest against election corruption, felt compelled to insult those who had no right to vote.
²⁷ Clive, [The Rehearsal], fol. 4r.
²⁸ *Ibid.*
²⁹ *Ibid.*, fol. 4v.

Witling also informs Hazard that the 'Ill Natur'd' among her acquaintances say that she has plagiarized her wordbook, which is precisely what Clive would later be accused of.[30] 'Why', asks Hazard, 'who's do they say it is pray?'[31] As Hazard justifies writing a Burletta, Clive has a go at tragedy, a genre from which she had generally been barred. At the time Clive wrote *The Rehearsal*, some playgoers were understood to attend tragedy mainly to demonstrate their sensibility, bursting into tears in a display as theatrical as the one on stage.[32] Alluding to this, Hazard explains that: 'My Motive for writing Wittling, was really Compassion: the Town has been so Overwhelmed with Tragedy lately, that their [sic] in one Entire Fit of the Vapours, they think they love it, but its no such thing.'[33] To substantiate her observation, she notes the 'Universal Yawn in the House' she has observed at a recent tragedy.[34] Only a 'great Quantity of Drums and Trumpets', she adds, kept the 'whole Audience' from falling asleep.[35] While this passage clearly promotes her own stagecraft – Clive had routinely joined vocal ensembles for music added to tragedies and to history plays – Clive also anticipates the extremes to which this practice would soon to be taken. Six months later, with Garrick and Rich both mounting nothing but rival productions of *Romeo and Juliet* for twelve nights, each manager added an elaborate funeral procession – music by Boyce for Garrick, by Arne for Rich – to help entice audiences. Boyce's music for Garrick went on to become a stage fixture.[36]

Hazard next takes would-be playhouse singers to task. 'Miss' arrives to audition for a vocal part. She has neither talent nor training, but lots of male sponsorship:

> Miss: So Mame, I have a Desire (not that I have any Occasion) but it's my fancy Mame, to Come and Sing upon the Stage.

---

[30] Ibid.
[31] Ibid.
[32] Ritchie, *Women and Shakespeare in the Eighteenth Century*, pp. 167–74.
[33] Clive, [The Rehearsal], fol. 5r.
[34] Ibid.
[35] '[I]f it had not been for a great Quantity of Drums and Trumpets, that must Judiciously came in that Instant, the whole Audience wou'd have fallen a Sleep'. Ibid.
[36] The defection of Drury Lane's principal tragedians Susannah Cibber and Spranger Berry to Covent Garden in the summer of 1750 sparked the competition that, to the Town's dismay, led to runs of *Romeo and Juliet* at both houses without interruption from 28 September until 12 October. Fiske notes that Boyce's music, with Garrick's words, 'was included in all productions of *Romeo and Juliet* until quite late in the nineteenth century'. Fiske, *English Theatre Music in the Eighteenth Century*, p. 217. Arne's score is compared to that of Boyce in Charles Haywood, 'William Boyce's "Solemn Dirge" in Garrick's *Romeo and Juliet* Production of 1750', *Shakespeare Quarterly*, vol. 11, no. 2 (1960), pp. 173–87. Details about Garrick's production are found in George Winchester Stone, Jr., '*Romeo and Juliet*: The Source of its Modern Stage Career', *Shakespeare Quarterly*, vol. 15, no. 2 (1964), pp. 191–206, and George C. Branam, 'The Genesis of David Garrick's *Romeo and Juliet*', *Shakespeare Quarterly*, vol. 35, no. 2 (1984), pp. 170–79.

Mrs. Hazard: And a very odd fancy I believe it is; well Miss, you say, 'tis your fancy to sing upon the Stage; but pray are you Qualified?
Miss: Oh Yes, Mame I've very good Friends.
Mrs. Hazard: This Girl's a Natural. Yes Miss but I believe a good voice, wou'd be more material to your fancy? I suppose you have a good Voice.
Miss: No Mame I can't say I have much Voice.
Mrs. Hazard: This Girl's delightful.[37]

Merit, Clive's invariable justification for the Town favour she enjoyed, is here the theme: Miss has none. Rather than a 'Voice', she has 'Friends', which in Miss's view is all she needs to procure a part and a career. Hazard then slyly asks Miss if she is 'Mistress', pretending to mean 'Mistress of Music' while implying that a lover-patron lurks in the background. Witling volunteers to fill this role: 'Miss is a very pretty Girl, I wish she'd take a fancy to me.'[38]

As the exchange continues, we discover that Miss cannot even read music, and has no ear. At Witling's request, she agrees to sing an air that she calls 'Pow'erful Guardians of ill Nature'[39] – an exquisitely mistitled reference to Handel's 'Pow'rful Guardians of all Nature' from his oratorio *Alexander Balus* (1748).[40] As Miss sings the air,[41] its words, which are not written out, become satirical in this context: 'Pow'rful Guardians of all Nature, / O preserve my beauteous Love; / Keep from Insult the dear Creature. – / Virtue sure hath Charms to move.'[42] Here Clive impishly borrows from a solemn work to damn Miss and the kind of favour she has garnered: the 'Pow'rful Guardians' are her patrons, and Miss is the 'beauteous Love' they preserve. This scene stages an argument that Clive had been making since 1736: unlike many playhouse sopranos, she had earned her success without recourse to sex, fashion, or patronage.

Clive next attacks Caterina Galli, who had premiered 'Pow'rful Guardians' under Handel's direction. Prints of this air had preserved the memory of Galli's performance, and she had been one of Handel's oratorio company members since.[43] Clive uses Hazard to protest against an Italian soprano being hired to sing English oratorio:

---

[37] Clive, [The Rehearsal], fol. 5v.
[38] Ibid., fols 5v–6r.
[39] Ibid., fol. 6r.
[40] Handel's *Alexander Balus*, HWV 65 opened at Covent Garden on 23 March 1748, receiving two performances. It was not revived again until 1754. The musical number is in Act III, Scene 2.
[41] '(Miss Sings)', Clive, [The Rehearsal], fol. 6r.
[42] [Thomas Morell], *Alexander Balus. An Oratorio.* (London, 1748), p. 19; see also George F. Handel, *Alexander Balus*, ed, F. Chrysander, Georg Friedrich Händels Werke, vol. 33 (Leipzig, 1870), pp. 171–73.
[43] The aria 'Pow'rful Guardians' is printed simply as 'Sung by Sig[ra] Galli' in George Frideric Handel, *Alexander Balus. An Oratorio* (London, [1748]), pp. 79–80. Galli made her name in Handel's Covent Garden oratorio seasons from 1747 to 1754. She appeared first in revivals of the *Occasional Oratorio* and *Joseph*. Winton Dean notes that, according

> Mrs. Hazard: Oh fie! Miss you speak your words as plain as a parish Girl, the Audience will never Endure you, in this kind of Singing if they understand what you say: You must give your words the Italian Accent Child, Come you shall hear me.[44]

Hazard's 'Italian Accent' will have combined Italian-accented English with Clive's own musical elaborations, likely during the melismatic turns sprinkled throughout 'Pow'rful Guardians', with its three-bar sequence on the word 'preserve'.[45] In taking off this music, Clive will have identified Galli as a source both of incomprehensible diction and of the diminutions festooning both Handel's score and Galli's extemporizations. Mocking Galli through song, Clive put her own vocal expertise on display.

In the second act, Hazard goes to Drury Lane and theatre personnel present themselves *in propria persona* – the prompter Cross, and the singers Beard and Norris – ready to rehearse Hazard's burletto. When Hazard orders tickets to Cross's benefit, she asks for 'all your side Boxes, and every first Row in the front; I may want more, but I shall certainly fill them'[46] – a statement about Hazard's many friends that is probably also a joke about Clive's bulk. When Cross informs Hazard that 'Mrs. Clive' cannot attend the rehearsal because she is calling on Town members to sell tickets to her own benefit, Hazard excoriates her in lines preserved uniquely in the 1750 *Rehearsal* playbook manuscript:

> Did you ever hear of a Paralell to this Insolence? ... I'll make Mrs. Clive repent treating me in this manner, if she had had the Modesty, to have sent word she had been Sick, tho I might have distrusted it? yet it wouldn't have been so provoking, but to have the Assurance to prefer her Interest to my Rehearsal; is a piece of Impudence I'll never forgive.[47]

Hazard objects because Mrs. Clive has failed to lie as the occasion demanded. What ends up being critiqued is the hypocrisy of Town manners that Mrs. Clive's candour prevents her from complying with. To allow the rehearsal to proceed, Hazard agrees to play Clive's role and don her shepherdess costume, which becomes the occasion for a last pair of quips about Clive's shortcomings. Witling urges Hazard to 'rehearse her part ... you'll do it better than she can';[48]

---

to Charles Burney, Galli's singing of 'Tis liberty alone' in *Judas Maccabaeus* (first performed 1 April 1747) was not only encored every night, but made her '"an important personage, among singers, for a considerable time afterwards"'. Dean, 'Galli, Caterina', *Handel's Dramatic Oratorios and Masques*, p. 655. A mezzo-soprano, Galli often sang male roles, and Handel's parts for her include Othniel in *Joshua* (1748), the title role of *Alexander Balus* (1748), Joachim in *Susanna* (1749), the title role of *Solomon* (1749), as well as Irene in *Theodora* (1750).

[44] Clive, [The Rehearsal], fol. 6r.
[45] Handel, *Alexander Balus*, p. 171.
[46] Clive, [The Rehearsal], fols 7r–7v.
[47] *Ibid.*, fol. 7v.
[48] *Ibid.*, fol. 8r.

Cross seconds Witling, begging Hazard to put on Clive's costume, since it will fit her 'Exactly as you're much of her Size'.[49] To this Hazard responds 'Yes to be sure it will fit me, because I happen to be a head taller, and I hope something better made, nay I may say Handsomer'.[50] Hazard goes off, and reappears dressed as a shepherdess.

Instead of a rehearsal, and instead of a burlettc, audiences in 1750 next saw an intact performance of Boyce's c.1740 pastoral *Corydon and Miranda*, without a whiff of comedy – at least on the page. Yet, with its action revolving around a jealous rich woman, an inserted final scene by Clive sufficed to turn a recycled Boyce masque into a current story about her. Because Clive chose *Corydon and Miranda* to close her career in serious song, I will treat this masque at some length, referring to both the manuscript score and the playbook manuscript.

The dramatis personae are two shepherdesses, Miranda (Norris) and Marcella (Clive), who compete for the love of Corydon (Beard). Miranda, singing alone in recitative, expresses her determination to win Corydon. She fears, however, that Marcella may prevail due to possessing 'wealth' as 'boundless as her Charms'.[51] Miranda sings an air about her love, a strophic, lightly ornamented gavotte, styled as a 'Scotch' ballad, which represents her simplicity and serenity (Ex. 12.1, 'If Cupid once the mind possess'). Its recurring motif is modally structured (ascent by a major third and major second concluding with two descending major seconds), each line features the middle cadence typical of traditional Scottish ballads, and its verses are in common meter (stanzas of four lines, alternately of four and three iambic feet).[52]

After this air Miranda is joined by Corydon. She tests his love by accusing him, in recitative, of favouring Marcella. Corydon protests: besides being 'capricious', Marcella has, by rebuffing another shepherd, caused his death, and he hates her.[53] Miranda insists that she heard Marcella boast of her power over Corydon.[54] Declaring his fidelity to Miranda and praising her virtues, Corydon sings an extended solo, 'In vain, Miranda, you complain'. This consists of a binary minuet air (AB) and a through-composed air. In the minuet's second section (Ex. 12.2), the drift away from the home key, from A major into B minor, captures the disorientation that Miranda, his 'sweetest Image' (bars 24–26), provokes in Corydon.[55] In the section following, the second stanza is a melting duple-meter air set against throbbing strings that represent the lover's

[49] *Ibid.*
[50] *Ibid.*
[51] *Ibid.*, fol. 9r; Boyce, 'Corydon and Miranda', fol. 44r.
[52] *Ibid.*, fol. 9r; *ibid.*, fols 44v–46r.
[53] *Ibid.*, fols 9r–9v; *ibid.*, fols 46r–47r.
[54] *Ibid.*, fol. 9v; *ibid.*, fol. 47r.
[55] *Ibid.*, fol. 9v; *ibid.*, fols 48r–49r.

Ex. 12.1 Words anonymous, music by William Boyce, 'If Cupid once the mind possess' in 'Corydon & Miranda, A Pastoral Interlude', 1750. Bodleian Libraries MSS Mus c.3, fol. 9r. Edited by Chris Gould.

heartbeat.[56] A violin obbligato weaves delicate patterns around a melody highlighting the verses' iambic meter ('if they can find an Equal fair') as loud and soft dynamics alternate with increasing rapidity.[57]

Unpersuaded, Miranda asks Corydon in recitative to abjure the vain Marcella. To prove himself, Corydon has Miranda secretly watch his interview with Marcella. Marcella approaches, assuring him (in recitative) that 'love is Come in sighs to breath its last'.[58] She follows her recitative with a limpid minuet air. Boyce dots quavers to highlight the pastoral images of 'silver rain' and 'pearly

---

[56] Boyce, 'Corydon and Miranda', fols 49r–51r.
[57] Clive, [The Rehearsal], fol. 9v. In Boyce's manuscript, the words differ from the playbook manuscript: instead of 'If they can find an Equal fair', the line in the Boyce manuscript is 'If you can spy an equal Fair'. The obbligato occurs when this line repeats. Boyce, 'Corydon and Miranda', fols 50r–51r.
[58] Clive, [The Rehearsal], fol. 9v; Boyce, 'Corydon and Miranda', fol. 52r.

Ex. 12.2 Words anonymous, music by William Boyce, 'In vain, Miranda, you complain' in 'Corydon & Miranda, A Pastoral Interlude', 1750. Bodleian Libraries MSS Mus c.3, fols 48r–49r. Edited by Chris Gould.

Ex. 12.3. Words anonymous, music by William Boyce, 'The silver rain, the pearly dew' in 'Corydon & Miranda, A Pastoral Interlude', 1750, Bodleian Libraries MSS Mus c.3, fols 52v–54r. Edited by Chris Gould.

dew' (Ex. 12.3, bars 8–12).[59] He gives Marcella the musical rhetoric to move Corydon, matching sighs, pauses, and repetitions (Ex. 12.4, 'Have pity', bars 30–35) with drooping figures, notated rests, and gestures that repeat when the word does.[60] The air's beauty is beguiling, as Marcella seeks to persuade

---

[59] *Ibid.*, fol. 10r; *ibid.*, fols 52v–54r.
[60] Boyce, 'Corydon and Miranda', fols 55r–56r.

Ex. 12.4 Words anonymous, music by William Boyce, 'The silver rain, the pearly dew' in 'Corydon & Miranda, A Pastoral Interlude', 1750. Bodleian Libraries MSS Mus c.3, fols 52v–54r. Edited by Chris Gould.

Corydon of her sweetness. Corydon rebukes her in recitative for causing the death of his fellow shepherd through her cruelty, and exits angrily.

Alone, Marcella – whose name, derived from Roman god Mars, means 'warlike one' – sings an abbreviated da capo rage aria, 'Rise, tempests, rise, cloud the skies!' At this juncture Clive likely used Boyce's music to mock her own now-legendary temper. The poetry's rhyming couplets and shifting meter flag this number's grandeur. Spondee meter that begins exclamations like 'Down, Down ye tow'rs of State!' (Ex. 12.5) trips up the established metric pattern preceding such exclamations, in this case a couplet in iambic tetrameter.[61] Boyce meticulously captures these shifts by pitting agitated strings, which alternate between tremolo semiquavers and accented quavers, against a vocal line that strides majestically up and down the triad to paint Marcella's words, such as 'Rise Tempest rise', in longer note values.[62]

In this number Boyce blends Italianate instrumental with native song composition, making this rage aria especially felicitous for Clive's self-representation. Apart from placing the melody within a modest range, he preserves word clarity and sense by treating the vocal line as a cantus firmus, a melody against which all other material is organized. He assigns storminess to the instruments, rather than to the voice, which is majestic in its fury. His compositional glue is species counterpoint – he was first and foremost a church musician – cunningly dressed in operatic idioms, which varies texture in an accompaniment derived from the loping melody. From the opening bars of Marcella's aria, soft and loud dynamics alternate, registering the affective extremes of the A section.

In accordance with convention, the middle (B) section of Marcella's da capo aria starkly contrasts the two outer sections. Here she shifts from a frantic duple-meter tempo to a lilting triple pulse (Ex. 12.6).[63] The oboe, which doubles the vocal part throughout, shines out clearly for the first time as the thick string accompaniment recedes. The poetic meter of each couplet calms, settling into a pattern. The scoring, tempo, soft dynamics, and slow harmonic rhythms represent a siciliano mood, but the restless quavers in the strings and the bass line signal Marcella's still-simmering anger. In another melody pitted against the strings, she pleads with nature to protect Corydon rather than destroy him. Clive almost certainly sang the B section of the da capo number straight. Pastoral images, such as 'feather'd Songsters', receive the requisite painting, such as flutters in the strings as the vocal line placidly unfolds with occasional instrumental interjections.[64]

---

[61] Clive, [The Rehearsal], fol. 10v.
[62] Boyce, 'Corydon and Miranda', fols 58r–61r.
[63] *Ibid.*, fols 61v–63v.
[64] *Ibid.*, fol. 63r; Clive, [The Rehearsal], fol. 10v.

Ex. 12.5 Words anonymous, music by William Boyce, 'Rise, tempests, rise, cloud the skies!' in 'Corydon & Miranda, A Pastoral Interlude', 1750.
Bodleian Libraries MSS Mus c.3, fols 58r–61r. Edited by Chris Gould.

With the return to the A section Marcella's rage again shatters the calm, whipping up musical forces in her calls to crush Corydon. The final stanza is truncated: its verse lines are shorter, and reduced from four to two couplets. Metric patterning dissolves in a hail of accented and unaccented syllables: 'No, no let him die … / Rain Vengeance from the sky'.[65] Boyce sets the verses as in the initial A section, but increases the response rate from the strings as they answer Marcella's expostulations with their own. The continuo part, whose relentless quavers have pushed the momentum throughout, now joins with the rest of the band. To conclude, Marcella declares: 'In pangs of passion let him be / In endless pangs, like me!'.[66] After this, scurrying accompaniment comes to a screeching halt, and against this sudden silence Marcella gathers her breath to spit out once more: 'like me!' (Ex. 12.7, bars 35–36). The band re-enters emphatically, leaping down more than an octave as Marcella exits, incandescent. This was a moment in which the legend of Clive's temper could nourish the audacity of her execution.

For the final number, Clive replaced Boyce's original chorus with recitative and a three-stanza duet for the lovers – possibly by Boyce, if advertisements

---

[65] *Ibid.*, fols 63v–64r; *ibid.*, fol. 10v. In the play manuscript, the phrase is 'Rain Vengeance from the Skie'.

[66] *Ibid.*, fols 65r–65v; *ibid.*, fol. 10v.

Ex. 12.6 Words anonymous, music by William Boyce, 'Rise, tempests, rise, cloud the skies!' in 'Corydon & Miranda, A Pastoral Interlude', 1750.
Bodleian Libraries MSS Mus c.3, fols 61v–63v. Edited by Chris Gould.

Ex. 12.7 Words anonymous, music by William Boyce, 'Rise, tempests, rise, cloud the skies!' in 'Corydon & Miranda, A Pastoral Interlude', 1750.
Bodleian Libraries MSS Mus c.3, fols 65r–v. Edited by Chris Gould.

for Clive's 1750 *Rehearsal* are wholly correct.[67] In doing so, she made Boyce's *Corydon* resemble *The Chaplet*, which closes with a lovers' duet after her final aria. In Clive's addition to Boyce's original, Miranda says she feels sorry for Marcella, but Corydon tells her not to, articulating for audiences this pastoral's lesson: 'Injurious Damsels well Deserve her woe.'[68] Instead of rejoicing, as is standard in pastoral masques, in this final duet Corydon and Miranda express their relief at being free of Marcella. Miranda revels in her release from Marcella's 'Subtile Care' which caused her 'Agonies'. Could this be a veiled reference to Clive's recently ended sponsorship of Mary Edwards?[69] Corydon rejoices that they are no longer 'Captive' to the 'Chain' that was Marcella.[70] For both Miranda and Corydon, Marcella stands for 'Pain', whose removal they jointly celebrate in their shared final stanza.[71]

As a platform for Clive's self-representation, Boyce's pastoral could fulfil multiple aims. His score, by virtue of its sensuality and innovative procedures, empowered her to shine as a first soprano. The coincidental fit between Marcella and Clive's own reputation – wealthy, vain, tyrannical, jealous, volatile – allowed Clive to work self-criticism into a display of her singing prowess. The masque's exalted sentiments also invite comic deflation. In her da capo rage aria, Clive may well have pivoted from hilarity in the A section to pastoral delicacy in the B section, and then back again. Such unexpected shifts spoke of Clive's own story ('like me') that she here told in song for one last time.

Clive's *Rehearsal*: Afterlife

Clive's *Rehearsal* has rightly earned her a place in studies of eighteenth-century comedy.[72] Yet its success was very local: of thirteen performances by 1762, all

---

[67] *General Advertiser*, issue 4487 (14 March 1750; the front page is dated 1749–50): 'For the Benefit of Mrs. CLIVE ... HAMLET ... To which will be added a Farce, never acted before, call'd The REHEARSAL; Or, BAYES in PETTICOATS. The Musick composed by Dr. BOYCE. The Principal Parts to be Performed by Mrs. CLIVE, Mr. Woodward, Mr Beard, Mr. Simpson, Mr. Cross, Mrs. Benner, Miss Cole, and Miss Norris.'

[68] Boyce, 'Corydon and Miranda', fols 65r–65v; Clive, [The Rehearsal], fol. 10v.

[69] Clive, [The Rehearsal], fol. 11r.

[70] *Ibid.*

[71] *Ibid.*

[72] Scholarly analyses of Clive's farces began with Crean, 'The Life and Times of Kitty Clive' (1933), and has advanced greatly thanks to the writings of Frushell and Nussbaum, cited above, and to the findings of Matthew Kinservik (see below). Clive's *Rehearsal* is mentioned by Hume and Love, who misrepresent its plot, asserting that her 'very bad pastoral burletta' is, according to Clive's plot, 'actually written by a man'. Hume and Love, ed., *Plays, Poems, and Miscellaneous Writings Associated with George Villiers*, p. 391. Clive's stage output is catalogued in Lorna Sage, Germaine Greer, and Elaine Showalter, ed., *The Cambridge Guide to Women's Writing in English* (Cambridge, 1999), p. 138.

but two were for benefits, and of these, eight were hers or her brother's.[73] *The Rehearsal* playbook, printed in 1753, is also misleading, suggesting as it does a fixed text, but in fact Clive repeatedly revised her *Rehearsal*, changing it in 1751, 1753, and 1762. The most extreme alteration came in 1753, when Clive made Boyce's music ludicrous. She did so almost certainly to fit her *Rehearsal* to her take-down of the tragedy *Zara*, which she led that evening for her mainpiece. Clive played Zara parodically and, by deflating a fictional she-queen, took aim against a live one: Susannah Cibber. As we've seen, in 1736 *Zara* had been Cibber's springboard to success; coached by Aaron Hill, who translated and adapted the tragedy for London audiences, Cibber rose overnight to be London's favourite new tragedienne. Clive seized on *Zara* partly to show that nothing – not even her own masque song, and certainly not *Zara* – escaped her scorching wit.

Already in 1751, Clive had revised *The Rehearsal* to conclude with insults to her surrogate, Hazard. Notices of her benefit on 12 March announced 'Alterations, and an additional Scene.'[74] Although managers sent no altered playbook to the censors, they did submit Clive's 'additional Scene'.[75] As it begins, the stage directions read: '(After Mr. Beard Miss Norris Duet / A Noise without)'.[76] That is, in 1751, Clive seems to have kept the 1750 masque, tacking on after its final duet her 'New Scene'. It ushers in new characters: Miss Giggle, Sir Albany Odelove, Miss Sidell, and Miss Daudle. As the new scene opens, Witling, to be 'Reveng'd' on Hazard, asks Giggle to 'burst into a violent Laugh' in which other company members will join, once Hazard recommences singing.[77] Giggle, however, proposes an alternative: to 'set Odelove upon [Hazard] to

---

[73] Benefit performances in 1750 were for Clive (15 May 1750), Miss Norris (3 April 1750), Clive's brother (26 April 1750), and the dance master Charles Leviez (27 April 1750). Benefit performances of 1751 were for Clive (12 March 1751), Sarah Ward (19 March 1751), and Clive's brother (3 May 1751). Benefit performances of 1753 were for Clive (22 March 1753), Mr. Dexter (3 April 1753), and Clive's brother (4 May 1753). There was one Clive-led performance during the regular season (31 October 1753) and one benefit performance in 1755, for Clive's brother (19 April 1755). During the 1762 benefit season Clive mounted her *Rehearsal* at her benefit of 22 March 1762, which was repeated 'by particular Desire' on 10 May 1762. There was a charity benefit without Clive on 22 (or 21) May 1753.

[74] 'The REHEARSAL; or, BAYS in PETTICOATS. With Alterations, and an additional Scene.' Clive's mainpiece was a revival of George Farquhar's *The Inconstant*. Earliest notice of her benefit appeared apparently in the *General Advertiser*, issue 5087 (15 February 1750).

[75] The insertion carries no date. It is, however, distinct from the original: the copyist's ink and hand are different, the pagination of its four leaves is independent of the 1750 manuscript, and a separate leaf gives the addition's title: 'The New Scene in Mrs. Clive's Farce'. Catherine Clive, 'No Title' [The Rehearsal; or, Bays in Petticoats; dated 5 March 1750], Huntington Library, John Larpent Plays, LA 86. The foliation of LA 86 changes to page numbering from what would be fol. 11v onwards. Consequently, citations below from this work use page numbers.

[76] Clive, [The Rehearsal], LA 86, p. 12.

[77] Ibid.

inquire into the plot of her play – he'll plague her to death, for he's immensely foolish'.[78] The plan works: Odelove's pedantic criticisms, together with Giggle talking just as Hazard begins to sing again, maddens Hazard. Her anger peaks when Odelove insists that Hazard seek advice from a 'Male Aquaintance, who will take some Care of your Diction', to which she retorts, 'Why thou Elaborate Ediat, how durst you venture to talk to any thing that's Rational?'[79] Declaring 'I cou'd tear these—',[80] a version of Clive's last line in *The Chaplet* ('My Rage into pieces could tear them'), Hazard ends the rehearsal.[81]

For two years, *The Rehearsal* lay fallow. Then, for her 1753 benefit, Clive gave what amounted to a meta-production of herself. Notices for this evening carry a blush of parody: 'For the Benefit of Mrs. CLIVE ... The MOURNING BRIDE. Osmyn, Mr. GARRICK; Zara, by Desire, by Mrs. CLIVE.[82] By deliberately miscasting herself in this title role, Clive cheekily kept the promise attributed to 'Mrs. Clive' in *The Rehearsal* to 'play a capital Tragedy Part for my own Benefit'.[83] But why would Clive go to the trouble of actually staging this elaborate joke? In the spring of 1753, Susannah Cibber was poised to return to Drury Lane after a three-year absence. With Cibber at Covent Garden, Clive had started routinely sharing the boards with Garrick, Cibber's favourite counterpart. Clive must have known that comedy's claim over Garrick would, with Cibber's return, yield to tragedy's graver charms. Clive's mock Zara reminded audiences of the Thalian gifts that she possessed and Cibber did not.

To make *The Rehearsal* fit with the evening's high jinx, Clive changed it in five ways: she cut down the masque; reordered its numbers; had Hazard, while singing Marcella, remain in Hazard's dress; had Hazard interrupt Miranda's singing; and almost certainly burlesqued the only air left to her. Together these changes erased the moments in the 1750 version during which London's first songster had resurfaced. *The Rehearsal* of 1753 therefore belongs wholly to Clive's line in self-parody that had begun in 1749 with *Lethe* and continued

---

[78] *Ibid.*

[79] *Ibid.*, p. 14.

[80] *Ibid.*

[81] Clive may have dropped her 'New scene' at her third and last performance in 1751, which was her brother's benefit; notices don't mention this 'Addition'. As usual, Jemmy Raftor shared his benefit with other players; on this evening the benefit was for 'Mr. SIMSON, Mr. RAFTOR, and Miss PITT'. The mainpiece was *Comus*, with Hannah Pritchard as the Lady, Miss Norris as Sabrina, and Beard and Clive in their standard roles. *General Advertiser*, issue 5159 (3 May 1751).

[82] *Public Advertiser*, issue 5740 (22 March 1753): 'For the Benefit of Mrs. CLIVE ... The MOURNING BRIDE. Osmyn, Mr. GARRICK; Zara, by Desire, by Mrs. CLIVE, *Being the First Time of her appearing in that Character* ... To which will be added, (not acted these two Years) a Farce, call'd The REHEARSAL; or, *Bayes in Petticoats*. With ALTERATIONS and an ADDITIONAL SCENE'. The first known notice for her benefit of 12 March 1753 is in the *Public Advertiser*, issue 5722 (1 March 1753).

[83] Clive, *The Rehearsal: Or, Bays in Petticoats. A Comedy in Two Acts ... The Music composed by Dr. Boyce* (1753), p. 15.

with *The Chaplet* (1750) and *The Shepherd's Lottery* (1751). Her 1753 changes to *The Rehearsal* showed Clive judging masque, and herself, as harshly in her afterpiece as she judged tragedy, and Susannah Cibber, in her mainpiece. Clive also treated her audience that evening to payback: just as Cibber had in 1746 briefly, and showily, co-opted Polly Peachum, so Clive in 1753 briefly, and ludicrously, stole Zara.

Clive's 1753 *Rehearsal* is preserved only in the playbook printed that year. The action begins to diverge substantively from her original when Hazard agrees to sing Clive's part. Whereas in 1750 and 1751 Clive had changed into a shepherdess costume, in the 1753 version Hazard decides 'No; hang it, I won't take the Trouble; I'll rehearse as I am.'[84] Dress keeps the foolish Hazard in character. After Miranda begins to sing, Hazard stops her after four lines with the correction '*Recitative* shou'd be spoken as plain as possible; or else you'll lose the Expression. — I'll shew you what I mean.'[85] Hazard's counsel is the opposite of the truth, and Clive will have demonstrated Hazard's ignorance by croaking out a 'spoken' recitative.

The masque seems then to start in earnest, as Miranda sings her air and Corydon responds. But because Clive had scrambled the order of Boyce's numbers, the masque quickly degenerates into a disjointed series of pastoral songs like those at the Ranelagh Garden concerts, which Clive mocks elsewhere in her dialogue.[86] As the pastoral lovers lurch unaccountably from sorrow to joyful duet,[87] Witling falls asleep.[88] Nonsense reigns fully when 'Marcella' (dressed as Hazard) steps in. The air she sings had in 1750 been Clive's first; now out of place, its verses will have allowed Clive to burlesque herself while singing: 'The weeping Rain, and sighing Wind, / All, all, but thee, some Mercy show. / Ah pity — if you scorn t'approve; / Have Pity, if thou hast not Love.'[89] The rehearsal is cut short when the unwanted visitors of the 1751 'New Scene' interrupt Hazard, instead of arriving after the masque is finished.

---

[84] *Ibid.*, p. 25.
[85] *Ibid.*, p. 26.
[86] On her arrival at the playhouse Miss Giggle observes: 'And so this is the Playhouse; I'll swear 'tis immensely pretty, and all the Music; well, if there was but a Scene of green Trees, we might fancy ourselves at Ranelagh, ha, ha, ha.' In the closing scene, as Hazard rants, she cries 'Go to —', to which Witling interjects, 'To Ranelagh—I knew you wou'd not name an ungenteel Place'. *Ibid.*, pp. 35, 40–41.
[87] *Ibid.*, pp. 27–30. The following numbers were cut: 'If Cupid once the Mind possess' (Air 1, Miranda); 'Recitative. / But see he comes …With Transport boast o'er Corydon her power' (Miranda and Corydon); 'In vain, my Fair One, you complain' (Air 2, Corydon); Recitative. / 'Well —wou'd you ease my Breast, and Peace restore, / Oh never see the vain Marcella more' (six other lines excised); 'At length return luxuriant Thought' (Air 5, duet).
[88] *Ibid.*, p. 30.
[89] *Ibid.*, p. 31.

Reviewing her playbook, a contributor to *The Gentleman's Magazine* observed that 'the spirit with which Mrs Clive must enter into a character of her own writing, cannot but render the representation highly entertaining'.[90] But the theatre critic Francis Gentleman objected to Clive's Zara:[91]

> We remember to have seen Mrs. CLIVE make a laughable assault upon Zara, which was nearer burlesque than could well be imagined. Had it not been to excite curiosity upon her night, it would have been one of the most unpardonable attempts that ever was made: exclusive of a voice dreadfully unfit for serious speaking, her person rendered all the King's amorous compliments ludicrous; and justified Osmyn's coldness, admitting he had no other engagement to warp his inclination. It is amazing that a principle of selfishness should cause people of great merit and good circumstances, for the sake of a few pounds, to exhibit themselves in a contemptible point of view.[92]

Gentleman charges Clive not just with greed – she sacrifices art to increase her benefit takings – but with 'selfishness', presumably for imposing on audience taste and travestying Susannah Cibber's most sacrosanct role. Indeed, Clive probably took off the vocal practices that Aaron Hill had drilled into Cibber. When Drury Lane mounted Clive's 1753 *Rehearsal* in October for the only time during a regular season, it was 'hiss'd a little'[93] – most likely by partisans of Cibber, who had just led that night's mainpiece.

Susannah Cibber was not Clive's only target in 1753. Pressing her point about Fielding's *Don Quixote*, Clive has Hazard observe that the Town will 'forgive an Author Stupidity, and overlook his being a Fool; provided he will do them the Favour not to be a Beast', implying that *Don Quixote* failed because of its vulgarity.[94] Swiping at John Rich, Clive has Hazard recoil at Witling's suggestion that she mount her stage work at Covent Garden. 'Lord, I wouldn't think of it,' says Hazard, as 'it stands in such a bad Air'.[95] The word 'air' here

---

[90] 'Register of Books and Pamphlets', *The Gentleman's Magazine and Historical Chronicle*, vol. 23 (March 1753), p. 150; cited in Frushell, 'An Edition of the Afterpieces of Mrs. Clive', p. lxvi.

[91] Gentleman's comments about Clive's Zara were published in 1770, but Gentleman may have written them in 1753 for Samuel Derrick's short-lived 'series' or periodical *The Dramatic Censor; Being Remarks upon the Conduct, Characters and Catastrophe of our most Celebrated Plays*. Only one issue ever appeared. In 1752 Gentleman was to supply the second issue. Notice that Gentleman was supposed in 1752 to contribute to Derrick's series appeared in *The Monthly Review* vol. 6 (March 1752), p. 234. In 1770 Gentleman used the same title as Derrick's series for his book, which begins with Gentleman's essay 'Richard the Third. As altered from Shakespeare by Cibber'.

[92] [Francis Gentleman], *The Dramatic Censor; Or, Critical Companion* (London, 1770), vol. 2, pp. 416–17.

[93] Afterpiece 'hiss'd a little': (MS Diary Richard) Cross, Folger Shakespeare Library. *The London Stage*, Part 4, vol. 1, p. 388 (under the entry for Drury Lane, 31 October 1753).

[94] Clive, *The Rehearsal*, p. 13.

[95] Ibid.

carries also the notion of manner. According to Hazard, Covent Garden is a toxic environment: its bad air keeps actors from playing there 'above three Days a Week' and puts players in 'more need of a Physician, than a Poet'.[96]

Clive had her 1753 *Rehearsal* playbook printed in time for her benefit. In its preface, Clive denies any personal desire to see her work published:

> This little Piece was written above three Years since, and acted for my Benefit. – The last Scene was an Addition the Year after. Whatever Faults are in it, I hope, will be pardoned, when I inform the Public, I had at first no Design of printing it; and do it now at the Request of my Friends, who (as it met with so much Indulgence from the Audience) thought it might give some Pleasure in the reading. – The Songs were written by a Gentleman.[97]

As ever in printed address, Clive denies any 'Design', despite rich evidence to the contrary.

One argument is common to all versions of Clive's *Rehearsal*: that men abuse and silence women. Nussbaum discusses the passages in Clive's *Rehearsal* expressing Clive's grievances.[98] We see men turn women into sexual objects; men use women either for sex or to increase their fortune; men deny that women are capable of intelligence; men bar female players from advancement on merit and promote pretty talentless girls. Garrick summed up Clive's moral in an epilogue that she spoke after *The Rehearsal* in 1751 and 1753:

> But pray, Sirs, why must we not write, nor think?
> Have we not Heads and hands, and Pen and Ink?
> Can you boast more, that are so wondrous wise?
> Have Women then no weapons but their Eyes?
> Were we, like you, to let our Genius loose
> We'd top your wit, and Match you for abuse.[99]

Henry Woodward, then known as Clive's co-principal in *Lethe*, attacked Clive's *Rehearsal* in his own 1751 benefit farce, *A Lick at the Town*.[100] Woodward, who as discussed previously was also the author of the Polly Row lampoon *The*

---

[96] *Ibid.*
[97] Clive, 'Advertisement', *ibid.*, page unnumbered.
[98] Nussbaum, 'The Actress and Performative Property: Catherine Clive', pp. 177–82.
[99] Nussbaum, 'The Actress and Performative Property: Catherine Clive', p. 175. Matthew Kinservik was the first to bring to print Garrick's unpublished 'Epilogue to Bayes in Petticoats' – identified earlier by Mary Knapp – that had been copied into two manuscripts dated 1751 at the Folger Shakespeare Library. Matthew Kinservik, 'Garrick's Unpublished Epilogue for Catherine Clive's "The Rehearsal: or, Bays in Petticoats" (1750)', *Études anglaises*, vol. 49 no. 3 (1996), pp. 320–26. He rightly emphasizes that Garrick's verses for Clive offer 'further satiric commentary on the status of the female playwright in general and of Kitty Clive in particular'. *Ibid.*, p. 321.
[100] Henry Woodward, 'A Lick at the Town' (dated 6 March 1751; first performed 16 March 1751), Huntington Library, John Larpent Plays, LA 92. For the first notice of Woodward's 1750 benefit, see the *General Advertiser,* issue 5107 (4 March 1750).

Beggar's Pantomime: Or, the Contending Colombines, was practised in the art of Clive-bashing. His animus towards Clive would become legendary: on 21 January 1756, playing opposite Woodward in David Garrick's version of *The Taming of the Shrew*, Clive would accuse him of making her fall on purpose;[101] later Thomas Davies would report that Woodward had on that same evening 'stuck a fork … in Mrs. Clive's finger' as well as 'pushing her off the stage' when he threw her down.[102] On 1 November 1756, the prompter Richard Cross recorded that Woodward, as Brisk in William Congreve's *The Double Dealer*, 'instead of observing, with the Author, that her Ladyship's Coachman, John, had a red Face, said *because Yr. Ladyship has a red face* … as Mrs Clive is of that Complexion the Audience burst into a loud roar, to her no small Mortification; but she behav'd well & took no Notice of it.'[103]

Clive, for whom self-abasement had become a marketing strategy, agreed to play herself in *A Lick at the Town*. In its action, *in propria persona* players – Clive, Jemmy Raftor, Sybilla Minors, Ann Pitt, James Taswell, and Ned Shuter – refuse to play the parts written for them by the Author (Woodward). Clive is the last and most loquacious player to appear.

> Clive: And this is the Author of the new Farce … ha! ha! ha! – You may judge of his Works by his Clothes. – take him away, Cross – the Audience have seen enough of him I believe.
> Author: Don't provoke me – don't provoke me, I say –
> Clive: Why you won't be quarrelsome, my Dear?[104]

She calls the Author 'pitiful, beggarly, impudent, ill-looking'; yet she repudiates him for calling 'Names'.[105] She prides herself on keeping her 'Temper', while indulging her rage;[106] his rejoinder, 'Dear, meek Mrs. Clive, proceed' drips with sarcasm.[107]

The Author accuses Clive of hypocrisy: she names him 'the lowest, scribbling Scavenger' for writing farces full of 'dull, gross, personal Abuse', yet she profits precisely from such entertainment: 'if it were not for Personal Abuse as you call it … Writers, Madam, in this Age wou'd have very little to say or do'.[108] 'I am', he tells Clive, 'for no Bridles upon free Britons' – a reference to her Patriot soprano line – instead he champions 'Liberty of Detraction, for

---

[101] 'Mrs Clive fell down in ye Farce, and accus'd Woodward wth doing it on purpose' ([Richard] Cross). *The London Stage*, Part 4, vol. 2, p. 521 (under the entry for Drury Lane, 21 January 1756).
[102] Davies, *Memoirs of the Life of David Garrick, Esq.*, vol. 1, p. 276.
[103] Cross, *The London Stage*, Part 4, vol. 2, p. 562 (under the entry for Drury Lane, 1 November 1756).
[104] Woodward, 'A Lick at the Town', fols 3r–3v.
[105] *Ibid.*, fol. 3v.
[106] *Ibid.*
[107] *Ibid.*
[108] *Ibid.*, fol. 4r.

ever – huzza! –'.[109] Clive is appalled. 'Have you no Regard to the Place you are in, and the Audience you are before?' His flippant response identifies what drives his success, and hers: 'I love Scandal … so if you and the rest will but serve it up, I believe the Town will have no Dislike to the Bill of Fare, nor to my Cookery of it'.[110]

Woodward then indicts Clive not just for writing and bringing out precisely such nonsense, but for judging it excellent:

> Mrs. Clive. I won't speak a Line, Sir, nor ever will of such low contemptible Stuff.
> Author. But yet you play'd in your own Farce, Madam.
> Clive. Flesh and Blood can't bear this – in spite of Nature I must exert myself a little – how dare you have the Impudence, sirrah, to compare your Composition with mine? Is Bays in Petticoats to be soild by your dirty Fingers, or Dirtier Tongue? – I'd have you to know, Wretch, that there is not such a Farce in the Language.
> Author. Nor in any Language, I believe.
> Clive. Nay, since I am provok'd, I'll venture to say & swear the Managers Farces themselves are contemptible to mine – I own, Gentlemen, I am indiscreet to say this – but as my Benefit for this Season is over, I have Time before the next to make it up with the Incomparable Author of those Pieces.
> Author. But how will you make it up with me, Mad^m? For by the sacred pine, Mrs. Clive, if you don't play the Part of Lady Firedrake, in my Piece, which fits you to a Hair, I'll issue forth a sixpenny Squib at you – I'll tear you to Pieces as an Actress – and demolish your Character as a Woman; for I'll not only publish all the Faults you have, but will add ten thousand more to the Catalogue.[111]

Could one express more clearly Clive's experience since 1743 than the closing sentence of this exchange? Woodward identifies not just how Clive lost her legitimacy as songster and actress, but how easily even her new burlesque self could lose Town favour. No wonder she agreed to play in *A Lick at the Town*; owning parody of herself was one of the very few means she had to steer her reception.

Clive mounted her last version of *The Rehearsal*, now lost, for her 1762 benefit, on 22 March. Advertisements suggest that Clive finally featured a 'Burletta' as the play within the play that she staged: 'The REHEARSAL; or, BAYES in PETTICOATS. With Alterations, and an additional Scene. In which will be introduced Part of an Italian Burletta.'[112] This time Clive's satiric butt was probably the singer and impresario Colomba Mattei, whose troupe briefly revitalized Italian burletta in London from 1760 to 1763.[113] From 27 February

---

[109] *Ibid.*
[110] *Ibid.*
[111] *Ibid.* fol. 4r.–fol.4v.
[112] The first known notice is in the *Public Advertiser*, issue 8524 (27 February 1762).
[113] Saskia Willaert, 'Colomba Mattei manages the King's Theatre, Autumn 1760–Summer 1763', 'Italian comic opera in London, 1760–1770' (PhD diss., King's College London,

until 20 March, ten notices of Clive's latest *Rehearsal* with 'an Italian Burletta' appeared, about one every two days. Clive repeated her 1762 *Rehearsal* on 10 May. It was the afterpiece to the late-season non-benefit revival of the 1716 comedy *Woman is a Riddle* 'To which (by particular Desire)' was 'added for that Night only' Clive's 1762 *Rehearsal* with its 'Italian Burletta'.[114]

Outside *The Rehearsal*, Clive's other farces typically met with the derision from critics that Hazard experiences. Of *Every Woman in her Humour*, written for her 1761 benefit, David Erskine Baker wrote decades later: 'This little piece has never yet appeared in print, but was performed … for Mrs. Clive's benefit, who it is therefore not improbable may be the author of it, as that lady had once before declaredly dipped her fingers in ink. (See *The Rehearsal, or Bayes in Petticoats*). There is no extraordinary merit, however, in any part of it, excepting in the character of an old maiden aunt, which Mrs. Clive performed herself.'[115] Later Baker added to his passage 'Mr. Wilkinson says this farce was d[amne]d.'[116]

Tate Wilkinson was wrong about this, and more complimentary about Clive's writing than Baker lets on. Baker's quote is from Wilkinson's story of 1790 about the premiere in 1760 of Clive's *Every Woman in her Humour*.[117] According to Wilkinson, while getting up productions in Portsmouth in March of that year, he convinced the actor Joseph Austin to stay in Portsmouth rather than return to London, where he was supposed to perform on 'Wednesday night, March 25, a new part wrote by Mrs. Clive for her own benefit; who at writing was … *a dead good one*'.[118] By Wilkinson's telling, Austin's absence led to the audience 'damning' Clive's farce. In fact, Clive's benefit was on 20 March; Austin was given out in the bills; and two days later a report ran that 'Every

---

1999), pp. 21–118. Willaert observes that Mattei's over-reliance on opera buffa and neglect of serious opera brought her financial problems, which then forced her to quit England. Mattei's achievements were, however, considerable: she introduced Goldoni's repertory to London, brought over leading singers, reinstated the post of house opera composer, and brought out strikingly original programmes that for the first time mixed serious with comic opera. Above all, Mattei was an efficient manager, raising subsidies from a board of directors and, unusually, balancing the house books.

[114] *Public Advertiser*, issue 8579 (3 May 1762). *Woman is a Riddle* is Christopher Bullock's adaptation of Calderón's *La dama duende* (*The Phantom Lady*); it 'enjoyed numerous runs' from its opening in 1716 until 1788. Bullock's adaptation was significantly altered in 1776, and mined before and after this date for slighter productions. 'Introduction: The Comedia in English', *The Comedia in English: Translation and Performance*, ed. S. Paun de García and D. R. Larson (Woodbridge and Rochester, 2008), p. 15.

[115] David E. Baker, *Biographia Dramatica, or, a Companion to the Playhouse* (London, 1782), vol. 2, p. 110.

[116] David E. Baker, *Biographia Dramatica: Or, a Companion to the Playhouse* (London, 1812), vol. 2, p. 206; cited in Frushell, 'An Edition of the Afterpieces of Mrs. Clive', p. lxviii.

[117] Catherine Clive, 'Every Woman in Her Humour' (undated; first performed 20 March 1760), Huntington Library, John Larpent Plays, LA 174.

[118] Wilkinson, *Memoirs* (1790), vol. 3, pp. 39–40.

Woman in her Humour, was performed on Thursday Night for Mrs. Clive's Benefit, to the most brilliant and crowded Audience that was ever seen there: and notwithstanding the Disadvantage of a crowded Stage, the new Piece was received with universal Approbation'.[119]

In 1763 another critic met Clive's *The Sketch of a Fine Lady's Return from a Rout*,[120] written for her benefit of 21 March, with a disdain akin to Baker's:

> This piece is said to be written by Mrs. Clive herself, with what degree of truth we know not; but, however, our regard to justice, and the favour of our readers, will not suffer us to sacrifice our judgment to our politeness, in recommending, or even passing uncommented, a performance we cannot approve, because it is the production of a Lady ... The Fable of this little piece, if tolerably handled, might afford no small entertainment [but] ... Lady Jenkins's reformation so suddenly, is monstrous and absurd; and Sir Jeremy's hasty forgiveness, no less injudicious.[121]

Note that the author of this passage maligns Clive just as Clive's *Rehearsal* characters malign Hazard: her authorship is first doubted, then slighted, as 'the production of a Lady', and the stage action is judged absurd and injudicious. When it came to anticipating her critics, Clive knew what she was about.

Clive's *Rehearsal* stands apart from her other farces. It alone was greeted warmly by players, audiences, and critics alike. It is also the only farce that captures Clive's shift, and her agency in effecting it, from serious first songster to burlesque comedienne and occasional singer. The various versions of Clive's *Rehearsal* register her history, ambition, searing wit, practice-driven writing, and above all business acumen. Only by appreciating Boyce's masque music can we grasp the vocal artistry that Clive integrated in her original *Rehearsal*. Only by recognizing the ways Clive nested herself within the character of Marcella can we hear Clive's farewell to serious vocal music and her embrace of self-parody. She bid adieu not just to a repertory, but to the moments when she could fascinate audiences while performing it. How many stars, once so revered, have had the courage to turn themselves into a joke?

Clive's break with her past attests to her commitment to, and financial dependence on, her profession: she knew the sacrifices required, and made them with flair. No writer is more cutting, witty, insightful, and just plain funny about herself, and about the monstrous prejudices she faced, than Clive. Her story continues after 1750, the career juncture where this book breaks off, and richly merits study. Clive was one of the century's great comic improvisors, constantly reinventing both herself and London's favourite characters.

---

[119] *Public Advertiser*, issue 7918 (22 March 1760).
[120] Catherine Clive, 'The Sketch of a Fine Lady's Return from a Rout' (dated 12 March 1763; first performed 21 March 1763), Huntington Library, John Larpent Plays, LA 220.
[121] *The Theatrical Review; Or, Annals of the Drama. Volume the First* (London, 1763), p. 145 (collected issues of semi-annual series, 1 January–1 June 1763).

Audiences couldn't stay away. In *The Rehearsal* Clive transcribed some of her stagecraft onto pages that, except in the very changed 1753 version, she never had printed. She went on to write other works that she alone could bring off. Reserved for benefits at which she led the afterpiece, Clive's live farces were isolated moments when, among well-wishers, the assembled players adopted her voice and she could make her audiences listen.

13

Conclusion: The Fair Songster

Who was Kitty Clive? Her very name suggests her elusiveness: was she baptized Ellenor, as Patrick J. Crean suggests, or Catherine? The former smacks of Ireland, the latter of England. Was she really 'Mrs. Clive'? Her marriage appears to have been a fiction. And then there's the propriety linked to the name 'Clive': was she a paragon of rectitude, as even her detractors long claimed, or was she a Sapphic lover, winking her same-sex loyalties even as she staged sneering mockery of the homosocial man? Clive's story confounds smooth telling.

Archival data apart, what is left to us of Clive are reports and representations. These clash constantly, because Clive was a celebrity of the first order. The business of stars is to create, destroy, elude, and constantly change what audiences think they know about them. Clive commanded these arts in the playhouse, where performer met audience nightly. Physically close, the playhouse star moved between familiarity and mystery: adopting a new dramatis persona on stage, acting and singing in a way that was familiar yet different, pointing up this familiarity and difference, and disappearing once the work ended. A Clive or a Garrick shape-shifted with great ease while being instantly recognizable, embodying a selfhood whose parameters were always fluid.

Voice was Clive's means to convey herself, first in music, then in stage speech, and ultimately in writing. Music schooled her in control – mental, physical, and emotional – and success showed her what audiences wanted. She was cherished for being original, yet her audiences admired not what she bared, but what she showed herself capable of hiding, and how. For Clive, as for many of her contemporaries, voice was a primary means of both concealment and confession. She keyed hers to social advancement, but possessed a unique sound, a distinct vocal grain with which audience identified her, regardless what character she played. In its poise, her voice dazzled, but left her open to charges of hypocrisy. In its boldness, her voice hooked listeners, but left her open to charges of impudence. When mimicking reigning Italian sopranos, she slipped between compliance with Town fashion and defiance of it, creating her own brand of vocal music. As she toggled between seeming polite and seeming frank, she sometimes succeeded in drowning out, to audience applause, the author's voice with her own.

This straddling of registers had been far beyond the capacities of the first ballad opera star, Lavinia Fenton. After witnessing the defamation of Fenton, and having other strengths at her disposal, Clive created alternatives. Clive appealed to intelligence rather than eroticism, deploying wit, spontaneity, native works, and vilification of the Other to her advantage. As Procris or Rosamond, her lamentations were heavenly; as Lucy or Euphrosyne, her song was wickedly funny; copying Italian sopranos, she was coruscating. In music and words, she made English works admirable. Yet she infused the production of even the greatest artists – Handel, Milton, Shakespeare – with her selfhood, shrugging off their greatness. Seizing comedy's prerogatives, she invited audience members to join in her fun and pretend, for a few hours at least, that liberty was real. Audiences watched her not only cut Worthies down to size while celebrating them, but also lend dignity to Henry Carey's lyrical sopranos – and to low stage characters, from Colley Cibber's anodyne rustics to Fielding's women of doubtful virtue. Regardless of provenance, her parts became means for self-projection. Phillida, Procris, Nell, Euphrosyne, Ophelia, Portia, the Jew-hating Harlot, the smart Chambermaid, the unruly Daughter, the Fine Lady: all contained aspects of the Clive that she variously assembled and challenged in each performance.

Her roles were overwhelmingly recuperative: the fools she bested, the authorities she defied, and the suitors she rejected re-asserted proper order in scenes in which she was strapped, silenced, and married off. Just as recuperative was her popular song, which bound her to conventions deemed native, and which constrained even the best composers – Carey, Arne, and Boyce – who wrote this music. Her serious song, by contrast, represented ideals of diction, gentility, pastoral charm, and subtle control whose attractions largely escape us today. Only in her mimic song, likewise lost in its dazzling waggishness, was she cut loose.

However transgressive she was on stage, Clive sought to project the greatest propriety off it. Seeming chaste and polite, she gave out that she knew her place; if she fought, it was only the better to serve her public and defend her rights, as befits a Briton. Disclosure of Clive's high earnings eventually meshed with media reports of her backstage temper and her visible weight gain to generate a much less favourable public image. Was Clive the Green Room scold – vain, arrogant, ambitious, jealous, controlling, excessive, demanding – that she was charged with being as early as 1733? Or was she the subtle first songster-comedienne of good judgment? She was clearly both, and more besides. From 1746, popular prejudice against a fleshy, ageing, rich woman with attitude took over. We see this bias today: the ire provoked when a woman's aptitudes are superior, the anxiety when a woman holds power, the shudder at the de-sexed older female body. Clive's very success energized the smashing of old views about her, and the cannibalism of the celebrity industry did the rest.

But Clive came back – as fallen stars very rarely do. Having mastered mimicry, making fun of the person she was held to be presented no technical problems, and live performance enabled her to persuade audiences that she thought them right. She was their servant; she submitted to and enacted their views, and they relished the gusto of her self-caricature. Enthusiasm was huge: Clive wasn't lost, she had merely changed to become what they wanted. Previously enigmatic, she had become knowable. Mrs. Riot became a collectible, not just as picture or figurine, but through the power of consumer choice to belittle. Clive put-downs were traded, deprecating anecdotes about her were passed down, and critics identified her defining negative characteristics; all of this tended to undermine the dignity and musicianship she had once possessed. Yet she had the last laugh, retiring at the age of fifty-eight to Horace Walpole's estate with enough money to socialize freely with Walpole's circle, and to support her own household.

Perhaps the main lesson of Clive's story is the extent to which sound could prevail over sight. Historians typically deal with residues of material culture; they tend especially to focus on the 'page', against which I have throughout this book attempted to argue the view from the 'stage'. The page was not the business of the playhouse, where productions were brought into being by their performers, who thereby acquired great agency over texts that were only partially fixed. To understand the genesis, fortunes, and significance of eighteenth-century stage works, we need to consider the ways in which players shaped their material. Sound was critical: it fuelled effervescence, and ignited the playgoer's imagination. Music, implicit declamation, and the cross-breeding of music with stage speech cling to the page still, inviting us to listen.

Of relevant contexts, the most important was the playhouse, where authors and managers, cabals and censors, aesthetes and publishers were in competition with players for control over what was heard. What stage work resulted from this tumult, and what audiences thought the stage work was 'about', is irreducible to a single author's intent, to the impact of one player, to a stylistic development on its own, or to any solitary aim political or commercial. Clive's story is also about the messiness of her workplace, where networks – of ethnicity or family, patrons or clients, critics or university affiliates – could decide what reached or got yanked off the boards. Finally, Clive's is a story about bias against the professional woman, the woman who performed, the woman who made good money. Understanding the obstacles she faced heightens our appreciation of her achievement, in particular the skill with which she negotiated with managers, and makes her mid-career crisis more readily comprehensible.

Catherine Clive was the first player to make song foundational to her stardom; others, starting with John Beard, would follow. In her case, stage masque powered her success in high-style repertory, first in staples like *Perseus and Andromeda*, then in vehicles like Carey's *Cephalus and Procris*, *The Fall of Phaeton*, and, most spectacularly, *Comus*. Clive stamped all three vehicles with her personal arts: her Purcellian repertory informed Carey's compositions, and *The Fall of Phaeton* and *Comus* welded Clive's impishness to her line in *galant* airs, thereby altering the masque's generic parameters. That Clive was groomed to be a first songster was due in part to John Gay's *The Beggar's Opera*. Of the several reactions this work unleashed, three especially affected Clive: public enthusiasm for singing that seemed natural, the publicity storm around Lavinia Fenton, and Colley Cibber's drive to expunge irony from ballad opera. Carey suddenly found his airs, and his pupil Clive, in demand. Able to sing ballads as persuasively as serious song, she could in her person resolve the conflict between low and high taste ignited by *The Beggar's Opera*. This took time: Cibber's first attempt to replace Gay's bottom-up taste-brokering with his own top-down version failed spectacularly. Cibber's *Love in a Riddle* (with Carey's airs) was as feeble as his untrained voice. It was Clive's singing that kept this production from being hooted off on its first night, and thereafter she helped sustain Cibber's push into the ballad opera market.

From Clive's perspective, Colley Cibber was a poor manager. Carey's *Damon and Phillida* and *Contrivances* were successful Clive vehicles that Cibber kept her from owning. The ballad opera parts he handed her were usually insipid. The Drury Lane summer company gave her relief, but only temporarily. Theophilus Cibber, while more flexible than his father, followed his own whims. Her defence was her stagecraft and her song, in which she could turn her part 'contrary to the Intention of the Author'.[1] The audience's focus on points, rather than the action as a whole, aided her in this. In August 1731 she transformed *The Devil to Pay*'s drab domestic-abuse victim Nell into a sentimental heroine. She was helped by the Irish playwright Charles Coffey, who almost certainly chose her tunes, and wrote verses co-extensive with her line elsewhere. As the sprightly Nell, Clive catapulted to fame. The mainpiece was changed to showcase her, and adorned with a climactic Handelian lovers' duet that paired Clive with her new singing partner, the Irish tenor Charles Stoppelaer. But her triumph meant that she lost a friend and ally at Drury Lane: Carey was sidelined, and Henry Fielding became Drury Lane's favoured writer of Clive vehicles.

The pairing with Stoppelaer, and Carey's retreat, highlight two practices that merit further study: star partnerships and vehicle-writing. Once Clive was renowned, managers repeatedly cast her opposite either a principal singer (Stoppelaer, then John Beard) or a principal actor (Theophilus Cibber, Hannah Pritchard, Charles Macklin, Henry Woodward). After James Miller first partnered Clive with Theophilus Cibber in *The Humours of Oxford* (1730), Fielding fit scenes to this comic duo, as did Miller in his later vehicles. Was this a general practice in casting? And if so, did stars then collaboratively produce each other? Clive's continued success despite Carey's exit forces us also to ask who really wrote her vehicles. Clearly she did to some extent, by what she

---

[1] Victor, *The History of the Theatres of London*, vol. 3, p. 145, cited at the start of Chapter 1.

CONCLUSION 413

did on stage. We can recognize Clive's hand in cousined roles such as Phillida and Pastora, in genres rejigged for her hybrid skills (in ballad-pantomime, serio-comic masque), and in the airs of *Cephalus and Procris, Comus, Samson, Joseph,* and her Shakespearean scenes.

And what of Fielding? Nowhere did Clive clash more strongly with authorial intent than in his works. We might picture his output for her on a sliding scale of the compromise required from him: from ignoring how audiences wished to see her, to pandering to it. His first vehicle, *The Lottery*, perked up her sagging line in Colley Cibber-style rustic heroines. But already here, as in the future, Fielding gave Clive the commonest tunes with the smuttiest associations. Writing for the Drury Lane summer company, Fielding indulged its manager, and his own obsession with sex.[2] For her straight comedy debut, Clive got a louche miss (in *The Old Debauchees*) as her mainpiece part, and a whore (in *The Covent Garden Tragedy*) as her afterpiece part; she also got an epilogue – the first of her career – that smacked of both characters. When critics recoiled, Fielding redeployed Clive's Nell in his *Mock Doctor*. He adapted the same Molière work, with wife-beating scenes, that she'd led weeks earlier as a ballad opera; within this, he crafted a part for manager Theophilus Cibber to play Clive's abuser. Happily, *The Mock Doctor* gave Clive the chance to blaze forth in French comedy; playwrights, even Fielding when it suited his aims, then fell into line.

Stage politics also shaped Clive's career. The 1733–34 actors' revolt pushed Clive and Fielding to make common cause. Trying to fill a house without a regular company, Fielding promoted Clive in parts, epilogues, and playbook introductions, and above all in his 'Epistle to Mrs. CLIVE'. Some have read this as evidence of Fielding's friendship towards Clive.[3] But even as Fielding praised her, he wrongly took credit for her success. His common tunes for her remained tawdry. Once running his own company, he disparaged her singing, reputation, and stage hits in his farce *Tumble-down Dick*. His parts for Clive in his later would-be vehicles reverted to insulting stereotypes – the gin-swilling *Eurydice*, the 'unscrupulous' *Miss Lucy in Town*, and the bawd in *The Wedding*

---

[2] See Chapter 4, pp. 159–61.
[3] 'Fielding's dedicatory "Epistle to Mrs. Clive" ... was so effusive it inspired one of the Grublings to compose what even Russel considered "a very vulgar Epigram," too naughty to publish. But we need not suppose that Fielding's fondness for this delightful actress, whose singing voice pleased even Handel, was at all improper. He admired her both as a person and as a performer.' Battestin, with Ruthe R. Battestin, *Henry Fielding: A Life*, p. 170. Rightly attributing to Clive the success of *The Intriguing Chambermaid*, in whose playbook Fielding had his 'Epistle' printed, Lockwood writes: 'Fielding himself would obviously not have begrudged her' this triumph. Lockwood, 'Introduction. The Intriguing Chambermaid', *Henry Fielding: Plays Volume II*, p. 570. See also Jane Spencer, 'Fielding and Female Authority', *The Cambridge Companion to Henry Fielding*, ed. C. Rawson (Cambridge, 2007), p. 126: 'Fielding's theatrical career was marked by a strong association with one actress in particular, Catherine Clive, née Raftor.'

Day – like those he had first imposed on her.[4] Fielding affirmed press reports of her arrogance during the 1743–44 actors' rebellion, and sided with Susannah Cibber during her provocation of Clive in 1746. Fielding may in passing have praised Clive in his novels,[5] but in his version of Juvenal's satires he wrote: 'Others, I say, themselves turn Players, / With Clive and Woffington's gay Airs; / Paint their fair Faces out like Witches, / And cram their Thighs into Fle[et] w[oo]d's Breeches'.[6] Is such commentary a mark of friendship?

While Fielding's importance to the stage waned after 1736, Clive's grew. The 1736 Polly Row registered not just her first rank, but Theophilus Cibber's decline, which modern scholars tend to pass over. Cibber started undermining Fleetwood soon after his return in March 1734; in response, Fleetwood quietly passed Cibber's duties to Charles Macklin, and to James Quin. Witnessing Cibber's missteps probably emboldened Clive. That Clive won the Polly Row was a *coup de théâtre* – meta-theatre, really, that combined live and press self-presentation. We can no more trust Clive's account of events – and in important respects she is the least trustworthy witness – than we can the accounts of her critics. What we can trust is that the campaign on her behalf was disciplined and at least co-led by her. Strengthening her hand were trade practices that the Polly Row laid bare: the distinction between principals who could choose parts and other players who could not, and principals' ownership of, and right to bequeath, their parts.

Another campaign of the 1730s, this one against James Miller, undercut Clive's progress. *The Humours of Oxford* (1730) was both Miller's breakthrough and his death warrant as a playwright. A professional translator, Miller mined for his Clive vehicles the kind of high-quality French comedy to which Fielding turned only when desperate. In contrast to Fielding, Miller forged bold yet polite characters in speech and song for Clive. Miller's afterpieces matched his

---

[4] 'Harold Pagliaro, adding up the marks of Lucy's character ("unselfconsciously desirous, unscrupulous, acquisitive and ambitious"), says that "Fielding pushes her self-indulgence to the limit".' Lockwood, 'Introduction. Miss Lucy in Town', *Henry Fielding: Plays Volume III*, p. 469. Lockwood cites Harold Pagliaro, *Henry Fielding* (New York, 1998), p. 101.

[5] For instance: 'Such indeed was her Image, that neither could Shakespeare describe, nor Hogarth paint, nor Clive act a Fury in higher Perfection.' Martin C. Battestin, ed., *Henry Fielding: Amelia* (Oxford, 1983), p. 43. Fielding also mentioned Clive in his first chapter of, and praised her in a footnote to, *Tom Jones*. Fredson Bowers and Martin C. Battestin, ed., *Henry Fielding, The History of Tom Jones, a Foundling*, p. 493. Battestin interprets Fielding's comment in *Amelia* as personal opinion: 'To the end of his life Fielding would praise "Kitty" Clive.' Battestin, with Ruthe R. Battestin, *Henry Fielding: a Life*, p. 170.

[6] Henry Fielding, *Miscellanies*, vol. 1, p. 85; repr. in Henry Knight Miller, ed., *Miscellanies. By Henry Fielding, Esq. Volume One* (Oxford, 1972), p. 93. Felicity Nussbaum believes the popularity of Fielding's translation was due to the piquancy of his topical references, and to the deftness with which he packaged negative stereotypes of public women. Felicity Nussbaum, *The Brink of all we Hate: English Satires on Women, 1660–1750* (Lexington, KY, 1984), pp. 85–87.

mainpieces in their ebullience; his spoken and sung parts were equally sophisticated; his experiments in epilogue-writing capitalized on Clive's facility to engage audiences. Eager to make best use of Miller's evident talent, deputy manager Theophilus Cibber tried without success to anonymize his playwriting. The determination of Miller's enemies to ruin him won out.

Miller was a target of a decade-long cabal, the evidence leaving little doubt that he fell victim to a network forged in hidden sexual politics. In like manner, Clive's choices, songs, and roles hint at necessarily muted London communities of same-sex lovers, especially among the elite. Her (probably) fake union to an (almost certainly) homosexual man, and her protection of a protégée who was (possibly) her lover – these were the feints of the privileged. Clive tapped into hostility towards what we today call homosexuality to sell herself, making the homophobic 'Life of a Beau' by Carey her signature song. Other networks – Clive's Irish peers, the Cibber-Arne clan – clearly both aided and blocked her progress. Chetwood's bias in Clive's favour, Thomas Arne's reservation in *Comus* of complex song for his wife, Macklin's handover to Clive of Oldfield's parts and his self-casting opposite her – all these suggest that families and peer groups were formative for the creation, production, and reception of stage works and player personae. Identifying and analyzing networks in Georgian London's entertainment industry might clarify many otherwise inexplicable developments beyond those relating to Clive.

Like the communities that helped or hindered her, Clive's agency in her self-production is largely undocumented. Aware of biases against public women, she covered her tracks, strategically concealing her power and how she obtained it. Benefit nights were an accepted means to stage one's selfhood, and Clive was a heavy user. Particularly before her star power enabled her contribution to press wars, she and the luckless Carey depended on benefits; even after the 1737 Licensing Act fixed the duopoly of patent playhouses, benefits at Prince Frederick's command could make Covent Garden manager John Rich think twice about messing her around. Patrons still had a role in playhouse politics. Through benefits – hers and those of her dependents – Clive reminded audiences of parts she owned, grabbed at the parts she wanted to own, promoted her protégées, staged her philanthropy, and introduced herself as a playwright. On such evenings she sometimes harnessed music to her cause, interpolating song, or showcasing herself as a high-style songster, for instance in Willem De Fesch's works.

As a comedienne, Clive was expected to question authority, and once the 1737 Licencing Act closed fringe theatres, her anti-establishment swagger became a selling point. Her parallel lines in serious and comic song intersected, to electrifying effect, in Milton's *Comus*, a work which exemplifies the promiscuity of eighteenth-century London stage entertainments. Into *Comus* flowed idolatry of Milton as both an artistic giant and nascent national hero, Milton's conscription to the Opposition cause through John Dalton's deft additions, and wordbook packaging that invoked Frederick, Prince of Wales as Opposition figurehead. All this politicking accompanied a plot about the defence of female chastity, and dollops of celebrity-mongering: the paired tragediennes James Quin and Susannah Cibber, the Beard-Clive singing dyad as Comus's followers, and Cecilia Arne displaying her husband's art. Then Clive, as Euphrosyne, stepped out with a string of song numbers that were all about herself, culminating in her show-stealing miming of the pastoral lamentations of Cecilia Arne.

Modern scholars tend to read a Georgian stage work to find one theme – Opposition politics, for instance – or to pick up a thread from the playwright's career, while passing over other referents. But eighteenth-century stage works aggregate multiple messages, and the disposition of referents, especially those about a production's star, depends on historical circumstances. For instance, after 1743, as braying nationalism replaced sly anti-Walpole entertainment, the utility and hence foregrounding of Clive's onstage Patriot feints diminished. And across her repertory, getting fatter, older, and richer were losing her public favour. After 1743 audiences wanted to believe the worst of her. As a star she had long been subject to 'peeps', starting with Edward Phillips' sketch of her as 'Miss Prudely Crotchet' in *The Stage Mutiny* (1733). By 1746, readers of broadsides were invited to laugh at the harridan of *The Green Room Scuffle*. Such seeming testimony tells us little about Clive, but much about fandom's cycle of worship, desire, resentment, putative revelation, and they-had-it-coming punishment – the last being often especially strong for the female star. Recognizing where she stood in this cycle, from 1747 Clive seized control of caricaturing herself. Clive then rose, phoenix-like, from the ashes of her reputation to reign for another twenty years, retiring only in 1769.

Clive's vocalism was the engine of her success. Even after 1750, she still used music, and a voice bred to sing, to woo audiences. To revisit Aaron Hill's 1735 encomium to Clive and her voice, quoted already in Chapter 6:

> The Stage's Acknowledgment.
> O NATURE! —where *thy* Sovereign POWER we see,
> How *poor* a *Thing* must AFFECTATION be! —
> While CLIVE, with beauteous *Ease*, the Audience *charms*,
> And, with the Fire of *native* Influence, *warms*;
> Pour'd from her Eyes, the meaning *Raptures* roll:
> And shoot the *laughing* GRACES through the *Soul*.
> Or, when the sprightly *Song* demands her *Aid*,
> How *pointed* are thy *Notes*, O MUSICK! made!
> Poets, and Masters, *careless*, may *compound*;
> Her Look is MEASURE: and Her Action, SOUND.[7]

---

[7] [Aaron Hill], 'The Stage's Acknowledgment', *The Prompter*, no. 99 (21 October 1735); repr. in the *London Magazine, or, Gentleman's Monthly Intelligencer* (1732–35), vol. 4 (October 1735), p. 566.

Fig. 13.1 Alexander van Aken after Joseph van Aken, *The FAIR SONGSTER* [original 1735], 1763–67. Mezzotint. © Trustees of the British Museum. Museum number: K,58.180.

Fig. 13.2 Robert Sayer, after Johann Ludwig Fäsch (?),
Mrs. CLIVE in the Character of Mrs. Heidelberg [in *The Clandestine Marriage*],
1769. Coloured engraving.
© Victoria and Albert Museum, London. Museum number: S.440-1997.

Hill turns the noun 'sound', representing Clive's voice, into an adjective. Adjectivally, 'sound' means true, correct, solid, honest, sincere, well-judged, wholesome. The double meaning here is that when Clive was on stage the sound of her voice proved the soundness of her performance.

Also in 1735, Alexander van Aken printed Clive's portrait along with rhapsodic verses about her singing – but the portrait bore no name (Fig. 6.6 in Chapter 6). The verses were printed immediately below Clive's picture, with no space left, so that when a title was later added (Fig. 13.1), it had to be squeezed into the margins to the left ('The FAIR') and right ('SONGSTER') of the verses. The seller is identified below the verses: 'Printed for C. Bowles in St Pauls Church Yard'. 'C. Bowles' was Carington Bowles, who in 1763 took over the

Fig. 13.3 Johann Ludwig Fäsch, *Mrs. CLIVE in the Character of Lady FUZ in a Peep behind Curtain*, c.1767. Print study.
© Trustees of the British Museum. Museum number: 1931,0509.252.

business of Thomas Bowles II, his uncle, who had issued the 1735 original.[8] In the 'Fair Songster' print, Carington Bowles does not give out his shop's street number; he would only after 1767.[9] We can therefore date this print's reissue to between 1763 and 1767.

---

[8] 'Thomas [ii] Bowles retired from business in 1763 ... He was succeeded in the shop (now numbered 69 St Paul's Churchyard) by his nephew Carington.' Timothy Clayton, 'Bowles family (per. c.1690–c.1830)', *Oxford Dictionary of National Biography*, Oxford University Press, 2004; *ODNB* online: accessed 4 August 2017. The mezzotint with verses only (Fig. 6.6) was 'Printed for T[homas] Bowles [the second] in St Pauls Church Yard'.

[9] From the seven catalogues that the Bowles' print shops issued from 1728 to 1785, a street number is first given out in *A Catalogue, for the Year M DCC LXVIII. of useful and*

This portrait captures not so much Clive's person as the mystery shrouding the first half of her career. In 1735, verses alone identified a sitter so celebrated she didn't need to be named: 'Of all the Arts that sooth the human Breast, / Music (blest Power) the sweetest is confest: / Heightens our Joys, suspends our fiercest Pains: / This each One proves who hears thy heavnly Strains'. But by 1763 these lines didn't necessarily conjure Clive's name any longer. Her 'heavnly Strains' had yielded to occasional song and musical burlesque, and her figure had ballooned out to that shown in the engravings after Johann Ludwig Fäsch (Fig. 13.2 and Fig. 13.3). Her lavish costumes in these portraits from the 1760s – square hoops, lace sleeve ruffle, frilled collar, elaborate head-dress, elbow-length mitts, ornate robings – helped represent the excesses of Clive and her 'Character'. Adding a title to the Van Aken print of 1735 restored dignity to Clive, relying on popular recollection that was, however, still deemed strong enough to obviate the need to name 'The Fair Songster'.

Who in the mid-1760s would have wished to preserve Clive's fading musical legacy? The only obvious suspect is Clive herself. She owned Jeremiah Davison's copy of Joseph van Aken's original oil that the 1735 mezzotint captures. Nearing retirement and faced daily with this image of her former self, Clive would have been more concerned than anyone else not to be forgotten. After her farewell night at Drury Lane on 24 April 1769 – a star-studded evening for which Clive chose Susannah Centlivre's feminist *The Wonder: A Woman keeps a Secret* (1714) and its smart chambermaid role, and for which Horace Walpole gifted her an epilogue[10] – the newly issued mezzotint preserved Clive's likeness as *The FAIR SONGSTER* for another quarter century. Clive's name was added to the engraving only after 1793, when Carington's son Henry began trading in partnership with Samuel Carver. The new title overwrites 'The Fair Songster' by likewise dividing itself in two on the mezzotint, with 'Mrs. CLIVE. / *from the*' to the left of the verses, and '*Picture at Strawberry Hill*' to the right of the verses (Fig. 13.4).[11] By the 1790s, most of those who had heard Clive's serious singing had passed away, so, when issuing the portrait in 1793, Henry Carington Bowles coupled Clive's name with the extra-urban celebrity colony at Twickenham where she had resided.

In this book I have focused on Clive, stardom, and her music until 1750, leaving her story unfinished. There's more to dig into. Until she retired in 1769,

---

correct Maps, ... Prints, Drawing-Books ... Copy-Books ... Printed for John Bowles, at No. 13, in Cornhill, London (London, [c.1768]).

[10] Clive played opposite David Garrick and Elizabeth Barry. For a full account of the evening, and a reprint of Walpole's epilogue, see Victor, *The History of the Theatres of London*, vol. 3, pp. 139–45. On the feminism in this comedy, see Nancy Copeland, 'The Wonder', *Staging Gender in Behn and Centlivre: Women's Comedy and the Theatre* (Burlington, VT, 2004), pp. 126–57.

[11] The mezzotint lettered 'Mrs. CLIVE' is held, *inter alia*, at the National Portrait Gallery, the Garrick Club of London, and the British Museum.

Fig. 13.4 Alexander van Aken after Joseph van Aken, *Mrs. CLIVE, from the Picture at Strawberry Hill* [original 1735], after 1793. Mezzotint. © Trustees of the British Museum. Museum number: 1902,1011.6028.

and during her retirement, Clive continued self-engineering of the kind I've probed. Some instances especially worthy of investigation include her 1761 press war with Ned Shuter over her patriotism, her response in 1760 to the accusation that she and Horace Walpole were lovers, and the way she wrote in her letters of gaming as a polite occupation. Looking more closely at her sexuality could illuminate particulars about the same-sex politics of her circles. A critical edition of her writings – her farces, private correspondence, and printed addresses to the public – is overdue. I'm sure Catherine Clive still has a lot to teach us.

Because Clive's voice was so vibrant yet is now so little known, this book will give her the last word. Below I quote Clive on matters relating to her career: securing earnings, defending professional rank, controlling publicity, mocking male learning, asserting female authority, and reflecting on the 'villany' of actors and managers. Against these writings I juxtapose a crayon portrait of the 25-year-old Clive, dated 1736 and entitled *Mrs. Clive in the Character of Philida* [sic] *Drury Lane*, by William Hoare (Fig. 13.5). Drawn the year of the Polly Row, this private view of Clive may evoke the distance she travelled from goddess to caricature. The young woman of 1736 and the embittered veteran of 1771 both knew all too well what managers exacted from a playhouse star.

On Financial Independence

Catherine Clive to Jane Pope, letter of 6 October 1773[12]

Mrs Hamilton wrote me a very long melancholly letter to tell me of her distress, that she was so poor as to want a dinner and how do you think she wanted to extricate herself by desiring me to go a strolling for her and act for her Benefit at Richmond; I don't believe there ever was an instance of such a piece of assurance[;] I answered her letter and told her she might with more propriety have asked Mr Garrick to have played for her there, as he continued on the stage and I had left – notwithstanding I am really sorry for her, this woman was but a few years ago in possession of nine pounds a week[,] had all the great characters both in comedy and tragedy and chose to give up an article with five years to come because she had quarrel[']d with Mr Beard. Mrs Yates has taken the Opera House. Oh Tempora [!]

Let this be a lesson to my dear Miss Pope not to enter into schemes and to save every shilling. I must say before I quit this subject that while the publick are contributing so largely in a Benefit at each house for the support of decayed actors, that Mrs Vincent should be discharged and Mrs Hamilton should want a dinner is a most infamous shame. I wish I could have an opportunity of speaking to Mr[s] Vincent, I think I could give her a piece of advice that might be of service to her, it is impossible to write upon that subject I would have no contention with people I have done with, and thank God, you will pay two

---

[12] Catherine Clive, Folger Shakespeare Library, W.b.73, 'Collection of Letters to Jane Pope', no. 7.

Fig. 13.5 William Hoare, *Mrs. Clive in the Character of Philida* [sic] *Drury Lane*, 1736. Red chalk on paper. Unknown collection.
Photograph National Portrait Gallery, London.

pence for these my Philosophical observations, which perhaps you will say is more than they are worth; the Post is going.

On being Worth as Much as Garrick

Thomas Davies, Memoirs of the Life of David Garrick (London, 1780), vol. 2, pp. 184–86

To Mr. George Garrick, whom he [David Garrick] afterwards deputed to wait on her on the same errand, this high-spirited actress was not much more civil; however she condescended to tell him, that if his brother wished to know her mind, he should have called upon her himself. When the manager and Mrs. Clive met, their interview was short, and their discourse curious. After some compliments on her great merit, Mr. Garrick wished, he said, that she would continue, for her own sake, some years longer on the stage. This civil suggestion she answered by a decisive negative. He asked how much she was worth; she replied briskly, as much as himself. Upon his smiling at her supposed ignorance or misinformation, she explained herself, by telling him, that *she* knew when she had enough, though *he* never would. He then entreated her to renew her agreement for three or four years; she peremptorily refused. Upon his renewing his regret at her leaving the stage, she frankly told him, that she hated hypocrisy; for she was sure that he would light up candles for joy of her leaving him, but that it would be attended with some expence [a reference to Garrick's reputed stinginess]. – Every body will see there was some unnecessary smartness in the lady's language; but however, it was her way, as her friend Mrs. Pritchard used to express it.

On being Advertised in the Playbills

Catherine Clive to Jane Pope, letter of 11 December 1777[13]

I feel great indignation at their [leaving?] your name out of the Bill <u>for the Puppet Show</u>. He [David Garrick] once served me so in *Lethe* there was only Lord Chalkstone[']s name [played by Garrick]. I sent my footman to the house to know if Mr Garrick intended my scene to be done, he was <u>frightened</u> and came to me himself I then told him if ever that happened again I would positively not come to the house and let the public know the reason thats the way to deal with such mean wretches[;] it never happened after[.]

---

[13] Catherine Clive, Folger Shakespeare Library, W.b.73, 'Collection of Letters to Jane Pope', no. 18.

On Male Academic Learning

Catherine Clive, Every Woman in her Humour *(1760)*[14]

Lady Di Clatter: Ah! dear, I am mighty sorry for that. Oh! Miss Gibberish, I have not seen you since you came from Oxford; how do you find yourself after having been at that frightfull, ridiculous place?

Miss Gibberish: For shame, for shame, Lady Di, how can you betray such an imbecility in the judicial faculty of your Intellects, as to rail at, and depreciate that Celestial nursery of Literature? from whence I may say are transplanted all those divine Luminaries that irradiate our Hemisphere.

Lady Di: Irradiate! O my Dear Ma'am, you have really set my teeth on edge by the delicacy of your Dialect. But as to Oxford, it is the most dismal place I ever was in, in my life; I hate it, and every Creature that's there.

Mrs. Croston: It is a wonder she shou'd not like Oxford, there are so many men. (*aside*)

Miss Gibberish: My Genius! sure you know nobody in it then; they are all men skill'd in the learned Sciences Ma'am, who can tell the number of the stars[,] their Gradations, Directions, Retrospections, can tell –

Lady Di: Fortunes by Coffee grounds I suppose ha! ha!

On Female Authority (while Taking off King George II)

William Henry Pyne, Wine and Walnuts; Or, After Dinner Chit-Chat *(London, 1823), pp. 318–20*[15]

[Clive, in company with Horace Walpole and his guests, mimicking a German-born courtier and the German-born King George's replies.]

'I am inform in Germany, dat dere is a law in England vot give the hospands the powers to pead [beat] his wive mid a gudgel as tick as his own thomb.'

'Shu! shu!' answered his Majesty, 'Dere shall be no such absurd law found in the English codes. For what shall the judges make a law so absurd, mine General, ven the English vives is the virtuous battern for all the vives in all the varld? Shu! shu! mine General, dat is a vulgar brejudice – noting in the varld put a vulgar brejudice!'

'I am moch honoured and moch opliged to your Majesdy. I voud not pote mine liddle finger upon a voman for to do her harm, for all the brecious chems in Colgonda.'

---

[14] Huntington Library, John Larpent Plays collection, 'Every Woman in her Humour' (undated; first performed 20 March 1760), LA 174, fols 17r–17v. This passage is also transcribed in Crean, 'The Life and Times of Kitty Clive', p. 506.

[15] This passage is cited in Crean, 'The Life and Times of Kitty Clive', pp. 388–89.

'God forbid, mine General!' responded the King. 'You are a brave man – you are a brave man – and the brave will never pud oud his littel finger for to do no violence to womans.'

'Den I am of obinions, your Majesdy, dat the English laidties are the habbiest wifes of all. For your Majesdy's Pritish subjecds he is prave to a mans. How well he foudght in Flanders! – how well he foudght in –'

'Shu! shu! mine goodt friend, he foudght well always, and in all the times. He is never known in fear pote of one power.'

'Andt, may I venture to askg your Majesdy, of whom is dat bower which he fears?'

'Well, will you keeb a secred?' said his Majesty, placing his finger on his lip: then whispering – 'Mine general, it is his wife!'

'Bravo! – bravo!' exclaimed Mister Horatio [Walpole] – 'Upon my honour, Madam, a most happy impromptu! – Prodigiously like the original, indeed! – Very like – very admirable – ha! ha! ha! ha! … Nay, nay, my dear Madam, do not close the book,' said Mr. Walpole – 'we must beg another scene. I do love to laugh at the humour of the worthy Hanoverian.'

'Hold, Sir!' said the witty puss, with mock solemnity – '*There's such divinity doth hedge a king, that treason can but peep to what it would!*'

On being a Stage Star

Catherine Clive to George Colman senior, 16 December (1771)[16]

The philosopher Stone, they say (when they can ketch it) will turn every thing into gould; but I am sure the theatres may truly be said to turn every body's happiness (who has anything to do there) into anxiety, wether it is owing to their vanity and avarice not being easily sattisfied I can't tell; than from the villany of managers to actors; and the villany of actors to managers, their anxiety is turnd into vexation, and that most excellent Docter Schomberg will tell you that vexation, and fretting are the great foundation for all Billous Complaints; I speak by experience; I have been fretted by managers, till my gaul has overflowd like the river Nile[.]

[16] Catherine Clive, Folger Shakespeare Library, W.b.472.

APPENDIX 1

Catherine Clive's Roles 1728–69

All performances at Drury Lane unless otherwise stated.

CG = Covent Garden, LIF = Lincoln Inn's Fields

Debut date stands for role and stage work unless stage work is listed with year, or is by Shakespeare.

Boldface = Song for Clive

Names and work titles follow either standardized usage, forms in *The London Stage*, or primary sources. Subtitles are included only where needed to help identify a stage work.

Further details on songs in spoken stage works are found in: Ian Bartlett with Robert J. Bruce, *William Boyce: a Tercentenary Sourcebook and Compendium* (Newcastle upon Tyne, 2013); Bernd Baselt, *Verzeichnis der Werke Georg Friedrich Händels (HWV): kleine Ausgabe* (Leipzig, 1986); Irena B. Cholij, 'Music in Eighteenth-Century London Shakespeare Productions' (PhD diss., University of London, 1995); Joseph N. Gillespie, 'The Life and Work of Henry Carey (1687–1743)' (PhD diss., University of London, 1982), vol. 2; Dennis R. Martin, 'Lampe's Books and Treatises, extant Operatic Music, and Song Collections', *The Operas and Operatic Style of John Frederick Lampe* (Detroit, 1985), pp. 179–81; John A. Parkinson, *An Index to the Vocal Music of Thomas Augustine Arne and Michael Arne* (Detroit, 1972); Franklin B. Zimmerman, *Henry Purcell, 1659–1695: An Analytical Catalogue of his Music* (London, 1963).

No.	Role Debut date	Work, Year	Genre	Dramatist / Composer, Arranger	Notice
1	Immenea, a Page 13 April 1728?	*Mithridates, King of Pontus*, 1678	Tragedy	Nathaniel Lee	William R. Chetwood, *A General History of the Stage* (London, 1749), p. 127
2	Bianca 12 October 1728	Othello	Tragedy	Shakespeare	*Daily Post*, issue 2827 (12 October 1728)
3	Minerva 15 November 1728	*Perseus and Andromeda: With the Rape*	Masque in pantomime	John Weaver / John Pepusch	*Daily Post*, issue 2856 (15 November 1728)

No.	Role, Debut date	Work, Year	Genre	Dramatist / Composer, Arranger	Notice
4	Dorinda, 2 January 1729	*The Tempest: Or, the Inchanted Island*, 1667	Comedy	William Davenant, John Dryden / John Weldon and others Adapted from Shakespeare	*Daily Post*, issue 2897 (2 January 1729): 'With all the Original Songs and Dances' *Daily Post*, issue 3155 (30 October 1729): 'The Song of —Dear, dear pretty Youth. Composed by the late Mr. Henry Purcell, to sung in the Character of Dorinda, by Miss Raftor'
5	Phillida, 7 January 1729	*Love in a Riddle*	Pastoral	Colley Cibber / Henry Carey	*Daily Post*, issue 2901 (7 January 1729)
6	Honoria, 20 January 1729	*Love Makes a Man*, 1700	Comedy	Colley Cibber	*Daily Post*, issue 2912 (20 January 1729)
7	Rosella, 6 February 1729	*The Village Opera*	Ballad opera	Charles Johnson after Dancourt, *Le Galant jardinier*, 1705, Lesage *Crispin rival de son maitre*, 1707	*Daily Post*, issue 2927 (6 February 1729)
8	Susan (vocal part), 10 April 1729	*The What D'ye Call It*, 1715	Farce	John Gay	*Daily Post*, issue 2981 (10 April 1729): 'With the usual Song by Miss Raftor' (Handel, 'Twas when the Seas were Roaring', HWV 228)
9	Valeria, 1 May 1729	*The Rover*, 1677	Comedy	Aphra Behn	*Daily Post*, issue 2999 (1 May 1729)
10	Flora, 14 May 1729	*The Lover's Opera*	Ballad opera	William R. Chetwood	*Daily Post*, issue 3010 (14 May 1729): 'For the Benefit of Mr. CHETWOOD … Intermixt with above 40 Airs, made to Old Ballad Tunes and Country Dances'
11	Amphitrite, 28 May (?) 1729	*Neptune and Amphitrite*, 1674	Masque in *The Tempest*	William Davenant, John Dryden / masque comp. Pelham Humfrey Adapted from Shakespeare	*Daily Post*, issue 3022 (28 May 1729): 'With new Scenes, Machines, and other Decorations, and all the Original Entertainments … The Vocal Parts to be perform'd by Mr. Boman … Miss Raftor … and others' *The London Stage*, Part 3, vol. 1, p. 145 (Drury Lane, 7 June 1731): 'Amphitrite – Miss Raftor'

429

No.	Role / Debut date	Work, Year	Genre	Dramatist / Composer, Arranger	Notice
12	Bonvica / 13 June 1729	*The History of Bonduca*, 1695	Tragedy	Francis Beaumont, John Fletcher / Henry Purcell	*Daily Post*, issue 3036 (13 June 1729): 'With the Original Songs set to Musick by Mr. H. Purcel' [sic]
13	Phebe / 13 June 1729	*Phebe: Or, the Beggar's Wedding*	Ballad Opera	Charles Coffey	*Daily Post*, issue 3036 (13 June 1729)
14	Maria / 25 July 1729	*Whig and Tory*	Comedy	Benjamin Griffin	*Daily Post*, issue 3072 (25 July 1729)
15	Arethusa / 5 August 1729	*The Contrivances: Or, More Ways than One*	Comedy with songs	Henry Carey / Henry Carey	*Country Journal or The Craftsman*, issue 161 (2 August 1729): 'several SONGS properly introduced in the Characters of ROVEWELL and ARETHUSA'
16	Phillida / 28 October 1729	*Damon and Phillida* Abridgement of *Love in a Riddle*, no. 5	Pastoral farce	Colley Cibber / Henry Carey	*Daily Post*, issue 3153 (28 October 1729): 'By his Majesty's Command … MACBETH … To which (by Command) will be added a Musical Entertainment, call'd DAMON and PHILLIDA'
17	Night / 10 December 1729	*Apollo and Daphne*, 1725	Masque	John Thurmond / Henry Carey	*Daily Post*, issue 3190 (10 December 1729): 'N. B. The Scene of Apollo and Daphne, reviv'd will open the whole Entertainment. The Part of Apollo by Mr. Thurmond … Night by Miss Raftor'
18	Miss Kitty / 9 January 1730	*The Humours of Oxford*	Comedy	James Miller / song by Richard Charke	*Daily Post*, issue 3216 (9 January 1730)
19	Rosella / 10 February 1730	*The Chambermaid* Abridgement of *The Village Opera*, no. 7	Ballad opera	Edward Phillips after Charles Johnson, *The Village Opera*, 1729; after Dancourt, *Le Galant Jardinier*, 1705; Lesage *Crispin rival de son maître*, 1707	*Daily Post*, issue 3243 (10 February 1730): '[A] Comedy of one Act call'd The CHAMBER-MAID Intermix'd with Songs made to old Ballad Tunes, for the Benefit of the Author'

No.	Role, Debut date	Work, Year	Genre	Dramatist / Composer, Arranger	Notice
20	Dulceda, 30 March 1730	*Bayes's Opera*	Ballad opera	Gabriel Odingsells	*Daily Post*, issue 3284 (30 March 1730)
21	Jenny, 11 April 1730	*The Provok'd Husband*, 1728	Comedy	Colley Cibber / Henry Carey (2 songs) Completion of Vanbrugh, *A Journey to London*, before 1726	*Daily Post*, issue 3295 (11 April 1730)
22	Serina, 16 April 1730	*The Orphan*, 1680	Domestic tragedy	Thomas Otway	*Daily Post*, issue 3299 (16 April 1730)
23	Prue, 18 April 1730	*Love for Love*, 1695	Comedy	William Congreve	*Daily Post*, issue 3301 (18 April 1730)
24	Peggy, 20 April 1730	*Patie and Peggy: Or, the Fair Foundling*	Ballad opera	Theophilus Cibber	*Daily Post*, issue 3302 (20 April 1730): '[A] New Scotch Ballad Opera'
25	Isabella, 13 May 1730	*The Stage Coach Opera*	Ballad opera	William R. Chetwood after Farquhar, after Motteux, 1704, after La Chappelle, *Les carosses d'Orléans*, 1680	*Daily Post*, issue 3322 (13 May 1730): 'With New Songs to old Ballad Tunes and Country Dances'
26	Fairy Queen, 15 May 1730	*The Fairy Queen: Or, Harlequin Turned Enchanter*	Pantomime (serious part)	Surel (choreographer)	*Daily Post*, issue 3324 (15 May 1730): 'For the Benefit of Mr. SUREL, the HARLEQUIN … A New Dramatic Entertainment of Dancing (never perform'd before)'
27	Procris, 28 October 1730	*Cephalus and Procris*	Masque	Henry Carey / Henry Carey	*Daily Post*, issue 3466 (28 October 1730): '[A] new Dramatic Masque'

No.	Role, Debut date	Work, Year	Genre	Dramatist / Composer, Arranger	Notice
28	Amie, 8 February 1731	*The Jovial Crew*	Ballad opera	after Brome, *A Jovial Crew*, 1641	*Daily Post*, issue 3554 (8 February 1731): '[A] Comic Opera'
29	Nanny, 20 March 1731	*The Highland Fair: Or, Union of the Clans*	Ballad opera	Joseph Mitchell	*Daily Post*, issue 3589 (20 March 1731): '[A] New Scot's Opera'
30	Kalid, 12 May 1731	*The Indian Emperor*, 1665	Tragedy	John Dryden / Henry Purcell	*Daily Advertiser*, issue 84 (11 May 1731): '*For the Benefit of Mrs. Roberts and Others* … The INDIAN EMPEROR … With all the Singing and Dancing proper to the Play'; *The London Stage*, Part 3, vol. 1, p. 138: "The Original Song ['I looked and saw within the Book of Fate'] set to Musick by Henry Purcell, perform'd in the Character of Kalid by Miss Raftor'
31	Jenny, 11 June 1731	*The Cobler's Opera*	Ballad opera	Lacy Ryan	*The London Stage*, Part 3, vol. 1, p. 146
32	Nell, 6 August 1731	*The Devil to Pay*	Ballad opera	Charles Coffey / Seedo after Jevon, *The Devil of a Wife*, 1686	*The London Stage*, Part 3, vol. 1, p.150: '[A] new Ballad-Opera. Taken from The Devil of a Wife. Written by Mr Jevon'
33	Kitty Carrot, 11 August 1731	*The What D'ye Cull It*, 1/15	Farce	John Gay / common tunes, one song by George F. Handel	*Daily Post*, issue 3712 (11 August 1731): 'At the particular Desire of several Persons of Quality and Distinction, and Eminent Merchants of the City of London. The FOURTEENTH DAY. … A New Play, call'd The LONDON MERCHANT … With the Prologue and Epilogue, and Singing by Miss Raftor … To which will be added, The WHAT D'YE CALL IT. Reviv'd. A Tragi-Comi-Pastoral-Farcical Ballad-Opera. Intermix'd with a Variety of new Songs made to old Ballad-Tunes and Country-Dances. The Part of Kitty Carrot by Miss Raftor'
34	Urania, 18 August 1731	*The Triumphs of Love and Honour*	Play	Thomas Cooke / Anon	*Daily Post*, issue 3718 (18 August 1731): 'A New Play (of Three Acts)'
35	Mrs. Littlewit, 30 October 1731	*Bartholomew Fair*, 1614	Comedy	Ben Jonson	*The London Stage*, Part 3, vol. 1, p. 164

No.	Role / Debut date	Work, Year	Genre	Dramatist / Composer, Arranger	Notice
36	Chloe / 1 January 1732	*The Lottery*	Farce	Henry Fielding / Seedo	*The London Stage*, Part 3, vol. 1, p. 180
37	Cast not listed / 17 April 1732	*The Ephesian Matron*	Ballad opera (all new songs)	Charles Johnson / Seedo after Chapman, *The Widow's Tears*, 1669?	*Daily Post*, issue 3926 (17 April 1732): '[A] new Ballad Opera, never Acted before, call'd The EPHESIAN MATRON. The Tunes all New; composed in the Old English, Scotch, and Irish Style, by Mr. Seedo' *Craftsman*, issue 300? (15 April 1732; excerpted notice from the Theatre & Performance Archive, Victoria & Albert Museum): 'The principal Parts to be performed by Mr. Bridgwater, Mr. Stoppelaer, Miss Raftor'
38	Busy / 20 April 1732	*The Man of Mode*, 1676	Comedy	George Etheridge	*Daily Post*, issue 3929 (20 April 1732) *Choice Ayres, Songs, & Dialogues* (1715, British Library R.M.15.c.8): 'Harriet's Waiting Woman … As Amoret'
39	Miss Sprightly / 3 May 1732	*The Tragedy of Tragedies*	Burlesque tragedy	Henry Fielding	*Daily Post*, issue 3940 (3 May 1732): 'For the Benefit of Mr. CHETWOOD … The TRAGEDY of TRAGEDIES … With a new Introduction, written by the Author of Tom Thumb: The Speakers, Lord Monkeytail, Mr. A. Hallam; Mr. Critick, Mr. Watson; Mr. Heroick Diction, Mr. Wetherilt; jun. Miss Sprightly, Miss Raftor; Mrs. Witwou'd, Mrs. Shireburn'
40	Margery / 8 May 1732	*The Country Wedding*	Ballad opera	Essex Hawker / John Pepusch	*Daily Post*, issue 3944 (8 May 1732): '[A] Tragi-Comi-Pastoral-Farcical Opera, (of one Act) call'd The COUNTRY WEDDING. The Part of Margery by Miss Raftor'
41	Martin's Wife / 12 May 1732	*The Comical Revenge*	Ballad Opera	after Susanna Centlivre after Molière, *Le Médecin malgré lui*, 1666	*Daily Post*, issue 3948 (12 May 1732): '[A] New Ballad Opera, never perform'd but once, call'd The COMICAL REVENGE: OR, A Doctor in Spight of his Teeth. Taken from MOLIERE … Martin's Wife, Miss Raftor'
42	Kissinda / 1 June 1732	*The Covent Garden Tragedy*	Comedy	Henry Fielding	*Daily Post*, issue 3965 (1 June 1732): '[A] new Comedy of three Acts'
43	Isabel	*The Old Debauchees*	Comedy	Henry Fielding	*Daily Post*, issue 3965 (1 June 1732): '[A] New Farce (of two Acts)'

No.	Role / Debut date	Work, Year	Genre	Dramatist / Composer, Arranger	Notice
44	Dorcas / 23 June 1732	*The Mock Doctor*	Comedy	Henry Fielding / Seedo after Molière, *Le Médecin malgré lui*, 1666	*Daily Post*, issue 3978 (23 June 1732): '[A] New Farce (never perform'd before) … done from the French of MOLIERE … N.B. The Company being busily employ'd in Rehearsing several New Pieces, &c.. could not perform till this Day, and they will positively continue to act twice a Week as usual'
45	Polly / 11 July 1732	*The Beggar's Opera*, 1728	Ballad opera	John Gay / John Pepusch	*Daily Post*, issue 3993 (11 July 1732)
46	Cast not listed / 4 August 1732	*Rural Love*	Pastoral	Anon	*The London Stage*, Part 3, vol. 1, p. 226: 'A new Pastoral Opera'
47	Flametta / 17 August 1732	*The Devil of a Duke*	Ballad opera	Robert Drury / Seedo after Tate, *A Duke and No Duke*, 1685	*Daily Post*, issue 4025 (17 August 1732): '[A] new Farcical Ballad Opera of One Act … Intermix'd with Songs set to Ballad Tunes, Country- Dances, &c.'
48	Vocal part / 28 September 1732	*Macbeth*	Tragedy	Shakespeare, adapted by Davenant, 1673 / music by Richard Leveridge, 1702	*Daily Post*, issue 4061 (28 September 1732): 'Original Musick, Songs and Dances, The Vocal Parts by Mr. Stoppelaer and Miss Raftor'
49	Silvia / 3 October 1732	*The Old Batchelor*, 1693	Comedy	William Congreve	*Daily Post*, issue 4065 (3 October 1732)
50	Vocal part / 13 November 1732	*King Henry the Eighth*	History play	Shakespeare / John F. Lampe	*Daily Post*, issue 4100 (13 November 1732): 'Containing, The Death of the Duke of Buckingham; the Fall of Cardinal Wosley; The Divorce and Death of Queen Katharine; the Coronation of Queen Anne Bullen, with the military Ceremony of the Champion in Westminster-Hall; the Christening of Queen Elizabeth; and many other Historical Passages … With Singing by Miss Raftor'
51	Betty / 6 December 1732	*Betty: Or, the Country Bumpkins*	Musical farce	Henry Carey / Henry Carey after Carey, *Hanging and Marriage*, 1722	*Daily Post*, issue 4120 (6 December 1732): '[A] New Ballad Opera'

434

No.	Role Debut date	Work, Year	Genre	Dramatist/ Composer, Arranger	Notice
52	Leonora 9 December 1732	*Sir Courtly Nice* 1683	Comedy	John Crowne	*Daily Post*, issue 4123 (9 December 1732) *Daily Post*, issue 3599 (1 April 1731): 'Sir COURTLY NICE … With the Original Dialogue sung by Mr. Charke and Miss Raftor'
53	Belinda 11 January 1733	*The Man of Mode*, 1676	Comedy	George Etheridge	*Daily Post*, issue 4157 (11 January 1733)
54	Cicely 19 January 1733	*Wat Tyler: Or, the State Menders*	Ballad opera?	Anon	*The London Stage*, Part 3, vol. 1, p. 267
55	Cydaria 20 January 1733	*The Indian Emperor*, 1665	Tragedy	John Dryden / Henry Purcell	*The London Stage*, Part 3, vol. 1, p. 267
56	Jenny 29 January 1733	*The Boarding School*	Ballad opera	Charles Coffey / Seedo after D'Urfey, *Love for Money: Or, the Boarding School*, 1691	*The London Stage*, Part 3, vol. 1, p. 267
57	Thalia 6 February 1733	*Judgment of Paris: Or, the Triumph of Beauty*	Masque	John Weaver / Seedo after Congreve, *Judgment of Paris*, 1701	*The London Stage*, Part 3, vol. 1, p. 269
58	Lappet 17 February 1733	*The Miser*	Comedy	Henry Fielding / Thomas Arne after Molière, *L'Avare*, 1668	*Daily Post*, issue 4189 (17 February 1733) *London Daily Post and General Advertiser*, issue 1252 (2 November 1738): "The MISER … the Part of Lappet, by Mrs. Clive, In which Character will be introduc'd a Song, call'd The Life of a Beau' (by Henry Carey, from James Miller, *The Coffee House*)
59	Kitty 31 March 1733	*The Harlot's Progress*	Ballad pantomime	Theophilus Cibber	*Daily Post*, issue 4225 (31 March 1733): '[A] New Grotesque Pantomime Entertainment'

435

No.	Role / Debut date	Work, Year	Genre	Dramatist / Composer, Arranger	Notice
60	Phillis 4 April 1733	*The Conscious Lovers*, 1722	Comedy	Richard Steele	*Daily Post*, issue 4225 (31 March 1733): '[O]n Wednesday next being the 4th Day of April … will be reviv'd a Comedy call'd The CONSCIOUS LOVERS'
61	**Deborah** 6 April 1733	***Deborah: Or, a Wife for You All***	Ballad opera?	Henry Fielding	*Daily Post*, issue 4224 (30 March 1733): '[O]n Friday the 6th Day of April, will be presented … a new Farce of one Act (never perform'd before) call'd A WIFE for YOU ALL'
62	Mrs. Fancifull 11 April 1733	*The Imaginary Cuckolds*	Ballad opera	after Molière, *Sganarelle, ou le cocu imaginaire*, 1660	*The London Stage*, Part 3, vol. 1, p. 286
63	Cast not listed 30 April 1733	*The Mock Countess*	Ballad opera	after Breval, *The Play is the Plot*, 1718?	*Daily Post*, issue 4250 (30 April 1733): '[A] New Ballad Opera of one Act, never performed before'
64	Phillis 5 May 1733	***The Livery Rake and The Country Lass***	Ballad opera	Thomas Phillips	*Daily Post*, issue 4255 (5 May 1733): '[A] New Ballad Opera of one Act (never perform'd before)'
65	[Venus] 7 May 1733	*Damon and Daphne*	Pastoral	Theophilus Cibber?	*The London Stage*, Part 3, vol. 1, p. 297: 'Benefit Mrs Charke … a new Pastoral of two Acts'
66	Venus 21 May 1733	*Venus, Cupid, and Hymen*	Masque	Anon / Seedo	*The London Stage*, Part 3, vol. 1, p. 302: 'Benefit Seedo … a new Masque. The Musick compos'd by Mr Seedo'
67	Doris 24 September 1733	*Aesop*, 1696	Comedy	John Vanbrugh after Boursault, *Les Fables d'Esope*, 1690	*The London Stage*, Part 3, vol. 1, p. 320
68	Estifania 1 October 1733	*Rule a Wife and Have a Wife*, 1624	Comedy	John Fletcher	*Daily Post*, issue 4381 (29 September 1733)
69	Cherry 5 October 1733	*The Beaux Strategem*, 1707	Comedy	George Farquhar	*The London Stage*, Part 3, vol. 1, p. 323
70	**Diana** 10 October 1733	***Harlequin Dr Faustus***	Pantomime (serious part)	John Thurmond, Barton Booth / Henry Carey	*The London Stage*, Part 3, vol. 1, p. 324: 'English Cantata composed by Carey, sung by Mrs Clive'
71	Elvira 19 October 1733	*The Spanish Fryar*, 1680	Comedy	John Dryden	*Daily Post*, issue 4398 (19 October 1733)

No.	Role, Debut date	Work, Year	Genre	Dramatist / Composer, Arranger	Notice
72	Queen Dollalolla 7 November 1733	*The Opera of Operas*	Burlesque opera	Henry Fielding / John F. Lampe after Fielding, *Tragedy of Tragedies*, 1731	*Daily Post*, issue 4414 (7 November 1733): 'In Three ACTS. Set to Musick after the Italian Manner by Mr. JOHN FREDERICK LAMPE'
73	Miranda 21 November 1733	*The Busy Body*, 1709	Comedy	Susanna Centlivre	*Daily Journal*, issue 4018 (21 November 1733)
74	Mercury or Aspasia 5 December 1733	*Timon in Love*	Comedy (with 17 songs)	John Kelly / Anon after Delisle de la Drévetière, *Timon misanthrope*, 1722	*Daily Journal*, issue 4020 (5 December 1733): '[A] new Comedy … In THREE ACTS'
75	Harriot 15 January 1734	*The Author's Farce*	Comedy	Henry Fielding / Seedo	*Daily Journal*, issue 4055 (15 January 1734): 'Never Acted there before.… The AUTHOR's FARCE. In which will be introduc'd an Operatical Puppet Show, call'd The Pleasures of the Town. With great Additions; and a new Prologue and Epilogue'
76	Lettice 15 January 1734	*The Intriguing Chambermaid*	Ballad opera	Henry Fielding after Regnard, *Le Retour imprévu*, 1700	*Daily Journal*, issue 4055 (15 January 1734): '[A] new Farce of two Acts, call'd The INTRIGUING CHAMBER-MAID. The Part of the Chamber-maid by Mrs. Clive'
77	Colombine 4 February 1734	*Cupid and Psyche: Or, Columbine-Courtezan*	Pantomime	Henry Carey / John F. Lampe, one song Carey	*Daily Journal*, issue 4072 (4 February 1734): '[A] New Pantomime Entertainment' *The British Musical Miscellany, or the Delightful Grove* (London, 1735), vol. 3, p. 9: 'Sung by Mrs. Clive at the Theatre in Drury Lane. The Words and Musick by Mr Carey'
78	Flippanta CG 11 March 1734	*The City Wives Confederacy*	Comedy	John Vanbrugh	*Daily Journal*, issue 4102 (11 March 1734): 'Never Acted there before. At the Desire of several Ladies of Quality. For the Benefit of Mrs. CLIVE, formerly Miss RAFTOR' *General Advertiser*, issue 3143 (10 December 1744): 'COVENT-GARDEN. Acted but Once these Five Years … The CITY WIVES CONFEDERACY … [T]he Part of Flippanta by Mrs. Clive, in which Character will be Introduc'd the Song call'd *The Life of a Belle* [by Henry Carey]'

437

No.	Role Debut date	Work, Year	Genre	Dramatist / Composer, Arranger	Notice
79	Edging 18 March 1734	*The Careless Husband*, 1704	Comedy	Colley Cibber	*Daily Journal*, issue 4108 (18 March 1734)
80	Cast not listed LIF 4 April 1734	*Love is the Doctor*	Comedy	Anon after Molière, *L'Amour médecin*, 1665	*Daily Journal*, issue 4123 (4 April 1734): '*At the Desire of several Ladies of Quality* … At the Theatre-Royal in Lincoln's-Inn-fields … The BEGGAR's OPERA. The Part of Polly by Mrs. Clive; Macheath by Mr. Stoppelaer. To which will be added, A New Comedy in one Act (never acted before) call'd LOVE is the DOCTOR. *From L'Amour Medicin of Moliere. For the Benefit of the* AUTHOR'
81	Desdemona 13 May 1734	**Othello**	Tragedy	Shakespeare	*The London Stage*, Part 3, vol. 1, p. 397
82	Primrose 19 October 1734	*The Mother-in-Law*	Comedy	James Miller after Molière, *La malade imaginaire*, 1673, *Monsieur de Pourceaugnac*, 1669 [James Miller], 'A DIALOGUE SONG [for Primrose, Belinda]', *The Mother-in-Law* (London, 1734), pp. 16–17	*The London Stage*, Part 3, vol. 1, p. 423 : 'Taken from the French of Moliere. With an additional Scene of a Consultation of Physicians from Moliere'
83	Hoyden 7 November 1734	*The Relapse*, 1696	Comedy	John Vanbrugh	*London Daily Post and General Advertiser*, issue 4 (7 November 1734)
84	Spirit Country Lass 12 December 1734	**Merlin: Or, the Devil of Stone-Henge**	Pantomime	Lewis Theobald / John Ernest Galliard	*London Daily Post and General Advertiser*, issue 34 (12 December 1734): '[A] new Pantomime Entertainment'

No.	Role, Debut date	Work, Year	Genre	Dramatist / Composer, Arranger	Notice
85	Miss Lucy, 6 January 1735	*An Old Man Taught Wisdom: Or, the Virgin Unmasked*	Ballad farce	Henry Fielding	*London Daily Post and General Advertiser*, issue 55 (6 January 1735): '[A] new Farce of one Act'
86	Mrs. Pinchwife, 4 February 1735	*The Country Wife*, 1675	Comedy	William Wycherly after Molière, *L'Ecole des Maris*, 1661	*London Daily Post and General Advertiser*, issue 80 (4 February 1735)
87	Peg, 25 February 1735	*A Cure for a Scold*	Ballad opera	James Worsdale after Shakespeare, *Taming of the Shrew*	*London Daily Post and General Advertiser*, issue 98 (25 February 1735): 'A New Farce of two Acts ... Taken from SHAKESPEAR. Intermix'd with SONGS'
88	Maria, 6 March 1735	*The Man of Taste*	Comedy	James Miller after Molière, *Les Précieuses ridicules*, 1659 [James Miller], [Maria sings] 'So the poor Sheep, with fragrant Flowers array'd', *The Man of Taste* (London, 1735), p. 31	*London Daily Post and General Advertiser*, issue 106 (6 March 1735). *London Daily Post and General Advertiser*, issue 1104 (13 May 1738): 'In which will be Introduc'd several Songs, to be sung by Mrs. Clive and Mr. Beard, particularly The Life of a Beau [by Henry Carey]. The Beaux Lamentation for the Loss of Farinelli [by Henry Carey]. And The Provident Damsel [Richard Charke]'
89	Ophelia, 10 March 1735	*Hamlet*	Tragedy	Shakespeare	*London Daily Post and General Advertiser*, issue 109 (10 March 1735)
90	Lady Woudbe, 13 March 1735	*Volpone*, 1606	Comedy	Ben Jonson	*The London Stage*, Part 3, vol. 1, p. 468

439

No.	Role Debut date	Work, Year	Genre	Dramatist / Composer, Arranger	Notice
91	Lady Fanciful 23 April 1735	*The Provok'd Wife*, 1697	Comedy	John Vanbrugh / Thomas Arne	*The London Stage*, Part 3, vol. 1, p. 482 *General Advertiser*, issue 4135 (21 March 1748): 'For the Benefit of Mrs. CLIVE … The PROVOK'D WIFE … With a new Scene restor'd, in which will be perform'd by Mr. LOWE and Mrs. CLIVE, the Original Dialogue Set to Musick by Mr. Arne. And (by particular Desire) the Irish Song of *Ellen a Roon* by Mrs. CLIVE'
92	Nell 6 May 1735	*The Merry Cobler*	Ballad farce	Charles Coffey	*The London Stage*, Part 3, vol. 1, p. 488: 'Benefit Coffey, Author of The Devil to Pay … A new Ballad Farce. Being the Second Part of the Devil to Pay'
93	Doll Common 15 September 1735	*The Alchymist*, 1610	Comedy	Ben Jonson	*London Daily Post and General Advertiser*, issue 271 (15 September 1735) *London Daily Post and General Advertiser*, issue 1375 (16 March 1739): 'For the Benefit of Mr. CIBBER … The ALCHYMIST … And Select Pieces of Musick. End of Act. I. A Ballad, call'd Advice to the Tatlers [by Henry Carey] [by Desire] by Mrs. Clive … Act III. Mary Scot, sung by Mrs. Clive'
94	Lady Froth 11 October 1735	*The Double Dealer*, 1693	Comedy	William Congreve	*London Daily Post and General Advertiser*, issue 294 (11 October 1735) *London Daily Post and General Advertiser*, issue 479 (14 May 1736): 'With the Original Song in Character, by Mrs. Clive'
95	Lady Sadlife 3 November 1735	*The Double Gallant*, 1707	Comedy	Colley Cibber after Burnaby, *The Reform'd Wife*, 1707	*London Daily Post and General Advertiser*, issue 313 (3 November 1735)
96	Aurelia 3 January 1736	*The Twin Rivals*, 1702	Comedy	George Farquhar	*London Daily Post and General Advertiser*, issue 366 (3 January 1736): 'Not Acted these Ten Years'
97	Flavia 20 February 1736	*The Connoisseur: Or, Every Man in his Folly*	Comedy	Joseph Connolly	*London Daily Post and General Advertiser*, issue 407 (20 February 1736): 'Never Acted before … At the Theatre-Royal in Drury Lane'

No.	Role, Debut date	Work, Year	Genre	Dramatist / Composer, Arranger	Notice
98	Clymene, 28 February 1736	**The Fall of Phaeton**	Dramatic masque	William Pritchard / Thomas Arne	*London Daily Post and General Advertiser*, issue 414 (28 February 1736): 'A New Dramatic Masque, call'd The FALL of PHAETON. Interspers'd with a Grotesque Pantomime'
99	Phaedra, 6 April 1736	Amphitryon, 1690	Comedy	John Dryden	*London Daily Post and General Advertiser*, issue 446 (6 April 1736): 'For the Benefit of Mr. HARPER … Phaedra, Mrs. Clive; being the first Time of her appearing in that Character. To which will be added, a Farce of One Act, call'd The CONTRIVANCES. The Part of Arethusa by Mrs. Clive'
100	Biddy, 12 April 1736	**The Tender Husband**	Comedy	Richard Steele / Thomas Arne	*London Daily Post and General Advertiser*, issue 451 (12 April 1736): 'The Part of Biddy to be perform'd by Mrs. Clive'. Thomas Arne, *Songs in As You Like It* (London, 1741): 'Sung by Mrs[.] Clive in the Tender Husband'
101	Principal Vocalist, 22 April 1736	**A Grand Epithalamium**	Musical entertainment	Anon / Thomas Arne	*London Daily Post and General Advertiser*, issue 460 (22 April 1736): 'For the Benefit of Mr. ARNE … The Principal Characters sung by Sig. Phillipo Palma, being the first Time of his performing here in Publick; Miss Isabella Young … Mrs. Clive. … An extraordinary Band of Musick is provided. The Chorus's will be perform'd by a great Number of Voices, the Stage illuminated, and the Performers rang'd in a particular Manner. N.B. An Organ will be erected, on which Mr. Roseingrave will accompany the Songs and Chorus's'
102	Isabella, 23 September 1736	The Squire of Alsatia	Comedy	Thomas Shadwell after Terence, *Adelphi*	*London Daily Post and General Advertiser*, issue 592 (23 September 1736): 'By Command of their Royal Highnesses the Prince and Princess of WALES. *Not acted these Nine Years*'
103	Arabella, 13 October 1736	The Wife's Relief	Comedy	Charles Johnson	*London Daily Post and General Advertiser*, issue 609 (13 October 1736): '*Not Acted these Twenty-four Years*'
104	Ghost of Statira (vocal part), 22 November 1736	**The Rival Queens: Or, the Death of Alexander**, 1677	Tragedy	Nathaniel Lee / Thomas Arne	*London Daily Post and General Advertiser*, issue 643 (22 November 1736): '*Not Acted these Twenty-five Years* … The RIVAL QUEENS. … The Ghosts of Darius and Statira, sung by Mr. Stoppelaer and Mrs. Clive'

441

No.	Role / Debut date	Work, Year	Genre	Dramatist / Composer, Arranger	Notice
105	Wanton Wife (Mrs. Brittle) / 7 December 1736	*The Amorous Widow: Or, the Wanton Wife*, 1668	Comedy	Thomas Betterton / Henry Carey after Molière, *George Dandin*, 1668	*London Daily Post and General Advertiser*, issue 656 (7 December [1736]): 'Not Acted these Three Years … Taken from the French of MOLIERE' *London Daily Post and General Advertiser*, issue 1422 (19 May 1739): 'The Part of the Wanton Wife, by Mrs. Clive, with a new Song [by Henry Carey] in Character, never perform'd before … End of the Play. The Life of a Beau [by Carey], sung by Mrs. Clive'
106	Eurydice / 19 February 1737	*Eurydice: Or, the Devil Henpeck'd*	Farce with 9 songs	Henry Fielding / Thomas Arne?	*Daily Post*, issue 544 (19 February 1737): 'This Evening will be perform'd … a new Entertainment call'd *Eurydice, or the Devil Hen-peck'd*'
107	Liberia / 28 February 1737	*The Universal Passion*	Comedy with 6 songs	James Miller / one song by Handel? (attribution doubtful) after Shakespeare, *Much Ado about Nothing*	*Daily Post*, issue 5449 (28 February 1737) *London Evening Post*, issue 1453 (8–10 March 1737): 'Next Week will be publish'd, THE UNIVERSAL PASSION; a COMEDY; is it is now acting at the Theatre-Royal in Drury Lane (with great Applause)'
108	Narcissa / 6 September 1737	*Love's Last Shift*, 1696	Comedy	Colley Cibber	*The London Stage*, Part 3, vol. 2, p. 682
109	Laetitia / 15 September 1737	*The Old Batchelor*, 1693	Comedy	William Congreve	*The London Stage*, Part 3, vol. 2, p. 682
110	Olivia / 14 January 1738	*The Plain Dealer*, 1676	Comedy	William Wycherley	*The London Stage*, Part 3, vol. 2, p. 695: 'Not Acted [there] these Fourteen Years'
111	Miss Kitty / 26 January 1738	*The Coffee-House*	Comedy with 5 songs	James Miller / Henry Carey, Henry Burgess after Rousseau's *Le Caffé*, 1695	*London Daily Post and General Advertiser*, issue 1012 (26 January 1738): 'A New Dramatick Piece (never acted before) call'd The COFFEE-HOUSE. Intermix'd with Songs in Character'

No.	Role / Debut date	Work, Year	Genre	Dramatist / Composer, Arranger	Notice
112	Violetta / 16 February 1738	*Art and Nature*	Comedy	James Miller after Delisle de la Drévetière, *L'Arlequin Sauvage*, pubd 1721, Rousseau, *Le Flatteur*, pubd 1697	*London Daily Post and General Advertiser*, issue 1030 (16 February 1738): 'Never Acted before … a New Comedy … BY HIS MAJESTY's COMMAND'
113	Miss Kitty / 23 February 1738	*Sir John Cockle at Court*	Comedy with 3 songs	Robert Dodsley / Thomas Arne?	*London Daily Post and General Advertiser*, issue 1036 (23 February 1738): 'A New Dramatic Piece of One Act (never perform'd before) call'd Sir JOHN COCKLE at COURT. Being the Sequel to the King and the Miller of Mansfield … Miss Kitty Cockle by Mrs. Clive'
114	Principal Vocalist / 3 March 1738	*Benefit Concert for Master Ferg*	Concert		*London Daily Post and General Advertiser*, issue 1043 (3 March 1738): 'For the Benefit of Master FERG. … *Scholar to Mons. Livier*. … a CONCERT of VOCAL and INSTRUMENTAL MUSIC. By the Best Hands. Consisting of … Mr. Handel and other Eminent Masters, taken from the most favourite Opera's. The Vocal Parts by Mr. Beard and Mrs. Clive, being several Favourite Songs in Italian and English … two French-Horns to be perform'd by two little Negro-Boys, Scholars to Mr. Charles, who never perform'd before. Concluding with the Anthem, God save the King, &c.'
115	Nymph Euphrosyne / 4 March 1738	*Comus*	Masque	John Dalton / Thomas Arne after Milton, *A Masque … at Ludlow Castle*, 1634	*London Daily Post and General Advertiser*, issue 1044 (4 March 1738): 'Never Acted before … [A] New Masque … Alter'd from Milton's Masque perform'd upwards of a Hundred Years since at Ludlow-Castle. And now adapted to the Stage'
116	Viletta / 14 November 1738	*She Wou'd and She Wou'd Not*, 1702	Comedy	Colley Cibber	*London Daily Post and General Advertiser*, issue 1262 (14 November 1738): 'Not Acted these Twelve Years'

No.	Role / Debut date	Work, Year	Genre	Dramatist / Composer, Arranger	Notice
117	Principal Vocalist 30 November 1738	*The Pilgrim*, 1700	Comedy	John Fletcher, altered by John Vanbrugh and John Dryden	*London Daily Post and General Advertiser*, issue 1276 (30 November 1738): 'Not Acted these Sixteen Years … The PILGRIM … In which will be introduc'd the Original Mad Dialogue, set to Musick by Mr. H. Purcel [sic], and performed by Mr. Beard and Mrs. Clive'
118	Hillaria 9 December 1738	*Tunbridge Walks*, 1703	Comedy	Thomas Baker	*London Daily Post and General Advertiser*, issue 1284 (9 December 1738): 'Not Acted these Six Years'
119	Anne Lovely 13 January 1739	*A Bold Stroke for a Wife*, 1718	Comedy	Susanna Centlivre	*London Daily Post and General Advertiser*, issue 1314 (13 January 1739): 'Never Acted there before … Written by the Late Mrs. Centlivre'
120	Mrs. Loveit 3 February 1739	*The Man of Mode*, 1696	Comedy	George Etheridge	*London Daily Post and General Advertiser*, issue 1332 (3 February 1739): 'Not Acted this Season … To which will be added a Ballad-Opera, call'd DAMON and PHILLIDA. The Part of Damon, by Mr. Beard; Phillida, Mrs. Clive'
121	Miss Notable 13 March 1739	*The Lady's Last Stake*, 1707	Comedy	Colley Cibber	*London Daily Post and General Advertiser*, issue 1364 (13 March 1739): 'By Command of their Royal Highnesses the Prince and Princess of WALES. Not Acted these Ten Years. For the Benefit of Mrs. CLIVE' *London Daily Post and General Advertiser*, issue 1709 (16 April 1740): 'For the Benefit of Mrs. BUTLER … The LADY'S LAST STAKE … The Part of Miss NOTABLE, by Mrs. CLIVE. In which Character will be perform'd a new Song'
122	Daughter 15 November 1739	*An Hospital for Fools*	Comedy with 5 songs	James Miller / Thomas Arne after William Walsh, *Aesculapius*, pubd 1714	*London Daily Post and General Advertiser*, issue 1578 (15 November 1739): 'A Dramatic Fable'
123	Second Constantia 23 November 1739	*The Chances*, 1683	Comedy	George Villiers, Duke of Buckingham after Fletcher, *The Chances*, c.1617	*Daily Post*, issue 6305 (23 November 1739)

No.	Role Debut date	Work, Year	Genre	Dramatist / Composer, Arranger	Notice
124	Kitty 31 December 1739	*Britons, Strike Home: Or, the Sailors' Rehearsal*	Farce with 18 songs	Edward Phillips / Henry Purcell, Thomas Arne, others	*London Daily Post and General Advertiser*, issue 1617 (31 December 1739): '[A] new Farce of one Act … And the Part of Miss Kitty (alias Donna Americana) by Mrs. Clive'
125	Allegro LIF 27 February, 6 March 1740 (one or both)	*L'Allegro, il Penseroso ed il moderato*	Ode	James Harris and Charles Jennens / George F. Handel after Milton, *L'Allegro* and *Il Penseroso*, pubd 1645	*London Daily Post and General Advertiser*, issue 1667 (27 February 1740): 'LINCOLN's-INN FIELDS. *Never perform'd before* … L'Allegro il Penseroso ed il Moderato' (no cast listed)
126	Rosamond 8 March 1740	*Rosamond*	Opera	Joseph Addison / Thomas Arne after Addison, *Rosamond*, 1707	*London Daily Post and General Advertiser*, issue 1676 (8 March 1740): 'An English Opera, written by the late Mr. Addison, and new set to Musick by Mr. Arne, reserving two or three Favourite Songs, out of his former Opera'
127	Millamant 17 March 1740	*The Way of the World*, 1699	Comedy	William Congreve / George F. Handel (one song)	*London Daily Post and General Advertiser*, issue 1683 (17 March 1740): 'At the particular Desire of several Ladies of Quality … For the Benefit of Mrs. CLIVE … The WAY of the WORLD. Written by the late Mr. Congreve. Part of Millamant, to be perform'd by Mrs. CLIVE; *In which Character will be introduced the Original Song, the Words by Mr. Congreve, and new set to Musick by Mr. Handel*'
128	Lucy 15 April 1740	*Lethe*	Dramatic satire	David Garrick / Thomas Arne after Miller, *An Hospital for Fools*, 1739	*London Daily Post and General Advertiser*, issue 1708 (15 April 1740): '[A] new Dramatic Satire, call'd LETHE … In which will be introduc'd Singing by Beard, and Mrs. Clive particularly 'The *Life of a Belle*, &c.. in Imitation of The *Life of Beau*, by Mrs. Clive. The Part of Aesop by Mr. Taswell … and the Part of Miss Lucy, by Mrs. Clive. With a PROLOGUE and EPILOGUE'

No.	Role Debut date	Work, Year	Genre	Dramatist / Composer, Arranger	Notice
129	30 April 1740?	'A Comic Chorus, or Interludes: to be sung between the Acts of Zara'	Intermezzo (duet with Beard)	Aaron Hill / Anon printed in Aaron Hill, *The Dramatic Works of Aaron Hill, Esq.* (1760), vol. 2, pp. 80–86	*London Daily Post and General Advertiser*, issue 1721 (30 April 1740): "The MOURNING BRIDE…. With Singing by Mr. Beard'
130	Emma, the Shepherdess 28 July 1740 Cliveden 1, 2 August 1740	*Alfred*	Masque	James Thomson, David Mallet / Thomas Arne	*The Gentleman's Magazine: and Historical Chronicle*, vol. 10 (July 1740), p. 356 (28 July): 'This day was rehears'd, at Drury-lane Theatre, a Masque entitled Alfred, in order to be represented before the Prince and Princess, at Cliefden-house, on the First of August'
131	Manto vocal part 19 November 1740	*Oedipus, King of Thebes*, 1678	Tragedy	John Dryden, Nathaniel Lee / Thomas Arne	*London Daily Post and General Advertiser*, issue 1895 (19 November 1740): 'Not Acted these Thirty Years … OEDIIPUS, King of THEBES. Written by Dryden and Lee. The Part of Oedipus, Mr. Milward … and the Part of Manto, with the Hymn to Apollo, by Mrs. Clive. With new Musick and Machinery. The Songs and Chorus's new set by Mr. Arne; and to be perform'd by Mr. Lowe, Mr. Savage, Mrs. Clive, and others…. N.B. The Performance of the Musick being greatly instrumental to the Play … Persons … cannot be admitted into the Orchestra'
132	Emilia 29 November 1740	*A Fond Husband*, 1677	Comedy	Thomas D'Urfey	*London Daily Post and General Advertiser*, issue 1904 (20 November 1740): 'Not Acted these Twenty Years … A FOND HUSBAND … The Part of the Fond Husband by Mr. Chapman … and the Part of Emilia, by Mrs. Clive, in which Character will introduced to new Songs'
133	Celia 20 December 1740	*As You Like It*	Comedy	Shakespeare / Thomas Arne	*London Daily Post and General Advertiser*, issue 1922 (20 December 1740): 'Not Acted these Forty Years … AS YOU LIKE IT. William Shakespear … Caelia, Mrs. Clive; Rosalind, Mrs Pritchard' (songs by Thomas Arne)

No.	Role / Debut date	Work, Year	Genre	Dramatist / Composer, Arranger	Notice
134	Olivia / 15 January 1741	*Twelfth Night*	Comedy	Shakespeare / Thomas Arne	*London Daily Post and General Advertiser*, issue 1944 (15 January 1741): 'Never Acted there before … TWELFTH NIGHT … The Part of Orsino by Mr. Mills … Viola, Mrs. Pritchard; and the Part of Olivia, by Mrs. Clive … the Songs new set by Mr. Arne'
135	Lady Townly / 2 February 1741	*The Provok'd Husband*, 1728	Comedy	Colley Cibber / Henry Carey (two songs for Jenny)	*London Daily Post and General Advertiser*, issue 1959 (2 February 1741): 'By Command of their Royal Highnesses the Prince and Princess of WALES'
136	Portia / 14 February 1741	*The Merchant of Venice*	Comedy	Shakespeare / Thomas Arne	*London Daily Post and General Advertiser*, issue 1970 (14 February 1741): '*Never acted there before* … The Merchant by Mr. Quin [replaced on that night by Charles Macklin] … Portia, Mrs. Clive'
137	Bessy / 3 April 1741	*The Blind Beggar of Bethnal Green*	Dramatic tale with 9 songs	Robert Dodsley / Thomas Arne	*London Daily Post and General Advertiser*, issue 2011 (3 April 1741): '[A] new Dramatick Tale, call'd, *The Blind Beggar of* Bethnal-Green. The Principal Parts to be perform'd by Mr. Lowe, Mr. Berry … and Mrs. Clive'
138	Lady Lurewell / 4 January 1742	*The Constant Couple*, 1700	Comedy	George Farquhar	*Daily Post*, issue 6967 (4 January 1742)
139	Principal Vocalist Cast not listed 12 March 1742	*Alexander's Feast*, 1697	Ode	John Dryden / George F. Handel	*The London Stage*, Part 3, vol. 2, p. 974–75: '[Benefit Thomas Arne] ALEXANDER'S FEAST [by Handel]. Also THE JUDGMENT OF PARIS. Written by Congreve and New Set by Mr Arne … Pallas – Mrs Clive; Juno – Mrs Edwards' *Ibid.*, p. 977, Drury Lane, 19 March 1742: 'Those Tickets that could not be admitted on Mr Arne's Benefit night will be taken'
140	Pallas / 12 March 1742	*The Judgment of Paris*, 1701	Masque	William Congreve / Thomas Arne	See row above.
141	Lucy / 6 May 1742	*Miss Lucy in Town*	Farce with 8 songs	Henry Fielding / Thomas Arne	*The London Stage*, Part 3, vol. 2, p. 991

No.	Role, Debut date	Work, Year	Genre	Dramatist / Composer, Arranger	Notice
142	Dalila CG 18 February 1743	*Samson*	Oratorio	Newburgh Hamilton / George F. Handel after Milton, *Samson Agonistes*, pubd 1671	*Daily Advertiser*, issue 3771 (18 February 1743): 'By SUBSCRIPTION … will be perform'd a new ORATORIO, call'd SAMPSON. With a new CONCERTO on the ORGAN'
143	Kitty 3 March 1743	*The Lying Valet*	Comedy	David Garrick after Motteux, *All Without Money*, 1697	*London Daily Post and General Advertiser*, issue 6030 (3 March 1743): '[A] Farce, never acted there before, call'd The LYING VALET. The Part of the Lying Valet by Mr. GARRICK; And the Part of Kitty Pry by Mrs. Clive'
144	Vocalist 18 March 1743	*L'Allegro ed Il Penseroso*	Ode	James Harris / George F. Handel after Milton, *L'Allegro* and *Il Penseroso*, pubd 1645	*The Daily Advertiser*, issue 3795 (18 March 1743): 'By SUBSCRIPTION. *The Eighth Night* … L'ALLEGRO ed il PENSEROSO. With ADDITIONS. And DRYDEN's ODE on St. CÆCILIA's DAY. A CONCERTO on the ORGAN. And a Solo on the Violin by Mr. DUBOURG'
145	Vocalist CG 23 March 1743	*Messiah*	Oratorio	Charles Jennens / George F. Handel	*Daily Advertiser*, issue 3799 (23 March 1743): 'By SUBSCRIPTION: *The Ninth Night* … A NEW SACRED ORATORIO. With a CONCERTO on the ORGAN. And a Solo on the Violin by Mr. DUBOURG'
146	Bayes 6 May 1743	*The Rehearsal*, 1671 / Thomas Arne (duet)	Comedy	George Villiers, Duke of Buckingham	*London Daily Post and General Advertiser*, issue 2665 (6 May 1743): 'For the Benefit of Mr. RAFTOR … The REHEARSAL. The Part of Bayes (by Desire) by Mrs. CLIVE … Act I. Singing by Mr. Beard … Act IV. Singing by Miss Edwards'
147	Shade of Hero CG 26 December 1743	*The Necromancer: Or, Harlequin Dr Faustus*, 1723	Pantomime	Lewis Theobald / John Galliard	*London Daily Post and General Advertiser*, issue 2843 (26 December 1743): 'COVENT-GARDEN … [A] Dramatick Entertainment … The Shade of Leander by Mr. BEARD; The Shade of Hero by Mrs. CLIVE'
148	Rhodope CG 14 February 1744	*Orpheus and Eurydice*	Dramatic entertainment	Lewis Theobald / John F. Lampe	*London Daily Post and General Advertiser*, issue 2886 (14 February 1744): 'COVENT-GARDEN … The last New Dramatick Entertainment of Musick, call'd ORPHEUS and EURYDICE. Intermix'd with a new Pantomime, in Grotesque Characters'

No.	Role Debut date	Work, Year	Genre	Dramatist / Composer, Arranger	Notice
149	Vocalist CG 8 March 1744	*Abramule*, 1704	Tragedy	Joseph Trapp	*London Daily Post and General Advertiser*, issue 2906 (8 March 1744): 'COVENT GARDEN … *Not Acted these Three Years*. The Benefit of Mr. RYAN … ABRAMULE … A Song proper to the Play, new set to Musick, and perform'd by Mr. Beard, Mrs. Clive, and others. Likewise (by particular Desire) *Genius of England by Mr. Beard*'
150	Morayma CG 12 March 1744	*Don Sebastian, King of Portugal*, 1689	Tragedy	John Dryden	*General Advertiser*, issue 2909 (12 March 1744): 'COVENT-GARDEN. By Command of their Royal Highnesses the Prince and Princess of WALES. *For the Benefit of Mr.* QUIN … will be a reviv'd a Play (not acted these Twenty Years) call'd Don SEBASTIAN … Written by Mr. Dryden'
151	Clorinda Crown and Anchor Tavern, 21 March 1744 CG 6 March 1745 DL 8 April 1746	*Love and Friendship*	Pastoral serenata	Anon / Willem De Fesch after *Love and Friendship*, 1734	*Daily Advertiser*, issue 4103 (12 March 1744): '*At the Desire of the several Ladies of Quality*. At the Crown and Anchor in the Strand, on Wednesday the 21st instant, will be perform'd, after the Manner of an Oratorio, a new English Pastoral Serenata, call'd LOVE and FRIENDSHIP. Set to Music by WILLIAM DEFESCH. The principal Vocal Parts will be perform'd by Mr. Beard, Mr. Savage, Mrs. Clive, and Miss Edwards'
152	Phillida CG 28 March 1744	*Damon and Phillida* (rev)	Ballad opera	Colley Cibber / William Boyce et al.	*General Advertiser*, issue 2923 (28 March 1744): 'COVENT-GARDEN. By Command of their Royal Highnesses the Prince and Princess of WALES. For the Benefit of Mr. BEARD … The OLD BATCHELOR … To which (by Command) will be added, a Ballad-Farce, not acted these Three Years, called DAMON AND PHILLIDA. Damon by Mr. BEARD; Phillida by Mrs. CLIVE. In which Characters will be introduced the favourite Duetto in Solomon, (composed by Mr. BOYCE)'.

No.	Role, Debut date	Work, Year	Genre	Dramatist / Composer, Arranger	Notice
153	Principal Vocalist Little Haymarket Theatre 2 November 1744	*Benefit Concert for Catherine Clive*	Concert		*General Advertiser*, issue 3111 (2 November 1744): 'By Command of their Royal Highnesses the Prince and Princess of WALES. For the Benefit of Mrs. CLIVE. At the New Theatre in the Haymarket, this Day, will be performed A CONCERT of Vocal and Instrumental MUSICK. By the BEST MASTERS. The Vocal Parts consisting of the most favourite Airs from the last new Operas and Oratorios to be performed by Mr. Lowe, Mrs. Clive, and Miss *Edwards*'
154	Vocalist CG 29 December 1744	*King Henry the Eighth*	History play	Shakespeare / John F. Lampe John F. Lampe, *THE GRAND CHORUS as Perform'd in the Representation OF THE CORONATION at the Theatre-Royal IN COVENT GARDEN* (London, n.d.)	*General Advertiser*, issue 3160 (29 December 1744): 'COVENT-GARDEN. ... King HENRY the Eighth. Written by Shakespear. Containing, The Death of the Duke of Buckingham ... Also a REPRESENTATION of the CORONATION of ANNE BULLEN. The Vocal Parts in the Procession to be perform'd by Mr. Leveridge, Mr. Beard ... Mrs. Clive, and Mrs. Lampe'
155	Potiphar's Wife CG 20 March 1745	*Joseph*	Oratorio	Anon / Willem De Fesch	*Daily Advertiser*, issue 4410 (5 March 1745): 'On the 20th instant, and the 3d of April, will be perform'd a New Oratorio, call'd JOSEPH, also set to Musick by Mr. De Fesch'
156	Berinthia CG 2 April 1745	*The Relapse*, 1696	Comedy	John Vanbrugh	*General Advertiser*, issue 3238 (2 April 1745): 'The Benefit of Mr. COOKE'
157	Kitty Carrot CG 4 April 1745	*The What D'ye Call It*, 1715	Farce with songs	John Gay / John F. Lampe	*Daily Advertiser*, issue 4436 (4 April 1745): 'The Musick entirely new, compos'd by Mr. Lampe'
158	Melissa CG 20 April 1745	*Timon of Athens*, 1678	Drama	Thomas Shadwell Adapted from Shakespeare	*General Advertiser*, issue 3254 (20 April 1745): 'TIMON of ATHENS ... With Entertainments of Singing and Dancing viz. In Act II. A Duet by Mr. Beard and Miss Edwards'

No.	Role / Debut date	Work, Year	Genre	Dramatist / Composer, Arranger	Notice
159	Ariel / 31 January 1746	*The Tempest*	Comedy	Shakespeare / Willem De Fesch, Thomas Arne / Willem De Fesch, [6] *Songs in the Tempest* (London, 1746)	*General Advertiser*, issue 3515 (31 January 1746): 'Never Acted there before … The TEMPEST. As Written by Shakespeare … The Part of Miranda, by Miss Edwards; and the Part of Ariel (with the proper Songs) by Mrs. Clive. With the Original Decorations, particularly the GRAND MASQUE new set to Musick by Mr. Arne. The Part of Juno by Mrs. Arne; Iris, Miss Young; Ceres, Mrs. Sibella; With proper Chorus's and Dances. Concluding with a Musical Entertainment by Mr. Arne'
160	Colombine / 3 March 1746	*Harlequin Incendiary: Or, Colombine Cameron*	Pantomime	Anon / Thomas Arne	*General Advertiser*, issue 3541 (3 March 1746): '[A] new Musical Pantomime … The Character of Colombine (with proper Songs) by Mrs[.] Clive'
161	Melantha / 10 March 1746	*The Comical Lovers: Or, Marriage A-la-Mode*, 1707	Comedy	Colley Cibber after Dryden, *Secret Love*, 1666, *Marriage à la Mode*, 1672	*General Advertiser*, issue 3547 (10 March 1746): '*Not Acted there Thirty Years*. For the Benefit of Mrs. CLIVE … The COMICAL LOVERS; Alter'd from Dryden by Colly Cibber, Esq; The Part of Melantha to be perform'd by Mrs. CLIVE, (*With Songs proper to the Character,*) particularly A Mimic Italian Song.… To which will be added a Farce, call'd DAMON and PHILLIDA'
162	Lucinda / 13 March 1746	*The She Gallant*, 1695	Comedy	George Granville / Thomas Arne	*General Advertiser*, issue 3550 (13 March 1746): '*Never acted there before* … For the Benefit of Mr. MACKLIN … The SHE GALLANTS … Written by the late Lord LANSDOW. With the Original Songs, new Set by Mr. Arne, and to be sung by Mr. Lowe and Mrs. Clive'
163	Victoria / 4 April 1746	*The Lying Lover*, 1703	Comedy	Richard Steele after Corneille, *Le Menteur*, 1644	*General Advertiser*, issue 3569 (4 April 1746): '*Not Acted these Forty Years*. For the Benefit of Mr. YATES … The LYING LOVER … With Entertainments of Singing and Dancing.… Act II. A Scotch Dialogue by Mr. Lowe and Miss Edwards'

No.	Role, Debut date	Work, Year	Genre	Dramatist / Composer, Arranger	Notice
164	Clarinda, 21 April 1746	*The Sea Voyage: Or, the Commonwealth of Women*, 1685	Comedy	after D'Urfey, 1685, after John Fletcher and Philip Massinger, 1667	*General Advertiser*, issue 3583 (21 April 1746): 'For the BENEFIT of Mr. BRIDGES, Mr. BLAKES, and Mr. CROSS, Prompter … will be reviv'd a Comedy, call'd THE SEA VOYAGE, OR, The COMMONWEALTH OF WOMEN. Alter'd from Beaumont and Fletcher. Capt. Marine, Mr. Delane … Clarinda, Mrs. Clive … Adriadne by Miss Edwards … With an EPILOGUE, recommending the Cause of Liberty to the Beauties of Great-Britain, by Mrs. Clive … Act I. A Scotch Dialogue by Mr. Lowe and Miss Edwards'
165	Sophronia, 28 November 1746	*The Refusal*, 1721	Comedy	Colley Cibber after Wright, *Female Virtuosos*, 1693, after Molière, *Les Femmes Savante*, 1672	*General Advertiser*, issue 3773 (28 November 1746): 'Not Acted these Twenty-five Years'
166	Vocalist, 15 December 1746	*Theodosius*, 1680	Tragedy	Nathaniel Lee / Thomas Arne	*General Advertiser*, issue 3787 (15 December 1746): 'Not Acted these Sixteen Years … this Day, will be reviv'd … THEODOSIUS … With the Original Songs new set by Arne To be sung by Mr. Lowe, Mr. Sullivan, Mr. Reinhold, Mrs. Clive, Mrs. Mozeen, and others'
167	Queen Elinor, 10 January 1747	*Rosamond*	Opera	Joseph Addison / Thomas Arne after Addison, *Rosamond*, 1707	*General Advertiser*, issue 3810 (10 January 1747): '[A]n Opera of Two Acts, call'd ROSAMOND … Queen Elinor by Mrs. CLIVE, (*Being the first time of her appearing in this Character.*) The Words by Mr. Addison; the Musick compos'd by Mr. Arne'
168	Lillia-Bianca, 7 March 1747	*The Wild Goose Chase*, 1652	Comedy	John Fletcher / Thomas Arne	*General Advertiser*, issue 3855 (4 March 1747): 'Never Acted there Before. *For the Benefit of Mrs. CLIVE …* on … the 7th of March … The WILD GOOSE CHASE. Written by Beaumont and Fletcher. The Part of Lilla Biancha to be perform'd by Mrs. CLIVE: In which Character will be introduced proper Songs, the Musick new composed by Mr. Arne'

No.	Role Debut date	Work, Year	Genre	Dramatist / Composer, Arranger	Notice
169	Margerina 7 March 1747	**The Dragon of Wantley**	Burlesque opera	Henry Carey / John F. Lampe	*General Advertiser*, issue 3855 (4 March 1747): '*For the Benefit of Mrs. CLIVE … The DRAGON OF WANTLEY. The Part of Margerina (in the Burlesque Manner) to be perform'd by Mrs. CLIVE; (Being the First Time of Her appearing in that Character.)*'
170	Betty Ruffle 30 March 1747	Marry or Do Worse: Or, No Wit like a Woman's, 1703	Comedy	William Walker	*General Advertiser*, issue 3849 (30 March 1747): '*Never Acted there. For the Benefit of Mr. YATES*'
171	Tag 24 October 1747	Miss in her Teens	Comedy	David Garrick after Dancourt, *La Parisienne*, 1691	*General Advertiser*, issue 4056 (14 October 1747): '*[A] Farce of Two Acts (never Acted there before)*'
172	Lady Wronghead 1 October 1748	The Provok'd Husband, 1728	Comedy	Colley Cibber / Thomas Arne	*General Advertiser*, issue 4348 (1 October 1748): '*Lady Wronghead by Mrs. CLIVE, (Being the first Time of her appearing this Character)*'
173	Vocal Part 14 November 1748	**Much Ado about Nothing**	Comedy	Shakespeare / Thomas Arne	*General Advertiser*, issue 4385 (14 November 1748): '*Never Acted there … MUCH ADO ABOUT NOTHING. Written by Shakespear … The Musical Parts by Mr. BEARD, Mr. RHEINHOLD, Mrs. CLIVE, and others*'
174	Mrs. Riot 2 January 1749	Lethe	Dramatic satire with 3 songs	David Garrick / Thomas Arne, William Boyce after Miller, *An Hospital for Fools*, 1739	*General Advertiser*, issue 4425 (2 January 1749): '*[A] Dramatick Satire call'd LETHE. The principal Parts to be perform'd by Mr. GARRICK; Mr. Woodward … And Mrs. CLIVE*'

No.	Role / Debut date	Work, Year	Genre	Dramatist / Composer, Arranger	Notice
175	Clarice / 14? February 1749	*Don Saverio*	Musical drama	Thomas Arne / Thomas Arne	*General Advertiser*, issue 4464 (14 February 1749; front page: 'The General Advertiser. WEDNESDAY, February 15, 1748–49'): *'Tomorrow at Twelve o'Clock will be publish'd, DON SAVERIO: A MUSICAL DRAMA. As it is perform'd at the Theatre-Royal in Drury-Lane. The Musick composed by Mr. ARNE'* (date in *The London Stage*, Part 4, vol. 1, p. 175 is 15 February 1750)
176	Shepherdess / 21 February 1749	*The Triumph of Peace*	Masque	Robert Dodsley / Thomas Arne	*General Advertiser*, issue 4470 (21 February 1749): '[A] Masque, never perform'd before, call'd The TRIUMPH of PEACE … Shepherdess Mrs. CLIVE … The Whole to conclude with a View of the TEMPLE of PEACE. *With New Scenes, Dresses, Musick and other Decorations*. The Musick compos'd by Mr. ARNE'
177	Clarinda / 13 March 1749	*The Suspicious Husband*	Comedy	Benjamin Hoadley	*General Advertiser*, issue 4486 (13 March 1749): '*At the Desire of several Ladies of Quality. For the Benefit of Mrs. CLIVE* … The SUSPICIOUS HUSBAND … The Part of Clarinda by Mrs. CLIVE, *Being the first Time of her appearing to that Character* … And (by particular Desire) *The Life of a Beau*, by Mrs. CLIVE'
178	Lady Harriet / 21 November 1749	*The Funeral: Or, Grief à la Mode*, 1702	Comedy	Richard Steele	*General Advertiser*, issue 4706 (21 November 1749): 'Lady Harriet, Mrs. CLIVE; *Being the First Time of appearing in that Character*'
179	Pastora / 2 December 1749	*The Chaplet*	Comic Pastoral	Moses Mendez / William Boyce	*General Advertiser*, issue 4715 (2 December 1749): '[A] New Musical Entertainment, in Two Interludes, call'd The CHAPLET. The Music composed by Dr. BOYCE. The Principal Parts to be performed by Mr. BEARD, Master MATTOCKS, Miss NORRIS and Mrs. CLIVE. To conclude with a Rural Dance'
180	Lady Squeamish / 22 January 1750	*Friendship in Fashion*, 1678	Comedy	Thomas Otway	*General Advertiser*, issue 4759 (22 January 1750; front page: 'The General Advertiser. MONDAY, January 22, 1749–50'): '*Not Acted these Thirty Years*'

No.	Role, Debut date	Work, Year	Genre	Dramatist / Composer, Arranger	Notice
181	Mrs. Hazard Marcella 15 March 1750	*The Rehearsal: Or, Bayes in Petticoats*	Comedy with masque	Catherine Clive / William Boyce	*General Advertiser*, issue 4487 (14 March 1750; front page): 'The General Advertiser. WEDNESDAY, March 14 1749–50': 'For the Benefit of Mrs. CLIVE … HAMLET … To which will be added a Farce, never acted before, call'd The REHEARSAL; Or, BAYES in PETTICOATS. The Musick composed by Dr. BOYCE. The Principal Parts to be Performed by Mrs. CLIVE, Mr. Woodward, Mr Beard, Mr. Simpson, Mr. Cross, Mrs. Benner, Miss Cole, and Miss Norris'
182	Vocal Part 1 October 1750	*Romeo and Juliet*	Tragedy	Shakespeare / William Boyce	*General Advertiser*, issue 4975 (1 October 1750): 'This Day, will be revived … ROMEO and JULIET … With the Additional Scene representing The FUNERAL PROCESSION of JULIET To the MONUMENT of the CAPULETS. Vocal Parts by Mr. Beard, Mr. Reinhold, Mr. Wilder, Master Mattocks, Mrs. Clive, Miss Norris, Mrs. Mathews, &c.. The Musick composed by Doctor BOYCE'
183	Diana 30 October 1750	*The Secular Masque*	Masque	John Dryden / William Boyce after masque in Fletcher, *The Pilgrim*, 1700	*General Advertiser*, issue 5000 (30 October 1750): 'The SECULAR MASQUE (Written by Mr. DRYDEN) The Musick composed by Dr. BOYCE. The Character of Memus [*sic*] by Mr. BEARD … and Diana, Mrs. Clive. With proper Dances, Chorusses, &c.. &c.'
184	Primrose 13 December 1750	*Robin Hood*	Burletta	Moses Mendez / Charles Burney	*General Advertiser*, issue 5038 (13 December 1750): '[A] New Musical Entertainment, call'd ROBIN HOOD. Principal Parts to be performed by Mr. BEARD … Mrs[.] CLIVE, &c.. To conclude with a New FOREST DANCE'
185	Vocalist 23 February 1751	*Alfred*	Masque	David Mallet / Thomas Arne after Mallet, Thomson, *Alfred*, 1740	*The London Stage*, Part 4, vol. 1, p. 238: 'Cast taken from 1st edn. The bill merely lists actors and notes "With proper Music, Scenes and Decorations. Never acted before" … *Prologue* – Garrick; *Epilogue* – Mrs. Clive'

455

No.	Role / Debut date	Work, Year	Genre	Dramatist / Composer, Arranger	Notice
186	Bisarre / 12 March 1751	The Inconstant: Or, the Way to Keep Him, 1699	Comedy	George Farquhar / Thomas Arne	*The London Stage*, Part 4, vol. 1, p. 238: 'Benefit for Mrs. Clive … Also THE REHEARSAL, or Bayes in Petticoats. Principal parts by Mrs Clive, Woodward, Beard, Shuter, Mrs Bennet, Miss Minors, Mrs Green, Miss Norris'
187	Mrs. Clive / 16 March 1751	A Lick at the Town	Farce	Henry Woodward	*General Advertiser*, issue 5116 (15 March 1751; front page: 'The General Advertiser. FRIDAY March 15, 1750–51'): '[A] New Dramatick Performance, call'd A LICK at the TOWN. The principal Parts to be performed by Mr. Woodward, Mr. Palmer … and Mrs. Clive'
188	Girtred / 29 October 1751	*Eastward Hoe,* 1605	Comedy	after George Chapman, Ben Jonson, and John Marston	*General Advertiser*, issue 5033 (29 October 1751): 'This day, will be reviv'd a Comedy, called EASTWARD-HOE … (Written by Ben Jonson, Chapman, Marston) The Part of Quicksilver to be performed by Mr. WOODWARD … And the Part of Girtred to be performed by Mrs. CLIVE'
189	Daphne / 19 November 1751	The Shepherd's Lottery	Comic pastoral	Moses Mendez / William Boyce	*General Advertiser*, issue 5303 (19 November 1751): '[A] new Musical Entertainment, call'd The SHEPHERD's LOTTTERY. (The Music composed by Dr. BOYCE.) The principal Parts to be performed by Mr. BEARD, Master VERNON, Mr. WILDER, Miss NORRIS, And Mrs. CLIVE. To conclude with a Pastoral Dance'
190	Mrs. Marwood / 10 October 1752	The Way of the World, 1699	Comedy	William Congreve	*General Advertiser*, issue 5600 (10 October 1752)
191	Lady Haughty / 26 October 1752	Epicoene: Or, the Silent Woman, 1609	Comedy	Ben Jonson	*General Advertiser*, issue 5614 (26 October 1752): 'Not Acted these Fifteen Years … (Written by BEN JOHNSON.). Sir John Daw, Mr. WOODWARD … Lady Haughty, by Mrs. Clive'
192	Zara / 22 March 1753	The Mourning Bride	Tragedy	Aaron Hill / Thomas Arne (instrumental) after Voltaire, *Zaïre*, 1732	*Public Advertiser*, issue 5740 (22 March 1753): 'For the Benefit of Mrs. CLIVE … The MOURNING BRIDE. Osmyn, Mr. GARRICK; Zara, by Desire, by Mrs. CLIVE, *Being the First Time of her appearing in that Character* … To which will be added, (not acted these two Years) a Farce, call'd The REHEARSAL; or, *Bayes in Petticoats*. With ALTERATIONS and an ADDITIONAL SCENE'

No.	Role / Debut date	Work, Year	Genre	Dramatist / Composer, Arranger	Notice
193	Mrs. Frail / 16 January 1754	*Love for Love*, 1695	Comedy	William Congreve	*Public Advertiser*, issue 5997 (16 January 1754)
194	Jacintha / 13 March 1755	*The Mistake*, 1705	Comedy	John Vanbrugh after Molière, *Le Dépit amoreux*, 1656	*Public Advertiser*, issue 6356 (13 March 1755)
195	Mrs. Kitely / 17 March 1755	*Every Man in his Humour*, 1751 version	Comedy	David Garrick Adapted from Jonson, 1598	*Public Advertiser*, issue 6359 (17 March 1755): 'For the Benefit of Mrs. CLIVE … EVERY MAN In His HUMOUR. Kitely, Mr. GARRICK … Mrs. Kitely, Mrs. CLIVE … To which will be added, an English Operetta, (never perform'd but twice) call'd The LONDON 'PRENTICE' (see below)
196	Princess Theoraze / 23 March 1754	*The London 'Prentice*	Comic opera?	Catherine Clive ? / William De Fesch	*Public Advertiser*, issue 6052 (23 March 1754): '[A] new English Operetta of Two Acts, call'd The LONDON 'PRENTICE. The principal Parts by Mr. Beard, Mr. Wilder, Mr. Venon, Miss Thomas, and Mrs. Clive. The Music composed by Mr. De FESCH'
197	Abigail / 3 October 1755	*The Drummer*, 1716	Comedy	Joseph Addison	*Public Advertiser*, issue 6541 (3 October 1755)
198	Margaret? / October? 1755	***King Pepin's Campaign***	Burlesque Opera	William Shirley / Thomas Arne William Shirley, 'Dramatis Personae … Margaret Pepin's mistress, beloved by Puff / Mrs. Clive', *King Pepin's Campaign. A Burlesque Opera … in Drury-Lane, in the Year 1745* (London, 1755)	*Public Advertiser*, issue 6562 (29 October 1755): '*This Days published*, Price 6d. KING PEPIN'S CAMPAIGN. A BURLESQUE OPERA, of TWO ACTS. Acted at the Theatre Royal in Drury-lane' (no performance advertised) *Daily Advertiser*, issue 4438 (6 April 1745): 'For the Benefit of Mr. ARNE. At … Drury-Lane … a new Burlesque Opera, of two Acts, call'd KING PEPIN's CAMPAIN. Set to Musick by Mr. ARNE … Margaret, Mrs. [Cecilia] Arne'

No.	Role, Debut date	Work, Year	Genre	Dramatist / Composer, Arranger	Notice
199	Mother, 28 November 1755	The Chances, 1683	Comedy	John Fletcher and George Villiers, Duke of Buckingham after Cervantes, La Señora Cornelia, 1613	Public Advertiser, issue 6579 (28 November 1755)
200	Catherine, 21 January 1756	Catherine and Petruchio	Comedy	David Garrick after Shakespeare, Taming of the Shrew	Public Advertiser, issue 6625 (21 January 1756): 'A COMEDY in THREE ACTS. (From SHAKESPEAR's Taming of the Shrew) … For the Benefit of a GENTLEWOMAN depriv'd of Sight'
201	Lady Wronglove, 27 March 1756	The Lady's Last Stake, 1707	Comedy	Colley Cibber	Public Advertiser, issue 6686 (27 March 1756): 'Not acted these Ten Years. For the Benefit of Mrs. CLIVE … The LADY's LAST STAKE … Lady Wronglove, Mrs. CLIVE, (Being the first Time of the their appearing in these Characters,) … To which will be added … LETHE … In which will be introduced a new Character to be perform'd by Mr. GARRICK … the Fine Lady, Mrs. Clive. In which will be introduc'd a new Mimic Italian Song'
202	Mrs. Cadwallader, 5 February 1757	The Author	Comedy	Samuel Foote	Public Advertiser, issue 6953 (5 February 1757): '[A] new Farce of Two Acts call'd The AUTHOR. The principal Characters by Mr. Foote, Mr. Ross … and Mrs. Clive'
203	Lady Wishfort, 16 March 1758	The Way of the World, 1699	Comedy	William Congreve	Public Advertiser, issue 9774 (16 March 1758): 'For the Benefit of Mrs. CLIVE … The WAY of the WORLD. Lady Wishfor't (by particular Desire) by Mrs. CLIVE, (Being the first Time of her appearing in that Character)'
204	Termagant, 30 March 1758	The Upholsterer	Comedy	Arthur Murphy	Public Advertiser, issue 7518 (2 December 1758): '[A] Farce of two Acts, never perform'd before'
205	Patch, 2 December 1758	The Busy Body, 1709	Comedy	Susanna Centlivre	Public Advertiser, issue 7518) 2 December 1758: 'The Busy Body by Mr. GARRICK … Patch by Mrs. CLIVE. (Being the 1st Time of her appearing in that Character)'
206	Lucy, 3 February 1759	The Guardian	Comedy	David Garrick after Fagan, La Pupille, 1734	Public Advertiser, issue 7564 (3 February 1759): '[A] new Comedy of two Acts'

No.	Role, Debut date	Work, Year	Genre	Dramatist / Composer, Arranger	Notice
207	Kitty, 31 October 1759	*High Life Below Stairs*	Comedy	James Townley, David Garrick / Jonathan Battishill	*Public Advertiser*, issue 7794 (31 October 1759): '[A] New Comedy of two Acts'; *Come Here fellow Servant. A New Song. Sung by Mrs. Clive, in the Farce of High Life below Stairs. Set by Mr. Battershill* (London, c.1760)
208	Muslin, 24 January 1760	*The Way to Keep Him*	Comedy	Arthur Murphy	*Public Advertiser*, issue 7848 (24 January 1760): 'Never acted before … a Comedy of three Acts, call'd The WAY TO KEEP HIM'
209	Mrs. Crostin, 20 March 1760	*Every Woman in her Humour*	Comedy	Catherine Clive	*Public Advertiser*, issue 7916 (20 March 1760): 'For the Benefit of Mrs. CLIVE … a new Comedy of two Acts, (never perform'd before) call'd EVERY WOMAN IN HER HUMOUR. The principal Characters by Mr. King, Mr. Yates … Mrs. Clive'
210	Lady Freelove, 12 February 1761	*The Jealous Wife*	Comedy	George Colman after Henry Fielding, *Tom Jones*, 1749	*Public Advertiser*, issue 8198 (12 February 1761): 'Never Acted before'
211	Euphrosine, 26 March 1761	*The Island of Slaves*	Comedy	Catherine Clive? after Marivaux, *L'île des esclaves*, 1725	*Public Advertiser*, issue 8234 (26 March 1761): 'At the Desire of several Persons of Quality. For the Benefit of Mrs. CLIVE … a new Dramatic Pieces (in two Acts) of a particular Species, call'd The ISLAND of SLAVES. The principal Characters by Mr. Havard, Mr. King … and Mrs. Clive. With a comic Opera Song in Character'
212	Lady Beverly, 10 February 1762	*The School for Lovers*	Comedy	William Whitehead after Fontenelle, *Le Testament*, 1758	*Public Advertiser*, issue 8509 (10 February 1762): 'Never acted before'
213	Old Maid, 7 January 1763	*The Old Maid*, 1756	Comedy	Arthur Murphy	*Public Advertiser*, issue 8794 (7 January 1763): 'The OLD MAID … Miss Harlow by Mrs. CLIVE: (Being her 1st Appearance in that Character.)'

459

No.	Role Debut date	Work, Year	Genre	Dramatist / Composer, Arranger	Notice
214	Lady Jenkings 21 March 1763	Sketch of a Fine Lady's Return from a Rout	Farce	Catherine Clive	*Public Advertiser*, issue 8856 (21 March 1763): 'For the Benefit of Mrs. CLIVE … a Farce in one Act (never performed before) called The SKETCH of a Fine LADY'S Return from a Rout. The Characters by Mr. KING, Mr. LOVE … And Mrs. CLIVE. At the End of the Farce, (by particular Desire) a mimic comic Italian Song, from the Opera of Philospho di Campagna [1754], by Mrs. Clive'
215	Mrs. Friendly 9 December 1763	The Dupe	Comedy	Frances Sheridan	*St. James's Chronicle or the British Evening*, issue 433 (10–13 December 1763): 'Drury-Lane. Yesterday, the Dupe. This Evening, the same'; *Ibid.*: "The Dupe is a very poor Performance, lame and defective, not to add gross and indelicate'
216	Lisetta 28 November 1764	**Capricious Lovers**	Comic opera	Robert Lloyd / George Rush after Favart, *Ninette à la Cour*, 1755	*Public Advertiser*, issue 9383 (28 November 1764): 'This Day will be presented, a New Comic Opera' *The London Stage*, Part 4, vol. 2, p. 1242 (Drury Lane, 4 May 1767): 'We had the *Capricious Lovers*, Lisetta by Mrs Clive, who took off the ridiculous sing-song at ye Opera House charmingly (Neville MS diary)'
217	Lady Fanshaw 24 January 1765	The Platonic Wife	Comedy	Elizabeth Griffith after Marmontel, *L'Heureux divorce in conges moraux*, 1758	*Public Advertiser*, issue 9432 (24 January 1765): 'Never Acted'
218	Irishwoman 18 March 1765	The Faithful Irishwoman	Farce	Catherine Clive after Clive, *Sketch of a Fine Lady's Return from a Rout*, 1763	*Public Advertiser*, issue 9467 (18 March 1765): 'For the Benefit of Mrs. CLIVE … a new Farce called The Faithful IRISHWOMAN. The principal Parts by Mr. LOVE Mr. PACKER … And the Irishwoman, by Mrs. CLIVE'
219	Widow Blackacre 7 December 1765	The Plain Dealer, 1676	Comedy	William Wycherly, Isaac Bickerstaff	*Public Advertiser*, issue 9704 (7 December 1765): NOT ACTED THESE TWENTY YEARS'
220	Mrs. Heidelberg 20 February 1766	The Clandestine Marriage	Comedy	George Colman, David Garrick	*Public Advertiser*, issue 9768 (20 February 1766): 'NEVER ACTED … a Comedy call'd The Clandestine MARRIAGE. The Principal Characters by Mr. HOLLAND, Mr. POWELL … And Mrs. CLIVE'

No.	Role Debut date	Work, Year	Genre	Dramatist / Composer, Arranger	Notice
221	Lady Fuz 23 October 1767	*A Peep behind the Curtain: Or, the New Rehearsal*	Farce	David Garrick after Clive, *The Rehearsal: Or, Bayes in Petticoats*, 1750 version	*Public Advertiser*, issue 10,290 (23 October 1767): '[A] Farce of Two Acts, never performed before'. Final scenes: 'BURLETTA OF ORPHEUS'; music by François-Hippolyte Barthélemon, principal vocalists, Joseph Vernon, James William Dodd, 'Mrs. Arne' (Mrs. Michael Arne, née Elizabeth Wright?); David Garrick, *A Peep behind the Curtain* (London, 1767), David Garrick, *The Songs and Recitative of Orpheus: An English Burletta* (London, 1767)
222	Mrs. Winifred 4 February 1769	*The School for Rakes*	Comedy	Elizabeth Griffiths	*Public Advertiser*, issue 10,693 (4 February 1769): 'FOR THE FIRST TIME'

APPENDIX 2

Lines in Catherine Clive's Repertory 1728–69

? = categorization is estimated; printed evidence missing
[SP] = sung part; [SPS] = spoken part with song; [OP] = Oldfield part

Season	Goddess (masque)	Pastoral, British rustic	Country girl in city	Defiant daughter	Sentimental heroine / spirited, abused wife	Fine Lady	Intriguing servant	Patriot soprano	Shakespeare	Vocal part	In propria persona / Burlesque
1727–28										**Immenea, a Page** [SP] *Mithridates, King of Pontus* 13 April 1728? **Minerva (?)** [SP] *Perseus and Andromeda* 15 November 1728	

Season	Goddess (masque)	Pastoral, British rustic	Sentimental heroine / spirited, abused wife	Country girl in city	Defiant daughter	Fine Lady	Intriguing servant	Patriot soprano	Shakespeare	Vocal part	In propria persona / Burlesque
1728–29	**Minerva** [SP] *Perseus and Andromeda* 15 November 1728 **Amphitrite** [SP] *Neptune and Amphitrite* 28 May (?) 1729	**Phillida** [SP] *Love in a Riddle* 7 January 1729	**Rosella** [SP] *The Village Opera* 6 February 1729 **Flora** [SP] *The Lover's Opera* 14 May 1729		**Phebe** [SP] *Phebe: Or, the Beggar's Wedding* 13 June 1729			**Bonvica** [SP] *The History of Bonduca* 13 June 1729	**Bianca** [SP] *Othello* 12 October 1728 **Dorinda** [SP] *The Tempest* 2 January 1729	**Susan** [SP] *The What D'ye Call It* 10 April 1729	
1729–30	**Night** [SP] *Apollo and Daphne* 10 December 1729 **Dulceda** [SP] *Bayes's Opera* 30 March 1730 **Fairy Queen** [SP] **Surel, Harlequin** *The Fairy Queen* 15 May 1730	**Peggy** [SP] *Patie and Peggy* 20 April 1730	**Rosella** [SP] *The Chambermaid* 10 February 1730 **Serina** [SP] *The Orphan* 16 April 1730 **Isabella** [SP] *The Stage Coach Opera* 13 May 1730	**Jenny** [SPS] *The Provok'd Husband* 11 April 1730 **Prue** [SP] *Love for Love* 18 April 1730			**Miss Kitty** [SPS] *The Humours of Oxford* 9 January 1730				**Miss Kitty** [SPS] *The Humours of Oxford* 9 January 1730

Season	Goddess (masque)	Pastoral, British rustic	Sentimental heroine / spirited, abused wife	Country girl in city	Defiant daughter	Fine Lady	Intriguing servant	Patriot soprano	Shakespeare	Vocal part	In propria persona / Burlesque
1730–31	**Procris** [SP] *Cephalus and Procris* 28 October 1730	**Nanny** [SP] *The Highland Fair* 20 March 1731 **Phillida** [SP] *Damon and Phillida* 7 June 1731 **Shepherdess** [SP] *The Triumphs of Love and Honour* 18 August 1731	**Jenny** [SP] *The Cobler's Opera* 11 June 1731 **Nell** [SP] (abused wife) *The Devil to Pay* 6 August 1731 **Urania** [SPS] *The Triumphs of Love and Honour* 18 August 1731		**Amie** [SP] *The Jovial Crew* 8 February 1731 **Kitty Carrot** [SP] *What D'ye Call It* 11 August 1731, ballad opera version					**Kalid** [SP] *The Indian Emperor* 12 May 1731	

Season	Goddess (masque)	Pastoral, British rustic	Sentimental heroine / spirited, abused wife	Country girl in city	Defiant daughter	Fine Lady	Intriguing servant	Patriot soprano	Shakespeare	Vocal part	In propria persona / Burlesque
1731–32		**Margery [SP]** *The Country Wedding* 8 May 1732 **Unkown [SP]** *Rural Love* 4 August 1732	**Unknown** (abused wife?) *The Ephesian Matron* 17 April 1732 **Martin's Wife [SP]** (abused wife) *The Comical Revenge* 12 May 1732 **Dorcas [SP]** (abused wife) *The Mock Doctor* 23 June 1732 **Polly [SP]** *The Beggar's Opera* 11 July 1732 **Flametta [SP]** *The Devil of a Duke* 17 August 1732	**Chloe [SP]** *The Lottery* 1 January 1732	**Isabel [SP]** *The Old Debauchees* 1 June 1732					**Busy [SPS]** *The Man of Mode* 20 April 1732	**Miss Sprightly [SP]** in lost intro to *The Tragedy of Tragedies* 3 May 1732

Season	Goddess (masque)	Pastoral, British rustic	Sentimental heroine / spirited, abused wife	Country girl in city	Defiant daughter	Fine Lady	Intriguing servant	Patriot soprano	Shakespeare	Vocal part	In propria persona / Burlesque
1732–33	**Thalia** [SP] *Judgment of Paris* 6 February 1733 **Venus** [SP] [lost] *Damon and Daphne* 7 May 1733 **Venus** [SP] *Venus, Cupid, and Hymen* 21 May 1733	**Cicely** [SP] *Wat Tyler* 19 January 1733	**Betty** [SP] *Betty: Or, the Country Bumpkins* 6 December 1732	**Phillis** [SP] *The Livery Rake* 5 May 1733	**Jenny** [SP] *The Boarding School* 29 January 1733 **Deborah** (?) [SP?] lost *Deborah: Or, a Wife for You All* 6 April 1733 **Mrs. Fancifull** [SP] *The Imaginary Cuckolds* 11 April 1733		**Lappet** [SPS] *The Miser* 17 February 1733 **Betty** (?) [SP?] lost *The Mock Countess* 30 April 1733			**Vocal part** [SP] *Macbeth* 28 September 1732 **Vocal part** [SP] *King Henry the Eighth* 13 November 1732 **Leonora** [SPS] *Sir Courtly Nice* 9 December 1732	**Miss Kitty** [SP] *The Harlot's Progress* 31 March 1733

Season	Goddess (masque)	Pastoral, British rustic	Sentimental heroine / spirited, abused wife	Country girl in city	Defiant daughter	Fine Lady	Intriguing servant	Patriot soprano	Shakespeare	Vocal part	In propria persona / Burlesque
1733–34	**Diana** [SP] *Harlequin Dr Faustus* 10 October 1733 **Mercury** [SP] *Timon in Love* 5 December 1733		**Miranda** [SP] *The Busy Body* 21 November 1733 **Aspasia** [SP] *Timon in Love* 5 December 1733 **Harriot** [SP] *The Author's Farce* 15 January 1734		**Elvira** [OP] *The Spanish Fryar* 19 October 1733		**Doris** [SP] *Aesop* 24 September 1733 **Estifania** [OP] *Rule a Wife and Have a Wife* 1 October 1733 **Cherry** [SP] *The Beaux Strategem* 5 October 1733 **Lettice** [SP] *The Intriguing Chambermaid* 15 January 1734 **Flippanta** [SPS] *The City Wives Confederacy* 11 March 1734 **Lisette** [?] lost *Love is the Doctor* 4 April 1734		**Desdemona** [SPS] *Othello* 13 May 1734		**Queen Dollalolla** [SP] *The Opera of Operas* 7 November 1733 **Columbine** [SP] [anti-Spanish] *Cupid and Psyche: Or, Columbine-Courtezan* 4 February 1734

467

Season	Goddess (masque)	Pastoral, British rustic	Sentimental heroine / spirited, abused wife	Country girl in city	Defiant daughter	Fine Lady	Intriguing servant	Patriot soprano	Shakespeare	Vocal part	In propria persona / Burlesque
1734–35	Spirit [SP] *Merlin: Or, the Devil of Stone-Henge* 12 December 1734		Nell [SP] (abused wife) *The Merry Cobler* 6 May 1735	Country Lass [SP] *Merlin: Or, the Devil of Stone-Henge* 12 December 1734 Mrs. Pinchwife [SP] *The Country Wife* 4 February 1735 Maria [SPS] *The Man of Taste* 6 March 1735	Hoyden [SP] *The Relapse* 7 November 1734 Miss Lucy [SP] *An Old Man Taught Wisdom* 6 January 1735 Maria [SPS] *The Man of Taste* 6 March 1735	Lady Woudbe [SP] ('learned' lady) *Volpone* 13 March 1735	Primrose [SPS] *The Mother-in-Law* 19 October 1734		Peg [SP] (abused wife) *A Cure for a Scold* 25 February 1735 Ophelia [SPS] *Hamlet* 10 March 1735	Lady Fanciful [SPS] *The Provok'd Wife* 23 April 1735	Country Lass [SP] *Merlin: Or, the Devil of Stone-Henge* 12 December 1734 (performs final song only, invokes 'Miss Kitty' *Harlot's Progress*)
1735–36	Clymene [SP] *The Fall of Phaeton* 28 February 1736				Aurelia [OP] *The Twin Rivals* 3 January 1736 Flavia [SP] *The Connoisseur* 20 February 1736 Biddy [OP] *The Tender Husband* 12 April 1736	Lady Froth [SPS] ('learned' lady) *The Double Dealer* 11 October 1735	Phaedra [SP] *Amphitryon* 6 April 1736	Clymene [SP] *The Fall of Phaeton* 28 February 1736 Vocalist [SP] *A Grand Epithalamium* 22 April 1736		Doll Common [SP] *The Alchymist* 15 September 1735 Vocalist [SP] *A Grand Epithalamium* 22 April 1736	

Season	Goddess (masque)	Pastoral, British rustic	Sentimental heroine/spirited, abused wife	Country girl in city	Defiant daughter	Fine Lady	Intriguing servant	Patriot soprano	Shakespeare	Vocal part	In propria persona/Burlesque
1736–37			**Isabella [SP]** *The Squire of Alsatia* 23 September 1736 **Arabella [SP]** *The Wife's Relief* 13 October 1736		**Wanton Wife [SPS]** *The Amorous Widow* 7 December 1736	**Eurydice [SP]** *Eurydice: Or, the Devil Henpeck'd* 19 February 1737 **Liberia [SP]** *The Universal Passion* 28 February 1737			**Liberia [SP]** *The Universal Passion* "Music by Handel" 28 February 1737	**Ghost of Statira [SP]** *The Rival Queens* 22 November 1736	**Ghost of Statira [SP]** *The Rival Queens* 22 November 1736
1737–38	**Euphrosyne [SP]** *Comus* 4 March 1738	**Nymph [SP]** *Comus* 4 March 1738	**Miss Kitty [SP]** *Sir John Cockle at Court* 23 February 1738	**Laetitia [OP]** *The Old Batchelor* 15 September 1737		**Narcissa [OP]** *Love's Last Shift* 6 September 1737	**Miss Kitty [SP]** *The Coffee-House* 26 January 1738 **Violetta [SP]** *Art and Nature* 16 February 1738	**Miss Kitty [SP]** *Sir John Cockle at Court* 23 February 1738		**Vocalist [SP]** Benefit Concert 3 March 1738	**Miss Kitty [SP]** *The Coffee-House* 26 January 1738 *Art and Nature* Epilogue scene 16 February 1738 **Miss Kitty [SP]** *Sir John Cockle at Court* 23 February 1738 **Euphrosyne [SP]** *Comus* 4 March 1738

Season	Goddess (masque)	Pastoral, British rustic	Sentimental heroine / spirited, abused wife	Country girl in city	Defiant daughter	Fine Lady	Intriguing servant	Patriot soprano	Shakespeare	Vocal part	In propria persona / Burlesque
1738–39			Anne Lovely [SP] *A Bold Stroke for a Wife* 13 January 1739			Hillaria [SP] *Tunbridge Walks* 9 December 1738 **Mrs. Loveit [OP]** *The Man of Mode* 3 February 1739				**Vocalist [SP]** *The Pilgrim* 30 November 1738 **Miss Notable [SPS]** *The Lady's Last Stake* 13 March 1739	
1739–40	Shepherdess [SP] *Alfred* 28 July, 1 & 2 August 1740		Miss Kitty [SP] *Britons, Strike Home* 31 December 1739		Daughter [SP] *An Hospital for Fools* 15 November 1739 **Miss Lucy [SP]** *Lethe* 15 April 1740 **Millamant [OP]** *The Way of the World* 17 March 1740			Rosamond [SP] *Rosamond* 8 March 1740 Shepherdess [SP] *Alfred* 28 July, 1 & 2 August 1740		**Vocalist [SP]** *L'Allegro, il Penseroso ed il moderato* 27 February, 6 March 1740 (one or both)	Miss Kitty [SP] *Britons, Strike Home* 31 December 1739 (Comus) 10 January 1740 **Vocalist [SP]** *L'Allegro, il Penseroso ed il moderato* 27 February, 6 March 1740 (one or both) **Miss Lucy [SP]** *Lethe* 15 April 1740 **Intermezzo with Beard [SP]** in *Zara* 30 April 1740?

Season	Goddess (masque)	Pastoral, British rustic	Sentimental heroine / spirited, abused wife	Country girl in city	Defiant daughter	Fine Lady	Intriguing servant	Patriot soprano	Shakespeare	Vocal part	In propria persona / Burlesque
1740–41			Bessy [SP] *The Blind Beggar of Bethnal Green* 3 April 1741			Lady Townly [OP] *The Provok'd Husband* 2 February 1741		Bessy [SP] *The Blind Beggar of Bethnal Green* 3 April 1741	Celia [SPS] *As You Like It* 20 December 1740 **Olivia** [SPS] *Twelfth Night* 15 January 1741 **Portia** [SP] *The Merchant of Venice* 14 February 1741	Manto(?) [SP] *Oedipus, King of Thebes* 19 November 1740 **Emilia** [SPS] *A Fond Husband* 29 November 1740	
1741–42	Pallas [SP] *The Judgment of Paris* 12 March 1742				Lady Lurewell [OP] *The Constant Couple* 4 January 1742 **Miss Lucy** [SP] *Lucy in Town* 6 May 1742					Vocalist(?) [SP] *Alexander's Feast* 12 March 1742 [Mimic Italian song] *Miss Lucy in Town* 6 May 1742	Miss Lucy [SP] *Miss Lucy in Town* 6 May 1742
1742–43		Vocalist [SP] *Messiah* [one arioso only] 23 March 1743						Dalila [SP] *Samson* [oratorio] 18 February 1743		Bayes (trousers role) *The Rehearsal* 6 May 1743	Miss Kitty [SP] *The Lying Valet* 3 March 1743

Season	Goddess (masque)	Pastoral, British rustic	Sentimental heroine / spirited, abused wife	Country girl in city	Defiant daughter	Fine Lady	Intriguing servant	Patriot soprano	Shakespeare	Vocal part	In propria personal / Burlesque
1743–44	**Shade of Hero [SP]** *The Necromancer: Or, Harlequin Dr Faustus* 26 December 1743 **Rhodope [SP]** *Orpheus and Eurydice* CG 14 February 1744	**Clorinda [SP]** *Love and Friendship* 21 March 1744								Vocalist [SP] *Abramule* 8 March 1744	
1744–45					Melissa *Timon of Athens* (Shadwell) 20 April 1745			Potiphar's Wife [SP] *Joseph* [oratorio, De Fesch] 20 March 1745			Benefit Concert for Catherine Clive [SP] 2 November 1744 Royal command, Prince of Wales
1745–46			**Melantha [SPS]** *The Comical Lovers* 10 March 1746 **Lucinda [SPS]** *The She Gallant* 13 March 1746 **Victoria** *The Lying Lover after Corneille Le Menteur* 4 April 1746		Clarinda *The Sea Voyage* 21 April 1746			Colombine [SP] *Harlequin Incendiary: Or, the Colombine Cameron* 3 March 1746	Ariel [SP] [De Fesch songs] *The Tempest* 31 January 1746	Lucinda [SPS] *The She Gallant* 13 March 1746	Colombine [SP] [anti-fop] *Harlequin Incendiary: Or, the Colombine Cameron* 3 March 1746

Season	Goddess (masque)	Pastoral, British rustic	Sentimental heroine/spirited, abused wife	Country girl in city	Defiant daughter	Fine Lady	Intriguing servant	Patriot soprano	Shakespeare	Vocal part	In propria persona/Burlesque
1746–47					Lillia-Bianca [SPS] *The Wild Goose Chase* 7 March 1747	Sophronia [satire, learning] *The Refusal* 28 November 1746	Betty Ruffle *Marry or Do Worse* 30 March 1747	Queen Elinor [SP] *Rosamond* 10 January 1747		Vocalist [SP] *Theodosius* 15 December 1746	Margerina [SP] [Mimic Italian] *The Dragon of Wantley* 7 March 1747
1747–48							Tag *Miss in her Teens* 24 October 1747				
1748–49		Shepherdess [SP] *The Triumph of Peace* 21 February 1749	Clarice [SP] *Don Saverio* 14? February 1749 Clarinda *The Suspicious Husband*, by Hoadley 13 March 1749			Lady Wronghead *The Provok'd Husband* 1 October 1748 Mrs. Riot [SPS] *Lethe* 2 January 1749		Shepherdess [SP] *The Triumph of Peace* 21 February 1749		Vocalist [SP] *Much Ado about Nothing* 14 November 1748	
1749–50		Pastora [SP] *The Chaplet* 2 December 1749			Lady Harriet *The Funeral: Or, Grief a la Mode* 21 November 1749	Lady Squeamish *Friendship in Fashion* 22 January 1750 Mrs. Hazard [SPS] *The Rehearsal: Or, Bayes in Petticoats* 15 March 1750				Vocal Part [SP] *Romeo and Juliet* 1 Oct 1750	Pastora [SP] *The Chaplet* 2 December 1749 Mrs. Hazard as Marcella [SP] *The Rehearsal: Or, Bayes in Petticoats* 15 March 1750

473

Season	Goddess (masque)	Pastoral, British rustic	Sentimental heroine/ spirited, abused wife	Country girl in city	Defiant daughter	Fine Lady	Intriguing servant	Patriot soprano	Shakespeare	Vocal part	In propria persona/ Burlesque
1750–51	Diana [SP] *The Secular Masque* 30 October 1750		Primrose [SP] *Robin Hood* 13 December 1750		Bisarre *The Inconstant* 12 March 1751					Vocal part [SP] *Alfred*, rev. 23 February 1751	Mrs. Clive *Alfred*, Epilogue-masque, with Euphrosyne's wand 23 February 1751
1751–52		Daphne [SP] *The Shepherd's Lottery* 19 November 1751			Girtred *Eastward Hoe* 29 October 1751						Daphne [SP] *The Shepherd's Lottery* 19 November 1751
1752–53							Mrs. Marwood *The Way of the World* 10 October 1752				
1753–54						Mrs. Frail *Love for Love* 16 January 1754		Princess Theoraze [SP] *The London 'Prentice* 23 March 1754			
1754–55					Jacintha [Dorcas, clashes w/ husband] *The Mistake* 13 March 1755	Mrs. Kitely *Every Man in his Humour* 17 March 1755	Jacintha *The Mistake* 13 March 1755				
1755–56			Catherine [SPS] [abused wife] *Catherine and Petruchio* 21 January 1756			Lady Wronglove [SPS] *The Lady's Last Stake* 27 March 1756	Abigail *The Drummer* 3 October 1755	Margaret [SP] [anti-French burlesque opera] *King Pepin's Campaign* October 1755?			Lady Wronglove [SPS] *The Lady's Last Stake* 27 March 1756

Season	Goddess (masque)	Pastoral, British rustic	Sentimental heroine/spirited, abused wife	Country girl in city	Defiant daughter	Fine Lady	Intriguing servant	Patriot soprano	Shakespeare	Vocal part	In propria persona/Burlesque
1756–57						Mrs. Cadwallader *The Author* 5 February 1757					Mrs. Cadwallader *The Author* 5 February 1757
1757–58						Lady Wishfort *The Way of the World* 16 March 1758	Termagant *The Upholsterer* 30 March 1758				
1758–59	Lucy *The Guardian* 3 February 1759						Patch [SPS] *The Busy Body* 2 December 1758				
1759–60						Mrs. Crostin *Every Woman in her Humour* 20 March 1760	Kitty [SPS] *High Life Below Stairs* 31 October 1759 Muslin *The Way to Keep Him* 24 January 1760				
1760–61	Euphrosine [SPS] *The Island of Slaves* 26 March 1761					Lady Freelove *The Jealous Wife* 12 February 1761 Euphrosine [SPS] *The Island of Slaves* 26 March 1761					Euphrosine [SPS] 'with comic opera song in character' *The Island of Slaves* 26 March 1761
1761–62						Lady Beverly *The School for Lovers* 10 February 1762					

Season	Goddess (masque)	Pastoral, British rustic	Sentimental heroine / spirited, abused wife	Country girl in city	Defiant daughter	Fine Lady	Intriguing servant	Patriot soprano	Shakespeare	Vocal part	In propria persona / Burlesque
1762–63						**Lady Jenkings** *Sketch of a Fine Lady's Return from a Rout* 21 March 1763 **Old Maid** *The Old Maid* 7 January 1763					
1763–64						**Mrs. Friendly** *The Dupe* 9 December 1763					
1764–65						**Lady Fanshaw** *The Platonic Wife* 24 January 1765	**Lisetta [SP]** *Capricious Lovers* 28 November 1764				
1765–66						**Widow Blackacre** *The Plain Dealer* 7 December 1765 **Mrs. Heidelberg** *The Clandestine Marriage* 20 February 1766					
1767–68						**Lady Fuz** *A Peep behind the Curtain* 23 October 1767					

Season	Goddess (masque)	Pastoral, British rustic	Sentimental heroine / spirited, abused wife	Country girl in city	Defiant daughter	Fine Lady	Intriguing servant	Patriot soprano	Shakespeare	Vocal part	In propria persona / Burlesque
1768–69						**Mrs. Winifred** *The School for Rakes* 4 February 1769					

APPENDIX 3

The Case of Mrs. CLIVE (1744)

THE
CASE
OF
Mrs. *CLIVE*
Submitted to the PUBLICK.

LONDON:
Printed for B. DOD at the *Bible* and *Key* in *Ave-Mary-Lane* near *Stationers-Hall*. MDCCXLIV.
[Price Six Pence.]

THE
CASE
OF
Mrs. *CLIVE*
Submitted to the PUBLICK.

IN order to put an End to some false Reports, which have been raised in Relation to my not acting this Season, as well as to bespeak the Favour of the Publick, I have, by the Advice of my Friends, ventured to address my self to them, from whom I have received many and great Marks of Favour, and whose further Protection I now stand in need of.

I know Appeals of this Nature, which relate to Disputes that happen at a Theatre, are by some thought presuming and impertinent, supposing they are too trifling to demand Attention: But, as I persuade my self, that Injustice and Oppression are by no means thought Matters of Indifference by any who have Humanity, I hope I shall not be thought to take too great a Liberty. I am the more encouraged to hope this from Experience; it having been observed, that those Performers, who have had the Happiness to please on the Stage, and who never did any thing to offend the Publick, whenever they have been injured by those who presided over Theatres, have seldom, if ever, failed of Redress upon representing the Hardships they met with: And, as I at this time, apprehend my self to be greatly oppressed by the Managers of both Theatres, I hope I shall be justified in taking this Method of acquainting the Publick with my Case, submitting it to their Determination.

Before the Disputes happened betwixt the Manager of *Drury-Lane* Theatre and his Actors, I had articled for Five Years to receive Three Hundred Pounds a Year, tho' another Performer on that Stage received for Seven Years Five Hundred Guineas, *per* Year; and at the Expiration of my Agreements the Manager offered me an additional Salary to continue at that Theatre.

And since I have mentioned those Disputes, which ended so greatly to the Disadvantage of the Actors, I must beg Leave to endeavour to set that Matter in a clear Light, which hitherto has been misrepresented to the Publick: I think my self obliged to this, as the Hardships I at present labour under are owing to that Disagreement; if any think I treat this Matter too seriously, I hope they will remember, that however trifling such Things may appear to them, to me, who am so much concerned in 'em, they are of great Importance, such as my Liberty and Livelihood depend on.

As only two Theatres were authorised, the Managers thought it was in their Power to reduce the Incomes of those Performers, who could not live independant [*sic*] of their Profession; but in order to make this appear with a better Face to the Town, it was agreed to complain of the Actors Salaries being too great, and accordingly a false Account was published of them in the daily Papers, by whom I will not say: Whether, or no, some particular Salaries were so, I will not pretend to determine; yet, in the whole, they did not amount to more than had been allowed for many Years, when the Theatre was under a frugal and exact Regulation; when the Managers punctually fulfilled, not only all Engagements to their Actors, but to every other Person concerned in the Theatre, and raised very considerable Fortunes for themselves.

But supposing the Expence of the Theatre too high, I am very certain it was not the Actors refusing to submit to a proper Reduction of them, which made so many of them quit the Stage, but from great Hardships they underwent, and greater which they feared would happen from an Agreement supposed to be concluded betwixt the two Managers, which made 'em apprehend, that if they submitted to act under such Agreements, they must be absolutely in the Managers Power; and the Event has proved that their Fears were not ill-grounded, as I doubt not but I shall make appear.

When the Actors Affairs obliged 'em to return to the Theatres last Winter, under such Abatements of their Salaries as hardly afforded the greater Part of them a Subsistence, I was offered, by the Manager of *Drury-Lane* Theatre, such Terms as bore no Proportion to what he gave other Performers, or to those he had offered me at the beginning of the Season. They were such as I was advis'd not to accept, because it was known they were proposed for no reason but to insult me, and make me seek for better at the other Theatre; for I knew it had been settled, by some dark Agreement, that Part of the Actors were to go to *Covent-Garden* Theatre, and others to *Drury-Lane*; I did, indeed, apprehend I should meet with better Terms at *Covent-Garden*, because that Manager had made many Overtures to get me into his Company the preceding Season, and many times before: But when I apply'd to him, he offered me exactly the same which I had refused at the other Theatre, and which I likewise rejected, but was persuaded to accept some very little better, rather than seem obstinate in not complying as well as others, and yielded so far to the Necessity of the Time, as to Act under a much less Salary than several other Performers on that Stage, and submitted to pay a Sum of Money for my Benefit, notwithstanding I had had one clear of all Expence for Nine Years before; an Advantage the first Performers had been thought to merit for near Thirty Years, and had grown into a Custom.

When I was fixed at that Theatre I determined to stay there; I did, in all things which related to my Profession, submit intirely to that Manager's Direction, and, with the help of other principal Performers, did greatly promote his Interest, as was evident from the Audiences after we went to Act there; but I found, by his Behaviour to me, it was designed I should not continue with him, but return the next Season to *Drury-Lane*.

The Agreements betwixt that Manager and me were verbal, but made before two Gentlemen of Character and Fortune, on whom I must depend for the fulfilling of them; they were for one Year. At the end of the Acting-season the Manager sent an Office-keeper to me with some Salary that was due, who required a Receipt in full; I told him a very great Part of my Agreements were yet due, and requested to see the Manager, who came and acknowledged them, and promised to bring one of the Gentlemen who was present at our Ingagements [*sic*] in a Day or two and pay me, and then he said he had done with me; but he has not paid me, nor have I ever seen him since, or as much as heard from him.

It has always been a Custom in Theatres, that if ever any Actor or Actress was to be discharged, or their Allowance lessen'd, they were acquainted with it at the End of the Season; the Reason of this will appear to be the giving them a proper Notice to provide for themselves: This the Manager of *Covent-Garden* did to all his Company whom he designed to discharge, or whose Allowance was to be lessen'd, except to me, which made me actually then conclude he determined I should continue with him, 'till I was undeceived by his Play-Bills with the Names of other Actresses in Parts I used to perform; so that he has not only broke thro' the Customs of the Theatre, but those in practice almost every where, in dismissing me, and has done me a real Injury in such an unprecedented Act of Injustice; for had I been informed of his Design at the End of the Season, I could have made Terms to have acted in *Ireland*, where I had met with most uncommon Civilities, and received very great Advantages, which I shall ever remember with the utmost Gratitude, and take this and every other Opportunity to acknowledge.

As I have said, it has been a Custom to give Actors Notice of a Discharge: I must at the same time observe, That it never was a Custom to discharge any, but upon Neglect of their Business, or such as were obnoxious to the Publick; this Maxim extended even to those of the lowest Class; but to those, on whose

Performances the Town had been pleased to stamp a Value, by their Indulgence and Applause, the Stage was always a Support, even after Age or any Accident had made 'em incapable of their Profession; for the then Patentees thought it as great a Piece of Insolence to deprive the Publick of their Pleasures, as of Cruelty and Injustice to deny those a Subsistence who had contributed towards 'em; for they knew and acknowledged, that the Publick was the only Support of all, consequently had an indisputable Right to be pleased in the best manner possible.

It is pretended by the Managers, that they have the same Right to discharge an Actor that a Master has to turn away a Servant, than which nothing can be more false and absurd; for, when a Master dismisses a Servant, there are many thousands besides to apply to; but when the Managers dismiss an Actor, where are they to apply? It is unlawful to act any where but with them; Necessity or Inclination brings every one to the Stage; if the former happens to be the Case, they will not readily find an Employment; and if the latter, they will not be fit for one; so that it will appear an Act of great Injustice and Oppression. If it should be objected, That the Actors Demands are so exorbitant, that the Managers cannot comply with 'em? I have already endeavoured to show, that tho' two or three Salaries might be thought so in general, they did not amount to more than had been allowed, and very considerable Profits arising to the Patentees. But there is a very melancholy Instance, that the Actors Demands is not the Reason of dismissing 'em, but the Will of the Manager alone; since last Season an Actor and Actress returned to *Drury-Lane* under such Abatements as that Manager thought proper, and such as were in no degree equal to their Merit; and yet, at the beginning of this Season, were dismissed, after having been from their Infancy on the Stage, and having no other Professions to live by, and very numerous Families to support.

The Manager of *Drury-Lane*, tho' he can't but know I am disengag'd from the other Theatre, has not made any Application to me to act with him, which he has done to several others who quitted that Stage at the Time I did: The Reasons which obliged me to leave him still subsist: He owes me a Hundred and Sixty Pounds, twelve Shillings, which he has acknowledged to be justly due, and promised Payment of it by last *Christmas* to a Person of too great Consequence for me to mention here, the greater Part of it Money I expended for Cloaths for his Use. He offer'd me, last Season, not near half as much as he afterwards agreed to give another Performer, and less than he then gave to some others in his Company; so that I must conclude, as every one knows there are Agreements betwixt the Managers, that there is a Design to distress me, and reduce me to such Terms as I cannot comply with.

I am sorry I am reduced to say any thing in favour of myself; but, as I think I merit as much as another Performer, and the Managers are so desirous to convince me of the contrary, I hope I shall be excused; especially when I declare, that at this time, I am not in the least vain of my Profession.

As to my Performances, the Audience are the only proper Judges: But I may venture to affirm, That my Labour, and Application, have been greater than any other Performers on the Stage. I have not only acted in almost all the Plays, but in Farces and Musical Entertainments; and very frequently two Parts in a Night, even to the Prejudice of my Health. I have been at a very great Expence in Masters for Singing; for which Article alone, the Managers now give five and six Pounds a Week. My additional Expences, in belonging to the Theatre, amount to upwards of one Hundred Pounds a Year, in Clothes, and other Necessaries; and the pretended great Salaries, of ten and twelve Pounds a Week, which have been so artfully, and falsly [sic] represented to the Town, to the Prejudice of the Actors, will, upon Enquiry, appear to be no more than half as much, since they performed last Season, at the Theatres, very seldom above three or four Days a Week; so taking in the long Vacation, when there are no Plays at all, to those Days the present Managers omit acting, a Salary which appears to be great, will be found, in effect, to be very moderate; and those which are less, not a Sufficiency.

I have now finished all I propos'd; I have shown in how aggravating a manner, without any Reason assigned, and at a Time a very considerable Sum of Money was owing to me, I have been turn'd out of *Covent-Garden* Theatre. The Manager of *Drury-Lane*, tho' he can't but know what just Reasons I had for quitting him, has never apply'd to me to return, nor made the least Excuse for not paying my Arrears, tho' due so long, and after promising Payment near a Year, notwithstanding I have, for many Years, not only endeavour'd, but succeeded, in greatly promoting that Manager's Interest, as is known to himself and his whole Company.

The Reason of my taking the Liberty to communicate these Things to the Publick, is most earnestly to interceed [sic] for their Favour and Protection, from whom I have always met with great Generosity and Indulgence: For, as I have already declared, in a Letter published by me last Year in the Daily Papers, that I had not a Fortune to support me, independent of my Profession, I doubt not but it will appear, I have not made any considerable Acquisition to it since, having not received two Hundred Pounds Salary for acting in Plays, Farces, and Singing; tho' other Performers have received more than twice that Sum. I have, in Consideration of these Hardships, been promised the Protection of many Ladies, to whom I have the Honour to be personally known, and will not doubt the Concurrence of the Publick, in receiving my Performance in the best manner I am, at present, capable of, which I shall always most gratefully Acknowledge.

C. CLIVE.

FINIS.

Select Bibliography

The bibliography includes details of the principal sources and literature (including music) that are referred to in the book but not the following:

1. Sources for illustrations, information on which is in each caption.
2. Class references to documentary manuscript sources, for which individual references are given in the footnotes.
3. Less significant manuscript and printed musical sources, for which individual references are given in the footnotes.
4. Class references to grangerized and extra-illustrated books, for which individual references are given in the footnotes.
5. Manuscript playbook sources for which individual references are given in the footnotes.
6. Editions of the Handel's music from the Hallische Händel-Ausgabe, for which individual references are given in the footnotes.
7. Online databases, for which access dates are given in the footnotes.
8. Dictionaries cited in the footnotes.
9. CD sleeve notes cited in the footnotes.
10. Variant titles of eighteenth-century newspapers or journals, whose date-specific version is cited in the footnotes.

EARLY SOURCES

Manuscript Sources

Arne, Thomas. British Library, Add MS 29370, 'Music in Rosamond 1733'.
Arne, Thomas. British Library, I.530.87, 'Sung by Mrs. Clive in Lethe'.
Boyce, William. British Library, MSS Mus c.3, 'Corydon and Miranda'.
[Carey, Henry, et al.]. British Library, R.M.21.c.44 (2.) [songs in *Damon and Phillida, The Devil to Pay,* and *The Lottery*].
Clive, Catherine. Bodleian Library, Toynbee b.1, 'Autograph letters from Catherine Clive to Jane Pope'.
Clive, Catherine. Folger Shakespeare Library. W.b.73, 'Collection of Letters to Jane Pope'.
Handel, Georg F. Gerald Coke Handel Foundation, Foundling Museum, Accession Number 1286, fols 137–39, 'Love's but the Frailty of the Mind'.

SELECT BIBLIOGRAPHY 483

Printed Music

The Agreeable Amusement, a Collection of Ancient & Modern Songs. [London], [1743–44].

Arne, [Thomas]. *The Songs, Duetto and Trio in the Masque of Comus ... dispos'd ... for a Harpsicord & Voice.* London, [c. 1738].

Arne, Thomas. *The Musick in the Masque of Comus. Written by Milton.* London, [1740].

Arne, Thomas. *The Songs in the Comedies called As You Like It, and Twelfth Night.* London, 1741.

Arne, Thomas. *A Favourite Collection of English Songs sung by Mr. Beard, Miss Young &c. at Ranelagh Gardens.* London, 1757.

Boyce, William. *The Chaplet. A Musical Entertainment ... Compos'd by Dr. Boyce.* London, [1750].

Boyce, William. *Numb: IV. Lyra Britannica: A Collection of English Songs ... In which are inserted some songs in Lethe.* London, 1754.

Boyce, William. *The Shepherds Lottery. A Musical Entertainment ... Compos'd by Dr. Boyce.* London, [1755].

Carey, Henry. *The Songs[,] Duett and Dialogue in The Contrivances w[i]th their Symphonies & Basses... The Words and Music by Mr Carey.* London, [1729].

Carey, Henry. *All the Songs in the new Entertainment of Cephallus and Procris: With their Symphonies & Basses.* London, [1731].

Carey, Henry. *The Musical Century.* 2 vols. London, 1737.

Carey, Henry. *Six Cantatas humbly dedicated to the Rt. Honbl Sackville Earl of Thanet The Words and Music by H: Carey.* London, 1732.

De Fesch, Willem. *The Songs in the Tempest or the Enchanted Isleland* [sic] *as they were perform'd at the Theatre Royal in Drury Lane by Mrs. Clive and Mrs. Mozeen. Set to Musick by W. Defesch.* London, [1746].

[De Fesch, Willem]. *Ye Medley of Mortals that make up this Throng: The Masquerade Song / Sung by Mr. Beard at Ranelagh.* [London, 1749?].

Four Songs in the Opera call'd Il Demofoonte sung by Sigra Mingotti. [London], [1755].

A General Collection of Minuets. London, 1729. [pubd by J. Walsh, J. Hare, and J. Young].

Handel, George F. [libretto by Thomas Morell]. *Alexander Balus, an Oratorio Set to Musick by Mr. Handel.* London, 1748.

Lampe, John. F. *A Collection of all the Aires, Pastorells, Chacoons, Entre, Jiggs, Minuets and Musette's in Columbine Courtezan.* London, 1735.

Select Minuets. Collected from the Castle Balls, and the Publick Assemblies in Dublin ... to which is added Eleena Roon by Mr. Dubourgh. Dublin, [1746].

Thumoth, Burk. *Twelve Scotch and Twelve Irish Airs with Variations set for the German Flute, Violin or Harpsichord.* London, [c.1742].

Newspapers and Journals

The Auditor
The Annual Biography and Obituary
British Journal
Common Sense
The Connoisseur

Country Journal or The Craftsman
Daily Advertiser
Daily Gazetteer
Daily Journal
Daily Post
Fog's Weekly Journal
General Evening Post
The Gentleman's Magazine
Grub-Street Journal
London and Country Journal
London Daily Post and General Advertiser
London Evening Post
London Journal
London Magazine, Or, Gentleman's Monthly Intelligencer
London Magazine: and Monthly Chronologer
Mist's Weekly Journal
The Monthly Review; or, Literary Journal
Old England or The Constitutional Journal
The Prompter
Public Advertiser
Read's Weekly Journal or British Gazetteer
The Records of Love: Or, Weekly Amusements for the Fair Sex
Scots Magazine
The Theatrical Review; Or, Annals of the Drama
Universal Spectator and Weekly Journal
Weekly Medley

Printed Sources

Forenames are given in full even when full forenames are not indicated in the original

[Addison, Joseph]. *Rosamond. An Opera. Humbly Inscrib'd to her Grace the Dutchess* [sic] *of Marlborough*. London, 1707.
Addison, Joseph. *Rosamond. An Opera ... Written by the late Mr. Addison, and new Set to Musick by Thomas Augustine Arne*. London, 1740.
An Answer to Polly Peachum's Ballad. London, 1728.
An Apology for the Life of Mr. T— C—, Comedian. Being a Proper Sequel to the Apology for the Life of Mr. Colley Cibber, Comedian ... Supposed to be written by himself. London, 1740.
Authentick Memoirs of the Life of the celebrated Actress Mrs. Anne Oldfield. 4th edn. London, 1730.
[Baker, David E]. *The Companion to the Play-house: Or, an Historical Account of all the Dramatic Writers (and their Works)*. 2 vols. London, 1764.
Baker, David E. *Biographia Dramatica, or, a Companion to the Playhouse*. 3 vols. London, 1782.
Bays in Council: Or, a Picture of a Green-Room: A Dramatic Poem. Dublin, 1751.

Bielfeld, Jacob Friedrich. *Letters of Baron Bielfeld, Secretary of Legation to the King of Prussia*. 4 vols. London, 1770.
Black, William Henry. *History and Antiquities of the Worshipful Company of Leathersellers of the City of London*. London, 1871.
Blackmore, Richard. *Alfred. An Epick Poem*. London, 1723.
Blackstone, William. *Commentaries on the Laws of England*. 4 vols. London, 1765–69.
Boaden, James, ed. *The Private Correspondence of David Garrick with the most Celebrated Persons of his Time*. 2 vols. London, 1831.
The Breeches, a Tale. Inscribed to the Fair of Great-Britain. With a Satyrical Introduction. London, 1738.
Burgh, Allatson. *Anecdotes of Music, Historical and Biographical: In a Series of Letters from a Gentleman to his Daughter*. 3 vols. London, 1814.
[Burgh, John]. *The Art of Speaking. Containing I. An Essay; in which are given Rules for expressing properly the principal Passions and Humours, which occur in Reading, or public Speaking; and II. Lessons taken from the Antients and Moderns (with Additions and Alterations, where thought useful) exhibiting a Variety of Matter for Practice; the emphatical Words printed in Italics; with Notes of Direction referring to the Essay*. London, 1761.
Burke, John Bernard. *A Genealogical and Heraldic Dictionary of the Peerage and Baronetage of the British Empire*. 7th edn. London, 1841.
Burney, Charles. *A General History of Music, from the Earliest Ages to the Present Period*. 4 vols. London, 1789.
Burney, Fanny. *Memoirs of Doctor Burney*. London, 1832.
Carey, Henry. *Six Ballads on the Humours of the Town*. London, 1728.
[Carey, Henry]. *The Contrivances: With the Songs, and other Additions, as now Acted at the Theatre-Royal in Drury-Lane*. London, 1729.
Carey, Henry. *Poems on Several Occasions … The Third Edition, much enlarged*. London, 1729.
[Carey, Henry]. *Cephalus and Procris. A Dramatic Masque. With a Pantomime Interlude, call'd, Harlequin Grand Volgi*. London, 1733.
Carey, Henry. *Of Stage Tyrants. An Epistle … Occasion'd by the Honest Yorkshire-Man being rejected at Drury-Lane Play-House, and since Acted at other Theatres with Universal Applause*. London, 1735.
Carey, Henry. *The Honest Yorkshire-Man. A Ballad Farce. Refus'd to be Acted at Drury-Lane Playhouse: But now Perform'd at the New Theatre in Goodman's-Fields, with great Applause*. London, 1736.
'Sig. Carini' [Carey, Henry]. *The Dragon of Wantley. A Burlesque Opera*. 4th edn. London, 1738.
Carrigan, William. *The History and Antiquities of the Diocese of Ossory*. 4 vols. Dublin, 1905.
The Case between the Proprietors of News-Papers … To which is annex'd … Polly Peachum's Child; its Name, Father, &c. London, [1729].
The Case between the Managers of the Two Theatres. London, [1743].
[Caulfield, James]. *Blackguardiana: Or, a Dictionary of Rogues, Bawds, Pimps, Whores … *. London, 1793.

[Centlivre, Susanna]. *Love's Contrivance, or, Le Medecin malgre Lui. A Comedy. As it is Acted at the Theatre Royal in Drury-Lane.* London, 1703.
Cephalus and Procris. A Dramatic Masque. With a Pantomime Interlude, call'd, Harlequin Grand Volgi. London, 1733.
Chalmers, Alexander, ed. *The Spectator. A corrected Edition.* 8 vols. London, 1806.
Chetwood, William R. *The Lover's Opera.* London, 1729.
[Chetwood, William R.]. *The Dramatic Congress. A Short State of the Stage under the Present Management. Concluding with a Dialogue.* London, 1743.
Chetwood, William R. *Kilkenny: Or, the Old Man's Wish.* Dublin, 1748.
Chetwood, William R. *A General History of the Stage, from its Origin in Greece down to the present Time. With the Memoirs of most of the principal Performers that have appeared on the English and Irish Stage for these last Fifty Years.* London, 1749.
[Chetwood, William R.]. *The British Theatre: Containing the Lives of the English Dramatic Poets ... Together with the Lives of Most of the Principal Actors, as well as Poets.* Dublin, 1750.
Churchill, Charles. *The Rosciad ... The Eighth Edition. With large Additions. To which is added, the Smithfield Rosciad.* Dublin, 1764.
Churchill, Charles. *The Rosciad. The Third Edition, Revised and Corrected.* London, 1761.
Cibber, Colley. *Venus and Adonis, a Masque: As it is Presented at the Theatre-Royal.* London, 1715.
[Cibber, Colley]. *Damon and Phillida: A Ballad Opera of One Act. As it is performed at the Theatre-Royal in Drury-Lane ... With the Musick prefix'd to each Song.* London, 1729.
Cibber, Colley. *Love in a Riddle.* London, 1729.
Cibber, Colley. *Venus and Adonis: A Masque.* London, 1736.
Cibber, Colley. *An Apology for the Life of Mr. Colley Cibber, Comedian.* 2nd edn. London, 1740.
Cibber, Theophilus. *The Lover. A Comedy.* London, 1730.
Cibber, Theophilus. *A Letter from Theophilus Cibber, Comedian, to John Highmore, Esq.* London, 1733.
Cibber, Theophilus. *A Serio-Comic Apology for Part of the Life of Mr. Theophilus Cibber, Comedian.* Dublin, 1748.
Cibber, Theophilus. *The Lives and Characters of the most Eminent Actors and Actresses of Great Britain and Ireland.* London, 1753.
Cibber, Theophilus. *The Lives of the Poets of Great-Britain and Ireland. By Mr. Cibber and other Hands.* 5 vols. London, 1753.
C.[ibber], T.[heophilus]. *Patie and Peggy: Or, The Fair Foundling. A Scotch Ballad Opera.* London, 1730.
Cibber, Theophilus, [and Henry Carey?]. *The Harlot's Progress; Or, the Ridotto al' fresco: A Grotesque Pantomime Entertainment ... The Songs made (to Old Ballad Tunes) by a Friend.* London, 1733.
Clayton, Thomas. *Songs in the new Opera called Rosamond.* (London, [1707]).
Clive, Catherine. *The Case of Mrs. Clive submitted to the Publick.* London, 1744.
Clive, Catherine. *The Rehearsal: Or, Bays in Petticoats. A Comedy in Two Acts ... The Music composed by Dr. Boyce.* London, 1753.

Coffey, Charles. *The Boarding-School: Or, the Sham Captain. An Opera*. London, 1733.
Coffey, Charles [and John Mottley]. *The Devil to Pay; Or, the Wives Metamorphos'd. An Opera*. London, 1731 [mainpiece].
Coffey, Charles [and John Mottley]. *The Devil to Pay; Or, the Wives Metamorphos'd. An Opera*. London, 1731 [afterpiece].
Coffey, Charles [and John Mottley]. *The Devil to Pay; Or, the Wives Metamorphos'd. An Opera*. London, 1732 [2nd afterpiece version].
A Collection of Letters ... Written by Alexander Pope, Esq; and Other Ingenious Gentlemen, to the Late Aaron Hill, Esq. London, 1751.
'Columbario, Christopher'. *The Pigeon-Pye, or, a King's Coronation*. London, 1738.
Congreve, Francis A. *Authentic Memoirs of the late Mr. Charles Macklin, Comedian*. London, 1798.
[Cooke, William]. *Memoirs of Charles Macklin, Comedian*. London, 1804.
The Country Correspondent ... with a Sketch of a Green Room. Number II. London, 1739.
A Critical Balance of the Performers at Drury-Lane Theatre. For the last Season 1765. London, 1765.
[Curll, Edmund]. *The Life of that eminent Comedian Robert Wilks, Esq*. London, 1733.
[Curll, Edmund, and William Oldys]. *The History of the English Stage ... by Mr. Thomas Betterton*. London, 1741.
[Cumberland, Richard]. *The Observer: Being a Collection of Moral, Literary and familiar Essays*. 5 vols. London, 1788.
[Dalton, John]. *Comus, A Mask: (now adapted to the Stage) as Alter'd from Milton's Mask at Ludlow-Castle*. 1st edn. London, 1738.
[Dalton, John]. *Comus, a Mask: (now adapted to the Stage) as Alter'd from Milton's Mask at Ludlow-Castle ... Second Edition*. London, 1738.
[Dalton, John]. *All the Songs of Comus a Mask, as sung at the Theatre in Aungier-street. By Mr. Worsdale, Mr. Layfield, Mrs. Clive, and Mrs. Reynolds*. [Dublin], [1741].
'D'Anvers, Caleb' [Nicholas Amhurst]. *The Twickenham Hotch-Potch ... a Sequel to the Beggars Opera*. London, 1728.
Davies, Thomas. *Memoirs of the Life of David Garrick, Esq*. 2 vols. London, 1780.
Davies, Thomas. *Dramatic Micellanies*. 3 vols. London, 1783–84.
Davies, Thomas. *Dramatic Miscellanies: Consisting of Critical Observations on several Plays of Shakspeare: With a Review of his Principal Characters ... a New Edition*. 2 vols. London, 1785.
[Derrick, Samuel]. *A General View of the Stage. By Mr. Wilkes*. London and Dublin, 1759.
Dodsley, Robert. *The Blind Beggar of Bethnal Green*. London, 1741.
The Dramatick Sessions: Or, the Stage Contest. London, 1734.
[Drury, Robert]. *The Devil of a Duke: Or, Trapolin's Vagaries. A (Farcical Ballad) Opera ... To which is prefix'd the Musick to each Song, set for the Spinnet, Harpsicord, German Flute, Violin, and Hautboy; with the Thorough Base to each Tune*. London, 1732.
D'Urfey, Thomas. *Love for Money: Or, the Boarding School: A Comedy*. London, 1691.
D'Urfey, Thomas. *Wit and Mirth: Or Pills to purge Melancholy*. 6 vols. London, 1698–1720.

'Egerton, William' [Edmund Curll]. *Faithful Memoirs of the Life, Amours and Performances, of that justly Celebrated, and most Eminent Actress of her Time, Mrs. Anne Oldfield.* London, 1731.

The Egotist: Or, Colley upon Cibber. London, 1743.

An Epilogue recommending the Cause of Liberty to the Beauties of Great Britain. Spoken by Mrs. Oldfield, at the Theatre-Royal. London, [1716].

A Faithful Narrative of the Proceedings in a late Affair between the Rev. Mr. John Swinton, and Mr. George Baker, both of Wadham College, Oxford. London, 1739.

[Fielding, Henry]. *The Mock Doctor: Or the Dumb Lady Cur'd. A Comedy. Done From Moliere. As it is acted at the Theatre-Royal In Drury-Lane, By His Majesty's Servants. With the Musick Prefix'd to each Song.* London, 1732.

[Fleetwood, Charles]. *A Full Answer to Queries upon Queries.* London, 1743.

Foote, Samuel. *The Roman and English Comedy consider'd ... and an Examen into the Merit of the present Comic Actors.* London, 1747.

[Garrick, David?]. *Queries to be Answer'd by the Manager of Drury-Lane Theatre.* London, 1743.

Garrick, David. *Lethe. A Dramatic Satire.* London, 1749.

[Garrick, David]. *Lethe Rehears'd: Or, a Critical Discussion of the Beauties and Blemishes of that Performance.* London, 1749.

[Gentleman, Francis]. *The Dramatic Censor; Or, Critical Companion.* 2 vols. London, 1770.

A Guide to the Stage: Or, Select Instructions and Precedents from the Best Authorities towards forming a Polite Audience; with some Account of the Players, &c. London, 1751.

[Hamilton, Newburgh]. *Samson. An Oratorio ... Alter'd and adapted to the Stage from the Samson Agonistes of John Milton.* London, 1743.

[Hill, Aaron]. *See and Seem Blind: Or, a Critical Dissertation on the Publick Diversions, &c.* London, [1732].

Hill, Aaron. *The Works of the Late Aaron Hill, Esq.* 4 vols. London, 1753.

Hill, Aaron. *The Insolvent.* London, 1758.

Hill, John. *An Answer to the many Plain and Notorious Lyes advanc'd by Mr. John Rich, Harlequin.* London, 1740.

Hill, John. *Orpheus: An English Opera ... With ... a fair and impartial Account of the Quarrel between the Author and Mr. Rich, who intends in a few Weeks to perform such an Entertainment without his Concurrence.* London, 1740 [sic].

[Hill, John]. *The Actor: A Treatise on the Art of Playing. Interspersed with Theatrical Anecdotes, Critical Remarks on Plays, and Occasional Observations on Audiences.* London, 1750.

[Hill, John]. *The Actor: Or, a Treatise on the Art of Playing. A new Work, written by the Author of the former, and Adapted to the Present State of the Theatres.* London, 1755.

Hogarth, George. *Memoirs of the Musical Drama.* 2 vols. London, 1838.

An Impartial State of the Present Dispute between the Patent and Players. [London], [1733].

Jevon, Thomas [and Thomas Shadwell?]. *The Devil of a Wife: Or, a Comical Transformation.* London, 1686.

Joe Miller's Jests: Or, the Wits Vade-Mecum. London, [1739].

[Kimber, Edward]. *The Peerage of Ireland: A Genealogical and Historical Account*. 2 vols. London, 1768.
Kirkman, James Thomas. *Memoirs of the Life of Charles Macklin, Esq. Principally compiled from his own Papers and Memorandums*. 2 vols. London, 1799.
The Laureat: Or, the Right Side of Colley Cibber, Esq. London, 1740.
A Letter to Polly. To one of her own Tunes. London, 1728.
A Letter of Compliment to the ingenious Author of a Treatise on the Passions ... with a critical Enquiry into the Theatrical Merit of Mr. G—k, Mr. Q—n, and Mr. B—y, &c. ... And a few Hints on our modern Actresses, particularly Mrs. C—r and Mrs. P—d. London, [1747].
Lewes, Charles L. *Memoirs of Charles Lee Lewes*. 4 vols. London, 1805.
The Life of Lavinia Beswick, alias Fenton, alias Polly Peachum. London, 1728.
The Life of Mr. James Quin, Comedian. London, 1766.
Love and Friendship. A Serenata. Set to Musick by Mr. W. Defesch. London, 1744.
Lynch, Francis. *The Independent Patriot: Or, Musical Folly. A Comedy*. London, 1737.
Macklin, Charles. *Mr. Macklin's Reply ... to which is prefix'd, All the Papers ... in regard to this Important Dispute*. London, 1743.
[Macklin, Charles]. *King Henry the VII. Or the Popish Imposter. A Tragedy*. London, 1746.
[Mallet, David]. *Alfred. A Masque. Represented before Their Royal Highnesses the Prince and Princess of Wales at Cliffden, on the First of August, 1740*. London, 1740.
[Mallet, David]. *Alfred: A Masque*. London, 1751.
[Mendez, Moses]. *The Chaplet. A Musical Entertainment ... The Music Compos'd by Dr. Boyce*. London, 1749.
[Mendez, Moses]. *The Shepherds Lottery. A Musical Entertainment ... The Music Compos'd by Dr. Boyce*. London, 1751.
[Mendez, Moses]. *The Double Disappointment: Or, the Fortune Hunters. A Comedy in Two Acts written by a Gentleman*. [London], 1755.
[Miller, James]. *The Humours of Oxford. A Comedy*. London, 1730.
[Miller, James]. *The Mother-in-Law: Or, the Doctor the Disease. A Comedy*. 2nd edn. London, 1734.
[Miller, James]. *The Man of Taste. A Comedy*. London, 1735.
[Miller, James]. *The Coffee-House. A Dramatick Piece*. London, 1737 [1738].
[Miller, James]. *The Universal Passion. A Comedy*. London, 1737.
[Miller, James]. *Art and Nature. A Comedy*. London, 1738.
[Miller, James]. *An Hospital for Fools. A Dramatic Fable*. London, 1739.
Miller, James. *Miscellaneous Works in Verse and Prose*. 3 vols. London, 1741.
[Morell, Thomas]. *Alexander Balus. An Oratorio*. London, 1748.
[Mottley, John?]. 'A Compleat List of all the English Dramatic Poets'. In Thomas Whincop [and John Mottley?], *Scanderbeg: Or, Love and Liberty. A Tragedy ... To which are added a List of all the Dramatic Authors*, [87]-320. London, 1747.
Mozeen, Thomas. *A Collection of Miscellaneous Essays*. London, 1762.
Murphy, Arthur. *The Apprentice. A Farce, in Two Acts*. London, 1756.
A New Ballad, Inscrib'd to Polly Peachum. To the Tune of Pretty Parrot say. London, [1728].
A New Theatrical Dictionary. London, 1792
Odell, Thomas. *The Patron: Or, the Statesman's Opera*. Dublin, [1729].

'Old Trader'. *The Female Glossary. Being a particular Description of the Principal Commodities of this Island*. London, [1732].
[Phillips, Edward]. *The Stage-Mutineers*. London, 1733.
Phillips, Edward. *Britons, Strike Home: Or, the Sailor's Rehearsal*. London, 1739.
Pinks and Lillies, or Phillis at a Nonplus. London, [1705?].
Poetical Miscellanies: The Sixth Part. containing a Collection of Original Poems ... By the most eminent Hands. London, 1709.
Polly Peachum on Fire, The Beggars Opera Blown Up, and Capt. Mackheath Entangled in his Bazzle-Strings. London, 1728.
Polly Peachum's Jests. London, 1728.
Pretty Doings in a Protestant Nation. Being a View of the present State of Fornication ... in Great-Britain ... Written originally in French by Father Poussin. London, 1734.
Pritchard, William. *The Fall of Phaeton ... Invented by Mr. Pritchard. The Musick compos'd by Mr. Arne; and the Scenes painted by Mr. Hayman*. London, 1736.
[William Henry Pyne]. *Wine and Walnuts; Or, After Dinner Chit-Chat. By Ephraim Hardcastle*. London, 1823.
Queries upon Queries, to be Answer'd by the Male-content Players. London, [1743?].
[Ralph, James]. *The Case of our Present Theatrical Disputes, fairly stated ... wherein, the only Method is Suggested, that can prevent all future Debate*. London, 1743.
Ray, James. *A Compleat History of the Rebellion*. Manchester, [1747].
Rees, Abraham. *The Cyclopaedia; Or, Universal Dictionary of Arts, Sciences, and Literature, by Abraham Rees ... with the Assistance of Eminent Professional Gentlemen*. 39 vols. London, 1819.
Rémond de Sainte-Albine, Pierre. *Le Comédien*. Paris, 1747.
Rich, John. *Mr. Rich's Answer to the many Falsities and Calumnies advanced by Mr. John Hill, Apothecary*. London, 1739.
Richardson, John. *An Essay on the Theory of Painting*. 2nd edn. London, 1725.
Robinson, Charles John. *A History of the Mansions and Manors of Herefordshire*. London, 1873.
Rolli, Paolo. *Sabrina. An Opera for the Theatre Royal in the Hay-Market*. London, [1737].
A Sapphick Epistle, from Jack Cavendish to the Honourable and most beautiful Mrs. D—. [London], [1778?].
Satan's Harvest Home: Or the present State of Whorecraft, Adultery, Fornication, Procuring, Pimping, Sodomy, and the Game at Flatts ... and other Satanic Works, daily propagated in this good Protestant Kingdom. London, 1749.
Shakespeare, William. *The Merchant of Venice*. London, 1745.
'Singleton, Mary' [Brooke, Frances]. *The Old Maid. By Mary Singleton, Spinster*. London, 1764.
[Smart, Christopher]. 'EPILOGUE written by a FRIEND, spoken by Mrs. CLIVE'. In *The Apprentice. A Farce, in Two Acts*, by Arthur Murphy. London, 1756.
The Smithfield Rosciad. London, 1763.
Songs in the Farce call'd the Mock Doctor ... The Tunes proper for the German Flute, Violin & Common Flute. To which is added ye Aires for the Violin & Harpsichord in the Opera call'd the Devil of a Duke. [London], [1732].
Stage Policy Detected; Or Some Select Pieces of Theatrical Secret History laid Open. London, 1744.

'Terrae-Filius' [Amhurst, Nicholas]. *Terrae-Filius: Or, the Secret History of the University of Oxford*. London, 1726.
The Theatre turned Upside Down: Or, the Mutineers. A Dialogue, occasioned by a Pamphlet, called, The Theatric Squabble. London, 1733.
The Theatric Squabble: Or, the P—ntees. A Satire. London, 1733.
The Theatrical Review: For the Year 1757, and Beginning of 1758. London, 1758.
The Theatrical Review; Or, Annals of the Drama. Volume the First. London, 1763.
Theatrical Biography: Or, Memoirs of the Principal Performers of the Three Theatres Royal. 2 vols. Dublin, 1772.
Theatrical Correspondence in Death. An Epistle from Mrs. Oldfield, in the Shades, to Mrs. Br--ceg---dle, upon Earth: Containing, a Dialogue between the most Eminent Players in the Shades, upon the late Stage Desertion. London, 1743.
[Theobald, Lewis]. *Orpheus and Eurydice; An Opera*. London, 1739.
Thievery A-la-mode: Or, the Fatal Encouragement. London, 1728.
[Thornton, Bonnell]. *Have at you all: Or, the Drury-Lane Journal. By Madam Roxana Termagant*. London, 1752.
Tyranny Triumphant! And Liberty Lost ... Or, Historical, Critical, and Prophetical Remarks on the Famous Cartel lately agreed on by the Masters of Two Theatres. In a Letter to a Friend in the Country. London, 1743.
The Usefulness of the Stage to Religion and to Government ... with Reflections on the Taste of the Times. London, 1738.
Victor, Benjamin. *The History of the Theatres of London and Dublin, from the Year 1730 to the present Time. To which is added, an Annual Register of all the Plays, &c. performed at the Theatres-Royal in London, from the Year 1712*. 2 vols. London, 1761.
Victor, Benjamin. *The History of the Theatres of London, from the Year 1760 to the present Time*. London, 1771.
[Voltaire], translated by Aaron Hill. *The Tragedy of Zara*. London, 1736.
Wakefield, Gilbert, ed. *The Poems of Mr. Gray*. London, 1786.
[Walker, Thomas]. *The Quaker's Opera. As it is Perform'd at Lee's and Harper's Great Theatrical Booth in Bartholomew-Fair. With the Musick prefix'd to each Song*. London, 1728.
Walpole, Horace. *Anecdotes of Painting in England*, repr. London, 1827. Twickenham, 1762.
Walpole, Horace. *A Description of the Villa of Horace Walpole, youngest Son of Sir Robert Walpole Earl of Orford, at Strawberry-Hill, near Twickenham*. Strawberry-Hill, 1774–86.
Walpole, Horace. *The Works of Horatio Walpole, Earl of Orford. In Five Volumes*. London, 1798.
[Ward, Edward]. *The Riddle. Or, a Paradoxical Character of a Hairy Monster often found in Holland*. London, 1706.
The Whole Life of Polly Peachum ... Written by one of her Companions. London, [1730?].
Wilkinson, Tate. *Memoirs of his own Life*. 4 vols. York, 1790.
Wilkinson, Tate. *Memoirs of his own Life, by Tate Wilkinson, Patentee of the Theatres-Royal, York and Hull*. 3 vols. Dublin, 1791.
Wilkinson, Tate. *The Wandering Patentee; Or, a History of the Yorkshire Theatres, from 1770 to the present Time*. 4 vols. York, 1795.

[Woodward, Henry]. *The Beggar's Pantomime: Or, the Contending Colombines*. 2nd edn. London, 1736.
[Woodward, Henry]. *The Beggar's Pantomime: Or, the Contending Colombines ... With New Songs, and several Alterations*. 3rd edn London, 1736.
Woodward, Henry. *A Letter from Henry Woodward ... to Dr. John Hill, Inspector-General of Great-Britain, the Greatest of all Characters*. London, 1752.
[Worsdale, James?]. *A Cure for a Scold. A Ballad Farce of Two Acts. (Founded upon Shakespear's Taming of a Shrew) .... By J. Worsdale, Portrait-Painter*. London, [1738].

MODERN SOURCES

Modern Scores

Arne, Thomas. *Masque of Comus*. Edited by J. Herbage. Musica Britannica, vol. 3. London, 1951, repr. 1965.
Arne, Thomas. *The Judgment of Paris*. Edited by I. Spink. Musica Britannica, vol. 42. London, 1978.
Bononcini, Giovanni. *Camilla*. Introduction and notes by L. Lindgren. Music for London Entertainment, series E, vol. 1. London, 1990 [facsimile edn].
Gluck, Christoph W. *Le Diable à Quatre, ou La Double Métamorphose*. Edited by B. A. Brown. Willibald Gluck Sämtliche Werke, series 4, vol. 3. Kassel, 1992.
Handel, George F. *Songs and Cantatas for Soprano and Continuo: Including the Complete English Songs for Soprano*. Edited by D. Burrows. Oxford, 1988.
Handel, George F. *Athalia: Oratorio in Three Parts, HWV 52*. Edited by S. Blaut. Hallische Händel-Ausgabe, series 1, vol. 12. Kassel, 2006.
Handel, George F. *Samson: Oratorio in Three Acts, HWV 57*. Edited by H. D. Clausen. Hallische Händel-Ausgabe, series 1, vol. 18. Kassel, 2011.
Leveridge, Richard. *Complete Songs (with the music in Macbeth) 1697–1770*. Introduction and notes by O. Baldwin and T. Wilson. Music for London Entertainment, series A, vol. 6. London, 1997 [facsimile edn].
Fesch, Willem de. *Joseph. Oratorio. 1745*. Edited by R. L. Tusler. Amsterdam, 1995.
Fesch, Willem de. *Willem de Fesch: The Tempest Songs or the Enchanted Island ... 1745*. Edited by R. L. Tusler. Amsterdam, 2003.
The Music of John Gay's The Beggar's Opera. Edited by J. Barlow. Oxford, 1990.

Printed Sources

Amory, Hugh, ed., with an introduction and commentary by Betrand A. Goldgar. *Henry Fielding: Miscellanies*. 3 vols. Oxford, 1993.
Anderson, Emily Hodgson. 'Celebrity Shylock'. *Publications of the Modern Language Association* 126, no. 4 (2011), 935–49.
Andrews, Richard. 'Molière, commedia dell'arte, and the Question of Influence in Early Modern European Theatre'. *The Modern Language Review* 100, no. 2 (2005), 444–63.
Appleton, William W. *Charles Macklin: An Actor's Life*. Cambridge, MA, 1960.
Ashton, Geoffrey. *Pictures in the Garrick Club: A Catalogue of the Paintings, Drawings, Watercolours and Sculpture*. Edited by K. A. Burnim and A. Wilton. London, 1997.

Aspden, Suzanne. 'Ballads and Britons: Imagined Community and the Continuity of "English" Opera'. *Journal of the Royal Musical Association* 122, no. 1 (1997), 24–51.
Austin-Leigh, Richard A. *The Eton College Register 1698–1752*. Eton, 1927.
Avery, Emmet. 'The Defense and Criticism of Pantomimic Entertainments in the Early Eighteenth Century'. *English Literary History* 5, no. 2 (1938), 127–45.
Avery, Emmett L. 'The Shakespeare Ladies Club'. *Shakespeare Quarterly* 7, no. 2 (1956), 153–58.
Baldwin, Olive, and Thelma Wilson. '"Heathen Gods and Heroes": Singers and John Rich's Pantomimes at Lincoln's Inn Fields'. In *"The Stage's Glory": John Rich, 1692–1761*, edited by B. Joncus and J. Barlow, 157–68. Newark, NJ, 2011.
Barber, Giles. 'Bolingbroke, Pope and the *Patriot King*'. *The Library* 19, no. 1 (1964), 67–89.
Barlow, Jeremy. 'The Beggar's Opera in London's Theatres, 1728–1761'. In *"The Stage's Glory": John Rich, 1692–1761*, edited by B. Joncus and J. Barlow, 169–83. Newark, NJ, 2011.
Barnett, Dean, and Jeanette Massy-Westropp. *The Art of Gesture: the Practice and Principles of Eighteenth-Century Acting*. Heidelberg, 1987.
Barthes, Roland. *Image, Music, Text*. Edited and translated by S. Heath. London, 1984.
Bartlett, Ian, with Robert J. Bruce. *William Boyce: A Tercentenary Sourcebook and Compendium*. Newcastle upon Tyne, 2013.
Barut, Philip E. *Introducing Charlotte Charke: Actress, Author, Enigma*. Urbana, IL, 1998.
Battestin, Martin C. *A Henry Fielding Companion*. Westport, CN and London, 2000.
Battestin, Martin C., with Ruthe R. Battestin. *Henry Fielding: A Life*. London, 1989.
Beherman, Thierry. *Gottfried Schalcken*. Paris, 1988.
Blouch, Christine. 'Eliza Haywood and the Romance of Obscurity'. *Studies in English Literature, 1500–1900* 31, no. 3 (1991), 535–52.
Bohlman, Philip. *Focus: Music, Nationalism, and the Making of the new Europe*. New York, 2011.
Bolton, Betsy. 'Theorizing Audience and Spectatorial Agency'. In *The Oxford Handbook of the Georgian Theatre, 1737–1832*, edited by J. Swindells and D. F. Taylor, 31–52. Oxford, 2013.
Boswell, James. *Life of Johnson*, edited by J. D. Chapman, introduction by Pat Rogers. Oxford, 1980.
Bowers, Terence. 'Universalizing Sociability: The Spectator, Civic Enfranchisement, and the Rule(s) of the Public Sphere'. In *The Spectator: Emerging Discourses*, edited by D. J. Newman, 150–74. Newark, NJ, 2005.
Boydell, Brian. *A Dublin Musical Calendar 1700–1760*. Dublin, 1988.
Boydell, Barra. '"Whatever has a Foreign Tone / We like much better than our own": Irish Music and Anglo-Irish Identity in the Eighteenth Century'. In *Music and Identity in Ireland and Beyond*, edited by M. Fitzgerald and J. O'Flynn, 19–38. Farnham, 2017.
Bradham, JoAllen. 'A Good Country Gentlewoman: Catherine Clive's Epistolary Autobiography'. *Biography* 19, no. 3 (1996), 259–82.
Bradshaw, Peter. *18th Century* [sic] *English Porcelain Figures 1745–1795*. Woodbridge, 1981.

Branam, George C. 'The Genesis of David Garrick's *Romeo and Juliet*'. *Shakespeare Quarterly* 35, no. 2 (1984), 170–79.
Brewer, David A. *The Afterlife of Character, 1726–1825*. Philadelphia, 2005.
Brooks, Helen. '"Your sincere Friend and humble Servant": Evidence of Managerial Aspirations in Susannah Cibber's Letters'. *Studies in Theatre and Performance* 28, no. 2 (2008), 147–59.
Brooks, Helen E. M. 'Negotiating Marriage and Professional Autonomy in the Careers of Eighteenth-Century Actresses'. *Eighteenth-Century Life* 35, no. 2 (2011), 40–57.
Brooks, Helen E. M. *Actresses, Gender, and the Eighteenth-Century Stage: Playing Women*. Basingstoke, 2014.
Burden, Michael. 'Britannia versus Virtue in the Harmony of the Spheres: Directions of Masque Writing in the Eighteenth Century'. *Miscellanea musicological* 17 (1990), 78–86.
Burden, Michael. 'The British Masque 1690–1800'. PhD diss., University of Edinburgh, 1993.
Burden, Michael. *Garrick, Arne and the Masque of 'Alfred': A Case Study in National, Theatrical and Musical Politics*. Lewiston, NY and Lampeter, 1994.
Burden, Michael. 'The Independent Masque 1700–1800: A Catalogue'. *Royal Musical Association Research Chronicle* 28 (1995), 59–159.
Burden, Michael. *Regina Mingotti: Diva and Impresario at the King's Theatre, London*. Farnham, 2013.
Burgess, Chester F., ed. *The Letters of John Gay*. Oxford, 1966.
Burling, William J. *Summer Theatre in London, 1661–1820, and the Rise of the Haymarket Theatre*. Madison, WI and London, 2000.
Burney, Charles. *A General History of Music: From the Earliest Ages to the Present Period (1789). Volume the Second. By Charles Burney*, edited by F. Mercer. New York, 1957.
Burnim, Kalman A. and John Baskett, with contributions by Edward A. Langhans. *Brief Lives: Sitters and Artists in the Garrick Club Collection*. London, 2003.
Burrows, Donald. 'Handel, the Dead March and a newly Identified Trombone Movement'. *Early Music* 18, no. 3 (1990), 408–16.
Burrows, Donald. *Handel: Messiah*. Cambridge, 1991.
Burrows, Donald. 'The Granville and Smith Collections of Handel Manuscripts'. In *Sundry Sorts of Music Books: Essays on the British Library Collections, Presented to O.W. Neighbour on his 70th Birthday*, edited by C. Banks, A. Searle, and M. Turner, 231–47. London, 1993.
Burrows, Donald. 'From Milton to Handel: the Transformation of Milton's *L'Allegro and Il Penseroso* into a Musical Work for Concert Performance in the London Theatres'. In *Musique et théâtralité dans les îles Britanniques*, edited by C. Bardelmann and P. Degott, 73–89. Metz, 2005.
Burrows, Donald. *Handel and the English Chapel Royal*. Oxford, 2005.
Burrows, Donald. 'The Word-books for Handel's Performances of *Samson*'. *Musical Times* 146, no. 1890 (2005), 9–12.
Burrows, Donald. *Handel*. 2nd edn. Oxford and New York, 2012.
Burrows, Donald. 'Reconstructing Handel's Performances of *L'Allegro*'. *The Musical Times* 154, no. 1922 (2013), 69–76.
Burrows, Donald, et al., eds. *George Frideric Handel: Collected Documents* 5 vols. Cambridge, 2013–.

Burrows, Donald, and Martha J. Ronish. *A Catalogue of Handel's Musical Autographs.* Oxford, 1994.
Burrows, Donald, and Rosemary Dunhill, eds. *Music and Theatre in Handel's World: The Family Papers of James Harris, 1732–1780.* Oxford and New York, 2002.
Burrows, Donald, and Berta Joncus, 'Music and Representation'. In *Enlightened Princesses: Caroline, Augusta, Charlotte, and the Shaping of the Modern World*, edited by J. Marschner with D. Bindman and L. L. Ford, 202–7. New Haven, CT, 2017.
Burwick, Frederick. 'Georgian Theories of the Actor'. In *The Oxford Handbook of the Georgian Theatre, 1737–1832*, edited by J. Swindells and D. F. Taylor, [177]–91. Oxford, 2013.
Buss, Robert Woodward. *Charles Fleetwood, Holder of the Drury Lane Theatre Patent ... Reprinted from Fleetwood Family Records.* [London], 1915.
Cable, Jennifer. '"Gods! I can never this endure": Madness made Manifest in the Songs of Henry Purcell (1659–1695) and Henry Carey (1689–1743)'. *Studies in Musical Theatre* 4, no. 1 (2010), 15–26.
Cable, Jennifer. 'How a Thrown Shooe Became a Tragedy and Other Funny Stories: A Study of the Three Burlesque Cantatas (1741) by Henry Carey (1689–1743)'. *ECHO: A Music-Centered Journal* 10, no. 1 (2012), 1–12.
Carlson, Marvin. *Theories of the Theatre: A Historical Survey, from the Greeks to the Present.* Ithaca, NY and London, 1984.
Casey, Nollaig. 'Eibhlin a Ruin and the Impact of Fashion in its Dissemination in Eighteenth and Nineteenth Century Ireland'. MA diss., Queen's University, Belfast, 2011.
Chapman, Clive G. 'English Pantomime and its Music, 1700–1730'. 2 vols. PhD diss., University of London, 1981.
Cholij, Irena. 'Defesch's "Tempest" Songs'. *The Musical Times* 127, no. 1719 (1986), 325–27.
Cholij, Irena. 'De Fesch and the Tempest'. In *Willem de Fesch (1687–c. 1760): voordrachten gehouden in Alkmaar, September 1987*, 61–68. Alkmaar, 1987.
Cholij, Irena. 'Music in Eighteenth-Century London Shakespeare Productions'. PhD diss., University of London, 1995.
Christmas, William J. '"From Threshing Corn, He Turns to Thresh His Brains": Stephen Duck as Laboring-Class Intellectual'. In *The Working-Class Intellectual in Eighteenth- and Nineteenth-century Britain*, edited by A. Krishnamurthy, 25–48. Farnham, 2009.
Cicali, Gianni. 'Roles and Acting'. In *The Cambridge Companion to Eighteenth-Century Opera*, edited by A. R. DelDonna and P. Polzonetti, 85–98. Cambridge, 2009.
Clayton, Timothy. *The English Print 1688–1802.* New Haven, CT, 1997.
Cleary, Thomas R. *Henry Fielding: Political Writer.* Waterloo, 1984.
Coke, David, and Alan Borg. *Vauxhall Gardens: A History.* New Haven, CT, 2011.
Coley, William B., ed. *Henry Fielding: The True Patriot and Related Writings.* Oxford, 1987.
Coley, William B., ed. *Henry Fielding: Contributions to The Champion and Related Writings.* Oxford, 2003.
Coppola, Al. *The Theater of Experiment: Staging Natural Philosophy in Eighteenth-Century Britain.* New York, 2016.
Cordner, Michael and Peter Holland, eds. *Players, Playwrights, Playhouses: Investigating Performance, 1660–1800.* Basingstoke, 2007.
Crawford, Katherine. *European Sexualities, 1400–1800.* Cambridge, 2007.

Crean, Patrick J. 'Kitty Clive'. *Notes and Queries* 162 (1932), 272–73.
Crean, Patrick J. 'The London 'Prentice'. *Notes and Queries* 163 (1932), 346–47.
Crean, Patrick J. 'The Life and Times of Kitty Clive'. PhD diss., University of London, 1933.
Crouch, Kimberly. 'Attitudes towards Actresses in Eighteenth-Century Britain'. PhD diss., University of Oxford, 1995.
Danchin, Pierre. *The Prologues and Epilogues of the Eighteenth Century: A Complete Edition*. Nancy, 1990.
Davis, Jim. *Comic Acting and Portraiture in late-Georgian and Regency England*. Cambridge, MA and New York, 2015.
Davis, Jim, and Daniel O'Quinn. 'Spectatorship'. In *The Cambridge Companion to British Theatre, 1730–1830*, edited by J. Moody, 57–70. Cambridge, 2007.
Dean, Winton. *Handel's Dramatic Oratorios and Masques*. London, 1959.
Dellaborra, Mariateresa. 'The Judgment of Paris (1740), pastorale di Giuseppe Sammartini', *Rivista Italiana di Musicologia* 48 (2013), 41–67.
Dennant, Paul. '"Barbarous Old English Jig": The "Black Joke" in the Eighteenth and Nineteenth Centuries'. *Folk Music Journal* 10, no. 3 (2013), 298–318.
Desmond, Marilynn. *Reading Dido: Gender, Textuality, and the Medieval Aeneid*. Minneapolis, 1994.
Dobson, Michael. *The Making of the National Poet: Shakespeare, Adaptation and Authorship, 1660–1769*. Oxford, 1992.
Donoghue, Emma. '"Random Shifts of Malice": The Outings of Anne Damer'. In *Lesbian Dames: Sapphism in the Long Eighteenth Century*, edited by J. C. Beynon and C. Gonda, 127–45. Farnham and Burlington, 2010.
Doran, John. *"Their Majesties' Servants": or, Annals of the English Stage, from Thomas Betterton to Edmund Kean*. London, 1897.
Downer, Alan S. 'Nature to Advantage Dressed: Eighteenth-Century Acting'. *Publications of the Modern Language Association* 58, no. 4 (1943), 1002–37.
Dugaw, Dianne. '"Critical Instants": Theatre Songs in the Age of Dryden and Purcell'. *Eighteenth-Century Studies* 23, no. 2 (1989), 157–81.
Dugaw, Dianne. *Deep Play: John Gay and the Invention of Modernity*. Newark, NJ, 2001.
Dunhill, Rosemary. *Handel and the Harris Circle*. Hampshire Papers 8. Hampshire County Council, 1995.
Dunhill, Rosemary, and Geoff Ridden. 'Milton's Nightcap: The Correspondence of James Harris'. *Milton Quarterly* 32, no. 3 (1998), 95–97.
Dyer, Richard, with Paul McDonald. *Stars*. 2nd rev. edn. London, 1998.
Edelstein, Teri J., ed. *Vauxhall Gardens*. New Haven, CT, 1983.
Edgerton, Michael. *The 21st-Century Voice: Contemporary and Traditional Extra-Normal Voice*. Lanham, MD, 2004.
Ellis, John. 'Stars as Cinematic Phenomenon'. In *Stardom and Celebrity: A Reader*, edited by S. Redmond and S. Holmes, 90–97. Los Angeles and London, 2007.
Endelman, Todd M. *The Jews of Georgian England, 1714–1830: Tradition and Change in a Liberal Society*. Ann Arbor, MI, 1999.
Evans, Jennifer. *Aphrodisiacs, Fertility and Medicine in Early Modern England*. Woodbridge, 2014.

Faller, Lincoln B. *The Popularity of Addison's Cato and Lillo's The London Merchant, 1700–1776*. New York, 1988.
Fawcett, Julia H. *Spectacular Disappearances: Celebrity and Privacy, 1696–1801*. Ann Arbor, MI, 2016.
Feldman, Martha. *The Castrato: Reflections on Natures and Kinds*. Oakland, CA, 2015.
Felsenstein, Frank. *Anti-Semitic Stereotypes: A Paradigm of Otherness in English Popular Culture, 1660–1830*. London and Baltimore, 1999.
Findlay, Robert R. 'Charles Macklin and the Problem of "Natural" Acting'. *Educational Theatre Journal* 19, no. 1 (1967), 33–40.
Fiske, Roger. *English Theatre Music in the Eighteenth Century*. New York, 1973, and 2nd edn (1986).
Fleming, Susannah. 'Frederick as Apollo at Vauxhall: A "Patriot" Project?'. *The London Gardener, or, The Gardener's Intelligencer* 13 (2007–8), 46–66.
Foyster, Elizabeth. *Marital Violence: An English Family History, 1660–1857*. Cambridge, 2005.
Freeman, Lisa. *Character's Theater: Genre and Identity on the Eighteenth-Century English Stage*. Philadelphia, 2001.
Frith, Simon. *Performing Rites: on the Value of Popular Music*. Cambridge, MA, 1996.
Frushell, Richard C. 'An Edition of the Afterpieces of Mrs. Clive'. PhD diss., University of Duquesne, 1968.
Frushell, Richard C. *The Case of Mrs. Clive*. Los Angeles, 1973.
Fuller-Maitland, John A. 'Some Theories about "God Save the King"'. *Proceedings of the Musical Association*, 43rd Sess. (1916–17), 123–38.
Fuller, John. *John Gay: Dramatic Works*. 2 vols. Oxford, 1983.
Gagey, Edmond. *Ballad Opera*. New York, 1937.
Garrioch, David. 'Sounds of the City: the Soundscape of Early Modern European Towns'. *Urban History* 30, no. 1 (2003), 5–25.
Gerbino, Giuseppe. *Music and the Myth of Arcadia in Renaissance Italy*. New York, 2009.
Gerrard, Christine. *The Patriot Opposition to Walpole: Politics, Poetry, and National Myth, 1725–1742*. Oxford, 1994.
Gerrard, Christine. *Aaron Hill: The Muses' Projector, 1685–1750*. Oxford, 2003.
Gillespie, Joseph N. 'The Life and Work of Henry Carey (1687–1743)'. 2 vols. PhD diss., University of London, 1982.
Gilman, Todd. *The Theatre Career of Thomas Arne*. Newark, NJ, 2013.
Gladfelder, Hal, ed. *The Beggar's Opera and Polly*. Oxford, 2013.
Godden, Geoffrey. *Eighteenth-Century English Porcelain, A Selection from the Godden Reference Collection*. London, 1985.
Goff, Moira. '"Art and Nature join'd": Hester Santlow and the Development of Dancing on the London Stage, 1700–1737'. PhD diss., University of Kent, 2000.
Goff, Moira. 'Weaver, Words, and Dancing in *The Judgment of Paris*'. In *On Common Ground 5: Dance in Drama, Drama in Dance: proceedings of the Fifth DHDS Conference*, edited by D. Parsons, 33–40. London, 2005.
Goff, Moira. *The Incomparable Hester Santlow: A Dancer-Actress on the Georgian Stage*. Aldershot, 2007.

Goggin, L. P. 'Fielding and the Select Comedies of Mr. de Moliere'. *Philological Quarterly* 31 (1952), 344–50.

Goldgar, Bertrand A. *Walpole and the Wits: The Relation of Politics to Literature, 1722–1742*. Lincoln, NE, 1976.

Goring, Paul. *The Rhetoric of Sensibility in Eighteenth-Century Culture*. Cambridge, 2005.

Gowing, Lawrence. 'Hogarth, Hayman and the Vauxhall Decorations'. *Burlington Magazine* 95 (1953), 6-13.

Greteman, Blaine. '"To secure our Freedom": How *A Mask presented at Ludlow-Castle* became Milton's *Comus*'. In *Milton in the Long Restoration*, edited by B. Hoxby and A. Baynes Coiro (Oxford and New York, 2016), 143–57.

Griffin, Dustin. *Regaining Paradise: Milton and the Eighteenth Century*. Cambridge, 1986.

Griffiths, Antony. 'Early Mezzotint Publishing in England – I. John Smith'. *Print Quarterly* 6, no. 3 (1989), 243–57.

Gross, John J. *Shylock: Four Hundred Years in the Life of a Legend*. London, 1992.

Haggerty, George E. *Men in Love: Masculinity and Sexuality in the Eighteenth Century*. New York, 1999.

Haggerty, George E. 'Horace Walpole's Epistolary Friendships'. *Journal for Eighteenth-Century Studies* 29, no. 2 (2006), 201–18.

Haggerty, George E. *Horace Walpole's Letters: Masculinity and Friendship in the Eighteenth Century*. Lewisburg, PA, 2011.

Halsband, Robert, ed. *The Complete Letters of Lady Mary Wortley Montagu*. 3 vols. Oxford, 1966.

Halsband, Robert. 'The Noble Lady and the Player'. *History Today* 18, no. 7 (1968), 464–72.

Halsband, Robert. 'A Prince, a Lord and a Maid of Honour: A Story of Amorous Intrigue at the Court of George II'. *History Today* 23, nos. 5–6 (1973), Part I, 305–12, Part II, 391–97.

Hammond, Brean. 'Joseph Addison's Opera "Rosamond": Britishness in the Early Eighteenth Century'. *English Literary History* 73, no. 3 (2006), 601–29.

Harris, Frances. *A Passion for Government: The Life of Sarah, Duchess of Marlborough*. Oxford, 1991.

Harris, Susan Cannon. 'Mixed Marriage: Sheridan, Macklin and the Hybrid Audience'. In *Players, Playwrights, Playhouses: Investigating Performance, 1660–1800*, edited by M. Cordner and P. Holland, 189–212. Basingstoke, 2007.

Harrison, Scott D., and Jessica O'Bryan Springer. *Teaching Singing in the 21st Century*. Dordrecht, 2014.

Haugen, Janine M. 'The Mimic Stage: Private Theatricals in Georgian Britain'. PhD diss., University of Colorado, 2014.

Haynes, Bruce, and Geoffrey Burgess. *The Pathetick Musician: Moving an Audience in the Age of Eloquence*. New York, 2016.

Haywood, Charles. 'William Boyce's "Solemn Dirge" in Garrick's *Romeo and Juliet* Production of 1750'. *Shakespeare Quarterly* 11, no. 2 (1960), 173–87.

Herbage, Julian. 'The Truth about Mrs. Cibber'. *The Monthly Musical Record* 78 (1948), 59–68.

Herissone, Rebecca. 'Performance History and Reception'. In *The Ashgate Research Companion to Henry Purcell*, edited by R. Herissone, 303–51. Farnham and Burlington, VT, 2012.
Highfill, Philip H., Kalman A. Burnim, and Edward A. Langhans, 'Mozeen, Mrs Thomas [Mary?], née Edwards'. In *A Biographical Dictionary of Actors, Actresses, Musicians, & Other Stage Personnel in London, 1660–1800*. 16 vols. vol. 10, 370–72. Carbondale, IL, 1984.
Highfill, Philip H., Kalman A. Burnim, and Edward A. Langhans. 'Woffington, Margaret'. *A Biographical Dictionary of Actors, Actresses, Musicians, & Other Stage Personnel in London, 1660–1800*. 16 vols. vol. 16, 195–225. Carbondale, IL, 1993.
Higney, John J. 'Henry Purcell: A Reception/Dissemination Study, 1695–1771'. PhD diss., University of Western Ontario, 2008.
Hoffbrand, Barry. 'John Misaubin, Hogarth's Quack: A Case for Rehabilitation'. *Journal of the Royal Society of Medicine* 94 (2001), 143–47.
Holland, Peter. *The Ornament of Action: Text and Performance in Restoration Comedy*. Cambridge, 1979.
Holland, Peter. 'Unpublished Scenes in David Garrick's "Lethe"'. *Huntington Library Quarterly* 57, no. 3 (1994), 300–11.
Holland, Peter. 'Hearing the Dead: The Sound of David Garrick'. In *Players, Playwrights, Playhouses: Investigating Performance, 1660–1800*, edited by M. Cordner and P. Holland, 248–70. Basingstoke, 2007.
Holman, Peter. 'Eighteenth-Century English Music: Past, Present, Future'. In *Music in Eighteenth-century Britain*, edited by D. Wyn Jones, 1–13. Burlington, VT, 2000.
Hopkins, D. and C. Martindale, eds. *The Oxford History of Classical Reception in English Literature: Volume 3 1660–1790*. Oxford and New York, 2012.
Hughes, Leo, and Arthur H. Scouten, eds. *Ten English Farces*. Austin, 1948.
Hume, Robert D. *Henry Fielding and the London Theatre, 1728–1737*. Oxford and New York, 1988.
Hume, Robert D. 'Drama and Theatre in the Mid and Later Eighteenth Century'. In *The Cambridge History of English Literature, 1660–1780*, edited by J. Richetti, 316–39. Cambridge, 2005.
Hume, Robert D., and Harold Love, eds. *Plays, Poems, and Miscellaneous Writings Associated with George Villiers, Second Duke of Buckingham*. 2 vols. Oxford, 2006.
Hume, Robert D. 'John Rich as Manager and Entrepreneur'. In *"The Stage's Glory": John Rich, 1692–1761*, edited by B. Joncus and J. Barlow, 29–60. Newark, NJ, 2011.
Hume, Robert D. 'Garrick in Dublin in 1745–46'. *Philological Quarterly* 93, no. 4 (2014), 508–33.
Hunter, David. *English Opera and Song Books 1703–1726*. Ann Arbor, MI, 1990.
Hunter, David. 'Patronizing Handel, Inventing audiences: The Intersections of Class, Money, Music and History'. *Early Music* 28, no. 1 (2000), 33–49.
Hunter, David. 'George Frideric Handel and the Jews: Fact, Fiction and the Tolerances of Scholarship'. *For the Love of Music: Festschrift in Honor of Theodore Front*, edited by D. F. Scott, 5–28. Lucca, 2002.
Hunter, David. *The Lives of George Frideric Handel*. Woodbridge, 2015.
Hutchinson, Gregory O. 'The Publication and Individuality of Horace's "Odes" Books 1–3'. *Classical Quarterly* 52, no. 2 (2002), 517–37.

Ingrassia, Catherine. 'Dissecting the Authorial Body: Pope, Curll, and the Portrait of a "Hack Writer"'. In *"More solid Learning": New Perspectives on Alexander Pope's Dunciad*, edited by C. Ingrassia and C. N. Thomas, 147–65. Lewisburg, PA, 2000.

Jenkins, Neil. *John Beard: Handel and Garrick's Favourite Tenor*. Bramber, 2012.

Joncus, Berta. 'A Star is Born: Kitty Clive and Female Representation in Eighteenth-Century English Musical Theatre'. PhD diss., University of Oxford, 2004.

Joncus, Berta. '"His Spirit is in Action Seen": Milton, Mrs. Clive and the Simulacra of the Pastoral in Comus'. *Eighteenth-Century Music* 2, no. 1 (2005), 7–40.

Joncus, Berta. 'Handel at Drury Lane: Ballad Opera and the Production of Kitty Clive'. *Journal of the Royal Musical Association* 131, no. 2 (2006), 179–226.

Joncus, Berta. 'Producing Stars in Dramma Per Musica'. In *Music as Social and Cultural Practice: Essays in Honour of Reinhard Strohm*, edited by M. Bucciarelli and B. Joncus, 275–93. Woodbridge, 2007.

Joncus, Berta. '"A Likeness where none was to be found": Imagining Kitty Clive (1711–1785)'. *Music in Art* 34 (2009), 89–106.

Joncus, Berta. '"In Wit Superior as in Fighting": Kitty Clive and the Conquest of a Rival Queen'. *Huntington Library Quarterly* 74, no. 1 (2011), 23–42.

Joncus, Berta. '"The Assemblage of every female Folly": Lavinia Fenton, Kitty Clive and the Genesis of Ballad Opera'. In *Women of Fashion: Popular Culture in the Eighteenth Century and the Eighteenth Century in Popular Culture*, edited by T. Potter, 25–51. Toronto, 2012.

Joncus, Berta. '"To propagate Sound for Sense": Music for Diversion and Seduction at Ranelagh Gardens'. *London Journal: A Review of Metropolitan Society Past and Present* 38, no. 1 (2013), 34–66.

Joncus, Berta. 'Ballad Opera: Commercial Song in Enlightenment Garb'. In *The Oxford Handbook of the British Musical*, edited by R. Gordon and O. Jubin, 31–63. Oxford, 2016.

Joncus, Berta. 'From "Ellen a Roon" to "Aileen aroon": Kitty Clive and the Irish Ballad'. Paper delivered at the conference, *The Irish and the London Stage: Identity, Culture, and Politics, 1680–1830*, Trinity College Dublin, 17–18 February 2017.

Joncus, Berta, and Jeremy Barlow, eds. *"The Stage's Glory": John Rich, 1692–1761*. Newark, NJ, 2011.

Joncus, Berta, and Vanessa Rogers. 'Beyond The Beggar's Opera: John Rich and English Ballad Opera'. In *"The Stage's Glory": John Rich, 1692–1761*, edited by B. Joncus and J. Barlow, 184–204. Newark, NJ, 2011.

Joncus, Berta, and Vanessa Rogers. '"United voices formed the very Perfection of Harmony": Music and the Invention of Harriett Abrams (c.1758–1821)'. In *Celebrity: The Idiom of a Modern Era*, edited by B. Czennia, 67–106. New York, 2013.

Joncus, Berta, and Vanessa Rogers. 'Ballad Opera and British double entendre: Henry Fielding's The Mock Doctor'. In *Die Praxis des Timbre in verschiedenen europäischen Kulturen: Eine musikalische Praxis zwischen Oralität und Schriftlichkeit*, edited by H. Schneider, 101–40. Hildesheim, 2013.

Joncus, Berta, et al., eds. *Love in a Village* (1762). OPERA – Spektrum des europäischen Musiktheaters in Einzeleditionen. Bärenreiter: Kassel, in press [hybrid hard copy and electronic critical music edition].

Jones, Vivien, ed. *Women in the Eighteenth Century: Constructions of Femininity*. London, 1990.
Joubert, Estelle. 'Genre and Form in German Opera'. In *The Cambridge Companion to Eighteenth-Century Opera*, edited by A. R. DelDonna and P. Polzonetti, 184–201. Cambridge, 2009.
Kennedy, Gwynne. *Just Anger: Representing Women's Anger in Early Modern England*. Carbondale, IL, 2000.
Kenny, Shirley Strum. 'Theatre, Related Arts and Profit Motive'. In *British Theatre and the Other Arts, 1660–1800*, edited by S. Strum Kenny, 15–38. Washington, 1984.
King, Kathryn R. *A Political Biography of Eliza Haywood*. London, 2012.
King, Richard G., and Saskia Willaert. 'Giovanni Francesco Crosa and the First Italian Comic Operas in London, Brussels and Amsterdam'. *Journal of the Royal Musical Association* 118, no. 2 (1993), 246–75.
Kinservik, Matthew. 'Benefit Play Selection at Drury Lane in 1729–1769: The Cases of Mrs. Cibber, Mrs. Clive, and Mrs. Pritchard'. *Theatre Notebook* 50, no. 1 (1996), 15–28.
Kinservik, Matthew. 'Garrick's Unpublished Epilogue for Catherine Clive's "The Rehearsal: or, Bays in Petticoats" (1750)'. *Études anglaises* 49, no. 3 (1996), 320–26.
Klein, Lawrence. 'Addisonian Afterlives: Joseph Addison in Eighteenth-Century Culture'. *Journal for Eighteenth-Century Studies* 35, no. 1 (2012), 101–18.
Knapp, Mary E. *Prologues and Epilogues of the Eighteenth Century*. New Haven, CT, 1961.
Koon, Helene. *Colley Cibber: A Biography*. Lexington, KY, 1986.
Lafler, Joanne. *The Celebrated Mrs. Oldfield: The Life and Art of an Augustan Actress*. Carbondale, IL, 1989.
Lancia, Séverine. 'The Actress and Eighteenth-Century Ideals of Femininity'. In *Invisible Woman: Aspects of Women's Work in Eighteenth-Century Britain*, edited by I. Baudino, J. Carré, and C. Révauger, 131–38. Abingdon, 2017.
Lanser, Susan S. *The Sexuality of History: Modernity and the Sapphic, 1565–1830*. Chicago, 2014.
Larson, Donald R. and Susan Paun de García, eds. *The Commedia in English: Translation and Performance*. Woodbridge and Rochester, 2008.
Laurie, Margaret. 'Did Purcell set *The Tempest?*'. *Proceedings of the Royal Musical Association* 90th Sess. (1963–64), 43–57.
Lawrence, W. J. 'Early Irish Ballad Opera and Comic Opera'. *The Musical Quarterly* 8, no. 3 (1922), 397–412.
Lee, Jonathan R. 'Virtue Rewarded: Handel's Oratorios and the Culture of Sentiment'. PhD diss., University of California, Berkeley, 2013.
Lee, Jonathan R. 'From Amelia to Calista and Beyond: Sentimental Heroines, "Fallen" Women and Handel's Oratorio Revisions for Susanna Cibber'. *Cambridge Opera Journal* 27, no. 1 (2015), 1–34.
Leppert, Richard. *Music and Image: Domesticity, Ideology and Socio-Cultural Formation in Eighteenth-Century England*. Cambridge, 1988.
Lewis, Peter. *Fielding's Burlesque Drama: Its Place in the Tradition*. Edinburgh, 1987.

Lewis, Wilmarth S., Warren Hunting Smith, and George L. Lam, eds. *Horace Walpole's Correspondence with Sir Horace Mann and Sir Horace Mann the Younger*. The Yale Edition of Horace Walpole's Correspondence. 11 vols. New Haven, CT, 1954–71.

Liesenfeld, Vincent J. *The Licensing Act of 1737*. Madison, WI and London, 1984.

Little, David M., and George M. Kahrl, eds. *The Letters of David Garrick*. 3 vols. Cambridge, MA, 1963.

Lockwood, Thomas. 'Fielding from Stage to Page'. In *Henry Fielding (1707–1754): Novelist, Playwright, Journalist, Magistrate: A Double Anniversary Tribute*, edited by C. Rawson, 21–39. Newark, NJ, 2008.

Lockwood, Thomas, ed. *Henry Fielding: Plays*. 3 vols. Oxford and New York, 2004–11.

The London Stage, 1660–1800: a Calendar of Plays, Entertainments and Afterpieces, together with Casts, Box-Receipts and Contemporary Comment, 5 parts, 11 vols; Part 2: 1700–1729, edited by E. L. Avery, 2 vols, Carbondale, IL, 1960; Part 3: 1729–1747, edited by A. H. Scouten, 2 vols, Carbondale, IL, 1961; Part 4: 1747–1776, edited by G. W. Stone, Jr., 3 vols, Carbondale, IL, 1962.

Lonsdale, Roger. *Dr. Charles Burney: A Literary Biography*. Oxford, 1965.

Luckett, Richard. '"Or Rather our Musical Shakespeare": Charles Burney's Purcell'. In *Music in Eighteenth-Century England: Essays in Memory of Charles Cudworth*, edited by C. Hogwood and R. Luckett, 59–77. Cambridge, 1983.

Mack, Robert L. *Thomas Gray*. London, 1996.

Mackenzie, Barbara D. 'The Creation of a Genre: Comic Opera's Dissemination in Italy in the 1740s'. PhD diss., University of Michigan, 1993.

Marschner, Joanna. *Queen Caroline: Cultural Politics at the Early Eighteenth-Century Court*. London and New Haven, 2014.

Marshall, P. David. *Celebrity and Power: Fame in Contemporary Culture*. Minneapolis, 2001.

Martin, Dennis R. *The Operas and Operatic Style of John Frederick Lampe*. Detroit, 1985.

Martinez, Marc. 'The Tricks of Lun: Mimesis and Mimicry in John Rich's Performance and Conception of Pantomimes'. *Theatre History Studies* 29 (2009), 148–70.

Mazella, David. '"Justly to Fall Unpitied and Abhorr'd": Sensibility, Punishment, and Morality in Lillo's *The London Merchant*'. *English Language History* 68, no. 4 (2001), 795–830.

McCreery, Cindy. *The Satirical Gaze: Prints of Women in Late Eighteenth-Century England*. Oxford, 2004.

McGeary, Thomas. 'Farinelli in Madrid: Opera, Politics, and the War of Jenkins' Ear'. *The Musical Quarterly* 82, no. 2 (1998), 383–421.

McGeary, Thomas. 'Farinelli's Progress to Albion: The Recruitment and Reception of Opera's "Blazing Star"'. *Journal for Eighteenth-Century Studies* 28, no. 3 (2005), 339–60.

McGeary, Thomas. *The Politics of Opera in Handel's Britain*. Cambridge, 2013.

McGirr, Elaine M. *Partial Histories: A Reappraisal of Colley Cibber*. Basingstoke, 2016.

McIntyre, Ian. *Garrick*. London, 1999.

McPherson, Heather. 'Theatrical Celebrity and Porcelain'. In *The Oxford Handbook of the Georgian Theatre, 1737–1832*, edited by J. Swindells and D. F. Taylor, 192–212. Oxford, 2013.

Meisel, Martin. *Realizations: Narrative, Pictorial, and Theatrical Arts in Nineteenth-Century England*. Princeton, 2014.
Milhous, Judith, and Robert D. Hume. 'David Garrick and Box Office Receipts at Drury Lane in 1742-43'. *Philological Quarterly* 67, no. 3 (1988), 323-44.
Milhous, Judith, and Robert D. Hume. 'The Drury Lane Actors' Rebellion of 1743'. *Theatre Journal* 42, no. 1 (1990), 57-80.
Milhous, Judith, and Robert D. Hume. 'Receipts at Drury Lane: Thomas Cross's Diary for 1746-47'. *Theatre Notebook* 49 (1995), 12-90.
Milhous, Judith, and Robert D. Hume. 'J. F. Lampe and English Opera at the Little Haymarket in 1732-3'. *Music & Letters* 78, no. 4 (1997), 502-31.
Moody, Jane. 'Stolen Identities: Character, Mimicry and the Invention of Samuel Foote'. In *Theatre and Celebrity in Britain, 1660-2000*, edited by M. Luckhurst and J. Moody, 65-89. New York, 2005.
Mullin, Janet E. *A Sixpence at Whist: Gaming and the English Middle Classes, 1680-1830*. Woodbridge, 2015.
Nash, Mary. *The Provoked Wife: Life and Times of Susannah Cibber*. Boston, 1977.
Newman, Steve. *Ballad Collection, Lyric, and the Canon: The Call of the Popular from the Restoration to the New Criticism*. Philadelphia, 2007.
Noble, Yvonne. 'Charles Coffey and John Mottley: An Odd Couple in Grub Street'. *Restoration and Eighteenth-Century Theatre Research* 16, no. 1 (2001), 1-12.
Noble, Yvonne. 'Attributions and Misattributions to Edward Phillips, Theatre Writer of the 1730s, with Some Remarks on Thomas Phillips, Theatre Writer of the 1730s'. *Restoration and Eighteenth-Century Theatre Research* 17, nos. 1-2 (2002), 71-83.
North, Roger. *Roger North on Music: Being a Selection from his Essays written during the years c.1695-1728*. Edited by J. Wilson. London, 1959.
Nussbaum, Felicity. *Rival Queens: Actresses, Performance, and the Eighteenth-Century British Theater*. Philadelphia, 2010.
O'Brien, Paula. 'The Life and Works of James Miller, 1704-1744'. PhD diss., University of London, 1979.
O'Brien, John. *Harlequin Britain: Pantomime and Entertainment, 1690-1760*. Baltimore, 2004.
O'Byrne, Alison. 'The Spectator and the Rise of the Modern Metropole'. In *The Cambridge Companion to the City in Literature*, edited by K. R. McNamara, 57-68. Cambridge, 2014.
O'Connor, John. 'Shylock in Performance'. In *The Merchant of Venice: New Critical Essays*, edited by J. W. Mahon and E. M. Mahon, 387-430. New York, 2002.
Pascoe, Judith. *The Sarah Siddons Audio Files: Romanticism and the Lost Voice*. Ann Arbor, MI, 2014.
Paulson, Ronald. *Hogarth's Graphic Works*. 3rd rev. edn. London, 1989.
Paulson, Ronald. 'Some Thoughts on Hogarth's Jew: Issues in Current Hogarth Scholarship'. In *Hogarth: Representing Nature's Machines*, edited by D. Bindman, F. Ogée, and P. Wagner, 219-263. Manchester and New York, 2001.
Paulson, Ronald, and Thomas Lockwood, eds. *Henry Fielding: The Critical Heritage*. London and New York, 1969.
Pearce, Charles E. *"Polly Peachum." Being the Story of Lavinia Fenton (Duchess of Bolton) and "The Beggar's Opera"*. London, 1913.

Pedicord, Harry William. *"By Their Majesties' Command": The House of Hanover at the London Theatres, 1714–1800.* London, 1991.
Pedicord, Harry William. *The Theatrical Public in the Time of Garrick.* New York, 1954.
Pedicord, Harry William, and Frederick Louis Bergmann. 'Commentary and Notes. Lethe; or, Esop in the Shades'. In *The Plays of David Garrick*, edited by H. W. Pedicord and F. L. Bergmann. 7 vols. vol. 1, *Garrick's Own Plays, 1740–1766.* Carbondale, IL, 1980.
Perry, Gill. *Spectacular Flirtations: Viewing the Actress in British Art and Theatre.* New Haven and London, 2007.
Perry, Gill, with Joseph Roach and Shearer West. *The First Actresses: Nell Gwyn to Sarah Siddons.* London and Ann Arbor, MI, 2011.
Petzold, Jochen. 'Polly Peachum, a "Model of Virtue"? Questions of Morality in John Gay's Polly'. *Journal for Eighteenth-Century Studies* 3, no. 3 (2012), 343–57.
Pilkington, Laetitia. *Memoirs of Laetitia Pilkington*, 2 vols. Edited by A. C. Elias Jr. Athens, GA, 1997.
Plank, Geoffrey. *Rebellion and Savagery: The Jacobite Rising of 1745 and the British Empire.* Philadelphia, 2005.
Pointon, Marcia. *Hanging the Head: Portraiture and Social Formation in Eighteenth-Century England.* New Haven, CT and London, 1993.
Porter, Roy. *Bodies Politic: Disease, Death and Doctors in Britain, 1650–1900.* Ithaca, NY, 2001.
Price, Curtis. *Music in the Restoration Theatre.* London, 1979.
Price, Curtis. *Henry Purcell and the London Stage.* Cambridge and New York, 1984.
Radzinowicz, Mary Ann. *Towards Samson Agonistes: The Growth of Milton's Mind.* Princeton, 1978.
Ragussis, Michael. *Figures of Conversion: "The Jewish Question" and English National Identity.* Durham, 1995.
Ragussis, Michael. 'Jews and Other "Outlandish Englishmen": Ethnic Performance and the Invention of British Identity under the Georges'. *Critical Inquiry* 26, no. 4 (2000), 773–97.
Ragussis, Michael. *Theatrical Nation: Jews and Other Outlandish Englishmen in Georgian Britain.* Philadelphia, 2010.
Redmond, Sean, and Su Holmes, eds. *Stardom and Celebrity: A Reader.* Los Angeles and London, 2007.
Richard, Jessica. 'Arts of Play: The Culture of Gambling in Eighteenth-Century Britain'. PhD diss., Princeton University, 2002.
Richards, Alfred E. 'A Literary Link between Thomas Shadwell and Christian Felix Weisse'. *Publications of the Modern Language Association* 21, no. 4 (1906), 808–30.
Ridel, Amanda-Nicole. 'Modification of Market: John Smith and the Mezzotint Print in Eighteenth-Century England'. MA diss., University of California, Riverside, 2011.
Ritchie, Fiona. *Women and Shakespeare in the Eighteenth Century.* New York, 2014.
Roach, Joseph. *The Player's Passion: Studies in the Science of Acting.* Newark, NJ and London, 1985.
Roach, Joseph. *It.* Ann Arbor, MI, 2007.
Roberts, Edgar V. 'Henry Fielding's Lost Play *Deborah, or A Wife for You All* (1733)'. *Bulletin of the New York Public Library* 66 (1962), 567–88.

Roberts, Edgar V. 'The Songs and Tunes in Henry Fielding's Ballad Operas'. In *Essays on the Eighteenth-Century English Stage: Proceedings of the 1971 Symposium of the Manchester University Department of Drama*, edited by K. Richards and P. Thomson, 29–49. Manchester, 1972.

Roberts, John L. *The Jacobite Wars: Scotland and the Military Campaigns of 1715 and 1745*. Edinburgh, 2002.

Rogers, Vanessa L. 'Writing Plays "In the Sing-Song Way": Henry Fielding's Ballad Operas And Early Musical Theater in Eighteenth-Century London'. PhD diss., University of Southern California, 2007.

Rogers, Vanessa L. 'Orchestra and Theatre Music'. In *The Oxford Handbook of the Georgian Theatre, 1737–1832*, edited by J. Swindells and D. F. Taylor, 304–20. Oxford, 2013.

Rogers, Vanessa L. 'John Gay, Ballad Opera and the Théâtres de la foire'. *Eighteenth-Century Music* 11, no. 2 (2014), 173–213.

Rojek, Chris. *Celebrity*. London, 2001.

Rojek, Chris. *Fame Attack: The Inflation of Celebrity and its Consequences*. London, 2012.

Rorschach, Kimerly. 'Frederick, Prince of Wales (1707–1751) as a Patron of the Visual Arts: Princely Patriotism and Political Propaganda', PhD diss., Yale University, 1985.

Rosenfeld, Sybil. *The Theatre of the London Fairs in the Eighteenth Century*. Cambridge, 1960.

Rosenthal, Laura J. 'Entertaining Women: The Actress in Eighteenth-Century Theatre and Culture'. In *The Cambridge Companion to British Theatre, 1730–1830*, edited by J. Moody and D. O'Quinn, 159–74. Cambridge, 2009.

Rousseau, George. *Children and Sexuality: From the Greeks to the Great War*. Basingstoke, 2007.

Rubini, Dennis. 'Sexuality and Augustan England: Sodomy, Politics, Elite Circles and Society'. In *The Pursuit of Sodomy: Male Homosexuality in Renaissance and Enlightenment Europe*, edited by K. Gerard and G. Hekma, 349–81. New York and London, 1989.

Rubsamen, Walter H. 'Mr. Seedo, Ballad Opera and the Singspiel'. In *Miscelánea En Homenaje a Monseñor Higinio Anglés*, 775–809. 2 vols. Barcelona, 1958–61.

Sage, Lorna, Germaine Greer, and Elaine Showalter, eds. *The Cambridge Guide to Women's Writing in English*. Cambridge, 1999.

Schechter, Joel. 'Treason, Wit and Scurrility: Fielding's Cibber Letter'. *Studies in Theatre and Performance*, 34, no. 1 (2014), 53–61.

Schneider, Jr., Ben Ross, foreword by George Winchester Stone, Jr. *Index to The London Stage, 1660–1800*. Carbondale, IL, 1979.

Schoch, Robert. *Writing the History of the British Stage: 1660–1900*. Cambridge, 2016.

Schultz, William. *Gay's Beggar's Opera: Its Content, History and Influence*. New Haven, CT, 1923.

Scouten, Arthur H. and Leo Hughes. 'The Devil to Pay: A Preliminary Check List'. *Library Chronicle of the Friends of the University of Pennsylvania Library* 15 (1948–49), 15–24.

Sechelski, Denise S. 'Garrick's Body and the Labor of Art in Eighteenth-Century Theater'. *Eighteenth-Century Studies* 29, no. 4 (1996), 369–89.

Seewald, Jan. *Theatrical Sculpture: Skulptiere Bildnisse berühmter englischer Schauspieler, 1750–1850, insbesondere David Garrick und Sarah Siddons*. Munich, 2007.
Semmens, Richard. *Studies in the English Pantomime, 1712–1733*. Hillsdale, NY, 2016.
Simon, Robin. 'Hogarth and Rich: Gesture and Expression in The Beggar's Opera'. In *"The Stage's Glory": John Rich, 1692–1761*, edited by B. Joncus and J. Barlow, 253–65. Newark, NJ, 2011.
Simpson, Claude M. *The British Broadside Ballad and its Music*. New Brunswick, 1966.
Smith, Dane Farnsworth. *Plays about the Theatre in England, from The Rehearsal in 1671 to the Licensing Act in 1737*. London, 1936.
Smith, Kent. 'Egidio Duni and the Development of opéra comique from 1753 to 1770'. PhD diss., Cornell University, 1980.
[Smith] Loewenthal, Ruth. 'Handel and Newburgh Hamilton: New References in the Strafford Papers'. *The Musical Times* 112, no. 1545 (1971), 1063–66.
Smith, Ruth. 'Intellectual Contexts of Handel's Oratorios'. In *Music in Eighteenth-Century England: Essays in Memory of Charles Cudworth*, edited by C. Hogwood and R. Luckett, 115–33. Cambridge, 1983.
Smith, Ruth. *Handel's Oratorios and Eighteenth-Century Thought*. Cambridge, 1995.
Smith, Ruth. 'Milton moderated: *Il moderato* and its Relation to *L'Allegro* and *Il Penseroso*'. *Händel-Jahrbuch* 56 (2010), 139–64.
Smith, Ruth. 'Milton Modulated for Handel's Music'. In *Milton in the Long Restoration*, edited by B. Hoxby and A. Baynes Coiro, 159–79. Oxford and New York, 2016.
Smith, William C. *Handel: A Descriptive Catalogue of the Early Editions*. 2nd edn. Oxford, 1970.
Solkin, David. 'The excessive Jew in *A Harlot's Progress*'. In *Hogarth: Representing Nature's Machines*, edited by D. Bindman, F. Ogée, and P. Wagner. Manchester and New York, 2001.
Solomon, Diana. 'Tragic Play, Bawdy Epilogue?'. In *Prologues, Epilogues, Curtain-Raisers, and Afterpieces: The Rest of the Eighteenth-Century London Stage*, edited by D. J. Ennis and J. Bailey, 155–78. Newark, NJ, 2007.
Solomon, Harry M. *The Rise of Robert Dodsley: Creating the New Age of Print*. Carbondale, IL, 1996.
Stephanson, Raymond. '"Epicoene Friendship": Understanding Male Friendship in the Early Eighteenth Century, with Some Speculations about Pope'. *The Eighteenth Century: Theory and Interpretation* 38, no. 2 (1997), 151–70.
Stern, Tiffany. *Rehearsal from Shakespeare to Sheridan*. Oxford, 2000.
Stewart, Powell, 'An Eighteenth-Century Adaptation of Shakespeare'. *Texas University Studies in English* 12 (1932), 98–117.
Stone Jr., George Winchester. '*Romeo and Juliet*: The Source of its Modern Stage Career'. *Shakespeare Quarterly* 15, no. 2 (1964), 191–206.
Straub, Kristina. *Sexual Suspects: Eighteenth-Century Players and Sexual Ideology*. Princeton, 1992.
Straub, Kristina. 'The Newspaper "Trial" of Charles Macklin's Macbeth and the Theatre as Juridicial Public Sphere'. *Eighteenth-Century Fiction* 27, nos. 3–4 (2015), 395–418.
Sturgess, H. A. C. *Register of Admissions to the Honourable Society of the Middle Temple, from the Fifteenth Century to the Year 1944*. 3 vols. London, 1949.

Sundberg, Johan. 'Where does the Sound come From?'. In *The Cambridge Companion to Singing*, edited by J. Potter, 231–47. Cambridge, 2000.
Tague, Ingrid H. *Women of Quality: Accepting and Contesting Ideals of Femininity in England*. Woodbridge, 2002.
Tave, Stuart M. *The Amiable Humorist: A Study in the Comic Theory and Criticism of the Eighteenth and early Nineteenth Centuries*. Chicago, 1960.
Taylor, Carole. 'Handel's Disengagement from the Italian Opera'. In *Handel: Tercentenary Collection*, edited by S. Sadie and A. Hicks, 165–81. Basingstoke, 1987.
Taylor, Gary, et al., eds. *The New Oxford Shakespeare: The Complete Works*. Oxford, 2016.
Thompson, Andrew C. *George II, King and Elector*. New Haven, CT, 2011.
Tobin, John. *Handel's Messiah: A Critical Account of the Manuscript Sources and Printed Editions*. London, 1969.
Tucker, Joseph E. 'The Eighteenth-Century English Translations of Molière'. *Modern Language Quarterly* 3 (1942), 83–103.
Tuppen, Sandra. 'Purcell in the 18th Century: Music for the "Quality, Gentry, and Others"'. *Early Music* 43, no. 2 (2015), 233–45.
Tusler, Robert L. *Willem de Fesch: 'An excellent Musician and a worthy Man'*. Den Haag, 2005.
Van Boer, Bertil H. 'Coffey's *The Devil to Pay*: The Comic War, and the Emergence of the German Singspiel'. *Journal of Musicological Research* 8, no. 1–2 (1988), 119–39.
Vandrei, Martha. '"Britons, strike Home": Politics, Patriotism and Popular Song in British Culture, c.1695–1900'. *Historical Research* 87, no. 238 (2014), 679–702.
Vaughan, Anthony. *Born to Please: Hannah Pritchard, Actress, 1711–1768: A Critical Biography*. London, 1979.
Vickers, David, ed. *Handel*. Farnham, 2011.
Viol, Claus-Ulrich. *Eighteenth-Century (sub)versions of Stage Irishness: Prevalent Anti-Irish Stereotypes and their Dramatic Functionalisation*. Trier, 1998.
Virgil, *Aeneid*, translated with notes by Frederick Ahl, with an introduction by Elaine Fantham. New York, 2007.
Vivian, Frances. *A Life of Frederick, Prince of Wales (1701–1751): A Connoisseur of the Arts*, edited by R. White. Lewiston, NY and Lampeter, 2007.
Wakely, Alice, ed. *Henry Fielding: The History of Tom Jones, a Foundling*. London, 2005.
Walpole, Horace. *Strawberry Hill Accounts: A Record of Expenditure in Building, Furnishing, &c., kept by Mr. Horace Walpole from 1747 to 1795 now first printed from the Original MS with notes and index by Paget Toynbee*. Oxford, 1927.
Wanko, Cheryl. *Roles of Authority: Thespian Biography and Celebrity in Eighteenth-Century Britain*. Lubbock, TX, 2003.
Wasserman, Earl R. 'The Sympathetic Imagination in Eighteenth-Century Theories of Acting'. *The Journal of English and Germanic Philology* 46 (1947), 264–72.
Watson, George, ed. *The New Cambridge Bibliography of English Literature*. 5 vols. London, 1969.
West, Shearer. *The Image of the Actor: Verbal and Visual Representation in the Age of Garrick and Kemble*. London, 1991.
Whinney, Margaret. *Sculpture in Britain, 1530 to 1830*. Harmondsworth, 1964.
White, Jerry. *London in the Eighteenth Century: A Great and Monstrous Thing*. London, 2012.

Whitworth, Rex. *William Augustus: Duke of Cumberland: A Life*. London, 1992.
Willaert, Saskia. 'Italian comic opera in London, 1760–1770'. PhD diss., King's College London, 1999.
Wilson, Brett D. *A Race of Female Patriots: Women and Public Spirit on the British Stage, 1688–1745*. Lewisburg, PA, 2012.
Wilson, Kathleen. 'Empire, Trade and Popular Politics in Mid-Hanoverian Britain: The Case of Admiral Vernon'. *Past & Present* 121 (1988), 74–109.
Wilson, Kathleen. *The Sense of the People*. Cambridge, 1998.
Woodfine, Philip. '"Suspicious Latitudes": Commerce, Colonies, and Patriotism in the 1730s'. *Studies in Eighteenth Century Culture* 27 (1998), 25–52.
Yarrington, Alison. 'The Female Pygmalion: Anne Seymour Damer, Allan Cunningham and the Writing of a Woman Sculptor's Life'. *Sculpture Journal* 5, no. 1 (1997), 32–44.
York, Richard, ed. *One Long Whitson Holyday: Country Dance Tunes from an 18th century* [sic] *Northamptonshire Hall*. Northampton, 1991.
Zon, Bennett. 'Histories of British Music and the Land without Music: National Identity and the Idea of the Hero'. In *Essays on the History of English Music in Honour of John Caldwell: Sources, Style, Performance, Historiography*, edited by E. Hornby and D. Maw, 311–24. Woodbridge, 2010.
Zunshine, Lisa, ed. *Acting Theory and the English Stage, 1700–1830*. 5 vols. London, 2009.

Index

A large amount of additional information is contained in footnotes. These are indicated in the index by the italicised letters *fn*. In, for instance, 25*fn*, the reference is to a footnote only. In 11 + *fn*, the reference is to both main text and footnote. In, say, 14–15 + *fn*, there is germane material in footnotes on both pages, as well as across the two pages of text. Illustrations are indicated by *ill*.

acting/drama styles, 11 + *fn*, 12–13, 25*fn*, 249*fn*
   application plays, 227, 244–60
   burlesque, 3, 6, 38*fn*, 63, 158
   farce, 11, 26, 42, 171
   harlequinade, 20, 57, 146
   interludes, 19, 21, 83 + *fn*, 106, 190, 192, 215, 249, 309, 349
   mainpiece comedy, 20
   masque, 20 + *fn*, 57–9, 57*fn*, 181–2, 275, 304–5, 399, 411–12
      types, 57*fn*
      see also Arne; Boyce; Carey; Clive: in masques; Congreve; Handel; Mallet; Pritchard, William; Purcell
   pantomime, 20, 26, 57, 146, 184, 232–3, 288, 297
   pastoral, 3, 41–2, 42*fn*, 52, 135, 160, 210, 252, 268, 292
      see also Boyce, William
   sentimental comedy, 11 + *fn*, 23–4, 42
   tragedy, 11 + *fn*, 23, 26
   vocal production, 5 + *fn*
actresses, reputation of, 14–15 + *fn*
Addison, Joseph, 10, 227, 244*fn*
   The Drummer, 219
   Rosamond, 179 + *fn*, 227, 241, 244–60, 249, 267
      'Beneath some hoary Mountain', 250, 252–60, 255–9*ill*
      different versions, 247–8
      'From Walk to Walk', 250–3, 253–5*ill*
      'Was ever Nymph like Rosamond', 249, 251–2*ill*
   The Spectator, 10 + *fn*, 244
   see also Steele, Richard
Amhurst, Nicholas: quoted, 39 + *fn*, 66*fn*
Arne, Cecilia, 209–10, 210*fn*, 211, 212, 261–2*fn*, 328 + *fn*, 415, 416
Arne, Susannah
   see Cibber, Susannah
Arne, Thomas, 161–2, 179, 193, 242, 328 + *fn*, 361 + *fn*, 410
   As You Like It
      'The Cuckow', 199–201, 199*fn*, 200*ill*, 226, 315
   borrowings from Shakespeare, 199
   'The Card invites', 341–2, 341*fn*, 343–7*ill*
   and Charles Burney, 328–9 + *fn*, 330
   compared with George F. Handel, 268, 270, 271
   compared with Henry Carey, 169–70, 180–1, 181*fn*
   An Hospital for Fools
      'How smoothly glides the Fool thro' Life', 225–6 + *fn*
   and Italianate style, 181 + *fn*
   The Judgement of Paris, 349 + *fn*, 350*fn*
      benefit, 349
   masques
      Alfred, 212, 227, 260 + *fn*
      'O Peace, thou fairest Child of Heav'n', 261*fn*, 262–3, 263*ill*

510 INDEX

Arne, Thomas (*continued*)
  masques (*continued*)
    Alfred (*continued*)
      'Rule Britannia', 261–2, 262–3
    Comus, 4, 195, 209–13, 211–12*fn*, 228 + *fn*, 263–4, 296, 309, 362, 415
    The Fall of Phaeton, 169–70, 181–4, 181*fn*, 209
    The Opera of Operas, 158 + *fn*
    Romeo and Juliet, 384
    Rosamond, 179 + *fn*, 227, 241, 244–60, 245*fn*, 247–9, 348
      'Beneath some hoary Mountain', 250, 252–60, 255–9*ill*
      different versions, 247–8
      'From Walk to Walk', 250–3, 253–5*ill*
      'Was ever Nymph like Rosamond', 249, 251–2*ill*
    setting of the National Anthem, 305–6, 305*fn*
    The Tempest, 21, 314 + *fn*, 315, 328
    at Vauxhall Gardens, 315
Arne family, 161, 179–80 + *fn*, 415
Ashley Cooper, Susanna (4th Countess of Shaftesbury), 195, 195–6*fn*
  see also Shaftesbury, 4th Earl of

Baker, David E.: quoted, 80
Barthes, Roland: quoted, 5–6 + *fn*, 26
Beard, John, 230–2, 265, 295, 348 + *fn*, 378–9*fn*, 422
  celebrity, 2*fn*, 33, 411
  in *The Coffee-House*, 213, 214 + *fn*, 215*fn*, 224*fn*
  in George F. Handel works, 194, 266*fn*, 269, 270*fn*, 271
  joins Drury Lane, 47*fn*, 192–3*fn*, 194, 266
  in *Joseph*, 271, 274
  in *L'Allegro ed il Penseroso*, 229, 230, 269, 270*fn*
  marriage to Lady Harriet, 265–6 + *fn*
  'Masquerade Song', 363 + *fn*
  move to Covent Garden, 288
  playing opposite Kitty Clive, 33, 69*fn*, 194, 230–2, 271, 290, 292–3 + *fn*, 296, 336, 412
  in *The Chaplet*, 361 + *fn*, 362–75, 380
  in *Comus*, 209–10, 212, 416
  in *Lethe*, 348
  in *The Rehearsal: Or, Bays in Petticoats*, 380, 381, 386, 399
    Corydon and Miranda, 387
  in *Rosamond*, 244, 245–6, 246–9, 249*fn*
  in *Samson*, 241, 267–8, 269, 271
  portrait painted, 249, 250*ill*
  in *The Shepherd's Lottery*, 375–6
Berry, Spranger, 376, 383, 384*fn*
Blackmore, Richard: *Alfred: An Epik Poem*, 196*fn*, 261 + *fn*
Blow, John, 78*fn*
Bolingbroke, 1st Viscount (Henry St John), 265
  The Idea of the Patriot King, 260 + *fn*
Bolton, 3rd Duke of (Charles Powlett), 37 + *fn*, 41
Bononcini, Giovanni: *Camilla*, 45 + *fn*, 49
Booth, Barton, 29*fn*, 72 + *fn*, 107*fn*, 145, 168, 232*fn*, 284
Booth, Hester (*née* Santlow), 72 + *fn*, 145 + *fn*, 168, 201 + *fn*
Booth, Thomas: *The Green Room Scuffle*, 319–23, 320*ill*
  quoted, 319, 321
Boswell, James: quoted, 34 + *fn*
Bowles, Thomas and John, 103, 104
Boyce, William, 6, 361*fn*, 407, 410
  The Chaplet, 361–75, 362*fn*, 368, 376, 398
    'From Flow'r to Flow'r', 364–7*ill*, 368
    'I know that my Person is charming', 371, 372–4*ill*
    'In vain I try my ev'ry Art', 368, 369–70*ill*
    'Masquerade Song', 363 + *fn*
  Lethe, 361 + *fn*
  masques
    Corydon and Miranda, 380 + *fn*, 381, 387–98
      'If Cupid once the mind possess', 387, 388–9*ill*, 401*fn*
      'In vain, Miranda, you complain', 387, 389*fn*, 390–1*ill*, 401*fn*
      quoted, 387, 393, 398

'Rise, tempests, rise, cloud the
skies!', 393, 394–5*ill*, 395,
396–7*ill*
'The silver rain, the pearly dew',
372–4*ill*, 389–91, 391–2*ill*
Romeo and Juliet, 384 + *fn*
The Shepherd's Lottery, 375–6, 375*fn*
Bridgewater, Roger, 125*fn*, 151*fn*
Buckingham, 2nd Duke of (George
Villiers),
The Chances, 72*fn*
The Rehearsal (after Molière), 294, 332,
349*fn*, 378 + *fn*, 379
Burgess, Henry,
'The Coffee-House Song', 215, 216*ill*
Burgh, John: quoted, 24–6
Burney, Charles, 4, 327–30
quoted, 83*fn*, 305*fn*, 328 + *fn*, 329 + *fn*,
361*fn*, 385–6*fn*
Butler, Elizabeth, 108, 149*fn*, 279

Carey, Henry, 29, 30*fn*, 59*fn*, 62–3, 114 +
fn, 410, 411–12
*Apollo and Daphne, or Harlequin
Mercury*, 33*fn*
benefits, 28, 54, 56, 59–62, 63, 140, 415
'Blundrella: Or, the Impertinent', 31–2
and Charles Fleetwood, 62
Colombine Courtezan, 30*fn*
compared with Thomas Arne, 169–70,
180–1, 181*fn*, 225–6
The Contrivances, 30*fn*, 52–4, 54*fn*,
55*ill*, 56, 63, 184, 309, 412
'Cease to perswade', 53, 54*ill*
playbook, 56
A Cure for a Scold (after Shakespeare),
196
Damon and Phillida, 45–9, 56, 63, 81,
309, 412
playbook, 47–9 + *fn*, 48*ill*, 103*fn*,
173
The Dragon of Wantley, 30–1, 30*fn*, 63 +
fn, 169, 219*fn*, 348
wordbook, 169*fn*
dropped by Drury Lane, 31, 62, 63, 169,
412
Harlequin Dr Faustus, 31
The Harlot's Progress (attributed),
146–7 + *fn*, 203, 309

his family, 30 + *fn*, 31 + *fn*, 33 + *fn*, 289,
290 + *fn*, 291 + *fn*
The Honest Yorkshire-Man, 169 + *fn*,
184, 316
indiscretion, 31
influence/possible authorship, 90, 108,
130, 225–6, 315
and Italian(ate) works, 30*fn*, 31–2, 32*fn*,
40, 53, 62, 315
'The Life of a Beau', 21, 30, 213 + *fn*,
217*ill*, 290, 415
'The Life of a Belle', 336, 337*ill*
Love in a Riddle, 30*fn*, 33, 41–5, 42*fn*,
45, 47, 412
masques, 6
Cephalus and Procris, 3–4, 20–1,
30*fn*, 58–9, 129*fn*, 411
sheet music, 60*ill*, 61*ill*
'Mocking is Catching', 31 + *fn*
as performer, 56, 61, 62
'Polly Peachum', 36 + *fn*, 40
quoted, 62, 169*fn*
The Records of Love, 46 + *fn*
'Sally in our Alley', 36*fn*, 40, 42*fn*,
79–80, 83, 146–7
Six Cantatas, 61–2, 62*fn*
'Go perjur'd Swain', 140–1, 140*ill*
suicide, 30–1 + 31*fn*, 290
support for women, 46, 62
teacher, friend and ally to Kitty Clive,
6, 21, 28, 30–1, 32–3, 52, 62,
290–1, 329*fn*
Centlivre, Susannah,
*The Comical Revenge/Love's
Contrivance*, 125, 128*fn*, 129 + *fn*
The Wonder: A Woman keeps a Secret,
420 + *fn*
Charke, Richard, 53
'The Provident Damsel', 67–9, 68*ill*,
140
Chetwood, William, 28–9, 29*fn*, 45*fn*,
164, 284, 415
The Dramatic Congress, 283, 318
quoted, 284, 307
The Lover's Opera, 49, 50 + *fn*, 160 + *fn*
quoted, 28, 29*fn*, 43, 62, 277, 323–4
on Jane Pope, 67*fn*
on Kitty Clive's reputation, 15, 153
+ *fn*

Chetwood, William (*continued*)
  quoted (*continued*)
    on Kitty Clive's singing, 5 + *fn*, 30, 240 + *fn*
    on Kitty Clive's spoken delivery, 17, 143
    on Mary Edwards, 348, 350–1
    on Susannah Cibber, 180
    on Theophilus Cibber, 67*fn*, 106 + *fn*
'Christopher Columbario': *The Pigeon-Pye*, 219–20 + *fn*
Churchill, Charles, 291
  quoted, 7, 13, 143
Churchill, Sarah (1st Duchess of Marlborough), 246 + *fn*
Cibber, Charlotte, 67 + *fn*
Cibber, Colley, 49, 51, 52, 64, 73, 160*fn*, 410, 412
  and Anne Oldfield, 65, 171
  and *The Beggar's Opera*, 29, 33–4, 41, 42
  The Careless Husband, 65
  The Comical Lovers (after Dryden), 309
  Damon and Phillida, 45–7, 51
  drops Henry Carey, 62–3
  as Drury Lane manager, 22, 28, 29–30, 29*fn*, 62, 145–6, 148, 160*fn*
  enemies (alleged), 44–5, 45*fn*
  and James Miller, 66
  and Kitty Clive, 28, 29–30, 33, 41, 49, 57–8, 98
  Love in a Riddle, 33, 41–5, 44*fn*, 47, 49, 51, 63, 114*fn*, 412
  quoted, 42
  as performer, 42–3, 43*fn*, 44, 63, 64, 66 + *fn*
  quoted, 22 + *fn*, 41
  reputation, 42–3, 44 + *fn*, 46–7, 63
  supposed enemies, 44–5, 45*fn*
  Venus and Adonis, 57
Cibber, Jane (née Johnson), 67 + *fn*, 106, 106–7*fn*, 157
  death, 106, 106–7*fn*, 149 + *fn*
Cibber, Susannah (née Arne), 12*fn*, 283, 300–1, 307–8, 308*fn*, 322, 414
  in *The Beggar's Opera*, 319, 349–50, 350*fn*
  'Polly Row', 35*fn*, 163, 185–93, 310–13, 315, 331, 376, 401

  benefits, 55*fn*
  in *Comus*, 209, 210 + *fn*, 212, 416
  in *Deborah*, 269 + *fn*
  earnings, 55*fn*
  engagement to/marriage/pregnancy with Theophilus Cibber, 161, 170, 178–9, 179*fn*, 186 + *fn*, 193, 194, 201, 225
  and William Sloper, 225
  good and bad notices, 179, 189, 269
  as Kitty Clive's rival, 180, 188–9, 191, 193, 201, 310, 322, 379, 399, 401–2
  leaves and returns to Drury Lane (or threatens to), 194, 225, 268–9, 296, 297, 306–8, 308*fn*, 376, 384*fn*, 400
  marketing of, 179*fn*, 180, 187, 188–9
  in *Messiah*, 268–9
  in the National Anthem, 305
  quoted, 304, 306, 307, 311, 312, 313*fn*, 322*fn*
  in *Rosamond*, 244, 245, 250
  in *Samson*, 268–9, 307*fn*
  and *The Theatrical Contest*, 300*ill*, 301
  voice, 24 + *fn*, 180, 192, 354–5
  in *Zara*, 180, 186, 399, 400, 402
  see also Veteran Scheme
Cibber, Theophilus, 83, 98, 166, 168, 170, 295, 311, 412
  An Apology for the Life of Mr. T– C–, 107–8 + *fn*, 149*fn*, 224 + *fn*, 325
  benefit, 106
  in *The Coffee-House*, 213–14
  (co-)manager at Drury Lane, 145 + *fn*, 146, 163, 169, 284, 415
  leads actors' rebellion from Drury Lane (1733) ... and returns, 106, 132*fn*, 138, 148–50, 158, 161–2, 167, 168
  leaves Drury Lane, 168, 194, 224–5, 225*fn*, 276–7, 297*fn*
  summer companies, 47*fn*, 51–3, 52*fn*, 73–4 + *fn*, 105, 127–8, 135, 136, 169*fn*, 413
  The Country Correspondent (attributed)
    quoted, 324–5, 331
  at Covent Garden, 296

INDEX 513

depicted in *The Coffee-House*, 213
The Harlot's Progress, 8, 146–8 + *fn*, 203
   quoted, 147
his marriages, 67 + *fn*, 106, 106–7*fn*,
   149 + *fn*, 179 + *fn*, 225
and Kitty Clive, 71, 108, 134, 135, 136,
   145, 146, 149, 167, 170
as 'Looby Headpiece', 162, 167
The Lover, 106 + *fn*
and money, 52
at New Haymarket, 158, 178
Patie and Peggy, 49, 160 + *fn*
as performer, 64–5, 66–7, 74–5, 105,
   106, 224
   in *The Lottery*, 109, 119
   in *The Man of Taste*, 165
   in *The Mock Doctor*, 129–30, 132–3,
     162, 413
   in *The Mother-in-Law*, 162
   in *The Old Debauchees*, 125–6
   Pistol (Shakespeare), 107, 151, 191–2,
     226
'Polly Row', 35*fn*, 163, 185–93, 414
quoted, 106–7*fn*, 107 + *fn*, 146, 148*fn*,
   221–2, 296 + *fn*, 311, 317
see also Cibber, Colley; Cibber,
   Susannah
Clayton, Thomas,
   Rosamond, 247–8
Clive, Catherine 'Kitty',
   in *As You Like It*, 163 + *fn*, 199, 201 + *fn*
   'The Cuckow', 199–201, 199*fn*, 200*ill*,
     212, 226, 315
   and the Actors' Rebellion (1733), 148–9,
     159–60, 413
   and the Actors' Rebellion (1743–44),
     275–7, 276*fn*, 278*fn*, 283, 284,
     288, 291, 301, 302, 349
   in *Alfred*, 260, 261–2 + *fn*
     'O Peace, thou fairest Child of
       Heav'n', 261*fn*, 262
   in *L'Allegro, il penseroso ed il moderato*,
     229–30 + *fn*, 232, 240–2. 270
     + *fn*
   and anti-Semitism, 148, 205–6, 213 + *fn*
   in *Art and Nature*: epilogue, 218–19,
     218*fn*
   and *Athalia*, 269–70, 270*fn*
   auditions for Drury Lane, 28

   in *The Author's Farce*, 159, 160, 165
   in *The Beggar's Opera*, 106, 107, 133–5,
     170, 185–93, 230, 297 + *fn*,
     349–50
     benefit, 134–5
     'Polly Row', 35*fn*, 163, 185–93, 197,
       275–6, 280–1, 310–13, 414, 422
   benefit concerts, 295, 295–6*fn*, 296
   benefits for her, 54–5, 55*fn*, 286, 289,
     318, 402, 415
   benefits for others, 240, 289, 309 + *fn*,
     338*fn*, 399*fn*, 400*fn*
     James Raftor (her brother), 289, 309,
       332, 338*fn*, 398–9, 400*fn*
     Mary Edwards, 289, 309, 349
   birth, 1
   in *The Camp Visitants*, 334
   and card gaming, 341–2, 342*fn*
   as Catherine 'Kitty' Clive/Mrs. Clive,
     15–16, 103*fn*, 153, 154, 165, 172*ill*,
     173, 240*fn*, 409
   as Catherine Rafter, 1–2*fn*, 50*ill*, 51, 169,
     178, 377
   as Catherine Rafto, 83*fn*
   as Catherine Raftor/Miss Raftor, 1,
     15–16, 28, 138, 153, 154, 172*ill*,
     173, 240*fn*, 316
     so billed, 61–2, 119, 127
     so named in the press/attacks and
       encomiums, 43, 80, 132, 133–4,
       150, 152, 316
     theoretically baptized as Ellenor
       Raftor, 1–2 + *fn*, 409
   in *Cephalus and Procris*, 30 + *fn*, 59,
     129*fn*, 182
   challenging convention, 3, 9, 32, 119,
     173, 368
   in *The Chaplet*, 362–75, 380, 383, 400–1
     benefit, 362
   in *The Coffee-House*, 140, 213–18
     anti-Semitism, 213 + *fn*
     homophobia, 214–15, 215*fn*, 415
     'The Life of a Beau', 144 + *fn*, 165,
       213, 215–18 + *fn*, 217*ill*, 290 + *fn*,
       296, 336
   in *The Comical Lovers*, 309
     benefit, 309
   compared to Anne Oldfield, 72, 148–9,
     152, 167, 168–9, 170–1

Clive, Catherine 'Kitty' (*continued*)
   in *Comus*, 3–4, 8, 148, 208–13, 226–7, 231–2*fn*, 267–8, 288, 331, 415–16
   in *The Contrivances*, 52–3, 54, 56, 67, 230–1
     benefit, 54, 56
     'Cease to perswade', 53
   at Covent Garden, 288–92, 296 + *fn*, 297
   in *The Covent Garden Tragedy*, 126–7, 138
   in *Damon and Phillida*, 45–9, 160 + *fn*, 165, 172*ill*, 176*ill*, 230–1, 309, 362, 422
   in *Deborah: Or, a Wife for you All*, 149
     benefit, 149, 240
   in *The Devil of a Duke*, 135–6
   in *The Devil to Pay*, 3–4, 8, 72, 74–104, 99–102*ill*, 288, 309, 322, 412
     breakthrough, 80
     differing versions, 84–9
   earnings, 52, 416
     comparable to men, 14–15, 424
     defended, 280, 286, 302, 477–81
     denied her just desserts, 280 + *fn*, 294–5
     reported, 276, 284–6, 291–2, 324, 376, 410
     "twenty shillings per week", 28, 29 + *fn*
     see also benefits
   encomiums, 90, 96*ill*, 97, 152, 178, 189, 416
   and epilogues, 18, 106, 413, 415
     The Author's Farce, 158–9, 165
     Britons, Strike Home, 226
     Comus, 211, 227
     The Covent Garden Tragedy, 413
     Lethe, 336–8, 338*fn*
     The Lottery, 119
     The Man of Taste, 165, 166
     The Universal Passion, 198
     The Wonder: A Woman keeps a Secret, 420
     Zara, 180
   in *Eurydice: Or, the Devil Henpeck'd*, 202
   as 'The Fair Songster', 169
   in *The Fall of Phaeton*, 182, 183, 230, 231
   figurines of, 326–7 + *fn*, 327*ill*, 354, 355, 360, 411
   and genius, 1, 8, 128, 159, 333, 340
   and *The Green Room Scuffle*, 318–24, 327, 329–30, 332, 416
   in *Hamlet*, 201–2, 308–9, 398*fn*
     benefit, 398
   in *The Harlot's Progress*, 8, 146–8, 230, 309
   and her audience/her public, 3, 8–9, 16, 26–7, 43, 65, 80, 98, 139, 143, 192, 205, 211, 410–11
   her own material, 7–8, 21, 378–9*fn*, 409, 422
     for benefits, 377, 378 + *fn*, 408
   Every Woman in her Humour:
     benefit, 406–7
     quoted, 425
   The London 'Prentice (attributed; benefit), 290 + *fn*
   The Rehearsal: Or, Bays in Petticoats (after Buckingham), 7–8, 8*fn*, 163, 377, 378–98, 398*fn*, 407–8
     benefits, 398–9
     incorporating *Corydon and Miranda*, 381, 387–98, 401
       'If Cupid once the mind possess', 387, 388–9*ill*, 401*fn*
     'In vain, Miranda, you complain', 387, 389*fn*, 390–1*ill*, 401*fn*
     'Rise, tempests, rise, cloud the skies!', 393, 394–5*ill*, 395, 396–7*ill*
     'The silver rain, the pearly dew', 372–4*ill*, 389–91, 391–2*ill*
     quoted, 381–7, 384*fn*, 399–400, 401 + *fn*, 402–3
     1750 version, 380–99, 401
       benefit, 378
     1751 version, 399–400 + *fn*, 401, 403
       benefit, 399
     1753 version, 399, 400–3, 400*fn*, 408
       benefit, 400 + *fn*, 403
     1762 version, 405–6
       benefit, 163*fn*, 405, 406
   The Sketch of a Fine Lady's Return from a Rout: benefit, 407
   her weight, 332, 377, 379, 410, 416, 420

in *An Hospital for Fools*, 140, 334–5
'The Prince, unable to conceal his
   pain', 335
in *The Humours of Oxford*, 64–5, 66–7,
   71, 109
   'The Provident Damsel', 67–9, 68*ill*,
      140, 143, 165
improvisation/extemporizing, 2–3, 6,
   7, 63
inspiring verse, 31–2
in *The Intriguing Chambermaid*, 138,
   140, 141 + *fn*, 142–3, 158, 160,
   230, 240, 309
Irish support, 28–9, 29*fn*, 212, 307, 415
in *The Island of Slaves*: benefit, 212,
   212–13*fn*
and Italian(ate) material, 21, 45, 53, 58,
   62, 181
   arias/ariosos, 3, 274
   and 'Burletto', 6, 379–82, 384, 386,
      398*fn*, 405–6
   mimicry/mockery of, 4–5, 19, 63,
      158, 164, 309, 340–1 + *fn*, 377,
      379–80, 409
   'The Merigghi Song'/'Son
      confusa pastorella', 83–90
      + *fn*, 106, 110–13*ill*, 114–19,
      115–18*ill*, 119*fn*
in *The Jealous Wife*: benefit, 163*fn*
in *Joseph*, 271–4
as 'Kitty Cuckoe', 283, 302
legacy, 13, 97–8
in *Lethe* (1740), 334–6, 400
   'Life of a Belle', 336, 337*ill*, 338*fn*
in *Lethe* (1749), 338–48, 355–60,
   357–9*ill*, 376
   'The Card invites', 341–2, 341*fn*,
      343–7*ill*, 348, 352
in *A Lick at the Town*, 404
loss of audience/critical support,
   3, 138, 148, 150, 304–5, 306,
   324, 327
in *The Lottery*, 108–24, 125–6, 130, 288,
   309, 313, 413
   'Alas! My Lord, you're too severe',
      120–4*ill*
in *Love and Friendship*, 292–3 + *fn*, 309
in *Love for Love*, 108, 309
in *Love in a Riddle*, 41–3, 47, 58

*Miss Rafter in the Character of
   Phillida* (portrait in oils,
   sold as a mezzotint), 50*ill*, 51
   + *fn*, 178
in *The Lover's Opera*, 49, 50 + *fn*
in *The Man of Taste*, 69 + *fn*, 140, 165
marriage and separation (alleged), 153,
   156, 157, 160, 409
marital law, 157 + *fn*
in masques, 3–4, 6, 11, 19, 20, 57–8, 62,
   271, 275, 411–12
   see also in *Comus*; her own
      material: *The Rehearsal*; in *The
      Tempest*
in *The Merchant of Venice*, 203, 204–6,
   205*fn*, 206, 292 + *fn*, 308–9,
   338–9
   benefit, 292, 294–5
in *Messiah*, 270–1 + *fn*
in *The Miser*, 138, 139, 141, 144 + *fn*, 288,
   290, 309
in *Miss Lucy in Town*, 334, 340*fn*
in *The Mock Doctor*, 130–33, 130*fn*, 138,
   143, 144, 163, 413
in *The Mother-in-Law*, 140
in *The Old Debauchees*, 125–6, 127, 128,
   138
in *An Old Man taught Wisdom*, 288,
   290
in *The Opera of Operas*, 158
in *Orpheus and Eurydice*, 288
as 'Patriot Soprano', 193, 195
and patronage, 9, 349, 385, 411
in *Phebe: Or, The Beggar's Wedding*,
   74*fn*
as a portrait sitter (sometimes
   apocryphally), 1, 19, 21–2,
   168–9, 170–6, 193, 241–4, 355–8,
   377, 422
portraits reproduced, 48, 50, 99, 100–3,
   172, 176, 177, 231, 356–9, 417–19,
   421, 423
in the press
   complaints in, 136
   letters to, 9*fn*, 187–8, 274, 280–1, 312
   quoted, 188, 280, 290
   pieces/pamphlets for quotation, 22
   The Case of Mrs. Clive, 274, 276,
      294, 339–40

Clive, Catherine 'Kitty' (*continued*)
in the press (*continued*)
pieces/pamphlets for quotation (*continued*)
The Case of Mrs. Clive (*continued*)
quoted, 290, 294–5, 295*fn*, 477–81
stories about, 22, 167, 170, 185–90, 192, 274, 276, 415, 421
see also pamphlets
quoted, 1*fn*, 8, 143*fn*, 157, 188, 335, 353, 422–6
in *The Rehearsal: Or, Bays in Petticoats*
see her own material (above)
in *The Rehearsal* (Buckingham), 332, 349*fn*, 379
benefit, 379
reputation, 106, 150, 151, 154, 159, 170, 187–9, 284–6, 331, 409–22
as a chaste woman, 13*fn*, 15, 18, 19, 136–7, 136*fn*, 295, 410
as 'Miss Prudely Crotchet', 15, 138, 151, 167, 292, 416
restored to status at Drury Lane, 306–7, 318
retirement, 260, 341, 420–1, 424
in *Rosamond*, 227, 241, 244–60, 253–5*ill*, 255–9*ill*, 267, 271, 348
in *Samson*, 241, 267–8, 271, 274, 309, 349 + *fn*
self-presentation, 1, 3, 7, 12–21, 46, 104, 143, 314, 376
sexual orientation/Sapphic proclivities (conjectured), 153, 348–53, 409, 415, 422
in *The Shepherd's Lottery*, 375–6, 400–1
singing in Gaelic, 317
in *Six Cantatas*, 61–2
'Go perjurd Swain', 140–1, 140*ill*
social influence, 14 + *fn*
and song, 3–5, 4*fn*, 7, 18–20, 28, 29–30, 104, 106, 124, 411–12
as a star and celebrity, 1, 2, 8–9, 139 + *fn*, 197, 210, 231, 240, 409, 426
precariousness of stardom, 26–7, 152
in *The Taming of the Shrew*, 404 + *fn*
technique, 58, 143–4
language/diction, 6, 24–5, 139, 142 + *fn*, 202, 409

voice, 2–6, 23–4, 25–6, 27, 32–3, 63, 166–7, 180, 317, 409
in *The Tempest* as a masque, 58
in *The Tempest* as a play, 33, 58, 308–9, 313–15, 328, 349, 350*fn*
and *The Theatrical Contest*, 299–301, 300*ill*
en travesti/trouser roles, 29–30, 332 + *fn*, 379
in *Twelfth Night*, 199, 308–9
in *The Universal Passion/Much Ado about Nothing*, 194–5, 197–9, 197*fn*, 198*fn*
benefit, 198 + *fn*, 202
in *The Virgin Unmask'd*, 163–4, 166 + *fn*, 222, 230, 297, 301, 309, 334
benefit, 166*fn*
in *The Way of the World*, 232–3, 233*fn*, 244
benefit, 232, 233, 244
'Love's but the Frailty of the Mind', 233–40, 233 + *fn*, 234–9*ill*
in *The Wonder: A Woman keeps a Secret*, 420 + *fn*
in *Zara*, 399, 402
Clive, George (Kitty Clive's supposed husband), 15–16, 138, 153–7, 167, 170, 191–2
cuts Kitty from his will, 153, 156–7
obituary quoted, 154–5, 155–6
sexual orientation, 138, 153, 155, 415
Cliveden, 260, 262*fn*, 263
Clive family of Shropshire, 153–4, 154*fn*
Coffey, Charles, 29, 316
The Beggar's Wedding, 74 + *fn*
The Boarding School, 144–5, 164 + *fn*, 165
The Devil to Pay, 73–104, 75*fn*, 76*fn*, 98*fn*, 100*ill*, 102*ill*, 107, 164 + *fn*, 382, 412
differing versions, 84–9
earnings, 81
influence, 109, 114, 129, 145, 184
playbook, 65, 77*fn*, 98, 99*ill*, 101*ill*
productions in Europe, 97
'Was ever Man possest', 92–5*ill*
Congreve, William, 6
The Double Dealer, 404
The Judgement of Paris, 349 + *fn*, 350*fn*

Love for Love, 108, 309
The Way of the World, 219, 232 + *fn*, 240
'Love's but the Frailty of the Mind', 233–40, 233 + *fn*, 234–9*ill*
Coprario, John, 78–9, 78*fn*
Covent Garden market, 60–1, 334
Covent Garden Theatre, 316
  built and managed by John Rich, 34, 150, 166*fn*, 280, 311, 415, 478–9
  defections from Drury Lane (and threats of), 232, 376, 384*fn*
  David Garrick, 278
  Kitty Clive (and Mary Edwards), 275, 349 + *fn*
  Susannah Cibber, 307–8, 308*fn*, 311–12, 319, 376, 384*fn*, 400
  Theophilus Cibber, 168
  and George F. Handel, 385–6*fn*
  and Kitty Clive, 288–97, 290*fn*, 292*fn*, 296 + *fn*, 301, 307, 309, 338*fn*, 362, 402–3
  rivalry with Drury Lane, 232–3, 276*fn*, 313, 330, 354
  and *The Theatrical Contest*, 300*ill*, 301
  see also pamphlets: *The Case between the Managers of the Two Theatres*
A Critical Balance of the Performers pamphlet, 13–14, 14*fn*
Crosa, Giovanni Francesco, 381–2, 381*fn*, 382
Cross, Richard, 309*fn*, 381, 386, 387
  quoted, 339, 362*fn*, 378, 398*fn*, 402, 404 + *fn*
Cumberland, Duke of (Prince William), 303–4, 304*fn*
Curll, Edmund, 170–1 + *fn*, 175
  quoted, 171 + *fn*, 291*fn*

Dalton, John, 208*fn*, 213
  Comus (after Milton), 208–13, 208*fn*, 210–13, 210*fn*, 211–12*fn*, 228, 415–16
  quoted, 209, 210, 211
Damer, Anne Seymour, 354 + *fn*
Davies, Thomas, 4, 22*fn*, 283, 318, 322
  quoted, 144, 162, 180, 205 + *fn*, 278 + *fn*, 283*fn*, 317, 323, 404, 424

Davison, Jeremiah, 175–6, 175*fn*, 176*ill*, 242–3, 243*fn*, 420
De Fesch, Willem, 21, 271, 275, 289–90, 289*fn*, 295, 295–6*fn*, 296, 349, 415
  The London 'Prentice, 290 + *fn*
  'Masquerade Song', 363 + *fn*
  masques, 271, 275
  oratorios, 271, 275, 289
  Joseph, 271–4 + 271*fn*
    'You see what I dare not say', 271–4, 272–3*ill*
  Judith, 289–90 + *fn*
  Love and Friendship, 292–3 + *fn*, 309
    quoted, 293
  patrons, 289–90, 289*fn*
  The Tempest, 314–15, 314*fn*, 328
Derrick, Samuel: quoted, 24, 139 + *fn*
Dodsley, Robert, 208–9, 209*fn*, 223 +*fn*, 477
  Toy-Shop, 335*fn*
Doggett, Thomas, 29*fn*
  Flora/The Country-Wake, 72–3, 74, 100*fn*
Drury, Robert,
  The Devil of a Duke, 135–6
Drury Lane (Queen's Theatre/Theatre Royal), 7, 9, 28–9, 29*fn*, 54, 56–7, 59, 65, 158, 224–5
  Actors' Rebellion (and settlement 1733), 106, 132*fn*, 138, 148, 149, 158, 161, 168, 170, 318
  bought by bankers, 298, 306
  history/nature, 2, 3
  summer company, 52*fn*, 74, 75*fn*, 81 + *fn*, 83, 114, 124, 125 + *fn*, 133
  The Beggar's Opera, 134–5, 134*fn*
  flagging/suspended, 129 + *fn*, 132, 139, 161
  under Theophilus Cibber, 47*fn*, 51–2, 52*fn*, 73–4 + *fn*, 105, 107–8, 136, 169*fn*, 412, 413
  schedule of performances, 134 + *fn*
  takings, 52, 81
  ticket prices, 297 + *fn*
  see also pamphlet: *The Case between the Managers of the Two Theatres*

Dryden, John, 6, 57, 309
  The Spanish Friar, 22*fn*
  and William Davenant: *The Tempest* (after Shakespeare), 33 + *fn*, 313–14, 314*fn*

Edwards, Mary, 240–1*fn*, 290, 295, 306–7
  in *The Beggar's Opera*, 193, 297 + *fn*, 309–11, 315, 349, 350
  benefits, 289, 297, 309 + *fn*, 349*fn*
  and George F. Handel, 232, 240–1, 241*fn*
  as Kitty Clive's protégée (and possible love object), 13, 192–3, 227, 240, 289, 292–3 + *fn*, 306–7, 309–10, 348–53, 398
  leaves Drury Lane, 350
  in *The Tempest*, 314–15
Ellys, John, 36*fn*, 145, 148, 149
  Miss Fenton (portrait in oils, sold as a mezzotint), 35*ill*, 36–7, 36*fn*, 40, 42
Etherege, Sir George: *The Man of Mode*, 124

Faber, John, 152, 171–5, 172*ill*
Farinelli, 31*fn*, 69*fn*, 165, 213, 214, 224 + *fn*
Farquhar, George,
  The Beaux' Stratagem, 29*fn*
  The Recruiting Officer, 283, 323–4
Fäsch, Johann Ludwig, 420
  'Mrs. Clive in *The Clandestine Marriage*' (attributed), 418*ill*
  'Mrs. Clive in a Peep behind the Curtain', 419*ill*
Fenton, Lavinia, 170, 410
  in *The Beggar's Opera*, 19, 34–41, 46, 80, 189
    'overnight star'/'media craze', 29, 33, 45
    retirement, 41 + *fn*
  earnings, 29*fn*
  influence of, 42–3
  Kitty Clive compared to, 42–3, 46, 51, 63, 64, 65, 80, 106, 134, 135
  portrait as a mezzotint, 35*ill*, 36–7, 36*fn*, 40, 42
  reputation, 34–40, 412
Fielding, Henry, 3–4, 6, 19, 69 + *fn*, 71, 73 + *fn*, 106, 107*fn*, 108, 114*fn*, 132 + *fn*, 136, 138, 151, 166, 379 + *fn*, 382–3, 410, 412, 413–14
  and actors' rebellion, 148 + *fn*
  after Juvenal: *Satires*, 414 + *fn*
  after Molière
    The Miser, 138, 139, 150 + *fn*, 288, 309, 316
    quoted, 139, 141
    The Mock Doctor, 105–6, 107, 128–33, 134, 138, 139, 162, 164, 413
    playbook, 129
    quoted, 130 + *fn*
  after Regnard
    The Intriguing Chambermaid, 138, 140, 141 + *fn*, 142, 158 + *fn*, 240, 291, 309
    playbook, 159 + *fn*
  Amelia, 105*fn*, 245*fn*, 414*fn*
  The Author's Farce, 73 + *fn*, 74, 138, 158–9, 160 + *fn*, 161, 162, 164
    quoted, 159
  The Covent Garden Tragedy, 105, 126 + *fn*, 127 + *fn*, 128, 136, 138
  Deborah: Or, a Wife for you All, 149, 240
  Don Quixote in England, 73, 108*fn*, 382–3, 383*fn*, 402
  eclipse at Drury Lane, 138–9, 161, 163
  'Epistle to Mrs. CLIVE' (attributed), 153, 167, 170, 413 + *fn*
    quoted, 159–60, 161
  Eurydice: Or, the Devil Henpeck'd, 202 + *fn*
  The Grub-Street Opera, 108*fn*, 109*fn*, 119*fn*, 131 + *fn*
  The Lottery, 105, 108–24, 108*fn*, 119*fn*, 147, 164, 180, 288, 309, 413
    'Alas! My Lord, you're too severe', 120–4*ill*
    'Some confounded Planet reigning', 110–13*ill*, 114–19, 115–18*ill*
  Miss Lucy in Town, 148*fn*, 166, 309, 334
  The Old Debauchees, 105, 125–6, 126*fn*, 127 + *fn*, 128, 138, 305 + *fn*
  An Old Man taught Wisdom, 288, 375*fn*
    quoted, 26, 128, 232–3, 295

The Theatre turned Upside Down: Or, the Mutineers (attributed), 152–3, 159
   quoted, 152, 171
The Tragedy of Tragedies, 124 + *fn*, 152, 158
The True Patriot, 313*fn*
   quoted, 313
Tumble-down Dick, 170, 184–5, 197–8
   quoted, 184–5
The Virgin Unmask'd, 163, 164–5, 166 + *fn*, 222, 309, 334, 335, 336
The Wedding Day, 136–7, 136*fn*
The Welsh Opera, 108*fn*, 124*fn*, 131 + *fn*
   as 'William Hint', 134, 295 + *fn*
Fisher, Edward, 172–3, 172*ill*, 173*fn*
Fleetwood, Charles
   and the Actors' Rebellion (1743–44), 275–86, 276*fn*, 278*fn*, 284*fn*, 288, 299, 301, 318
   'Estimates of the Salaries and Benefits', 284–6, 284*fn*, 285*ill*
   cartel with John Rich, 161, 180 + *fn*, 275, 279 + *fn*, 281, 294–5
   and Charles Macklin, 168, 187 + *fn*, 276–7, 293, 297, 301, 414
   and the Cibbers, 170, 179–80, 187 + *fn*, 224–5, 225*fn*, 414
   and David Garrick, 293, 297 + *fn*, 301, 306
   and the Drury Lane patent, 161, 298, 306
   and Henry Carey, 62, 63, 169 + *fn*
   and Kitty Clive, 167, 186, 188, 192, 202, 274, 275–6, 291, 302, 307
   leaves Drury Lane, 298, 306
   and the Lord Chamberlain, 275, 278*fn*, 279 + *fn*, 281*fn*, 282, 283 + *fn*, 284, 299, 301, 306
   manager of Drury Lane, 163, 168, 222*fn*, 224–5, 266–7, 267*fn*, 297–9, 298*fn*, 325*fn*, 383*fn*
   and *The Theatrical Contest*, 299–301, 300*ill*
   unreliability, 167, 169*fn*, 275, 298, 306, 318
   see also pamphlet war
Foote, Samuel, 331–2, 332*fn*
   quoted, 332–3

Frederick, Prince of Wales
   see Prince of Wales, Frederick

Galli, Caterina, 385–6 + *fn*
Garrick, David, 204, 277, 321 + *fn*, 380*fn*, 384 + *fn*, 422
   and the Actors' Rebellion (1743–44), 275–80, 276*fn*, 279*fn*, 283, 288, 293, 301
   (co-)actor-manager at Drury Lane, 166*fn*, 181*fn*, 330, 333, 354 + *fn*, 361, 376, 383, 384 + *fn*
   and the Drury Lane patent, 278*fn*, 306, 308 + *fn*, 338, 354
   in Dublin, 288, 306, 308, 311
   earnings, 284, 286, 306, 424
   Kitty Clive as "the Garrick of the ladies", 139 + *fn*
   Lethe (1740), 215*fn*, 333–4 + *fn*, 335
   quoted, 335, 336, 338
   Lethe (1749), 338–9*fn*, 338–48, 341–2 + *fn*, 353, 354, 376, 380, 424
   puffing (attributed), 339, 354, 360
   quoted, 339, 340, 342, 360
   'The Card invites', 341–2, 341*fn*, 343–7*ill*, 348, 352
   A Peep behind the Curtain, 303
   playing opposite Kitty Clive, 400, 403 + *fn*, 420 + *fn*, 424
   quoted, 308, 403
   star quality/technique/box office appeal, 11, 12 + *fn*, 23*fn*, 24, 25*fn*, 277 + *fn*, 377, 409
   and *The Theatrical Contest*, 299–301, 300*ill*
   as a tragedian, 11 + *fn*, 23*fn*, 306, 400
   as a wine merchant, 333–4
   see also Macklin, Charles; pamphlet war
Garrick Club, 243*fn*
Gay, John, 19 + *fn*, 39, 73, 189
   The Beggar's Opera, 34–41, 36*fn*, 38*fn*, 39*fn*, 97–8*fn*, 124*fn*, 131, 190, 319, 349
   at Drury Lane, 106, 107, 133–4 + *fn*, 170
   founding ballad opera, 3
   and Kitty Clive, 30, 32–3, 106, 349
   opens at Lincoln's Inn Fields, 29 + *fn*

Gay, John (*continued*)
  The Beggar's Opera (*continued*)
    opportunities furnished to Polly Peachum players, 19–20, 80, 412
    'Polly Row', 35*fn*, 163, 185–93, 319
    rejected by/countered by Colley Cibber, 29, 33, 34, 72–3
    and Italian opera, 34
    What d'ye call it, 81 + *fn*, 83, 296
Gentleman, Francis: quoted, 204, 206, 317, 402
Giffard, Henry, 145, 191, 224, 312*fn*, 333–4, 338 + *fn*
Glynn, Eleanor: quoted, 18*fn*
Goodman's Fields Theatre, 73*fn*, 145, 166*fn*, 208*fn*, 277*fn*, 334, 338*fn*
Grace, Ann, 277 + *fn*, 294
Grafton, 2nd Duke of (Charles Fitzroy) *see* Lord Chamberlain
Gray, Thomas, 156 + *fn*
Green, Jane (Jane Hippisley), 142 + *fn*, 338*fn*
Griffin, Benjamin, 149*fn*, 150 + *fn*
The Grub-street Journal, 71 + *fn*, 151, 199*fn*, 208*fn*
  quoted, 22–3, 126 + *fn*, 127–8, 127*fn*, 132, 134, 190

Hale, Sacheverel: quoted, 290–1
Hamilton, Newburgh,
  Samson, 264 + *fn*, 265, 266, 267, 268
  quoted, 265, 267
Handel, George Frideric, 24, 43, 82, 220 + *fn*, 310, 315, 410, 412
  'I like the am'rous Youth' (misattributed to Handel), 202 + *fn*
  and James Harris, 196 + *fn*, 228–9 + *fn*
  and Kitty Clive (and Mary Edwards), 240–1, 241*fn*, 289, 329, 349
  'Love's but the Frailty of the Mind', 233–40, 233 + *fn*, 234–9*ill*
  masques
    Acis and Galatea, 266*fn*
    Alexander's Feast
      'The Prince, unable to conceal his pain', 335
  operas
    Berenice
      Minuet, 45
    Deidamia, 240 + *fn*
    Floridante, 109 + *fn*
    Imeneo, 240 + *fn*
  oratorios
    Alexander Balus, 385–6 + *fn*
    L'Allegro ed il Penseroso, 229–30 + *fn*, 232, 266*fn*, 269, 270
      'Sweet Bird', 241–2, 242*fn*
    Athalia, 220*fn*, 269–70 + *fn*
    company/seasons of, 229 + *fn*, 241, 266, 268–71, 289, 293, 296, 304, 307, 385
    Deborah, 149, 179, 220*fn*, 240, 269 + *fn*, 307*fn*
    Esther, 220 + *fn*, 289*fn*
    favourably compared to *The Beggar's Opera*, 38*fn*, 40
    Joseph and his Brethren, 271, 296
    Judas Maccabaeus, 304*fn*
    Messiah, 241 + *fn*, 268–9, 270
    Samson, 227, 241, 263–4, 266–8, 293, 296, 307*fn*, 309, 310, 349
    Saul, 240, 266*fn*, 335 + *fn*
  Ottone, 83 + *fn*
    'Nò, non temere', 83 + *fn*, 90, 91–5*ill*
  Partenope, 135, 136
  patrons, 228*fn*, 289
  Poro/'*Porus*', 83 + *fn*, 119*fn*
    'Son confusa pastorella', 83–90 + *fn*, 106, 110–13*ill*, 114–19, 115–18*ill*
  quoted, 308*fn*
  royal family support, 209 + *fn*
  Siroe: 'Dimmi, cara', 164, 240
  'Twas when the Seas', 83
Hanoverian succession, 182
Harper, John, 98, 108*fn*, 109, 129 + *fn*, 149*fn*, 158, 163
  en travesti, 145
Harris, James, 196 + *fn*, 198, 220, 228 + *fn*, 264
  L'Allegro ed il Penseroso, 228–9
Harris, Thomas, 243*fn*
  quoted, 240 + *fn*, 269
Hayman, Francis, 98–102, 99*ill*, 100–1*fn*, 100*ill*, 101*ill*, 102*ill*, 103*ill*, 132*fn*, 183–4, 201*fn*
Haymarket (the street), 59–60, 60*fn*

Herbert, Lady Henrietta (Lady
    Powis/'Lady Harriet'), 265–6
    + *fn*
Heron, Mary, 71, 71–2*fn*, 148, 149*fn*, 151*fn*,
    162, 167
    retirement, 168 + *fn*
Hertford, Countess of (Frances Seymour,
    later 7th Duchess of Somerset),
    319
    quoted, 318
Highmore, John, 138, 145 + *fn*, 148 + *fn*,
    149, 151, 161, 167, 168
Hill, Aaron, 25 + *fn*, 72, 139, 178 + *fn*, 186,
    189, 203*fn*, 212*fn*, 290, 399
    quoted, 52, 72*fn*, 80, 98, 317
    'The Stage's Acknowledgment', 419
        quoted, 178, 416
    Zara, 33*fn*, 180, 186, 399, 402
    See and Seem Blind (attributed):
        quoted, 179
Hill, John, 13*fn*, 22, 66, 141–2 + *fn*, 203*fn*
    Orpheus and Eurydice, 141–2*fn*, 232–3
    quoted, 13, 22, 142 + *fn*, 143 + *fn*
Hoare, William: 'Mrs. Clive in the
    Character of Philida', 422,
    423*ill*
Hogarth, George: quoted, 361
Hogarth, William, 36*fn*, 37*fn*, 38 + *fn*,
    146–7, 146*fn*, 148*fn*, 289*fn*
homosexuality (male), 155–6, 156*fn*,
    214–15, 215*fn*, 409, 415
    see also Clive, George; Gray, Thomas;
        Ince, Richard; Walpole, Horace
Horton, Christiana, 71, 72*fn*, 148, 151*fn*,
    167, 168, 232 + *fn*, 261*fn*
    benefit, 72*fn*

Ince, Richard, 154–5
influences on English music and drama
    (actual and alleged),
    French, 57, 181, 198, 279, 315, 414–15
    German, 181
    Italian, 30*fn*, 32 + *fn*, 34, 42*fn*, 44, 45 +
        fn, 198, 279, 315, 393
        burlettas, 6, 379–80, 381–2, 386,
            405–6
        castrato singing, 31, 159, 213
        emerging as masques, 3, 20, 57–8,
            57*fn*

improvisation, 141
out of favour, 38*fn*, 159
performers in London, 279, 328, 340
    + *fn*
see also Clive, Catherine 'Kitty': and
    Italian(ate) material

Jacobites, 2, 208*fn*, 221, 264
    Jacobite Rebellion, 303–4, 304*fn*, 309
    see also Cumberland, Duke of;
        Stuart, Charles Edward
Jennens, Charles, 228–9 + *fn*, 233 + *fn*,
    240, 308*fn*
    quoted, 240, 266–7, 267*fn*
Jevon, Thomas: *The Devil of a Wife*, 73–4,
    76 + *fn*, 77*fn*, 80, 82
Johnson, Samuel, 338 + *fn*
'joke' (lewd meaning), 109–14 + *fn*
Jommelli, Niccolò,
    *Four Songs in the Opera call'd Il
        Demofoonte*, 341 + *fn*
Jonson, Ben: *Volpone*, 283

Kimberley, Richard: quoted, 14
King George II, 182–3, 194, 208*fn*, 304,
    425–6
    quoted, 203
King James II, 2, 2*fn*, 265, 304, 305 + *fn*
King's Theatre, Haymarket, 60, 240, 308
King William III, Prince of Orange, 2,
    305*fn*
    Glorious Revolution, 156*fn*, 223*fn*,
        249*fn*, 305

Lacy, James, 312 + *fn*, 313 + *fn*, 314, 322
    assistant manager at Covent Garden,
        283 + *fn*
    commissions the National Anthem,
        305
    and *The Green Room Scuffle*, 318–24,
        416
    manager at Drury Lane, 298, 306–7,
        310–11, 313, 314, 338 + *fn*
    paying his players (and not), 307
        + *fn*
    quoted, 313
    and *The Theatrical Contest*, 300–1,
        300*ill*
Laguerre, John, 72–3, 163

Laguerre, John (*continued*)
  The Stage Mutiny, 150 + *fn*
Lampe, John F., 6, 296 + *fn*
  Amelia, 178–9
  The Dragon of Wantley, 63 + *fn*, 169
  The Opera of Operas, 30*fn*, 158 + *fn*
  Orpheus and Eurydice, 288
Lee, Nathaniel,
  Mithridates, 29–30, 29*fn*, 30*fn*
  The Rival Queens, 190*fn*, 319
Lee and Harper's Booth, 80 + *fn*
Leveridge, Richard, 78 + *fn*, 83 + *fn*, 90
Licensing Act (of Theatres 1737), 194, 208, 213, 214*fn*, 224, 275, 307, 415
  see also Lord Chamberlain
Lichtenberg, Georg: quoted, 206 + *fn*
Lillo, George: *The London Merchant*, 83–90 + *fn*, 107
Lincoln's Inn Fields playhouse, 29, 41*fn*, 58–9, 59*fn*, 191, 278, 289*fn*
Little Haymarket Theatre
  see New Haymarket
Lord Chamberlain (Duke of Grafton), 2, 166*fn*, 225*fn*, 306
  and the Actors' Rebellion (1743–44), 275, 279–83, 279*fn*, 280*fn*, 281*fn*, 284–6
  Examiner of Plays/'censor' (office under the Lord Chamberlain), 136, 214 + *fn*, 218*fn*, 338*fn*, 339–40*fn*, 399
  bans plays outright, 195, 222
  and *The Theatrical Contest*, 299–301, 300*ill*
  see also Licensing Act

Macklin, Charles, 25*fn*, 141*fn*, 203*fn*, 205–6 + *fn*, 277 + *fn*, 297, 301, 312*fn*, 415
  and the Actors' Rebellion (1743–44), 275–8, 276*fn*, 277 + *fn*, 282, 283, 288, 301
  in *Britons, Strike Home*, 225, 226
  and David Garrick, 276*fn*, 277–9, 278–9*fn*, 282, 283, 288, 293–4, 295, 297, 301
  in *The Harlot's Progress*, 203, 205
  in *The Intriguing Chambermaid*, 168 + *fn*
  kills Thomas Hallam, 205, 276–7
  King Henry the VII, 322 + *fn*
  and Kitty Clive, 277, 306, 308, 412
  in *The Merchant of Venice*, 203–4 + *fn*, 205–6, 206*fn*, 207*ill*, 277, 299, 308, 338–9
  quoted, 225, 278*fn*, 279*fn*
  (re)joins Drury Lane (and leaves), 151, 168, 306, 376
  as deputy manager, 168–9, 187 + *fn*, 277 + *fn*, 414
  and *The Theatrical Contest*, 299–301, 300*ill*
  in *The Virgin Unmask'd*, 163
Mallet, David,
  masque: *Alfred*, 212 + *fn*, 227, 260 + *fn*, 262–3, 263*ill*, 265
Marivaux, Pierre: *L'Île des esclaves (The Island of Slaves)*, 212, 212–13*fn*
Marlborough, 1st Duke of (John Churchill, and his wife), 244
  see also Churchill, Sarah
Mathews, Charles, 243 + *fn*
Mattei, Colomba, 405, 405–6*fn*
Mattocks, George, 362, 363
Mendez, Moses,
  The Chaplet, 361–75, 362*fn*, 376, 380
  'From Flow'r to Flow'r', 364–7*ill*, 368
  'I know that my Person is charming', 371, 372–4*ill*
  'In vain I try my ev'ry Art', 368, 369–70*ill*
  quoted, 362, 363, 368, 371, 400
  The Shepherd's Lottery, 375–6, 375*fn*
  quoted, 375, 376
Miller, James, 65–6, 128 + *fn*, 138–9, 161, 163, 166, 167, 196 + *fn*, 334, 412
  after Molière, 165 + *fn*, 166
  The Humours of Oxford, 64, 66, 109, 162 + *fn*, 219, 221, 412, 414
  earnings, 69
  makes enemies, 69–71, 69*fn*, 162 + *fn*, 194, 198–9
  'The Provident Damsel', 67–9, 68*ill*, 140, 165
  The Man of Taste, 69 + *fn*, 140, 163, 165, 166, 221
  benefit, 215*fn*
  after Shakespeare

Much Ado about Nothing (as *The Universal Passion*), 194–5, 196–9, 197*fn*, 228
  quoted, 197 + *fn*
  after William Walsh's *Aesculapius An Hospital for Fools*, 140, 222, 225, 240, 334–5, 334*fn*
  'How smoothly glides the Fool thro' Life', 225–6 + *fn*
Art and Nature, 218–19, 218*fn*
  quoted, 218, 219
The Camp Visitants, 195, 222 + *fn*, 334
  quoted, 222–3
The Coffee-House (after Rousseau), 21, 140, 213–18, 214*fn*, 224
  anti-Semitism, 213 + *fn*
  homophobia, 214–15, 215*fn*
  quoted, 214–15, 215*fn*
  'Song', 215, 216*ill*
  downfall, 195, 199 + *fn*, 218–23, 335, 414–15
Harlequin-Horace, 49*fn*
The Mother-in-Law, 140, 161, 162 + *fn*
  earnings, 162
  pamphlets against him, 199
  quoted, 219–21
Miller, Joe, 291–2
Mills, John, 52*fn*, 149*fn*
Milton, John, 6, 209*fn*, 227, 244, 410
  L'Allegro, 210, 211, 228, 265
  Comus, 195, 208–13, 351, 415–16
    quoted, 213, 351
  Paradise Lost, 209, 228*fn*
    quoted, 331
  Il Penseroso, 228, 265
  Samson Agonistes, 264–5, 264*fn*, 267, 268
Milward, William, 149*fn*, 240
Mingotti, Regina, 328, 340–1, 341*fn*
Molière, 105–6, 132, 162 + *fn*, 165 + *fn*, 167
  L'Avare (The Miser), 138
  and commedia dell'arte, 141 + *fn*, 379
  L'Impromptu de Versailles, 379–80
  Le Médecin malgré lui, 125, 128–9, 128*fn*
  La Princesse d'Élide, 197 + *fn*
Monro, George: *A New Song*, 90, 96*ill*, 97
Mosley, Charles, 355, 357–9*ill*, 358*fn*, 360, 377
Mottley, John, 74, 78*fn*
  quoted, 43 + *fn*, 65*fn*, 74, 81*fn*
  see also Coffey, Charles: *The Devil to Pay*
Mozeen, Thomas, 350, 351
  The Heiress, 351–2
  quoted, 351, 352
Murphy, Arthur: *The Apprentice*, 32

New Haymarket Theatre, 124*fn*, 158, 161*fn*, 340
  agreement with Drury Lane, 180 + *fn*
  hosts *Damon and Phillida*, 47 + *fn*, 49*fn*
  hosts *Don Quixote in England*, 383*fn*
  hosts *The Author's Farce*, 73 + *fn*, 74, 108
  hosts *The Beggar's Wedding*, 74
  hosts *The Contrivances*, 53 + *fn*
  hosts *The Honest Yorkshire-Man*, 184
  Little Haymarket, 133*fn*, 295 + *fn*
  Theophilus Cibber's company, 158, 162, 178–9, 311
Norris, Miss (first name unrecorded), 362–3, 362*fn*, 375, 380
  in *The Rehearsal; Or, Bays in Petticoats*, 380, 381, 386, 399
  Corydon and Miranda, 387
North, Roger: quoted, 32 + *fn*

Odingsells, Gabriel: *Bays's Opera*, 73 + *fn*
Oldfield, Anne, 65–6, 67, 71, 171, 172 + *ill*, 176*fn*, 177*ill*, 232 + *fn*
  benefits, 286
  death, 71 + *fn*, 72*fn*, 170–1
  earnings, 171*fn*, 286 + *fn*
  and Lavinia Fenton, 40 + *fn*
  legacy of image, 168, 169, 170–7, 193, 291 + *fn*
  legacy of roles
    to Kitty Clive, 148–9, 152, 167, 168–9, 171, 232 + *fn*, 291, 295, 309 + *fn*, 415
    to others, 71–2 + *fn*, 105, 148–9, 232
  power and influence, 64, 66
  self-presentation, 16*fn*, 65, 171 + *fn*, 176
opera, 2, 3, 49, 179
  ballad opera, 2*fn*, 3, 19–20, 26, 97–8, 183, 412

opera (*continued*)
  ballad opera (*continued*)
    at Drury Lane, 30, 33, 41–2, 51–2, 57, 58, 65, 72–4, 97–8, 144
  comic opera, 2*fn*
  interpolated song, 3
  see also acting/drama styles: burlesque, masque, pastoral; Handel: operas
oratorio, 3, 6, 169, 219, 275, 289, 295, 296
  see also De Fesch: oratorios; Handel: oratorios
oysters (as aphrodisiac), 353 + *fn*

pamphlets/broadside/periodical/ newspaper war (1743–44), 421
  The Case between the Managers of the Two Theatres, 281 + *fn*
    quoted, 281
  The Case of Mrs. Clive, 274, 276, 294, 339–40
    quoted, 290, 294–5, 295*fn*, 477–81
  The Dramatic Congress (Chetwood), 275, 279–83, 279*fn*, 281*fn*
    quoted, 284
  'Estimates of the Salaries and Benefits', 284–6, 284*fn*, 285*ill*
  The Green Room Scuffle, 319–23, 320*ill*, 416
  'Historical Chronicle', 286, 287*ill*
  Queries to be Answer'd (attributed to Garrick), 279, 281*fn*, 282
  Queries upon Queries (Fleetwood), 282 + *fn*
  A Sapphick Epistle, 353–4
  Satan's Harvest Home, 352 + *fn*
  Socius, 312–13
  Theatrical Correspondence in Death, 324
    quoted, 291–2, 291*fn*, 295, 302 + *fn*
  The Theatric Squabble: Or, the P–ntees, 152–3, 162
    quoted, 150, 151*fn*
  Tyranny Triumphant! And Liberty Lost
    quoted, 281–2
  'Veteran Protestant', 312 + *fn*
  see also Fielding, Henry: *The Theatre turned Upside Down*
Parr, Richard, 103–4, 103*ill*

Phillips, Edward, 138, 150–1*fn*
  Britons, Strike Home, 223–4, 225, 292 + *fn*
    quoted, 224, 225, 226, 277
  The Rival Theatres, 316
  The Stage-Mutineers, 150–2, 170, 225, 416
    quoted, 151 + *fn*
playhouses, 8–9, 26, 411
  audience behaviour, 9, 16*fn*, 17, 43 + *fn*, 126 + *fn*, 294, 297–8, 298*fn*
  configuration, 9
  receipts, 9*fn*
  royal patronage, 9 + *fn*, 20, 43–4, 44*fn*, 82, 107*fn*, 186*fn*, 202, 415
  see also Covent Garden; Drury Lane; Goodman's Fields; King's Theatre; Lee and Harper's Booth; Lincoln's Inn Fields; New Haymarket
Pope, Alexander, 156*fn*, 209*fn*, 260 + *fn*
  The Dunciad, 170–1*fn*, 221*fn*
    quoted, 36 + *fn*
Pope, Jane,
  as Kitty Clive's protégée (and possible love object), 13, 98 + *fn*, 206, 207*ill*, 243, 353
  letters from Kitty Clive, 1*fn*, 8 + *fn*, 143 + *fn*, 153 + *fn*, 157, 341, 353 + *fn*, 422–4, 424
Pope, Susanna, 243
Prince of Wales, Frederick, 182–3, 182 *fn*, 185, 246 + *fn*, 249, 260 + *fn*, 262–3, 310 + *fn*, 324
  and *Alfred the Great*, 260–1 + *fn*, 262*fn*
  banishment from court, 194, 208
  as dedicatee, 295–6*fn*
  Histoire du Prince Titi (attributed), 182 + *fn*
  and John Milton, 209 + *fn*
  as patron, 209 + *fn*, 246, 260, 289
  as performer, 260*fn*
  popular following/opposition figurehead, 194, 195 + *fn*, 196*fn*, 208 + *fn*, 223 + *fn*, 227, 245 + *fn*, 304, 306, 415–16
  as theatre-goer, 43–4, 44*fn*, 209 + *fn*
  command performances, 82, 202, 260, 292, 415

en famille/en masse, 47 + *fn*, 147, 292*fn*, 295
Prince William
  see Cumberland, Duke of
Pritchard, Hannah, 12*fn*, 55*fn*, 192, 201*fn*, 278*fn*, 349*fn*, 412
  benefit, 163 + *fn*
  compared to Susannah Cibber, 24*fn*
  and Kitty Clive, 162–3, 163*fn*, 165, 181, 424
  in *The Mock Doctor*, 132 + *fn*, 163
  and *The Theatrical Contest*, 300 + *ill*
Pritchard, William, 181*fn*
  masque: *The Fall of Phaeton*, 181–5, 209
  quoted, 182–3, 183*fn*
Purcell, Henry, 6, 33, 58–9 + *fn*, 61, 62, 78, 79 + *fn*, 315, 411–12
  The History of Bonduca, 58
  'Britons, Strike Home', 223–4, 223*fn*, 225, 305–6
  masques, 6, 315
  The Tempest, 58

Queen Caroline, 183 + *fn*, 208 + *fn*, 221 + *fn*, 304–5
Queen's Theatre/Theatre Royal, Drury Lane
  see Drury Lane
Quin, James, 29, 292, 306, 324*fn*
  characterised as Sir John Falstaff, 324–5
  and Charles Fleetwood's Drury Lane, 225, 232, 261, 414
  in *Comus*, 209, 210, 211–12
  at Covent Garden, 278, 292, 308*fn*
  and Frederick, Prince of Wales, 209, 261, 292
  leaves Drury Lane, 203, 277
  as sex pest (alleged), 325–6, 325*fn*
  and *The Theatrical Contest*, 300*ill*, 301

Raftor, Catherine
  see Clive, Catherine 'Kitty'
Raftor, Elizabeth (*née* Daniell; Kitty Clive's mother), 1–2
Raftor, James ('Jemmy', Kitty Clive's brother), 335–6, 404
  fight with Owen Swiney, 318, 321, 322, 323

his benefit performances, 289, 297, 309, 332, 338*fn*, 349*fn*, 398–9, 399*fn*, 400*fn*
his estate, 243 + *fn*
Raftor, William (Kitty Clive's father), 1–2, 2*fn*, 29 + *fn*, 159, 170
Ralph, James, 107*fn*
  The Fashionable Lady, 73*fn*
  quoted, 286
Ranelagh Gardens, 348*fn*, 362, 363*fn*, 371, 401
Raymond, James Grant, 243 + *fn*
Regnard, Jean-François,
  Le Retour imprévu (as *The Intriguing Chambermaid*), 138, 141
Restoration comedy, 11, 20
Rich, John, 134, 184, 260, 283, 324*fn*
  and Theophilus Cibber, 158
  builds and runs Covent Garden Theatre, 34, 125*fn*, 150, 209*fn*, 308*fn*, 415
  cartel with Charles Fleetwood, 161, 180 + *fn*, 275, 279 + *fn*, 281, 294
  and David Garrick, 354, 354–5*fn*, 384
  and Edward Phillips, 150–1 + *fn*
  and John Beard, 295
  and John Hill, 141–2 + *fn*
  and Kitty Clive, 166*fn*, 288–9, 294–5, 296, 376, 402, 415
  and Lavinia Fenton, 29*fn*, 39
  manager at Lincoln's Inn Fields, 29 + *fn*, 125*fn*, 278
  rivalry with Drury Lane, 52, 72, 133, 134, 136, 384
  summer companies in Richmond, 51–2, 52*fn*, 150–1
  and Susannah Cibber, 311–12 + *fn*, 313*fn*
  and *The Theatrical Contest*, 300–1, 300*ill*
Richardson, Jonathan, 172–3, 172*ill*, 175–6, 177*ill*
  quoted, 174 + *fn*
Rolli, Paolo: *Sabrina* (after Milton), 209 + *fn*
Rousseau, Jean-Baptiste: *Le Caffé*, 213 + *fn*
Russel, Richard, 71 + *fn*
  see also The Grub-street Journal

Santlow, Hester
    see Booth, Hester
Sayer, Robert: 'Mrs. Clive in *The Clandestine Marriage*', 418*ill*
Schalcken, Godfried: *Miss Rafter in the Character of Phillida* (portrait in oils, sold as a mezzotint), 50*ill*, 51 + *fn*, 169, 172
'Seedo'/'Mr Seedo', 125*fn*, 136*fn*
    The Author's Farce, 108*fn*
    The Devil to Pay, 74 + *fn*, 83, 91–5*ill*, 97, 108
    Don Quixote in England, 108*fn*
    The Grub-Street Opera, 108*fn*
    The Judgment of Paris, 144
    The Lottery, 108 + *fn*, 114, 119, 124, 375
        'Alas! My Lord, you're too severe', 120–4*ill*
        'Some confounded Planet reigning', 110–13*ill*, 115–18*ill*
    The Mock Doctor, 130–1
    The Welsh Opera, 108*fn*
Shaftesbury, 4th Earl of (Anthony Ashley Cooper, and his wife), 195, 196, 228*fn*, 263
    see also Ashley Cooper, Susanna
Shakespeare, William, 6, 57, 100*fn*, 196–7, 208, 228, 279, 281, 410
    As You Like It, 163 + *fn*, 199, 308–9
    Hamlet, 193, 201 + *fn*, 308–9, 398*fn*
    Henry IV Part 1, 318, 322–3
    Henry IV Part 2 (character of Pistol), 107
    King Lear: quoted, 350 + *fn*
    Love's Labour's Lost, 199
    Macbeth, 47 + *fn*
    The Merchant of Venice, 199, 203–4, 292 + *fn*, 308–9, 318, 338–9
    Much Ado about Nothing, 194–5, 198
    Othello, 196
    Romeo and Juliet, 384 + *fn*
    Shakespeare Ladies' Club, 194, 195–7, 195*fn*, 202, 314
    as a speciality of Kitty Clive, 6, 195–6, 199, 201, 202, 203–4, 205*fn*, 283, 288, 413
    The Taming of the Shrew, 196 + *fn*, 404
    The Tempest, 33, 58, 308–9, 313–15, 314*fn*
    Timon of Athens, 58*fn*, 240

Twelfth Night, 199, 308–9
Siddons, Sarah, 23*fn*, 330 + *fn*
Smart, Christopher: epilogue, 32–3, 33*fn*, 173
Smith, John, 36*fn*, 51*fn*
Steele, Richard, 29*fn*, 145
    The Conscious Lovers, 1*fn* + 11*fn*
    quoted, 11
    The Spectator, 10*fn*, 154–5, 155*fn*
    Tatler, 10*fn*
Stoppelaer, Charles, 119*fn*, 135, 149
    in *The Beggar's Opera*, 133
    in *The Comical Revenge*, 129 + *fn*
    in *The Devil to Pay*, 82–3, 109, 114, 129, 412
    in *The Lottery*, 108, 109, 114
    in *The Mock Doctor*, 130, 131
Strawberry Hill, 341, 342*fn*, 352–3*fn*, 353–4, 354*fn*, 355–8*fn*, 421*ill*
Stuart, Charles Edward ('the Young Pretender'/'Bonnie Prince Charlie'), 304
Swiney, Owen, 318, 321, 322, 323

Temple Bar, 60
theatre conventions, 8–13, 16–21, 23–7, 57
    benefits, 21, 54–6, 56*fn*, 125*fn*, 282, 284, 309
    seasons, 55, 124–5, 149, 232, 292, 296, 308, 349*fn*, 351, 399*fn*
    generic characters, 10–11 + *fn*
    green room, 150, 151, 302–3, 303*fn*, 311, 318, 410
    mechanical devices, 288
    patronage, 14*fn*, 16, 29*fn*, 30, 69*fn*, 145*fn*, 175*fn*, 209, 220, 283*fn*
    royal, 183*fn*, 209 + *fn*, 246, 261*fn*, 289
    prologues and epilogues, 16–18, 17–18*fn*, 26, 53, 158–9, 211, 218
    'puffing', 22–3, 106, 128–9, 132–5, 150, 186–7, 232, 261, 296
        at length, 335*fn*, 339, 354
    rehearsal/preparation, 12
    'returning the ball', 205
The Theatrical Contest engraving, 299–301, 299*fn*, 300*ill*, 302
Thistlethwayte, Robert, 69–71, 69*fn*, 71*fn*, 222 + *fn*
Thomson, James: *Alfred*, 196*fn*, 227, 260, 261–3, 263*ill*, 265

INDEX

Thornton, Bonnell, 16*fn*, 23
  quoted, 23, 24 + *fn*
'Tom Cynick': quoted, 145
Twickenham, 163 + *fn*

Van Aken, Alexander,
  'The Fair Songster', 417*ill*, 418–20
  'Mrs. Clive', 421*ill*
  'Of all the Arts …', 177*ill*, 178, 418, 420
Van Aken, Joseph, 175–7, 175*fn*, 176 +
    177*ill*, 242–3, 420
  'Mrs. Clive', 421*ill*
  'The Fair Songster', 417*ill*, 420
Van Bleeck, Pieter, 169, 172–5, 172*ill* + *fn*,
    176*ill*, 355, 356–9*ill*, 358*fn*, 360
Vanbrugh, Sir John,
  Aesop, 335 + *fn*
  The Provok'd Husband, 33*fn*, 65, 219
  The Provok'd Wife, 309
  The Relapse, 66*fn*, 163, 309
Vandergucht, Gerard, 48*ill*, 49 + *fn*, 101*ill*,
    102–3, 103*fn*, 173
Vane, Anne, 183 + *fn*, 185
Vauxhall Gardens, 99–100, 102, 132*fn*, 147
    + *fn*, 195*fn*, 314*fn*, 315, 348*fn*
Verelst, William, 243*fn*
  Portrait of Catherine Clive, 231*ill*, 232,
    241–4
Vernon, Admiral Edward, 224, 246 + *fn*,
    264, 306
Veteran Scheme, benefits for, 308, 310 +
    fn, 311, 312, 313 + *fn*, 315, 319
Victor, Benjamin, 8, 145, 213
  quoted, 1, 45, 107, 145–6, 187 + *fn*,
    204–5, 213, 305*fn*, 412

Waldegrave, James, 1st Earl, 265–6 + *fn*
Walker, Thomas,
  The Quaker's Opera, 37 + *fn*
Walpole, Horace, 156 + *fn*, 243*fn*, 260, 298
    + *fn*, 341, 352, 352–3*fn*, 411, 420
    + *fn*, 421
  quoted, 14*fn*, 242*fn*, 290*fn*, 340*fn*,
    341–2, 342*fn*, 425–6
Walpole, Sir Robert (1st Earl of Orford),
    36*fn*, 39*fn*, 203, 208, 260*fn*
  attacked from the stage, 34, 183, 194–5,
    208*fn*, 214*fn*, 416

Excise Tax, 246
and war with Spain (War of Jenkins'
  Ear), 194, 222–3, 224, 246,
  264*fn*
see also Licensing Act (of Theatres
  1737)
Watts, John, 84–9
  Damon and Phillida, 47–9 + *fn*, 63, 173
  The Devil to Pay, 81*fn*, 82*fn*, 102–3,
    103*fn*
  The Humours of Oxford, 49, 69, 162
  The Intriguing Chambermaid, 159 + *fn*
  Molière, 128 + *fn*, 162 + *fn*, 165
  Musical Miscellany, 114*fn*
  The Old Debauchees, 69*fn*
  playbooks/wordbooks, 49
Wilkinson, Tate, 406–7
  quoted, 201, 316, 324*fn*, 350, 376, 406
Wilks, Mary, 145, 161
Wilks, Robert, 36*fn*, 67*fn*, 291 + *fn*
  as actor, 39*fn*, 42, 70*fn*, 145, 232*fn*, 284
  death, 145
  as Drury Lane manager/patent holder,
    29*fn*, 36*fn*, 42, 73, 107, 145, 284
Woffington, Margaret 'Peg', 12*fn*, 277, 283,
    296, 306, 316–24
  copying Kitty Clive, 316
  figurine of, 326–7 + *fn*, 327*ill*
  and *The Green Room Scuffle*, 274 + *fn*,
    318–24, 329–30, 331, 376
  image/reputation, 15, 16*fn*, 316
  and *The Theatrical Contest*, 300 + *ill*
  women in society, 14, 14–15*fn*, 194, 195–6,
    195*fn*
Woodward, Henry, 354–5, 354*fn*, 403–4,
    412
  *The Beggar's Pantomime: Or, the
    Contending Colombines*, 170,
    185, 190–3, 318, 319, 354–5,
    403–4
  figurine of, 354–5, 360
  A Lick at the Town, 403–5
  quoted, 404–5
  quoted, 142, 191
Worlidge, Thomas, 355–8 + *fn*
Worsdale, James,
  A Cure for a Scold (after Shakespeare),
    196